COMPUTER SCIENCE
A Structured Programming Approach Using C
Second Edition

COMPUTER SCIENCE
A Structured Programming Approach Using C
Second Edition

Behrouz A. Forouzan
De Anza College

Richard F. Gilberg
De Anza College

Brooks/Cole
Thomson Learning™

Australia • Canada • Mexico • Singapore • Spain • United Kingdom • United States

Sponsoring Editor: *Kallie Swanson*
Marketing Team: *Nathan Wilbur and Christina De Veto*
Editorial Assistant: *Grace Fujimoto*
Production Coordinator: *Mary Vezilich*
Production Service: *Carlisle Publishers Services*
Print Buyer: *Vena Dyer*

Cover Designer: *Denise Davidson*
Cover Photo: *Lightsource Images/Lois Stanfield*
Design Coordinator: *Roy Neuhaus*
Typesetting: *Carlisle Communications, Ltd.*
Cover Printing: *Phoenix Color*
Printing and Binding: *Courier—Kendallville*

Library of Congress Cataloging-in-Publication Data

Forouzan, Behrouz A.
    Computer science: a structured programming approach using C / Behrouz A. Forouzan,
    Richard F. Gilberg.—2nd ed.
        p.   cm.
    Includes index.
    ISBN 0-534-37482-4
    1. C (Computer program language) 2. Structured programming. I. Gilberg, Richard F.
II. Title.

QA76.73.C15 F662 2001
005.13'3—dc21   99-087765
                                                        CIP

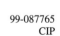

To my family
> Behrouz Forouzan

To Evelyn
> Richard Gilberg

Preface

This text has two primary objectives: to teach the basic principles of programming as outlined in the ACM curriculum for a CS1 class and to teach the basic constructs of the C Language. Our text puts these objectives in the context of good software engineering concepts that we have developed through over thirty years of experience in industry and academia.

A C LANGUAGE PERSPECTIVE

While C is a complex and professional language, our classroom experience using the first edition of this book has shown that beginning students can easily understand it. We believe that if the language is put into a perspective that allows the student to understand its design, C is not a difficult language.

There are two aspects of C that separate it from most other languages: expressions and pointers. The concept of expressions, as used in C, is unique. For this reason, we felt this book had to be built for C from the ground up, not based on a book that used Pascal. The first half of this text builds a firm understanding of expressions. We introduce pointers only to the extent necessary to cover passing addresses in Chapter 4 and arrays in Chapter 8. Our experiences have shown that with a firm grasp of the expression concept, much of the mystery of C disappears.

In Chapter 9, we begin to develop the concept of pointers, culminating with a simple introduction to linked lists. While not all courses will have time to cover linked lists, those that do will give the students a head start into data structures. Motivated students will find that they can study the linked lists material as a preview to data structures. The last chapter of the text covers bitwise operators, a subject that is beyond the CS 1 curriculum, but is needed to make the book complete. The appendices at the end of the text comprise a rich set of references to subjects required in the complete C language. These will be of use to students who go on to take other courses in the C language.

FEATURES OF THE BOOK

Several features of this book make it unique and easy for beginning students to understand.

STRUCTURE AND STYLE

One of our basic tenets is that good habits are formed early. The corollary is that bad habits are hard to break. Therefore, we consistently emphasize the principles of structured programming and software engineering. Every complete program in the book uses a consistent style. As programs are analyzed, style and standards are further explained. While we acknowledge that there are many good styles, our experience has shown that if students are exposed to one good style and adopt it, they will be better able to adapt to other good styles. On the other hand, unlearning sloppy short-cut habits is very difficult.

PRINCIPLE BEFORE PRACTICE

Whenever possible, we develop the principle of a subject before we introduce the language implementation. For example, in Chapter 5 we first introduce the concept of logical data and selection and then we introduce the *if . . . else* and *switch* statements. This approach gives the student an understanding of selection before introducing the nuances of the language.

VISUAL APPROACH

A brief scan of the book will demonstrate that our approach is visual. There are over 400 figures, plus over 70 tables and 180 program examples. While this amount of material tends to create a large book, the visual approach makes it easy for students to follow the material.

EXAMPLES

While the programming examples vary in complexity, each uses a consistent style. Our experience working with productional programs that live for 10 to 20 years convinced us that readable and understandable programs are easier to work with than programs written in a terse, cryptic manner. For that reason, and to emphasize the structure of the language, we label the sections in a function with comments. We consistently follow a style that places only one declaration, definition, or statement on a line. The source code for these programs is available on the Brooks/Cole Web site (**www.brookscole.com/ compsci/forouzan/c2**). Students are able to run these programs and to explore related topics through modification and experimentation.

CODING TECHNIQUES

Throughout the text we include coding techniques that make programs more readable and often more efficient. For example, in Chapter 5 on page 185 you will find the following discussion:

Where do we check for *greater than*? The answer is that we default the *greater than* condition to the outer *else.* . . .When coding a two-way selection statement, try to code the most probable condition first; with nested selection statements, code the most probable first and the least probable last.

These techniques, drawn from our extensive industry and classroom experience, are not found in most texts.

SOFTWARE ENGINEERING

A discussion of software engineering principles concludes each chapter. Our intent is not to replace a separate course in software engineering. Rather, we firmly believe that by incorporating basic software engineering principles early in their studies, students will be better prepared for a formal treatment of the subject. Even more important, by writing well-engineered programs from the beginning, students will not be forced to unlearn and relearn. They will better understand software discussions in their subsequent classes.

While the software engineering sections are found at the end of each chapter, they are most successfully taught by introducing them as the chapter unfolds. Then, a short review at the end of the chapter summarizes the principles that have been demonstrated during the lectures.

These sections are visually distinguishable from the rest of the chapter. They have been set apart for several reasons. First, they are in reality a small book within a book. While these sections contain important material, the book stands on its own without them. You may, therefore, decide to cover the software engineering sections as formal lecture topics or informally while the chapter material is being covered. You may decide to assign them to the student as additional reading, or, you may decide to exclude them entirely from the course.

In all but two chapters, software engineering sections directly or indirectly pertain to the chapter material. In Chapter 9 ("Pointers") the software engineering section covers an important general topic—software quality. The software engineering section for Chapter 15 develops a system design case study that builds a structure chart.

PEDAGOGICAL MATERIAL

End chapter material meets two pedagogical objectives: first, it helps the students to review or summarize what they have learned, and second, it tests the students' mastery of the chapter material.

REVIEW MATERIAL

Tips and Common Programming Errors points out helpful hints and possible problem areas.

Key Terms provides a list of the important terms introduced in the chapter.

Summary contains a concise overview of the key points for students to understand in the chapter.

PRACTICE SETS

Review Questions contain several multiple choice questions that are similar to the questions found in the examination data base. The answers to the odd numbered questions are included in the solutions at the back of the book.

Exercises are short questions covering the material in the chapter. The answers to the odd-numbered exercises are also included in the solutions at the back of the book.

Problems are short coding problems, generally intended to be run on a computer. They can usually be developed in two to three hours.

Projects are longer, major assignments that may take the average student six to nine hours to develop.

The Instructor's solutions manual contains a complete set of solutions to all review questions, exercises and problems.

APPENDIXES AND COVER MATERIAL

The appendixes are intended to provide quick reference material, such as the ANSI Character Set, or a review of material, such as numbering systems, usually covered in a general computer class. An appendix is also included that discusses the standards and guidelines used throughout the book. The inside covers contain two important figures that are used continually throughout the course—the Precedence Table and the Formatted I/O Codes.

CHANGES IN THE SECOND EDITION

We have made some changes based on reader input and our experiences with the first edition. The more important changes are summarized here.

- Basic C expression concepts in Chapter 3 have been simplified and clarified.
- All programs were reviewed and run on at least two compilers, including Microsoft's Visual C.

- New programming examples were added to selected chapters.
- New exercises, projects, and problems were added to end material of selected chapters.
- New section entitled "Review Questions" was added at the end of each chapter.
- New online Powerpoint transparencies are available at **www.brookscole.com/compsci/forouzan/c2**
- Linked lists (Chapter 14) have been extensively revised to provide a more simplified and logical introduction.
- Chapter 15 has been extensively rewritten and retitled "Bitwise Operators." The other first edition material from this chapter has moved to appendices.
- Three new appendices have been added:
  - Appendix I—Command-Line Arguments
  - Appendix J—Pointers to Functions
  - Appendix K—Storage Classes and Type Qualifiers
- The index has been rebuilt to include additional terms and appendix materials.
- All identified errata have been incorporated.

ACKNOWLEDGMENTS

No book of this scope can be developed without the support of many people. This is especially true for this text which was "field tested" for two years by our students at De Anza College. Our first acknowledgment, therefore, has to be to the hundreds of students who by using the text and commenting on it made a vital contribution. In addition to the students who contributed so much to the first edition, Madeline Damiano, Sophia Fegan, Shouli Tiechman, and Tomo Nagai, we would like to acknowledge the support of Scott DeMouthe who worked so diligently to re-read the text and verify the solutions to all of the problems. We would also like to acknowledge the support of the De Anza staff for their continuing encouragement and their insightful comments.

To anyone who has not been through the process, the value of peer reviews cannot be appreciated enough. Writing a text rapidly becomes a myopic process. The important guidance of reviewers who can stand back and review the text as a whole cannot be measured. To twist an old cliche, "They are not valuable, they are priceless." We would especially like to acknowledge the contributions of the reviewers of this second edition including: Mary Astone, *Troy State University*; Henry Gordon, *Kutztown University*; Kara Nance, *University of Alaska—Fairbanks*; Ali Nikzad, *Huston-Tillotson College*; and K.C. Wong, *Fayetteville State University*.

We gratefully acknowledge the initial work done by the reviewers of the first edition, including:

Stephen Allen, *Utah State University*
Ali Behforooz, *Towson State University*
George Berry, *Wentworth Institute of Technology*
Ernest Carey, *Utah Valley State College*
Constance Conner, *City College of San Francisco*
John S. DaPonte, *Southern Connecticut State University*
Maurice L. Eggen, *Trinity University*
Peter Gabrovsky, *CSU Northridge*

Robert Gann, *Hartwick College*
Rick Graziani, *Cabrillo College*
Jerzy Jaromczyk, *University of Kentucky*
John Kinio, *Humber College*
Roberta Klibaner, *College of Staten Island*
Joseph A. Konstan, *University of Minnesota*
Krishna Kulkarni, *Rust College*
John Lowther, *Michigan Technological University*
Mike Michaelson, *Palomar College*
Jo Ann Parikh, *Southern Connecticut State University*
Mark Parker, *Shoreline Community College*
Oskar Reiksts, *Kutztown University*
Jim Roberts, *Carnegie Mellon University*
Ali Salenia, *South Dakota State University*
Larry Sells, *Oklahoma City University*
Shashi Shekhar, *University of Minnesota*
Robert Signorile, *Boston College*
Brenda Sonderegger, *Montana State University*
Deborah Sturm, *College of Staten Island*
Venkat Subramanian, *University of Houston*
John B. Tappen, *University of Southern Colorado*
Marc Thomasm, *California State University, Bakersfield*
John Trono, *St. Michael's College*

Two key people in the development of any text are its acquisition and production editors. Our thanks to our editors, Kallie Swanson and Mary Vezilich, for helping us produce the best book possible. We would also like to thank the staff at Carlisle Publishers Services, especially Kelli Jauron, who ably guided the book through production.

Last, and most obviously not the least, is the support of our families and friends. Many years ago an author described writing a text as a "locking yourself in a room" process. While the authors suffer through the writing process, families and friends suffer through their absence. We can only hope that as they view the final product, they feel that their sacrifices were worth it.

Behrouz A. Forouzan
Richard F. Gilberg

Contents

Introduction to Computers 1

Welcome to computer science! You are about to explore a wonderful and exciting world—a world that offers many challenging and exciting careers.

You should be aware that computer jobs demand a lot from you. If you want to succeed in the computing field, you must be a planner: someone who can work precisely with an often overwhelming amount of detail and, at the same time, who can see and understand the environment in which he or she works.

In this chapter, we introduce you to the concepts of computer science, especially as they pertain to computer programming. You will study the concept of a computer system and how it relates to computer hardware and software. We will also present a short history of computer programming languages so that you understand how they have evolved and how C fits into the picture.

We will then describe how to write a program, first with a review of the tools and steps involved, and then with a review of a system development methodology.

1-1   COMPUTER SYSTEMS

Today computer systems are found everywhere. Computers have become almost as common as televisions. But what is a computer? A computer is a system made of two major components: hardware and software. The computer hardware is the physical equipment. The software is the collection of programs (instructions) that allow the hardware to do its job. Figure 1-1 represents a **computer system**.

Figure 1-1   A computer system

1-2   COMPUTER HARDWARE

The **hardware** component of the computer system contains five parts: input devices; central processing unit (CPU); primary storage, or main memory; output devices; and auxiliary storage devices (Figure 1-2).

Figure 1-2   Basic hardware components

The **input device** is usually a keyboard where programs and data are entered into the computer. Examples of other input devices include a mouse, a pen or stylus, a touch screen, or an audio input unit.

The **central processing unit (CPU)** is responsible for executing instructions such as arithmetic calculations, comparisons among data, and movement of data inside the system. **Primary storage**, also known as **main memory**, is a place where the programs and data are stored temporarily during processing. The data in primary storage are erased when you turn off a personal computer or when you log off from a time-sharing computer.

The **output device** is usually a monitor or a printer to show output. If the output is shown on the monitor, we say we have a **soft copy**. If it is printed on the printer, we say we have a **hard copy**.

Auxiliary storage, or **secondary storage**, is used for both input and output. It is the place where the programs and data are stored permanently. When you turn off the computer, your programs and data remain in the secondary storage ready for the next time you need them.

1-3 COMPUTER SOFTWARE

Computer **software** is divided into two broad categories: system software and application software. This is true regardless of the hardware system architecture. System software manages the computer resources. It provides the interface between the hardware and the users but does nothing to directly serve the users' needs. Application software, on the other hand, is directly responsible for helping users solve their problems. Figure 1-3 shows this breakdown of computer software.

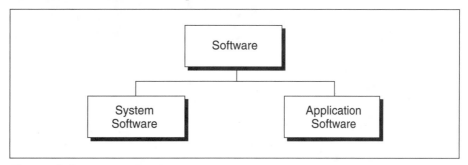

Figure 1-3 Types of software

SYSTEM SOFTWARE

System software consists of programs that manage the hardware resources of a computer and perform required information processing tasks. These programs are divided into three classes: the operating system, system support, and system development.

The **operating system** provides services such as a user interface, file and database access, and interfaces to communication systems such as Internet protocols. The primary purpose of this software is to keep the system operating in an efficient manner while allowing the users access to the system.

System support software provides system utilities and other operating services. Examples of system utilities are sort programs and disk format programs. Operating services consist of programs that provide performance statistics for the operational staff and security monitors to protect the system and data.

The last system software category, **system development software**, includes the language translators that convert programs into machine language for execution, debugging tools to ensure that the programs are error-free, and computer-assisted software engineering (CASE) systems that are beyond the scope of this book.

APPLICATION SOFTWARE

Application software is broken into two classes: general-purpose software and application-specific software. **General-purpose software** is purchased from a software developer and can be used for more than one application. Examples of general-purpose software include word processors, database management systems, and computer-aided design systems. They are called general purpose because they can solve a variety of user computing problems.

Application-specific software can be used only for its intended purpose. A general ledger system used by accountants and a material requirements planning system used by a manufacturing organization are examples of application-specific software. They can be used only for the task they were designed for; they cannot be used for other generalized tasks.

The relationship between system and application software is seen in Figure 1-4. In this figure, each circle represents an interface point. The inner core is the hardware. The user is represented by the outer layer. To work with the system, the typical user uses some form of application software. The application software in turn interacts with the operating system, which is a part of the system software layer. The system software provides the direct interaction with the hardware. Note the opening at the bottom of the figure. This is the path followed by the user who interacts directly with the operating system whenever necessary.

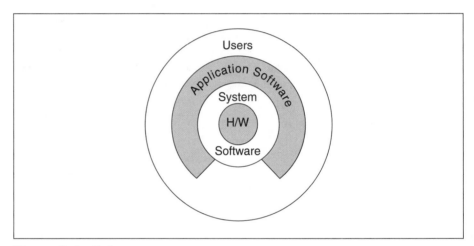

Figure 1-4   Software

If users cannot buy software that supports their needs, then a custom-developed application must be built. In today's computing environment, one of the tools used to develop software is the C language that you will be studying in this text.

1-4   COMPUTING ENVIRONMENTS

PERSONAL COMPUTING ENVIRONMENT

In 1971, Marcian E. Hoff, working for Intel, combined the basic elements of the central processing unit into the microprocessor. This first computer on a chip was the Intel 4004 and was the great-great-great grandparent of Intel's Pentium system.

If you are using a personal computer, all of the computer hardware components are tied together in your **personal computer** (or **PC** for short). In this situation, you have the whole computer for yourself; you can do whatever you want to do. A typical personal computer is shown in Figure 1-5.

TIME-SHARING ENVIRONMENT

Employees in large companies often work in what is known as a **time-sharing environment**. In the time-sharing environment, many users are connected to one or more computers.

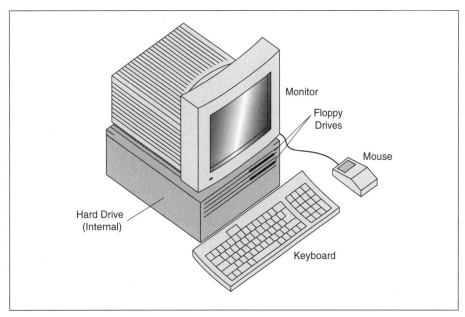

Figure 1-5 Personal computing environment

These computers may be minicomputers or central mainframes. The terminals they use are often nonprogrammable, although today we see more and more microcomputers being used to simulate terminals. Also, in the time-sharing environment, the output devices (such as printers) and auxiliary storage devices (such as disks) are shared by all of the users. A typical college lab in which a minicomputer is shared by many students is shown in Figure 1-6.

Figure 1-6 Time-sharing environment

In the time-sharing environment, all computing must be done by the central computer. In other words, the central computer has many duties: It must control the shared resources; it must manage the shared data and printing; and, it must also do the computing. All of this work tends to keep the computer busy. In fact, it is sometimes so busy that the user becomes frustrated by the computer's slow responses.

CLIENT/SERVER ENVIRONMENT

A **client/server** computing environment splits the computing function between a central computer and users' computers. The users are given personal computers or workstations so that some of the computation responsibility can be moved from the central computer and assigned to the workstations. In the client/server environment, the users' microcomputers or workstations are called the **client**. The central computer, which may be a powerful microcomputer, minicomputer, or central mainframe system, is known as the **server**. Because the work is now shared between the users' computers and the central computer, response time and monitor display are faster and the users are more productive. Figure 1-7 shows a typical client/server environment.

Figure 1-7 The client/server environment

1-5 COMPUTER LANGUAGES

To write a program for a computer, you must use a **computer language**. Over the years computer languages have evolved from machine language to natural languages. A summary of computer languages is seen in Figure 1-8.

MACHINE LANGUAGES

In the earliest days of computers, the only programming languages available were machine languages. Each computer has its own **machine language**, which is made of streams of 0s and 1s. Program 1-1 shows an example of a machine language. This program multiplies two numbers and prints the results.

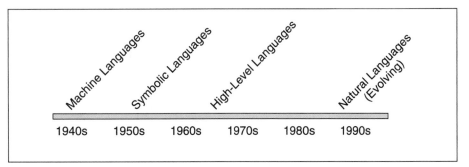

Figure 1-8 Computer language evolution

1		00000000	00000100	0000000000000000
2	01011110	00001100	11000010	0000000000000010
3		11101111	00010110	0000000000000101
4		11101111	10011110	0000000000001011
5	11111000	10101101	11011111	0000000000010010
6		01100010	11011111	0000000000010101
7	11101111	00000010	11111011	0000000000010111
8	11110100	10101101	11011111	0000000000011110
9	00000011	10100010	11011111	0000000000100001
10	11101111	00000010	11111011	0000000000100100
11	01111110	11110100	10101101	
12	11111000	10101110	11000101	0000000000101011
13	00000110	10100010	11111011	0000000000110001
14	11101111	00000010	11111011	0000000000110100
15		01010000	11010100	0000000000111011
16			00000100	0000000000111101

Program 1-1 The multiplication program in machine language

The instructions in machine language must be in streams of 0s and 1s because the internal circuits of a computer are made of switches, transistors, and other electronic devices that can be in one of two states: off or on. The off state is represented by 0; the on state is represented by 1.

> The only language understood by a computer is machine language.

SYMBOLIC LANGUAGES

It became obvious that not many programs would be written if programmers continued to work in machine language. In the early 1950s, Grace Hopper, a mathematician and U.S. Navy admiral, developed the concept of a special computer program that would convert programs into machine language. These early programming languages simply mirrored the machine languages using symbols, or mnemonics, to represent the various machine language instructions. Because they used symbols, these languages were known as **symbolic languages**. Program 1-2 shows the multiplication program in a symbolic language.

Because a computer does not understand symbolic language, it must be translated to the machine language. A special program called an assembler translates symbolic code into machine language. Because symbolic languages had to be assembled into machine language, they soon became known as **assembly languages**. This name is

```
 1       entry    main,^m<r2>
 2       subl2    #12,sp
 3       jsb      C$MAIN_ARGS
 4       movab    $CHAR_STRING_CON
 5
 6       pushal   -8(fp)
 7       pushal   (r2)
 8       calls    #2,SCANF
 9       pushal   -12(fp)
10       pushal   3(r2)
11       calls    #2,SCANF
12       mull3    -8(fp),-12(fp),-
13       pusha    6(r2)
14       calls    #2,PRINTF
15       clrl     r0
16       ret
```

Program 1-2 The multiplication program in a symbolic language

still used today for symbolic languages that closely represent the machine language of their computer.

HIGH-LEVEL LANGUAGES

Although symbolic languages greatly improved programming efficiency, they still required programmers to concentrate on the hardware that they were using. Working with symbolic languages was also very tedious because each machine instruction had to be individually coded. The desire to improve programmer efficiency and to change the focus from the computer to the problem being solved led to the development of **high-level languages**.

High-level languages are portable to many different computers, allowing the programmer to concentrate on the application problem at hand rather than the intricacies of the computer. High-level languages are designed to relieve the programmer from the details of the assembly language. High-level languages share one thing with symbolic languages: They must be converted to machine language. The process of converting them is known as **compilation**.

The first widely used high-level language, FORTRAN,[1] was created by John Backus and an IBM team in 1957; it is still widely used today in scientific and engineering applications. Following soon after FORTRAN was COBOL.[2] Admiral Hopper was again a key figure in the development of the COBOL business language.

Today, one of the most popular high-level languages for system software and new application code is C. Program 1-3 shows the multiplication program as it would appear in the C language.

```
 1   /* This program reads two integer numbers from the
 2       keyboard and prints their product.
 3         Written by:
```

Program 1-3 The multiplication program in C

---

[1]FORTRAN is an acronym for FORmula TRANslation.

[2]COBOL is an acronym for COmmon Business-Oriented Language.

```
 4        Date:
 5  */
 6  #include <stdio.h>
 7
 8  int main (void)
 9  {
10  /* Local Definitions */
11      int number1;
12      int number2;
13      int result;
14
15  /* Statements */
16      scanf   ("%d", &number1);
17      scanf   ("%d", &number2);
18      result = number1 * number2;
19      printf ("%d", result);
20      return 0;
21  }  /* main */
```

Program 1-3 The multiplication program in C (continued)

NATURAL LANGUAGES

Ideally, we could use our **natural language** (such as English, French, or Chinese) and the computer would understand it and execute our requests immediately. Although this may sound like something out of science fiction, considerable work on natural language is being done in labs today. So far, its use in industry is still quite limited.

1-6 WRITING, EDITING, COMPILING, AND LINKING PROGRAMS

As we learned in the previous section, a computer understands a program only if the program is coded in its machine language. In this section, we explain the procedure for turning a program written in C into machine language. The process is presented in a straightforward, linear fashion, but you should recognize that these steps are repeated many times during development to correct errors and make improvements to the code.

It is the job of the programmer to write the program and then to turn it into an **executable** (machine language) **file**. There are three steps in this process: (1) writing and editing the program, (2) compiling the program, and (3) linking the program with the required library modules. These steps are seen in Figure 1-9.

STEP 1: WRITING AND EDITING PROGRAMS

The software used to write programs is known as a **text editor**. A text editor helps you enter, change, and store character data. Depending on the editor on your system, you could use it to write letters, create reports, or write programs. The main difference between text processing and program writing is that programs are written using lines of code, while most text processing is done with characters and lines.

Your text editor could be a generalized word processor, but it is more often a special editor provided by the same company that supplies your compiler. Some of the features you

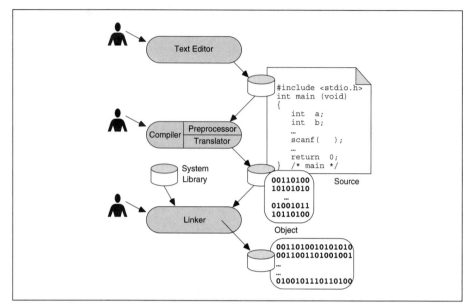

Figure 1-9   Building a C program

should look for in your editor are search commands to locate and replace statements, copy and paste commands to copy or move statements from one part of your program to another, and formatting commands that allow you to set tabs to align statements.

After you complete a program, you save your file to disk. This file will be input to the compiler; it is known as a **source file**.

STEP 2: COMPILING PROGRAMS

The code in a source file stored on the disk must be translated into machine language. This is the job of the **compiler**. The C compiler is actually two separate programs: the **preprocessor** and the **translator**.

The preprocessor reads the source code and prepares it for the translator. While preparing the code, it scans for special commands known as **preprocessor directives**. These directives tell the preprocessor to look for special code libraries, make substitutions in the code, and in other ways prepare the code for translation into machine language. The result of preprocessing is called the **translation unit**.

After the preprocessor has prepared the code for compilation, the translator does the actual work of converting your program into machine language. The translator reads the translation unit and writes the resulting **object module** to a file that can then be combined with other precompiled units to form the final program. An object module is the code in machine language. Even though the output of the compiler is machine language code, it is not yet ready to run; that is, it is not yet executable, because it does not have the required C and other functions included.

STEP 3: LINKING PROGRAMS

As we will see later, a C program is made up of many functions. Some of these functions are written by you and are a part of your source program. However, there are other functions, such as input/output processes and mathematical library functions, that exist elsewhere and must be attached to your program. The **linker** assembles all of these functions, yours and the system's, into your final executable program.

1-7 PROGRAM EXECUTION

Once your program has been linked, it is ready for execution. To execute your program, use an operating system command, such as run, to load your program into primary memory and execute it. Getting the program into memory is the function of an operating system program known as the **loader**. It locates the executable program and reads it into memory. When everything is loaded, the program takes control and it begins execution.

In a typical program execution, the program reads data for processing, either from the user or from a file. After the program processes the data, it prepares the output. Data output can be to the user's monitor or to a file. When the program has finished its job, it tells the operating system, which then removes the program from memory. A program execution in a personal computer environment is seen in Figure 1-10.

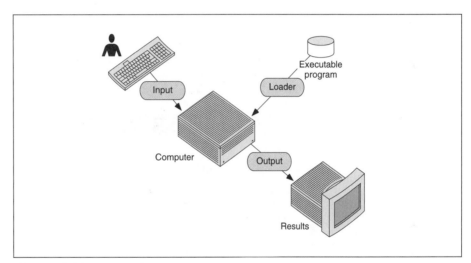

Figure 1-10 Executing programs

1-8 SYSTEM DEVELOPMENT

We've now seen the steps that are necessary to build your program. In this section, we discuss *how* you go about developing a program. This critical process determines the overall quality and success of your program. If you carefully design each program using good structured development techniques, your programs will be efficient, error-free,[3] and easy to maintain.

---

[3]Many computer scientists believe that all programs contain at least one *bug* that is just waiting to cause problems, given the right set of circumstances. Programs have run for years without problems only to fail when an unusual situation occurs. Perhaps the most famous bug is the one known as Y2K because it can't handle programs run after January 1, 2000.

SYSTEM DEVELOPMENT LIFE CYCLE

Today's large-scale, modern programming projects are built using a series of interrelated phases commonly referred to as the **system development life cycle**. Although the exact number and names of the phases differ depending on the environment, there is general agreement as to the steps that must be followed. Whatever the methodology, however, today's software engineering concepts require a rigorous and systematic approach to software development.[4]

One very popular development life cycle is the *waterfall model*. Depending on the company and the type of software being developed, this model consists of between five and seven phases. Figure 1-11 is one possible variation on the model.

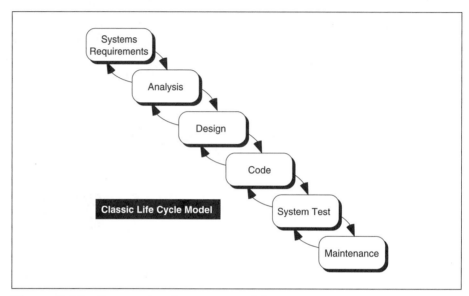

Figure 1-11 System development model

The waterfall model starts with *systems requirements*. In this phase, the systems analyst defines requirements that specify what the proposed system is to accomplish. The requirements are usually stated in terms that the user understands. The *analysis* phase looks at different alternatives from a systems point of view, while the *design* phase determines how the system will be built. In the design phase, the functions of the individual programs that will make up the system are determined and the design of the files and/or the databases is completed. Finally, in the fourth phase, *code*, we write the programs. This is the phase that is explained in this book. After the programs have been written and tested to the programmer's satisfaction, the project proceeds to *system test*. All of the programs are tested together to make sure the system works as a whole. The final phase, *maintenance*, keeps the system working once it has been put into production.

Although the implication of the waterfall approach is that the phases flow in a continuous stream from the first to the last, this is not really the case. Note the iteration as indicated by the backward-flowing arrows in Figure 1-11. As each phase is developed, errors and omissions will often be found in the previous work. When this happens, it is necessary to go back to the previous phase to rework it for consistency and to analyze the impact caused by the changes. Hopefully, this is a short rework. We are aware of at least three major projects, however, that were in the code and test

---

[4]For a discussion of various models, see *Software Engineering: A Practitioner's Approach,* 2nd ed. by Roger S. Pressman, (New York, NY: McGraw-Hill, 1982).

phases when it was determined that they could not be implemented and had to be canceled. When this happens, millions of dollars and years of development are lost.

PROGRAM DEVELOPMENT

Program Development is a multi step process that requires you to understand the problem, develop a solution, write the program, and then test it. When you are given the assignment to develop a program, you will be given a program requirements statement and the design of any program interfaces. You should also receive an overview of the complete project so that you will understand how your part fits into the whole. Your job is to determine how to take the inputs you are given and convert them into the outputs that have been specified. This is known as *program design*. To give you an idea of how this process works, let's look at a simple problem.

```
Calculate the square footage of your house.
```

How do you go about doing this?

Understand the Problem

The first step in solving any problem is to understand it. Begin by reading the requirements statement carefully. When you think that you fully understand it, review your understanding with the user and the systems analyst. Often this involves asking questions to confirm your understanding.

For example, after reading our simple requirements statement, you should ask several clarifying questions.

```
What is the definition of square footage?
How is the square footage going to be used?
• for insurance purposes?
• to paint the inside or outside of the house?
• to carpet the whole house?
Is the garage included?
Are closets and hallways included?
```

Each of these potential uses requires a different measure. If you don't clarify the exact purpose—that is, if you make assumptions about how the output is going to be used—you could supply the wrong answer.

As this example shows, even the simplest problem statements need clarification. Imagine how many questions must be asked for a programmer to write a program that will contain hundreds or thousands of detailed statements.

Develop the Solution

Once you fully understand the problem and have clarified any questions you may have, you need to develop your solution. Three tools will help you in this task: (1) structure charts, (2) pseudocode, and (3) flowcharts. Generally you will use only two of them—a structure chart and either pseudocode or a flowchart.

The structure chart is used to design the whole program. Pseudocode and flowcharts, on the other hand, are used to design the individual parts of the program. These parts are known as modules in pseudocode or functions in the C language.

Structure Chart A **structure chart**, also known as a hierarchy chart, shows the functional flow through your program. Large programs are complex structures consisting of many interrelated parts; thus, they must be carefully laid out. This task is similar to that of a design engineer who is responsible for the operational design of any complex item. The major difference between the design built by a programmer and the design built by an engineer is that the programmer's product is software that exists only inside the computer, whereas the engineer's product is something that can be seen and touched.

The structure chart shows how you are going to break your program into logical steps; each step will be a separate module. The structure chart shows the interaction between all the parts (modules) of your program.

It is important to realize that the design, as represented by the structure chart, is done before you write your program. In this respect, it is like the architect's blueprint. You would not start to build a house without a detailed set of plans. Yet one of the most common errors of both experienced and new programmers alike is to start coding a program before the design is complete and fully documented.

This rush to start is due in part to programmers' thinking they fully understand the problem and also due to their excitement about solving a new problem. In the first case, what they find is that they did not fully understand the problem. By taking the time to design the program, they will raise more questions that must be answered and therefore will gain a better understanding of the problem.

> An old programming proverb:
> Resist the temptation to code.

The second reason programmers code before completing the design is just human nature. Programming is a tremendously exciting task. To see your design begin to take shape, to see your program creation working for the first time, brings a form of personal satisfaction that is a natural high.

In the business world, when you complete a structure chart design, you will convene a review panel for a *structured walk-through* of your program. Such a panel usually consists of a representative from the user community, one or two peer programmers, the system analyst, and possibly a representative from the testing organization. In the review, you will walk your review team through your structure chart to show how you plan to solve the objectives of your program. The team will then offer constructive suggestions as to how to improve your design.

The primary intent of the review is to increase quality and save time. The earlier a mistake is detected, the easier it is to fix it. If you can eliminate only one or two problems with the structured walk-through, the time will be well spent. Naturally, in a programming class, you will not be able to convene a full panel and conduct a formal walk-through. What you can do, however, is review your design with some of your classmates and with your professor.

Looking again at our problem to calculate the square footage of a house, let's assume the following answers to the questions raised in the previous section.

1. The purpose of calculating the square footage is to install new floor covering.
2. Only the living space will be carpeted. The garage and closets will not be considered.
3. The kitchen and bathrooms will be covered with linoleum; the rest of the house is to be carpeted.

With this understanding, we decide to write separate modules for the kitchen, bathroom(s), bedrooms, family room, and living room. We use separate modules because the various rooms may require a different quality of linoleum and carpeting. The structure chart for our design is shown in Figure 1-12.

Whether you use a flowchart or pseudocode to complete the design of your program will depend on your experience, the difficulty of the process you are designing, and the culture and standards of the organization where you are working. We believe that new programmers should first learn program design by flowcharting because a flowchart is a visual tool that is easier to create than pseudocode. On the other hand, pseudocode is more common among professional programmers.

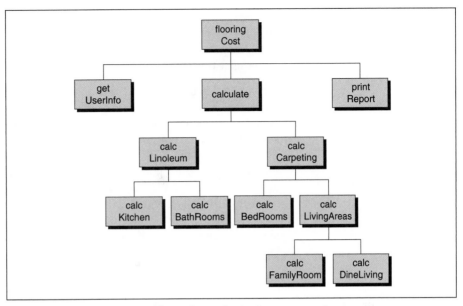

Figure 1-12   Structure chart for calculating square footage

Pseudocode   **Pseudocode** is part English, part program logic. Its purpose is to describe, in precise algorithmic detail, what the program being designed is to do. This requires defining the steps to accomplish the task in sufficient detail so that they can be converted into a computer program. Pseudocode excels at this type of precise logic. The pseudocode for determining the linoleum for the bathroom is shown in Program 1-4.

Pseudocode

English-like statements that follow a loosely defined syntax and are used to convey the design of an algorithm.

```
Algorithm Calculate BathRooms
1 prompt user and read linoleum price
2 prompt user and read number of bathrooms
3 set total bath area and baths processed to zero
4 while ( baths processed < number of bathrooms )
   1 prompt user and read bath length and width
   2 total bath area =
        total bath area + bath length * bath width
   3 add 1 to baths processed
5 bath cost = total bath area * linoleum price
6 return bath cost
end Algorithm Calculate BathRooms
```

Program 1-4   Pseudocode for `calcBathrooms`

Most of the statements in the pseudocode are easy to understand. A prompt is simply a displayed message telling the user what data are to be entered. The *while* is a loop that repeats the three statements that follow it and uses the number of bathrooms read in statement 2 to tell when to stop. Looping is a programming concept that allows you to repeat a block of code. We will study it in Chapter 6. In this case, it allows us to process the information for one or more bathrooms.

Flowchart   A **flowchart** is a program design tool in which standard graphical symbols are used to represent the logical flow of data through a function. Appendix C contains complete instructions for creating flowcharts. If you are not familiar with flowcharts, we suggest you read it now.

The flowchart in Figure 1-13 shows the design for obtaining the area and cost for the bathrooms. A few points merit comment here. This flowchart is basically the same as the pseudocode. We begin with prompts for the price of the linoleum and the number of bathrooms and read these two pieces of data. (As a general rule, flowcharts do not explicitly show standard concepts such as prompts.) The loop reads the dimensions for each bathroom. Finally, when we know the total area, we calculate the price and return to `calcLinoleum`.

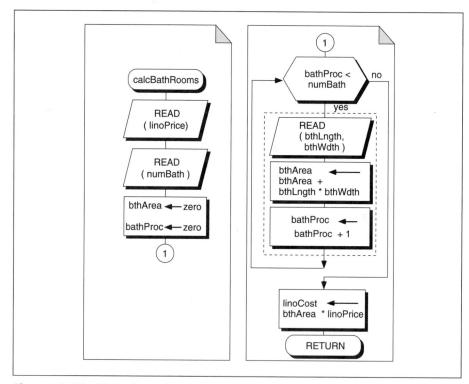

Figure 1-13   Flowchart for `calcBathRooms`

Write the Program   Now it's time to write the program! But first, let's review the steps that we've used.

1. Understand the problem.
2. Develop a solution.
    a. Design the program—create the structure chart.
    b. Design the algorithms for the program using either flowcharting or pseudocode or both.
3. Write the program.

When you write a program, you start with the top box on the structure chart and work your way to the bottom. This is known as top–down implementation. You will find that it is a very easy and natural way to write programs, especially if you have done a solid job on your design.

For your first few programs, there will be only one module, representing the top box of the structure chart. The first programs are quite simple and do not require subdivision. When we get to Chapter 4, however, you will begin to write functions and your structure charts will get larger. At that time we will point out some more techniques for writing structured programs. In the meantime, concentrate on writing good pseudocode or flowcharts for the main part of your programs.

Test the Program

After you've written your program, you must test it. Program testing can be a very tedious and time-consuming part of program development. As the programmer, you are responsible for completely testing your program. In large development projects, there are often specialists known as test engineers who are responsible for testing the system as a whole—that is, for testing to make sure all the programs work together.

There are two types of testing, blackbox and whitebox. Blackbox testing is done by the system test engineer and the user. Whitebox testing is the responsibility of the programmer.

Blackbox Testing

Blackbox testing gets its name from the concept of testing the program without knowing what is inside it—without knowing how it works. In other words, the program is like a black box that you can't see into.

Blackbox test plans are developed by looking only at the requirements statement (this is only one reason why it is so important to have a good set of requirements). The test engineer uses these requirements and his or her knowledge of systems development and the user working environment to create a test plan that will then be used when the system is tested as a whole. You should ask to see this test plan before you write your program. The test engineer's plan will help you make sure you fully understand the requirements and also help you create your own test plan.

Whitebox Testing

Whereas blackbox testing assumes that the tester knows nothing about the program, **whitebox testing** assumes that the tester knows everything about the program. In this case, the program is like a glass house in which everything is visible.

Whitebox testing is your responsibility. As the programmer, you know exactly what is going on inside the program. You must make sure that every instruction and every possible situation have been tested. That is not a simple task!

Experience will help you design good test data, but one thing you can do from the start is to get in the habit of writing test plans. Start your test plan when you are in the design stage. As you build your structure chart, ask yourself what situations, especially unusual situations, you need to test for and make a note of them immediately because you won't remember them an hour later.

When you are writing your flowcharts or pseudocode, review them with an eye toward test cases and make additional notes of the cases you need. Finally, while you are coding, keep paper handy (or a test document open in your word processor) to make notes about test cases you need.

> Except for the most simple program, one set of test data
> will not completely validate a program.

When it is time to construct your test cases, review your notes and organize them into logical sets. Except for very simple student programs, one set of test data will never completely validate a program. For large-scale development projects, 20, 30, or even more test cases may need to be run to validate a program.

Finally, while you are testing, you will think of more test cases. Again, write them down and incorporate them into your test plan. After your program is finished and in production, you will need the test plan again when you make modifications to the program.

How do you know when your program is completely tested? In reality, there is no way to know for sure. But there are a few things you can do to help the odds. While some of these concepts will not be clear until you have read other chapters, we include them here for completeness.

1. Verify that every line of code has been executed at least once. Fortunately, there are programming tools on the market today that will do this for you.

2. Verify that every conditional statement in your program has executed both the true and false branches, even if one of them is null. (See Chapter 5.)

3. For every condition that has a range, make sure the tests include the first and last items in the range, as well as items below the first and above the last. For example, the most common mistakes in array range tests occur at the extremes of the range. (See Chapter 8.)

4. If error conditions are being checked, make sure all error logic is tested. This may require you to make temporary modifications to your program to force the errors (for instance, an input/output error usually cannot be created—it must be simulated).

1-9 SOFTWARE ENGINEERING AND PROGRAMMING STYLE

Software engineering is the establishment and use of sound engineering methods and principles to obtain software that is reliable and that works on real machines.[5] This definition, from the first international conference on software engineering in 1969, was proposed 30 years after the first computer was built. During that period, software was more of an art than a science. In fact, one of the most authoritative treatments of programming describes it as an art: *The Art of Computer Programming*. This three-volume series, originally written by Donald E. Knuth in the late 1960s and early 1970s,[6] is considered the most complete discussion of many computer science concepts.

The computing field is relatively young. It took time and study to begin to formulate concepts that would make reliable and efficient software. To understand the background of structured programming, it is necessary to understand some of the history of computing.

Because the science and engineering base for building reliable software did not yet exist, programs written in the 1950s and 1960s were a maze of complexity known as "spaghetti code." It was not until Edsger Dijkstra wrote a letter to the editor of the *Communications of the ACM* (Association of Computing Machinery)[7] in 1968 that the concept of structured programming began to emerge.

Dijkstra was working to develop algorithms that would mathematically prove program accuracy. He proposed that any program could be written with only three constructs or types of instructions: (1) sequences, (2) the *if . . . else* selection statement, and (3) the *while* loop. As we will see, language developers have added constructs, such as the *for* loop and the *switch* in C. These additional statements are simply enhancements to Dijkstra's basic constructs that make programming easier. Today, virtually all programming languages offer structured programming capabilities. Some older languages, such as FORTRAN, COBOL, and BASIC, have even been reworked to include structured programming capabilities.

Throughout this text we will be emphasizing the concepts of good software engineering. Chief among them is the concept of structured programming and a sound programming style. A section in each chapter will include a discussion of these concepts with specific emphasis on the application of the material in the chapter.

The tools of programming design have also changed over the years. In the first generation of programming, one primary tool was a block diagram. This tool provided boxes, diamonds, and other flowchart symbols to represent different instructions in a program. Each instruction was contained in a separate symbol. This concept allowed programmers to write a program on paper and check its logic flow before they entered it in the computer.

---

[5]F. L Bauer, Technical University, Munich, Germany (1969).

[6]Donald E. Knuth, *The Art of Computer Programming*, vols. 1, 2, 3d ed. (Reading, Mass.: Addison-Wesley, 1977); vol. 3, 2d ed. (1998).

[7]Edsger W. Dijkstra, "Goto Statement Considered Harmful," *Communications of the ACM* 11, no. 3 (March 1968).

With the advance of symbolic programming, the block diagram gave way to the flowchart. Although the block diagram and flowchart look similar, the flowchart does not contain the detail of the block diagram. Many instructions are implied by the descriptive names put into the boxes; for example, the read statements in "Flowchart for calcBathRooms" in Figure 1-13 (page 16) imply the prompt. Flowcharts have largely given way to other techniques in program design, but they are still used today by many programmers for working on a difficult logic problem.

Today's programmers are most likely to use a high-level design tool such as tight English or pseudocode. These design tools were made possible by the emergence of structured programming concepts. We will use pseudocode throughout the text to describe many of the algorithms we will be developing.

Finally, the last several years have seen the automation of programming through the use of computer-assisted software engineering (CASE) tools. These tools make it possible to determine requirements, design software, and develop and test software in an automated environment using programming workstations. Much work still needs to be done on CASE tools, but their use is firmly established in industry. The discussion of the CASE environment is beyond the scope of this text and is left for courses in systems engineering.

1-10   TIPS AND COMMON PROGRAMMING ERRORS

You will find this section at the end of each chapter. It lists some tips to help you program better and some common errors that you should try to avoid. Most of them will be specific to the C language, although some that apply to the algorithms or program design may apply to all languages. Not all of the errors we describe in this section will generate compiler syntax messages. We will indicate those that do. It is impossible to specify the exact error, however, for two reasons. First, there is no standard set of error messages used by all compilers. Second, the error message may vary depending on unrelated factors in your program.

1. Become familiar with the text editor in your system so you will be able to create and edit your programs efficiently. The time spent learning different techniques and shortcuts in a text editor will save time in the future.

2. Also, become familiar with the compiler commands and keyboard shortcuts. On most computers, a variety of options are available to be used with the compiler. Make yourself familiar with all of these options.

3. Read the compiler's error messages. Becoming familiar with the types of error messages and their meanings will be a big help as you learn C.

4. Remember to save and compile your program each time you make changes or corrections in your source file. When your program has been saved, you won't lose your changes if a program error causes the system to fail during testing.

5. Run your program many times with different sets of data to be sure it does what you want.

6. The most common programming error is not following the old proverb to "resist the urge to code." Make sure you understand the requirements and take the time to design a solution before you start writing code.

1-11   KEY TERMS AND CONCEPTS

application software
application-specific software
assembly language
auxiliary storage
blackbox testing
central processing unit (CPU)
client
client/server
compilation
compiler
computer language
computer system
executable program
flowchart
general-purpose software
hard copy
hardware

high-level language
input device
linker
loader
machine language
main memory
natural language
object module
operating system
output device
personal computer (PC)
preprocessor
preprocessor directives
primary storage
program development
pseudocode

secondary storage
server
soft copy
software
source file
structure chart
symbolic language
system development life cycle
system development software
system software
system support software
text editor
time-sharing environment
translation unit
translator
whitebox testing

1-12   SUMMARY

■ A computer system consists of hardware and software.

■ Computer hardware consists of a central processing unit (CPU), primary memory, input devices, output devices, and auxiliary storage.

■ Software consists of two broad categories: system software and application software.

■ The primary components of system software are system management (operating system), system support, and system development.

■ Application software is divided into general purpose applications and application-specific software.

■ Over the years, programming languages have evolved from machine language, to symbolic language, and to high-level languages. Research is currently under way to develop the next generation of programming languages, the natural language.

■ The C language is considered to be a high-level language.

■ The system development life cycle is a series of interrelated steps that provide a rigorous and systematic approach to software development.

■ To develop a program, a programmer must complete the following steps:

   a. Understand the problem.

   b. Develop a solution using structure charts and either flowcharts or pseudocode.

   c. Write the program.

   d. Test the program.

■ The development of a test plan starts with the design of the program and continues through all steps in program development.

■ Blackbox testing consists primarily of testing based on user requirements.

■ Whitebox testing, executed by the programmer, tests the program with full knowledge of its operational weaknesses.

■ Testing is one of the most important parts of your programming task. You are responsible for whitebox testing; the systems analyst and user are responsible for blackbox testing.

■ Software engineering is the application of sound engineering methods and principles to the design and development of application programs.

1-13   PRACTICE SETS

REVIEW QUESTIONS

1. Computer software is divided into two broad categories: system software and operational software.
   a. True   b. False

2. The operating system provides services such as a user interface, file and database access, and interfaces to communications systems.
   a. True   b. False

3. The first step in system development is to create a source program.
   a. True   b. False

4. The programmer design tool used to design the whole program is the flowchart.
   a. True   b. False

5. Blackbox testing gets its name from the concept that the program is being tested without knowing how it works.
   a. True   b. False

6. Which of the following is a component(s) of a computer system?
   a. Hardware
   b. Software
   c. Both hardware and software
   d. Pseudocode
   e. System test

7. Which of the following is an example of application software?
   a. Database management system
   b. Language translator
   c. Operating system
   d. Sort
   e. Security monitor

8. Which of the following is not a computer language?
   a. Assembly/symbolic language
   b. Binary language
   c. High-level languages
   d. Machine language
   e. Natural language

9. The computer language that most closely resembles machine language is
   a. Assembly/symbolic   d. High-level
   b. COBOL   e. Natural
   c. FORTRAN

10. The tool used by a programmer to convert a source program to a machine language object module is a
    a. Compiler   d. Preprocessor
    b. Language translator   e. Text editor
    c. Linker

11. The _____ contains the programmer's original program code.
    a. Application file   d. Source file
    b. Executable file   e. Text file
    c. Object file

12. The series of interrelated phases that is used to develop computer software is known as
    a. Program development
    b. Software engineering
    c. System development life cycle
    d. System analysis
    e. System design

13. The _____ is a program design tool that is a visual representation of the logic in a function within a program.
    a. Flowchart   d. Structure chart
    b. Program map   e. Waterfall model
    c. Pseudocode

14. The test that validates a program by ensuring that all of its statements have been executed—that is, by knowing exactly how the program is written—is
    a. Blackbox testing   d. System testing
    b. Destructive testing   e. Whitebox testing
    c. Nondestructive testing

EXERCISES

15. Describe the two major components of a computer system.

16. Computer hardware is made up of five parts. List and describe them.

17. Describe the major differences between a time-sharing and a client/server environment.

18. Describe the two major categories of software.

19. What is the purpose of an operating system?

20. Identify at least two types of system software that you will use when you write programs.

21. Give at least one example of general-purpose and one example of application-specific software.

22. List the levels of computer languages discussed in the text.

23. What are the primary differences between symbolic and high-level languages?

24. What is the difference between a source program and an object module?

25. Describe the basic steps in the system development life cycle.

26. What documentation should a programmer receive to be able to write a program?

27. List and explain the steps that a programmer follows in writing a program.

28. Describe the three tools that a programmer may use to develop a program solution.

29. What is meant by the old programming proverb, "Resist the temptation to code"?

30. What is the difference between blackbox and white-box testing?

31. What is software engineering?

PROBLEMS

32. Write pseudocode for `calcLivingAreas`, Figure 1-12, "Structure Chart for Calculating Square Footage," on page 15.

33. Create a flowchart for a routine task, such as calling a friend, that you do on a regular basis.

34. Write pseudocode for the flowchart you created in Problem 33.

Introduction to the C Language

₂

In Chapter 1, we traced the evolution of computer languages from the original machine languages to the latest language concept, natural languages. As mentioned, **ANSI/ISO C** (the language used exclusively in this book) is a high-level language. Since you are going to spend considerable time working with the language, you should have some idea of its origins and evolution.

In this chapter we introduce the basics of the C language. You will write your first program, what is known traditionally in C as the "Hello World," or "Greeting" program. Along the way we will introduce you to the concepts of data types, constants, and variables. Finally, you will see two C functions that read and write data. Since this is just an introduction to C, most of these topics are covered only in sufficient detail to enable you to write your first program. They will be fully developed in future chapters.

2-1 BACKGROUND

C is a structured programming language which is one of the reasons that it is so popular. It is considered a high-level language because it allows the programmer to concentrate on the problem at hand and not worry about the machine that the program will be using. While many languages claim to be machine independent, C comes the closest to achieving that goal. That is another reason it is so popular, especially among software developers whose applications have to run on many different hardware platforms.

ANSI/ISO C, like most modern languages, is derived from ALGOL, the first language to use a block structure. ALGOL never gained wide acceptance in the United States, but it was widely used in Europe.

ALGOL's introduction in the early 1960s paved the way for the development of structured programming concepts. Some of the first work was done by two computer scientists, Corrado Bohm and Guiseppe Jacopini, who published a paper in 1966 that defined the concept of structured programming. Another computer scientist, Edsger Dijkstra, popularized the concept. His letter to the editors of the *Communications of the ACM* (Association of Computing Machinery) brought the structured programming concept to the attention of the computer science community.

Several obscure languages preceded the development of C. In 1967, Martin Richards developed a language he called Basic Combined Programming Language, or BCPL. Ken Thompson followed in 1970 with a similar language he simply called B. B was used to develop the first version of UNIX, one of the most popular network operating systems in use today and the heart of the Internet data superhighway. Finally, in 1972, Dennis Ritchie developed C, which took many concepts from ALGOL, BCPL, and B and added the concept of data types. This path, along with several others, is shown in Figure 2-1.

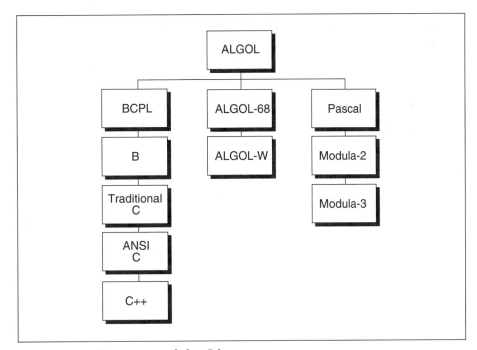

Figure 2-1   Taxonomy of the C language

What is known as traditional C is this 1972 version of the language, as documented and popularized in a 1978 book by Brian W. Kernighan and Dennis Ritchie.[1] In 1983, the American National Standards Institute (ANSI) began the definition of a standard for C. It was approved in December 1989. In 1990, the International Standards Organization (ISO) adopted the ANSI standard. We use the ANSI standard in this book. Every program in this text has been compiled and run on at least two, and in most cases three, different compilers.

The history of ANSI/ISO C is summarized in Table 2-1.

---

1. In 1960 a block-structured language emerged, which was called ALGOL (ALGOrithmic Language).

2. In 1967, Martin Richards invented BCPL (Basic Combined Programming Language), which was a typeless language. It permitted only one data object (the machine word).

3. In 1970, Ken Thompson invented the typeless system programming language B.

4. In 1972, working at Bell Laboratories, Dennis Ritchie designed C, a combination of BCPL and B but with data types.

5. In 1978, Brian Kernighan and Dennis Ritchie published the ad hoc standard for traditional C.

6. In 1989, the American National Standards Institute approved ANSI/ISO C.

7. In 1990, the ISO standard for C was approved.

Table 2-1   History of the C Language

2-2 C PROGRAMS

It's time to write your first C program! This section will take you through all the basic parts of a C program so that you will be able to write it.

STRUCTURE OF A C PROGRAM

Every C program is made of a global declaration section and one or more **functions**. The **global declaration section** comes at the beginning of the program. We will talk more about it later, but the basic idea of global declarations is that they are visible to all parts of the program. (The term *global* comes from the concept that your program is a little world. Anything that is global, therefore, pertains to the whole world—to the whole program.)

One, and only one, of the functions in the program must be named `main`. The `main` function is the starting point for the program. All functions in a program, including `main`, are divided into two sections, the definition section and the statement section. The **definition section** is at the beginning of the function. It describes the data that you will be using in the function. Definitions in a function are known as local definitions (as opposed to global definitions) because they are visible only to the function that contains them.

---

[1]Brian Kernighan and Dennis Ritchie, *The C Programming Language,* 2nd ed. (Englewood Cliffs, N.J.: Prentice Hall, 1988).

The **statement section** follows the definition section. It contains the instructions to the computer that cause it to do something, such as add two numbers. In C, these instructions are written in the form of **statements**, which gives us the name for the section.

A SIMPLE PROGRAM

Figure 2-2 shows the parts of a simple C program. In this example, the program is made up of only one function, `main`. We have explained everything in this program but the **preprocessor directives**. A better name for these statements would be precompiler directives. They are special instructions to the preprocessor that tell it how to prepare your program for compilation. One of the most important of the preprocessor directives, and one that is used in virtually all programs, is **include**. The include command tells the preprocessor that you need information from selected libraries known as header files. In today's complex programming environments, it is almost impossible to write even the smallest of programs without at least one library system. In your first program, you will use one include command to tell C that you need the input/output library to write data to the monitor.

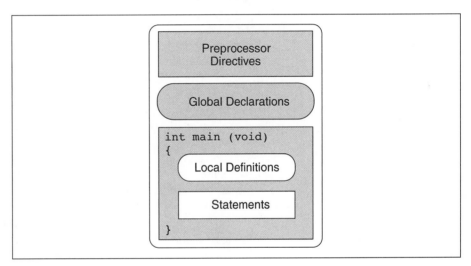

Figure 2-2   Structure of a C program

YOUR FIRST PROGRAM

Your first C program will be very simple (Figure 2-3). It will have only one preprocessor command, no global declarations, and no local definitions. Its purpose will be simply to print a greeting to the user. Therefore, its statement section will have only two statements, one that prints a greeting and one that stops the program.

The preprocessor directive comes at the beginning of the program. All preprocessor directives start with a pound sign (#). Ritchie could have chosen any of several different symbols to identify the preprocessor directives; he chose the pound sign. This is just one of the rules of C known as its **syntax**. Preprocessor directives can start in any column, but they traditionally start in column 1. In fact, some nonstandard compilers insist that they start in column 1, so it's a good idea to code them that way.

In "Hello World" your preprocessor directive says that you will need to have the standard input/output header file included in your program. You need this header file because you will be printing a message to the monitor. Printing is one of the input/output processes identified in this header file. The complete syntax for this directive is shown below.

```
#include <stdio.h>
```

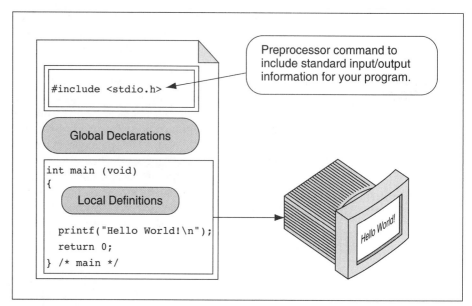

Figure 2-3 The greeting program

The format, or syntax, of this directive must be exact. Since it is a preprocessor directive, it starts with the pound sign. There can be no space between the pound sign and the keyword, *include*. Include means just what you would think it does. It tells the preprocessor that you want the header file in the pointed brackets (< >) added to your program. The name of the header file is stdio.h. This is an abbreviation for standard input/output. The suffix .h is short for **header file** and is a traditional C convention. All system header files, and by convention all user header files, are suffixed by .h.

The executable part of your program begins with the function main, which is identified by the function header shown below. We explore the meaning of the function syntax in Chapter 4. For now, all you need to understand is that *int* says that the function will return an integer value to the operating system, that the function's name is main, and that it has no parameters (the parameter list is *void*). Note that there is no punctuation after the function header.

```
int main ( void )
```

Within main there are two statements, one to print your message and one to terminate the program. The print statement uses another function to do the actual writing to the monitor. To invoke or execute this print function, you *call* it. All function call statements consist of the name of the function, in this case *printf*, followed by a **parameter list** enclosed in parentheses. For your simple program, the parameter list simply contains what you want displayed, enclosed in double quote marks ("). The \n at the end of the message tells the computer to advance to the next line in the output.

The last statement in your program, return 0, terminates the program and returns control to the operating system. One last thing: The function starts with an open brace ({)and terminates with a close brace (}).

COMMENTS

Although it is reasonable to expect that a good programmer should be able to read code, sometimes the meaning of the code is not entirely clear. This is especially true in C. Thus, it is helpful if the person who writes the code adds some documentation comments in the code to help the reader. Such **comments** are merely internal program documentation. The compiler ignores these comments when it translates the program into executable code.

To identify a comment, C uses opening and closing comment tokens. A **token** is one or more symbols understood by the compiler that help it interpret your code. Each comment token is made of two characters that, taken together, form the token; there can be no space between them. The opening token is /*, and the closing token is */. Everything between the opening and closing comment tokens is ignored by the compiler. The tokens can start in any column, and they do not have to be on the same line. The only requirement is that the opening token must precede the closing token. Figure 2-4 shows several examples of comments.

```
/*  This is a comment. */


/*  This is a comment that
    covers two lines.        */


/*
    It is a very common style to put the opening token
    on a line by itself, followed by the documentation
    and then the closing token on a separate line. Some
    programmers also like to put asterisks at the beginning
    of each line to clearly mark the comment.
*/
```

Figure 2-4   Examples of comments

Comments can appear anywhere in a program. In good programming style, a program starts with a series of comments that document its purpose. Comments are also found wherever it is necessary to explain a point about the code. We will demonstrate the use of comments throughout the text. You should note, however, that many of our comments would not appear in programs written by professional programmers, because many of our comments are intended to explain code to you, the student, that would be obvious to professionals.

Although they can appear anywhere, comments cannot be nested in C. That means that you cannot have comments inside comments. Once the compiler sees an opening token, it ignores everything it sees until it finds a closing token. Therefore, the opening token of the nested comment is not recognized, and the ending token that matches the first opening token is left standing on its own. This error is shown in Figure 2-5.

Program 2-1 shows the `greeting` program just as you should write it. We have included some comments at the beginning that explain what the program is going to do. Each program you write should begin with documentation explaining the purpose of the program. We have also shown comments to identify the definitions and statement sections of your program. The numbers on the left in Program 2-1 and the other programs in the text are for discussion reference. You do not enter them.

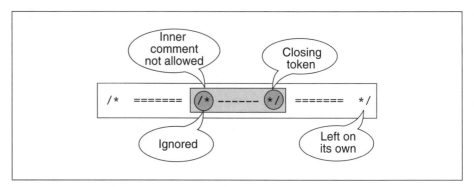

Figure 2-5 Nested comments problem

```
 1  /* The greeting program. This program demonstrates
 2     some of the components of a simple C program.
 3        Written by:   your name here
 4        Date:         date program written
 5  */
 6  #include <stdio.h>
 7
 8  int main (void)
 9  {
10  /* Local Definitions */
11
12  /* Statements */
13
14     printf("Hello World!\n");
15
16     return 0;
17  } /* main */
```

Program 2-1 The greeting program

2-3 IDENTIFIERS

One feature present in all computer languages is the **identifier**. Identifiers allow us to name data and other objects in the program. Each piece of data in the computer is stored at a unique address. If we didn't have identifiers that we could use to symbolically represent data locations, we would have to know and use data addresses to manipulate them. Instead, we simply give data identifiers and let the compiler keep track of where they are physically located.

Different programming languages use different syntactical rules to form identifiers. In C, the rules for identifiers are very simple. The only valid name symbols are the capital letters *A* through *Z*, the lowercase letters *a* through *z*, the digits 0 through 9, and the underscore. The first character of the identifier cannot be a digit. By custom, applications do not use the underscore for the first character either, because many of the identifiers in the system libraries that support C start with an underscore. In this way, we make sure that our names do not duplicate system names, which could become very confusing. The last rule is that the name you create cannot be any of the 30-plus special names, known as **reserved words**, or **keywords**, that are contained in the language itself. For a list of the reserved words, see Appendix B.

Good identifier names are descriptive but short. To make them short, we often use abbreviations[2]. ANSI/ISO C allows names to be up to 31 characters long. If the names are longer than 31 characters, then only the first 31 are used. Table 2-2 summarizes the rules for identifiers.

---

1. First character must be alphabetic character or underscore.
2. Must consist only of alphabetic characters, digits, or underscores.
3. First 31 characters of an identifier are significant.
4. Cannot duplicate a reserved word.

Table 2-2 Rules for identifiers

You might be curious as to why the underscore is included among the possible characters that can be used for an identifier. It is there so that we can separate different parts of an identifier. To make identifiers descriptive, we often combine two or more words. When the names contain multiple words, the underscore makes it easier to read the name. Another way to separate the words in a name is to capitalize the first letter in each word. The traditional method of separation in C uses the underscore. A growing group of programmers, however, prefer to capitalize the first letter of each word. Table 2-3 contains examples of valid and invalid names.

Two more comments about names. Note that `TRUE` and `FALSE` in Table 2-3 are capitalized. By tradition, capitalized names are reserved for preprocessor-defined names. The second comment is that C is case sensitive. This means that even though two identifiers are spelled the same, if the case of each corresponding letter doesn't match, C thinks of them as different names. Under this rule, `TRUE`, `True`, and `true` are three different identifiers.

Valid Names		Invalid Names–Comment	
a	a1	$sum	$ is illegal
student_name	stdntNm	2names	First char digit
_aSystemName	_anthrSysNm	stdnt Nmbr	Contains spaces
TRUE	FALSE	int	Reserved word

Table 2-3 Examples of valid and invalid names

2-4 TYPES

A **type** defines a set of **values** and a set of **operations** that can be applied on those values. The set of values for each type is known as the domain for the type. For example, a light switch can be compared to a computer type. It has a set of two values, on and off. Since the domain of a light switch consists of only these two values, its size is 2. Only two operations can be applied to a light switch: turn-on and turn-off.

---

[2]One way to abbreviate an identifier is to remove any vowels in the middle of the word. For example, *student* could be abbreviated *stdnt*.

Functions also have types. The type of a function is determined by the data it returns. We will talk about the operators and functions later. In this section, we just define the different **data types** available in C using only the first characteristic, the set of values.

C contains four **standard types**: *void*, *char* (short for character), *int* (short for integer), and *float* (short for floating point). These types are shown in Figure 2-6. Standard types are atomic: They cannot be broken down. They also serve as the basic building blocks for the derived types. **Derived types** are complex structures that are built using the standard types. The derived types are pointer, enumerated type, union, array, and structure. In this chapter we discuss only the standard types; the derived types appear in later chapters.

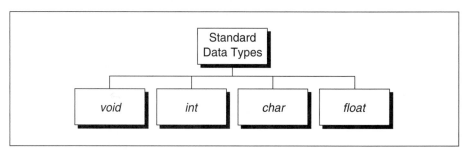

Figure 2-6   Standard data types

VOID

The **void** type has no values and only one operation, assignment. Although this might seem unusual, we will see later that it is a very useful data type. For instance, it can play the role of a generic type—that is, a type that can represent any of the other standard types.

INTEGER

An **integer** (*int*) type is a number without a fraction part. It is also known as an integral number. C supports three different sizes of the integer data type: *short int, int,* and *long int*. A *short int* can also be referred to as **short**, and *long int* can be referred to as **long**. ANSI/ISO C defines these data types so that they can be organized from the smallest to the largest, as shown in Figure 2-7 .

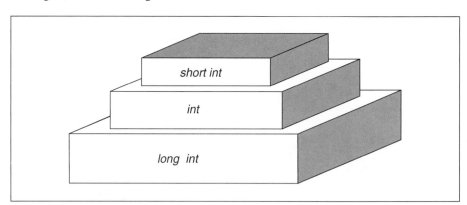

Figure 2-7   Integer types

The type also defines the size of the field in which data can be stored. In C, this is true even though the size is machine dependent and varies from computer to computer. Most microcomputers, minicomputers, and mainframes use the integer sizes shown in Table 2-4.

If you need to know the size of any data type, C provides an operator, *sizeof*, that will tell you the exact size in bytes. We will discuss this operator in detail in Chapter 3. Although the size is machine dependent, ANSI/ISO C requires that the following relationship always be true:

> sizeof (short int) <= sizeof (int) <= sizeof (long int)

Each integer data type can be further divided into two different subtypes depending on whether the number stored in the variable is considered as a signed integer or an unsigned integer. If the integer is *signed*, then one bit must be used for the sign (0 is plus, 1 is minus). The *unsigned* integer can store a positive number that is twice as large as the signed integer of the same size (see Table 2-4).[3]

Type	Sign	Byte Size	Number of Bits	Minimum Value	Maximum Value
short int	*Signed* *Unsigned*	2	16	−32,768 0	32,767 65,535
int (16 bit)	*Signed* *Unsigned*	2	16	−32,768 0	32,767 65,535
int (32 bit)	*Signed* *Unsigned*	4	32	−2,147,483,648 0	2,147,483,647 4,294,967,295
long int	*Signed* *Unsigned*	4	32[a]	−2,147,483,648 0	2,147,483,647 4,294,967,295

[a]Some computers use 48, 64, or more bits

Table 2-4   Typical integer sizes

You must be careful about choosing the correct type for integers, especially if you want to run your program on different hardware platforms. Many personal computers use a 16-bit word size for both integer and short integer. By referring to Table 2-4, you can see that the maximum signed value you can store in 16 bits is +32,767. If your numeric value will always be less than this maximum, use *short*. On the other hand, if your value can be larger than 32,767, you should use *long* on a personal computer.

On large computers, most systems use a 32-bit word for both *int* and *long*. To provide maximum flexibility, therefore, we recommend that you also use *int* and *long* when you may be running on large computers.

To provide flexibility across different hardware platforms, C has a library, limits.h, that contains size information about integers. For example, the minimum integer value for the computer is defined as INT_MIN, and the maximum value is defined as INT_MAX. See Appendix E, "Standard Libraries" for a complete list of these named values.

CHARACTER

The third type is **character** (*char*). Although we think of characters as the letters of the alphabet, a computer has another definition. To a computer, a character is any value that can be represented in the computer's alphabet. Most computers use the American Standard Code for Information Interchange (**ASCII**—pronounced "ask-key") alphabet. You do not need to memorize this alphabet as you did when you learned

---

[3]For a complete discussion, see Appendix D, "Numbering Systems."

your natural languages; you will learn many of the special values by using them. The ASCII code is included in Appendix A.

Most of the personal, mini-, and mainframe computers use 1 byte to store the *char* data types. A byte is 8 bits. With 8 bits, there are 256 different values in the *char* set. (Note in Appendix A that ASCII uses only half of these possible values.) Although the size of *char* is machine dependent and varies from computer to computer, normally it is 1 byte, or 8 bits.

If you examine the ASCII code carefully, you will notice that there is a pattern to its alphabet that corresponds to the English alphabet. All the lowercase letters are grouped together, as are all the uppercase letters and the digits. Many of the special characters are grouped together, but some are found spread throughout the alphabet.

What makes the letter *a* different from the letter *x*? In English, it is the visual formation of the graphic associated with the letter. In the computer, it is the underlying value of the bit configuration for the letter. The letter *a* is binary 0110 0001. The letter *x* is 0111 1000. The decimal values of these two binary numbers are 97 and 120, respectively.

A character is stored in a computer's memory as an integer representing the ASCII code of the corresponding character.[4] For this reason, it is possible—although not necessarily arithmetically consistent—to perform arithmetic operations on characters.[5]

> A character in C can be interpreted as a small integer (between 0 and 255). For this reason, C often treats a character like an integer.

FLOATING POINT

A **floating-point** (*float*) type is a number with a fractional part, such as 43.32. The C language supports three different sizes of floating-point data types: *float*, **double**, and *long double*. As was the case for the *int*, *float* types are defined so that they can be organized from smallest to largest. The relationship among the floating-point types is seen in Figure 2-8.

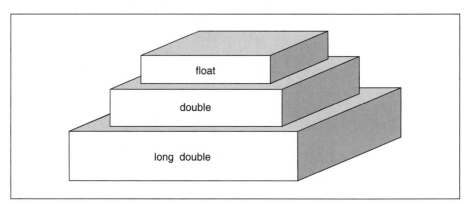

Figure 2-8   Floating-point types

Although the physical size of floating-point types is machine dependent, many computers support the sizes shown in Table 2-5. Regardless of machine size, ANSI/ISO C requires that the following relationship must be true:

---

[4]For more information, refer to Appendix D, "Numbering Systems."

[5]For example, any arithmetic operation that results in a value less than 0 or greater than 255 is invalid.

```
sizeof (float) <= sizeof (double) <= sizeof (long double)
```

Another difference between floating-point and integer types is that floating-point is always signed. A final point to remember about characters, integers, floating-point numbers, and any other type we may discuss is that each type has its own internal format. Therefore, when the same number value is stored in different types, the internal bit configuration will be different. For example, the ASCII character plus (+) has a value of 43. Its bit configuration is different from the integer 43, which is also different from the float 43.0. One of your jobs as a programmer is to use these different types consistently in your programs.

Type	Byte Size	Number of Bits
float	4	32
double	8	64
long double	10	80

Table 2-5 Typical floating-point sizes

A summary of the four standard data types is shown in Table 2-6.

Data Type	C-Implementation
void	*void*
character	*char*
integer	*unsigned short int*
	unsigned int
	unsigned long int
	short int
	int
	long int
floating point	*float*
	double
	long double

Table 2-6 Type summary

Like the limits library for integer values, there is a standard library, `float.h`, for the floating-point values (see Appendix E, "Standard Libraries").

LOGICAL DATA

A logical type can represent only two values, usually referred to as true and false, or on and off. Many languages have a data type for **logical data**, often called **Boolean**. Although C does not have a logical data type, it supports the concept through the integer type. In C any nonzero number (positive or negative) can be used to represent **true,** and zero is used to represent **false.**

> In C any nonzero number is considered true;
> zero is considered false.

2-5   VARIABLES

Variables are named memory locations that have a type, such as integer or character, and consequently a size, which is inherited from their type. And of course, since variables have a type, they have a set of operations that can be used to change or manipulate them.

VARIABLE DECLARATION AND DEFINITION

Each variable in your program must be declared and defined. In C, a **declaration** is used to name an object, such as a variable. **Definitions** are used to create the object. With one exception, a variable is declared and defined at the same time. The exception, which we will see later, declares them first and then defines them at a later time. In the common use of the terms, *definition* assumes that the declaration has been done or is being done at the same time. While this distinction is somewhat of an oversimplification, it works in most situations. We won't worry about the exception at this time.

When we create variables, the declaration gives them a symbolic name and the definition reserves memory for them. Once defined, variables are used to hold the data that are required by the program for its operation. Generally speaking, where the variable is located in memory is not a programmer's concern; it is a concern only of the compiler. From our perspective, all we are concerned with is being able to access the data through their symbolic names, their identifiers. The concept of variables in memory is illustrated in Figure 2-9.

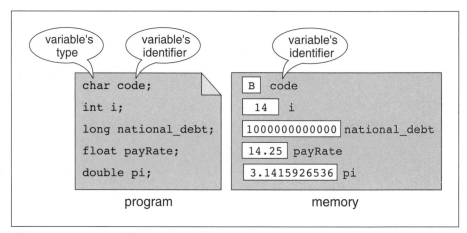

Figure 2-9   Variables in memory

A variable's type can be any of the data types, such as *char*, *int*, and *float*. The one exception to this rule is the type *void*; a variable cannot be type *void*. To create a variable, you first specify the type and then its identifier, as shown below in the definition of a floating-point variable named `price`.

```
float price;
```

Table 2-7 shows some examples of variable declarations and definitions. As you study the variable identifiers, note the different styles used to make them readable. You should select a style and use it consistently. We prefer the use of an uppercase letter to identify the beginning of each word after the first one.

```
short int    maxItems;              /* Word separator: Capital */
long int     national_debt;         /* Word separator: underscore */
float        payRate;               /* Word separator: Capital */
double       tax;
char         code, kind;            /* Poor style—see text */
int          a, b;                  /* Poor style—see text */
```

Table 2-7 Examples of variable declarations and definitions

C allows multiple variables of the same type to be defined in one statement. The last two entries in Table 2-7 use this format. Even though many professional programmers use it, we do not consider it to be good programming style. It is much easier to find and work with variables if they are defined on separate lines. This makes the compiler work a little harder, but the resulting code is no different. This is one situation in which ease of reading the program and programmer efficiency are more important than the convenience of coding multiple declarations on the same line.

VARIABLE INITIALIZATION

We can initialize a variable at the same time that we declare it by including an initializer. When present, the **initializer** establishes the first value that the variable will contain. To initialize a variable when it is defined, the identifier is followed by the assignment operator[6] and then the initializer, which is the value the variable is to have when the function starts. This simple initialization format is shown below.

```
int count = 0;
```

Every time the function containing count is entered, count is set to zero. Now, what will be the result of the following initialization? Are both count and sum initialized or is just sum initialized?

```
int count, sum = 0;
```

The answer is that the initializer applies only to the variable defined immediately before it. Therefore, only sum is initialized! If you wanted both variables initialized, you would have to provide two initializers.

```
int count = 0, sum = 0;
```

Again, to avoid confusion and error, we prefer using only one variable definition to a line. The preferred code in this case would be

```
int count  = 0 ;
int  sum   = 0 ;
```

It is important to remember that with a few exceptions that we will see later, variables are not initialized automatically. When variables are defined, they usually contain garbage (meaningless values left over from a previous use), so we need to initialize them or store data in them (using run-time statements) before accessing their values.

---

[6]The assignment operator is the equal sign (=).

> When a variable is defined, it is not initialized. The programmer must initialize any variable requiring prescribed data when the function starts.

One final point about initializing variables when they are defined: Although the practice is convenient and saves you a line of code, it also can lead to errors. It is better, therefore, to initialize the variable with an assignment statement at the proper place in the body of the code. This may take another statement, but the efficiency of the resulting program is exactly the same, and you will make fewer errors in your code.

Print Sum   At this point you might like to see what a more complex program looks like. As you read Program 2-2, note the blank lines to separate different groups of code. This is a good technique for making programs more readable. You should use blank lines in your programs the same way you use them to separate the paragraphs in a report.

```
 1  /* This program calculates and prints the sum of
 2      three numbers input by the user at the keyboard.
 3         Written by:
 4         Date:
 5  */
 6  #include <stdio.h>
 7
 8  int  main  (void)
 9  {
10  /* Local Definitions */
11     int  a;
12     int  b;
13     int  c;
14     int  sum;
15
16  /* Statements */
17     printf("\nWelcome. This program adds\n");
18     printf("three numbers. Enter three numbers\n");
19     printf("in the form: nnn nnn nnn <return>\n");
20
21     scanf("%d %d %d", &a, &b, &c);
22
23     /* Numbers are now in a, b, and c. Add them. */
24     sum = a + b + c;
25
26     printf("The total is: %d\n\n", sum);
27
28     printf("Thank you. Have a good day.\n");
29     return 0;
30  }  /*  main  */
```

```
    Results:
    Welcome. This program adds
```

Program 2-2   Print sum of three numbers

```
three numbers. Enter three numbers
in the form: nnn nnn nnn <return>
11 22 33

The total is: 66

Thank you. Have a good day.
```

Program 2-2   Print sum of three numbers (continued)

2-6   CONSTANTS

Constants are data values that cannot be changed during the execution of a program. Like variables, constants have a type. In this section, we will discuss character, integer, floating-point, and string constants.

INTEGER CONSTANTS

Although integers are always stored in their binary form, they are simply coded as you would use them in everyday life. Thus, the value 15 is simply coded as 15.

If you code the number as a series of digits, its type is signed integer, or signed long integer if the number is large. You can override this default by specifying unsigned (u or U) and long (1 or L) after the number. The codes may be combined and may be coded in any order. Note that there is no way to specify a *short int* constant. When you omit the suffix on a literal, it defaults to *int*. While both upper- and lowercase codes are allowed, we recommend that you always use uppercase to avoid confusion (especially with the lowercase letter *l*, which in many cases looks like the number 1). Table 2-8 shows several examples of **integer constants**. The default types are typical for a personal computer.

Literal	Value	Type
+123	123	int
−378	−378	int
−32271L	−32,271	long int
76542LU	76,542	unsigned long int

Table 2-8   Examples of integer constants

FLOATING-POINT CONSTANTS

Floating-point constants are numbers with decimal parts. They are stored in memory as two parts: the significand and the exponent. The default form for float constants is *double*. If you want the resulting data type to be *float* or *long double*, you must use a code to specify the desired data type. As you might anticipate, f and F are used for *float* and l and L are used for *long double*. Do not use the lowercase l for *long double*; it is too easily confused with the number 1.

Table 2-9 shows several examples of float constants.

Literal	Value	Type
0.	0.0	double
.0	0.0	double
2.0	2.0	double
3.1416	3.1416	double
−2.0f	−2.0	float
3.1415926536L	3.1415926536	long double

Table 2-9   Examples of float constants

CHARACTER CONSTANTS

Character constants are enclosed between two single quotes (apostrophes). In addition to the character, there can be a backslash (\) between the quote marks. The backslash is known as the **escape character**. It is used when the character you need to represent does not have any graphic associated with it—that is, when it cannot be printed or when it cannot be entered from the keyboard. The escape character says that what follows is not the normal character but something else. For example, to represent the newline character (line feed), we code \n. So, even though there may be multiple symbols in the character constant, they always represent only one character.

> A character constant is enclosed in single quotes.

Character Sets

The character in the character constant comes from the **character set** supplied by the hardware manufacturer. Most computers use the ASCII character set, or as it is sometimes called, the ASCII alphabet. The ASCII character set is shown in Appendix A.

The other common alphabet, usually found only on IBM mainframes and their clones, is the Extended Binary Coded Decimal Interchange Code (**EBCDIC**—pronounced "ebb-see-dic"). This book uses the ASCII set in all its examples. This is not a major problem if you are working on an EBCDIC computer, however, because C has named all the critical character values so that we can refer to them symbolically. They are shown in Table 2-10.

ASCII Character	Symbolic Name
null character	'\0'
alert (bell)	'\a'
backspace	'\b'
horizontal tab	'\t'
newline	'\n'
vertical tab	'\v'
form feed	'\f'
carriage return	'\r'
single quote	'\''
double quote	'\"'
backslash	'\\'

Table 2-10   Symbolic names for special characters

STRING CONSTANTS

A **string constant** is a sequence of zero or more characters enclosed in double quotes. You used a **string** in your first program without even knowing that it was a string! Look at Program 2-1 on page 30 to see if you can identify the string.

Listed in Figure 2-10 are several strings, including the one from your first program. The first example, an empty string, is simply two double quotes in succession. The second example, a string containing only the letter h, differs from a character constant in that it is enclosed in double quotes. When we study strings, we will see that there is also a big difference in how h is stored in memory as a character and as a string.

```
""                                    /* A null string */
"h"
"Hello World\n"
"HOW ARE YOU"
"Good Morning!"
```

Figure 2-10 Some strings

It is important to understand the difference between the null character (see Table 2-10) and an empty string. The null character represents no value. As a character, it is 8 zero bits. An empty string, on the other hand, is a string containing nothing. Figure 2-11 shows the difference between these two constant types.

```
'\0'    ⮂   Null character
""      ⮂   Empty string
```

Figure 2-11 Null characters and null strings

At this point, this is all you need to know about strings. We will talk more about them and how they are stored in the computer when we study strings in Chapter 11.

> Use single quotes for character constants.
> Use double quotes for string constants.

2-7 CODING CONSTANTS

In this section we discuss three different ways to code constants in our programs: literal constants, defined constants, and memory constants.

LITERAL CONSTANTS

A **literal** is an unnamed constant used to specify data. If we know that the data cannot be changed, then we can simply code the data value itself in a statement.

The literal is by far the most common form of constant. You used literals in your first program. Table 2-11 shows several examples of literals.

```
'A'                          /* a character literal */
5                            /* numeric literal 5 */
a + 5                        /* another numeric literal (5) */
3.1416                       /* a float literal */
"Hello"                      /* a string literal */
```

Table 2-11 Examples of literals

DEFINED CONSTANTS

Another way to designate a constant is to use the preprocessor command **define**. Like all preprocessor commands, it is prefaced with the pound sign (#). A typical define command might be

```
#define SALES_TAX_RATE .0825
```

The *define* commands are usually placed at the beginning of the program, although they are legal anywhere. Placing them at the beginning of the program makes them easy to find and change. In the preceding example, for instance, the sales tax rate changes more often than we would like. By placing it and other similar constants at the beginning of the program, we can find and change them easily.

The way *define* works is that the expression that follows the name (in this case, .0825) replaces the name wherever it is found in the source program. This action is just like the search-and-replace command found in your text editor. The preprocessor does not evaluate the code in any way—it just blindly makes the substitution. For a complete discussion of defined constants, see Appendix G, "Preprocessor Directives."

MEMORY CONSTANTS

The third way to use a constant is with memory constants. **Memory constants** use a C **type qualifier** to indicate that the data cannot be changed. We have seen how to define a variable, which does nothing more than give a type and size to a named object in memory. Now let us assume that we want to fix the contents of this memory location so that they cannot be changed. This is exactly the concept of a constant, only now we have stored it in memory and given it a name.

C provides the capability to define a named constant. We simply add the type qualifier, *const*, before the definition as shown below.

```
const float pi = 3.14159;
```

Three points merit discussion: (1) The type qualifier comes first. (2) Then there must be an initializer. If we didn't have an initializer, then our named constant would be whatever happened to be in memory at pi's location when our program started. (3) Finally, since we have said that pi is a constant, we cannot change it.

Program 2-3 demonstrates the three different ways to code pi as a constant.

```
1   /* This program demonstrates three ways to use constants.
2        Written by:
3        Date:
4   */
5   #include <stdio.h>
```

Program 2-3 Memory constants

```
 6  #define PI 3.1415926536
 7
 8  int main (void)
 9  {
10  /* Local Definitions */
11      const double pi = 3.1415926536;
12
13  /* Statements */
14      printf("Defined constant PI: %f\n", PI);
15      printf("Memory constant pi:  %f\n", pi);
16      printf("Literal constant:    %f\n", 3.1415926536);
17      return 0;
18  } /* main */
```

```
Results:
Defined constant PI:   3.141593
Memory constant pi:    3.141593
Literal constant:      3.141593
```

Program 2-3 Memory constants (continued)

2-8 FORMATTED INPUT/OUTPUT

C uses two functions for formatted input and output. The first reads formatted data from the keyboard; the second writes formatted data to the monitor. We will study these two functions here very briefly. We will also discuss standard input and output files. We will discuss all of them again when we study the rest of the input/output functions in Chapter 7.

STANDARD FILES

In C, data must be input to and output from a program through a file. The keyboard is considered the **standard input file**. The monitor is considered the **standard output file**.

We enter input data on the keyboard, and our C program receives them. The keyboard represents a text file (a file of characters). Everything entered into the C program through the keyboard must be in the form of a sequence of characters. To enter other types of data, such as integer, we simply enter them as a sequence of characters and let the C program change them into the appropriate form and store them into the variables we specify. That is, C interprets program formatting instructions that we provide and changes the data into the appropriate form.

The standard input file is usually **buffered**. In other words, a temporary storage area holds the input character sequence until one complete line has been received. Thus, we can backspace and change the input sequence before pressing the enter key. The concept of keyboard input is shown in Figure 2-12.

The standard output file is the monitor. Like the keyboard, it is a text file. When you need to display data that is not text, it must be converted to text before it is written. Fortunately, there is also a standard function to convert and display data. The concept of monitor output is also shown in Figure 2-12.

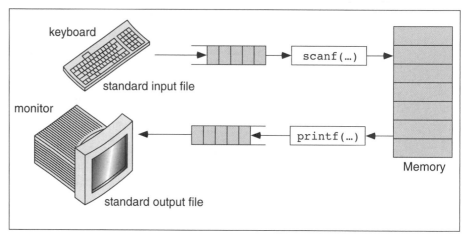

Figure 2-12   Formatted input and output

FORMATTED OUTPUT

The standard formatted output function in C is *printf* (print formatted). It is called a formatted output function because it can convert binary and text data in memory into data formatted for people to read. To print data, *printf* needs two things: instructions for formatting the data and the actual data to be printed. We tell it these things with parameters. **Parameters** are simply values passed to a function. They are coded in the parentheses after the function name. For *printf*, the first parameter is a **format string** that contains any text data to be printed and instructions for formatting the data, if any. The format string may be followed by a list of the data to be printed. When the only thing to be printed is a text message, the data list is empty.

The format string is enclosed in a set of quotation marks ("...") and contains constant text to be output and zero or more field specifications. Constant text could be any message, such as *"Hello World!"* A field specification describes the data to be printed. Each field specification begins with a percent sign (%) and describes exactly one piece of data that is to be printed. The first field specification matches the first parameter in the data list, the second matches the second parameter, and so forth. The *printf* format, with an example containing two variables to be printed on separate lines, is shown in Figure 2-13.

Field Specification

To describe a field, we use a field specification that contains a percent-sign token, a conversion code, and up to four optional modifiers as shown below. Only the field-specification token (%) and the conversion code are required.

```
%<flag><minimum width><precision><size>conversion-code
```

Approximately 30 different conversion codes are used to describe data types. For now, however, we are concerned with only three: character (c), integer (d), and floating point (f). These codes with some examples are shown in Table 2-12.

The **size** is used to modify the type specified by the conversion code. There are three different sizes: h, l, and L. The h is used with the integer codes to indicate that the variable is a short integer. The l is used with integer to indicate the variable is a long integer. And the L is used with floating-point numbers to indicate that the type is long double. Note that there is no size for character, integer, float, and double.

The **width modifier** is used to specify the minimum number of positions in the output. (If the data require using more space to print everything, then *printf* will override the width.) It is very useful to align output in columns, such as when you need to print

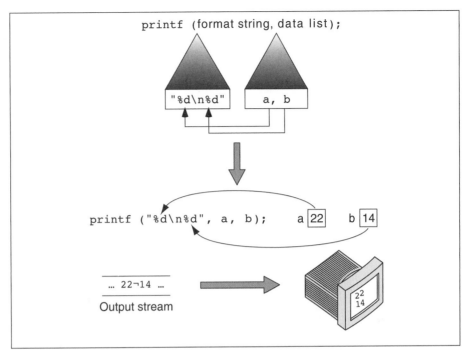

Figure 2-13 Format of *printf* statement

Size	Code	Type	Example
none	c	char	%c
h	d	short int	%hd
none	d	int	%d
l or L	d	long int	%Ld
None	f	float	%f
None	f	double	%f
L	f	long double	%Lf

Table 2-12 Format codes for output and input

a column of numbers. If you don't use a width modifier, each output value will take just enough room for the data. Table 2-13 shows the result of printing integers without a width and then with a width. Note that when the width is exceeded, *printf* will use whatever it needs to print all the data. This case is seen in the last example.

Value	%d	%4d
12	12	12
123	123	123
1234	1234	1234
12345	12345	12345

Table 2-13 *printf* with and without the width modifier

If a floating-point number is being printed, then we specify the number of decimal places to be printed with the **precision modifier**. The precision modifier has the format

.m

where m is the number of decimal digits. If no precision is specified, *printf* prints six decimal positions. This is often more than is necessary.

When both width and precision are used, the width must be large enough to contain the integral value of the number, the decimal point, and the number of digits in the decimal position. Thus, a field specification of %7.2f is designed to print a maximum value of 9999.99. Some examples of width specifications and precision are shown in Table 2-14.

```
%2hd          /* short integer—2 print positions */
%4d           /* integer—4 print positions */
%8ld          /* long int—8 (not 81) positions */
%7.2f         /* float—7 print positions: nnnn.dd */
%10.3Lf       /* long double—10 positions: nnnnnn.ddd */
```

Table 2-14 Floating-point width and precision

The last modifier is the **flag**. The flag can be used to specify two print modifications. If the flag is zero and there is a width specification, then a number will be printed with leading zeros. If the flag is a minus sign (−), then the data are formatted left justified—that is, with the data pushed to the left and spaces used to fill in the right portion of the width specification. Two examples are shown in Table 2-15.

```
%-8d          /* decimal—8 print positions, left justify */
%08d          /* decimal—8 print positions, leading zeros */
```

Table 2-15 Examples of *printf* flag modifier

Format String Text

The format string may also contain text to be printed, such as instructions to the user, variable captions or other identifiers, and other text intended to make the output more readable. In fact, as we have already seen, the format string may contain nothing but text, in which case the text will be printed exactly as shown. We used this concept when we wrote the greeting program. In addition, we can also print control characters, such as tabs (\t), newlines (\n), and alerts (\a), by including them in the format string. These control characters are seen in Table 2-10 on page 40.

Output Examples

This section contains several output examples. We show the *printf* statement, followed by what would be printed. Cover up the solution and try to predict the results.

1. printf("%d%c%f", 23, 'z', 4.1);

```
23z4.100000
```

Note that because there are no spaces between the field specifications, the data are formatted without space between the values.

2. printf("%d %c %f", 23, 'z', 4.1);

```
23 z 4.100000
```

This is a repeat of Output Example 1 with spaces between the field specifications.

3. ```
int   num1 = 23;
char zee = 'z';
float num2 = 4.1;
printf("%d %c %f", num1, zee, num2);
```

```
    23 z 4.100000
```

Again, the same example, this time using variables.

4. ```
printf("%d\t%c\t%5.1f\n", 23, 'Z', 14.2);
printf("%d\t%c\t%5.1f\n", 107, 'A', 53.6);
printf("%d\t%c\t%5.1f\n", 1754, 'F', 122.0);
printf("%d\t%c\t%5.1f\n", 3, 'P', 0.1);
```

```
    23    Z    14.2
    107   A    53.6
    1754  F    122.0
    3     P     0.1
```

In addition to the field specifications, note the tab character (\t) between the first and second, and second and third field specifications. Since the data are to be printed in separate lines, each format string ends with a newline (\n).

5. ```
printf("The number%dis my favorite number.", 23);
```

```
    The number23is my favorite number.
```

Since there are no spaces before and after the format code (%d), the number 23 is run together with the text before and after.

6. ```
printf("The number is %6d", 23);
```

```
    The number is     23
    ^^^^^^^^^^^^^^^^^^^^^
```

If you count the spaces carefully, you will note that five spaces follow the word is. The first space comes from the space after is and before the % in the format string. The other four come from the width in the field specification.

7. ```
printf("The tax is %6.2f this year.", 233.12);
```

```
    The tax is 233.12 this year.
```

In this example, the width is six and the precision two. Since the number of digits printed totals five (three for the integral portion and two for the decimal portion), and the decimal point takes one print position, the full width is filled with data. The only spaces are the spaces before and after the conversion code in the format string.

8. ```
printf("The tax is %8.2f this year.", 233.12);
```

```
    The tax is   233.12 this year.
    ^^^^^^^^^^^^^^^^^^^^^^^^^^^^^^^^
```

9. ```
printf("The tax is %08.2f this year.", 233.12);
```

```
    The tax is 00233.12 this year.
    ^^^^^^^^^^^^^^^^^^^^^^^^^^^^^^^^
```
```

This example uses the zero flag to print leading zeros. Note that the width is eight positions. Three of these positions are taken up by the precision of two digits and the decimal point. This leaves five positions for the integral portion of the number. Since there are only three digits (233), *printf* inserts two leading zeros.

10. ```
printf("\"%8c   %d\"", 'h', 23);
```

```
"        h    23"
 ^^^^^^^^^^^^^^^^
```

In this example, we want to print the data within quotes. Since quotes are used to identify the format string, we can't use them as print characters. To print them, therefore, we must use the escape character with the quote (\"), which tells *printf* that what follows is not the end of the string but a character to be printed, in this case, a quote mark.

11. ```
printf ("This line that disappears.\r...A new line\n");
printf ("This is the bell character \a\n");
printf ("A null character\0kills the rest of the line\n");
printf ("\nThis is \'it\' in single quotes\n");
printf ("This is \"it\" in double quotes\n");
printf ("This is \\ the escape character itself\n");
```

```
...A new line
This is the bell character
A null character
This is 'it' in single quotes
This is "it" in double quotes
This is \ the escape character itself
```

These examples use some of the special names found in Table 2-10 on page 40. Two of them give unexpected results. The return character (\r) repositions the output at the beginning of the current line without advancing the line. Therefore, all data that were placed in the output stream are erased.

The null character effectively kills the rest of the line. Had we not put a new-line character (\n) at the beginning of the next line, it would have started immediately after `character`.

Common Output Errors　Each of the following examples has at least one error. Try to find it before you look at the solution. Your results may vary depending on your compiler and hardware.

1. ```
printf ("%d %d %d\n", 44, 55);
```

```
44 55 0
```

This example has three field specifications but only two values.

2. ```
printf ("%d %d\n", 44, 55 , 66);
```

```
44 55
```

This example has two field specifications with three values. In this case, *printf* ignores the third value.

3. ```
long int x = 444446766;
printf("%d\n", x);
```
```

```
444446766           (if sizeof (int) is four bytes)
-18386              (if sizeof (int) is two bytes)
```

This is a very common problem with older computers in which the size of an integer is only 2 bytes. Because *printf* thinks the value is only 2 bytes when it is actually 4 (a long integer), it prints only the first 2 bytes of the value.

FORMATTED INPUT

The standard formatted input function in C is *scanf* (scan formatted). Like *printf*, it consists of two parts: a format string that describes the data and an **address list** that identifies where data are to be placed in memory. The *scanf* format is seen in Figure 2-14.

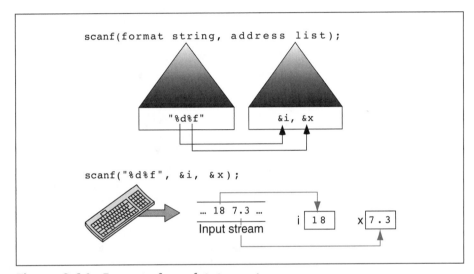

Figure 2-14 Format of *scanf* statement

Like the format string for *printf*, the format string for *scanf* is enclosed in a set of quotation marks ("...") and contains one or more field specifications that describe the data types and indicate any special formatting rules and/or characters. Characters in the format string represent input delimiters and show their exact placement and format in the input stream. Generally speaking, you should not use delimiters in the *scanf* input stream, because if the user does not input them exactly as coded in the format string, they are considered errors. The format for the *scanf* function is shown below

```
%<flag><maximum width><size>conversion-code
```

A field specification begins with a percent sign (%) and describes exactly one field or variable. With a few exceptions that we will show later, the same format codes are used for *scanf* that we used for *printf* (see Table 2-12 on page 45). Each specification describes how text data read from the keyboard or file are to be formatted for storage in memory. For example, the *float* format (%f) specifies that a number is to be input and converted to a floating-point value stored in memory.

With the exception of the character format code (c), the *scanf* function *skips leading whitespace*. That means that the *scanf* function will ignore leading spaces, tabs, or newlines in an input stream. On the other hand, if the format code is character, then *scanf* will read exactly one character, which can be any of the valid codes for the system, including the whitespace characters. If you want to skip leading whitespace before a character, place a space before the field specification.

> To skip leading whitespace when reading character data, code a space before the field specification as shown below:
>
> " %c"

Once it starts reading numeric data, *scanf* will read until it finds a trailing whitespace character. This rule can be overridden by using a width modifier. The width modifier specifies the *maximum* number of characters that are to be read for one format code. When a width specification is included, therefore, *scanf* reads until the maximum number of characters have been processed or until *scanf* finds a whitespace character. If *scanf* finds a whitespace character before the maximum is reached, it stops.

In addition to whitespace and width specifications, two other things will stop the *scanf* function. If the user signals that there is no more input by keying **end of file (EOF)**, then *scanf* terminates the input process. While there is no EOF on the keyboard, it can be simulated in most systems. Digital Equipment MVS systems and most IBM-compatible microcomputers use the `<ctrl + z>` key combination to signal EOF. Unix and Apple Macintosh use `<ctrl + d>` for EOF. The C user's manual for your system should specify the key sequence for EOF. Within your C program, you can symbolically indicate end of file by the declared constant EOF. On most systems, EOF is an integer value of –1.

Second, if *scanf* encounters an invalid character when it is trying to convert the input to the stored data type, it stops. The most common error is finding a nonnumeric character when it is trying to read a number. The valid characters are leading plus or minus, digits, and one decimal point. Any other combination, including any alphabetic characters, will cause an error. Although it is possible to detect this error and ask the user to re-input the data, we will not be able to cover the conventions for this logic until Chapter 7. Until then, be very careful when you enter data into your program.

For every field specification there must be a matching variable in the address list. The address list contains the address of the matching variable. How do you specify an address? It's quite simple: Addresses are indicated by prefixing the variable name with an ampersand (`&`). In C, the ampersand is known as the **address operator**. Using the address operator, if the variable name is `price`, then the address is `&price`. Forgetting the ampersand is one of the most common errors for beginning C programmers, so you will have to concentrate on it when you use the *scanf* function.

> `scanf` requires that the variables in the address list be represented by their addresses. To specify an address, you prefix the variable name with the address operator, the ampersand (`&`).

Remember that the first field specification matches the first variable address, the second field specification matches the second variable address, and so on. This correspondence is very important.

Another very important point: Never end the format string with whitespace. If the last character in the format string is whitespace, the computer will hang up when you try to run your program and you will have to abort your program. This is a fatal error!

Table 2-16 summarizes the rules for using *scanf.*

> 1. The conversion operation processes until:
>   a. End of file is reached.
>   b. The maximum number of characters have been processed.
>   c. A whitespace character is found after a digit in a numeric specification.
>   d. An error is detected.
> 2. There must be a field specification for each variable to be read.
> 3. There must be a variable address of the proper type for each field specification.
> 4. Any character in the format string other than whitespace or a field specification must be exactly matched by the user during input. If the input stream does not match the character specified, an error is signaled and *scanf* stops.
> 5. It is a fatal error to end the format string with a whitespace character. Your program will not run if you do.

Table 2-16 *scanf* rules

Input Examples

This section contains several examples. We list the data that will be input first. This allows you to cover up the function and try to formulate your own *scanf* statement.

1. 214 156 14Z

```
scanf("%d%d%d%c", &a, &b, &c, &d);
```

Note that a space between the 14 and the Z would create an error, because %c does not skip whitespace! To prevent this problem, put a space before the %c code as shown below. This will cause it to skip leading whitespace.

```
scanf("%d%d%d %c", &a, &b, &c, &d);
```

2. 2314 15 2.14

```
scanf("%d %d %f",  &a, &b, &c);
```

Note the whitespace between the field specifications. These spaces are not necessary with numeric input, but it is a good idea to include them.

3. 14/26 25/66

```
scanf("%2d/%2d %2d/%2d",
      &num1, &den1, &num2, &den2);
```

Note the slashes (/) in the format string. Since they are not a part of the field specification, the user must enter them exactly as shown or *scanf* will stop reading.

4. 11–25–56

```
scanf ("%d-%d-%d", &a, &b, &c);
```

Again, we see some required user input, this time dashes between the month, day, and year. While this is a common date format, it can cause problems. A better solution would be to prompt the user separately for the month, the day, and the year.

Common Input Errors

Each of the following examples has at least one error. Try to find it before you look at the solution. Your results may vary depending on your compiler and hardware.

1.
```c
int  a = 0;
scanf ("%d",    a);
printf("%d\n", a);
```

234	(Input)
0	(Output)

This example has no address token on the variable (`&a`). If the program runs at all, the data are read into an unidentified area in memory. What is printed is the original contents of the variable, in this case 0.

2.
```c
float a = 2.1;
scanf  ("%5.2f", &a);
printf ("%5.2f",  a);
```

74.35	(Input)
2.10	(Output)

This example has no precision in the input field specification. When *scanf* finds a precision, it stops processing and returns to the function that called it. The input variable is unchanged.

3.
```c
int a;
int b;
scanf  ("%d%d%d", &a , &b);
printf ("%d %d\n", a ,  b);
```

5 10	(input)
5 10	(output)

This example has three field specifications but only two addresses. Therefore, *scanf* reads the first two values and quits because no third address if found.

4.
```c
int a = 1;
int b = 2;
int c = 3;
scanf  ("%d%d",    &a , &b, &c);
printf ("%d %d\n", a ,  b,  c);
```

5 10 15	(input)
5 10 3	(output)

This example has only two field specifications, but it has three addresses. Therefore, *scanf* reads the first two values and ignores the third address. The value 15 is still in the input stream waiting to be read.

2-9 PROGRAMMING EXAMPLES

PRINT "Nothing!"   Program 2-4 is a very simple program that prints "Nothing!"

```
 1  /* Prints the message "Nothing!".
 2       Written by:
 3       Date:
 4  */
 5  #include <stdio.h>
 6  int main (void)
 7  {
 8  /* Statements */
 9     printf("This program prints\n\n\t\"Nothing!\"");
10     return 0;
11  }  /* main */
```

```
Results:
    This program prints

        "Nothing!"
```

Program 2-4 A program that prints "Nothing!"

PRINT CHARACTER VALUES   Program 2-5 demonstrates that all characters are stored in the computer as integers. We define some character variables and initialize them with values, and then we print them as integers. As you study the output, note that the ASCII values of the characters are printed. The program also shows the value of some nonprintable characters. All values can be verified by referring to Appendix A.

```
 1  /* Display the decimal value of selected characters,
 2       Written by:
 3       Date:
 4  */
 5  #include <stdio.h>
 6  int main (void)
 7  {
 8  /* Local Definitions */
 9     char A          = 'A';
10     char a          = 'a';
11     char B          = 'B';
12     char b          = 'b';
13     char Zed        = 'Z';
14     char zed        = 'z';
15     char zero       = '0';
16     char eight      = '8';
17     char NL         = '\n';          /* newline */
```

Program 2-5 Print value of selected characters

```
18    char HT        = '\t';         /* horizontal tab */
19    char VT        = '\v';         /* vertical tab */
20    char SP        = ' ';          /* blank or space */
21    char BEL       = '\a';         /* alert (bell). */
22    char dblQuote  = '"';          /* double quote */
23    char backSlash = '\\';         /* backslash itself */
24    char oneQuote  = '\'';         /* single quote itself */
25
26 /* Statements */
27    printf("\nASCII for char 'A'  is: %d",  A);
28    printf("\nASCII for char 'a'  is: %d",  a);
29    printf("\nASCII for char 'B'  is: %d",  B);
30    printf("\nASCII for char 'b'  is: %d",  b);
31    printf("\nASCII for char 'Z'  is: %d",  Zed);
32    printf("\nASCII for char 'z'  is: %d",  zed);
33    printf("\nASCII for char '0'  is: %d",  zero);
34    printf("\nASCII for char '8'  is: %d",  eight);
35    printf("\nASCII for char '\\n' is: %d", NL);
36    printf("\nASCII for char '\\t' is: %d", HT);
37    printf("\nASCII for char '\\v' is: %d", VT);
38    printf("\nASCII for char ' '  is: %d", SP);
39    printf("\nASCII for char '\\a' is: %d", BEL);
40    printf("\nASCII for char '\"'  is: %d", dblQuote);
41    printf("\nASCII for char '\\'  is: %d", backSlash);
42    printf("\nASCII for char '\''  is: %d", oneQuote);
43
44    return 0;
45 }  /* main */
```

```
Results:
    ASCII for character 'A'  is: 65
    ASCII for character 'a'  is: 97
    ASCII for character 'B'  is: 66
    ASCII for character 'b'  is: 98
    ASCII for character 'Z'  is: 90
    ASCII for character 'z'  is: 122
    ASCII for character '0'  is: 48
    ASCII for character '8'  is: 56
    ASCII for character '\n' is: 10
    ASCII for character '\t' is: 9
    ASCII for character '\v' is: 11
    ASCII for character ' '  is: 32
    ASCII for character '\a' is: 7
    ASCII for character '"'  is: 34
    ASCII for character '\'  is: 92
    ASCII for character '''  is: 39
```

Program 2-5   Print value of selected characters (continued)

DEFINE CONSTANTS   Write a program that calculates the area and circumference of a circle. Use a preprocessor-defined constant for π. Although we haven't shown you how to make calculations in C, if you know algebra you will have no problem reading the code in Program 2-6.

```
 1  /* This program calculates the area and circumference
 2     of a circle using PI as a defined constant.
 3        Written by:
 4        Date:
 5  */
 6  #include <stdio.h>
 7  #define PI  3.1416
 8
 9  int main (void)
10  {
11  /* Local Definitions */
12     float circ;
13     float area;
14
15     float radius;
16
17  /* Statements */
18
19     printf("\nPlease enter the value of the radius: ");
20     scanf("%f", &radius);
21
22     circ  = 2  * PI     * radius;
23     area  = PI * radius * radius;
24
25     printf("\nRadius is :        %10.2f", radius);
26     printf("\nCircumference is : %10.2f", circ);
27     printf("\nArea is :          %10.2f", area);
28
29     return 0;
30  }  /* main */
```

```
Results:
   Please enter the value of the radius: 23

   Radius is :           23.00
   Circumference is :    144.51
   Area is :             1661.91
```

Program 2-6 Calculate a circle's area and circumference

PRINT A REPORT

You are assigned to a new project that is currently being designed. To give the customer an idea of what a proposed report might look like, the project leader has asked you to write a small program to print a sample. The specifications for the report are shown in Figure 2-15, and the code is shown in Program 2-7.

The report contains four fields: a part number, which must be printed with leading zeros; the current quantity on hand; the current quantity on order; and the price of the item, printed to two decimal points. All data should be aligned in columns with captions indicating the type of data in each column. The report should be closed with an "End of Report" message.

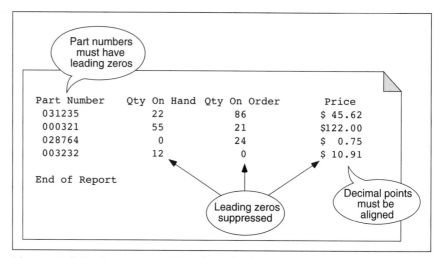

Figure 2-15   Output specifications for inventory report

```c
1   /* This program will print four lines of inventory data
2      on an inventory report to give the user an idea of
3      what a new report will look like. Since this is not a
4      real report, no input is required. The data are all
5      specified as constants
6          Written by:
7          Date:
8   */
9   #include <stdio.h>
10
11  int main (void)
12  {
13  /* Statements */
14     /* Print captions */
15     printf("\tPart Number\tQty On Hand");
16     printf("\tQty On Order\tPrice\n");
17
18     /* Print data */
19     printf("\t %06d\t\t%7d\t\t%7d\t\t $%7.2f\n",
20             31235, 22, 86, 45.62);
21     printf("\t %06d\t\t%7d\t\t%7d\t\t $%7.2f\n",
22             321, 55, 21, 122.);
23     printf("\t %06d\t\t%7d\t\t%7d\t\t $%7.2f\n",
24             28764, 0, 24, .75);
25     printf("\t %06d\t\t%7d\t\t%7d\t\t $%7.2f\n",
26             3232, 12, 0, 10.91);
27
28     /* Print end message */
29     printf("\n\tEnd of Report\n" );
30     return 0;
31  }   /* main */
```

Program 2-7   A sample inventory report

Program 2-7 Analysis   There are a few things about Program 2-7 that you should note. First, it is fully documented. Professional programmers often ignore documentation on "one-time-only" programs, thinking they will throw them away, only to find that they end up using them over and over. It only takes a few minutes to document a program, and it is always time well spent. If nothing else, it helps clarify the project in your mind.

Next, look carefully at the formatting for the print statements. Spacing is controlled by a combination of tabs and format code widths. The double spacing for the end of report message is controlled by placing a newline command ($\backslash$n) at the beginning of the message in Statement 29.

Finally, note that the program concludes with a return statement that informs the operating system that it concluded successfully. Attention to details, even in small programs, is the sign of a good programmer.

2-10 SOFTWARE ENGINEERING AND PROGRAMMING STYLE

Although this chapter introduces only a few programming concepts, there is still much to be said from a software engineering point of view. We will discuss the concepts of program documentation, data naming, and data hiding.

PROGRAM DOCUMENTATION

There are two levels of program documentation. The first is the general documentation at the start of the program. The second level is found within each function.

General Documentation

Program 2-8 shows what we recommend for **program documentation.** Each program should start with a general description of the program. Following the general description is the name of the author and the date the program was written. Following the date is the program's change history, which documents the reason and authority for all changes. For a production program whose use spans several years, the change history can become extensive.

```
1   /* A sample of program documentation. Each program
2       starts with a general description of the program.
3       Often, this description can be taken from the
4       requirements specification given to the programmer.
5         Written by: original author
6         Date:        Date first released to production
7       Change History:
8         <date> Included in this documentation is a short
9                 description of each change.
10  */
```

Program 2-8   Sample of general program documentation

Module Documentation

Whenever necessary, you should include a brief comment for blocks of code. A block of code is much like a paragraph in a report. It contains one thought—that is, one set of statements that accomplish a specific task. Blocks of code in your program should be separated by blank program lines, just as you skip blank lines in your reports between paragraphs.

If the block of code is difficult, or if the logic is especially significant, then you may choose to give the reader a short—one- or two-line—description of the block's purpose and/or operation. We will provide many examples of this type of documentation throughout the text.

Sometimes you will find a textbook suggesting that you document each variable in a program. We disagree with this approach. In the first place, the proper location for variable documentation is in a data dictionary. A data dictionary is a system documentation tool that contains standard names, descriptions, and other information about data used in a system.

Second, good data names eliminate the need for variable comments. In fact, if you think you need to document the purpose of a variable, check your variable name. You will usually find that improving the name eliminates the need for the comment.

DATA NAMES

Another principle of good structured programming is the use of **intelligent data names**. This means that the variable name itself should give the reader a good idea about what data it contains and maybe even an idea about how the data are used.

Although there are obvious advantages to keeping names short, the advantage is quickly lost if the names become so cryptic that they are unintelligible. We have seen programmers struggle for hours to find a bug, only to discover that the problem was use of the wrong variable. The time saved keying short, cryptic names is often lost ten- or a hundredfold in debugging time.

We have formulated several guidelines to help you construct good, intelligent data names.

1. The name should match the terminology of the user as closely as possible.

   Let's suppose that you are writing a program to calculate the area of a rectangle. Mathematicians often label the sides of a rectangle *a* and *b*, but their real names are length and width. Therefore, your program should call the sides of the rectangle `length` and `width`. These names are commonly used by anyone describing a rectangle.

2. When necessary for readability, and to separate similar variables from each other, combine terms to form a variable name.

   Suppose that you are working on a project to compute a payroll. There are many different types of taxes. Each of the different taxes should be clearly distinguished from the others by good data names. Table 2-17 shows both good and bad names for this programming situation. Most of the poor names are either too abbreviated to be meaningful (such as `ftr`) or are generic names (such as `rate`) that could apply to many different pieces of data.

Good Names	Poor Names			
`ficaTaxRate` `fica_tax_rate`	rate	ftr	frate	fica
`ficaWitholding` `fica_witholding`	fwh	ficaw	wh	
`ficaWthldng` `fica_wthldng`	fcwthldng	wthldng		
`ficaMax` `ficaDlrMax`	max	fmax		

Table 2-17 Examples of good and poor data names

Note the two different concepts for separating the words in a variable's name demonstrated in Table 2-17. In the first example, we capitalized the first letter of each word. In the second example, we separated the words with an underscore. Both are good techniques for making a compound name readable. If you use capitalization, keep in mind that C is case sensitive, so you must be careful to use the same cases for the name each time you use it.

3. Do not create variable names that are different by only one or two letters, especially if the differences are at the end of the word. Names that are too similar create confusion. On the other hand, a naming pattern makes it easier to recall the names. This is especially true when user terminology is being used. Thus we see that the good names in Table 2-17 all start with fica.

4. Abbreviations, when used, should clearly indicate the word being abbreviated.

   Table 2-17 also contains several examples of good abbreviations. Whenever possible, use abbreviations created by the users. They will often have a glossary of abbreviations and acronyms that they use.

   Short words are usually not abbreviated. If they are short in the first place, they don't need to be made shorter.

5. Avoid the use of generic names.

   Generic names are programming or user jargon. For example, count and sum are both generic names. They tell you their purpose but don't give you any clue as to the type of data they are associated with. Better names would be emplyCnt and ficaSum. Programmers are especially fond of using generic names, but they tend to make the program confusing. Several of the poor names in Table 2-17 are generic.

6. Use defined constants for constants that are hard to read or that might change from system to system.

   Some constants are just about impossible to read. We pointed out the space earlier. If you need a space often, create a defined constant for it. Table 2-18 contains several examples of constants that are better when coded as defined constants.

```
#define SPACE      ' '        #define BANG     '!'
#define DBL_QTE    '"'        #define QUOTE    '\''
#define COMMA      ','        #define COLON    ':'
```

Table 2-18   Examples of defined constants

Another advantage of defined constants over literals and memory constants is consistency. Since they are coded only once in the program, they will be the same throughout the program.

DATA HIDING

In "Structure of a C Program" on page 26 we discussed the concept of global and local variables. We pointed out that anything placed before main was said to be in the global part of the program. With the exception of data that must be visible to other programs, no data must be placed in this section.

One of the principles of structured programming states that the data structure should be hidden from view. The two terms you usually hear in connection with this concept are **data hiding** and **data encapsulation**. Both of these principles have as their objective protecting data from accidental destruction by parts of your program that don't require access to the data. In other words, if a part of your program doesn't require data to do its job, it shouldn't be able to see or modify the data. Until you learn to use functions in Chapter 4, however, you will not be able to provide this data-hiding capability.

Nevertheless, you should start your programming with good practices. And since our ultimate objective is good structured programming, we now formulate our first programming standard:

> **Programming Standard**
> No variables are to be placed in the global area of a program.

Any variables placed in the global area of your program—that is, before `main`—can be used and changed by every part of your program. This is undesirable and is in direct conflict with the structured programming principles of data hiding and data encapsulation. For a complete overview of programming style, refer to Appendix H, "Program Standards and Styles."

2-11   TIPS AND COMMON PROGRAMMING ERRORS

1. Always use ANSI/ISO C. Avoid nonstandard C.
2. Unless you specifically want to read a whitespace character, put a space before the character field specification in a *scanf* statement.
3. Well-structured programs use global (defined) constants but do not use global variables.
4. The function header for `main` should be complete. We recommend the following format:

```
int main (void)
```

   a. If you forget the parentheses after `main`, you will get a compile error.
   b. If you put a semicolon after the parentheses, you will get a compile error.
   c. If you misspell `main` you will not get a compile error, but you will get an error when you try to link the program. All programs must have a function named `main`.
5. If you forget to close the format string in the *scanf* or *printf* statement, you will get a compile error.
6. Using an incorrect conversion code for the data type being read or written is a run-time error. You can't read an integer with a *float* conversion code. Your program will compile with this error, but it won't run correctly.
7. Not separating read and write parameters with commas is a compile error.
8. Forgetting the comma after the format string in a read or write statement is a compile error.
9. Not terminating a comment with a close token (`*/`) is a compile error.
10. Not including required libraries, such as `stdio.h`, at the beginning of your program is a linker error. Your program will compile, but the linker cannot find the required functions in the system library.

11. If you misspell the name of a function, you will get an error when you link the program. For example, if you misspell *scanf* or *printf*, your program will compile without errors, but you will get a linker error. Using the wrong case is a form of spelling error. For example, each of the following function names are different:

```
scanf, Scanf, SCANF     printf, Printf, PRINTF
```

12. Forgetting the address operator (&) on a *scanf* parameter is a logic (run-time) error.

13. Do not use commas or other characters in the format string for a *scanf* statement. This will most likely lead to a run-time error when the user does not enter matching commas or characters. For example, the comma in the following statement will create a run-time problem if the user doesn't enter it exactly as coded.

```
scanf ("%d, %d", &a, &b);
```

14. Using an address operator (&) with a variable in the *printf* statement is usually a run-time error.

15. Do not put a trailing whitespace at the end of a format string in *scanf*. This is a fatal run-time error.

2-12 KEY TERMS AND CONCEPTS[7]

address list	flag	program documentation
address operator	*float*	reserved words
ANSI/ISO C	floating-point	*return*
ASCII	format string	*scanf*
Boolean	function	*short*
buffered	global declaration section	*signed*
call	header file	size
char	identifier	standard input file
character constant	include	standard output file
character set	initializer	standard types
comment	*int*	statement
constant	integer	statement section
data encapsulation	integer constant	stdio.h
data hiding	intelligent data name	string
data type	keywords	string constant
declaration	literal	syntax
define	logical data	token
definition section	*long*	true
definitions	memory constant	type
derived types	operation	type qualifier
double	parameter	*unsigned*
EBCDIC	parameter list	values
end of file (EOF)	precision modifier	variables
escape character	preprocessor directives	*void*
false	*printf*	width modifier

---

[7]Note: Italic terms are C keywords or standard function names.

2-13   SUMMARY

- In 1972, Dennis Ritchie designed C at Bell Laboratories.

- In 1989, the American National Standards Institute (ANSI) approved ANSI C; in 1990, the ISO standard was approved.

- The basic component of a C program is the function.

- Every C function is made of declarations, definitions, and one or more statements.

- One and only one of the functions in a C program must be called `main`.

- To make a program more readable, use comments in your program. A comment in C is a sequence of characters ignored by the compiler. It starts with the token `/*` and ends with the token `*/`.

- Identifiers are used in a language to name objects.

- We have two general categories of data types in C: standard and derived.

- The standard data types are void, character, integer, and floating point.

- The derived data types are arrays, pointers, structures, unions, and enumerated.

- Character data represents a character from the alphabet used by the computer, which is normally the ASCII alphabet. In C, the character data type is called *char*.

- The integer data type represents a number without a fraction. The integer data type in C is called *int*. There are three sizes of integer: *short int, int,* and *long int*.

- The floating-point data type represents a number with fraction. The floating point data type in C is called *float*. There are three sizes of float: *float, double,* and *long double*.

- Logical data are data that evaluate to either true or false. C does not have an explicit logical data type. It uses other standard data types (except *void*) to represent logical values. If a data variable is zero, it is false. If it is nonzero (positive or negative), it is true.

- A constant is data whose value cannot be changed.

- There are four kinds of constants in C: integer constant, floating-point constant, character constant, and string constant.

- Constants can be coded in three different ways: as literals, as define commands, and as memory constants.

- Variables are named areas of memory used to hold data.

- Variables must be declared and defined before being used in C.

- To input data through the keyboard and to output data through the monitor (or printer), you can use the standard formatted input/output functions.

- *scanf* is a standard input function for inputting formatted data through the keyboard.

- *printf* is a standard output function for outputting formatted data to the monitor.

- As necessary, programs should contain comments that provide the reader with in-line documentation for blocks of code.

- Programs that use "intelligent" names are easier to read and understand.

2-14   PRACTICE SETS

REVIEW QUESTIONS

1. The purpose of a header file, such as `stdio.h`, is to store a program's source code.
   a. True   b. False

2. Any valid printable ASCII character can be used in an identifier.
   a. True   b. False

3. Logical data in C is generally represented by integer values.
   a. True   b. False

4. The C standard function that receives data from the keyboard is *printf*.
   a. True   b. False

5. Which of the following statements about the structure of a C program is false?
   a. A C program starts with a global declaration section.
   b. Declaration sections contain instructions to the computer.
   c. Every program must have at least one function.
   d. One and only one function may be named `main`.
   e. Within each function there is a local declaration section.

6. Which of the following statements about comments is false?

   a. Comments are internal documentation for programmers.

   b. Comments are used by the preprocessor to help format the program.

   c. Comments begin with a /* token

   d. Comments cannot be nested.

   e. Comments end with a */ token

7. Which of the following identifiers is not valid?

   a. _option   d. salesAmount

   b. amount   e. $salesAmount

   c. sales_amount

8. Which of the following is not a standard data type?

   a. char   c. int   e. void

   b. float   d. logical

9. Which of the following statements about characters is true?

   a. Each character has a unique binary value.

   b. In C, characters are normally stored in 2 bytes (16 bits).

   c. Lowercase and uppercase values are organized as value pairs, such as aAbBcC.

   d. Most computers use the American Standard Code for Computer Information (ASCCI) for their alphabet.

   e. The special characters are found grouped together between uppercase and lowercase letters.

10. The code that establishes the original value for a variable is known as a(n):

    a. assignment   c. initializer   e. value

    b. constant   d. originator

11. Which of the following statements about a constant are true?

    a. Character constants are coded using double quotes (").

    b. It is impossible to tell the computer that a constant should be a *float* or a *long double*.

    c. Like variables, constants have a type and may be named.

    d. Only integer values can be used in a constant.

    e. The value of a constant may be changed during a program's execution.

12. Which of the following statements about files is false?

    a. The keyboard is a file.

    b. The keyboard is usually not buffered.

    c. The standard input file is usually the keyboard.

    d. The standard output file is a text file.

    e. The standard output file is usually the monitor.

13. The _____ field specification is used to read or write a short integer.

    a. %c   c. %f   e. %lf

    b. %d   d. %hd

14. To print data left justified, you would use a _____ in the field specification.

    a. flag   d. width

    b. precision   e. width and precision

    c. size

15. The _____ function reads data from the keyboard.

    a. displayf   c. read   e. write

    b. printf   d. scanf

16. One of the most common errors for new programmers is forgetting to use the address operator for variables in a *scanf* statement. What is the address operator?

    a. The address modifier (@) in the field specification

    b. The ampersand (&)

    c. The caret (^)

    d. The percent (%)

    e. The pound sign (#)

EXERCISES

17. Which of the following are *not* character constants in C?

    a. 'C'   c. "C"   e. ' '

    b. 'bb'   d. '?'

18. Which of the following are *not* integer constants in C?

    a. -320   c. -31.80   e. 2,456

    b. +45   d. 1456

19. Which of the following are *not* floating-point constants in C?

    a. 45.6   c. 'a'   e. 40

    b. -14.05   d. pi

20. What is the type of each of the following constants?
    a. 15   c. 'b'   e. "16"
    b. -14.24   d. "1"

21. Which of the following are *not* valid identifiers in C?
    a. A3   c. if   e. tax-rate
    b. 4A   d. IF

22. What is the type of each of the following constants?
    a. "7"   c. "3.14159" e. 5.1
    b. 3   d. '2'

23. What is the type of each of the following constants?
    a. "Hello"   c. 8.5L   e. '\a'
    b. 15L   d. 8.5f

24. Which of the following identifiers are valid and which are invalid? Explain your answer.
    a. num   c. 2dNum   e. num#2
    b. num2   d. 2d_num

25. Which of the following identifiers are valid and which are invalid? Explain your answer.
    a. num-2   c. num_2   e. _num_2
    b. num 2   d. _num2

26. What is output from the following program fragment? To show your output, draw a grid of at least 8 lines with at least 15 characters per line.
    ```
    /* Local Definitions */
    int   x = 10;
    char  w = 'Y';
    float z = 5.1234;
    /* Statements */
    printf("\nFirst\nExample\n:");
    printf("%5d\n, w is %c\n", x, w);
    printf("\nz is %8.2f\n", z);
    ```

27. Find any errors in the following program:
    ```
    /* This program does nothing
    int main
    {
     return 0;
    }
    ```

28. Find any errors in the following program:
    ```
    #include (stdio.h)
    int main (void)
    {
            print ("Hello World");
            return 0;
    {
    ```

29. Find any errors in the following program:
    ```
    include <stdio>
    int main (void)
    {
      printf('We are to learn correct');
      printf('C language here');
      return 0;
    }       /* main /*
    ```

30. Find any errors in the following program:
    ```
    /* This is a program with some errors
       in it to be corrected.
    */
    int main (void)
    {
    /* Local Definitions */
        integer         a;
        floating-point  b;
        character       c;

    /* Statements */
        printf("The end of the program.");
        return 0;
    }  /* main */
    ```

31. Find any errors in the following program:
    ```
    /* This is another program with some
       errors in it to be corrected.
    */
    int main (void)
    {
    /* Local Definitions */
            a  int;
            b  float, double;
            c, d char;

    /* Statements */
            printf("The end of the program.");
            return 0;
    } /* main */
    ```

32. Find any errors in the following program:
    ```
    /* This is the last program to be
       corrected
    ```

```
        in these exercises.
*/
int main (void)
{
/* Local Definitions */
        a   int;
        b : c : d char;
        d , e, f double float;

/* Statements */
printf("The end of the program.");
return 0;
} /* main */
```

PROBLEMS

33. Code the variable definitions for each of the following:
    a. a character variable named `option`.
    b. an integer variable, `sum`, initialized to 0.
    c. a floating-point variable, `product`, initialized to 1.

34. Code the variable definitions for each of the following:
    a. a short integer variable named `code`.
    b. a constant named `salesTax` initialized to .0825.
    c. a floating-point named `sum` of size double initialized to 0.

35. Write a statement to print the following line. Assume the total value is contained in a variable named `cost`.
    ```
    The sales total is: $    172.53
    ^^^^^^^^^^^^^^^^^^^^^^^^^^^^^^^^^^
    ```

36. Write a program that uses four print statements to print the pattern of asterisks shown next:
    ```
    ******

    ******

    ******

    ******
    ```

37. Write a program that uses four print statements to print the pattern of asterisks shown next:
    ```
    *

    **

    ***

    ****
    ```

38. Write a program that uses defined constants for the vowels in the alphabet and memory constants for the even-numbered decimal digits (0, 2, 4, 6, 8). It then prints the following three lines using literal constants for the odd digits:

a	e	i	o	u
0	2	4	6	8
1	3	5	7	9

39. Write a program that defines five float variables and initializes them to 1, 10, 100, 1000, and 10000. It then prints them on a single line separated by space characters using the decimal conversion code (`%d`), and on the next line with the float conversion code (`%f`). Note the differences between the results. How do you explain them?

40. Write a program that prompts the user to enter a quantity and a cost. The values are to be read into an integer named `quantity` and a float named `unitPrice`. Define the variables, and use only *one statement* to read the values. After reading the values, skip one line and print each value, with an appropriate name, on a separate line.

41. Write a program that prompts the user to enter an integer and then prints the integer first as a character, then as a decimal, and finally as a float. Use separate print statements. A sample run is shown below.
    ```
    The number as a character: K
    The number as a decimal  : 75
    The number as a float    : 0.000000
    ```

PROJECTS

42. Write a C program using *printf* statements to print the three first letters of your first name in big blocks. This program does not read anything from the keyboard. Each letter is formed using seven rows and five columns using the letter itself. For example, the letter *B* is formed using 17 B's, as shown below as part of the initials BEF:
    ```
    BBB    EEEEE  FFFFF
    B  B   E      F
    B  B   E      F
    BBB    EEE    FFF
    B  B   E      F
    B  B   E      F
    BBB    EEEEE  F
    ```

This is just an example. Your program must print the first three letters of your first name. Design your *printf* statements carefully to create enough blank lines at the beginning and end to make your initials readable. Use comments in your program to enhance readability as shown in this chapter.

43. Write a program that reads a character, an integer, and a floating-point number. It then prints the character, first using a character format specification (%c) and then using an integer specification (%d). After printing the character, it prints the integer and floating-point numbers on separate lines. Be sure to provide complete instructions (prompts) for the user.

44. Write a program that prompts the user to enter three numbers and then prints them vertically (each on one line), first forward and then reversed (the last one first), as shown below.

```
Please enter three numbers: 15 35 72

Your numbers forward:
       15
       35
       72
Your numbers reversed:
       72
       35
       15
```

45. Write a program that reads 10 integers and prints the first and the last on one line, the second and the ninth on the next line, the third and the seventh on the next line, and so forth. Sample input and the results are shown below.

```
Please enter 10 numbers:
10 31 2 73 24 65 6 87 18 9

Your numbers are:
       10          9
       31         18
        2         87
       73          6
       24         65
```

46. Write a program that reads nine integers and prints them three in a line separated by commas as shown below.

```
Input:
    10 31 2 73 24 65 6 87 18
Output
    10, 31,  2
    73, 24, 65
     6, 87, 18
```

Structure of a
C Program

Two features set the C language apart from many other languages: expressions and pointers. Both of these concepts lie at the very heart of the language, giving C its unique look and feel.

This chapter explores the first of these concepts: expressions. Expressions are not new to you; you have used them in mathematics. However, C's use of expressions is unique to the C language.

Closely tied to the concept of expressions are operators, precedence and associativity, and statements, all of which are discussed in this chapter. This chapter also introduces a concept known as side effects and explains in detail how it affects statements in C.

3-1 EXPRESSIONS

An **expression** is a sequence of operands and operators that reduces to a single value. For example,

```
2 + 5
```

is an expression whose value is 7. The value can be any type other than *void*.

An **operator** is a language-specific syntactical token that requires an action to be taken. The most familiar operators are drawn from mathematics. For example, multiply (*) is an operator. It indicates that two numbers are to be multiplied. Every language has operators, and their use is rigorously specified in the syntax, or rules, of the language.

An **operand** receives an operator's action. Any given operator may have one, two, or more operands. In our arithmetic example, the operands of multiply are the multiplier and the multiplicand.

There is no limit to the number of operator and operand sets that you can combine to form an expression. The only rule is that, when they have all been evaluated, the result is a single value that represents the expression.

> Expressions always reduce to a single value.

As illustrated in Figure 3-1, C implements seven different expression formats. We discuss five of them in this chapter; the comma and ternary expressions are discussed in Chapters 5 and 6 respectively. The various types of operands are shown as rectangles; the operators are shown as ovals.

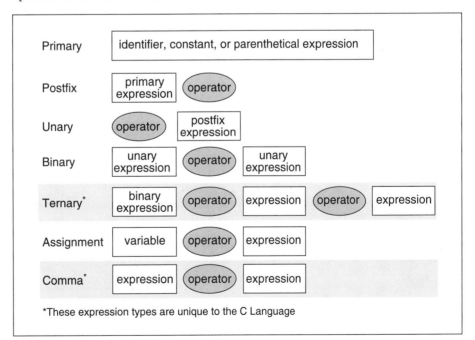

Figure 3-1 C expression formats

Now, look at Table 3-1. This is an abbreviated version of the complete Precedence Table and contains only those expressions we discuss in this chapter. The complete

Precedence Table is found inside the front cover. Table 3-1 groups expressions by the expression formats shown in Figure 3-1. By the time you finish this book, you will be quite familiar with all the different expressions, but it will take the whole book to get to that point.

Type	Description		Side Effects[a]	Pr	Assoc
Primary	Identifier Constant Parenthetical expression		N	18	
Postfix	Function Postfix increment Postfix decrement	(...) ++ – –	Y Y	17 16	Left
Unary	Prefix increment Prefix decrement Size in bytes Plus, Minus	++ – – sizeof + –	Y N N	15	Right
Binary	Multiply, Divide, Modulus Addition, Subtraction	* / % + –	N N	13 12	Left
Assignment	Assignment = += –= *= /= %=		Y	2	Right

[a]Y = Yes, N = No.

Table 3-1   Partial precedence table for C expressions

Although the table is easy to use, a brief explanation of its contents is in order. The first column indicates the **expression type.** The expressions are listed in priority order (Pr, column 4) from the highest (18) to the lowest (2). The numbers are important because they indicate which expressions are evaluated first; that is, they indicate **precedence.** The higher the number, the earlier the evaluation. In examining the priority column, you will see that many expressions are missing (the priorities run consecutively from 18 to 1). We will fill in the missing expressions as we progress through the text.

The first column indicates the type of expression. Note that even within some types there are different levels of evaluation. Thus, within the binary expressions, multiply, divide, and modulus (13) are evaluated before add and subtract (12). This is what you would expect, since it corresponds to the algebraic ordering of expressions.

Associativity (column 5) determines how operators with the same precedence are grouped together to form an expression. In other words, associativity determines how C would use parentheses to group the different expressions at the same level. "Left" indicates the expression is evaluated from the left; "right" indicates that it is evaluated from the right.

PRIMARY EXPRESSIONS

The most elementary type of expression is a primary expression. A **primary expression** consists of only one operand with no operator. In C, the operand in the primary expression can be a name, a constant, or a parenthetical expression. These formats are seen in Figure 3-2.

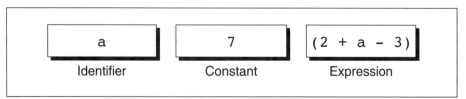

a	7	(2 + a – 3)
Identifier	Constant	Expression

Figure 3-2   Primary expressions

Names

A **name** is any identifier for a variable, a function, or any other object in the language. The following are examples of some names used as primary expressions:

```
a    b12    price    calc    INT_MAX    SIZE
```

Constants

The second type of primary expression is the constant. A constant is a piece of data whose value can't change during the execution of the program. The following are examples of constants used as primary expressions:

```
5    123.98    'A'    "Welcome"
```

Parenthetical Expressions

The final type of primary expression is the parenthetical expression. Any value enclosed in parentheses must be reducible to a single value and is therefore a primary expression. This includes any of the complex expression formats when they are enclosed in parentheses. Thus, a complex expression can be enclosed in parentheses to make it a primary expression. The following are primary expressions:

```
( 2 * 3 + 4 )       ( a = 23 + b * 6 )
```

BINARY EXPRESSIONS

Binary expressions are formed by an operand-operator-operand combination. They are perhaps the most common type. Any two numbers added, subtracted, multiplied, or divided are usually formed in *infix* or algebraic (with the operator between its two operands) notation, which is a binary expression. There are many binary expressions. We will cover the first two in this chapter. A binary plus expression is seen in Figure 3-3.

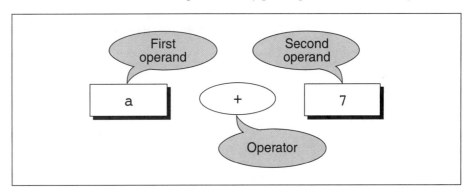

Figure 3-3 Binary expressions

Multiplicative Expressions

The first level of binary expressions, **multiplicative expressions**, takes its name from the first operator, multiply. Multiply, divide, and modulus operators have the highest priority (13) among the binary expressions and are therefore evaluated first among the binary expressions.

The value of a multiply (*) expression is the product of the two operands. The value of a divide (/) expression is a little more complex. If both operands are integers, then the result of the division is the integral value of the quotient, expressed as an integer. If either operand is a floating-point number, then the result of the division is a floating-point number in a type that matches the higher format of the operands (*float, double,* or *long double*). The following expression is a binary multiply:

```
10 * 12
```

Multiply and divide are well known, but you may not be familiar with the modulus operator (%), more commonly known as modulo. This operator divides the first operand by the second and returns the remainder rather than the quotient. For example,

```
5 % 2 evaluates to 1
5 % 3 evaluates to 2
```

Both operands must be integer types, and the operator returns the remainder as an integer type. Because the division and modulus operators are related, they are often confused. Remember: The value of an expression with the division operator is the quotient; the value of a modulus operator is the remainder. Study the effect of these two operators in the following expressions:

```
3 / 5 evaluates to 0
3 % 5 evaluates to 3
```

The multiplicative expressions are summarized in Table 3-2.

*	Result is algebraic multiplication of two operands.
/	Result is algebraic division of first operand by second operand: • Integer quotient if both operands are integer. • Floating-point quotient if either operand is a floating-point number.
%	Result is integer remainder after first operand is divided by second operand. Both operands must be integer types.

Table 3-2 Multiplicative binary operators

Table 3-3 contains several examples of the multiplicative binary expressions.

Integer		Float	
Multiplication: Value:	3 * 5 15	Multiplication: Value:	3.1 * 5.2 16.12
Division: Value:	20 / 6 3	Division: Value:	20 / 6 3.333333
Modulo: Value:	20% 6 2		

Table 3-3 Examples of multiplicative binary expressions

Additive Expressions

The second level of binary expressions contains the **additive expressions**. The second operand is added to or subtracted from the first operand, depending on the operator used. Additive expressions are evaluated after multiplicative expressions. Their use parallels algebraic notation. Two simple examples are shown below:

```
a + 7          b - 11
```

Now let's look at a little program that uses some of these expressions. Program 3-1 contains several binary expressions.

```
 1 │ /* This program demonstrates binary expressions.
 2 │       Written by:
 3 │       Date:
 4 │ */
 5 │ #include <stdio.h>
 6 │ int main (void)
 7 │ {
 8 │ /* Local Definitions */
 9 │    int a = 17;
10 │    int b = 5;
11 │
12 │ /* Statements */
13 │    printf("%d + %d = %d\n",  a, b, a + b);
14 │    printf("%d - %d = %d\n",  a, b, a - b);
15 │    printf("%d * %d = %d\n",  a, b, a * b);
16 │    printf("%d / %d = %d\n",  a, b, a / b);
17 │    printf("%d %% %d = %d\n", a, b, a % b);
18 │    printf("Hope you enjoyed the demonstration.\n");
19 │    return 0;
20 │ }  /* main */
```

```
Results:
    17 + 5 = 22
    17 - 5 = 12
    17 * 5 = 85
    17 / 5 = 3
    17 % 5 = 2
    Hope you enjoyed the demonstration.
```

Program 3-1   Binary expressions

Program 3-1 Analysis   This simple program requires only three comments by way of explanation. (1) Note that even for a simple program we include all of the standard documentation comments. (2) We do not recommend that you include calculations in your print statements as we have done in this program—it is not a good structured programming technique. We include them in this program because we haven't yet shown you how to save the results of a calculation. (3) Study the format string in Statement 17. To print a percent sign as text in the format string, we need to code two percent signs.

ASSIGNMENT EXPRESSIONS

The **assignment expression** evaluates the operand on the right side of the operator (=) and places its value in the variable on the left. The assignment expression has a value and a result.

■ The value of the total expression is the value of the expression on the right of the assignment operator (=).

■ The result places the expression value in the operand on the left of the assignment operator.

There are two forms of assignment: simple and compound. The format of the simple assignment expression is seen in Figure 3-4.

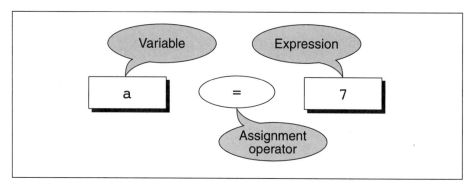

Figure 3-4   Assignment expression

Simple Assignment

Simple assignment is the assignment form found in algebraic expressions. Three examples of simple assignments are shown below.

```
a = 5          b = x + 1          i = i + 1
```

The value of the expression on the right of the assignment operator is evaluated and becomes the value of the total expression. The assignment expression then places the value in the left operand. Of course, for the effect to take place, the left operand must be able to receive it; that is, it must be a variable, not a constant. If the left operand cannot receive a value and you assign one to it, you will get a compile error.

> The left operand in an assignment expression must be a single variable.

Several examples of assignments are shown in Table 3-4.

Contents of Variable x	Contents of Variable y	Expression	Value of Expression	Result of Expression
10	5	x = y + 2	7	x = 7
10	5	x = x / y	2	x = 2
10	5	x = y % 4	1	x = 1

Table 3-4   Examples of assignment expressions

Compound Assignment

A compound assignment is a shorthand notation for a simple assignment. It requires that the left operand be repeated as a part of the right expression. Five compound assignment operators are discussed in this chapter: *=, /=, %=, +=, and -=.

To evaluate a compound assignment expression, first change it to a simple assignment, as shown in Table 3-5. Then perform the operation to determine the value of the expression.

Compound Expression	Equivalent Simple Expression
x *= y	x = x * y
x /= y	x = x / y
x %= y	x = x % y
x += y	x = x + y
x -= y	x = x - y

Table 3-5   Expansion of compound expressions

Examples of the five basic compound assignment expressions are seen in Table 3-6. You may find it helpful to convert each expression to its simple form to see how the result is determined.

Contents of Variable x	Contents of Variable y	Expression	Value of Expression	Result of Expression
10	5	x *= y	50	x = 50
10	5	x /= y	2	x = 2
10	5	x %= y	0	x = 0
10	5	x += y	15	x = 15
10	5	x -= y	5	x = 5

Table 3-6 Examples of compound assignment expressions

If a compound assignment is used with a binary expression, the binary expression is evaluated first. Thus, the expression

```
x *= y + 3
```

is evaluated as

```
x = x * (y + 3)
```

which, given the values in Table 3-6, evaluates to 80—not 53, as most people would assume. This is not an intuitive format and appears to violate the normal precedence rules of both algebra and C. For that reason, we recommend that you never code a compound expression with more than two operands.

Program 3-2 demonstrates the first three examples in Table 3-6. You may want to copy it and add the last two.

```
1  /* Demonstrate examples of compound assignments.
2        Written by:
3        Date:
4  */
5  #include <stdio.h>
6
7  int main (void)
8  {
9  /* Local Definitions */
10     int x;
11     int y;
12
13  /* Statements */
14     x = 10;
15     y = 5;
16
17     printf("x: %2d  |  y: %2d ",    x, y);
18     printf(" |   x *= y: %2d ",     x *= y);
19     printf(" |   x is now: %2d\n", x);
```

Program 3-2 Demonstration of compound assignments

```
20
21     x = 10;
22     printf("x: %2d  |   y: %2d ",    x, y);
23     printf("  |   x /= y: %2d ",    x /= y);
24     printf("  |   x is now: %2d\n", x);
25
26     x = 10;
27     printf("x: %2d  |   y: %2d ",    x, y);
28     printf("  |   x %%= y: %2d ",    x %= y);
29     printf("  |   x is now: %2d\n", x);
30
31     return 0;
32 }  /* main */
```

```
Results:
    x: 10  |  y:  5  |  x *= y: 50  |  x is now: 50
    x: 10  |  y:  5  |  x /= y:  2  |  x is now:  2
    x: 10  |  y:  5  |  x %= y:  0  |  x is now:  0
```

Program 3-2 Demonstration of compound assignments (continued)

Program 3-2 Analysis   Note that we have used an assignment statement in the *printf* statements to demonstrate that an assignment expression has a value. As we said before, this is not good programming style, but we use it here to match the format we used in Program 3-1. *Do not hide calculations in print statements.* Also, since we are changing the value of x with each assignment, even though it is in a *printf* statement, we need to set it to 10 again for each of the print series.

POSTFIX EXPRESSIONS

The **postfix expression** operates at the second level of the Precedence Table (see inside front cover), immediately after primary expressions. It consists of one operand followed by one operator. Its format is shown in Figure 3-5.

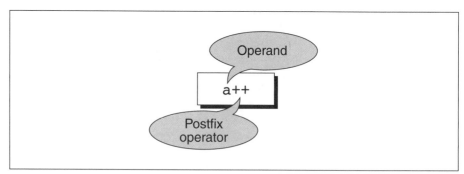

Figure 3-5 Postfix expressions

Function Call

You have already used a postfix expression from the C language. In your first program, you wrote a message on the monitor by using the *printf* function. Function calls are postfix expressions. When you called the *printf* function, it displayed your message and then returned to continue your program. The function name is the operand and the operator is the parentheses that follow the name.

**Postfix Increment/
Decrement**

The **postfix increment** and **postfix decrement** are also postfix operators. Virtually all programs require somewhere in their code that the value 1 be added to a variable. In most languages, this additive operation can only be represented as a binary expression. C provides the same functionality, however, in both the postfix and the unary expressions.

In the postfix increment, the variable is increased by 1. Thus, a++ results in the variable a being increased by 1. The effect is the same as the assignment expression a = a + 1.

(a++) has the same effect as (a = a + 1)

Although the result of both expressions is that a is incremented by 1, there is a major difference. The *value* of the postfix increment expression is determined *before* the variable is increased. For instance, if the variable a contains 4 before the expression is evaluated, the value of the expression a++ is 4. As a result of evaluating the expression and its side effect, a contains 5. The value and effect of the postfix increment are graphically shown in Figure 3-6.

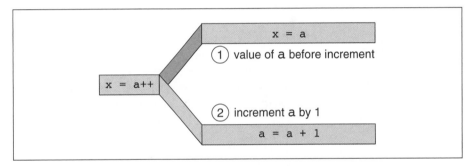

Figure 3-6   Result of postfix a++

The postfix decrement (a−−) also has a value and a result. In this case, the value is the value of a before the evaluation and results in a being decremented by 1. Table 3-7 shows examples of these two expressions.

Contents of a Before	Expression	Value of Expression	Contents of a After
10	a++	10	11
10	a--	10	9

Table 3-7   Examples of postfix expressions

Program 3-3 demonstrates the effect of the postfix increment expression.

```
1   /* Example of postfix increment.
2         Written by:
3         Date:
4   */
5   #include <stdio.h>
6   int main (void)
```

Program 3-3   Demonstrate postfix increment

```
 7  {
 8  /* Local Definitions */
 9     int a;
10
11  /* Statements */
12     a = 4;
13     printf("value of a    : %2d\n", a);
14     printf("value of a++  : %2d\n",    a++);
15     printf("new value of a: %2d\n\n", a);
16     return 0;
17  }  /* main */
```

```
Results:
   value of a    :  4
   value of a++  :  4
   new value of a:  5
```

Program 3-3 Demonstrate postfix increment (continued)

UNARY EXPRESSIONS

Unary expressions consist of one operator and one operand. Many of the unary expressions are also familiar to you from mathematics and will require little explanation. In this chapter we discuss only the prefix increment/decrement, the *sizeof* operator, and the plus/minus operators. The others will be discussed in later chapters. The format of the unary expressions is demonstrated by the prefix increment seen in Figure 3-7.

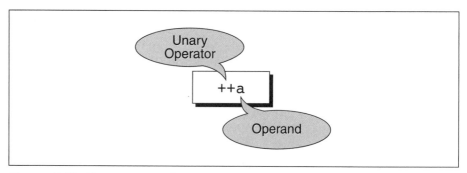

Figure 3-7 Unary expressions

Prefix Increment/ Decrement

Just like the postfix increment and postfix decrement operators, the **prefix increment** and **prefix decrement** operators are shorthand notations for adding or subtracting 1 from a variable. There is one major difference between the postfix and prefix operators, however: With the prefix operators, the effect takes place *before* the expression that contains the operator is evaluated. Note that this is the reverse of the postfix operation. Figure 3-8 shows the operation graphically.

The effect of both the postfix and prefix increment is the same: The variable is increased by 1. If you don't actually require the value of the expression—that is, if all you need is the effect of increasing the value of a variable by 1—then it makes no difference which one you use. You will find that programmers use the postfix increment and decrement more often, if for no other reason than that the variable is shown first and is therefore easier to read.

On the other hand, if you require both the value and the effect, then your application will determine which one you want to use. When you need the value to be the *current*

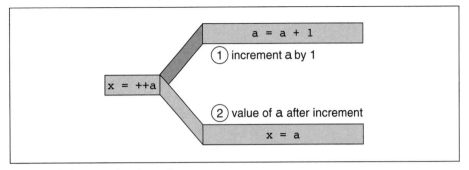

Figure 3-8 Result of prefix ++a

(++a) has the same effect as (a = a + 1)

---

contents of the variable, use the postfix operator; when you need the value to be the *new contents* of the variable (after it has been incremented or decremented), use the prefix operator. Table 3-8 shows examples of the prefix increment and decrement expressions.

Contents of a Before	Expression	Contents of a After	Value of Expression
10	++a	11	11
10	--a	9	9

Table 3-8 Examples of prefix operator expressions

If the ++ is before the operand, the addition takes place before
the value is determined; if it is after the operand, the addition
takes place after the value is determined.

Program 3-4 demonstrates the prefix increment expression. Study it carefully, and compare it to the results from Program 3-3.

```
 1  /* Example of prefix increment.
 2       Written by:
 3       Date:
 4  */
 5  #include <stdio.h>
 6  int main (void)
 7  {
 8  /* Local Definitions */
 9     int a;
10
11  /* Statements */
12     a = 4;
13     printf("value of a     : %2d\n", a);
14     printf("value of ++a   : %2d\n", ++a);
```

Program 3-4 Demonstrate prefix increment

```
15 ||    printf("new value of a: %2d\n", a);
16 ||    return 0;
17 || }  /* main */
```

```
Results:
   value of a    :   4
   value of ++a  :   5
   new value of a:   5
```

Program 3-4   Demonstrate prefix increment (continued)

Program 3-4 Analysis   The only difference in the printouts between Program 3-3 and Program 3-4 is the use of the increment operators. The first program uses the postfix increment; the second uses the unary prefix increment. In both cases, we start with the same value for a and it has the same value at the end. But the value of the expression itself is different. To help remember the difference, use this rule: If the ++ is *before* the operand, the addition takes place *before* the value is determined; if it is *after* the operand, the addition takes place *after* the value is determined.

sizeof

The *sizeof* operator looks like a function, but it is actually an operator. Its purpose matches its name: It tells you the size, in bytes, of whatever type is specified. By specifying the size of an object during execution, you make your program more portable to other hardware. A simple example will illustrate the point. On most personal computers, the size of the integer type is 2 bytes. On most mainframe computers, it is 4 bytes. On the very large supercomputers, it can be as large as 16 bytes. If it is important to know exactly how large (in bytes) an integer is, you can use the *sizeof* operator, as shown below.

```
sizeof (int)
```

Remember that all expressions have a value and that the value can be assigned to a variable. It is therefore possible to save the result of the *sizeof* operator if you like. The following use of the expression saves the value in an integer type:

```
x = sizeof (int)
```

It is also possible to find the size of a primary expression. The value is the size of memory in bytes required to hold the expression. Here are two examples.

```
sizeof (-345.23)
sizeof (x)
```

Unary Plus/Minus

The **unary plus** and **unary minus** operators are what we think of as simply the plus and minus signs. In C, however, they are actually operators. Because they are operators, they can be used to compute the arithmetic value of an operand.

The plus operator actually does nothing but yield the value of the operand. Its primary purpose is to provide symmetry with the minus operator. The minus operator can be used to change the sign of a value algebraically—that is, to change it from plus to minus or minus to plus. Note, however, that the value of the stored variable is unchanged. The operation of these operators is seen in Table 3-9.

Expression	Contents of a Before *and* After Expression	Expression Value
+a	3	+3
−a	3	−3
+a	−5	−5
−a	−5	+5

Table 3-9   Examples of unary plus and minus

3-2   PRECEDENCE AND ASSOCIATIVITY

Precedence is used to determine the order in which different operators in a complex expression are evaluated. **Associativity** is used to determine the order in which operators with the same precedence are evaluated in a complex expression. Another way of stating this is that associativity determines how operators *with the same precedence* are grouped together to form nested expressions. As its name implies, precedence is applied before associativity to determine the order in which expressions are evaluated. Associativity is then applied, if necessary.

PRECEDENCE

The concept of precedence is well founded in mathematics. For example, in algebra, multiplication and division are performed before addition and subtraction. C extends the concept to 18 levels, as shown in the Precedence Table inside the front cover of this textbook.

The following is a simple example of precedence:

```
2 + 3 * 4
```

This expression is actually two binary expressions, a binary addition and a binary multiplication. Binary addition has a precedence of 12. Binary multiplication has a precedence of 13. This results in the multiplication being done first, followed by the addition, as shown below in the same expression with the default parentheses added. The value of the complete expression is 14.

```
( 2 + (3 * 4) )
```

As another example consider the following expression:

```
-b++
```

Two different operators are in this expression. The first is the unary minus, the second is the postfix increment. The postfix increment has the higher precedence (16), so it is evaluated first. Then the unary minus, with a precedence of 15, is evaluated. To reflect the precedence, we have recoded the expression using parentheses.

```
( -(b++) )
```

Assuming that the value of b is 5 initially, the expression is evaluated as shown at the top of page 82. What is the value of the expression?

```
( -(5++) )
```

Did you get –5? Now another question: What is the value of **b** after the expression is complete? (It is 6, but it was created as an effect that is separate from the value of the expression.)

Program 3-5 demonstrates precedence by printing the same expression, once without parentheses and once with parentheses to change the precedence. Because the parentheses create a primary expression that must be evaluated before the binary multiply, the answer is different.

```c
1   /* Examine the effect of precedence on an expression.
2          Written by:
3          Date:
4   */
5   #include <stdio.h>
6
7   int main (void)
8   {
9   /* Local Definitions */
10     int a = 10;
11     int b = 20;
12     int c = 30;
13
14   /* Statements */
15     printf ("a *  b + c  is: %d\n", a *  b + c);
16     printf ("a * (b + c) is: %d\n", a * (b + c));
17     return 0;
18  }  /* main */
```

```
Results:
   a *  b + c  is: 230
   a * (b + c) is: 500
```

Program 3-5 Precedence

ASSOCIATIVITY

Associativity can be from either the left or the right. **Left associativity** evaluates the expression by starting on the left and moving to the right. Conversely, **right associativity** evaluates the expression by proceeding from the right to the left. Remember, however, that associativity is used only when the operators all have the same precedence (Figure 3-9).

Associativity is applied when we have more than one operator of the same precedence level in an expression.

ASSOCIATIVITY

Figure 3-9 Associativity

Left Associativity

The following shows an example of left-to-right associativity. Here we have four operators of the same precedence (* / % *).

```
3 * 8 / 4 % 4 * 5
```

Associativity determines how the subexpressions are grouped together. All of these operators have the same precedence (13). Their associativity is from left to right. So they are grouped as follows:

```
((((3 * 8) / 4) % 4) * 5)
```

What is the value of this expression? Did you get 10? A graphical representation of this expression is shown in Figure 3-10.

Figure 3-10   Left associativity

Right Associativity

Only three types of expressions associate from the right: the unary expressions, the conditional ternary expression, and the assignment expressions.

When more than one assignment operator occurs in an assignment expression, the assignment operators must be interpreted from right to left. This means that the rightmost expression will be evaluated first; then its value will be assigned to the operand on the left of the assignment operator and the next expression will be evaluated. Under these rules, the expression

```
a += b *= c -= 5
```

is evaluated as

```
(a += (b *= (c -= 5)))
```

which is expanded to

```
(a = a + (b = b * (c = c - 5)))
```

If a has an initial value of 3, b has an initial value of 5, and c has an initial value of 8, these expressions become

```
(a = 3 + (b = (5 * ( c =  8 - 5)))
```

which results in c being assigned a value of 3, b being assigned a value of 15, and a being assigned a value of 18. The value of the complete expression is also 18. A diagram of this expression is shown in Figure 3-11.

A simple but common form of assignment is shown below. Suppose that you have several variables that all need to be initialized to zero. Rather than initializing each separately, you can form a complex statement to do it.

Figure 3-11   Right associativity

```
a = b = c = d = 0;
```

3-3   SIDE EFFECTS

A **side effect** is an action that results from the evaluation of an expression. For example, in an assignment expression, C first evaluates the expression on the right of the assignment operator and then places its value in the variable on the left of the assignment operator. Changing the value of the variable is a side effect. Consider the following expression:

```
x = 4;
```

This simple expression has three parts. First, on the right of the assignment operator is a primary expression that has the value 4. Second, the whole expression (**x** = 4) also has a value of 4. And third, as a side effect, **x** receives the value 4.

Let's modify the expression slightly and see the same three parts.

```
x = x + 4;
```

Assuming that **x** has an initial value of 3, the value of the expression on the right of the assignment operator has a value of 7. The whole expression also has a value of 7. And as a side effect, **x** receives the value of 7. To prove these three steps to yourself, write and run the following code fragment:

```
x = 3;
printf("Step 1--Value of x: %d\n", x);
printf("Step 2--Value of x = x + 4: %d\n", x = x + 4);
printf("Step 3--Value of x now: %d\n", x);
```

Now, let's consider the side effect in the postfix increment expression. This expression is typically coded as shown below.

```
a++
```

As we saw earlier, the value of this expression is the value of **a** before the expression is evaluated. As a side effect, however, the value of **a** is incremented by 1.

C has six different side effects: four pre-effects and two posteffects. The four pre-effect side effects are the unary prefix increment and decrement operators (**++a** and **−−a**), the function call, and the assignment. The side effect for these expressions takes place *before* the expression is evaluated.

The posteffect operators are the postfix increment and decrement. The side effect takes place *after* the expression has been evaluated. Therefore, the variable value is not changed until after it has been used in the expression. These six operators are shown in Table 3-10.

Type of Side Effect	Expression Type	Example
Pre-effect	Unary prefix increment	++a
Pre-effect	Unary prefix decrement	--a
Pre-effect	Function call	scanf(...)
Pre-effect	Assignment	a = 1 a += y
Posteffect	Postfix increment	a++
Posteffect	Postfix decrement	a--

Table 3-10   Pre-effect and posteffect side effects

3-4   EVALUATING EXPRESSIONS

Now that we have introduced the concepts of precedence, associativity, and side effects, let's work through a couple of examples. The first expression is shown below. It has no side effects, so the values of all of its variables are unchanged.

```
a * 4 + b / 2 - c * b
```

For this example, assume that the values of the variables are

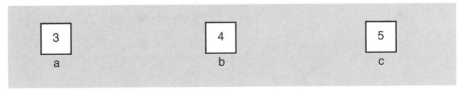

To **evaluate an expression** *without side effects,* follow the simple rules shown below.

1. Replace the variables by their values. This gives us the following expression:

```
3 * 4 + 4 / 2 - 5 * 4
```

2. Evaluate the highest precedence operators, and replace them with the resulting value.

   In the above expression, the operators with the highest precedence are the multiply and divide (13). We therefore evaluate them first from the left and replace them with the resulting values. The expression is now

```
(3 * 4) + (4 / 2) - (5 * 4)  �  12 + 2 - 20
```

3. Repeat step 2 until the result is a single value.

In this example, there is only one more precedence, binary addition and subtraction. After they are evaluated, the final value is –6.

Since this expression had no side effects, all of the variables have the same values after the expression has been evaluated that they had at the beginning.

Now let's look at the rules for an expression that has side effects and parenthetical expressions. For this example, consider the expression

```
--a * (3 + b) / 2 - c++ * b
```

Assume that the variables have the values used above, a = 3, b = 4, c = 5.
To evaluate this expression, use the following rules:

1. Rewrite the expression as follows:

    a. Copy any prefix increment or decrement expressions, and place them *before* the expression being evaluated. Replace each removed expression with its variable.

    b. Copy any postfix increment or decrement expressions, and place them *after* the expression being evaluated. Replace each removed expression with its variable.

    After applying this rule, the expression now reads

    ```
    --a
    a * (3 + b) / 2 - c * b
    c++
    ```

    Evaluate any pre-effect expressions, determining the effect on the variables. After you evaluate ──a, the variables are now

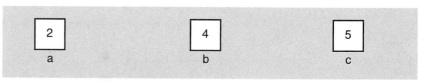

2. Replace the variables in the expression with their values. The modified expression is now

    ```
    2 * ( 3 + 4) / 2 - 5 * 4
    c++
    ```

3. Evaluate the parenthetical expression(s) first, and discard the parentheses. Our expression now reads

    ```
    2 * 7 / 2 - 5 * 4
    c++
    ```

4. Evaluate the highest precedence operators, and replace them with the resulting value, repeating until the result is a single value. The result of each step in this rule is shown below.

    ```
    14 / 2 - 5 * 4 ➡ 7 - 5 * 4 ➡ 7 - 20 ➡ -13
    c++
    ```

5. Evaluate the posteffect expressions, and replace their values with the new value. In this example, the resulting values are

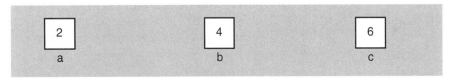

Program 3-6 evaluates these two expressions.

```c
 1  /* Evaluate two complex expressions.
 2         Written by:
 3         Date:
 4  */
 5  #include <stdio.h>
 6  int main (void)
 7  {
 8  /* Local Definitions */
 9     int a = 3;
10     int b = 4;
11     int c = 5;
12     int x;
13     int y;
14
15  /* Statements */
16     printf("Initial values of the variables: \n");
17     printf("a = %d\tb = %d\tc = %d\n\n", a, b, c);
18
19     x = a * 4 + b / 2 - c * b;
20     printf("Value of   a *  4 + b  / 2 - c   * b: %d\n", x);
21
22     y = --a * (3 + b) / 2 - c++ * b;
23     printf("Value of --a * (3 + b) / 2 - c++ * b: %d\n", y);
24     printf("\nValues of the variables are now: \n");
25     printf("a = %d\tb = %d\tc = %d\n\n", a, b, c);
26
27     return 0;
28  }  /* main */
```

```
Results:
   Initial values of the variables:
   a = 3   b = 4   c = 5

   Value of   a *  4 + b  / 2 - c   * b: -6
   Value of --a * (3 + b) / 2 - c++ * b: -13

   Values of the variables are now:
   a = 2   b = 4   c = 6
```

Program 3-6 Evaluating expressions

WARNING

A warning is in order: In ANSI/ISO C, if an expression variable is modified more than once in an expression, the result is undefined. ANSI C has no specific rule to cover this situation, and compiler writers can implement the expression in different ways. The result is that different compilers will give different expression results. For example, consider the following rather simple expression:

```
(b++ - b++)
```

In this expression, b is modified twice. Three interpretations of this expression are possible, all correct. Given that b is initially 4, one evaluation is

```
((4++) - (b++))
(  4   - (5++))
(  4   -   5  )
(       -1    )
     b is 6
```

Two other interpretations are

```
((b++) - (4++))        ((4++) - (4++))
((5++) -   4  )        ((4  ) - (4  ))
(  5   -   4  )        (  4   -   4  )
(      +1     )        (       0     )
      b is 6                 b is 6
```

Although the side effect is the same in all cases—b is 6—the value of the expression differs. In the first case, the value is −1; in the second case, the value is +1; and, in the last case, the value is 0. *Never use a variable affected by a side effect more than once in an expression.*

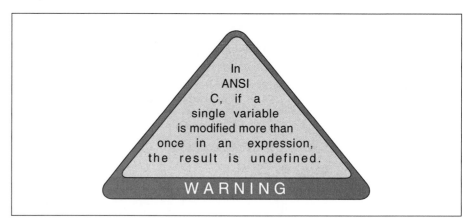

3-5 MIXED TYPE EXPRESSIONS

Up to this point, we have assumed that all of our expressions involved data of the same type. But, what happens when you write an expression that involves two different data types, such as multiplying an integer and a floating-point number? These type expressions are known as mixed type expressions, and C has rules for handling them.

The first rule is that, in an assignment expression, the final expression value must have the same type as the left operand, the operand that receives the value. This makes sense: You can't store a float in an integer variable.

IMPLICIT TYPE CONVERSION

C will automatically convert any intermediate values to the proper type so that the expression can be evaluated. When C automatically converts a type from one format to another, it is known as **implicit type conversion**. Of course, during all of these conversions, we don't want to lose any significance. Therefore, we shouldn't convert an integer into a short integer, except in the final assignment step; the maximum value that can be stored in a short integer is potentially smaller than the maximum value that can be stored in an integer.

To cover the situation, C uses the rule that, in all expressions except assignments, any implicit type conversions will always be made to the more general type according to the promotion order shown in Figure 3-12.

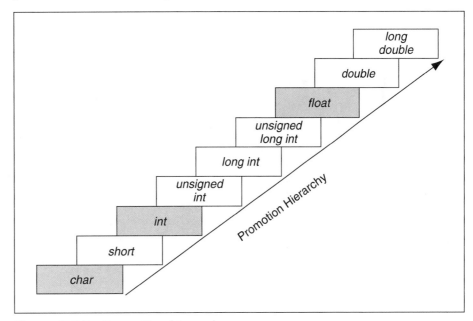

Figure 3-12   Promotion hierarchy

Using this hierarchy, if we were to add an integer and a floating-point number and store the result in an integer, we would first convert the integer to a floating-point value—because *float* is higher in the promotion hierarchy—and then, after the addition, we would convert the result back into an integer for assignment to the integer variable. Fortunately, all of this work is done for us by the compiler. Table 3-11 gives several examples of the intermediate type in a mixed type operation.

Expression	Intermediate Type
char + float	float
int – long	long
int * double	double
float / long double	long double
(short + long) / float	long *then* float

Table 3-11   Examples of implicit conversions

Let's look at a small program to see the effect of implicit conversions. In Program 3-7 we add a character, an integer, and a float. We can add characters to integers and floating-point values because all characters have a numeric value.

```
1  /* Demonstrate automatic promotion of numeric types.
2        Written by:
3        Date:
4  */
5  #include <stdio.h>
6
7  int main (void)
8  {
9  /* Local Definitions */
10    char    aChar   = 'A';
11    int     intNum  = 200;
12    double  fltNum  = 245.3;
13
14  /* Statements */
15    printf("aChar contains : %c\n", aChar);
16    printf("aChar numeric  : %d\n", aChar);
17    printf("intNum contains: %d\n", intNum);
18    printf("fltNum contains: %f\n", fltNum);
19
20    intNum = intNum + aChar;   /* aChar promoted to int   */
21    fltNum = fltNum + aChar;   /* aChar promoted to float */
22
23    printf("\nAfter additions...\n");
24    printf("aChar numeric  : %d\n", aChar);
25    printf("intNum contains: %d\n", intNum);
26    printf("fltNum contains: %f\n", fltNum);
27
28    return 0;
29  } /* main */
```

```
Results:
aChar contains :  A
aChar numeric  :  65
intNum contains:  200
fltNum contains:  245.300000

After additions...
aChar numeric  :  65
intNum contains:  265
fltNum contains:  310.300000
```

Program 3-7   Implicit type conversion

EXPLICIT TYPE CONVERSION (CAST)

Rather than let the compiler implicitly convert data, you can convert data from one type to another yourself using **explicit type conversion**. Explicit type conversion uses the **cast** expression operator. You will find the cast operator at Priority 14 in the Precedence Table (see inside front cover). To cast data from one type to another, you specify the new type in parentheses before the value you want converted. For example, to convert an integer, a, to a float, you code the expression shown below.

```
(float) a
```

The operand must be a unary expression. Therefore, if you want to cast another format, such as a binary expression, you must put it in parentheses to get the correct conversion. For example, to cast the sum of two integers to a *float*, you code

```
(float) (x + y)
```

One use of the cast is to ensure that the result of a divide is a floating-point number. For example, if you calculated the average of a series of integer test scores without a cast, the result would be an integer. To force a floating-point result, you cast the calculation as shown below.

```
average = (float) totalScores / numScores;
```

In this statement, there is an explicit conversion of totalScores to *float*, and then an implicit conversion of numScores so that it will match. The result of the divide is then a floating-point number to be assigned to average.

But beware! What would be the result of the following floating-point expression when a is 3?

```
(float) (a / 10)
```

Are you surprised to find that the result is 0.0? Since no conversions are required to divide integer 3 by integer 10, C simply divides with an integer result, 0. The integer 0 is then explicitly converted to the floating-point 0.0. To get a float result, you must cast one of the numbers as shown below.

```
(float) a / 10
```

One final thought about casts: Even when the compiler can correctly cast for you, it is sometimes better to code the cast explicitly to remind yourself that the cast is taking place.

Program 3-8 demonstrates the use of explicit casts. In this program, we divide several mixed types. While the results are nonsense, they demonstrate the effect of casting.

```
 1  /* Demonstrate casting of numeric types.
 2         Written by:
 3         Date:
 4  */
 5  #include <stdio.h>
 6
 7  int main (void)
 8  {
 9  /* Local Definitions */
10      char    aChar    = '\0';
11      int     intNum1  = 100;
```

Program 3-8   Explicit casts

```
12    int    intNum2   =   45;
13    double fltNum1   = 100.0;
14    double fltNum2   =  45.0;
15    double fltNum3;
16
17 /* Statements */
18    printf("aChar numeric   :   %3d\n",   aChar);
19    printf("intNum1 contains: %3d\n",   intNum1);
20    printf("intNum2 contains: %3d\n",   intNum2);
21    printf("fltNum1 contains: %6.2f\n", fltNum1);
22    printf("fltNum2 contains: %6.2f\n", fltNum2);
23
24    fltNum3 = (double)(intNum1 / intNum2);
25    printf
26       ("\n(double)(intNum1 / intNum2): %6.2f\n",  fltNum3);
27
28    fltNum3 = (double)intNum1 / intNum2;
29    printf("(double) intNum1 / intNum2 : %6.2f\n", fltNum3);
30
31    aChar = (char)(fltNum1 / fltNum2);
32    printf("  (char)(fltNum1 / fltNum2): %3d\n",   aChar);
33
34    return 0;
35 }  /* main */
```

```
Results:
    aChar numeric   :    0
    intNum1 contains:  100
    intNum2 contains:   45
    fltNum1 contains:  100.00
    fltNum2 contains:   45.00

    (double)(intNum1 / intNum2):   2.00
    (double) intNum1 / intNum2 :   2.22
      (char)(fltNum1 / fltNum2):   2
```

Program 3-8   Explicit casts (continued)

Program 3-8 Analysis   Study the casts carefully. The only difference between State-ments 24 and 28 is the use of parentheses around the calculation. In Statement 24, both operands are integers so the result of the division is integer, which is then cast to a *double*. In Statement 28, intNum1 is cast to a double. The compiler automatically casts intNum2 to a double before the division. The result is therefore a double. Finally, in Statement 31, we cast the result of the integer division into a character.

3-6   STATEMENTS

A **statement** causes an action to be performed by the program. It translates directly into one or more executable computer instructions. ANSI/ISO C defines six types of statements, which are shown in Figure 3-13. In this chapter, we will discuss the first two, the expression statement and the compound statement. The other types—labeled, selection, iterative, and jump—will be covered in chapters 5 and 6.

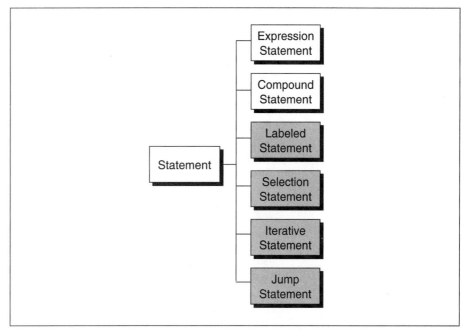

Figure 3-13 Types of statements

EXPRESSION STATEMENTS

An **expression** is turned into a statement by placing a semicolon (;) after it. When C sees the semicolon, it completes any pending side effects and discards the expression value before continuing with the next statement. An expression without side effects does not cause an action. Its value exists and it can be used, but unless a statement has a side effect, it does nothing.

Let us look at some **expression statements**. First, consider the expression statement

```
a = 2;
```

The effect of the expression statement is to store the value, 2, in the variable a. The value of the expression is 2. After the value has been stored, the expression is terminated (because there is a semicolon), and the value is discarded. C then continues with the next statement.

The next expression statement is a little more complex.

```
a = b = 3;
```

This statement actually has two expressions. If we put parentheses around them, you will be able to see them clearly.

```
a = (b = 3);
```

The parenthetical expression, (b = 3), has a side effect of assigning the value 3 to the variable b. The value of this expression is 3. The expression statement now results in the expression value 3 being assigned to the variable a. Since the expression is terminated by the semicolon, its value, 3, is discarded. The effect of the expression statement, therefore, is that 3 has been stored in both a and b.

In Chapter 2 we examined the *scanf* and *printf* functions. These statements present interesting insights into the concepts of expressions and side effects. Consider the following *scanf* function call:

```
ioResult = scanf("%d", &x);
```

This satement has two side effects. The first is found in the *scanf* function. Reading an integer value from the keyboard and placing it into the variable **x** (note the address operator before the variable) is a side effect. The second side effect is storing the value returned by *scanf*, which represents the number of values that were converted correctly. In this case, the return value could be EOF, 0, or 1. Assuming that the user correctly keys the integer, the value will be 1. The assignment operator stores the return value in **ioResult**. The expression then terminates, and the *scanf* value is discarded.

In a similar fashion, *printf* has the effect of displaying data on the monitor and returning a value, the number of characters displayed. This is seen in the statement below.

```
numDisplayed = printf
     ("x contains %d, y contains %d\n", x, y);
```

As a general rule, however, the number of characters displayed is discarded without being stored. Therefore, we normally code the above statement as shown below.

```
printf("x contains %d, y contains %d\n", x, y);
```

Now consider the following expression statement. Assume that **a** has a value of 5 before the expression is evaluated.

```
a++;
```

In this postfix expression, the value of the expression is 5, the value of the variable, a, before it is changed by the side effect. Upon completion of the expression statement, a is incremented to 6. The value of the expression, which is still 5, is discarded since the expression is now complete.

Although they are useless, the following are also expression statements. They are useless because they have no side effect and their values are not assigned to a variable. We usually don't use them, but it is important to know they are syntactically correct expression statements. C will evaluate them, determine their value, and then discard the value.[1]

```
b ;                 3 ;                 ;
```

The third expression above, the semicolon, is an example of a null expression statement. The null expression statement has no side effect and no value, but it is useful in some complex statements.

> An expression statement is terminated with a semicolon. The semicolon is a terminator, and it tells the compiler that the statement is finished.

---

[1]In an optimized compiler, the translator determines that there is no effect and generates no code.

COMPOUND STATEMENTS

A **compound statement** is a unit of code consisting of zero or more statements. It is also known as a **block**. The compound statement allows a group of statements to become one single entity. You used a compound statement in your first program when you formed the body of the function `main`. All C functions contain a compound statement known as the function body.

A compound statement consists of an opening brace, an optional declaration and definition section, and an optional statement section, followed by a closing brace. Although both the declaration–definition section and the statement section statements are optional, one should be present. If neither is present, then you have a null statement, which doesn't make much sense. Figure 3-14 shows the makeup of a compound statement.

Figure 3-14 Compound statement

One important point to remember is that a compound statement does not need a semicolon. If you put a semicolon after the closing brace, the compiler thinks that you have put an extra null statement after the compound statement. This is poor style, but it does not generate any code or give you a compile error.

C requires placement of the declaration and definition code before any statements within a compound statement block. The code in the declaration section and statement section cannot be intermixed.

STATEMENTS AND DEFINED CONSTANTS

When you use preprocessor-defined commands, be very careful to make sure that you do not create an error. Remember that the defined constant is an automatic substitution. This can cause subtle problems. One common mistake is to place a semicolon at the end of the definition. Since the preprocessor uses a simple text replacement of the name with whatever expression follows, the compiler will generate a compile error if it finds a semicolon at the end of the definition. This problem is seen in the following example:

```
#define SALES_TAX_RATE 0.825;
...
salesTax = SALES_TAX_RATE * salesAmount;
```

After the substitution, the following erroneous code occurs because the programmer coded a semicolon after the constant value:

```
salesTax = 0.0825; * salesAmount;
```

This can be an extremely difficult compile error to figure out because you see the original statement and not the erroneous substitution error. One of the reasons programmers use uppercase for defined constant identifiers is to provide an automatic warning to readers that they are not looking at the real code.

3-7 SAMPLE PROGRAMS

This section contains several programs that you should study for programming technique and style.

EXAMPLE: CALCULATE QUOTIENT AND REMAINDER

Let's write a program that calculates and prints the quotient and remainder of two integer numbers. The code is shown in Program 3-9.

```
1   /* Calculate and print quotient and remainder of two numbers.
2         Written by:
3         Date:
4   */
5   #include <stdio.h>
6
7   int main (void)
8   {
9   /* Local Definitions */
10     int   intNum1;
11     int   intNum2;
12     int   intCalc;
13
14  /* Statements */
15     printf("Enter two integral numbers: ");
16     scanf ("%d %d", &intNum1, &intNum2);
17
18     intCalc = intNum1 / intNum2;
19     printf("%d / %d is %d", intNum1, intNum2, intCalc);
20
21     intCalc = intNum1 % intNum2;
22     printf(" with a remainder of: %d\n", intCalc);
23
24     return 0;
25  }  /* main */
```

```
Results:
   Enter two integral numbers: 13 2
   13 / 2 is 6 with a remainder of: 1
```

Program 3-9   Calculate quotient and remainder

Program 3-9 Analysis   Using good programming style, the program begins with documentation about what it does, who created it, and when it was created.

Program 3-9 has no global variable declarations, so after including the standard input/output library, we start immediately with main. Following main is the opening brace. The matching closing brace is found on line 25.

The most difficult part of this program is figuring out how to get the remainder. Fortunately, C has a modulo operator (%) that does the job for us. The rest of the problem is straightforward.

EXAMPLE: PRINT RIGHT DIGIT

Another problem that requires the use of the modulo operator is to print a digit contained in an integer. Program 3-10 prints the least significant (rightmost) digit of an integer.

```
 1  /* Print rightmost digit of an integer.
 2         Written by:
 3         Date:
 4  */
 5  #include <stdio.h>
 6
 7  int main (void)
 8  {
 9  /* Local Definitions */
10     int   intNum;
11     int   oneDigit;
12
13  /* Statements */
14     printf("Enter an integral numbers: ");
15     scanf ("%d", &intNum);
16
17     oneDigit = intNum % 10;
18     printf("\nThe right digit is: %d", oneDigit);
19
20     return 0;
21  }   /* main */
```

```
Results:
   Enter an integral numbers: 185

   The right digit is: 5
```

Program 3-10   Print right digit of integer

EXAMPLE: CALCULATE AVERAGE

Program 3-11 reads four integers from the keyboard, calculates their average, and then prints the numbers with their average and the deviation (not the standard deviation, just the difference plus or minus) from the average.

```
 1  /* This program calculates the average of four integers and
 2         prints the numbers and their deviation from the average.
 3         Written by:
 4         Date:
 5  */
 6  #include <stdio.h>
 7  int main (void)
 8  {
 9  /* Local Definitions */
```

Program 3-11   Calculate average of four numbers

```
10    int     num1;
11    int     num2;
12    int     num3;
13    int     num4;
14    int     sum;
15
16    float   average;
17
18 /* Statements */
19    printf("\nEnter the first number  : ");
20    scanf("%d", &num1);
21    printf("Enter the second number : ");
22    scanf("%d", &num2);
23    printf("Enter the third  number : ");
24    scanf("%d", &num3);
25    printf("Enter the fourth number : ");
26    scanf("%d", &num4);
27
28    sum     = num1 + num2 + num3 + num4;
29    average = sum / 4.0;
30
31    printf("\n ******** average is %6.2f ******** ",
32            average);
33    printf("\n");
34
35    printf("\nfirst number:  %6d -- deviation: %8.2f",
36            num1, num1 - average);
37    printf("\nsecond number: %6d -- deviation: %8.2f",
38            num2, num2 - average);
39    printf("\nthird number:  %6d -- deviation: %8.2f",
40            num3, num3 - average);
41    printf("\nfourth number: %6d -- deviation: %8.2f",
42            num4, num4 - average);
43
44    return 0;
45 }  /* main */
```

```
Results:
   Enter the first number:  23
   Enter the second number: 12
   Enter the third  number: 45
   Enter the fourth number: 23

   ******** average is 25.75   ********

   first number:       23 -- deviation:     -2.75
   second number:      12 -- deviation:    -13.75
   third number:       45 -- deviation:     19.25
   fourth number:      23 -- deviation:     -2.75
```

Program 3-11   Calculate average of four numbers (continued)

Program 3-11 Analysis   Program 3-11 is a little more complex than the previous ones. At the beginning of `main` are several variable definitions, five integers, and a float. The first four are for the variables read from the keyboard, the fifth is for the sum, and the *float* is for the average.

The statements section starts by reading the data. Each read is preceded by a display so the user will know what to do. The specific instructions about what to input are known as **user prompts**. You should always tell the user what input is expected from the keyboard. After the user has keyed the data, the program continues by adding the numbers, placing the total in `sum`, and computing `average`. It then displays the results. Notice that the program displays the results in a format that allows the user to easily verify that the program ran correctly. The program not only prints the average but also repeats each input with its deviation from the average. After completing its work, the program concludes by returning to the operating system.

Look at the results carefully. Note how each series of numbers is aligned so that they can be easily read. Taking the time to align output is one of the things that distinguishes a good programmer from an average programmer. Always pay attention to how your program presents its results to the user. Paying attention to these little details pays off in the long run.

EXAMPLE: DEGREES TO RADIANS

One way to measure an angle in a circle is in degrees. For example, the angle formed by a clock at 3 o'clock is 90°. Another way to measure the angle is in radians. One radian is equal to 57.295779 degrees. In Program 3-12 we ask the user to input an angle in radians, and we convert it to degrees.

```
 1  /* This program prompts the user to enter an angle measured
 2     in radians and converts it into degrees.
 3        Written by:
 4        Date:
 5  */
 6  #include <stdio.h>
 7
 8  #define DEGREE_FACTOR 57.295779
 9
10  int main (void)
11  {
12  /* Local Definitions */
13     double  radians;
14     double  degrees;
15
16  /* Statements */
17     printf("Enter the angle in radians: ");
18     scanf("%lf", &radians);
19
20     degrees = radians * DEGREE_FACTOR;
21
22     printf("%6.3f radians is %6.3f degrees\n",
23             radians, degrees);
24     return 0;
```

Program 3-12   Convert radians to degrees

```
25 }  /* main */
```

```
Results:
    Enter the angle in radians: 1.57080
    1.571 radians is 90.000 degrees
```

Program 3-12 Convert radians to degrees (continued)

Program 3-12 Analysis   In this short program we introduce the defined constant. Defined constants are an excellent way to document factors in a program. We could have just as easily used a memory constant. Because factors are usually placed at the beginning of the program where they can easily be found and changed as necessary, they should not be variables. Remember that the area before main is global and that variables should be protected in functions.

EXAMPLE: FAHRENHEIT TO CELSIUS

Program 3-13 changes a temperature reading from Fahrenheit to Celsius using the following formula:

Celsius = (100 / 180) * (Fahrenheit - 32)

```
 1 /* This program shows how to change a temperature in
 2    Fahrenheit to Celsius
 3       Written by:
 4       Date:
 5 */
 6 #include <stdio.h>
 7
 8 #define CONVERSION_FACTOR (100.0 / 180.0)
 9
10 int main (void)
11 {
12 /* Local Definitions */
13    float cel;
14    float fah;
15
16 /* Statements */
17    printf("Enter the temperature in Fahrenheit: ");
18    scanf("%f", &fah);
19
20    cel = CONVERSION_FACTOR * (fah - 32);
21
22    printf("Fahrenheit temperature is: %5.1f\n", fah);
23    printf("Celsius temperature is:    %5.1f\n", cel);
24
25    return 0;
26 }  /* main */
```

```
Results:
    Enter the temperature in Fahrenheit: 98.6
    Fahrenheit temperature is:  98.6
    Celsius temperature is:     37.0
```

Program 3-13 Fahrenheit to Celsius

Program 3-13 Analysis   Notice how we used the defined constant for the conversion factor in this program. First, the expression is enclosed in parentheses. This is always a good idea. It ensures that the constant, when combined with other expressions, will be evaluated properly. Second, notice how we coded the expression: (100.0 / 180.0). The decimals ensure that the result will be a floating-point number, not an integer. Then, the expression is coded in user terminology. We could have reduced the expression to 5.0 / 9.0, and while it would be mathematically correct, it is potentially confusing because the user specification stated the formula as 100 / 180. Whenever possible, keep user terminology and algorithms consistent in your programs.

EXAMPLE: CALCULATE SALES TOTAL

Program 3-14 calculates a sale given the unit price, quantity, discount rate, and sales tax rate.

```
 1  /* Calculates the total sale given the unit price,
 2     quantity, discount, and tax rate.
 3        Written by:
 4        Date:
 5  */
 6  #include <stdio.h>
 7
 8  #define TAX_RATE 8.50
 9
10  int main (void)
11  {
12  /* Local Definitions */
13     int     quantity;
14
15     float   discountRate;
16     float   discountAm;
17     float   unitPrice;
18     float   subTotal;
19     float   subTaxable;
20     float   taxAm;
21     float   total;
22
23  /* Statements */
24     printf("\nEnter number of items sold:         ");
25     scanf("%d", &quantity);
26
27     printf("Enter the unit price:              ");
28     scanf("%f", &unitPrice);
29
30     printf("Enter the discount rate (per cent): ");
31     scanf("%f", &discountRate);
32
33     subTotal    = quantity * unitPrice;
34     discountAm  = subTotal * discountRate / 100.0;
35     subTaxable  = subTotal - discountAm;
36     taxAm = subTaxable * TAX_RATE/ 100.00;
```

Program 3-14   Calculate sales total

```
37    total = subTaxable + taxAm;
38
39    printf("\nQuantity sold:         %6d\n", quantity);
40    printf("Unit Price of items: %9.2f\n", unitPrice);
41    printf("                      ------------\n");
42
43    printf("Subtotal :           %9.2f\n", subTotal);
44    printf("Discount:           -%9.2f\n", discountAm);
45    printf("Discounted total:    %9.2f\n", subTaxable);
46    printf("Sales tax:          +%9.2f\n", taxAm);
47    printf("Total sale:          %9.2f\n", total );
48
49    return 0;
50 } /* main */
```

```
Results:
    Enter number of items sold:        34
    Enter the unit price:              12.89
    Enter the discount rate (per cent): 7

    Quantity sold:            34
    Unit Price of items:      12.89

                          ------------
    Subtotal :                438.26
    Discount:             -    30.68
    Discounted total:         407.58
    Sales tax:            +    34.64
    Total sale:               442.23
```

Program 3-14   Calculate sales total (continued)

Program 3-14 Analysis   Look at the results of this program carefully. Do you see any problems? Just because a program runs doesn't mean that it is running correctly. In this case, the total is incorrect (407.58 + 34.64 is not equal to 442.23). The problem is created by the floating-point arithmetic and rounding errors. If we wanted absolute accuracy, we would have to do the arithmetic in integer (cents) and then divide by 100 to print the report.

EXAMPLE:
CALCULATE
STUDENT SCORE

Program 3-15 calculates the average score for a student. The class has four quizzes (30%), two midterms (40%), and a final (30%). The maximum score for all quizzes and exams is 100 points.

```
1 /* Calculate a student's average score for a course
2    with 4 quizzes, 2 midterms, and a final. The quizzes
3    are weighted 30%, the midterms 40%, & the final 30%.
4       Written by:
5       Date:
6 */
7 #include <stdio.h>
```

Program 3-15   Calculate student score

```
 8
 9   #define QUIZ_WEIGHT      30
10   #define MIDTERM_WEIGHT   40
11   #define FINAL_WEIGHT     30
12   #define QUIZ_MAX        400.00
13   #define MIDTERM_MAX     200.00
14   #define FINAL_MAX       100.00
15
16   int main (void)
17   {
18   /* Local Definitions */
19      int     quiz1;
20      int     quiz2;
21      int     quiz3;
22      int     quiz4;
23      int     totalQuiz;
24      int     midterm1;
25      int     midterm2;
26      int     totalMidterm;
27      int     final;
28
29      float   quizPercent;
30      float   midtermPercent;
31      float   finalPercent;
32      float   totalPercent;
33
34   /* Statements */
35      printf("=========== QUIZZES ================\n");
36      printf("Enter the score for the first quiz:  ");
37      scanf("%d", &quiz1);
38      printf("Enter the score for the second quiz: ");
39      scanf("%d", &quiz2);
40      printf("Enter the score for the third quiz:  ");
41      scanf("%d", &quiz3);
42      printf("Enter the score for the fourth quiz: ");
43      scanf("%d", &quiz4);
44
45      printf("============= MIDTERM  =============\n");
46      printf("Enter the score for the first midterm:  ");
47      scanf("%d", &midterm1);
48      printf("Enter the score for the second midterm: ");
49      scanf("%d", &midterm2);
50
51      printf("=============== FINAL =============\n");
52      printf("Enter the score for the final: ");
53      scanf("%d", &final);
54      printf("\n");
55
56      totalQuiz = quiz1 + quiz2 + quiz3 + quiz4;
```

Program 3-15 Calculate student score (continued)

```
57        totalMidterm = midterm1 + midterm2;
58
59        quizPercent =
60           (float)totalQuiz * QUIZ_WEIGHT / QUIZ_MAX;
61        midtermPercent =
62           (float)totalMidterm * MIDTERM_WEIGHT / MIDTERM_MAX;
63        finalPercent =
64           (float)final * FINAL_WEIGHT / FINAL_MAX;
65
66        totalPercent =
67             quizPercent + midtermPercent + finalPercent;
68
69        printf("First Quiz  %4d\n",   quiz1);
70        printf("Second Quiz %4d\n",   quiz2);
71        printf("Third Quiz  %4d\n",   quiz3);
72        printf("Fourth Quiz %4d\n",   quiz4);
73        printf("Quiz Total  %4d\n\n", totalQuiz);
74
75        printf("First Midterm  %4d\n",   midterm1);
76        printf("Second Midterm %4d\n",   midterm2);
77        printf("Total Midterms %4d\n\n", totalMidterm);
78
79        printf("Final          %4d\n\n", final);
80
81        printf("Quiz    %6.1f%%\n" , quizPercent);
82        printf("Midterm %6.1f%%\n" , midtermPercent);
83        printf("Final   %6.1f%%\n" , finalPercent);
84        printf("--------------\n");
85        printf("Total   %6.1f%%\n" , totalPercent);
86
87        return 0;
88  }  /* main */
```

```
Results
    =========== QUIZZES ================
    Enter the score for the first quiz:  98
    Enter the score for the second quiz: 89
    Enter the score for the third quiz:  78
    Enter the score for the fourth quiz: 79
    ============= MIDTERM  ============
    Enter the score for the first midterm:  90
    Enter the score for the second midterm: 100
    =============== FINAL ============
    Enter the score for the final: 92

    First Quiz     98
    Second Quiz    89
    Third Quiz     78
    Fourth Quiz    79
    Quiz Total    344
```

Program 3-15 Calculate student score (continued)

```
First Midterm      90
Second Midterm    100
Total Midterms    190

Final              92

Quiz      25.8%
Midterm   38.0%
Final     27.6%
--------------
Total     91.4%
```

Program 3-15   Calculate student score (continued)

Program 3-15 Analysis   This rather long program contains several points to consider. First, note how the program starts with a series of defined constants. Putting the definitions of constant values at the beginning of the program does two things: (1) It gives them names that we can use in the program. (2) It makes them easy to change.

Now study the statements. Notice how they are grouped? By putting a blank line between a group of related statements, you separate them, much as you would separate paragraphs in a report. This makes it easy for the user to follow the program.

Finally, study the input and output. Notice that the user was prompted for all input with clear instructions. We even divided the input with headings.

The output is also divided, making it easy to read. It would be even easier to read if we aligned all the amounts, but the techniques for doing so will not be introduced until Chapter 7.

3-8 SOFTWARE ENGINEERING AND PROGRAMMING STYLE

In this section we discuss three concepts that, although technically not engineering principles, are important to writing clear and understandable programs.

KISS

Keep It Simple and Short (**KISS**[2]) is an old programming principle. Unfortunately, many programmers tend to forget it, especially the simple part. They seem to feel that just because they are working on a complex problem, the solution must be complex, too. That is simply not true. Good programmers solve the problem in the simplest possible way; they do not contribute to a complex situation by writing obscure and complex code.

A trivial example will make the point. If you were writing a program that reads floating-point numbers from the keyboard, you would not program it so that the user had to enter the integral portion of the number first and then the fractional part. Although this would work, it is unnecessarily complex, even though it might be a fun way to solve the problem.

Unfortunately, C provides many operators and expression rules that make it easy for a programmer to write obscure and difficult to follow code. Your job as a programmer is to make sure that your code is always easy to read. Your code should be unambiguous: It should not be written so that it is easy to misread it.

Another old structured programming principle is that a function should not be larger than one page of code. Now, for online programming in a workstation environment, a function should be no longer than one screen—about 20 lines of code. By breaking a problem down into small, easily understood parts, we simplify it. Then we reassemble the simple components into a simple solution to a complex problem.

> Blocks of code should be no longer than one screen.

One element of the C language that tends to complicate programs, especially for new programmers, is side effects. We explained in "Evaluating Expressions," on page 85, that side effects can lead to confusing and different results depending on the code. You need to fully understand the effects when you write C code. If you are unsure of the effects, then simplify your logic until you are sure.

PARENTHESES

One programming technique to simplify code is to use parentheses, even when unnecessary. While this may lead to a few extra keystrokes, it can save hours of debugging time created by a misunderstanding of the precedence and associativity rules. If a statement contains more than one expression type, use parentheses to ensure that the compiler will interpret it as you intended.

---

[2]KISS originally had a different, rather insulting, meaning. We prefer this interpretation.

> Computers do what you *tell* them to do, not what you *intended* to tell them to do. Make sure your code is as clear and simple as possible.

USER COMMUNICATION

You should always make sure you communicate with your user from the very first statement in your program to the very last. As mentioned previously, we recommend that you start your program with a message that identifies the program and end with a display that says the program is done.

When you give your user instructions, make sure that they are clear and understandable. In Program 3-14, on page 101, we used three statements to give the user complete and detailed instructions on what we wanted entered. We could have simply said

```
"Enter data"
```

but that would have been vague and subject to interpretation. How would the user know what specific data were required? For each input in Program 3-14, we told the users exactly what data we needed in terms that they understand. If you don't tell users exactly what data to input, they may do anything they feel like, which is usually not what you wanted or expected.

One common mistake made by new programmers is to forget to tell the user anything. What do you think would be the user's response to Program 3-16 when confronted with a blank screen and a computer that is doing nothing?

```
1   #include <stdio.h>
2   int main (void)
3   {
4      int  i;
5      int  j;
6      int  sum;
7
8      scanf("%d%d", &i, &j);
9      sum = i + j;
10     printf("The sum of %d & %d is %d\n", i, j, sum);
11     return 0;
12  }  /*  main  */
```

Program 3-16 Program that will confuse the user

We will return to these three concepts from time to time when we introduce new structures that tend to be confusing or misunderstood.

3-9   TIPS AND COMMON PROGRAMMING ERRORS

1. Be aware of expression side effects. They are one of the main sources of confusion and logical errors in a program.

2. Use decrement/increment operators wisely. Understand the difference between postfix and prefix decrement/increment operators before using them.

3. Add parentheses in your program everywhere you feel they will help to make the purpose clear.

4. It is a compile error to use a variable that has not been defined.

5. It is a compile error to forget the semicolon at the end of an expression statement.

6. It is a compile error to code a variable declaration or definition once you have started the statement section. Therefore, you should use comments to separate these two sections within a function.

7. It is most likely a compile error to terminate a defined constant (*#define*) with a semicolon. This is an especially difficult error to decipher because you will not see it in your code—you see the code you wrote, not the code that the preprocessor substituted.

8. It is a compile error when the operand on the left of the assignment operator is not a variable. For example, a + 3 is not a variable and cannot receive the value of b * c.

```
(a + 3) = b * c;
```

9. It is a compile error to use the increment or decrement operators with any expression other than a variable identifier. For example, the following code is an error:

```
(a + 3)++
```

10. It is a compile error to use the modulus operator (%) with anything other than integers.

11. It is a logic error to use a variable before it has been assigned a value.

12. It is a logic error to modify a variable in an expression when the variable appears more than once. For example, the following code compiles and runs but will give inconsistent results:

```
a++ * (a + b)
a = a++ + b
```

3-10   KEY TERMS AND CONCEPTS[3]

additive expression
assignment expression
associativity
binary expression
block
cast
compound statement
evaluating expressions
explicit type conversion
expression
expression statement
expression type

implicit type conversion
KISS
left associativity
multiplicative expression
name
operand
operator
precedence
postfix decrement
postfix expression
postfix increment

prefix decrement
prefix increment
primary expression
right associativity
side effect
sizeof
statement
unary expression
unary minus
unary plus
user prompts

[3]Note: Italic terms are C keywords or standard function names.

3-11   SUMMARY

- An expression is a sequence of operators and operands that reduces to a single value.

- An operator is a language-specific token that requires an action to be taken.

- An operand is the recipient of the action.

- C has seven kinds of expressions: primary, postfix, unary, binary, ternary, assignment, and comma.

- The most elementary type of expression is a primary expression. A primary expression is an expression made up of only one operand. It can be a name, a constant, or a parenthetical expression.

- A postfix expression is an expression made up of an operand followed by an operator. C has five different postfix expressions. You studied function call and postfix increment/decrement expressions in this chapter.

- A unary expression is an expression made up of an operator followed by an operand. C has eight kinds of unary expressions. You studied only five in this chapter: prefix increment/decrement, *sizeof*, and plus/minus expressions.

- A binary expression is an expression made up of two operands with an operator between them. Although C has ten different categories of binary expressions, you studied only two in this chapter: multiplicative and additive.

- An assignment expression is made up of two operands with the assignment operator (=) between them.

- Precedence is a concept that determines the order in which different operators in a complex expression act on their operands.

- Associativity defines the order of evaluation when operators have the same precedence.

- The side effect of an expression is one of the unique phenomena in C. An expression can have a side effect in addition to a value. The side effect can be pre-effect or posteffect.

- To evaluate an expression, we must follow the rules of precedence and associativity.

- A statement causes an action to be performed by the program.

- Although C has six different types of statements, you studied only two types in this chapter: expression and compound statements.

- An expression statement is an expression converted to a statement by keeping the side effect and discarding the value.

- A compound statement is a combination of statements enclosed in two braces.

- KISS means "Keep It Simple and Short."

- One of the important recommendations in software engineering is the use of parentheses when they can help clarify your code.

- Another recommendation in software engineering is to communicate clearly with the user.

3-12 PRACTICE SETS

REVIEW QUESTIONS

1. A unary expression consists of only one operand with no operator.
   a. True   b. False

2. The left operand in an assignment expression must be a single variable.
   a. True   b. False

3. Associativity is used to determine which of several different expressions is evaluated first.
   a. True   b. False

4. Side effect is an action that results from the evaluation of an expression.
   a. True   b. False

5. An expression statement is terminated with a period.
   a. True   b. False

6. A(n) _____ is a sequence of operands and operators that reduces to a single value.
   a. expression   d. function
   b. format   e. value
   c. formula

7. C contains seven different expression formats. Which of the following is not an expression format?
   a. assignment   c. conditional
   b. binary   d. primary

8. Which of the following expressions has the highest precedence?
   a. assignment   c. conditional
   b. binary   d. primary

9. Which of the following is a unary expression?
   a. `i + j`   d. `scanf(…)`
   b. `++a`   e. `x *= 5`
   c. `c++`

10. The _____ expression evaluates the operand on the right side of the operator and places its value in the variable on the left side of the operator.
    a. additive   d. postfix
    b. assignment   e. primary
    c. multiplicative

11. _____ is used to determine the order in which different operators in a complex expression are evaluated.
    a. associativity   d. precedence
    b. evaluation   e. side effect
    c. format

12. _____ is an action that results from the evaluation of an expression.
    a. associativity   d. precedence
    b. evaluation   e. side effect
    c. format

13. Which of the following statements about mixed expressions is false?
    a. A cast cannot be used to change an assigned value.
    b. An explicit cast can be used to change the expression type.
    c. An explicit cast on a variable changes its type in memory.
    d. An implicit cast is generated by the compiler automatically when necessary.
    e. Constant casting is done by the compiler automatically.

14. A(n) _____ causes an action to be performed by the program.
    a. expression   d. operand
    b. function   e. statement
    c. operator

15. Which of the following statements about compound statements is false?
    a. A compound statement is also known as a block.
    b. A compound statement is enclosed in a set of braces.
    c. All compound statements must be terminated by a semicolon.
    d. The declaration and definition section in a compound statement is optional.
    e. The statement section in a compound statement is optional.

EXERCISES

16. Which of the following expressions are not postfix expressions?
    a. `x++`   d. `x * y`
    b. `--x`   e. `++x`
    c. `scanf (…)`

17. Which of the following are not unary expressions?
    a. `++x`   d. `+5`
    b. `--x`   e. `x = 4`
    c. `sizeof (x)`

18. Which of the following is not a binary expression?
    a. 3 * 5
    b. x += 6
    c. y = 5 +2
    d. z - 2
    e. y % z

19. Which of the following is not a valid assignment expression?
    a. x = 23
    b. 4 = x
    c. y % = 5
    d. x = 8 = 3
    e. x = r = 5

20. If originally x = 4, what is the value of x after the evaluation of the following expression?
    a. x = 2
    b. x += 4
    c. x + = x +3
    d. x * = 2
    e. x / = x +2

21. If originally x = 3 and y = 5, what is the value of x and y after each of the following expressions?
    a. x++ + y
    b. ++x
    c. x++ + y++
    d. ++x + 2
    e. x- - - y- -

22. What is the value of each of the following expressions?
    a. 24 - 6 * 2
    b. -15 * 2 + 3 + 15 % 4
    c. 72 / 5
    d. 72 % 5
    e. 5 * 2 / 6 +

23. What is the value of each of the following expressions?
    a. 6.2 + 5.1 * 3.2
    b. 2.0 + 3.0 / 1.2
    c. 4.0 * (3.0 + 2.0 / 6.0)
    d. 6.0 / (2.0 + 4.0 * 1.2)
    e. 2.7 + 3.2 - 5.3 * 1.1

24. Given the following definitions, which of the following statements are valid assignments?
    ```
    #define NUM10 10
        int   x;
        int   y = 15;
    ```
    a. x = 5;
    b. y = 5;
    c. x = y = 50;
    d. x = 50 = y;
    e. x = x + 1;
    f. y = 1 + NUM10;
    g. 5 = y;

25. If originally x = 2, y = 3, and z = 2, what is the value of each of the following expressions?
    a. x++ + y++
    b. ++x - - -z
    c. - -x + y++
    d. x- - + x- - - - y- -
    e. x + y - - -x + x++ - - -y

26. If originally x = 2, y = 3, and z = 1, what is the value of each of the following expressions?
    a. x + 2 / 6 + y
    b. y - 3 * z+2
    c. z - (x + z) % 2 + 4
    d. x - 2 * (3 + z) + y
    e. y++ + z- - + x++

27. If x = 2945, what is the value of each of the following expressions?
    a. x % 10
    b. x / 10
    c. (x / 10) % 10
    d. x / 100
    e. (x / 100) % 10

28. What is the output from the following code fragment?
    ```
    int a;
    int b;
    a = b = 50;
    printf ("%4d %4d", a, b);
    a = a * 2;
    b = b / 2;
    printf ("%4d %4d", a, b);
    ```

PROBLEMS

29. Given the following pseudocode, write a program that executes it. Use floating-point types for all values.

    ```
    1 read x
    2 read y
    3 compute p = x * y
    4 compute s = x + y
    5 total = s² + p * (s - x) * (p + y)
    6 print total
    ```

30. Write a program that reads two integers from the keyboard, multiplies them, and then prints the two numbers and their product.

31. Write a program that extracts and prints the rightmost digit of the integral portion of a *float*.

32. Write a program that extracts and prints the second rightmost digit of the integral portion of a *float*.

33. Write a program that calculates the area and perimeter of a rectangle from a user-supplied (*scanf*) length and width.

34. We are all familiar with the fact that angles are measured in degrees, minutes, and seconds. Another measure of an angle is a radian. A radian is the angle formed by two radii forming an arc that is equal to the radius of their circle. One radian equals 57.295779 degrees. Write a program that converts degrees into radians. Provide good user prompts. Include the following test data in your run:

> 90° is 1.57080 radians

35. The formula for converting centigrade temperatures to Fahrenheit is :

$$F = 32 + \left(C \times \frac{180.0}{100.0}\right)$$

Write a program that asks the user to enter a temperature reading in centigrade and then prints the equivalent Fahrenheit value. Be sure to include at least one negative centigrade number in your test cases.

36. Write the C code for each of the following formulas. Assume that all variables are defined as double.
    a.

    $$KinEn = \frac{mv^2}{2}$$

    b.

    $$res = \frac{b+c}{2bc}$$

37. Write the C code to calculate and print the next two numbers in each of the following series. You may use only one variable in each problem.
    a. 0, 5, 10, 15, 20, 25, ?, ?
    b. 0, 2, 4, 6, 8, 10, ?, ?
    c. 1, 2, 4, 8, 16, 32, ?, ?

PROJECTS

38. Write a program that converts and prints a user-supplied measurement in inches into
    a. foot (12 inches)   c. centimeter (2.54/inch)
    b. yard (36 inches)   d. meter (39.37 inches)

39. A Fibonacci number is a member of a set in which each number is the sum of the previous two numbers. (The Fibonacci series describes a form of a spiral.) The series begins

> 0, 1, 1, 2, 3, 5, 8, 13, 21, …

Write a program that calculates and prints the next three numbers in the Fibonacci series. You are to use only three variables, `fib1`, `fib2`, and `fib3`.

40. Write a program that prompts a user for an integer value in the range 0 to 32,767 and then prints the individual digits of the numbers on a line with three spaces between the digits. The first line is to start with the leftmost digit and print all five digits; the second line is to start with the second digit from the left and print four digits, and so forth. For example, if the user enters 1234, your program should print

> 0   1   2   3   4
> 1   2   3   4
> 2   3   4
> 3   4
> 4

41. Write a program to create a customer's bill for a company. The company sells only five different products: TV, VCR, Remote Controller, CD Player, and Tape Recorder. The unit prices are $400.00, $220, $35.20, $300.00, and $150.00, respectively. The program must read the quantity of each piece of equipment purchased from the keyboard. It then calculates the cost of each item, the subtotal, and the total cost after an 8.25% sales tax.

The input data consist of a set of integers representing the quantities of each item sold. These integers must be input into the program in a user friendly way; that is, the program must prompt the user for each quantity as shown below. The numbers in boldface show the user's answers.

> How Many TVs Were Sold? **3**
> How Many VCRs Were Sold? **5**
> How Many Remote Controllers Were Sold? **1**
> How Many CDs Were Sold? **2**
> How Many Tape Recorders Were Sold? **4**

The format for the output from the program follows:

QTY	DESCRIPTION	UNIT PRICE	TOTAL PRICE
---	-----------	----------	-----------
XX	TV	400.00	XXXX.XX
XX	VCR	220.00	XXXX.XX
XX	REMOTE CTRLR	35.20	XXXX.XX
XX	CD PLAYER	300.00	XXXX.XX
XX	TAPE RECORDER	150.00	XXXX.XX

		SUBTOTAL	XXXXX.XX
		TAX	XXXX.XX
		TOTAL	XXXXX.XX

Use either defined constants or memory constants for the unit prices and the tax rate. Use integer variables to store the quantities for each item. Use floating-point variables to store the total price for each item, the bill subtotal, the tax amount, and the total amount of the bill. Run your program twice with the following data:

```
SET 1 ⇨ 2   1   4   1   2
SET 2 ⇨ 3   0   2   0  21
```

Functions 4

The programs we have presented so far have been very simple. They solved problems that could be understood without too much effort. As we consider larger and larger programs, however, you will discover that it is not possible to understand all aspects of such programs without somehow reducing them to more elementary parts.

Breaking a complex problem into smaller parts is a common practice. For example, suppose that for your vacation this year you decide to drive in a circular route that will allow you to visit as many national parks as possible in 2 weeks. Your requirements for this problem are very simple: Visit as many parks as possible in 2 weeks. But how will you do it? You might first gather some data about national parks and then you calculate the distance between each of them to figure out the travel time. Next, you would estimate how much time it would take to visit each park. Finally, you would put all your data together to plan your itinerary. Then you would make your motel and camp reservations and any other arrangements that had to be in place in advance.

The planning for large programs is similar. First, you must understand the problem as a whole; then you must break it into simpler, understandable parts. We call each of these parts of a program a *module* and the process of subdividing a problem into manageable parts **top–down design**. The implementation of the resulting design using the three basic constructs—sequence (Chapter 3), selection (Chapter 5), and repetition (Chapter 6)—popularized by Edsger Dijkstra[1] is known as *structured programming*.

---

[1]Dijkstra's work was based on earlier research by two Italian computer scientists, Corrado Bohm and Guiseppe Jacopini. They proved that any algorithm could be written with only these three constructs.

4-1 DESIGNING STRUCTURED PROGRAMS

The principles of top–down design and structured programming dictate that a program should be divided into a main module and its related modules. Each module should also be divided into submodules according to software engineering principles that we will discuss in "Software Engineering and Programming Style" on page 154. The division of modules proceeds until the module consists only of elementary processes that are intrinsically understood and cannot be further subdivided. This process is known as *factoring*.

> In top-down design, a program is divided into a main module and its related modules. Each module is in turn divided into submodules until the resulting modules are intrinsic; that is, until they are implicitly understood without further division.

Top–down design is usually done using a visual representation of the modules known as a **structure chart**. The structure chart shows the relation between each module and its submodules. The rules for reading and creating structure charts are also covered in "Software Engineering and Programming Style," but at this point, you only need a few simple rules. First, the structure chart is read top–down, left–right. Referring to Figure 4-1, first we read Main Module. In this case, Main Module represents our entire set of code to solve the problem.

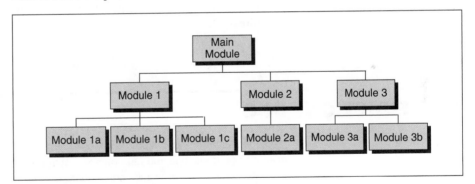

Figure 4-1 Structure chart

Going down and left, we then read Module 1. On the same level with Module 1 are Module 2 and Module 3. The main module consists of three submodules. At this point, however, we are dealing only with Module 1. We now note that Module 1 is further subdivided into three modules, Module 1a, Module 1b, and Module 1c. To write the code for Module 1, therefore, we will need to write code for its three submodules. What does this concept say about writing the code for the Main Module?

Now for some more terminology. The Main Module is known as a *calling* module because it has submodules. Each of the submodules is known as a *called* module. But, because Modules 1, 2, and 3 also have submodules, they are also calling modules; they are both called and calling modules.

Communication between modules in a structure chart is allowed only through a calling module. If Module 1 needs to send data to Module 2, the data must be passed through the calling module, Main Module. No communication can take place directly between modules that do not have a calling–called relationship.

> In a structure chart, a module can be called
> by one and only one higher module.

With this understanding, how can Module 1a send data to Module 3b? It first sends the data to Module 1, which in turn sends it to the Main Module, which passes it to Module 3, and then on to Module 3b. Although this sounds complex, you will find that it is easily done.

The technique used to pass data to a function is known as **parameter passing**. The parameters are contained in a list that is a definition of the data passed to the function by the caller. The list serves as the formal declaration of the data types and names.

Data are passed to a function using one of two techniques: **pass by value** or **pass by reference**. In pass by value, a copy of the data is made and the copy is sent to the function. This technique results in the parameters being copied to variables in the called function and also ensures that the original data in the calling function cannot be changed accidentally.

The second technique, pass by reference, sends the address of the data rather than a copy. In this case, the called function can change the original data in the calling function. Although changing data is often necessary, it is one of the common sources of errors; it is also one of the most difficult errors to trace. As you will see, the C language does not have a true pass by reference. It is simulated by what we call pass by address.

4-2 FUNCTIONS IN C

In C, the idea of top–down design is done using **functions**. A C program is made of one or more functions, one and only one of which must be named `main`. The execution of the program always starts and ends with `main`, but it can call other functions to do special tasks. Figure 4-2 shows a C program structure chart.

A function in C (including `main`) is an independent module that will be called to do a specific task. A **called function** receives control from a **calling function**. When the called function completes its task, it returns to the calling function. It may or may not return a value to the caller. The function `main` is called by the operating system; `main` in turn calls other functions. When `main` is complete, control returns to the operating system.

> In C, a program is made of one or more functions, one
> and only one of which must be called `main`. The execution
> of the program always starts with `main`, but it can call
> other functions to do some part of the job.

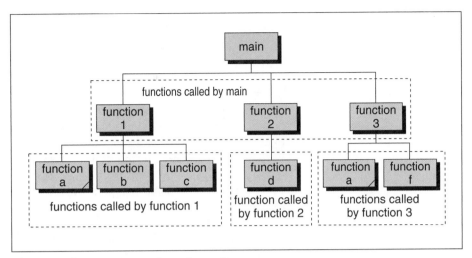

Figure 4-2 Structure chart for a C program

In general, the purpose of a function is to receive zero or more pieces of data, operate on them, and return at most one piece of data. At the same time, a function can have a **side effect**. A function side effect is an action that results in a change in the state of the program. If a side effect occurs, it occurs while the function is executing and before the function returns. The side effect can involve accepting data from outside the program, sending data out of the program to the monitor or a file, or changing the value of a variable in the calling function. The function concept is shown in Figure 4-3.

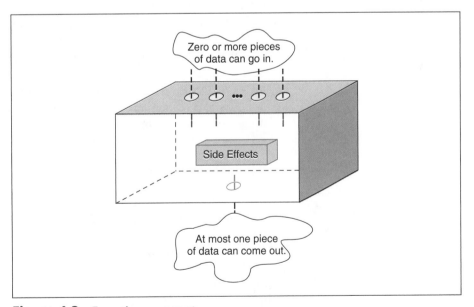

Figure 4-3 Function concept

Several advantages are associated with the use of functions in C or any other language: (1) As already described, problems can be factored into understandable and

> A function in C can have a value, a side effect, or both. The side effect occurs before the value is returned. The function's value is the value in the expression of the return statement. A function can be called for its value, its side effect, or both.

manageable steps. (2) Functions provide a way to reuse code that is required in more than one place in your program. Assume, for instance, that your program requires you to compute the average of a series of numbers in five different parts of the program. Each time the data are different. You could write the code to compute the average five times, but this would take a lot of effort. Also, if you needed to change the calculation, you would have to find all five places that use it to change each of them. It is much easier to write the code once as a function and then call it whenever you need to compute the average.

(3) This advantage to using functions is closely tied to reusing code. Like many languages, C comes with a rich and valuable library. For example, there is a math library, `math.h`, that contains almost any mathematical or statistical function that you will ever need. These C libraries provide standard functions that make your work as a programmer much easier. You can also create personal and project libraries that make developing systems easier. Appendix F, "Function Prototypes," documents many of the functions included with the C language.

(4) We use functions to protect data. This is a rather complex idea that centers around the concept of *local* data. Local data consist of data described in a function. These data are available only to the function and only while the function is executing. When the function is not running, the data are not accessible. Data in one function, then, cannot be seen or changed by a function outside of its scope.

You have already used several functions, such as *scanf* and *printf*, in your programs. These functions, however, were written by the creator of the C environment, not by you. Now you will start writing your own functions. Before we discuss the details, however, Program 4-1 demonstrates how you write and call a function.

```
 1   /* This program demonstrates function calls by calling
 2      a small function to multiply two numbers.
 3         Written by:
 4         Date:
 5   */
 6   #include <stdio.h>
 7
 8   /* Prototype Declarations */
 9   int multiply (int num1, int num2);
10
11   int main (void)
12   {
13   /* Local Definitions */
14      int multiplier;
15      int multiplicand;
16      int product;
```

Program 4-1   Sample program with subfunction

```
17
18   /* Statements */
19      printf("Enter two integers: ");
20      scanf ("%d%d", &multiplier, &multiplicand);
21
22      product = multiply (multiplier, multiplicand);
23
24      printf("Product of %d & %d is %d\n",
25               multiplier, multiplicand, product);
26      return 0;
27   }  /* main */
28   /* =================== multiply ===================
29      Multiples two numbers and returns product.
30          Pre    num1 & num2 are values to be multiplied
31          Post   product returned
32   */
33   int multiply (int num1,
34                 int num2)
35   {
36   /* Statements */
37      return (num1 * num2);
38   }  /* multiply */
```

```
Results:
Enter two integers: 17 21
Product of 17 & 21 is 357
```

Program 4-1   Sample program with subfunction (continued)

4-3   USER-DEFINED FUNCTIONS

Like every other object in C, functions must be both declared and defined. The **function declaration** is done first with a prototype statement. You use the function by calling it from the statement section. The **function definition**, which is traditionally coded after the function that makes the call, contains the code needed to complete the task. Figure 4-4 shows the interrelationships among these function components. When you study Figure 4-4, note that the function name is used three times: when the function is declared, when it is called, and when it is defined.

Before looking at how we write functions, let's look at examples of the three general function designs: *void* functions with no parameters, *void* functions with parameters, and functions that return values.

> The name of a function is used in three ways: for
> **declaration**, in a **call**, and for **definition**.

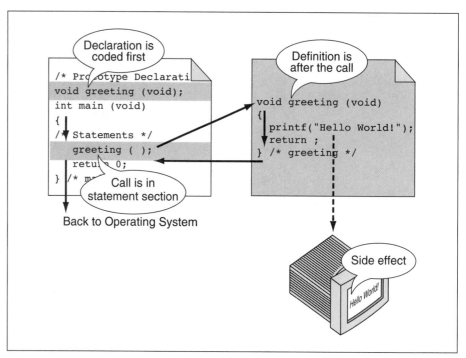

Figure 4-4 Declaring, calling, and defining functions

VOID FUNCTIONS WITH NO PARAMETERS

A function can be written with no parameters. The greeting function in Figure 4-4 receives nothing and returns nothing. It has only a side effect, display the message, and is called only for that side effect.

The call still requires parentheses, however, even when no parameters are present. When you make a call to a function with no parameters, it is tempting to leave the parentheses off the call. Although this is valid syntax, it is not what you intended. Without the parentheses, it is not a function call.

Because a *void* **function** does not have a value, it can be used only as a statement; it cannot be used in an expression. Examine the call to the greeting function in Figure 4-4. This call stands alone as a statement. Including this call in an expression, as shown below, would be an error.

```
result = greeting();           /* Error. Void function */
```

VOID FUNCTIONS WITH PARAMETERS

Now let's call a function that has parameters but still returns *void*. The function printOne, as seen in Figure 4-5, receives an integer parameter. Since this function returns nothing to the calling function, main, its return type is *void*. As with the greeting function discussed previously, this function must be coded as a stand-alone call because it does not return a value; it cannot be included as part of another expression. Note, however, that while printOne returns no values, it does have a side effect: The parameter value is printed to the monitor.

As you study Figure 4-5, note that the name of the variable in main (a) and the name of parameter in printOne (x) do not have to be the same. On the other hand, there is no reason why they can't be the same if that makes it easier to understand the code.

In Program 4-2 we use printOne to demonstrate that a function can be called multiple times.

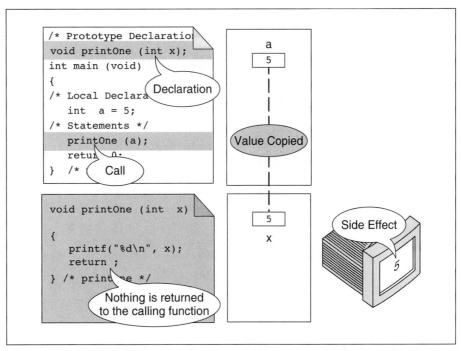

Figure 4-5   *void* function with parameters

```
 1  /* This program demonstrates that one function can be called
 2     multiple times.
 3        Written by:
 4        Date:
 5  */
 6  #include <stdio.h>
 7
 8  /* Prototype Declarations */
 9  void printOne (int x);
10
11  int main (void)
12  {
13  /* Local Definitions */
14     int a;
15
16  /* Statements */
17     /* First call */
18     a = 5;
19     printOne (a);
20
21     /* Second call */
22     a = 33;
23     printOne (a);
24
25     /* Done. Return to operating system. */
```

Program 4-2   *void* function with a parameter

```
26    return 0;
27  }  /* main */
28
29  /* ================== printOne ==================
30     Print one integer value.
31         Pre    x contains number to be printed
32         Post   value in x printed
33  */
34  void printOne (int x)
35  {
36  /* Statements */
37     printf("%d\n", x);
38     return;
39  }  /* printOne */
```

```
Results:
  5
  33
```

Program 4-2   *void* func*tion* with a parameter (continued)

FUNCTIONS THAT RETURN VALUES

Figure 4-6 contains a function that passes parameters and returns a value—in this case, the square of the parameter. Note how the returned value is placed in the variable, b. This is not done by the call; it is a result of expression evaluation. Since the call is a postfix expression, it has a value—whatever is returned from the function. After the function has been executed and the value returned, the value on the right side of the assignment expression is the returned value, which is then assigned to b. Thus, again we see the power of expressions in the C language. Note that the function, sqr, has no side effect.

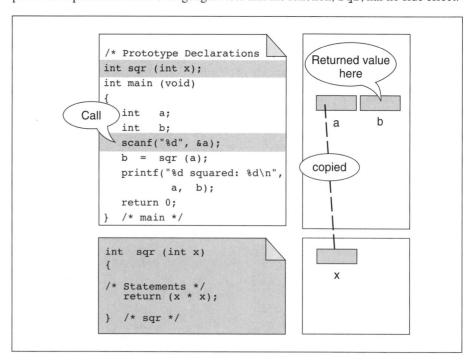

Figure 4-6   Calling a function that returns a value

We saw previously that when a function returns *void*, it cannot be used in an expression. Functions that return values are often found in an expression. In fact, if we didn't assign the return value in Figure 4-6 to the variable **b**, we would have lost it. C would have discarded it, and it would not have been available to be printed.

---

void functions cannot be used in an expression; they must be a separate statement.

Functions that return a value may be used in an expression or as a separate statement.

In large programs, `main` is written with only function calls. To demonstrate how this would be done with our simple example, we combine our square and print functions into Program 4-3.

```
1   /* This program reads a number and prints its square.
2          Written by:
3          Date:
4   */
5   #include <stdio.h>
6
7   /* Prototype Declarations */
8   int  getNum   (void);
9   int  sqr      (int x);
10  void printOne (int x);
11
12  int main (void)
13  {
14  /* Local Definitions */
15     int a;
16     int b;
17
18  /* Statements */
19     /* Get number and square it */
20     a = getNum ();
21
22     /* Square the number just read */
23     b = sqr (a);
24
25     /* Now print it */
26     printOne(b);
27
28     /* Done. Return to operating system. */
29     return 0;
30  } /* main */
31
32  /* ================== getNum ==================
33     Read number from keyboard and return it.
```

Program 4-3 Read a number and square it

```
34        Pre    nothing
35        Post   number read and returned
36  */
37  int getNum (void)
38  {
39  /* Local Definitions */
40     int numIn;
41
42  /* Statements */
43     printf("Enter a number to be squared: ");
44     scanf ("%d", &numIn);
45     return numIn;
46  }  /* getNum */
47
48  /* =================== sqr ===================
49     Return the square of the parameter.
50        Pre    x contains number to be squared
51        Post   squared value returned
52  */
53  int sqr (int x)
54  {
55  /* Statements */
56     return (x * x);
57  }  /* sqr */
58
59  /* =================== printOne ===================
60     Print one integer value.
61        Pre    x contains number to be printed
62        Post   value in x printed
63  */
64  void printOne (int x)
65  {
66  /* Statements */
67     printf("The value is: %d\n", x);
68     return;
69  }  /* printOne */
```

```
Results:
   Enter a number to be squared: 81
   The value is: 6561
```

Program 4-3   Read a number and square it (continued)

Program 4-3 Analysis   Our simple program has grown to four functions, including main. This is an example of **decomposition**, the process of breaking a complex problem into simple parts. While our example is not really complex, it still demonstrates the concept.

We made one slight modification to printOne in this program. To make the output a little more meaningful, we added The value is: to the print statement. As a general principle, the person at the monitor should not have to guess what the output is.

FUNCTION DEFINITION

Now that we have seen examples of the basic function formats, let's look at functions in more detail. We begin with the function definition.

The function definition contains the code for a function. It is made up of two parts: the function header and the function body, which is a compound statement. Remember that a compound statement must have opening and closing braces, and it has declaration and statement sections. The function definition format is shown in Figure 4-7.

```
              function
              header

return_type function_name (formal parameter list)


{
/* Local Definitions */
   …
/* Statements */
   …
}  /* function_name */

              function
              body
```

Figure 4-7 Function definition

Function Header

A **function header** consists of three parts: the *return* type, the function name, and the formal parameter list. A semicolon is not used at the end of the function definition header.

If the *return* type is not explicitly coded, C will assume that it is an integer. If you are returning nothing, you need to code the *return* type as *void*. You should always explicitly code the *return* type, even when it is an integer. The consistency of this practice eliminates confusion and errors.

Function Body

The **function body** contains the declarations and statements for the function. The body starts with local definitions that specify the variables needed by the function. After the local definitions, the function statements, terminating with a *return* statement, are coded. If a function *return* type is *void*, it can be written without a *return* statement. Because we believe that *default* statements should be explicitly coded for clarity, we strongly recommend that every function, even *void* functions, have a *return* statement.

Figure 4-8 shows two functions, `first` and `second`. The function `first` has been declared to return an integer value. Its *return* statement therefore contains the expression x + 2. When the *return* statement is executed, the expression is evaluated and the resulting value is returned. The function `second` returns nothing; its *return* type is *void*. It therefore needs no *return* statement—the end of the function acts as a *void return*. Again, we strongly recommend that you include a *return* statement even for *void* functions. In this case, the *return* statement has no expression; it is just completed with a semicolon.

Formal Parameter List

In the definition of a function, the **parameters** are contained in the **formal parameter list**. This list defines and declares the variables that will contain the data received by the function. The parameter list is always required. If the function has no parameters—that is, if it does not receive any data from the calling function—then the fact that the parameter list is empty is declared with the keyword *void*.

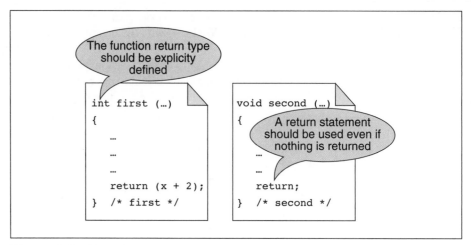

Figure 4-8 Function return statements

In ANSI C each variable must be defined and declared fully with multiple parameters separated by commas. In addition, we recommend that, to make the code more readable, each parameter be defined on a separate line *in the function definition*. To make the parameter list much easier to read, align the parameter types and their names with tabs. Attention to these little details makes the code much easier to read and understand.

In Figure 4-9, the variables x and y are formal parameters that receive data from the calling function's parameters. Since they are value parameters, copies of the values being passed are stored in the called function's memory area. If the function changes either of these values, only the copies will be changed. The original values in the calling function remain unchanged.

Local Variables

A **local variable** is a variable that is defined inside a function and used without having any role in the communication between functions. Figure 4-9 shows an example of a function with both formal parameters and a local variable, sum.

![Figure showing function local variables with annotations. The code reads: double average (int x, int y) { double sum; sum = x + y; return (sum / 2); } /* average */. A speech bubble at top reads "Two values are received from the calling function". A speech bubble at bottom reads "One value is returned to the calling function". On the right side: "parameter variables" with boxes labeled x and y, and "local variable" with a box labeled sum.]

Figure 4-9 Function local variables

PROTOTYPE DECLARATION

Prototype declarations consist only of a function header; they contain no code. Like function definition headers, prototype headers consist of three parts: the return type, the function name, and the formal parameter list. Unlike the header for the function definition, prototype declarations are terminated with a semicolon.

As we discussed with function definitions, the return type does not need to be included, but we recommend that you always use it. Likewise, the parameter list must always be present. If the program has no parameters, code *void* in the parentheses. If the program has multiple parameters, separate each type-identifier set with commas. Unlike the function definition, the prototype declaration's parameters are coded on one line.

The ANSI/ISO standard does not require identifier names for the prototype declaration's formal parameters. This does not prevent your using names in a prototype statement, however. In fact, readability and understandability are improved if names are used. One point to note, however, is that the names do not need to be the same in the prototype declaration and the function definition; on the other hand, if the types are not the same, you will get a compile error. The compiler checks the types in the prototype statements with the types in the call to ensure that they are the same or at least compatible.

The major reason to include the identifiers is documentation; thus, their names should be meaningful. Don't use generic identifiers such as `a` or `x`.

When you use a prototype declaration, place it in the global declaration section before `main`. Grouping all prototype statements at the beginning of the program makes them available whenever they are needed. Prototype statements also provide an excellent quick reference for functions used in the program, making them excellent documentation.

Another important point is that prototype declarations are not required. If a function has not been declared or defined before it is used, C will assume that you will provide it when you link your program. Since there are no specifications, C will also assume that the return type is an integer and that the parameter types correctly match the formal definitions. These assumptions may be right or they may be wrong. If they are wrong, the linker will fail, and you will have to change your program. We therefore highly recommend that you always include prototype statements.

- Formal parameters are variables that are declared in the header of the function definition.
- Actual parameters are the expressions in the calling statement.
- The formal and actual parameters must match exactly in type, order, and number. Their names, however, do not need to match.

Figure 4-10 demonstrates several of these concepts. The prototype declaration tells the program that a function named `multiply`, which accepts two integers and returns one integer, will be called. That is all the compiler needs; it does not need to know anything else to evaluate the call.

Figure 4–10 also demonstrates that the formal parameter names in the declaration do not need to be the same as the actual parameter names. In this case, the names in the prototype declarations are much more meaningful and therefore should have been used in the function definition. It also would have been possible to default the *return* type in this case, since it is an integer. As we continue to emphasize, however, this is not good style.

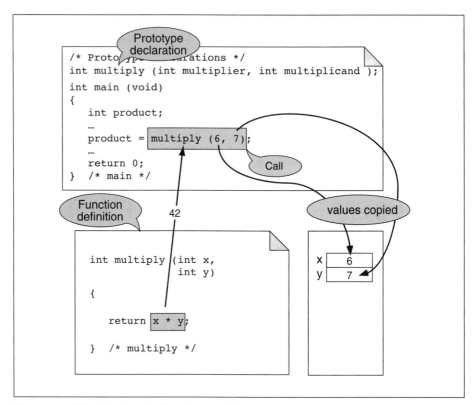

Figure 4-10 Parts of a function call

THE FUNCTION CALL

A **function call** is a postfix expression. The postfix operators are at a very high level (17) in the Precedence Table (see inside front cover). In fact, the only thing higher is the primary expression. Therefore, when a function is used as a part of a larger expression, it will be evaluated first unless parentheses are used to specify a different evaluation order.

The operand in a function call is the function name; the operator is the parentheses set, (...), which contains the **actual parameters**. The actual parameters identify the values that are to be sent to the called function. They match the function's formal parameters in type and order in the parameter list. If the program has multiple actual parameters, they are separated by commas.

There are many different ways to call a function. In Figure 4-11, `multiply` is called six different ways. The first three show calls with primary expressions. The fourth uses a binary expression, `a + 6`, as the first parameter value, and the fifth shows the function `multiply (a, b)` as its own first parameter. The last example sums it all up: Any expression that reduces to a single value can be passed as a parameter.

Functions can be classified by the presence or absence of a return value. Functions that cannot return a value have a return type of *void*. Since these types of functions do not have a value, they can be used only as a stand-alone statement; that is, they cannot be included as part of an expression. All other functions return a value and can be used either as part of an expression or as a stand-alone statement, in which case the value is simply discarded.

Figure 4-11   Examples of function calls

FUNCTION EXAMPLES

This section contains four examples of programs in which functions call functions. Look for the points they demonstrate.

Print Least Significant Digit

Program 4-4 prints the least significant (rightmost) digit of any integer read from the keyboard.

```
1   /* This program prints the first digits of an integer
2      read from the keyboard
3         Written by:
4         Date:
5   */
6   #include <stdio.h>
7
8   /*  Prototype Declarations */
9      int firstDigit (int num);
10
11  int main (void)
12  {
13  /* Local Definitions */
14     int number;
15     int digit;
16
17  /* Statements */
18     printf("Enter an integer: ");
19     scanf ("%d", &number);
20
21     digit = firstDigit (number);
22     printf("\nLeast significant digit is: %d\n", digit);
23
24     return 0;
25  } /* main */
26
```

Program 4-4   Print least significant digit

```
27 | /* ================= firstDigit ===================
28 |    This function extracts the least significant digit
29 |    of an integer.
30 |       Pre    num contains an integer
31 |       Post   Returns least significant digit.
32 | */
33 | int firstDigit (int num)
34 | {
35 | /* Statements */
36 |    return (num % 10);
37 | }  /* firstDigit */
```

```
    Results:
       Enter an integer: 27

       Least significant digit is: 7
```

Program 4-4   Print least significant digit (continued)

Program 4-4 Analysis   This extremely simple program demonstrates how to call a function from main. Note that even though firstDigit is used only in main, its prototype declaration is at the global level. In the sample run, when firstDigit was executed, it returned 7, which was then put into digit and printed.

Add Two Digits

Let's write a function that extracts and adds the two least significant digits of any integer number. In Program 4-5 the function addTwoDigits, which in turn calls two other functions—firstDigit and secondDigit, is called by main. Its design is shown in Figure 4-12. (Turn to "Software Engineering and Programming Style" on page 154 if you have trouble understanding the structure charts.)

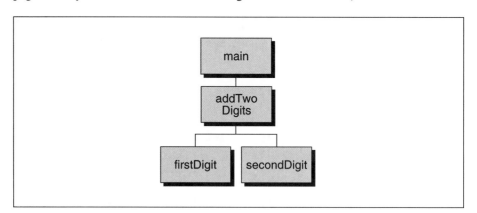

Figure 4-12   Design for addTwoDigits

```
1 | /* This program extracts and adds the two least
2 |    significant digits of an integer.
3 |       Written by:
4 |       Date:
```

Program 4-5   addTwoDigits

```
 5  */
 6  #include <stdio.h>
 7
 8  /*  Prototype Declarations */
 9  int addTwoDigits (int num);
10  int firstDigit   (int num);
11  int secondDigit  (int num);
12
13  int main (void)
14  {
15  /* Local Definitions */
16     int   number;
17     int   sum;
18
19  /* Statements */
20     printf("\nEnter an integer: ");
21     scanf ("%d", &number);
22
23     sum = addTwoDigits (number);
24     printf ("\nSum of last two digits is: %d", sum);
25
26     return 0;
27  }  /* main */
28
29  /* ================== addTwoDigits ==================
30      Adds the first two digits of an integer.
31          Pre   num contains an integer
32          Post returns sum of two least significant digits
33  */
34  int addTwoDigits (int number)
35  {
36  /* Local Definitions */
37     int   result;
38
39  /* Statements */
40     result = firstDigit(number) + secondDigit(number);
41     return result;
42  }  /* addTwoDigits */
43
44  /* ================== firstDigit ==================
45     Extract the least significant digit of an integer.
46         Pre    num contains an integer
47         Post   Returns least significant digit.
48  */
49  int firstDigit (int num)
50  {
51  /* Statements */
52     return (num % 10);
```

Program 4-5 addTwoDigits (continued)

```
53 | }   /* firstDigit */
54 |
55 | /* ================== secondDigit ==================
56 |     Extract second least significant (10s) digit
57 |         Pre   num is an integer
58 |         Post  Returns digit in 10s position
59 | */
60 | int secondDigit (int num)
61 | {
62 | /* Local Definitions */
63 |     int   result;
64 |
65 | /* Statements */
66 |     result = (num / 10) % 10;
67 |     return result;
68 | }   /* secondDigit */
```

```
Results:
    1. Enter an integer: 23

       Sum of last two digits is: 5

    2. Enter an integer: 8

       Sum of last two digits is: 8
```

Program 4-5 addTwoDigits (continued)

Program 4-5 Analysis   A natural question asked by students when they first read this program is, "Why not put firstDigit and secondDigit as in-line code in addTwoDigits?" This may seem to be an obvious way to code the problem. And after all, each of the called functions is *only one statement*.

The answer is that, although each function is only one statement, it does a job that can be used in other places. One of the principles of structured programming is that processes should appear in a program in only one place. For example, we have used the same code for firstDigit that we used in the first program. If a function is to be reusable in this way, it must do only one thing. The short answer, then, is that it is better structured programming. It is the nature of the task to be performed, not the amount of code, that determines if a function should be used.

An interesting point to note is the way these two different digits were calculated. To get the least significant digit, we took the 10's modulus of the number. But to get the second digit, we had to divide by 10. Can you figure out how to sum the digits in a three-digit number? We will give you a chance to do this in the problems at the end of the chapter.

Note that we tested the program with two different numbers, one containing only one digit. It is often necessary to run the program with more than one test case. Another test case that should be run is a negative number. What do you think would happen? As a programmer, not only should you run several tests but you should predict the results before you run the program.

Format
Long Integer

Program 4-6 reads a long integer and prints it with a comma after the first three digits, such as 123,456. The number is printed with leading zeros (see field specification %03d in Statement 40) in case the value is less than 100,000.

```
1  /* This program reads long integers from the keyboard
2     and prints them with leading zeros in the form
3     123,456 with a comma between 3rd & 4th digit.
4        Written by:
5        Date:
6  */
7  #include <stdio.h>
8  /* Prototype Declarations */
9  void printWithComma (long num);
10
11 int main (void)
12 {
13 /* Local Definitions */
14    long   number;
15
16 /* Statements */
17    printf("\nEnter a number with up to 6 digits: ");
18    scanf ("%ld", &number);
19    printWithComma (number);
20
21    return 0;
22 }  /* main */
23
24 /* =============== printWithComma ================
25    This function divides num into two three-digit
26    numbers and prints them with a comma inserted.
27        Pre    num is a six digit number
28        Post   num has been printed with a comma inserted
29 */
30 void printWithComma (long num)
31 {
32 /* Local Definitions */
33    int   thousands;
34    int   hundreds;
35
36 /* Statements */
37    thousands  = num / 1000;
38    hundreds   = num % 1000;
39
40    printf("\nThe number you entered is \t%03d,%03d",
41            thousands, hundreds);
42    return;
43 }  /* printWithComma */
```

```
Results:
  Run 1.
```

Program 4-6 Print six digits with comma

```
        Enter a number with up to 6 digits: 123456

        The number you entered is        123,456

    Run 2.
        Enter a number with up to 6 digits: 12

        The number you entered is        000,012
```

Program 4-6   Print six digits with comma (continued)

Program 4-6 Analysis   Once again, we have a simple program that has the makings of a very useful function. C has no built-in functions that will provide number formatting like commas and dollar signs. You have to program these details. And since this logic will be used over and over again, it must be in its own function. Note, however, that more work is needed to print numbers less than 100,000 correctly. However, we have not yet introduced the tools to do the complete job.

Again, we have used two test cases to show that more work must be done. An even bigger problem occurs if we try to format a small negative number. Can you see what the problem is? If not, code the problem and run it to see. We will explain how to handle these problems in the next chapter.

Print Tuition for Strange College

Program 4-7 calculates and prints the annual tuition for a student enrolled in Strange College. In this college, students can take an unlimited number of units each term. Each term, the students are charged $10 per unit plus a $10 registration fee. To discourage them from overloading, the college charges $50 extra for each 12 units, or fraction thereof, a student takes after the first 12 units. For example, if a student takes 13 units, the tuition is $190 ($10 for registration, plus 13 times $10 for units, plus a $50 penalty for the one extra unit). If a student takes 25 units, the tuition is $360 ($10 for registration, plus 25 times $10 for units, plus $100 for two penalty fees). The design for this problem is shown in Figure 4-13.

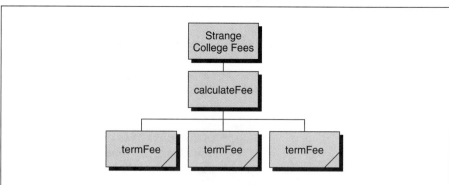

Figure 4-13   Design for Strange College fees

```
1   /* This program prints the tuition at Strange College.
2       Strange charges $10 for registration, plus $10 per
3       unit and a penalty of $50 for each 12 units, or
4       fraction of 12, over 12.
```

Program 4-7   Strange College fees

```
 5          Written by:
 6          Date:
 7  */
 8  #include <stdio.h>
 9
10  #define REG_FEE     10
11  #define UNIT_FEE    10
12  #define EXCESS_FEE 50
13
14  /* Prototype Declarations */
15  int calculateFee (int firstTerm,
16                     int secondTerm,
17                     int thirdTerm);
18  int termFee       (int units);
19
20  int main (void)
21  {
22  /* Local Definitions */
23     int   firstTerm;
24     int   secondTerm;
25     int   thirdTerm;
26     int   totalFee;
27
28  /* Statements */
29     printf("Enter units for first term:   ");
30     scanf ("%d", &firstTerm);
31
32     printf("Enter units for second term: ");
33     scanf ("%d", &secondTerm);
34
35     printf("Enter units for third term:   ");
36     scanf ("%d", &thirdTerm);
37
38     totalFee = calculateFee
39               (firstTerm, secondTerm, thirdTerm);
40     printf("\nThe total tuition is : %8d\n", totalFee);
41
42     return 0;
43  }  /* main */
44
45  /* ================= calculateFee ================
46     Calculate the total fees for the year.
47        Pre   The number of units to be taken each term.
48        Post  Returns the annual fees.
49  */
50  int calculateFee (int firstTerm,
51                     int secondTerm,
52                     int thirdTerm)
53  {
```

Program 4-7 Strange College fees (continued)

```
54  /* Local Definitions */
55     int  fee;
56
57  /* Statements */
58     fee = termFee    (firstTerm)
59           + termFee (secondTerm)
60           + termFee (thirdTerm);
61     return fee;
62  }  /* calculateFee */
63
64  /* ==================== termFee ====================
65     Calculate the tuition for one term
66         Pre   units contains units for the term
67         Post  The fee is calculated and returned
68  */
69  int   termFee (int units)
70  {
71  /* Local Definitions */
72     int   totalFees;
73
74  /* Statements */
75     totalFees = REG_FEE
76               + ((units - 1)/12 * EXCESS_FEE)
77               + (units * UNIT_FEE);
78     return (totalFees);
79  }  /* termFee */
```

```
Results:
    Enter units for first term:   10
    Enter units for second term: 20
    Enter units for third term:  30

    The total tuition is :       780
```

Program 4-7   Strange College fees (continued)

Program 4-7 Analysis   The most interesting aspect of Program 4-7 is how we call
termFee three different times in one function. Let's look at how it works. The key
statement is shown below.

```
fee = termFee    (firstTerm)
      + termFee (secondTerm)
      + termFee (thirdTerm);
```

A function call is a postfix expression. Therefore, it evaluates from the left. To evaluate the expression (three function calls) on the right of the assignment operator, we first
evaluate the first expression, the call to termFee with the number of units for the first
term. When termFee completes the first time, the return value (110) replaces the call.
At this point, we have the expression shown below.

```
110 + termFee (secondTerm) + termFee (thirdTerm)
```

When `termFee` is executed a second time, its return value (260) becomes the value of the second expression and we have

```
110 + 260 + termFee (thirdTerm)
```

After the third call to `termFee`, the expression on the right of the assignment operator is ready for evaluation. Its value is 780, which is assigned to `fee`.

At least two more tests are needed to completely evaluate this program. We would run it with all three terms having 0 units and then do another test of 11, 12, and 13 units.

PARAMETER PASSING

Now that you have seen how function parameters work, let's look more closely at how parameters are passed.

Pass by Value

In all the examples up to this point, we have passed data values to the called functions. When you pass by value, a copy of the data is created and placed in a local variable in the called function. This means of passing data ensures that regardless of how the data are manipulated and changed in the called function, the original data in the calling function are safe and unchanged. Because passing the value protects the data, it is the preferred passing technique. This is demonstrated in Figure 4-14. Even after the call to `fun`, the value of `a` is unchanged.

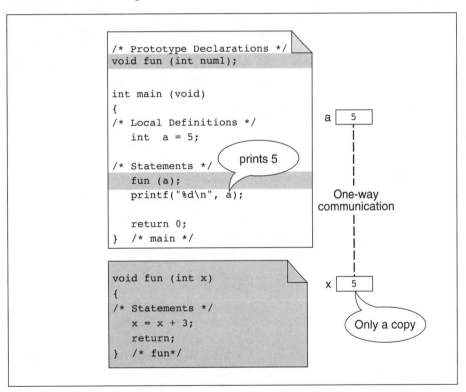

Figure 4-14   Pass by value—One-way communication

Pass by Reference

In some cases, however, it is necessary to pass by reference. Pass by reference links the variable identifiers in the calling function to their corresponding parameters in the called function. Any reference to a parameter is therefore the same as a reference to the variable in the calling function. Thus, when the called function changes a value, it actually changes the variable in the calling function. Once the parameters are identified as reference parameters, the link between the variables and the parameter identifiers is automatically established.

Unfortunately, C does not have pass by reference. Whenever the data in the calling function must be changed, therefore, we must pass the variable's address and use it to change the value. While pass by reference is automatic, pass by address is not. We must use special code to tell C that we want to change the value. It is not automatic.

Pass by Address

Pass by address uses C pointers. Pointers are a rather complex aspect of the language. Chapters 9 and 10 are devoted entirely to pointers. In the next section we discuss only the pointer operators required to implement pass by address.

Pointer Operators

Consider this case: We need to write a function that processes two data values and "returns" them to the calling function; that is, the function changes their values in the calling program. Obviously, since a function can return only one value, we have a problem. The solution is to pass the addresses of the variables and let the subfunction use the addresses to store the values directly in the calling function's variables. To pass an address, we use the **address operator** (&). To tell the compiler that we want to store data at an address, we use the **indirection operator** (*).

You have used the address operator since you first read data using the *scanf* function. The indirection operator is the opposite of the address operator. Whereas the address operator says "Give me the address of this data," the indirection address says "Use this value as an address to find the data." The address operator is an indirect reference to a variable through an address. When we use the indirection operator to reference an address, we are **dereferencing** the address. We use the indirection operator to dereference data.

> Indirection is an indirect reference
> to a variable through its address.

Indirection is a unary operator found at priority 15 in the Precedence Table (see inside front cover). As a unary operator, it is evaluated from the right, meaning that it is put *before* the address to be dereferenced. If numAddr is a variable that contains the address of a number, we will find the data by dereferencing the variable as shown below.

```
*numAddr
```

Figure 4-15 revisits the fun function from Figure 4-14, this time using pass by address. Note that when a is printed now, its value has been changed to 8.

Study the use of the address and dereference operators in Figure 4-15 carefully. In main, and only in main, we need to use the address operator to turn the parameter into an address for the variable a. In both function headers, we use an asterisk to indicate that the parameter is an address. Then, in the function definition, whenever we use the parameter x, we must include the dereference operator to refer back the variable a in main.

Let's look at a program that uses the indirection operator to dereference data. One common process that occurs often in programming is exchanging two pieces of data. Let's write a function that, given two integer variables, exchanges them. Since two variables are being changed, we cannot use the *return* statement. Instead, we will use pass by address to make the changes.

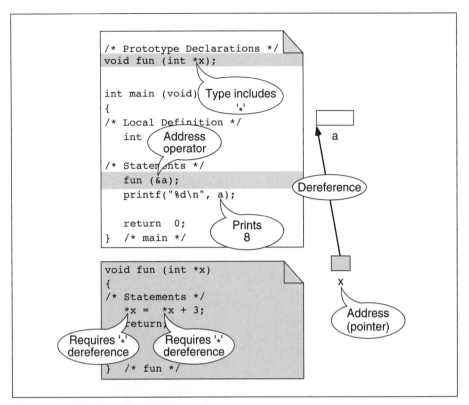

Figure 4-15 Pass by address

> *x in fun is a reference to the variable a in main.

First, make sure you understand how to exchange two variables: You cannot simply assign variables to each other, as shown below.

```
x = y;                    /* This won't work */
y = x;                    /* Result is y in both */
```

If you carefully trace these two statements, you will see that the original value of **y** ends up in both variables. Therefore, to exchange variables, you need to create a temporary variable to hold the first value while the exchange is being made. The correct logic is shown below.

```
hold = y;                 /* value of y saved */
y    = x;                 /* x now in y */
x    = hold;              /* original y now in x */
```

The exchange function and its data flow are shown in Figure 4-16. First, examine the prototype statement in Figure 4-16 carefully. Note the asterisk in the declaration of num1 and num2. The asterisk is used with the type declaration to specify that the type is an address—in this case, the address of an integer. Now, look at the call statement in main. Since we will change the values of a and b in main, we need to pass their addresses. The address operators (&) tell the compiler that we want their addresses passed, not their values.

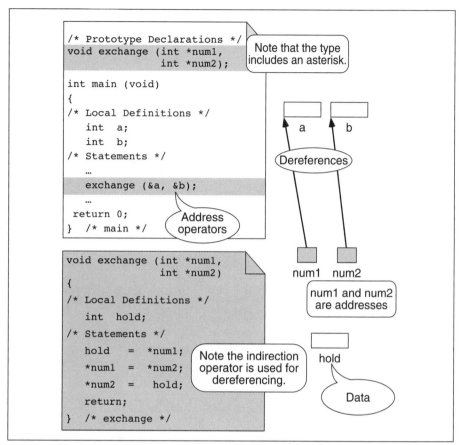

Figure 4-16 Exchange function

Now, look at the statements in `exchange`. First, we copy `num1`'s value to `hold`. Since `hold` is a local variable, it is treated the same as any local variable—no special operators are required. However, `num1` contains the address of the data we want, not the data itself. To get the value it is referring to, we must dereference it. This is done with the indirection operator, the asterisk (`*`). The statement is shown below.

```
hold = *num1;
```

In the same manner, we can now dereference `num2` and copy it to `num1` and then complete the exchange by copying `hold` to `num2`. These statements are seen below.

```
*num1 = *num2;
*num2 =  hold;
```

Note that with the exception of `hold`, all of the data movement is done in the calling program's area. This is the power of the indirection operator.

Here is another simple example, one that uses both pass-by-value and pass-by-address parameters. We need to write a function that, given two numbers, calculates both the quotient and the remainder. Since we can't return two values, we will pass the addresses where we want the quotient and remainder stored. This problem is shown in Figure 4-17.

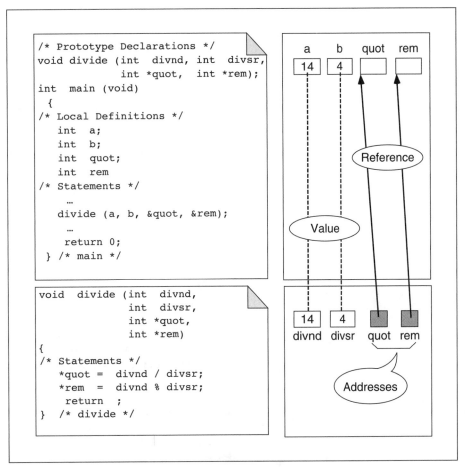

```
/* Prototype Declarations */
void divide (int   divnd, int  divsr,
               int *quot,  int *rem);
int  main (void)
 {
/* Local Definitions */
   int   a;
   int   b;
   int   quot;
   int   rem
/* Statements */
     ...
   divide (a, b, &quot, &rem);
     ...
    return 0;
 } /* main */
```

```
void   divide (int   divnd,
               int   divsr,
               int *quot,
               int *rem)
{
/* Statements */
   *quot =  divnd / divsr;
   *rem  =  divnd % divsr;
    return  ;
 }  /* divide */
```

Figure 4-17   Calculate quotient and remainder

Let's examine `divide` first. Note that the first two parameters are pass by value. You can tell this because their types are just *int;* there are no asterisks indicating that they are addresses. The last two parameters are addresses. Their types are `int *`; therefore, any references to them in the function must use the indirection operator.

Now look at the call in `main`. Note that a and b are simply passed by using their identifiers. They are primary expressions whose value is the contents of the variable. On the other hand, `quot` and `rem` are passed as addresses by using the address operator. In this case, the value of the primary expression created by the address operator and the identifier is the address of the variable. Therefore, we pass an address value rather than a data value.

As the programmer, it is your job to know what needs to be passed, a value or an address, when you write a call. Similarly, when you use the parameters in the called program, you must remember to use the indirection operator when you have an address.

Let's use `divide` in a program that reads two integers, divides them, and then prints the quotient and the remainder. The design for this program is shown in Figure 4-18, and the code is shown in Program 4-8.

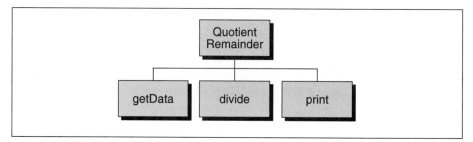

Figure 4-18   Quotient and remainder design

```
1  /* This program reads two integers and then prints the
2     quotient and remainder of the first number divided
3     by the second.
4        Written by:
5        Date:
6  */
7  #include <stdio.h>
8
9  /* Prototype Declarations */
10    void divide  (int  dividend, int  divisor,
11                  int *quotient, int *remainder);
12    void getData (int *dividend, int *divisor);
13    void print   (int  quotient, int  remainder);
14
15 int main (void)
16 {
17 /* Local Definitions */
18 int  dividend;
19 int  divisor;
20 int  quot;
21 int  rem;
22
23 /* Statements */
24    getData (&dividend, &divisor);
25    divide  ( dividend,  divisor, &quot, &rem);
26    print   ( quot,        rem);
27
28    return 0;
29 }  /* main */
30
31 /* ================== getData ==================
32    This function reads two numbers into variables
33    specified in the parameter list.
34        Pre   Nothing.
35        Post  Data read and placed in calling function.
36 */
37 void getData  (int *dividend,
38                int *divisor)
39 {
```

Program 4-8   Quotient and remainder

```
40    /* Statements */
41       printf("Enter two integers and return: ");
42       scanf ("%d%d", dividend, divisor);
43       return;
44    }  /* getData */
45
46    /* ==================== divide ====================
47       This function divides two integers and places the
48       quotient/remainder in calling program variables
49          Pre    dividend & divisor contain integer values
50          Post   quotient & remainder calc'd
51    */
52    void divide (int   dividend,
53                 int   divisor,
54                 int  *quotient,
55                 int  *remainder)
56    {
57    /* Statements */
58       *quotient  = dividend / divisor;
59       *remainder = dividend % divisor;
60
61       return;
62    }  /* divide */
63    /* ==================== print ====================
64       This function prints the quotient and the remainder
65          Pre    quot contains the quotient
66                 rem contains the remainder
67          Post   Quotient and remainder printed
68    */
69    void print (int quot,
70                int rem)
71    {
72    /* Statements */
73       printf ("Quotient : %3d\n", quot);
74       printf ("Remainder: %3d\n", rem);
75       return;
76    }  /* print */
77    /* =============== End of Program =============== */
```

Program 4-8 Quotient and remainder (continued)

Program 4-8 Analysis   First, look at the design of this program. Note how main contains only calls to subfunctions. It does no work itself; like a good manager, it delegates all work to lower levels in the program. This is how you should design your programs.

Study the getData function carefully. First note that the parameters identify the variables as addresses. Verify that they contain an asterisk as a part of their type. Now look at the *scanf* statement carefully. What is missing? There are no address operators for the variables! We don't need the address operators because the parameters are already addresses. We have used the address operator (&) up to this example to tell the compiler that we want the address of the variable, not its contents. Since the parameters were passed as addresses (see Statement 24), we don't need the address operator.

Now study the way we use `quot` and `rem` in `divide`. In Statement 25, we pass them as addresses by using the address operator. Since we are passing addresses, we can change their values in `main`. In the function definition, the formal parameters show these two parameters to be addresses to integers by showing the type as `int *` (see Statements 54 and 55). To change the value back in `main`, we use the indirection operator in Statements 58 and 59 when we assign the results of the divide and modulo operations.

4-4 STANDARD LIBRARY FUNCTIONS

C++ provides a rich collection of standard functions whose definitions have been written and are ready to be used in our programs. To use these functions, you must include their prototype declarations. The prototypes for these functions are grouped together and collected in several header files. Instead of adding the individual prototypes of each function, therefore, we simply include the headers at the top of our programs. Appendix F contains the prototype declarations for most standard library functions.

Figure 4-19 shows how two of the **C standard library** functions that you have used several times are brought into your program. The *include* statement causes the library header file for standard input and output (`stdio.h`) to be copied into your program. It contains the prototype statements for *printf* and *scanf*. Then, when your program is linked, the object code for these functions is combined with your code to build the complete program.

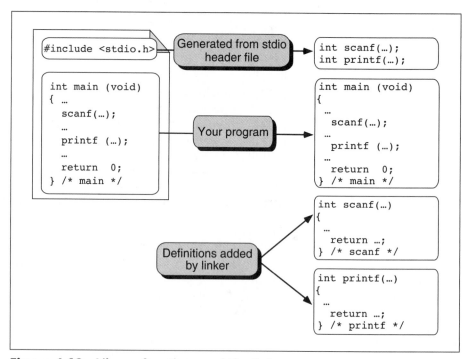

Figure 4-19 Library functions and the linker

STANDARD FUNCTIONS FOR MATHEMATICAL MANIPULATION

Many important library functions are available for mathematical calculations. Most of the prototypes for these functions are in a header file called `math.h`. Two of them, *abs* and *labs*, are found in `stdlib.h`.

abs/fabs/labs

The functions called **abs**, **fabs**, and **labs** return the absolute value of a number. An absolute value is the positive rendering of the value regardless of its sign. For *abs* the parameter must be an integer, and it returns an integer. For *labs* the parameter must be a long integer, and it returns a long integer. For *fabs* the parameter is a double, and it returns a double. The *f* stands for floating-point; its type is *double*.

The prototype statements for these three functions are shown below. The `abs` and `labs` functions are found in `stdlib.h`. The `fabs` function is found in `math.h`.

```
int    abs  (int    number);
long   labs (long   number);
double fabs (double number);
```

Examples:

```
abs  (3)      ⇒ returns 3
fabs (-3.4)   ⇒ returns 3.4
```

ceil

A ceiling, or *ceil*, is the smallest integral value greater than or equal to a number. For example, the ceiling of 3.0000001 is 4. If we consider all numbers as a continuous range from minus infinity to plus infinity (Figure 4-20), this function moves the number right to an integer value.

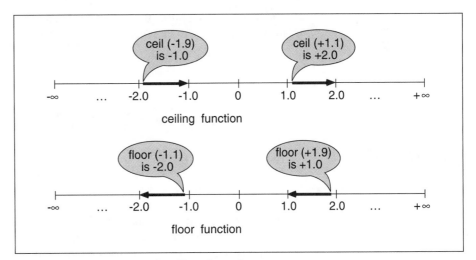

Figure 4-20 Floor and ceiling functions

Although the ceiling function (*ceil*) returns an integral value, note that the return type is *double*. The ceiling prototype is

```
double ceil (double number);
```

Examples:

```
ceil (-1.9)   ⮂ returns -1.0
ceil ( 1.1)   ⮂ returns  2.0
```

floor

A *floor* is the largest integral value that is equal to or less than a number (see Figure 4-20). For example, the floor of 3.99999 is 3.0. Again, looking at numbers as a continuum, this function moves the number left to an integer value. Its prototype is

```
double floor (double number);
```

Examples:

```
floor (-1.1)   ⮂ returns -2.0
floor ( 1.9)   ⮂ returns  1.0
```

pow

The *pow* function returns the value of the x raised to the power y— that is, x^y. An error occurs if the base (x) is negative and the exponent (y) is not an integer, or if the base is zero and the exponent is not positive. The power prototype is

```
double pow (double x, double y);
```

Examples:

```
pow (3.0, 4.0)   ⮂ returns 81.0
pow (3.4, 2.3)   ⮂ returns 16.687893
```

sqrt

The *sqrt* function returns the non-negative square root of number. An error occurs if number is negative. The square root prototype is

```
double sqrt (double number);
```

Example:

```
sqrt (25.0)   ⮂ returns 5.0
```

GENERAL LIBRARY FUNCTIONS

Many important general library functions are available in C. We mention only two of them here that we will be using in future chapters. The prototypes for these functions are in the stdlib.h header file.

srand

The seed random function, coded *srand*, creates the first seed for a pseudorandom number series. A pseudorandom series is a repeatable series of numbers with random properties. The seed is the variable used by the random number generator to calculate the next number in the series. Each seed produces a different series when the random number generator (rand—see following discussion) is called. Note that as each number is generated, it becomes the seed for the next number in the series. Figure 4-21 demonstrates how the seed works.

To generate a truly random number series, therefore, the seed must be a random number. The most common technique for generating a random number is to use a seed that is a function of the current date or time of day.

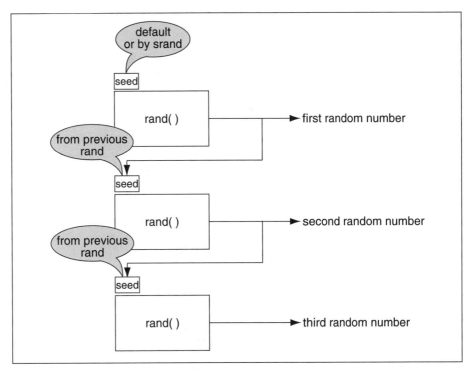

Figure 4-21   The random number seed

The seed random prototype is

```
void srand (unsigned int seed);
```

Example: To generate random numbers, use the following call before your first call to *rand.* (The time requires the `time.h` header file.)

```
srand(time (NULL));
```

To generate a pseudorandom number series, seed random is called with a constant, preferably a large prime number, such as 997.

```
srand (997);
```

Whichever series you want, *srand* should be *called only once* for each random number series, usually only once in your program.

rand

The *rand* function returns a pseudorandom integer between 0 and **RAND_MAX**, which is defined in the standard library as the largest number that *rand* can generate. The ANSI/ISO standard requires that it be at least 32,767. Each call generates the next number in a random number series.

The random number prototype is

```
int rand (void);
```

If *srand* is not called before the first call to *rand,* the series will be based on the seed 1. Thus, the same series of numbers will always be generated (see Figure 4-21).

Program 4-9 generates three random numbers and prints them. Because we use the time of day as a seed, we get a different series each time we run the program.

```
1   /* Demonstrate random number generation
2       Written by:
3       Date:
4   */
5
6   #include <stdio.h>
7   #include <stdlib.h>
8   #include <time.h>
9
10  int main (void)
11  {
12  /* Local Definitions */
13     int   rand1;
14     int   rand2;
15     int   rand3;
16
17  /* Statements */
18     printf("Begin random number generation\n");
19
20     srand (time (NULL));
21     rand1 = rand();
22     rand2 = rand();
23     rand3 = rand();
24
25     printf("The random numbers are: %d %d %d\n",
26             rand1, rand2, rand3);
27     return 0;
28  }  /* main */
```
```
Results
   Begin random number generation
   The random numbers are: 31277 16136 26092
```

Program 4-9   Generate random numbers

SCALING RANDOM NUMBERS

Often you will need to generate a series of numbers in a narrower range than provided by the standard library. To create your own range, you must scale what is returned from *rand*. The **scaling** is done by the modulus operator. For example, to produce a random number in the range 0 . . . 50, you simply scale the random number as shown below.

```
rand ( ) % 51
```

Modulus works well when your range starts at 0. But what if you need a different range? In that case, you must shift the result. For example, suppose you want a random number between 3 and 7 (Figure 4-22). If you call *rand* and then use modulus 8, your range will be 0 through 7. To convert to the correct range, you first determine your modulus factor by subtracting the starting point (3) from the modulus divisor (8) and then adding the starting point to the resulting number. Thus, for our example, we subtract 3 from 8, which makes the modulus divisor 5.

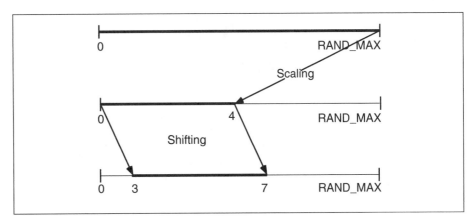

Figure 4-22 Random number scaling for 3–7

Generalizing the algorithm, we get

```
rand () % ((max + 1) - min) + min
```

where `min` is the minimum number and `max` is the maximum number in the desired range. Of course, if a range starting at zero is desired, then the minimum value (`min`) is zero and therefore ignored. For example, to create a random number in the range 20–30, we would use the following expression:

```
rand() % ((30 + 1) - 20) + 20 ⇔ rand() % 11 + 20
```

Program 4-10 demonstrates the generation and scaling of random numbers.

```c
 1  /* Demonstrates the generation of random numbers in
 2     three different series:
 3         03 and 07
 4         20 and 50
 5         -6 and 15
 6     After generating three numbers, it prints them.
 7     The seed for the series is 997.
 8         Written by:
 9         Date:
10  */
11  #include <stdio.h>
12  #include <stdlib.h>
13  int main (void)
14  {
15  /* Local Definitions */
16     int   a;
17     int   b;
18     int   c;
19
20  /* Statements */
21     srand (997);
```

Program 4-10 Scaling for random number generation

```
22      /* range is 3 through 7 */
23      a = rand () % 5  + 3;                /* 8 - 3 = 5 */
24
25      /* range is 20 through 50*/
26      b = rand () % 31 + 20;               /* 51 - 20 = 31 */
27
28      /* range is -6 through 15*/
29      c = rand () % 22  - 6;               /* 16 - (-6) = 22 */
30      printf ("Range  3 to 7:  %2d\n", a);
31      printf ("Range 20 to 50: %2d\n", b);
32      printf ("Range -6 to 15: %2d\n", c);
33      return 0;
34  }  /* main */
```

```
Results:
    Range  3 to 7:   3
    Range 20 to 50: 34
    Range -6 to 15:  2
```

Program 4-10   Scaling for random number generation (continued)

Program 4-10 Analysis   Note that we have used *srand* to generate pseudorandom numbers. The seed we used, 997, is a prime number. Generally speaking, prime numbers generate better random number series than nonprime numbers. However, the fact that we used a seed does not guarantee that you will get the same results if you run the program on a different computer. It only guarantees that when the program is run repetitively on the same computer, you will always get the same set of random numbers. Given the same seed, different compilers may generate different random series depending on their random number algorithm.

4-5 SCOPE

Scope determines the region of the program in which a defined object is *visible*—that is, the part of the program in which you can use the object's name. Scope pertains to any object that can be defined, such as a variable or a function prototype statement. It does not pertain directly to precompiler directives, such as define statements; they have separate rules. Scope is a source program concept: It has no direct bearing on the run-time program.

To discuss the concept of scope, we need to review two concepts. A **block** is zero or more statements enclosed in a set of braces. Recall that a function's body is enclosed in a set of braces; thus, a body is also a block. A block has a declarations section and a statement section. This concept gives us the ability to nest blocks within the body of a function and allow each block to be an independent group of statements with its own isolated definitions.

The global area of your program consists of all statements that are outside functions. Figure 4-23 is a graphical representation of the concept of global area and blocks.

An object's scope extends from its declaration until the end of its block. A variable is in scope if it is visible to the statement being examined. Variables are in scope from their point of declaration until the end of their function or block.

```
/*  This is a sample to demonstrate scope. The techniques
    used in this program should never be used in practice.
*/
#include  <stdio.h>                         Global area
int fun (int a, int b);

  int    main  ( void )
  {
    int    a;                               main's area
    int    b;
    float  c;
    ...
        {  /* Beginning of nested block */
        float  a = y  / 2;
        float  y;                           Nested block
        float  z;                               area
        ...
        z = a * b;
        ...
        }  /* End of nested block */
    ...

  }  /* End of Main */

  int fun (int  i,
           int  j)                          fun's area
  {
     int  a;
     int  y;
     ...
  }  /* fun */
```

Figure 4-23 Scope for global and block areas

GLOBAL SCOPE

The global scope is easily defined. Any object defined in the global area of a program is visible from its definition until the end of the program. Referring to Figure 4-23, the prototype statement for fun is a global definition. It is visible everywhere in the program.

LOCAL SCOPE

Variables defined within a block have local scope. They exist only from the point of their declaration until the end of the block (usually a function) in which they are declared. Outside the block they are invisible.

In Figure 4-23, we see two blocks in main. The first block is all of main. Since the second block is nested within main, all definitions in main are visible to the block unless local variables with an identical name are defined. In the inner block, a local version of a has been defined; its type is float. Under these circumstances, the integer variable a in main is visible from its declaration until the declaration of the floating-point variable a in the nested block. At that point, main's a can no longer be referenced in the nested block. Any statement in the block that references a will get the float version. Once we reach the end of the nested block, the float a is no longer in scope and the integer a becomes visible again.

> Variables are in scope from their point of definition
> until the end of their function or block.

We have also defined a new variable y. Note, however, that before we defined the local y, we used main's y to set the initial value for a. Although this is flagrant disregard for structured programming principles and should never be used in practice, it demonstrates that a variable is in scope until it is redefined. Immediately after using y, we defined the local version, so main's version of y is no longer available. Since the variable b is not redeclared in the block, it is in scope throughout the entire block.

> It is poor programming style to reuse
> identifiers within the same scope.

Although main's variables are visible inside the nested block, the reverse is not true. The variables defined in the block, a, y, and z, exist only for the duration of the block and are no longer visible after the end of the block.

Within the function fun, which is coded after main, only its variables and any global objects are visible. Thus, we are free to use any names we want. In Figure 4-23, we chose to use the names a and y even though they had been used in main. This is an acceptable practice; there is nothing wrong with it.

4-6 A PROGRAMMING EXAMPLE—CALCULATOR PROGRAM

Program 4-11 asks the user to input two numbers. The program then calls one function that adds the numbers and another function that subtracts them. It concludes by displaying the sum and difference of the two numbers. The pseudocode for this program is seen in Algorithim 4-1.

```
1 Prompt and Read x and y
2 sum   = add       (x, y)
3 diff  = subtract (x, y)
4 print sum, diff
```

Algorithm 4-1 Pseudocode for calculator program

The complete code to implement this program is seen in Program 4-11.

```
1   /* This program adds and subtracts two integers read
2      from the keyboard.
3         Written by:
4         Date:
5   */
6   #include <stdio.h>
7
8   /*  Prototype Declarations */
9   int   add  (int a, int b);
10  int   subt (int a, int b);
11
12  int main (void)
13  {
14  /* Local Definitions*/
15     int   a;
```

Program 4-11 Calculator program

```
16      int  b;
17      int  sum;
18      int  diff;
19
20  /* Statements */
21      /* Prompt user for input and get data */
22      printf("\nPlease enter two integer numbers: ");
23
24      /* Read numbers into a and b */
25      scanf("%d %d", &a, &b);
26
27      /* Calculate the sum and difference */
28      sum  = add (a, b);
29      diff = subt(a, b);
30
31      printf("\n%4d + %4d = %4d\n", a, b, sum);
32      printf("%4d - %4d = %4d\n",    a, b, diff);
33
34      /* Close program */
35      printf("\nThank you for using my calculator\n");
36      return 0;
37  } /* main */
38  /* ===================== add =====================
39      This function adds two integers and returns the sum.
40         Pre    Parameters a and b.
41         Post   Returns a + b.
42  */
43  int add (int a,
44           int b)
45  {
46      return (a + b);
47  } /* add */
48  /* ===================== subt =====================
49      Return the difference of two integers
50         Pre    Parameters a and b.
51         Post   Returns a - b.
52  */
53  int subt (int a,
54           int b)
55  {
56      return (a - b);
57  } /* subt */
```

```
Results
    Please enter two integer numbers: 8 23

        8 +   23 =   31
        8 -   23 =  -15

    Thank you for using my calculator
```

Program 4-11 Calculator program (continued)

4-7 SOFTWARE ENGINEERING AND PROGRAMMING STYLE

In this section we discuss three different but related aspects of software engineering design: the structure chart, functional cohesion, and top–down development.

STRUCTURE CHARTS

The structure chart is the primary design tool for a program. You therefore create it before you start writing your program. An analogy will help you understand the importance of designing before you start coding.

Assume that you have decided to build a house. You will spend a lot of time thinking about exactly what you want. How many rooms will it need? Do you want a family room or a great room? Should the laundry be inside the house or in the garage? To make sure everyone understands what you want, you will prepare formal blueprints that describe everything in detail. Even if you are building something small, like a dollhouse for a child or a tool shed for your back yard, you will make some sketches or plans.

Figuring out what you want in your house is comparable to determining the requirements for a large system. Drawing up a set of blueprints parallels the structure chart in the design of a program. All require advance planning; only the level of detail changes.

Professional programmers use the structure chart for another purpose. In a project team environment, before programmers start writing a program, they must have its design reviewed. This review process is called a structured walk-through. The review team consists of the systems analyst responsible for the area of the project, a representative of the user community, a system test engineer, and one or two programmers from the project.

The design walk-through serves three purposes: First, it ensures that you understand how your program fits into the system by communicating your design to the team. If the design has any omissions or communication errors, the team should detect them now. If you invite programmers who must interface with your program, you will also ensure that the interprogram communication linkages are correct.

Second, the walk-through validates your design. In creating your design, you will have considered several alternative approaches to writing your program. The review team will expect to see and understand the different designs you considered and hear why you chose the design you are proposing. They will challenge aspects of the design and suggest approaches you may not have considered. The result of the review will be the best possible design.

Finally, the walk-through gives the test engineer the opportunity to assess your program's testability. This in turn ensures that the final program will be robust and as error-free as possible.

STRUCTURE CHART RULES AND SYMBOLS

Figure 4-24 shows the various symbols that you use to write a structure chart. Although we include all symbols here for completeness, we will discuss only the two colored symbols. We discuss the other symbols in Chapters 5 and 6. In addition to the symbols, we will discuss several rules that you should follow in your structure chart.

Function Symbol

Each rectangle in a structure chart (see Figure 4-24) represents a function *that you write*. Functions found in the standard C libraries are not shown. The name in the rectangle is the name you will give to the function. It should be meaningful. The software engineering principle known as *intelligent names* states that the names used in a program should be self-documenting; that is, they should convey their intended usage to the reader. You should use intelligent names for both functions and for data names within your program.

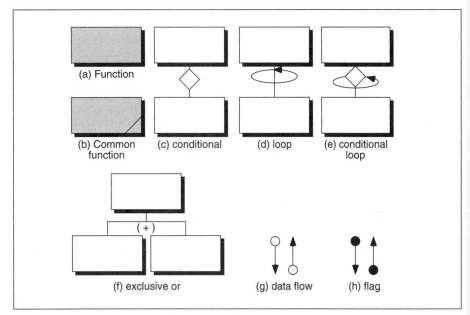

Figure 4-24   Structure chart symbols

Now that we have explained that all names should be descriptive, we will break our own rule because we want to concentrate on the format of a structure chart rather than a particular program. The names you see in Figure 4-25 identify the various modules for discussion.

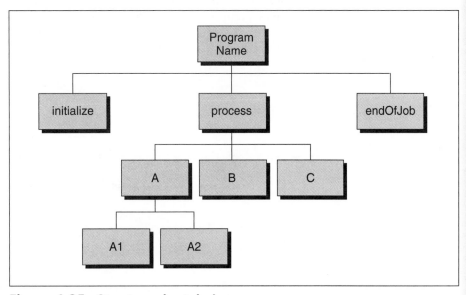

Figure 4-25   Structure chart design

Structure charts are read *top–down, left–right.* In Figure 4-25, Program-Name (`main`) consists of three subfunctions: `initialize`, `process`, and `endOfJob`. According to the left–right rule, the first call in the program is to `initialize`. After `initialize` is complete, the program calls `process`. When `process` is complete, the program calls `endOfJob`. The functions on the same level of a structure chart are called in order from the left to the right.

The concept of top–down is demonstrated by `process`. When `process` is called, it calls `A`, `B`, and `C` in turn. Function `B` does not start running, however, until `A` is finished. While `A` is running, it calls `A1` and `A2` in turn. In other words, all functions in a line from `process` to `A2` must be called before Function `B` can start.

Now you need to know the next rule of structure charts: No code is contained in a structure chart. A structure chart shows only the function flow through the program. It is not a block diagram or a flowchart. As a map of your program, the structure chart shows only the logical flow of the functions. Exactly how each function does its job is shown by algorithm design (flowchart or pseudocode). A structure chart shows the big picture; the details are left to algorithm design.

> Structure charts show only function flow; they contain no code.

Often a program contains several calls to a common function (see Figure 4-24b). These calls are usually scattered throughout the program. The structure chart shows the call wherever it logically occurs in the program. To identify common structures, the lower right corner of the rectangle contains a cross-hatch or is shaded. If the common function is complex and contains subfunctions, these subfunctions must be shown only once. An indication that the incomplete references contain additional structure should be shown. This is usually done with a line below the function rectangle and a cut (~) symbol. This concept is shown in Figure 4-26, which uses a common function, `average`, in two different places in the program. Note, however, that you never graphically show a function connected to two calling functions.

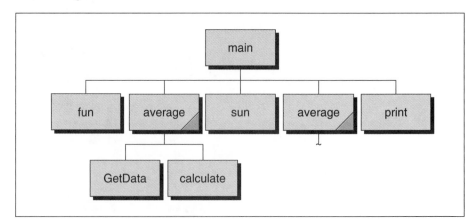

Figure 4-26 Common functions in a structure chart

It is not necessary to show **data flows** (Figure 4-24g) and **flags** (see Figure 4-24h), both of which represent parameters, although it may be helpful in certain circumstances. If they are shown, inputs are on the left of the vertical line and outputs are on the right. When they are included, the name of the data or flag should also be indicated.

The structrure chart rules described in this section are summarized in Table 4-1.

1. Each rectangle in a structure chart represents a function written by the programmer. Standard C functions are not included.
2. The name in the rectangle is an intelligent name that communicates the purpose of the function. It is the name that will be used in the coding of the function.
3. The function chart contains only function flow. No code is indicated.
4. Common functions are indicated by a cross-hatch or shading in the lower right corner of the function rectangle.
5. Common calls are shown in a structure wherever they will be found in the program. If they contain subfunction calls, the complete structure need be shown only once.
6. Data flows and flags are optional. When used, they should be named.
7. Input flows and flags are shown on the left of the vertical line; output flows and flags are shown on the right.

Table 4-1   Structure chart rules

FUNCTIONAL COHESION

One of the most difficult structured programming concepts for new programmers is knowing when and how to create a function.

Functional cohesion is a measure of how closely the processes in a function are related. A function that does one and only one process is functionally cohesive. A function that contains totally unrelated processes is coincidentally cohesive. We provide a few rules here to help you write cohesive functions. For a complete discussion of the topic, see Page-Jones.[2]

Before we discuss the rules, however, you should understand why the concept is important. Following are the three primary reasons for using structurally cohesive functions:

1. *Correctness*: If you are concentrating on only one thing as you write a function, you will be less apt to make an error. It is much easier to get a simple task right than a complex task.
2. *Maintainability*: Production programs can live for years. The better structured a program, the easier it is to change. When programs are not well structured, making a change in one part of the program often leads to errors in other parts.
3. *Reusability*: Some processes are so common that they are found in many programs. Good programmers build libraries of these functions so that they don't have to reinvent the function each time it is

---

[2]Meilir Page-Jones, *The Practical Guide to Structured Systems Design*, 2nd ed,. Chap. 6. (Englewood Cliffs, N.J.: Prentice Hall, 1988).

needed. This not only leads to quicker program development but also reduces debugging time, since the library functions have already been debugged.

Only One Thing

Each function should do only one thing. Furthermore, all of the statements in the function should contribute only to that one thing. For example, assume that you are writing a program that requires the statistical measures of average and standard deviation. The two statistical measures are obviously related, if for no other reason than they are both measures of the same series of numbers. But you would not calculate both measures in one function. That would be calculating two things, and each function should do only one thing.

One way to determine if your function is doing more than one thing is to count the number of *objects* that it handles. An object in this sense is anything that exists separately from the other elements of the function. In the previous example, the average and the standard deviation are two different objects.

As another example, to compute the taxes for a payroll program in the state of California, you would deal with FICA taxes, state disability insurance, state unemployment taxes, state withholding taxes, and federal withholding taxes. Each of these is a different object. Your design should group all of these taxes together in a function to calculate taxes, and it should call subfunctions to calculate each individual tax. This design is seen in Figure 4-27.

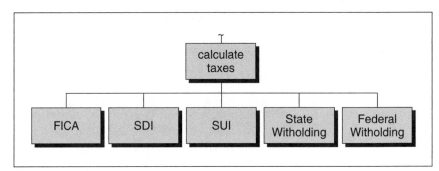

Figure 4-27   Calculate taxes design

In One Place

The corollary rule is that the one thing a function does should be done in only one place. If the code for a process is scattered in several different and unrelated parts of the program, it is very difficult to change. Therefore, all the processing for a task should be placed in one function and, if necessary, its subfunctions. This is the reason we created the function `calculate taxes` in Figure 4-27.

An example of scattered code common among programmers is found in printing reports. Suppose that we needed to write a program that, among other things, prints a report that includes a heading, some data with a total, and then an end-of-report message. A well-structured solution is seen in Figure 4-28. It is quite common, however, to find the statements for each of these subtasks scattered in `main` and other parts of the program.

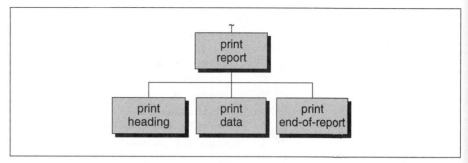

Figure 4-28 Design for `print report`

As a final measure of your program's structure, you should be able to test program functions independently. We will discuss a technique for this in the next section. Let us simply say here that **testability** is an attribute of a well-designed and well-structured program allows each section of the program to be tested separately from the rest of the program.

TOP–DOWN DEVELOPMENT

If you have designed your program using structured programming concepts and a structure chart, you can then proceed to implement it in a top–down fashion.

Referring again to Figure 4-25, on page 155, a top–down implementation starts with the code for `main` only, shown in the structure chart as `Program-Name`. The code for the first compile and test is shown in Program 4-12.

```
1   /* Sample of top-down development using stubs.
2          Written by:
3          Date:
4   */
5   #include <stdio.h>
6
7   /*  Prototype Declarations */
8      int initialize (void);
9      int process    (void);
10     int endOfJob   (void);
11
12  int main (void)
13  {
14  /* Statements */
15     printf("Begin program \n\n");
16
17     initialize ();
18     process ();
19     endOfJob ();
20     return 0;
21  } /* main */
22  /* ================= initialize =================
23     Stub for initialize.
```

Program 4-12 Top–down development example

```
24   */
25   int initialize (void)
26   {
27      /* Statements */
28      printf("In initialize: \n");
29      return 0;
30   }  /* initialize */
31   /* =================== process ===================
32      Stub for process
33   */
34   int process (void)
35   {
36      /* Statements */
37      printf("In process: \n");
38      return 0 ;
39   }  /* process */
40   /* ================= endOfJob =================
41      Stub for endOfJob
42   */
43   int endOfJob (void)
44   {
45      /* Statements */
46      printf("In endOfJob: \n");
47      return 0 ;
48   }  /* endOfJob*/
```

```
Results
   Begin program
   In initialize:
   In process:
   In endOfJob:
```

Program 4-12 Top–down development example (continued)

Program 4-12 Analysis   Note that this program has only the first four boxes from the structure chart: ProgramName (main), initialize, process, and endOfJob. For each of main's subfunctions, all that is included is a **stub**. A stub is the skeleton of a function that is called and immediately returns. Although it is a complete function, it does nothing other than to establish and verify the linkage between the caller and itself. But this is a very important part of testing and verifying a program. At this point the program should be compiled, linked, and run. Chances are that you will find some minor problems, such as missing semicolons or errors between the prototype declarations and the function definitions. Before you continue with the program, you should correct these problems.

The top–down development then continues with the coding of initialize, process, or endOfJob. Normally, you develop the functions left to right, but it is not necessary to do so. To develop process, you again stub its subfunctions, A, B, and C, and then test the program. This top–down development continues until the complete program has been coded and tested.

4-8 TIPS AND COMMON PROGRAMMING ERRORS

1. Several possible errors are related to passing parameters.

   a. It is a compile error if the types in the prototype declaration and function definition are incompatible. For example, the types in the following statements are incompatible:

   ```
   double divide (int dividend, int divisor);
       ...
   double divide (float dividend,
                  float divisor)
   {
       ...
   }    /* divide */
   ```

   b. It is a compile error to have a different number of actual parameters in the function call than there are in the prototype statement.

   c. It is a logic error if you code the parameters in the wrong order. Their meaning will be inconsistent in the called program. For example, in the following statements, the types are the same but the meaning of the variables is reversed:

   ```
   double divide (float dividend, float divisor);
       ...
   double divide (float divisor,
                  float dividend)
   {
       ...
   }    /* divide */
   ```

2. It is a compile error to define local variables with the same identifiers as formal parameters, as shown below.

   ```
   double divide (float dividend,
                  float divisor)
   {
   /*    Local Definitions */
       float dividend;
       ...
   }    /* divide */
   ```

3. Using a *void* return with a function that expects a return value or using a return value with a function that expects a *void* return is a compile error.

4. Each parameter's type must be individually specified; you cannot use multiple definitions like you can in variables. For example, the following is a compile error because y does not have a type:

   ```
   double fun (float x, y);
   ```

5. Forgetting the semicolon at the end of a function prototype statement is a compile error. Similarly, using a semicolon at the end of the header in a function definition is a compile error.

6. It is most likely a logic error to call a function from within itself or one of its called functions. (This is known as recursion, and its correct use is covered in Chapter 6.)

7. It is a compile error to attempt to define a function within the body of another function.

8. It is a run-time error to code a function call without the parentheses, even when the function has no parameters.

```
printHello;                    /* Not a call */
printHello ( );                /* A valid call */
```

9. It is a compile error if the type of data in the return statement does not match the function return type.

10. It is a logic error to call *srand* every time you call *rand*.

4-9 KEY TERMS AND CONCEPTS[3]

abs	function	*rand*
actual parameters	function body	RAND_MAX
address operator	function call	random number
block	function declaration	*return*
C standard library	function definition	scaling (with random numbers)
called function	function header	scope
calling function	indirection operator	side effect
ceil	*labs*	*sqrt*
data flow	local variables	*srand*
decomposition	parameter	structure chart
dereferencing	parameter passing	stub
fabs	pass by reference	testability
flag	pass by value	top–down design
floor	*pow*	*void* functions
formal parameter list	prototype declaration	

[3]Note: Italic terms are C keywords or standard function names.

4-10 SUMMARY

- In structured programming, a program is divided into modules.
    a. Each module is designed to do a specific task.
    b. Modules in C are written as functions.
- Each C program must have one and only one function called `main`.
- A function can return only one value.
- A function can be called for its returned value or for its side effect.
- The function call includes the function name and the values of the actual parameters to provide the called function with the data it needs to perform its job.

- Each actual parameter of the function is an expression. The expression must have a value that can be evaluated at the time the function is called.
- A local variable is known only in a function definition. The local variables do not take part in communication between the calling and the called functions.
- The general format for a function definition is

```
return_type function_name (parameter list)
{
/* Local Definitions */

/* Statements */
}  /* function_name */
```

- If a function returns no value, the return type must be declared as *void*.
- If a function has no parameters, the parameter list must be declared *void*.
- The actual parameters passed to a function must match in number, type, and order with the formal parameters in the function definition.
- When a function is called, control is passed to the called function. The calling function "rests" until the called function finishes its job.
- We highly recommend that every function have a *return* statement. A *return* statement is required if the return type is anything other than *void*.
- Control returns to the caller when the *return* statement is encountered.
- A function prototype requires only the return type of the function, the function name, and the number, types, and order of the formal parameters. Parameter identifiers may be added for documentation but are not required.
- The scope of a parameter is the block following the header.
- A local variable is a variable declared inside a block. The scope of a local variable is the block in which it is declared.

4-11   PRACTICE SETS

REVIEW QUESTIONS

1. The principles of top–down design and structured programming dictate that a program should be divided into a main module and its related modules.
   a. True   b. False

2. The function definition contains the code for a function.
   a. True   b. False

3. Function calls that return *void* may not be used as a part of an expression.
   a. True   b. False

4. The address operator (&) is used to tell the compiler to store data at an address.
   a. True   b. False

5. Variables defined within a block have global scope.
   a. True   b. False

6. The process of dividing a program into functions—which in turn are divided into functions until they consist of only elementary processing that is intrinsically understood and cannot be further subdivided—is known as
   a. charting   c. factoring   e. structuring
   b. flow charting   d. programming

7. Which of the following statements about function declaration and definition is true?
   a. The function call is found in the called function.
   b. The function declaration requires that the parameters be named.
   c. The function definition is done with a prototype statement.
   d. The function definition contains executable statements that perform the function's task.
   e. The function definition header concludes with a semicolon (;).

8. Which of the following is not a part of a function header?
   a. name
   b. parameter list
   c. return type
   d. title

9. Which of the following statements about function parameters is true?
   a. Empty parameter lists are declared with the keyword *void*.
   b. If there is only one parameter, the function list parentheses are not required.
   c. In the definition of a function, the parameters are known as actual parameters.
   d. Parameters are separated by semicolons.
   e. The parameters in a function definition are defined in the function's body (local declaration section).

10. Which of the following statements about local variables is false?
   a. A local variable's value may be returned through a *return* statement.
   b. Local variables are defined inside a function.
   c. Local variables cannot be referenced through their identifiers outside the function.
   d. Local variables may be initialized with an initializer.
   e. Local variables' names can be the same as the function's parameter names.

11. To tell the compiler to store data at an address, use the
   a. address operator (&)
   b. array operator ([ ])
   c. dereference operator (#)
   d. indirection operator (*)
   e. pointer operator (^)

12. The function that returns the absolute value of a long integer is
   a. `abs`
   b. `dabs`
   c. `fabs`
   d. `labs`
   e. `tabs`

13. Which of the following statements will generate a random number in the range 30–50?
   a. `rand (33)`
   b. `(rand () % 20) + 1`
   c. `(rand () % 21) + 20`
   d. `(rand () % 21) + 30`
   e. `(rand () % 51) + 1`

14. Which of the following statements about structure charts is false?
   a. Structure charts are a replacement for flowcharts.
   b. Structure charts are the primary design tool for a program.
   c. Structure charts are used in a structured walkthrough to validate the design.
   d. Structure charts can be used to assess the testability of a program.
   e. Structure charts should be created before you start writing a program.

EXERCISES

15. Find any errors in the following function definition:
```
void fun (int x, int y)
{
  int z;
  ...
  return z;
}  /* fun */
```

16. Find any errors in the following function definition:
```
int fun (int x, y)
{
    int z;
    ...
    return z;
}  /* fun */
```

17. Find any errors in the following function definition:
    ```
    int fun (int x, int y)
    {
       ...
       int sun (int t)
          {
             ...
             return (t + 3);
          }
       ...
       return z;
    } /* fun */
    ```

18. Find any errors in the following function definition:
    ```
    void fun (int, x)
    {
       ...
       return;
    } /* fun */
    ```

19. Find any errors in the following prototype statements:
    ```
    a. int sun (int x, y);
    b. int sun (int x, int y)
    c. void sun (void, void);
    d. void sun (x int, y float);
    ```

20. Find any errors in the following function calls:
    ```
    a. void fun ( );
    b. fun ( void );
    c. void fun (int x, int y);
    d. fun ( );
    ```

21. Evaluate the value of the following expressions:
    ```
    a. fabs (9.5)      c. fabs (−3.4)     e. fabs (7)
    b. fabs (−2.4)     d. fabs (−7)
    ```

22. Evaluate the value of the following expressions:
    ```
    a. floor ( 9.5 )    c. floor ( −3.4 )    e. ceil ( −2.4 )
    b. floor ( −2.4 )   d. ceil ( 9.5 )      f. ceil ( −3.4 )
    ```

23. Evaluate the value of the following expressions when x is 3.5, 3.45, 3.76, 3.234, and 3.4567:
    ```
    a. floor (x * 10 + 0.5) / 10
    b. floor (x * 100 + 0.5) / 100
    c. floor (x * 1000 + 0.5) / 1000
    ```

24. Define the range of the random numbers generated by the following expressions:
    ```
    a. rand( ) % 10    c. rand( ) % 52      e. rand( ) % 2 +1f
    b. rand( ) % 4     d. rand( ) % 10 +1   f. rand( ) % 52 − 5
    ```

25. What would be printed from Program 4-13 when run using 3   5 as data?

```
 1 | #include <stdio.h>
 2 |
 3 | /* Prototype Declarations */
 4 | int strange (int x, int y);
 5 |
 6 | int main (void)
 7 | {
 8 | /* Local Definitions */
 9 |    int  a;
10 |    int  b;
11 |    int  r;
12 |    int  s;
13 |
14 | /* Statements */
15 |    scanf("%d %d", &a, &b);
16 |    r = strange (a, b);
17 |    s = strange (b, a);
18 |    printf("%d %d", r, s);
19 |    return 0;
20 | }  /* main */
21 | /* ================= strange ================= */
22 | int strange (int x,
23 |             int y)
24 | {
25 | /* Statements */
26 |    return (x - y);
27 | }  /* strange */
```

Program 4-13   Program for Exercise 25

26. What would be printed from Program 4-14 when run using 3   5   4   6 as data?

```
 1 | #include <stdio.h>
 2 |
 3 | /* Prototype Declarations */
 4 | int strange (int x, int y);
 5 |
 6 | int main (void)
 7 | {
 8 | /* Local Definitions */
 9 |    int  a;
10 |    int  b;
11 |    int  c;
12 |    int  d;
13 |    int  r;
```

Program 4-14   Program for Exercise 26

```
14      int   s;
15      int   t;
16      int   u;
17      int   v;
18
19   /* Statements */
20      scanf("%d %d %d %d", &a, &b, &c, &d);
21
22      r = strange (a, b);
23      s = strange (r, c);
24      t = strange (strange (s, d), strange (4, 2));
25      u = strange (t + 3, s + 2);
26      v = strange (strange (strange (u, a), b), c);
27
28      printf("%d %d %d %d %d", r, s, t, u, v);
29      return 0;
30   }  /* main */
31   /* ================= strange ================= */
32   int strange (int x,
33               int y)
34   {
35   /* Local Definitions */
36      int   t;
37      int   z;
38
39   /* Statements */
40      t = x + y;
41      z = x * y;
42      return (t + z);
43   }  /* strange */
```

Program 4-14   Program for Exercise 26 (continued)

27. Draw the structure chart for the following program. What output does it produce?

```
1    #include <stdio.h>
2
3    /* Prototype Declarations */
4    int  funA (int x);
5    void funB (int x);
6
7    int main (void)
8    {
9    /* Local Definitions */
10      int   a;
11      int   b;
12      int   c;
13
14   /* Statements */
```

Program 4-15   Program for Exercise 27

```
15    a = 10;
16    funB (a);
17    b = 5;
18    c = funA (b);
19    funB(c);
20    printf("%3d %3d %3d", a, b, c);
21    return 0;
22 }  /* main */
23
24 int funA (int x)
25 {
26 /* Statements */
27    return x * x;
28 }  /* funA */
29
30 void funB (int x)
31 {
32 /* Local Definitions */
33    int y;
34
35 /* Statements */
36    y  = x % 2;
37    x /= 2;
38    printf ("\n%3d %3d\n", x, y);
39    return;
40 }  /* funB */
```

Program 4-15 Program for Exercise 27 (continued)

PROBLEMS

28. Write a function to print your name, as shown below. Write a call as it would be coded in a calling function, such as `main`.

```
        *****************************
        *                           *
        *       Your Name Here       *
        *                           *
        *****************************
```

29. Write a program that generates a random number from the following set:
    ```
    1, 2, 3, 4, 5, 6
    ```

30. Write a program that generates a random number from the following set:
    ```
    1, 4, 7, 10, 13, 16
    ```

31. Explain the difference between pass by value, pass by reference, and pass by address.

32. Draw the structure chart for the calculator program on page 152.

33. Explain what is meant by the statement "a function should do only one thing."

34. Code and run Program 4-12, on page 159, to demonstrate how stubs work.

35. Write a function to convert inches into centimeters. (One inch is 2.54 centimeters.) Then write a program that prompts the user to input a measure in inches, calls the conversion function, and prints out the measurement in centimeters.

36. Write a program that reads three integers and then prints them in the order read and reversed. Use three functions, one to read the data, one to print them in the order read, and one to print them reversed.

37. Expand the calculator program, Program 4-11, on page 152, to calculate the product, quotient, and modulus of the number. Calculate the quotient and modulus in one function using pass by address.

38. Modify Program 4-5, `addTwoDigits`, on page 130, to add the least significant three digits (hundreds, tens, and ones).

39. Write a function that receives a positive floating-point number and rounds it to two decimal places. For example, 127.565031 rounds to 127.570000. Hint: To round, you must convert the floating-point number to an integer and then back to a floating-point number. Print the rounded numbers to six decimal places. Test the function with the following data:

    123.456789   123.499999 123.500001

40. Write a program that reads a floating-point number and prints the ceiling, floor, and rounded value. Use the function in Problem 39. Test it with the same values as Problem 39.

41. Write a function to compute the perimeter and area of a right triangle (Figure 4-29) when given the length of the two sides (a and b).

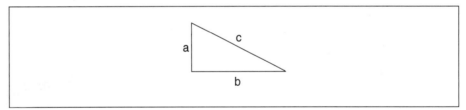

Figure 4-29   Problem 41

The following formulas may be helpful:
$$c^2 = a^2 + b^2$$
$$area = .5 * (a * b)$$

PROJECTS

42. Prepare a payroll earnings statement for the sales force at the Arctic Ice Company. All of Arctic's employees are on a straight commission basis of 12.5% of sales. Each month, they also receive a bonus that varies depending on the profit for the month and their length of service. The sales manager calculates the bonus separately and enters it with the salesperson's total sales for the month. Your program is also to calculate the withholding taxes and retirement for the month based on the following rates:

    a. Federal withholding: 25%

    b. State withholding: 10%

    c. Retirement plan: 8%

    Use the test data in Table 4-2 to test the program.

Salesperson	Sales	Bonus
1	53,500	425
2	41,300	300
3	56,800	350
4	36,200	175

Table 4-2   Test data for Project 42

43. Write a program that, given a beginning balance in your savings account, calculates the balance at the end of 1 year. The interest is 5.3% compounded quarterly. Show the interest earned and balance at the end of each quarter. Present the data in tabular columns with appropriate headings. Use separate functions to compute the interest and print the balance.

44. The formula for converting centigrade temperatures to fahrenheit is

$$F = 32 + C\frac{180.0}{100.0}$$

Write a program that asks the user to enter a temperature reading in centigrade and then prints the equivalent fahrenheit value. It then asks the user to enter a fahrenheit value and prints out the equivalent centigrade value. Run the program several times. Be sure to include at least one negative temperature reading in your test cases. Provide separate functions as needed by your design. One possible design is shown in Figure 4-30. (Your `main` function should have only function calls.)

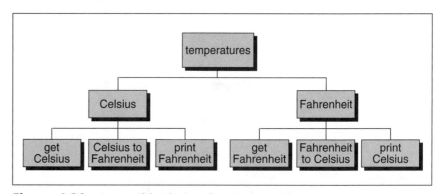

Figure 4-30   A possible design for Project 44

45. Write a program that uses standard functions. The program may be written entirely in `main` and must follow the pseudocode shown in Algorithm 4-2. Give the output appropriate captions, and align the data.

```
1 Prompt the user to enter a number.
2 Read number.
3 Display number.
4 Get a random number and scale to range 3...37.
```

Algorithm 4-2   Pseudocode for Project 45

```
 5 Display random number.
 6 Set product to number * random number.
 7 Display product.
 8 Display ceiling of product.
 9 Display floor of product.
10 Display number raised to power 5.
11 Display square root of random number.
```

Algorithm 4-2 Pseudocode for Project 45 (continued)

46. Write a C program that creates customers' bills for a carpet company when the following information is given:

a. the length and the width of the carpet in feet

b. the carpet price per square foot

c. the percent of discount for each customer

The labor cost is fixed at $0.35 per square foot. It is to be defined as a constant. The tax rate is 8.5% applied after the discount. It is also to be defined as a constant. The input data consist of a set of three integers representing the length and width of the room to be carpeted, the percentage of the discount the owner gives to a customer, and a floating-point number representing the unit price of the carpet. The program is to prompt the user for this input as shown below. (Bold numbers are typical responses.)

```
Length of room (feet)?        30
Width of room (feet)?         18
Customer discount (percent)?   9
Cost per square foot (xxx.xx)? 8.23
```

The output is shown below. Be careful to align the decimal points.

```
                    MEASUREMENT


         Length                      XXX ft
         Width                       XXX ft
         Area                        XXX square ft


                      CHARGES

         DESCRIPTION  COST/SQ.FT.  CHARGE/ROOM
         -----------  -----------  -----------

         Carpet         XXX.XX      $XXXX.XX
         Labor           0.35        XXXX.XX
                                    -----------
         INSTALLED PRICE            $XXXX.XX
         Discount        XX.X%       XXXX.XX
                                    -----------
         SUBTOTAL                   $XXXX.XX
         Tax                         XXXX.XX
         TOTAL                      $XXXX.XX
```

The program's design should use `main` and at least the six functions described below:

a. Read data (`getData`) from the keyboard. This function is to use addresses (pass-by-address concept) to read all data and place it in the calling function's variables.

b. Calculate values (`calculate`). This function calls three subfunctions.
   - Calculate the installed price (`calcInstall`). The installed price is the cost of the carpet and the cost of the labor.
   - Calculate the subtotal (`calcSubTotal`).
   - Calculate the total price with discount and tax (`calcTotal`).

c. Print the result (`printResult`). Use two subfunctions to print the results: one to print the measurements, and one to print the charges.

Test your program with the test data shown in Table 4-3.

Test	Length	Width	Discount	Price
1	23	13	12	$14.20
2	35	8	0	$ 8.00
3	14	11	10	$22.25

Table 4-3   Test data for Project 46

Selection—Making Decisions

The second of the structured programming constructs is **selection**. Selection allows you to choose between two or more alternatives: It allows you to make decisions.

What a dull world it would be if we didn't have any choices. Vanilla ice cream for everybody! Uniforms all around! And no debates or arguments to keep things interesting. Fortunately, our world is filled with choices. And since our programs must reflect the world in which they are designed to operate, they, too, are filled with choices and opportunities for decision making.

How are decisions made by a computer? In this chapter, you will find out. One of the main points to keep in mind is that the decisions made by a computer must be very simple, since everything in the computer ultimately reduces to either true (1) or false (0). If complex decisions are required, it is the programmer's job to reduce them to a series of simple decisions that the computer can handle.

5-1 LOGICAL DATA AND OPERATORS

A piece of data is called logical if it conveys the idea of true or false. We need logical data in real life as well as in programming. In real life, **logical data** (true or false) are created in answer to a question that needs a yes–no answer. For example, we ask if an item is on sale or not. We ask if a business is open or not. The answer to these questions is a piece of data that is usually yes or no. We can also ask questions like "Is **x** greater than **y**?" The answer is again yes or no. In computer science, we do not use yes or no, we use true or false.

LOGICAL DATA IN C

C has no logical data type; C programmers use other data types (such as *int* and *char*) to represent logical data. If a data item is zero, it is considered false. If it is nonzero, it is considered true. This concept of true and false on a numeric scale is seen in Figure 5-1.

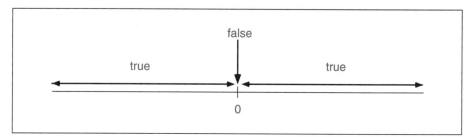

Figure 5-1 True and false on the arithmetic scale

LOGICAL OPERATORS

C has three **logical operators** for combining logical values and creating new logical values: *not*, *and*, and *or*. These operators are seen in Table 5-1. A common way to show logical relationships is in truth tables. Truth tables list the values that each operand can assume and the resulting value.

Operator	Meaning	Precedence
!	*not*	15
&&	Logical *and*	5
||	Logical *or*	4

Table 5-1 Logical operators

not

The *not* operator (!) is a unary operator with precedence 15 in the Precedence Table (see inside front cover). It changes a true value (nonzero) to false (zero) and a false value (0) to true (1). The truth table for *not* is shown in Figure 5-2.

and

The *and* operator (&&) is a binary operator with a precedence of 5. Since *and* is a binary operator, four distinct combinations of values in its operands are possible. The result is true only when both operands are true; it is false in all other cases. This relationship is shown in the *and* truth table in Figure 5-2.

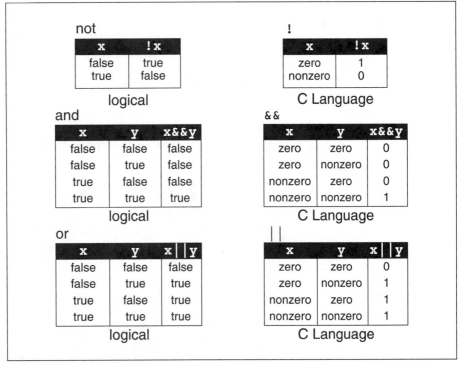

Figure 5-2 Logical operators truth table

or

The *or operator* (||) is a binary operator with a precedence of 4. Again, since it is a binary operator, four distinct combinations of values in its operands are possible. The result is false if both operands are false; it is true in all other cases. The *or* truth table is also shown in Figure 5-2.

EVALUATING LOGICAL EXPRESSIONS

Computer languages can use two methods to evaluate the binary logical relationships. They deal with whether or not the complete expression needs to be evaluated.

In the first method, the expression must be completely evaluated before the result is determined. This means that the *and* expression must be completely evaluated, even when the first operand is false and it is therefore known that the result must be false. Likewise, in the *or* expression, the whole expression must be evaluated even when the first operand is true and the obvious result of the expression must be true. The Pascal language uses this method.

The second method sets the resulting value as soon as it is known. It does not need to complete the evaluation. In other words, it operates in a short-circuit fashion and stops the evaluation when it knows for sure what the final result will be. Under this method, if the first operand of a logical *and* expression is false, the second half of the expression is not evaluated because it is apparent that the result must be false. Again, with the *or* expression, if the first operand is true, there is no need to evaluate the second half of the expression, so the resulting value is set true immediately. C uses this short-circuit method, which is graphically shown in Figure 5-3.

Although the C method is more efficient, it can cause problems when the second operand contains side effects, which is poor programming practice. Consider for example, the following expression in which a programmer wants to find the value of the logical expression and at the same time wants to increment the value of the second operand:

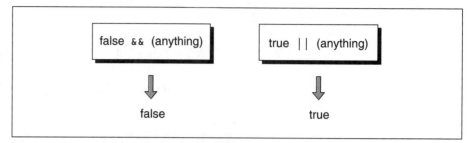

Figure 5-3 Short-circuit methods for *and/or*

```
x && y++
```

Everything works fine when the first operand is nonzero. But if the first operand is zero, the second operand will never be evaluated and therefore will never be incremented. It is the same with the next example. If the first operand is nonzero, the second operand will never be incremented.

```
x || y++
```

Program 5-1 demonstrates the use of logical data in expressions.

```
1   /* Demonstrate the results of logical operators.
2          Written by:
3          Date:
4   */
5   #include <stdio.h>
6
7   int main (void)
8   {
9   /* Local Definitions */
10      int a = 5;
11      int b = -3;
12      int c = 0;
13
14  /* Statements */
15      printf(" %2d &&  %2d is %2d\n", a, b,  a &&  b);
16      printf(" %2d &&  %2d is %2d\n", a, c,  a &&  c);
17      printf(" %2d &&  %2d is %2d\n", c, a,  c &&  a);
18      printf(" %2d ||  %2d is %2d\n", a, c,  a ||  c);
19      printf(" %2d ||  %2d is %2d\n", c, a,  c ||  a);
20      printf(" %2d ||  %2d is %2d\n", c, c,  c ||  c);
21      printf("!%2d && !%2d is %2d\n", a, c, !a && !c);
22      printf("!%2d &&  %2d is %2d\n", a, c, !a &&  c);
23      printf(" %2d && !%2d is %2d\n", a, c,  a && !c);
24      return 0;
25  }   /* main */
```

```
   Results:
        5 &&  -3 is  1
        5 &&   0 is  0
```

Program 5-1 Logical expressions

```
    0 &&    5 is   0
    5 ||    0 is   1
    0 ||    5 is   1
    0 ||    0 is   0
  ! 5 && ! 0 is   0
  ! 5 &&   0 is   0
    5 && ! 0 is   1
```

Program 5-1   Logical expressions (continued)

Program 5-1 Analysis   Each print statement in Program 5-1 contains a logical expression that evaluates either to 1 (true) or 0 (false). The print statements have been written to display the data as an expression and the results. Make sure you understand why each of the expressions evaluates as shown in the results.

RELATIONAL OPERATORS

Six **relational operators** support logical relationships. They are all binary operators that accept two operands and compare them. The result is logical data—that is, the result is always true (1) or false (0). The operators are shown in Figure 5-4.

Operator	Meaning	Precedence
<	less than	
<=	less than or equal	10
>	greater than	
>=	greater than or equal	
==	equal	9
!=	not equal	

Figure 5-4   Relational operators

If you examine Figure 5-4 carefully, you will note that the first four operators—**less than, less than or equal, greater than, greater than or equal**—have a higher priority (10) in the Precedence Table (see inside front cover) than the **equal** and **not equal operators** (9). This means that they will be evaluated before the equal operators when they appear together in the same expression.

It is important to recognize that each operator is a complement of another operator in the group. But, surprisingly, the complement is not the one that you might expect. Figure 5-5 shows each operator and its complement.

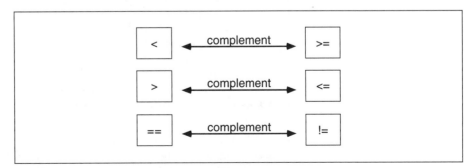

Figure 5-5   Logical operator complements

If we want to simplify an expression involving the *not* and the *less than* operator, we use the *greater than* or *equal* operator. This concept is important for simplifying expressions and coding expressions in good, clear style. Table 5-2 shows an example of each expression and its complement.

Original Expression	Simplified Expression
!(x < y)	x >= y
!(x > y)	x <= y
!(x != y)	x == y
!(x <= y)	x > y
!(x >= y)	x < y
!(x == y)	x != y

Table 5-2 Examples of relational operator complements

Program 5-2 demonstrates the use of relational operators.

```
 1  /* Demonstrates the results of relational operators.
 2         Written by:
 3         Date:
 4  */
 5  #include <stdio.h>
 6  int main (void)
 7  {
 8  /* Local Definitions */
 9     int a = 5;
10     int b = -3;
11
12  /* Statements */
13     printf(" %2d <  %2d is %2d\n", a, b,  a <  b);
14     printf(" %2d == %2d is %2d\n", a, b,  a == b);
15     printf(" %2d != %2d is %2d\n", a, b,  a != b);
16     printf(" %2d >  %2d is %2d\n", a, b,  a >  b);
17     printf(" %2d <= %2d is %2d\n", a, b,  a <= b);
18     printf(" %2d >= %2d is %2d\n", a, b,  a >= b);
19     return 0;
20  }   /* main */
```

```
Results:
    5 <  -3 is  0
    5 == -3 is  0
    5 != -3 is  1
    5 >  -3 is  1
    5 <= -3 is  0
    5 >= -3 is  1
```

Program 5-2 Relational operators

Program 5-2 Analysis   Program 5-2 follows the same patterns we saw in Program 5-1. Once again, make sure that you understand why each of the representations in the results evaluates to true or false.

5-2   TWO-WAY SELECTION

The basic decision statement in the computer is the **two-way selection**. The decision is described to the computer as a conditional statement that can be answered either true or false. If the answer is true, one or more action statements are executed. If the answer is false, then a different action or set of actions is executed. Regardless of which set of actions is executed, the program continues with the next statement after the selection. The flowchart for two-way decision logic is shown in Figure 5-6.

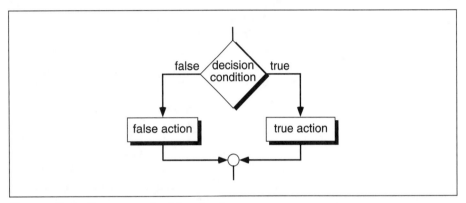

Figure 5-6   Two-way decision logic

if . . . else

C implements two-way selection with the *if...else* statement. An *if...else* statement is a composite statement used to make a decision between two alternatives. Figure 5-7 shows the logic flow for an *if...else*. The expression can be any C expression. After it has been evaluated, if its value is true (not zero), `statement1` is executed: otherwise, `statement2` is executed. It is impossible for both statements to be executed in the same evaluation.

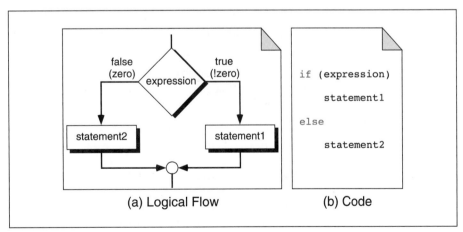

Figure 5-7   *if...else* logic flow

There are some syntactical points you must remember about *if...else* statements. These points are summarized in Table 5-3.

De Morgan's Rule

When we design the logical flow of our program, we often have a situation in which the *not* operator is in front of a logical expression enclosed in the parentheses. Human engineering studies tell us, however, that positive logic is easier to read and understand than negative logic. In these cases, therefore, if we want to make the total expression positive by removing the parentheses, we apply the *not* operator directly to each operand. **De Morgan's rule** governs the complementing of operators in this situation. This rule is defined as follows:

> When we remove the parentheses in a logical expression preceded by the *not* operator, we must apply the *not* operator to each expression component while complementing the relational operators—that is, changing *and* (&&) to *or* (||) while changing *or* (||) to *and* (&&).

To demonstrate De Morgan's rule, consider the expression shown below.

If the expression has been properly complemented, then the result (true or false) will be the same given a set of values for x, y, z, t, and u.

---

1. The expression must be enclosed in parentheses.

2. No semicolon (;) is needed for an *if...else* statement; `statement1` and `statement2` may have a semicolon as required by their types.

3. The expression can have a side effect.

4. Both the true and the false statements can be any statement (even another *if...else* statement) or can be a null statement.

5. Both `statement1` and `statement2` must be one and only one statement. Remember, however, that multiple statements can be combined into a compound statement through the use of braces.

6. We can swap the position of `statement1` and `statement2` if we use the complement of the original expression.

Table 5-3   Syntactical rules for *if...else* statements

The first rule in Table 5-3—that the expression must be enclosed in parentheses—is simple and needs no further discussion. The second rule is also simple, but it tends to cause more problems. We have therefore provided an example in Figure 5-8. In this example, each action is a single statement that either adds or subtracts 1 from the variable a. Note that the semicolons belong to the arithmetic statements, not the *if...else.*

The third rule in Table 5-3 requires more discussion. It is quite common in C to code expressions that have side effects. For example, you will find expressions

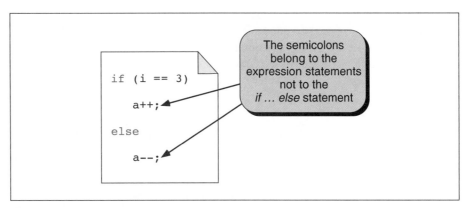

Figure 5-8 A simple *if...else* statement.

that read data as a side effect. As an example, consider what happens when we are writing a series of numbers, and when we have written ten numbers we want to go to a new line. A simple solution increments a line count and tests the limit in the same statement. The code for this logic could be written as shown below.

```
if (++lineCnt > 10)
   {
   printf("\n");
   lineCnt = 0;
   } /* end true */
else
   printf( … );
```

Rules 4 and 5 in Table 5-3 are closely related. The fact that any statement can be used in an *if...else* is straightforward, but often new C programmers will forget to use a compound statement for complex logic. The use of compound statements is seen in Figure 5-9. The first example shows a compound statement only for the true condition. The second example shows compound statements for both conditions. Note that the compound statements begin with an open brace and end with a close brace.

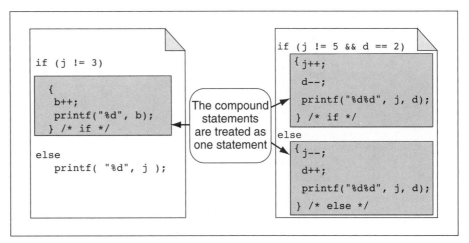

Figure 5-9 Compound statements in an *if...else*

The sixth rule states that the true and false statements can be exchanged by complementing the expression. Recall from our discussion of relational operators on page 177 that any expression can be complemented. When we find that we need to complement an *if...else* statement, all we have to do is to switch the true and false statements. An example of this operation is shown in Figure 5-10.

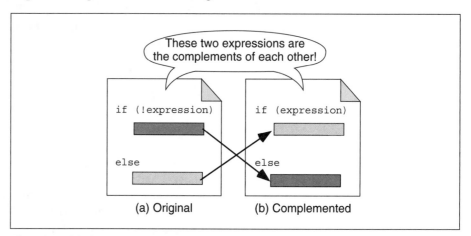

Figure 5-10 Complemented *if...else* statements

NULL *else* STATEMENT

Although there are always two possible actions after a decision, sometimes we do not care about both of them. In this case, the false action is usually left out. For example, assume you are averaging numbers as they are being read. However, for some reason, the logic requires that you average only numbers greater than zero. As you read the number, you test it for greater than zero. If the test is true, you include it in the average. If it is false, you do nothing.

If the false condition is not required—that is, if it is null—it can be omitted. This omission can be shown as a **null *else*** statement (a null statement consists of only a semicolon); more commonly, the else statement is simply omitted entirely, as shown in Figure 5-11.

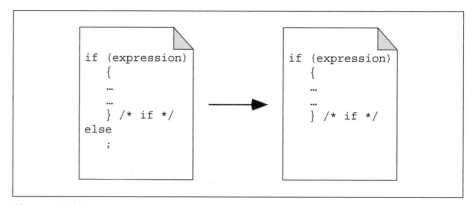

Figure 5-11 A null *else* statement

It is possible to omit the false action, but the true statement cannot be omitted. It can be coded as a null statement; normally, however, we do not use null in the true branch of an *if...else* statement. To eliminate it, we can use Rule 6 in Table 5-3, on page 180, which allows us to complement the expression and swap the two statements. This is shown in Figure 5-12.

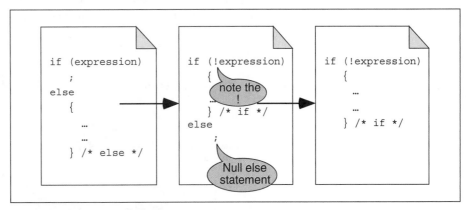

Figure 5-12   A null *if* statement

Program 5-3 contains an example of a simple two-way selection. It displays the relationship between two numbers read from the keyboard.

```
 1   /* Two-way selection.
 2         Written by:
 3         Date:
 4   */
 5   #include <stdio.h>
 6
 7   int main (void)
 8   {
 9      /* Local Definitions */
10      int a;
11      int b;
12
13      /* Statements */
14      printf("Please enter two integers: ");
15      scanf ("%d%d", &a, &b);
16
17      if (a <= b)
18         printf("%d <= %d\n", a, b);
19      else
20         printf("%d > %d\n", a, b);
21      return 0;
22   }  /* main */
```

```
Results:
   Please enter two integers: 10 15
   10 <= 15
```

Program 5-3   Two-way selection

NESTED *if* STATEMENTS

As we stated previously, for the *if...else,* the statements may be any statement, including another *if...else.* When an *if...else* is included within an *if...else,* it is known as a **nested if statement**. Figure 5-13 shows a nested *if* statement. There is no limit to how many levels can be nested, but if there are more than three, they can become difficult to read.

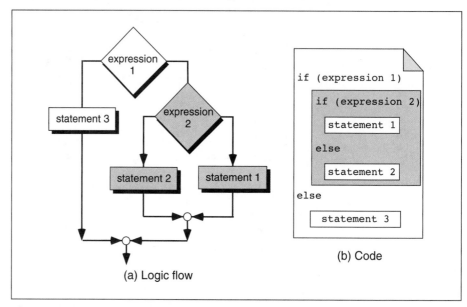

(a) Logic flow

(b) Code

Figure 5-13 Nested *if* statements

Program 5-4 is a modification of Program 5-3. It uses a nested *if* statement to determine if a is less than, equal to, or greater than b.

```
1   /* Nested if in two-way selection.
2          Written by:
3          Date:
4   */
5   #include <stdio.h>
6
7   int main (void)
8   {
9   /* Local Definitions */
10      int a;
11      int b;
12
13  /* Statements */
14      printf("Please enter two integers: ");
15      scanf ("%d%d", &a, &b);
16
17      if (a <= b)
18         if (a < b)
19            printf("%d < %d\n", a, b);
20         else
21            printf("%d == %d\n", a, b);
```

Program 5-4 Nested *if* statements

```
22      else
23          printf("%d > %d\n", a, b);
24      return 0;
    }  /* main */
```

```
Results:
    Please enter two integers: 10 10
    10 == 10
```

Program 5-4   Nested *if* statements (continued)

Program 5-4 Analysis   You should be able to follow this simple program with relative ease. However, it does contain a subtle software engineering principle. Study the *if* statements (17 and 18) carefully. Where do we check for *greater than*? The answer is that we default the *greater than* condition to the outer *else* (see Statement 22). When coding a two-way selection statement, try to code the most probable condition first; with nested selection statements, code the most probable first and the least probable last.

DANGLING *else* PROBLEM

Once you start nesting *if...else* statements, however, you encounter a classic problem known as the **dangling *else***. This problem is created when there is no matching *else* for every *if*. C's solution to this problem is a simple rule: *Always pair an* else *to the most recent unpaired* if *in the current block*. This rule may result in some *if* statement's being left unpaired. Since such an arbitrary rule often does not match your intent, you must

> *else* is always paired with the most recent unpaired *if*.

take care to ensure that the resulting code is what you need. Take, for instance, the example shown in Figure 5-14. From the code alignment, we conclude that the programmer intended the *else* statement to be paired with the first *if*. However, the compiler will pair it with the second *if*, as shown in the flowchart.

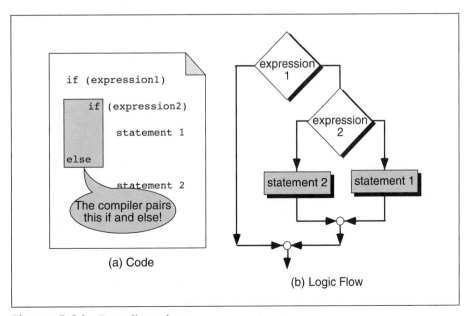

Figure 5-14   Dangling *else*

Figure 5-15 shows a solution to the dangling *else* problem, a compound statement. In the compound statement, you simply enclose the true actions in braces to make the second *if* a compound statement. Since the closing brace completes the body of the compound statement, the *if* statement is also closed from further consideration and the *else* is automatically paired with the correct *if*.

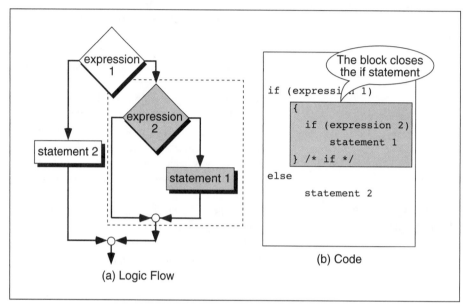

(a) Logic Flow

(b) Code

Figure 5-15   Dangling *else* solution

SIMPLIFYING *if* STATEMENTS

By now you should recognize that *if...else* statements can become quite complex. This discussion will give you some ideas on how to simplify them. Usually, the purpose of simplification is to provide more readable code.

Another reason for **simplifying *if...else* statements** is to eliminate bad code. For example, look at the code in Table 5-4. Although you would not write this code to begin with, often, modifications to your program result in exactly the same kind of logic. It is obvious that the *else* statement can never be executed—because the constant 5 is always true—so why have it? In this case, simply eliminate the *if...else*. Would the same simplifying concept work if the conditional expression (5) were a variable instead of a constant? No.

Original Statement	Simplified Statement
```if (5) printf("Hello"); else printf("Bye");```	```printf("Hello");```

Table 5-4   Eliminating the *else* statement

Sometimes the control expression itself can be simplified. For example, the two statements in Table 5-5 are exactly the same. The simplified statements, however, are much preferred by experienced C programmers. When the simplified code becomes a natural way of thinking, you have begun to internalize the C concepts; that is, you are beginning to think in C!

Original Statement	Simplified Statement
`if (a != 0)` `    statement`	`if (a)` `    statement`
`if (a == 0)` `    statement`	`if (!a)` `    statement`

Table 5-5   Simplifying the condition

Since the simplified statements in Table 5-5 are new, let's look at them a little more carefully. The expression `a != 0` evaluates to either true or false. If `a` is anything other than zero, then the expression is true and `statement` is executed. However, any integer can be used to represent true or false. In this case, if `a` contains any value other than zero, it is true; otherwise, it is false. Therefore, since we want to execute `statement` whenever `a` is not zero, and since anything other than zero is true, we code the expression as `(a)`—that is, as "a is true." Similarly, if we want to test for `a` equal to zero, we simply complement the expression, making it `!a`.

CONDITIONAL EXPRESSIONS

C provides a convenient alternative to the traditional *if...else* for two-way selection—the ternary conditional expression found at priority 3 in the Precedence Table (see inside front cover).

The **conditional expression** has three operands and two operators. Each operand is an expression. The first operator, a question mark (`?`), separates the first two expressions. The second operator, a colon (`:`), separates the last two expressions. This gives it the following format:

```
expression ? expression1 : expression2
```

To evaluate this expression, C first evaluates the leftmost expression. If the expression is true, then the value of the conditional expression is the value of `expression1`. If the expression is false, then the value of the conditional expression is the value of `expression2`.

Let's look at an example.

```
a == b ? c-- : c++;
```

In this expression, only one of the two side effects will take place. If `a` is equal to `b`, `c--` will be evaluated and one will be subtracted from `c`; `expression2` will be ignored. On the other hand, if `a` is not equal to `b`, then `c++` will be evaluated and 1 will be added to `c`; `expression1` will be ignored. If this sounds much like a simplified *if...else*, it's because it is! Figure 5-16 shows the flowchart for the expression, which could easily be coded as an *if...else*.

The results of a conditional expression can be assigned. Suppose that we have a program that can write either to a printer or to the system monitor. When we write to the monitor, we can write ten numbers to a line. When we write to the printer, we can write 15 numbers to a line. Given that `fileFlag` is a variable that indicates either the monitor (`M`) or printer (`P`), we could set the numbers per line as shown below. (The parentheses are not necessary but make the statement more readable.)

```
numPerLine = (fileFlag == 'M' ? 10 : 15);
```

One final note: Although you can nest conditional expressions, it is not recommended. If the logic begins to get complex, remember the KISS principle and use nested *if* statements.

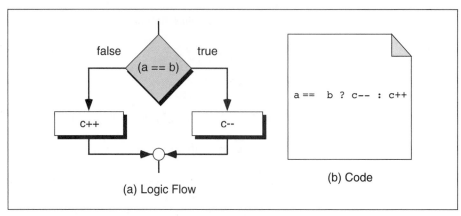

Figure 5-16 Conditional expression

HANDLING MAJOR ERRORS

One of the better known computer acronyms is GIGO—garbage in, garbage out. In writing programs, we must decide how to handle errors to prevent garbage from corrupting the data. Sometimes, as we will see in the next chapter, we can recover from the error by having the user re-enter it. Other times, there is no way to recover.

When we can't recover, C provides two functions that allow us to terminate the functions: *exit* and *abort*. Both functions are found in the standard library (`stdlib.h`).

exit

Whereas *return* terminates a function, *exit* terminates the program regardless of where in the program it is executed. While we use it to terminate the program because we detected an error, C considers it a normal termination. For this reason, the termination is orderly; any pending file stream writes are first completed and all streams are closed. The exit prototype statement is shown below.

```
void exit (int completionStatus);
```

There is one parameter to the *exit* call, an integer value to be passed to the operating system. While any integer is acceptable, it is usually a nonzero, indicating that the program did not complete successfully. We demonstrate the exit function in Program 5-11 on page 207.

abort

The *abort* function is used to terminate a program abnormally. It is considered a nonorderly termination because the output streams are not flushed and they are not closed. It is like drawing the "Go to Jail" card in Monopoly—you go directly to jail, you do not pass go, and you do not collect $200. When *abort* is called, the program immediately goes to the operating system.

The abort function has no parameters. Its prototype statement is shown below.

```
void abort (void);
```

TWO-WAY SELECTION EXAMPLE

To demonstrate two-way selection, let's look at a program that calculates income taxes. A brief explanation of progressive tax brackets may be helpful. In a progressive bracket system, the higher the income, the higher the tax rate. However, the higher rates are applied only to the income in the bracket level. Thus, if you examine two incomes, they will both pay the same amount of taxes at the lower rates. This concept of marginal tax rates is shown in Table 5-6.

The design for the program to calculate taxes is shown in the structure chart in Figure 5-17. The design has only four functions besides `main`. The notation for `bracketTax` is somewhat unusual: In the final code, it is called five times in one expression. Therefore, we show it as a nested set of calls.

Case 1: Total Income 23,000			Case 2: Total Income 18,000		
Income in Bracket	Tax Rate	Tax	Income in Bracket	Tax Rate	Tax
(1) 10,000	2%	200	(1) 10,000	2%	200
(2) 10,000	5%	500	(2) 8,000	5%	400
(3) 3,000	7%	210	(3) none	7%	0
Total Tax		910	Total Tax		600

Table 5-6 Examples of marginal tax rates

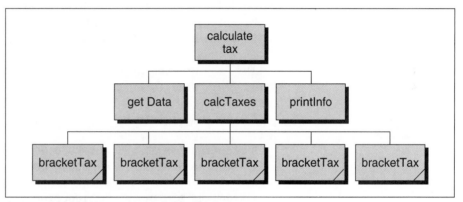

Figure 5-17 Design for calculate taxes

The pseudocode for the program is shown in Figure 5-18. Since the logic for reading and printing data is rather straightforward, it is not included in the pseudocode. The logic for calculating the tax information requires three major steps: (1) Calculate the taxable

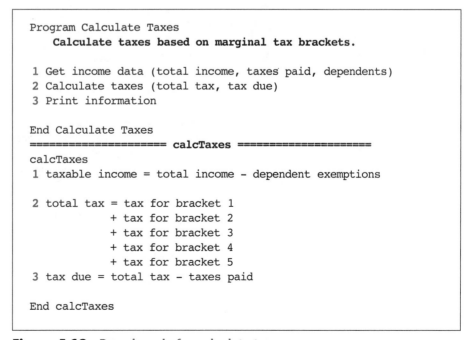

Figure 5-18 Pseudocode for calculate taxes

income. (2) Calculate the taxes. (3) Calculate the taxes due or to be refunded. Note that if more taxes were withheld than are due, the taxes due will be a negative number, indicating a refund. The coding is seen in Program 5-5.

```
 1  /* Calculate the tax due or the refund for a family based
 2     on the following imaginary formula.
 3     1. For each dependent deduct $1,000 from income.
 4     2. Determine tax rate from the following brackets:
 5           bracket      taxable income        tax rate
 6             1                <= 10000           2%
 7             2            10001 - 20000          5%
 8             3            20001 - 30000          7%
 9             4            30001 - 50000         10%
10             5            50001 and up          15%
11     Then print the amount of tax or the refund.
12
13        Written by:
14        Date:
15  */
16  #include <stdio.h>
17
18  #define LOWEST        0000000.00
19  #define HIGHEST       1000000.00
20
21  #define LIMIT1          10000.00
22  #define LIMIT2          20000.00
23  #define LIMIT3          30000.00
24  #define LIMIT4          50000.00
25
26  #define RATE1         02
27  #define RATE2         05
28  #define RATE3         07
29  #define RATE4         10
30  #define RATE5         15
31
32  #define DEDN_PER_DPNDNT 1000
33
34  /* Prototype Declarations */
35  void getData    (double *totalIncome,
36                   double *taxPaid,
37                   int    *numOfDpndnts);
38
39  void calcTaxes (double  totalIncome,
40                  double  taxPaid,
41                  int     numOfDpndnts,
```

Program 5-5   Calculate taxes

```
42                     double *taxableIncome,
43                     double *totalTax,
44                     double *taxDue);
45
46   void printInformation (double totalIncome,
47                          double taxPaid,
48                          int    numOfDpndnts,
49                          double totalTax,
50                          double paidTax,
51                          double taxDue);
52
53   double bracketTax (double income,
54                      double startLimit,
55                      double stopLimit,
56                      int    rate);
57
58   int main (void)
59   {
60   /* Local Definitions */
61      int numOfDpndnts;
62
63      double taxDue;
64      double taxPaid;
65      double totalIncome;
66      double taxableIncome;
67      double totalTax;
68
69   /* Statements */
70      getData    (&totalIncome, &taxPaid, &numOfDpndnts);
71      calcTaxes ( totalIncome,
72                  taxPaid,
73                  numOfDpndnts,
74                 &taxableIncome,
75                 &totalTax,
76                 &taxDue);
77      printInformation (totalIncome,
78                        taxableIncome,
79                        numOfDpndnts,
80                        totalTax,
81                        taxPaid,
82                        taxDue);
83      return 0;
84   }  /* main */
85
86   /* =================== getData ==================
```

Program 5-5 Calculate taxes (continued)

```
 87        This function reads tax data from the keyboard.
 88           Pre    Nothing
 89           Post   Reads totalIncome, taxPaid, & numOfDpndnts
 90  */
 91  void getData ( double *totalIncome,
 92                 double *taxPaid,
 93                 int    *numOfDpndnts)
 94  {
 95  /* Statements */
 96     printf("Enter your total income for last year: ");
 97     scanf ("%lf", totalIncome);
 98
 99     printf("Enter total of payroll deductions    : ");
100     scanf ("%lf", taxPaid);
101
102     printf("Enter the number of dependents       : ");
103     scanf ("%d", numOfDpndnts);
104
105     return;
106  }  /* getData */
107
108  /* ================= calcTaxes =================
109     This function calculates the taxes due.
110         Pre    Given-income, numOfDpndnts, & taxPaid
111         Post   Tax income, total tax, and tax due
112                calculated.
113  */
114  void calcTaxes (double  totInc,
115                  double  taxPaid,
116                  int     numOfDpndnts,
117                  double *taxableInc,
118                  double *totTax,
119                  double *taxDue)
120  {
121  /* Statements */
122     *taxableInc = totInc - (numOfDpndnts * DEDN_PER_DPNDNT);
123
124     *totTax = bracketTax (*taxableInc, LOWEST, LIMIT1, RATE1)
125            + bracketTax (*taxableInc, LIMIT1, LIMIT2, RATE2)
126            + bracketTax (*taxableInc, LIMIT2, LIMIT3, RATE3)
127            + bracketTax (*taxableInc, LIMIT3, LIMIT4, RATE4)
128            + bracketTax (*taxableInc, LIMIT4, HIGHEST, RATE5);
129
130     *taxDue = *totTax - taxPaid;
131     return;
132  }  /* calcTaxes */
133
```

Program 5-5 Calculate taxes (continued)

```
134   /* ================= printInformation ================= *
135   /* This function prints a table showing all information.
136      Pre    The parameter list.
137      Post   Prints the table.
138   */
139   void printInformation (double totalIncome,
140                          double income,
141                          int    numDpndnts,
142                          double totalTax,
143                          double paidTax,
144                          double dueTax)
145   {
146   /* Statements */
147      printf("\nTotal income          :%10.2f\n", totalIncome);
148      printf("Number of dependents  :%7d\n",    numDpndnts);
149      printf("Taxable income        :%10.2f\n", income);
150      printf("Total tax             :%10.2f\n", totalTax);
151      printf("Tax already paid      :%10.2f\n", paidTax);
152
153      if (dueTax >= 0.0)
154         printf("Tax due               :%10.2f\n", dueTax);
155      else
156         printf("Refund                :%10.2f\n", -dueTax);
157      return;
158   }  /* printInformation */
159
160   /* ================= bracketTax =================
161      Calculates the tax for a particular bracket.
162         Pre    The taxableIncome
163         Post   Returns the tax for a particular bracket
164   */
165   double bracketTax (double income,
166                      double startLimit,
167                      double stopLimit,
168                      int    rate)
169   {
170   /* Local Definitions */
171      double tax;
172
173   /* Statements */
174      if (income <= startLimit)
175         tax = 0.0;
176      else
177         if (income > startLimit && income <= stopLimit)
178            tax = (income - startLimit) * rate / 100.00;
179         else
180            tax = (stopLimit - startLimit) * rate / 100.00;
```

Program 5-5   Calculate taxes (continued)

```
181
182     return tax;
183 }   /* bracketTax */
```

Program 5-5 Calculate taxes (continued)

Program 5-5 Analysis   Note that Program 5-5 contains extensive internal documentation. This documentation includes a series of comments at the beginning of the program, the define statements used to set some of the key values in the program, and the prototype statements.

Next examine the structure of the program; `main` contains no detail code; it simply calls three functions to get the job done. Since two of the functions must pass data back to `main`, they use the address (`&`) and indirection (`*`) operators. The call to `getData` in Statement 70 uses the address operator to pass the address of the three variables that need to be read from the keyboard. Then, Statements 91–93 in the `getData` header statement use the asterisk to specify that the type is an address. Because the parameters are already addresses, the *scanf* statements do not need an address operator. You must always consider what type of parameter you are using, data or address, and use the correct operators for it. Do not automatically use the address operator with *scanf*.

Now examine the code for `calcTaxes`. The function header (starting at Statement 114) specifies that the first three formal parameters are passed as values and the last three are passed by address. The last three are address parameters because they are calculated values that need to be passed back to `main` for later printing. Note that all references to them in the function are prefaced with the indirection operator, which tells the compiler that it must use the variables in `main`.

Now note the use of the type *double* throughout the program. If you examine the conversion specifications in the format strings, you will note that they are `lf` for input and `f` for output.

Finally, and the main point of this example, note how we used the function `bracket-Tax` to calculate the tax. This function was designed so that it could calculate the tax for any bracket. This is a much simpler design than writing complex code for different brackets and demonstrates how keeping it simple and short (KISS) makes for better programs.

5-3 MULTIWAY SELECTION

In addition to two-way selection, most programming languages provide another selection concept known as **multiway selection**. Multiway selection chooses among several alternatives.

C has two different ways to implement multiway selection. The first is by using the *switch* statement. The other is a programming technique known as the *else-if* that provides a convenient style to nest *if* statements. The *switch* statement can be used only when the selection condition reduces to an integral expression. Many times, however, such as when the selection is based on a range of values, the condition is not an integral. In these cases, we use the *else-if*.

THE *switch* STATEMENT

Switch is a composite statement used to make a decision between many alternatives. The selection condition must be one of the C integral types. Although you can use any expression that reduces to an integral value, the most common is a unary expression in the form of an integral identifier. The decision logic for the multiway statement is seen in Figure 5-19.

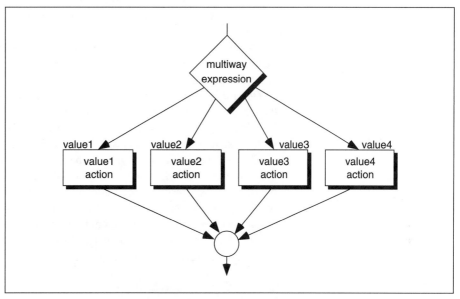

Figure 5-19 *switch* decision logic

The *switch* expression contains the condition that is evaluated. For every possible value that can result from the condition, a separate *case* constant is defined. Associated with each possible *case* is zero or more statements.

Figure 5-20 shows the *switch* format. Note several syntactical elements in this figure. First, the format must include at least one *case* statement. Of course, if you had only one value to evaluate, you would not use a *switch* statement; you would use a simple *if...else*.

```
switch (expression)
  {
  case constant-1: statement
                   ...
                   statement
  case constant-2: statement
                   ...
                   statement
  case constant-n: statement
                   ...
                   statement
  default        : statement
                   ...
                   statement
  } /* end switch */
```

Figure 5-20 *switch* statement

Second, each *case* expression is associated with a constant. The keyword *case* together- er with its constant are known as a ***case*-labeled statement**. The label is a syntactical identifier that C uses to determine which statement is the starting point in the *switch* statement. The *case* expression is followed by a colon (**:**) and then the statement with which it is associated.

Each *case* may have zero or more statements. Everything from a *case*-labeled state- ment to the next *case* statement is a sequence. The ***case*** **label** simply provides an entry point to start executing the code.

Default is a special form of the labeled statement. It is executed whenever none of the other *case* values matches the value in the *switch* expression. Note, however, that *de- fault* is not required. If you do not provide a default, the compiler will simply continue with the statement after the closing brace in the *switch*.

The *switch* statement is a puzzle that must be solved carefully to avoid confusion. Think of the *switch* statement as a series of drawbridges, one for each case and one for the default. As a result of the *switch* evaluation, one and only one of the drawbridges will be closed, so that there will be a path for the program to follow. (If none of the draw- bridges is closed, then the statement is skipped and the program continues with the next statement after the *switch*.) The *switch* flow is shown in Figure 5-21.

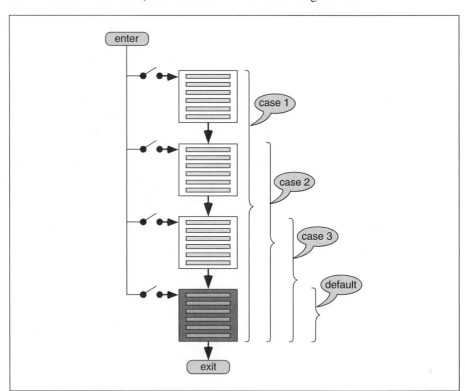

Figure 5-21 *switch* flow

Pay careful attention to what happens once the program flow enters a *case* statement. When the statements associated with one *case* have been executed, the program flow continues with the statements for the next *case*. In other words, once the program enters through a closed *switch*, it executes the code for all of the following *cases* until the end.

While you occasionally need this flexibility, it is not always what you want. We will show you how to break the flow shortly, but let's look at an example first. Program 5-6 demonstrates the *switch* statement. Can you figure out what it prints?

```
1  /* Program fragment to demonstrate switch */
2     switch (printFlag)
3        {
4         case 1:  printf("This is case 1\n");
5
6         case 2:  printf("This is case 2\n");
7
8         default: printf("This is default\n");
9        } /* switch */
```

Program 5-6 Demonstrate the *switch* statement

Program 5-6 has three different *case*-labeled statements. The first *case* statement identifies the entry point to be used when `printFlag` is 1. The second *case* statement identifies the entry point when `printFlag` is a 2. And finally, the third *case* statement identifies the entry point when `printFlag` is neither a 1 nor a 2. While *default* is not a required condition in a *switch* statement, it should be included when all possible situations have not been covered by the *case* statements.

Have you figured out what is printed by Program 5-6? The answers are in Figure 5-22. Three results are possible, depending on the value in `printFlag`. If `printFlag` is a 1, then all three print statements are executed. If `printFlag` is a 2, then the first print statement is skipped and the last two are executed. Finally, if `printFlag` is neither a 1 nor a 2, then only *default* is executed. This results in the first two print statements being skipped and only the last one being executed.

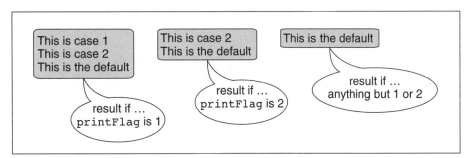

Figure 5-22 *switch* results

But what if we want to execute only one of the *case* statements? To do so, we must use *break* statements. The **break statement** causes the program to jump out of the *switch* statement—that is, to go to the closing brace and continue with the code that follows the *switch*. If we add a *break* as the last statement in each *case*, we have Figure 5-23. Now, only one print statement will be executed, regardless of the value of `printFlag`.

Two or more *case* expression values can belong to the same *case* statement. In Program 5-7, for example, we print a message depending on whether `printFlag` is even or odd.

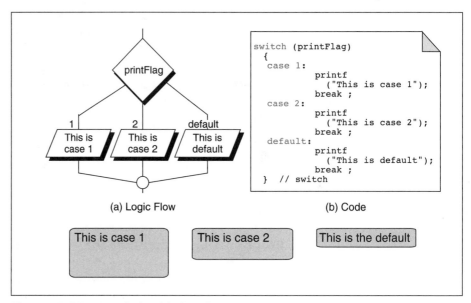

Figure 5-23 A *switch* with *break* statements

```
 1  /* Program fragment that demonstrates multiple
 2     cases for one set of statements
 3  */
 4  switch (printFlag)
 5     {
 6       case 1:
 7       case 3:  printf("Good Day\n");
 8                printf("Odds have it!\n");
 9                break;
10       case 2:
11       case 4:  printf("Good Day\n");
12                printf("Evens have it!\n");
13                break;
14      default: printf("Good Day, I'm confused!\n");
15                printf("Bye!\n");
16                break ;
17     } /* switch */
```

Program 5-7 Multivalued *case* statements

As a matter of style, the last statement in the *switch* does not require a *break*. We recommend, however, that you get in the habit of using it, especially when the last statement is not the *default*. This good habit will eventually save you hours of debugging time because you will not forget to add it when you add a new *case* to the statement.

Table 5-7 summarizes some points you must remember about the *switch* statement.

1. The control expression that follows the keyword *switch* must be an integral type.

2. The expression followed by each *case* label must be a constant expression. A constant expression is an expression that is evaluated at compilation time, not run time.

3. No two *case* labels can have the same value.

4. But two *case* labels can be associated with the same statements.

5. The *default* label is not required. If the value of the expression does not match with any label, the control transfers outside of the *switch* statement.

6. The *switch* statement can include at most one *default* label. The *default* label may be coded anywhere, but it is traditionally coded last.

Table 5-7   Summary of *switch* statement rules

switch **Example**

Program 5-8 converts a numeric score to a letter grade. The grading scale is the rather typical "absolute scale," in which 90% or more is an A, 80%–90% is a B, 70%–80% is a C, and 60%–70% is a D. Anything below 60% is an F.

```
1   /* This program reads a test score, calculates the letter
2       grade for the score, and prints the grade.
3          Written by:
4          Date:
5   */
6   #include <stdio.h>
7
8   /* Prototype Declarations */
9      char scoreToGrade (int score);
10
11  int main (void)
12  {
13  /* Local Definitions */
14     int   score;
15     char grade;
16
17  /* Statements */
18     printf("Enter the test score (0-100): ");
19     scanf ("%d", &score);
20
21     grade = scoreToGrade (score);
22     printf("The grade is: %c\n", grade);
23
24     return 0;
25  }  /* main */
26  /* =================== scoreToGrade ===================
```

Program 5-8   Student grading

```
27        This function calculates the letter grade for a score.
28            Pre    the parameter score
29            Post   returns the grade
30   */
31   char scoreToGrade (int score)
32   {
33   /* Local Definitions */
34      char grade;
35
36      int temp;
37
38   /* Statements */
39      temp = score / 10;
40      switch (temp)
41          {
42          case 10:
43          case 9 : grade = 'A';
44                   break;
45          case 8 : grade = 'B';
46                   break;
47          case 7 : grade = 'C';
48                   break;
49          case 6 : grade = 'D';
50                   break;
51          default: grade = 'F';
52          } /* switch */
53
54      return grade;
55   }/* scoreToGrade*/
```

```
Results
    Enter the test score (0–100): 89
    The grade is: B
```

Program 5-8   Student grading (continued)

Program 5-8 Analysis   This example shows how we can use the integer division operator (/) to change a range of numbers to individual points to be used by the *switch* statement. The problem definition requires that if the score is between 80% and 90%, it must be changed to letter grade 'B'. This condition cannot be used in a *switch* statement. But if we divide the score by 10 (integer division), the entire range (such as 80–89) can be changed to one single number (8), which can be used as a constant in the *case*-labeled statement.

Note how the *break* statement works. This is an important part of the logic for *switch* statements. Without the *break*, we would have determined and assigned the score, and then proceeded to assign all of the lower scores down to 'F', with the result that everyone would have failed. The *break* allows us to leave the body of the *switch* as soon as we have completed the grade assignment.

One word of caution. If the user enters an invalid score, such as 110, this program gives invalid results. We will describe how to prevent this problem in the next chapter.

THE *else-if*

The *switch* statement only works when the *case* values are integral. What if we need to make a multiway decision on the basis of a value that is not integral? The answer is the *else-if.* There is no such C construct as the *else-if.* Rather, it is a style of coding that you use when you need a multiway selection based on a value that is not integral.

Suppose we need a selection based on a range of values. We code the first *if* condition and its associated statements, and then we follow it with all other possible values using *else-if.* The last test in the series concludes with an *else.* This is the default condition; that is, it is the condition that is to be executed if all other statements are false. A sample of the *else-if* logic design is shown in Figure 5-24.

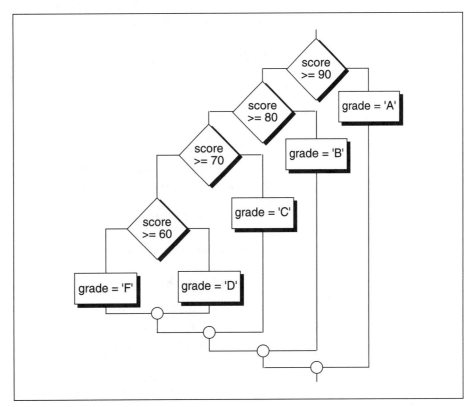

Figure 5-24 The *else-if* logic design for Program 5-9

What is different about the *else-if* code? As we said, it is really nothing more than a style change. Rather than indenting each *if* statement, we code the *else-if* on a single line and align it with the previous *if.* In this way we simulate the same formatting that you see in the *switch* and its associated *case* expressions. This style format is shown below.

```
if (score >= 90)
        grade = 'A';
else if (score >= 80)
        grade = 'B';
```

One important point about the *else-if:* Use it *only* when the same basic expression is being evaluated. In Figure 5-24, the expressions are all based on the variable `score`. If different variables were being evaluated, we would use the normal nesting associated with the *if...else* statement. Do not use the *else-if* format with nested *if* statements.

> The *else-if* is an artificial C construct that is only used when
> 1. The selection variable is not an integral, and
> 2. The same variable is being tested in the expressions.

else-if **Example**

Program 5-9 is the same as the *switch* example on page 199, but this time we use the *else-if* to solve the problem. It shows how we can use multiway selection and the *else-if* construct to change a numeric score to a letter grade.

```c
 1  /* This program reads a test score, calculates the letter
 2     grade based on the absolute scale, and prints it.
 3        Written by:
 4        Date:
 5  */
 6  #include <stdio.h>
 7
 8  /* Prototype Declarations */
 9   char scoreToGrade (int score);
10
11  int main (void)
12  {
13  /* Local Definitions */
14     int   score;
15     char grade;
16
17  /* Statements */
18     printf("Enter the test score (0-100): ");
19     scanf ("%d", &score);
20
21     grade = scoreToGrade (score);
22     printf("The grade is: %c\n", grade);
23
24     return 0;
25  }  /* main */
26
27  /* ===================== scoreToGrade ====================
28     This function calculates the letter grade for a score.
29        Pre    the parameter score
30        Post   returns the grade
31  */
32  char scoreToGrade (int score)
33  {
34  /* Local Definitions */
35     char grade;
36
37  /* Statements */
```

Program 5-9 Convert score to grade

```
38     if (score >= 90)
39         grade = 'A';
40     else if (score >= 80)
41         grade = 'B';
42     else if (score >= 70)
43         grade = 'C';
44     else if (score >= 60)
45         grade = 'D';
46     else
47         grade = 'F';
48     return grade;
49  }/* scoreToGrade*/
```

```
Results
    Enter the test score (0-100): 90
    The grade is: A
```

Program 5-9 Convert score to grade (continued)

Program 5-9 Analysis   We used the *else-if* construct because our condition was not an integral; rather, it tested several ranges of the same variable, `score`. Study the code carefully. Note that, once the correct range is located, none of the following conditions will be tested. For instance, if a score of 85 is entered, the test against 90% is false, so we execute the *else-if* test for a score greater than 80%. Since this condition is true, we set grade to `'B'` and skip all the remaining tests.

Also, note how the tests are ordered. In this case we first eliminate those scores equal to or greater than 90%; then we check 80%, 70%, and 60% in turn. Since we were checking for greater than, we could not have coded it in the reverse, 60% first. This is an important design concept: When checking a range using greater than, start with the largest value; when checking a range using less than, start with the lowest value.

5-4   MORE STANDARD LIBRARY FUNCTIONS

One of the assets of the C language is its rich set of standard functions that make programming much easier. In Chapter 4 we introduced some of these standard functions. Now that we have studied selection, we can discuss two other groups of standard functions that are closely related to selection statements.

STANDARD CHARACTERS FUNCTIONS

Many important library functions are available in C for manipulating characters. They are divided into two major groups: classifying functions and converting functions. The prototypes of these functions are in the `ctype.h` header file (character type). Before looking at these functions, make sure you understand the classification of characters that ANSI/ISO C uses. This breakdown of classes is shown in Figure 5-25, which uses a tree to show how characters are classified. You read the tree much like a structure chart, starting at the top and following the branches to the bottom.

Characters are first broken down into control characters, such as carriage return and end of file, or into printable characters. This tells us that control characters are not printable. The printable characters are either a space or the rest of the printable characters, which are classified as graphical. In turn, the graphical characters are broken down into

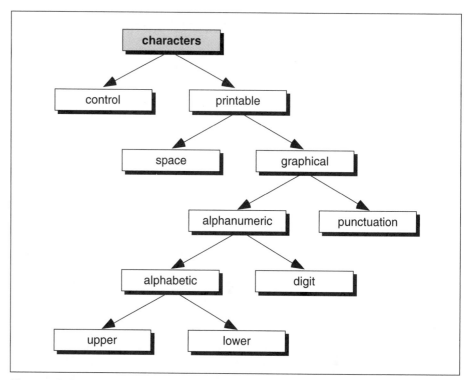

Figure 5-25 Classifications of the character type

alphanumeric and punctuation characters. Alphanumeric means either an alphabetic character or a digit. Finally, alphabetic characters are either upper- or lowercase.

Classifying Functions

Classifying functions examine a character and tell if it belongs to a given classification as described above. They all start with the prefix "`is`" and return true (integer 1) if the actual parameter is in the specified class and false (0) if it is not. The prototypes of these functions are found in the `ctype.h` file.

The general form of the prototype function is

```
int  is… (int testChar);
```

where the function name starts with `is`; for example, `iscntrl`, which stands for "is a control character." Listed below is a brief explanation of each function's operation and an example of how it is coded. For each example, we use a variable, `testChar`, that is defined as type *char*. One final point: Even though the function type is integer, you don't need to worry about it. C automatically casts characters to integers and back for you.

iscntrl The ASCII control characters are all the values below space (decimal 32) and the delete character (decimal 127). If `testChar` is one of these values, *iscntrl* returns true; otherwise, *iscntrl* returns false.

isprint Is printable, *isprint,* is the complement of *iscntrl.* It returns true if the value in `testChar` is greater than 31 and less than 127; otherwise it returns false.

isspace Is space, *isspace,* checks for whitespace. Recall that whitespace consists of the space character (32), horizontal tab (9), line feed (10), vertical tab (11), form feed (12), and carriage return (13). If `testChar` is any of these values, *isspace* returns true; otherwise it returns false.

The *isspace* function sometimes causes confusion because it deals with two types of characters: control characters and printable characters. Four of the whitespace characters are control characters (line feed, vertical tab, horizontal tab, and form feed); the space is a printable character. The name of this function would be better phrased as *is_whitespace,* but we must live with the name given it long ago.

isgraph　Is graphic, *isgraph,* tests for a graphic character. All of the ASCII values greater than the space (decimal 32) and less than the delete (decimal 127) are considered graphic characters. If `testChar` is in this range, *isgraph* returns true; otherwise it returns false.

isalnum　The alphanumeric characters are the sets {A, B…Y, Z}, {a, b…y, z}, and {0, 1…8, 9}; in other words, they are the alphabetic letters and the numeric digits. If `testChar` is one of these characters, *isalnum* returns true; otherwise it returns false.

ispunct　The punctuation characters are the graphic complement of the alphanumeric characters. Therefore, if `testChar` is greater than a space (32) and less than a delete (127), but not an alphanumeric character, *ispunct* returns true; otherwise it returns false.

isalpha　The alphabetic set consists of the characters {A, B…Y, Z, a, b…y, z}. If `testChar` is one of these values, *isalpha* returns true; otherwise it returns false.

islower　If `testChar` is in the set {a, b…y, z}, *islower* returns true; otherwise it returns false.

isupper　If `testChar` is in the set {A, B…Y, Z}, *isupper* returns true; otherwise it returns false.

isdigit　If `testChar` is a decimal digit {0, 1…8, 9}, *isdigit* returns true; otherwise it returns false.

isxdigit　This is a special test for hexadecimal digits. The hexadecimal digits are the decimal digits plus the first six alphabetic characters, both upper- and lowercase {0, 1…8, 9, a…f, A…F}. If `testChar` is in this set, *isxdigit* returns true; otherwise it returns false.

Character Conversion Functions

Two **converting functions** in ANSI/ISO C are used to convert a character from one class to another. These functions start with prefix *to* and return an integer that is the value of the converted character. Their basic format is

```
int to… (int oldChar);
```

toupper　This function converts `oldChar` to an uppercase letter {A, B…Y, Z} if it is in the lowercase set {a, b…y, z}. If it is not in the lowercase set, *toupper* simply returns `oldChar`.

tolower　This function converts `oldChar` to a lowercase letter {a, b…y, z} if it is in the uppercase set {A, B…Y, Z}. If it is not in the uppercase set, *tolower* simply returns `oldChar`.

A CLASSIFICATION PROGRAM

Let's write a program that uses classification functions to examine a character input from the keyboard. If you study Figure 5-25 on page 204, carefully, you will note that most characters fall into more than one classification. For instance, a digit is printable, graphical, alphanumeric, and a digit.

Our program tests from the bottom up, so that only one classification will be printed for each character. For a digit, only the fact that it is a digit will be printed. Because it is a relatively simple demonstration of the classification functions, we wrote it using only `main`. The solution is shown in Program 5-10.

```c
 1  /* This program demonstrates the use of the character
 2     classification functions found in the c-type library.
 3     Given a character, it displays the highest classification
 4     for the character.
 5        Written by:
 6        Date:
 7  */
 8
 9  #include <stdio.h>
10  #include <ctype.h>
11
12  int main (void)
13  {
14  /* Local Definitions */
15     char charIn;
16
17  /* Statements */
18     printf("Enter a character to be examined: ");
19     scanf ("%c", &charIn);
20
21     if (islower(charIn))
22         printf("You entered a lowercase letter.\n");
23     else if (isupper(charIn))
24         printf("You entered an uppercase character.\n");
25     else if (isdigit(charIn))
26         printf("You entered a digit.\n");
27     else if (ispunct(charIn))
28         printf("You entered a punctuation character.\n");
29     else if (isspace(charIn))
30         printf("You entered a whitespace character.\n");
31     else
32         printf("You entered a control character\n");
33
34     return 0;
    }  /* main */
```

```
Results
   Enter a character to be examined: a
   You entered a lowercase letter.
```

Program 5-10 Demonstrate classification functions

Program 5-10 Analysis   Note the use of the *else-if* in this program. While it may not appear so at first analysis, this is actually a range analysis problem, which makes it suitable for multiway selection.

5-5 A MENU PROGRAM

The menu program in Program 5-10 uses a somewhat oversimplified example to illustrate how you can communicate with a user through a menu. Figure 5-26 shows the design of the program.

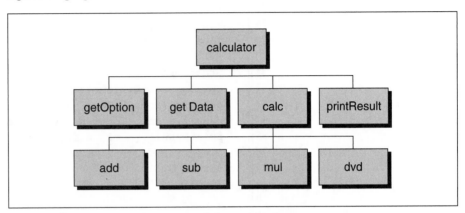

Figure 5-26 Design for menu-driven calculator

Good structured programming requires that each function do only one thing. In this program, we are doing four different things. (1) We must ask the user what function is desired. Then we need to (2) get the data for the operation, (3) make the calculation, and finally (4) print the result. These four processes are seen as called functions in main. In its turn, calc calls one of four functions to perform an arithmetic operation. Finally, printResult displays the result. Program 5-11 shows the complete solution.

```
 1  /* This program uses a menu to allow the user to add,
 2     multiply, subtract, or divide two integers.
 3         Written by:
 4         Date:
 5  */
 6  #include <stdio.h>
 7  #include <stdlib.h>
 8
 9  /* Prototype Declarations */
10  void  getData      (float *num1, float *num2);
11  void  printResult  (float num1,
12                      float num2,
13                      float result,
14                      int   option);
15  int   getOption    (void);
16  float calc         (int option, float num1, float num2);
17  float add          (float num1, float num2);
18  float sub          (float num1, float num2);
19  float mul          (float num1, float num2);
20  float dvd          (float num1, float num2);
```

Program 5-11 Code for menu-driven calculator

```
21
22    int main (void)
23    {
24    /* Local Definitions */
25       int option;
26
27       float num1;
28       float num2;
29       float result;
30
31    /* Statements */
32       option = getOption();
33       getData (&num1, &num2);
34       result = calc (option, num1, num2);
35       printResult (num1, num2, result, option);
36
37       return 0;
38    }  /* main */
39
40    /* ==================== getOption ====================
41       This function shows a menu and reads the user option.
42          Pre    Nothing
43          Post   returns the option
44    */
45    int getOption (void)
46    {
47    /* Local Definitions */
48       int option;
49
50    /* Statements */
51       printf  ("\t********************************");
52       printf("\n\t*              MENU             *");
53       printf("\n\t*                              *");
54       printf("\n\t*   1. ADD                     *");
55       printf("\n\t*   2. SUBTRACT                *");
56       printf("\n\t*   3. MULTIPLY                *");
57       printf("\n\t*   4. DIVIDE                  *");
58       printf("\n\t*                              *");
59       printf("\n\t********************************");
60
61       printf("\n\nPlease type your choice ");
62       printf("and key return: ");
63       scanf ("%d", &option);
64       return option;
65    }  /* getOption */
66
67    /* ==================== getData ====================
68       This function reads two numbers from the keyboard.
69          Pre   Nothing
```

Program 5-11 Code for menu-driven calculator (continued)

```
 70           Post    Two numbers read into variables in main
 71     */
 72     void getData (float *num1,
 73                   float *num2)
 74     {
 75     /* Statements */
 76        printf("Enter two numbers separated by a space: ");
 77        scanf ("%f %f", num1, num2);
 78        return;
 79     }/* getData */
 80
 81     /* ==================== calc ====================
 82        This function determines the type of operation
 83        and calls a function to perform it.
 84            Pre    option contains the operation
 85                   num1 & num2 contains data
 86            Post   returns the results
 87     */
 88     float calc (int    option,
 89                 float  num1,
 90                 float  num2)
 91     {
 92     /* Local Definitions */
 93     float result;
 94
 95     /* Statements */
 96        switch (option)
 97           {
 98           case 1:  result = add (num1, num2);
 99                    break;
100           case 2:  result = sub (num1, num2);
101                    break;
102           case 3:  result = mul (num1, num2);
103                    break;
104           case 4:  if (num2 == 0.0)
105                       {
106                        printf("\n\a\aError: ");
107                        printf("division by zero ***\n");
108                        exit (1);
109                       } /* if */
110                    else
111                        result = dvd (num1, num2);
112                    break;
113           /* Better structured programming would validate the
114              option in getOption. However, we have not yet
115              learned the technique to put it there.
116           */
117           default: printf("\aOption not available\n");
118                    exit (1);
```

Program 5-11   Code for menu-driven calculator (continued)

```
119        } /* switch */
120     return result;
121  } /* calc */
122
123  /* ===================== add =====================
124     This function adds two numbers.
125         Pre   The two numbers are given as parameters.
126         Post  returns the results.
127  */
128  float add (float num1,
129             float num2)
130  {
131  /* Local Definitions */
132     float res;
133
134  /* Statements */
135     res = num1 + num2;
136     return res;
137  } /* add */
138  /* ===================== sub =====================
139     This function subtracts two numbers.
140         Pre   The two numbers are given as parameters
141         Post  returns the results
142  */
143  float sub (float num1,
144             float num2)
145  {
146  /* Local Definitions */
147     float res;
148
149  /* Statements */
150     res = num1 - num2;
151     return res;
152  } /* sub */
153  /* ===================== mul =====================
154     This function multiplies two numbers.
155         Pre   The two numbers are given as parameters
156         Post  returns the results
157  */
158  float mul (float num1,
159             float num2)
160  {
161  /* Local Definitions */
162     float res;
163
164  /* Statements */
165     res = num1 * num2;
166     return res;
167  } /* mul */
```

Program 5-11 Code for menu-driven calculator (continued)

```
168  /* ===================== dvd =====================
169     This function divides two numbers.
170        Pre    The two numbers are given as parameters
171        Post   returns the results
172  */
173  float dvd (float num1,
174             float num2)
175  {
176  /* Local Definitions */
177     float res;
178
179  /* Statements */
180     res = num1 / num2;
181     return res;
182  }  /* dvd */
183  /* ==================== printResult ====================
184     This function prints the result of calculation.
185        Pre    The two numbers, result, and option are given
186        Post   Prints the numbers and the result
187  */
188  void printResult (float num1,
189                    float num2,
190                    float res,
191                    int   option)
192  {
193  /* Statements */
194     printf("\n%8.2f ", num1);
195     switch (option)
196        {
197        case 1: printf(" + ");
198                break;
199        case 2: printf(" - ");
200                break;
201        case 3: printf(" * ");
202                break;
203        case 4: printf(" / ");
204                break;
205        } /* switch option */
206     printf(" %.2f = %.2f\n", num2, res);
207
208     return;
209  }  /* printResults */
210  /* ================= End of Program ================= */
```

Results:
```
    *******************************
    *            MENU             *
    *                             *
    *  1. ADD                     *
```

Program 5-11 Code for menu-driven calculator (continued)

```
    *   2.  SUBTRACT                        *
    *   3.  MULTIPLY                        *
    *   4.  DIVIDE                          *
    *                                       *
    *************************************

    Please type your choice and key return: 3
    Enter two numbers separated by a space: 5 7

        5.00  *  7.00 = 35.00
```

Program 5-11   Code for menu-driven calculator (continued)

Program 5-11 Analysis   Spend some time studying Program 5-11. It has several techniques that you will use again and again.

First, study the menu display function, getOption. This is a common technique when you have to interact with users. It allows them to select from a set of prescribed options. In the next chapter, you will learn how to validate the options in getOption, which will make it a much more powerful function.

Then note how we give users detailed instructions on how to enter the numbers. We also make sure they know when something has gone wrong, such as when a zero divisor is entered. These are some of the little user communication techniques that make for a user-friendly system.

Finally, study the *switch* statements in calc and in printResults. Note how they are formatted for readability. Note also that with the exception of the test for divide by zero, we have kept the *case* options as simple as possible. Generally speaking, you want to keep the code in a *case* option simple.

5-6   SOFTWARE ENGINEERING AND PROGRAMMING STYLE

DEPENDENT STATEMENTS

Several statements in the C language control other statements that follow them. The *if...else* is the first of these statements that we have seen. Whenever one statement controls or influences statements that follow it, good structured programming style indents the dependent statements to show that the indented code is dependent on the controlling statement. The compiler does not need the **indentation**—it follows its syntactical rules regardless of how a program is formatted—but good style makes for readable programs.

To illustrate the point, consider the two versions of the code for the function in Program 5-12. They both accomplish the same task. To make this exercise even more meaningful, cover up the right half of the program and predict the results that will be produced when the ill-formed code executes. Then look at the well-structured code.

	Poor Style	Good Style
1	`int someFun (int a,`	`int someFun (int a,`
2	`            int b)`	`                int b)`
3	`{`	`{`
4	`int x;`	`    int x;`
5		
6	`    if ( a < b )`	`    if ( a < b )`
7	`    x = a;`	`        x = a;`
8	`    else`	`    else`
9	`        x = b;`	`        x = b;`
10	`        x *= .5f;`	`    x *= .5f;`
11	`    return x;`	`    return x;`
12	`}   /* someFun */`	`}   /* someFun */`

Program 5-12   Examples of poor and good nesting styles

Assume that in this example, a has a value of 10 and b has a value of 20. What value will be returned? First, look at Statement 7. The assignment of x in this example is dependent on the *if* in Statement 6. Since Statement 7 is not indented, however, it is difficult to see the dependency. Because the value of a (10) is less than the value of b (20), x will be assigned the value 10.

Now examine Statement 10. It is indented and therefore appears to be dependent on the *else* statement. But is it? The answer is no. It just looks that way and is therefore misleading. Statement 10 will therefore execute regardless of the expression in the *if* statement. This relationship is much more clearly seen in the well-styled code on the right. The code on the right is properly indented to show the relationships among the statements, and therefore the chance of misreading the code is minimal.

The indentation rules are summarized in Table 5-8.

1.	Indent statements that are dependent on previous statements. The indentations are at least three spaces from the left end of the controlling statement.
2.	Align *else* statements with their corresponding *if* statement. (See Figure 5-13 on page 184.)
3.	Place the opening brace identifying a body of code on a separate line. Indent the statements in the body of the code one space to the right of the opening brace.
4.	Align the closing brace identifying a body of code with the opening brace, and place the closing brace on a separate line. Use a comment to identify the block being terminated.
5.	Align all code on the same level, which is dependent on the same control statement.
6.	Further indent nested statements according to the above rules.
7.	Surround operators with whitespace.
8.	Code only one definition or statement on a single line.
9.	Make your comments meaningful at the block level. Comments should not simply parrot the code.

Table 5-8   Indentation rules

NEGATIVE LOGIC

In the discussion of Figure 5-12, on page 183, and in the section on simplifying the *if* statement, one technique that we proposed was complementing a conditional statement. This requires making a positive statement negative and a negative statement positive. This can be done by following Rule 6 in Table 5-3, on page 180, which states that the positions of the statements in an *if...else* can be swapped if the original control expression is complemented. The concept of complementing the *if* statement was shown in Figure 5-10 on page 182.

Remember, however, that simple code is the clearest code. This concept has been formulated into an acronym: KISS, which stands for "Keep It Simple and Short!" (see Chapter 3). Unfortunately, **negative logic** is not always simple. In fact, it can get extremely confusing. We have seen professional programmers work for hours trying to debug negative logic.

> Avoid compound negative statements!

When you complement an expression, make sure that the resulting statement is easily readable. Complementing an expression can be more difficult than simply making the condition negative. Examine the third statement in Table 5-9 carefully. Note that the complement of the *not* (!) is *not-not* (! !), which in effect cancels the *not*. In general, you should avoid compound negative statements. In this case, therefore, the complemented statement is greatly preferred.

Original Statement	Complemented Statement
if (x <= 0)	if (x > 0)
if (x != 5)	if (x == 5)
if (!(x <= 0 || !flag))	if (x > 0 && flag)

Table 5-9   Complementing expressions

RULES FOR SELECTION STATEMENTS

For selection statements, you need to consider three other rules, shown in Table 5-10. Since these rules are sometimes conflicting, they are listed in their order of importance.

---

1. Code positive statements whenever possible.

2. Code the normal/expected condition first.

3. Code the most probable conditions first.

Table 5-10   Selection rules

Human engineering studies have shown that people make fewer errors when reading positive statements than when reading negative statements. This is especially true when complex, compound Boolean statements are involved. Therefore, the first rule in Table 5-10 is, whenever possible, code your selection statements using positive conditions.

The second rule concerns the human expectations about what will follow. People have a tendency to anticipate things. They will therefore be less confused if what follows is what they expect. In most cases, this means coding the anticipated condition first.

Finally, the third rule concerns the efficiency of the resulting program. Coding the most probable conditions first is especially important in a multiway selection, such as the *else-if*. When you code the most probable test first, then the program can skip the rest of the statements. Obviously, the more statements skipped, the more efficient the resulting program.

As we mentioned previously, these rules often conflict with each other. We have listed them in their order of importance from a human engineering point of view. Unless there are overriding circumstances, you should select the higher option (Rule 1 before Rule 2 before Rule 3) in case of conflicts. But remember the overriding principle: KISS—Keep It Simple and Short.

SELECTION IN STRUCTURE CHARTS

We introduced the basic concepts of structure charts in Chapter 4. Figure 4-24, on page 155 shows two symbols for a function that is called by a selection statement, the condition and the exclusive *or*. We repeat them in Figure 5-27 for your convenience.

In Figure 5-27(a), the function doIt contains a conditional call to a subfunction, fun. If the condition in the *if* statement is true, we call doIt. If it is not true, we skip doIt. This situation is represented in a structure chart as a small diamond on the vertical line between the two function blocks.

Figure 5-27(b) represents the selection between two different functions. In this example, the function select chooses between doA and doB. One and only one of them will be called each time the conditional statement is exe-

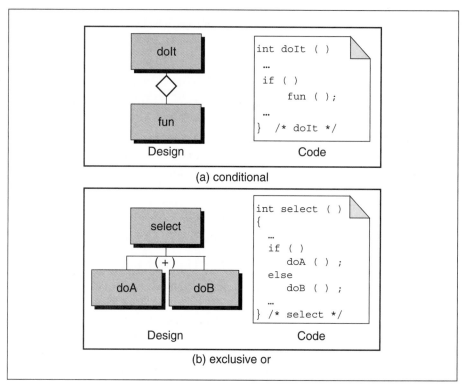

Figure 5-27 Structure chart symbols for selection

cuted. This is known as an **exclusive or**; one of the two alternatives is executed to the exclusion of the other. The exclusive or is represented by a plus sign between the processes.

Now consider the design found when a series of functions can be called exclusively. This occurs when a multiway selection contains calls to several different functions. Figure 5-28 contains an example of a *switch* statement that calls different functions based on color.

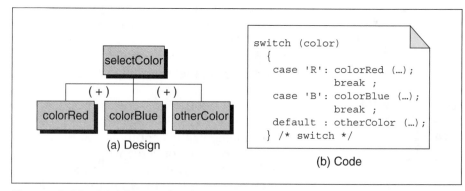

Figure 5-28 Multiway selection in a structure chart

The structure chart rules described in this section follow:

1. Conditional calls are indicated by a diamond above the function rectangle.

2. Exclusive or calls are indicated by a (+) between functions.

5-7   TIPS AND COMMON PROGRAMMING ERRORS

1. The complement of < is >=, and the complement of > is <=.

2. Dangling *else* statements are easily created and difficult to debug. One technique for avoiding dangling *else* statements is to use braces, even when they are not needed.

3. The expression in the control expression in the *if...else* statement may have a side effect, as shown below.

```
if(a++)
```

4. Encapsulate the statements inside braces if you have more than one statement after *if* or *else* in an *if...else* statement.

5. Do not use the equal operator with a floating-point number. Floating-point numbers are seldom exactly equal to a required value. When you need to test for equality, such as a == b, use the expression shown below.

```
if (fabs (a - b) < .0000001)
```

6. Do not forget to use a *break* statement when the cases in a *switch* statement are exclusive.

7. While not necessarily an error, it is poor programming practice to write a *switch* statement without a *default*. If the logic doesn't require one, code it with an error message to guard against unanticipated conditions. This is shown below.

```
default: printf("\aImpossible default\n");
         exit (100);
```

8. The most common C error is using the assignment operator (=) in place of the equal operator (==). One way to minimize this error is to get in the habit of using the term "assignment operator" when reading the code. For example, say "a is assigned b," not "a equals b."

9. It may be an error to place a semicolon after the *if* expression.

   a. The semicolon terminates the *if* statement, and any statement that follows it is not part of the *if*.

   b. It is a compile error to code an *else* without a matching *if*. This error is most likely created by a misplaced semicolon.

```
if (a == b);                    /* If terminated here
*/
    printf(…);
else                            /* No matching if */
    printf(…);
```

10. It is a compile error to forget the parentheses in the *if* expression.

11. It is a compile error to put a space between the following relational operators: ==, !=, >=, <=. It is also a compile error to reverse them.

12. It is a compile error to use a variable rather than an integral constant as the value in a *case* label.

13. It is a compile error to use the same constant in two *case* labels.

14. The logical operators require two ampersands (&&) or two bars (||). It is a logic error to code them with only one. (Single operators are bitwise operators and are therefore valid code.)

15. It is generally a logic error to use side effects in the second operand in a logical binary expression, as shown below, because the second operand may not be evaluated.

```
(a++ && --b)
```

5-8   KEY TERMS AND CONCEPTS[1]

and operator (&&)	*else-if*	negative logic
break statement	equal operator (==)	nested *if* statement
case	exclusive or	not equal operator (!)
case label	greater than operator (>)	*not* operator (!)
case-labeled statement	greater than or equal operator (>=)	null *else*
classifying function	*if...else*	*or* operator (||)
complemented *if . . .else*	indentation	relational operator
conditional expression	less than operator (<)	selection
converting function	less than or equal operator (<=)	selection in structure chart
dangling *else*	logical data	simplifying *if...else* statements
default	logical operator	*switch*
De Morgan's rule	multiway selection	two-way selection

---

[1]Note: Italic terms are C keywords or standard function names.

5-9   SUMMARY

- Data are called logical if they convey the idea of true or false.

- C has no explicit logical type. C programmers use other data types to represent logical data. If a data item is nonzero, it is considered true; if it is zero, it is considered false.

- C has three operators for combining logical values to create new values: *not, and, or*.

- Six relational operators are used in C: <, <=, >, >=, ==, and !=.

- Selection in C is done using two statements: *if...else* and *switch*.

- The *if...else* construct is used for selection between two alternatives.

- You can swap the statements in the true and false branches if you use the complement of an expression in an *if...else* statement.

- If the false statement is not required in an *if...else,* it is omitted and the keyword *else* dropped.

- If an *else* is dangling, it will be paired with the last unpaired *if.*

- Multiway selection can be accomplished using either the *switch* statement or an *else-if* format.

- The *switch* statement is used to make a decision between many alternatives when the different conditions can be expressed as integral values.

- The *else-if* format is used to make multiple decisions when the item being tested is not an integral and therefore a *switch* statement cannot be used.

- A *case*-labeled statement is used for selection in a switch statement.

- A *default*-labeled statement is used as the last statement in a *switch* statement, to be executed when none of the *case* alternatives match the tested value.

- Indenting the controlled statements in C is good style that enhances the readability of a program.
- Selection is used in a structure chart only when it involves a call to another function.
- The structure chart for selection shows the paths taken by the logic flow. You cannot always tell by looking at the structure chart which selection will be used (two-way or multiway).
  - a. A simple *if* is indicated by a diamond below the calling function.
  - b. An *if...else* and *switch* are indicated by the exclusive or (+).

5-10 PRACTICE SETS

REVIEW QUESTIONS

1. Logical data are data that can be interpreted as true or false.
   - a. True
   - b. False

2. The expression in a selection statement can have no side effects.
   - a. True
   - b. False

3. Each case-labeled statement may identify one or more statements.
   - a. True
   - b. False

4. The character classification functions are found in the standard library (`stdlib.h`).
   - a. True
   - b. False

5. To ensure that a character is uppercase, the *toupper* conversion function is used.
   - a. True
   - b. False

6. The _____ logical operator is true only when both operands are true.
   - a. and (&&)
   - b. greater than (>)
   - c. less than (<)
   - d. or (||)
   - e. not (!)

7. Which of the following is not a relational operator in C?
   - a. <
   - b. <=
   - c. =
   - d. >
   - e. >=

8. Two-way selection is implemented with the _____ statement.
   - a. *case*
   - b. *else if*
   - c. *switch*
   - d. *the if...else and the switch*
   - e. *if...else*

9. Which of the following is not a syntactical rule for the *if...else* statement?
   - a. Any expression can be used for the *if* expression.
   - b. Only one statement is allowed for the true and the false actions.
   - c. The true and the false statements can be another *if...else* statement.
   - d. The expression must be enclosed in parentheses.
   - e. The selection expression cannot have a side effect.

10. Which of the following statements creates the "dangling *else* problem"?
    - a. a nested *if* statement without a false statement
    - b. a nested *if* statement without a true statement
    - c. a *switch* statement without a default
    - d. an *if* statement without a true or a false statement
    - e. any nested *if* statement

11. There are two different ways to implement a multiway selection in C. They are
    - a. *if...else* and *switch*
    - b. *if...else* and *else if*
    - c. *else-if* and *case*
    - d. *else-if* and *switch*
    - e. *switch* and *case*

12. Which of the following statements about *switch* statements is false?
    - a. No two *case* labels can have the same value.
    - b. The *switch* control expression must be an integral type.
    - c. The *case*-labeled expression can be a constant or a variable.
    - d. Two *case* labels can be associated with the same statement series.
    - e. A *switch* statement can have at most one *default* statement.

13. Which of the following statements about the *else-if* is false?
    - a. Each expression in the *else-if* must test the same variable.
    - b. The *else-if* is a coding style rather than a C construct.
    - c. The *else-if* requires integral values in its expression.
    - d. The *else-if* is used for multiway selections.
    - e. The last test in the *else-if* series concludes with a single *else*, which is the default condition.

14. Which of the following is not a character classification in the C language?
    - a. ascii
    - b. control
    - c. digit
    - d. graphical
    - e. space

EXERCISES

15. Evaluate the following expressions to true or false. Show how you arrived at your answer by first adding the default parentheses and then showing the value of each expression as it would be evaluated by C, one expression to a line.

    a. `!(3 + 3 >= 6)`
    b. `1 + 6 == 7 || 3 + 2 == 1`
    c. `1 > 5 || 6 < 50 && 2 < 5`
    d. `14 != 55 && !(13 < 29) || 31 > 52`
    e. `6 < 7 > 5`

16. If $x = 0$, $y = 5$, $z = 5$, what is the value of x, y, and z for each of the following code fragments? (Assume that x, y, and z are their original values for each fragment.)

    a. ```
    if (z != 0)
        y = 295;
    else
        x = 10;
    ```
    b. ```
    if (y + z > 10)
        y = 99;
        z = 8;
    x = ++z;
    ```
    c. ```
    if (x = 1)
        {
            x = x - 3;
            z = z + 3;
        }
    else
        y = 99;
    ```

17. If $x = 3$, $y = 0$, and $z = -4$, what is the value of the following expressions?

    a. `x && y || z`
    b. `x || y && z`
    c. `(x && y) || z`
    d. `(x || y) && z`
    e. `(x && z) || y`

18. Simplify the following expressions by removing the `!` operator and the parentheses:

    a. `!(x < y)`   c. `!(x == y)`   e. `!(!(x > y))`
    b. `!(x >= y)`  d. `!(x != y)`

19. If $x = -2$, $y = 5$, $z = 0$, and $t = -4$, what is the value of each of the following expressions?

    a. `x + y < z + t`
    b. `x - 2 * y + y < z * 2 / 3`
    c. `3 * y / 4 % 5 && y`
    d. `t || z < (y + 5) && y`
    e. `!(4 + 5 * y >= z - 4) && (z - 2)`

20. If originally $x = 4$, $y = 0$, and $z = 2$, what is the value of x, y, and z after executing the following code?
    ```
    if (x != 0)
        y = 3;
    else
        z = 2;
    ```

21. If originally $x = 4$, $y = 0$, and $z = 2$, what is the value of x, y, and z after executing the following code?
    ```
    if (z == 2)
        y = 1;
    else
        x = 3;
    ```

22. If originally $x = 4$, $y = 0$, and $z = 2$, what is the value of x, y, and z after executing the following code?
    ```
    if (x && y)
        x = 3;
    else
        y = 2;
    ```

23. If originally $x = 4$, $y = 0$, and $z = 2$, what is the value of x, y, and z after executing the following code?
    ```
    if (x || y || z)
        y = 1;
    else
        z = 3;
    ```

24. If originally $x = 0$, $y = 0$, and $z = 1$, what is the value of x, y, and z after executing the following code?
    ```
    if (x)
        if (y)
            z = 3;
    else
        z = 2;
    ```

25. If originally $x = 4$, $y = 0$, and $z = 2$, what is the value of x, y, and z after executing the following code?
    ```
    if (z == 0 || x && !y)
        if (!z)
            y = 1;
    else
        x = 2;
    ```
    ```

26. If originally x = 0, y = 0, and z = 1, what is the value of x, y, and z after executing the following code?
```
if (x)
    if (y)
        if (z)
            z = 3;
        else
            z = 2;
```

27. If originally x = 0, y = 0, and z = 1, what is the value of x, y, and z after executing the following code?
```
if (z < x || y >= z && z == 1)
    if (z && y)
        y = 1;
else
    x = 1;
```

28. If originally x = 0, y = 0, and z = 1, what is the value of x, y, and z after executing the following code?
```
if (z = y )
    {
    y++;
    z--;
    }
else
    --x;
```

29. If originally x = 0, y = 0, and z = 1, what is the value of x, y, and z after executing the following code?
```
if (z = x < y)
    {
    x += 3;
    y -= 1;
    }
else
    x = y++;
```

30. If originally x = 0, y = 0, and z = 1, what is the value of x, y, and z after executing the following code?
```
switch (x)
    {
    case 0  : x = 2;
              y = 3;
    case 1  : x = 4;
    default : y = 3;
              x = 1;
    }
```

31. If originally x = 2, y = 1, and z = 1, what is the value of x, y, and z after executing the following code?
```
switch (x)
    {
    case 0 : x = 2;
             y = 3;
    case 1 : x = 4;
             break;
    default:
             y = 3;
             x = 1;
    }
```

32. If originally x = 1, y = 3, and z = 0, what is the value of x, y, and z after executing the following code?
```
switch ( x )
    {
    case 0 : x = 2;
             y = 3;
             break;
    case 1 : x = 4;
             break;
    default: y = 3;
             x = 1;
    }
```

33. Evaluate the value of the following expressions:
    a. tolower ('C')   b. tolower ('?')
    c. tolower ('c')   d. tolower ('5')

34. Evaluate the value of the following expressions:
    a. toupper ('c')   b. toupper ('C')
    c. toupper ('?')   d. toupper ('7')

35. Use De Morgan's rule to simplify the following expressions:
    a. !(x && y || !z)
    b. !(y || !z && !x)
    c. !(x || y || !z)
    d. !(!(x && y) && !(z|| y))
    e. !(x && y && z && !(y || z))

PROBLEMS

36. Write an *if* statement that will assign the value 1 to the variable `best` if the integer variable `score` is 90 or greater.

37. Repeat Problem 36 using a conditional expression.

38. Write the code to add 4 to an integer variable, `num`, if a float variable, `amount`, is greater than 5.4.

39. Print the value of the integer `num` if the variable `flag` is true.

40. Write the code to print either `zero` or `not zero` based on the integer variable `num`.

41. If the variable `divisor` is not zero, divide the variable `dividend` by `divisor`, and store the result in `quotient`. If `divisor` is zero, assign it to `quotient`. Then print all three variables. Assume that `dividend` and `divisor` are integers and `quotient` is a double.

42. If the variable `flag` is true, read the integer variables `a` and `b`. Then calculate and print the sum and average of both inputs.

43. Rewrite the following code using one *if* statement:
```
if (aChar == 'E')
    c++;

if (aChar == 'E')
    printf ("Value is E\n");
```

44. Rewrite the following code fragment using one *switch* statement:
```
if (ch == 'E' || ch == 'e')
    countE++;
else if (ch == 'A' || ch == 'a')
    countA++
else if (ch == 'I' || ch == 'i')
    countI++;
else
    print ("Error--Not A, E, or I\a\n");
```

45. Write a code fragment that tests the value of an integer num1. If the value is 10, square num1. If it is 9, read a new value into num1. If it is 2 or 3, multiply num1 by 99 and print out the result. Implement your code using nested *if* statements, not a *switch.*

46. Rewrite Problem 45 using a *switch* statement.

47. Write a code fragment for the flowchart shown in Figure 5-29. Assume that the variables `x` and `y` are integers and `z` is a float-point number.

48. Write a function called `smallest` that, given three integers, returns the smallest one.

49. Write a function called `day_of_week` that, given an integer between 0 and 6, prints the corresponding day of the week. Assume that the first day of the week (0) is Sunday.

50. Write a function called `month_of_year` that, given an integer between 1 and 12, prints the corresponding month of the year.

51. Write a function called `parkingCharge` that, given the type of vehicle (`'c'` for car, `'b'` for bus, `'t'` for truck) and the hours a vehicle spent in the parking lot, returns the parking charge based on the rates shown below.

car	$2 per hour
bus	$3 per hour
truck	$4 per hour

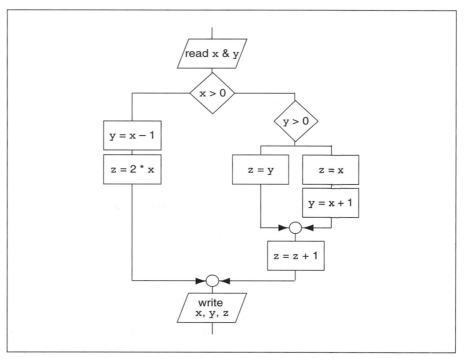

Figure 5-29 Flowchart for Problem 47

52. Write a function to find the smallest of four integers.

PROJECTS

53. Write a program that determines a student's grade. It reads three test scores (between 0 and 100) and calls a function that calculates and returns a student's grade based on the following rules:

   a. If the average score is 90% or more, the grade is `'A'`.

   b. If the average score is 70% or more and less than 90%, it checks the third score. If the third score is more than 90%, the grade is `'A'`, otherwise, the grade is `'B'`.

   c. If the average score is 50% or more and less than 70%, it checks the average of the second and third scores. If the average of the two is greater than 70%, the grade is `'C'`, otherwise, it is `'D'`.

   d. If the average score is less than 50 percent, then the grade is `'F'`.

   The program's `main` is to contain only call statements. At least three subfunctions are required: one to read scores, one to determine the grade, and one to print the results.

54. In Program 4-7, "Strange College Fees," page 134, we wrote a program to calculate college fees. Modify this program for Typical College. At Typical College, the students pay a fee of $10 per unit for up to 12 units; once they have paid for 12 units, they have no additional per-unit fee. The registration fee remains $10 but is assessed only if courses are taken in the term.

55. Given a point, a line from the point forms an angle with the horizontal axis to the right of the line. The line is said to terminate in one of four quadrants based on its angle (a) from the horizontal, as shown in Figure 5-30.

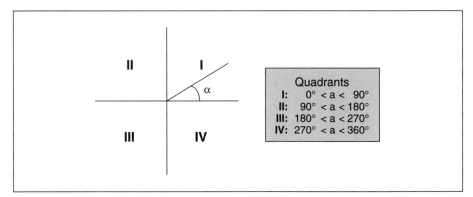

Figure 5-30   Quadrants for Project 55

Write a program that determines the quadrant, given a user-input angle. Use a function to read and validate the angle. Note: If the angle is exactly 0°, it is not in a quadrant but lies on the positive X-axis; if it is exactly 90°, it lies on the positive Y-axis; if it is exactly 180°, it lies on the negative X-axis; and if it is exactly 270°, it lies on the negative Y-axis. Test your program with the following data:

0°, 48.3°, 90°, 179.8°, 180°, 186°, 270°, 300°, and 360°

56. How many values of the variable num must be used to completely test all branches of the following code fragment?

```
if (num > 0)

   if (value < 25)

      {

        value = 10 * num;

        if (num < 12)

            value = value / 10;

      } /* if sum */

   else

      value = 20 * num;

else

   value = 30 * num;
```

57. Write a program that asks the user to enter the current date and a person's birth date in the form month, day, year. The program then calculates the person's age in integral years. Use separate functions to enter the dates (pass by address), calculate the person's age, and print the results. Test your program with the following dates: 11/14/1957, 5/10/1989, and 1/5/2000.

58. Write a C program to calculate the parking fare for customers who park their cars in a parking lot when the following information is given:

    a. A character showing the type of vehicle: 'C' for car, 'B' for bus, 'T' for truck.

    b. An integer between 0 and 24 showing the hour the vehicle entered the lot.

    c. An integer between 0 and 60 showing the minute the vehicle entered the lot.

    d. An integer between 0 and 24 showing the hour the vehicle left the lot.

    e. An integer between 0 and 60 showing the minute the vehicle left the lot.

This is a public lot. To encourage people to park for a short period of time, the management uses two different rates for each type of vehicle, as shown in Table 5-11.

	First Rate	Second Rate
CAR	$0.00/hr first 3 hr	$1.50/hr after 3 hr
TRUCK	$1.00/hr first 2 hr	$2.30/hr after 2 hr
BUS	$2.00/hr for first hr	$3.70/hr after first hr

Table 5-11 Rates for Project 58

No vehicle is allowed to stay in the parking lot later than midnight; it will be towed away.

The input data consist of a character and a set of four integers representing the type of vehicle and the entering and leaving hours and minutes. But these pieces of data must be input into the computer in a user-friendly way. In other words, the computer must prompt the user to enter each piece of data as shown below. (Bold indicates typical data.)

```
Type of vehicle? C
Hour vehicle entered lot    (0 - 24)?  14
Minute vehicle entered lot (0 - 60)?  23
Hour vehicle left lot       (0 - 24 )? 18
Minute vehicle left lot     (0 - 60)?   8
```

The output format is shown below.

```
                 PARKING LOT CHARGE


        Type of vehicle: Car or Bus or Truck
            TIME-IN              XX : XX
            TIME-OUT             XX : XX

                              --------

            PARKING TIME           XX:XX
            ROUNDED TOTAL            XX

                              --------

            TOTAL CHARGE          $XX.XX
```

This program must first calculate the actual time spent in the parking lot for each vehicle. This means using modulo arithmetic to handle time calculation. We can calculate this in many ways, one of which is shown below. To calculate the time spent in the parking lot, use the following algorithm:

a. Compare the minute portion of the leaving and the entering time.
   If the first one is smaller than the second,
   • Add 60 to the minute portion of the leaving time.
   • Subtract 1 from the hour portion of the leaving time.

b. Subtract the hour portions.

c. Subtract the minute portions.

d. Since there are no fractional hour charges, the program must also round the parking time up to the next hour before calculating the charge. The program should use the *switch* statement to distinguish between the different types of vehicles.

A well-structured program design is required. A typical solution will use several functions besides main. Before you start programming, prepare a structure chart. Run your program six times with the data shown in Table 5-12.

Test	Type	Hour In	Minute In	Hour Out	Minute Out
1	C	12	40	14	22
2	B	8	20	8	40
3	T	2	0	3	59
4	C	12	40	16	22
5	B	8	20	14	20
6	T	2	0	12	0

Table 5-12   Test data for Project 58

59. This program is a simple guessing game. The computer is to generate a random number between 1 and 20. The user is given up to five tries to guess the exact number. After each guess, you are to tell the user if the guessed number is greater than, less than, or equal to the random number. If it is equal, no more guesses should be made. If the user hasn't guessed the number after five tries, display the number with a message that the user should know it by now and terminate the game.

A possible successful dialog:

```
I am thinking of a number between 1 and 20.
    Can you guess what it is?        10
    Your guess is low. Try again:    15
    Your guess is low. Try again:    17
    Your guess is high. Try again:   16


          Congratulations! You did it.
```

A possible unsuccessful dialog:

```
I am thinking of a number between 1 and 20.
    Can you guess what it is?        10
    Your guess is low. Try again:    20
    Your guess is high. Try again:   10
    Your guess is low. Try again:    18
    Your guess is high. Try again:   12


    Sorry. The number was 15.
    You should have gotten it by now.
    Better luck next time.
```

Your design for this program should include a separate function to get the user's guess, a function to print the unsuccessful message, one to print the successful message, and one to print the sorry message.

60. Write a program that, given a person's birth date (or any other date in the Gregorian calendar), will display the day of the week the person was born.

To determine the day of the week, you will first need to calculate the day of the week for December 31 of the previous year. To calculate the day for December 31, use the formula shown below.

$$\left((\text{year} - 1) * 365 + \left\lfloor \frac{(\text{year} - 1)}{4} \right\rfloor - \left\lfloor \frac{\text{year} - 1}{100} \right\rfloor + \left\lfloor \frac{\text{year} - 1}{400} \right\rfloor \right) \% 7$$

The formula determines the day based on the values as shown below.

Day 0:   Sunday
Day 1:   Monday
Day 2:   Tuesday
Day 3:   Wednesday
Day 4:   Thursday
Day 5:   Friday
Day 6:   Saturday

Once you know the day for December 31, you simply calculate the days in the year before the month in question. Use a *switch* statement to make this calculation. (Hint: Use *case* 12 first, and then fall into *case* 11, 10 . . . 2.) If the desired month is 12, add the number of days for November (30). If it is 11, add the number of days for October (31). If it is 3, add the number of days for February (28). If it is 2, add the number of days for January (31). If you do not use a *break* between the months, the *switch* will add the days in each month before the current month.

To this figure, add the day in the current month and then add the result to the day code for December 31. This number modulo seven is the day of the week.

There is one more refinement. If the current year is a leap year, and if the desired date is after February, you need to add 1 to the day code. The following formula can be used to determine if the year is a leap year.

```
(!(year % 4) && (year % 100) ) || !(year % 400)
```

Your program should have a function to get data from the user, another to calculate the day of the week, and a third to print the result.

To test your program, run it with the following dates:

a. February 28, 1900, and March 1, 1900

b. February 28, 1955, and March 1, 1955

c. February 28, 1996, and March 1, 1996

d. February 28, 2000, and March 1, 2000

e. December 31, 1996

f. The first and last dates of the current week.

61. Write a program that calculates the change due a customer by denomination; that is, how many pennies, nickels, dimes, etc. are needed in change. The input is to be the purchase price and the size of the bill tendered by the customer ($100, $50, $20, $10, $5, $1).

62. Write a menu-driven program that allows a user to enter five numbers and then choose between finding the smallest, largest, sum, or average. The menu and all the choices are to be functions. Use a *switch* statement to determine what action to take. Provide an error message if an invalid choice is entered.

    Run the program five times, once with each option and once with an invalid option. Each run is to use the following set of data:

    18, 21, 7, 54, 9

63. Write a program that tests a user-entered character and displays its classification according to the ASCII classifications shown in Figure 5-25 on page 204. Write the program starting at the top of the classification tree and display all classifications that the character belongs to. For instance, if the user enters a digit, you should display that it is printable, graphical, alphanumeric, and a digit.

64. Write a program to compute the real roots of a quadratic equation ($ax^2 + bx + c = 0$). The roots can be calculated using the following formulas:

$$x1 = -b + \frac{\sqrt{b^2 - 4ac}}{2a}$$

and

$$x2 = -b - \frac{\sqrt{b^2 - 4ac}}{2a}$$

Your program is to prompt the user to enter the constants (a, b, c). It is then to display the roots based on the following rules:

a. If both a and b are zero, there is no solution.

b. If a is zero, there is only one root (−c / b).

c. If the discriminate ($b^2 - 4ac$) is negative, there are no real roots.

d. For all other combinations, there are two roots.

Test your program with the following data:

a	b	c
3	8	5
−6	7	8
0	9	−10
0	0	11

Repetition 6

The real power of computers is in their ability to repeat an operation or a series of operations many times. This repetition, called looping, is one of the basic structured programming concepts. In this chapter, we discuss looping and introduce different looping constructs. First we define the basic concepts of loops, including a most important concept: how to stop a loop. We then present the three different loop constructs and take you through the C implementation of these three constructs. In this discussion, we include some basic loop applications. We conclude with a discussion of some of the software engineering implications of loops.

6-1 CONCEPT OF A LOOP

The concept of a loop is shown in the flowchart in Figure 6-1. In this flowchart, the action is repeated over and over again. It never stops.

Since the loop in Figure 6-1 never stops, it is the computer version of the perpetual motion machine. The action (or actions) will be repeated forever. We definitely do not want this to happen. We want our loop to end when the work is done. To make sure that it ends, we must have a condition that controls the loop. In other words, we must design the loop so that before or after each **iteration**, it checks to see if it is done. If it is not done, it repeats one more time; if it is done, it exits the loop. This test is known as a **loop control expression**.

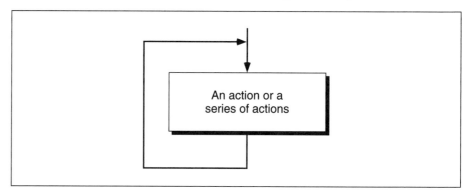

Figure 6-1 The concept of a loop

6-2 PRETEST AND POST-TEST LOOPS

We have established that we need a loop control test, but where should we check it—before or after each iteration? Programming languages allow us to check the loop control expression either before *or* after each iteration of the loop. In other words, we can have either a pre- or a post-test terminating condition. In a **pretest loop**, the condition is checked before we start and at the beginning of each iteration after the first. If the test condition is true, we execute the code; if the test condition is false, we terminate the loop.

> Pretest Loop
>
> In each iteration, the loop control expression is tested first. If it is true, the loop action(s) are executed; if it is false, the loop is terminated.
>
> Post-test Loop
>
> In each iteration, the loop action(s) are executed. Then the loop control expression is tested. If it is true, a new iteration is started; otherwise, the loop terminates.

In the **post-test loop**, we always execute the code at least once. At the completion of the loop code, the loop control expression is tested. If the expression is true, the loop repeats; if the expression is false, the loop terminates. The flowcharts in Figure 6-2 show these two loop types.

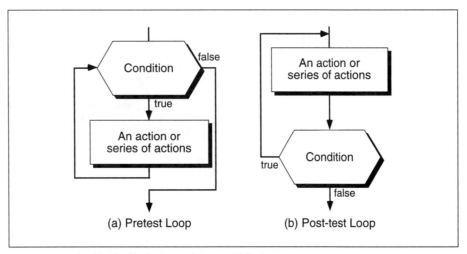

Figure 6-2   Pretest and post-test loops

Consider this example of pretest and post-test looping. Imagine that you are ready to start your daily exercises. Your exercise program requires you to do as many push-ups as possible. You can check your limit using either a pretest or a post-test condition. In the pretest strategy, you first check to see if you have enough energy to start. In the post-test strategy, you do one push-up and then you test to see if you have enough energy to do another one. Note that in both cases the question is phrased so that if the answer is true you continue the loop. The two strategies are shown in Figure 6-3.

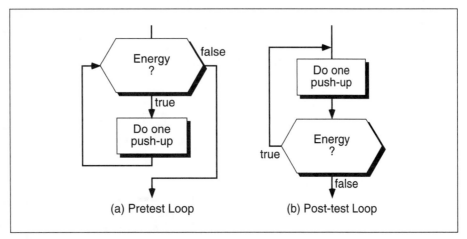

Figure 6-3   Two different strategies for doing exercises

As you can see, in the first strategy, you may not do any push-ups. If you are tired when you start and don't have the energy for at least one push-up, you are done. In the second strategy, you must do at least one push-up. In other words, in a pretest loop, the action may be done zero, one, or more times; in a post-test loop, the action is done one or more times. This major difference between a pretest and a post-test loop, which you must clearly understand, is shown in Figure 6-4.

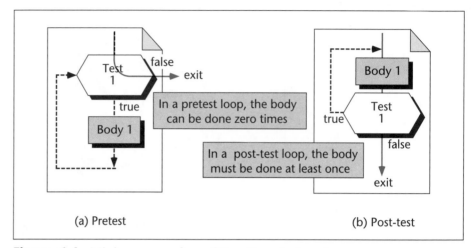

Figure 6-4 Minimum number of iterations in two loops

6-3 INITIALIZATION AND UPDATING

In addition to the loop control expression, two other processes are associated with almost all loops, initialization and updating.

LOOP INITIALIZATION

Before a loop can start, some preparation is usually required. We call this preparation loop **initialization**. Initialization must be done before the first execution of the body. It sets the stage for the loop actions. Figure 6-5 shows the initialization as a process box before the loop.

Initialization may be explicit or implicit. Explicit initialization is much more common. When the initialization is explicit, you include code to set the beginning values of

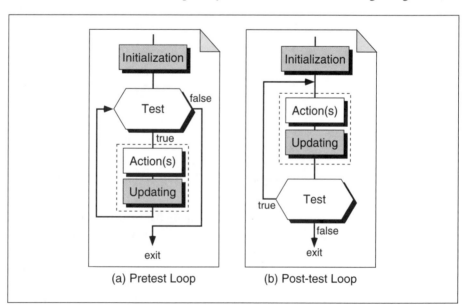

Figure 6-5 Loop initialization and updating

key loop variables. Implicit initialization provides no direct code to set the starting values but, rather, relies on a preexisting situation, such as values passed to the function that controls a loop.

LOOP UPDATE

How can the condition that controls the loop be true for a while and then change to false? The answer is that something must happen inside the body of the loop to change the condition. Otherwise, we would have an **infinite loop**. For example, in the loops shown in Figure 6-3, you gradually lose your energy until a point comes when you cannot continue the push-ups. This changes the resulting condition from true to false. The actions that cause these changes are known as **loop update**. Updating is done in each iteration, usually as the last action. If the body of the loop is repeated m times, then the updating is also done m times.

The concepts of initialization and updating can be applied to our previous push-up example. In this case, initialization is created by nutrition, an implicit initialization. During each push-up, some of the initial energy is consumed in the process and your energy is reduced, which updates your energy level. This is shown in Figure 6-6.

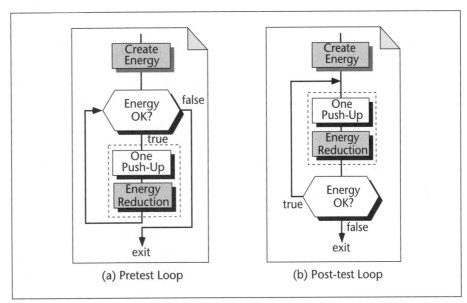

Figure 6-6 Initialization and updating for exercise

6-4   EVENT-CONTROLLED AND COUNTER-CONTROLLED LOOPS

All the possible expressions that can be used in a loop limit test can be summarized into two general categories: event-controlled loops and counter-controlled loops.

EVENT-CONTROLLED LOOPS

In an **event-controlled loop**, an event changes the loop control expression from true to false. For example, when reading data, reaching the end of the data changes the loop control expression from true to false. In event-controlled loops, the updating process can be explicit or implicit. If it is explicit, such as finding a specific piece of information, it is controlled by the loop. If it is implicit, such as the temperature of a batch of chemicals reaching a certain point, it is controlled by some external condition. The event-controlled loop is shown in Figure 6-7.

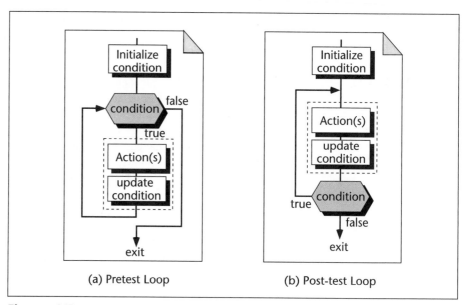

Figure 6-7   Event-controlled loop concept

COUNTER-CONTROLLED LOOPS

When we know the number of times an action is to be repeated, we use a **counter-controlled loop**. We must initialize, update, and test the counter. Although we need to know the number of times we want to execute the loop, the number does not need to be a constant. It can also be a variable or a calculated value. The update can be an increment, in which case we are counting up, or a decrement, in which case we are counting down. The counter-controlled loop is shown in Figure 6-8.

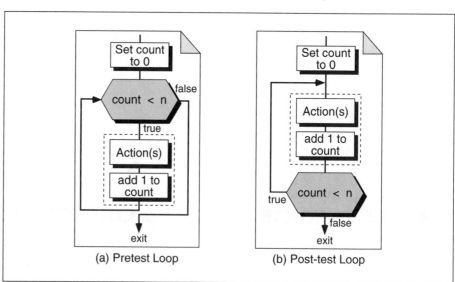

Figure 6-8   Counter-controlled loop concept

LOOP COMPARISON

Note that in the pretest loop, when we come out of the loop, the limit test has been done $n + 1$ times. In the post-test loop, when we come out of the loop, the limit test has been done only n times. A summary of the two different loop concepts is shown in Table 6-1.

Pretest Loop	Executions	Post-test Loop	Executions
Initialization:	1	Initialization:	1
Number of tests:	$n + 1$	Number of tests:	n
Action executed:	n	Action executed:	n
Updating executed:	n	Updating executed:	n
Minimum iterations:	0	Minimum iterations:	1

n is the number of iterations

Table 6-1   Loop comparisons

6-5   LOOPS IN C

C has three loop statements: the *while,* the *for,* and the *do...while.* The first two are pretest loops, and the *do...while* is a post-test loop. We can use all of them for event-controlled and counter-controlled loops. The *while* and *do...while* are most commonly used for event-controlled loops, and the *for* is usually used for counter-controlled loops. These loop constructs are shown in Figure 6-9.

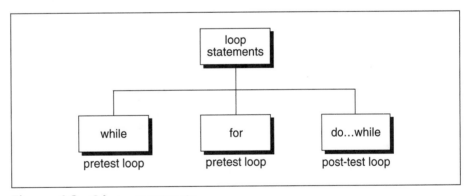

Figure 6-9   C loop constructs

Note that all three of these three loop constructs continue when the limit control test is true and terminate when it is false. This consistency of design makes it easy to write the limit test in C. On the other hand, general algorithms are usually written just the opposite because analysts tend to think about what will terminate the loop rather than what will continue it. In these cases, you must complement or otherwise modify the limit test when you write your program. This is one place where De Morgan's rule, see page 180, is very handy.

THE *while* LOOP

The *while* statement is the pretest loop. It uses an expression to control the loop. Since it is a pretest loop, it tests the expression before every iteration of the loop. The basic syntax of the *while* statement is shown in Figure 6-10. No semicolon is needed at the end of the *while* statement. When you see a semicolon, it actually belongs to the statement within the *while* statement.

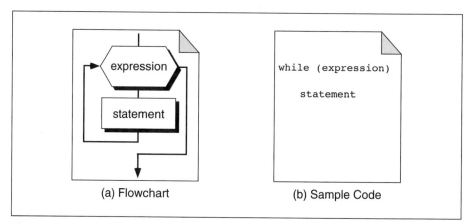

Figure 6-10   The *while* statement

Note that the sample code in Figure 6-10 shows that the loop body is a single statement; that is, the body of the loop must be one, and only one, statement. If we want to include multiple statements in the body, we must put them in a compound statement (block). This concept is shown in Figure 6-11.

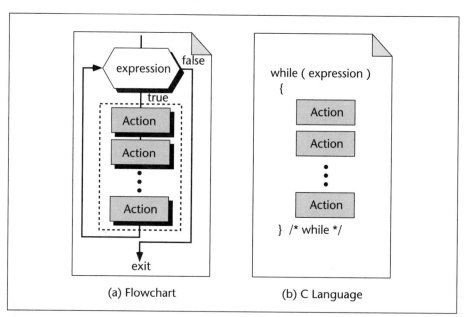

Figure 6-11   Compound *while* statement

Process Control Loops

Perhaps the simplest loop is the loop that never ends. While it is virtually never used in data processing, it is common in **process-control loops** such as network servers, environmental systems, and manufacturing systems. A simple process-control system that might be used to control the temperature in a building is shown in Program 6-1.

```
1   while (1)
2     {
3       temp = getTemperature();
4       if (temp < 68)
5           turnOnHeater();
6       else if (temp > 78)
7           turnOnAirCond();
8       else
9           {
10          turnOffHeater();
11          turnOffAirCond();
12          } /* else */
13    } /* while 1 */
```

Program 6-1   Process-control system example

Program 6-1 Analysis   The limit test in this simple program is a literal constant. It cannot be changed. Therefore, no update is required. Because the limit test in the *while* statement is always true, it will never stop. We must emphasize, however, that this is not a good construct for anything other than a loop that truly never ends.

As an aside, what would be the effect in Program 6-1 if the following *while* statement were used?

```
while (0)
```

Because the limit condition is a constant false, the loop would never start. Obviously, this would be a logic error.

Print Loops

A more common *while* loop is shown in Program 6-2. In this case we want to print a series of numbers. To keep from running off the end of the line, we have added a test to write a newline when ten numbers have been written.

```
1   /* Simple while loop that prints numbers 10 per line.
2         Written by:
3         Date:
4   */
5   #include <stdio.h>
6
7   int main (void)
8   {
9   /* Local Definitions */
10     int num;
11     int lineCount;
12
```

Program 6-2   A *while* loop to print numbers

```
13   /* Statements */
14      printf ("Enter an integer between 1 and 100: ");
15      scanf  ("%d", &num);
16
17      /* Test number */
18      if (num > 100)
19          num = 100;
20
21      lineCount = 0;
22      while (num > 0)
23          {
24           if (lineCount < 10)
25               lineCount++;
26           else
27               {
28                printf("\n");
29                lineCount = 1;
30               } /* else */
31           printf("%4d", num--);
32          } /* while */
33      return 0;
34   }  /* main */
```

```
Results:
    Enter an integer between 1 and 100: 15
        15   14   13   12   11   10    9    8    7    6
         5    4    3    2    1
```

Program 6-2   A *while* loop to print numbers (continued)

Program 6-2 Analysis   Find the basic elements of a loop in this program. First, look for loop initialization, then the limit test, and finally the update.

The initialization is done by asking the user to enter num in Statement 14. Note how we make sure that the user enters a number that is not too large. If the number is over 100, we simply set it to 100, which is the maximum we told the user to enter. The limit test is in Statement 22. As long as num is greater than 0, we continue printing out the number series. The update is hidden in Statement 31; after printing num, we subtract 1 from it. Although this is a common C programmer trick, the program would have been easier to read if we had put the update (num--) on the line after the print. That way it would have been obvious.

File Looping

One of the most common loop applications in any language is reading data until all the data have been processed—that is, until the end-of-file. In C, the *scanf* function returns the system constant **EOF** when it detects an end-of-file.

Consider this application of the *scanf* feature: Suppose you want to read and process a list of numbers from the keyboard. You type all the numbers, each one on a separate line. At the end, you can type end-of-file (<ctrl+d> in UNIX or <ctrl+z> in DOS). This loop logic is shown in the first example on the next page.

But no one codes a *while* loop like this. Let's simplify it. In the revised version of the loop, we have moved the *scanf* to the conditional expression in the *while* statement itself. We can do this because the initialization and the update are identical. The initialization

```
ioResult = scanf ("%d", &a);
while (ioResult != EOF)
   {
   /* Action: Process the number */
   ...
   ioResult = scanf ("%d", &a) ;
}  /* while */
```

and updating are now both self-contained parts of the *while* statement. This change is shown below.

```
while ((ioResult = scanf ("%d", &a)) != EOF)
   {
   /* Process the number */
   ...
   }  /* while */
```

But we can simplify this loop even further. Since the *scanf* function returns a value, we can test for end-of-file in the *while* expression. We don't need the variable, ioResult, so we can simply use the function value and discard it after it has been checked. The result is the standard C loop for reading and processing data from a file shown in Program 6-3, which adds a list of integers read from the keyboard and displays their sum.

```
 1  /* Add a list of integers from the standard input unit
 2     Written by:
 3     Date:
 4  */
 5  #include <stdio.h>
 6  int main (void)
 7  {
 8  /* Local Definitions */
 9     int x;
10     int sum = 0;
11
12     /* Statements */
13     printf("Enter your numbers: <EOF> to stop.\n");
14     while (scanf("%d", &x) != EOF)
15        sum += x;
16     printf ("\nThe total is: %d\n", sum);
17     return  0;
18  }  /* main */
```

```
Results:
   Enter your numbers: <EOF> to stop
   15
   22
   3^d
   The total is: 40
```

Program 6-3   Adding a list of numbers

Program 6-3 Analysis   Note that a compound statement (block) is not needed in the *while* loop, because the addition can be done in one statement. Another important point is that the statement to print the sum is outside the loop. Since the user can see the input values on the screen, all we need to show is the sum.

THE *for* LOOP

The *for* statement is a pretest loop that uses three expressions. The first expression contains any initialization statements, the second contains the **limit-test expression**, and the third contains the updating expression. Figure 6-12 shows a flowchart, and an expanded interpretation, for a sample *for* statement. Expression 1 is executed when the *for* starts. Expression 2 is the limit test expression. As shown in the expanded flowchart, it is executed *before* every iteration. Remember that since the *for* is a pretest loop, the body is not executed if the limit condition is false at the start of the loop. Finally, Expression 3 is the update expression. It is executed at the end of each loop. Note that the code in the *for* statement must be expressions. This means that you cannot use statements, such as *return,* in the *for* statement itself. Like the *while* statement, the *for* statement does not need a semicolon.

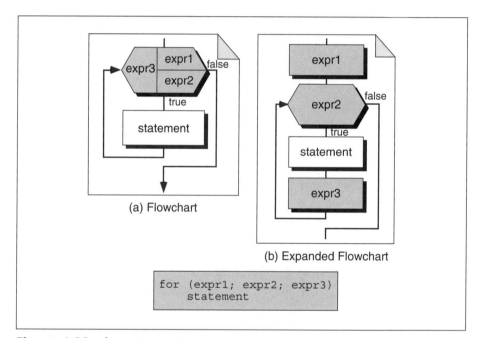

(a) Flowchart

(b) Expanded Flowchart

```
for (expr1; expr2; expr3)
    statement
```

Figure 6-12   *for* statement

The **body** of the *for* loop must be one, and only one, statement. If we want to include more than one statement in the body, we must code them in a compound statement. A *for* statement with a compound statement is shown in Figure 6-13.

Unlike some languages, C allows the loop control expression to be controlled inside the *for* statement itself. Therefore, the updating of the limit condition can also be done in the body of the *for* statement. In fact, Expression 3 can be null and the updating controlled entirely within the body of the loop. This is not a recommended structured programming coding technique.

Although the *for* loop can be used anywhere a pretest loop is required, it is most naturally used for counter-controlled loops (see page 234). Its self-contained design makes it ideal for count logic.

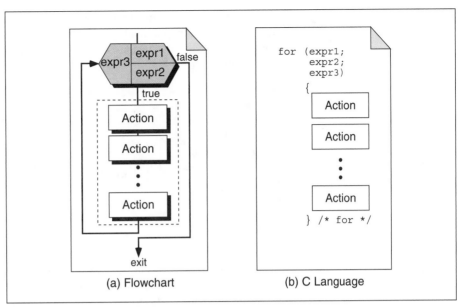

Figure 6-13 Compound *for* statement

A *for* loop is used when your loop is to be executed a known number of times. You can do the same thing with a *while* loop, but the *for* loop is easier to read and more natural for counting loops.

Let's compare the *while* and the *for* loops. Figure 6-14 shows a graphical representation of each side by side. Note that the *for* loop contains the initialization, update code, and limit test in one statement. This makes for very readable code. All the control steps, initialization, end-of-loop test, and updating are done in one place. This is a variation of the structured programming concepts of encapsulation, in which all code for a process is placed in one module. Another way of looking at it is that a *for* loop communicates better and is more compact.

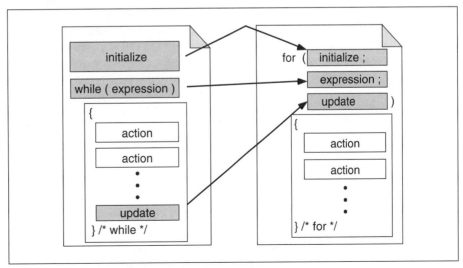

Figure 6-14 Comparing *for* and *while* loops

Now let's solve the same problem using both a *while* and a *for* loop. The code shown below contains a loop to read 20 numbers from the keyboard and find their sum. This can be done both in a *while* loop and a *for* loop. But as you can see, the *for* loop is more self-documenting.

```
i = 1;
sum = 0;                          sum = 0;
while (i <= 20)                   for (i = 1; i <= 20; i++)
  {                                 {
    scanf("%d", &a);                  scanf ("%d", &a);
    sum += a;                         sum += a;
    i ++;                           } /* for */
  } /* while */
```

Example: Print Number Series

To demonstrate the *for* loop, let's write a program that asks the user for a number and then prints the series of numbers starting at one and continuing up to and including the user-entered number. The code is in Program 6-4.

```
 1  /* Print number series from 1 to user-specified limit.
 2         Written by:
 3         Date:
 4  */
 5  #include <stdio.h>
 6  int main (void)
 7  {
 8  /* Local Definitions */
 9     int i;
10     int limit;
11
12  /* Statements */
13     printf ("\nPlease enter the limit: ");
14     scanf ("%d", &limit);
15     for (i = 1; i <= limit; i++)
16        printf("\t%d\n", i);
17
18     return 0;
19  }  /* main*/
```

```
Results:
Please enter the limit: 3
    1
    2
    3
```

Program 6-4 Example of a *for* loop

Program 6-4 Analysis   This simple program is the model for many looping functions. Let's look at three simple modifications to it. First, how would you print only odd numbers? This requires a change only to the update in the *for* statement.

```
for (i = 1; i <= limit; i += 2)
```

Now let's change it to print the numbers backward. In this case, all the statements in the *for* statement must be changed, but the rest of the program is still unchanged.

```
for (i = limit; i >= 1; i--)
```

For the final example, let's print the numbers in two columns, the odd numbers in the first column and the even numbers in the second column. We must modify the update statement in the *for* statement and also the print statement as shown below.

```
for (i = 1; i <= limit; i += 2)
    printf("\t%2d\t%2d\n", i, i + 1);
```

We have used tabs and width specifications to align the output in columns. Note that the second print value ($i + 1$) is an expression. It does *not* change the value of i. There is no side effect, it is just a value.

Nested *for* Loops

Any statement, even another *for* loop, can be included in the body of a *for* statement. Using nested loops can create some interesting applications. Let's look at a very simple one here. We will give other examples in "Looping Applications," page 263.

Program 6-5 uses a nested loop to print a series of numbers on multiple lines.

```
 1  /* Print numbers on a line.
 2        Written by:
 3        Date:
 4  */
 5  #include <stdio.h>
 6
 7  int main (void)
 8  {
 9  /* Local Definitions */
10     int i;
11     int j;
12
13  /* Statements */
14     for (i = 1; i <= 3; i++)
15        {
16         printf("Row %d: ", i);
17         for (j = 1; j<= 5; j++)
18             printf("%3d", j);
19         printf("\n");
20        } /* for i */
21     return 0;
22  }  /* main */
```

```
Results:
Row 1:   1  2  3  4  5
Row 2:   1  2  3  4  5
Row 3:   1  2  3  4  5
```

Program 6-5 A simple nested *for* loop

THE *do...while* LOOP

The *do...while* statement is a post-test loop. Like the *while* and *for* loops, it also uses an expression to control the loop, but it tests this expression *after* the execution of the body. The format of the *do...while* statement is shown in Figure 6-15.

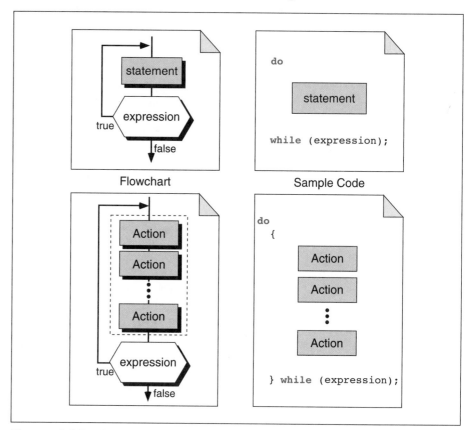

Figure 6-15   *do...while* statement

The body of the *do...while* loop must be one, and only one, statement. If we need to include multiple statements in the body, we must put them in a compound statement. The second example in Figure 6-15 shows the logic flow and code for a *do...while* statement that uses a compound statement. Look carefully at the code block in the second example. Note that the *do* and the *while* braces are aligned. Note also that the *while* expression follows the brace on the same line. This is a good style because it makes it easy for the reader to see the statement. Finally, note that the *do...while* is concluded with a semicolon. This differs from the other looping constructs that you have seen.

Let's look at a simple program that uses a loop to print five numbers. We code two loops, first a *while* loop and then a *do...while*. Although one loop is a pretest and the other is a post-test, both print the same series. The code is seen in Program 6-6.

```
1   /* Demonstrate while and do...while loops.
2          Written by:
3          Date:
4   */
```

Program 6-6   Two simple loops

```
 5   #include <stdio.h>
 6
 7   int main (void)
 8   {
 9   /* Local Definitions */
10      int loopCount;
11
12   /* Statements */
13      loopCount = 5;
14      printf("while loop      : ");
15      while (loopCount > 0)
16         printf ("%3d", loopCount--);
17      printf("\n\n");
18
19      loopCount = 5;
20      printf("do...while loop: ");
21      do
22         printf ("%3d", loopCount--);
23      while (loopCount > 0);
24      printf("\n");
25      return 0;
26   }  /* main */
```

```
     Results
        while loop      :  5  4  3  2  1

        do...while loop:  5  4  3  2  1
```

Program 6-6 Two simple loops (continued)

Because the *do...while* limit test isn't done until the end of the loop, we use it when we know that the body of the loop must be done at least once. To demonstrate the impact of the two loops, study the code in Figure 6-16. In the *while* loop, the message is not printed, because the limit condition is tested first. In the *do...while* loop, even though the limit test is false, the message is printed because the message is printed before the limit test.

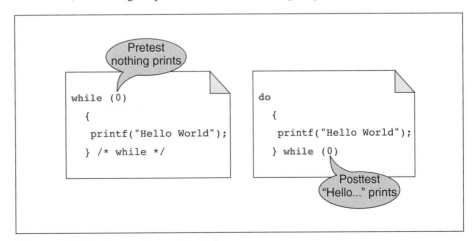

Figure 6-16 Pre- and post-test loops

Programmers commonly use the *do...while* loop in data validation to make the program robust. For example, imagine we want to read an integer that must be between 10 and 20. We can use the *do...while* loop as shown below.

```
do
    {
     printf ("Enter a number between 10 & 20: ");
     scanf ("%d", &a);
    } while (a < 10 || a > 20);
```

To demonstrate the *do...while,* let's rewrite Program 6-3, "Adding a list of numbers," on page 239. The modified code is shown in Program 6-7.

```
 1  /* Add a list of integers from the standard input unit
 2         Written by:
 3         Date:
 4  */
 5  #include <stdio.h>
 6
 7  int main (void)
 8  {
 9  /* Local Definitions */
10     int x;
11     int sum = 0;
12     int testEOF;
13
14     /* Statements */
15     printf("Enter your numbers: <EOF> to stop.\n");
16     do
17        {
18          testEOF = scanf("%d", &x);
19          if (testEOF != EOF)
20              sum += x;
21        } while (testEOF != EOF);
22     printf ("\nTotal: %d\n", sum);
23     return  0;
24  }  /* main */
```

```
Results:
    Run 1:
    Enter your numbers: <EOF> to stop.
    10 15 20 25 ^d
    Total: 70

    Run 2:
    Enter your numbers: <EOF> to stop.
    ^d
    Total: 0
```

Program 6-7   Adding a list with the *do...while*

Program 6-7 Analysis   Since the *do...while* always executes the body of the loop at least once, we had to make some changes. Compare Program 6-3 and Program 6-7 carefully. Note that the *scanf* is no longer in the loop limit test. Since the limit test is after the loop body, the *scanf* must be moved to the beginning of the loop. The result of the input is saved in a new variable, `testEOF`. Finally, before we can add the value we read to the accumulator, we must ensure we are not at the end of the file. The add statement is therefore guarded by an *if* statement. Although Program 6-7 is a little less efficient than Program 6-3, it does the same job.

THE COMMA EXPRESSION

A **comma expression** is a complex expression made up of two expressions separated by commas. Although it can legally be used in many places, it is most often used in *for* statements. The expressions are evaluated left to right. The value and type of the expressions are the value and type of the right expression; the other expression is included for its side effect. The comma expression has the lowest priority of all expressions, priority 1.

The following statement is a modification of the *for* statement code shown on page 242. It uses a comma expression to initialize the accumulator, `sum`, and the index, `i`, in the loop. In this example, the value of the comma expression is discarded. This is a common use of the **comma operator.**

```
for (sum = 0, i = 1; i <= 20; i++)
    {
    scanf("%d", &a);
    sum += a;
    } /* for */
```

Comma expressions can be nested. When they are nested, all expression values other than the last are discarded. Figure 6-17 shows the format of a nested comma expression.

Figure 6-17   Nested comma expression

A final word of caution. Remember that the value of the expression is the value of the rightmost expression. Although it is not recommended, if you use a comma expression for the second expression in a *for* loop, make sure that the loop control is the last expression.

Let's use the comma expression to demonstrate the difference between the *while* and the *do...while*. As shown in Table 6-1, "Loop comparisons," on page 235, the only difference is the number of limit tests that are made. Program 6-6 shows that the same job can be done by either loop. Program 6-8 uses both loops to count from 1 to 10. It uses the comma expression to count the number of limit tests in each loop.

```
1 | /* Demonstrate while and do…while loops.
2 |      Written by:
3 |      Date:
```

Program 6-8   Comparison of *while* and *do...while*

```
 4  */
 5  #include <stdio.h>
 6
 7  int main (void)
 8  {
 9  /* Local Definitions */
10     int loopCount;
11     int testCount;
12
13  /* Statements */
14     loopCount = 1;
15     testCount = 0;
16     printf("while loop:         ");
17     while (testCount++, loopCount <= 10)
18        printf("%3d", loopCount++);
19     printf("\nLoop Count:        %3d\n", loopCount);
20     printf("Number of tests:  %3d\n", testCount);
21
22     loopCount = 1;
23     testCount = 0;
24     printf("\ndo...while loop:  ");
25     do
26        printf("%3d",    loopCount++);
27     while (testCount++,  loopCount <= 10);
28
29     printf("\nLoop Count:        %3d\n", loopCount);
30     printf("Number of tests:  %3d\n", testCount);
31
32     return 0;
33  }  /* main */
```

```
Results:
   while loop:          1  2  3  4  5  6  7  8  9 10
   Loop Count:         11
   Number of tests:    11

   do...while loop:     1  2  3  4  5  6  7  8  9 10
   Loop Count:         11
   Number of tests:    10
```

Program 6-8 Comparison of *while* and *do...while* (continued)

Program 6-8 Analysis Look at Statements 17 and 27 carefully. They both contain comma expressions. This technique of combining the counter and the limit test in one expression ensures that the count will be accurate. Because the value of the whole comma expression is the value of its last expression, however, the limit test must be coded last.

The results demonstrate that both loops count from one to ten. Since they are doing exactly the same job, we expect that the loop bodies would also execute the same number of times. As predicted in Table 6-1 on page 235, the only difference is in the number of tests: The *while* loop control expression was evaluated 11 times; the *do...while* control expression was evaluated only 10 times.

6-6   LOOP EXAMPLES

This section contains several short examples of loop applications. Each program demonstrates one or more programming concepts that you will find helpful in solving other problems.

for LOOPS

Example: Compound Interest

One classic loop problem is calculating the value of an investment. Suppose that we want to know the value of an investment over time, given its initial value and annual interest rate. Program 6-9 displays a compound interest table.

```c
 1  /* Print report showing value of investment.
 2         Written by:
 3         Date:
 4  */
 5  #include <stdio.h>
 6
 7  int main (void)
 8  {
 9  /* Local Definitions */
10     double presVal;
11     double futureVal;
12     double rate;
13
14     int years;
15     int looper;
16
17  /* Statements */
18     printf("Enter value of investment:   ");
19     scanf ("%lf", &presVal);
20     printf("Enter rate of return (nn.n): ");
21     scanf ("%lf", &rate);
22     printf("Enter number of years:       ");
23     scanf ("%d", &years);
24
25     printf("\nYear    Value\n");
26     printf("====  ========\n");
27     for (futureVal = presVal, looper = 1;
28          looper <= years;
29          looper++)
30        {
31         futureVal = futureVal * (1 + rate/100.0);
32         printf("%3d%11.2lf\n", looper, futureVal);
33        } /* for */
34     return 0;
35  }  /* main */
```

Program 6-9   Compound interest

```
Results:
   Enter value of investment:    10000
   Enter rate of return (nn.n): 7.2
   Enter number of years:        5

   Year        Value
   ====      ========
    1        10720.00
    2        11491.84
    3        12319.25
    4        13206.24
    5        14157.09
```

Program 6-9   Compound interest (continued)

Program 6-9 Analysis   This program uses a *for* loop to calculate the value of the investment at the end of each year. Each iteration adds the current year's interest to the investment and then prints its current value.

Note how we prompted the user for input, especially the decimal return rate. Things like percentage rates can be confusing to enter. Is 7.2% entered as 7.2 or .072? Make sure you give the user a sample of how the data should be entered.

Now study the way we created a caption for the reports, using equal signs to underscore the captions and spaces with width specifications to align the values in columns. This rather simple technique makes the results quite readable.

Example: Right Triangle

Let's write a program that will print a series of numbers in the form of a right triangle. Ask the user to enter a one-digit number. Each line, from the first to the limit entered by the user, is to print a number series from one to the current line number. For example, if a user enters 6, the program prints

```
1
12
123
1234
12345
123456
```

The flowchart and pseudocode for the loop are shown in Figure 6-18. The completed program is shown in Program 6-10.

Program 6-10 Analysis   Program 6-10 (see opposite page) demonstrates the concept of a loop within a loop (see page 243). Note how we use two *for* loops to print the triangle. The first or outer *for* controls how many lines we will print. The second or inner *for* writes the number series on one line. This concept of nested loops is a very important programming concept.

Also note the name we used in the loops. Often programmers will use i and j to control *for* loops. We often do ourselves. But notice how much more meaningful the code is when meaningful names are used. When we use lineCtrl rather than i in the outer loop, we know that this *for* is controlling the number of lines we are printing. Likewise, the name numCtrl clearly tells the reader that the *for* loop is controlling the numbers.

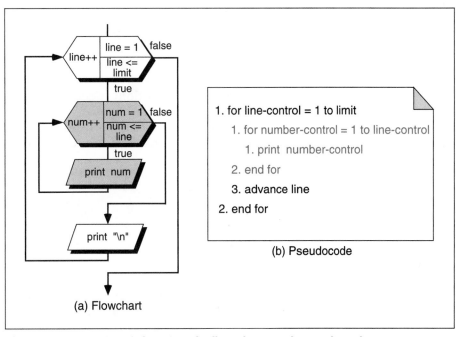

1. for line-control = 1 to limit
    1. for number-control = 1 to line-control
        1. print number-control
    2. end for
    3. advance line
2. end for

(b) Pseudocode

(a) Flowchart

Figure 6-18   Print right triangle flowchart and pseudocode

```
1   /* Print a number series from 1 to a user-specified limit
2      in the form of a right triangle.
3          Written by:
4          Date:
5   */
6   #include <stdio.h>
7   int main (void)
8   {
9   /* Local Definitions */
10     int lineCtrl;
11     int numCtrl;
12     int limit;
13
14  /* Statements */
15     /* Read limit */
16     printf("\nPlease enter a number between 1 and 9: ");
17     scanf("%d", &limit);
18
19     for (lineCtrl = 1; lineCtrl <= limit; lineCtrl++)
20        {
21         for (numCtrl = 1;
22              numCtrl <= lineCtrl;
23              numCtrl++)
24           printf("%1d", numCtrl);
25
```

Program 6-10   Print right triangle using nested *for*

```
26          printf("\n");
27          } /* for lineCtrl */
28      return 0;
29  }   /* main */
```

Program 6-10 Print right triangle using nested *for* (continued)

Example: Print Rectangle

Now let's write a program that prints the triangle pattern in the previous example filled out with asterisks to form a rectangle. For example, if a user enters 6, Program 6-11 prints

```
1*****
12****
123***
1234**
12345*
123456
```

```
1   /* Print number series from 1 to a user-specified limit
2      in the form of a rectangle.
3          Written by:
4          Date:
5   */
6   #include <stdio.h>
7
8   int main (void)
9   {
10  /* Local Definitions */
11     int row;
12     int col;
13     int limit;
14
15  /*Statements */
16     /* Read limit */
17     printf("\nPlease enter a number between 1 and 9: ");
18     scanf("%d", &limit);
19
20     for (row = 1; row <= limit; row++)
21         {
22         for (col = 1; col <= limit; col++)
23             if (row >= col)
24                 printf("%d", col);
25             else
26                 printf("*");
27         printf("\n");
28         } /* for row ... */
29
30     return 0;
31  }   /* main */
```

Program 6-11 Print rectangle using nested *for* loops

Program 6-11 Analysis This program is an interesting variation of the previous program. Compare the inner loop in this program to the inner loop in the previous one. This is the only part of the program that is different. The first thing you should note is that the limit test expression is different; it always goes to the maximum number of print positions. Within the inner loop, we test the column number (col) to determine how many digits we print on the line. If the expression is true, we print a digit. If it is false, we print an asterisk.

Example: Print Month

As a final example of a *for* loop, let's print a calendar month. In Program 6-12, the function printMonth receives only the start day of the month—Sunday is 0, Monday is 1... Saturday is 6—and the number of days in the month. This is all that the program needs to print any month of the year.

```c
 1  /* Test driver for function to print a calendar month.
 2         Written by:
 3         Date:
 4  */
 5  #include <stdio.h>
 6
 7  /* Prototype Declarations */
 8  void printMonth (int startDay, int days);
 9
10  int main (void)
11  {
12  /* Statements */
13      printMonth (2, 29);                 /* Day 2 is Tuesday */
14      return 0;
15  }  /* main */
16
17  /* ================= printMonth =================
18      Print one calendar month.
19         Pre    startDay is day of week relative
20                   to Sunday (0)
21                days is number of days in month
22         Post   Calendar printed
23  */
24  void printMonth (int startDay,
25                    int days)
26  {
27  /* Local Definitions */
28      int dayCount;
29      int weekDay;
30
31  /* Statements */
32      /* print day header */
33      printf("Sun Mon Tue Wed Thu Fri Sat\n");
34      printf("--- --- --- --- --- --- ---\n");
35
36      /* position first day */
```

Program 6-12 Print calendar month

```
37      for (weekDay = 0; weekDay < startDay; weekDay++)
38          printf("    ");
39
40      for (dayCount = 1; dayCount <= days; dayCount++)
41          {
42           if (weekDay > 6)
43              {
44               printf("\n");
45               weekDay = 1;
46              } /* if */
47           else
48               weekDay++;
49           printf("%3d ", dayCount);
50          } /* for */
51      printf("\n--- --- --- --- --- --- ---\n");
52      return;
53  }  /* printMonth */
```

```
Results:
Sun Mon Tue Wed Thu Fri Sat
--- --- --- --- --- --- ---
             1   2   3   4   5
  6   7   8   9  10  11  12
 13  14  15  16  17  18  19
 20  21  22  23  24  25  26
 27  28  29
--- --- --- --- --- --- ---
```

Program 6-12   Print calendar month (continued)

Program 6-12 Analysis   This program is interesting for two reasons: First, it requires two for loops, one to position the printing for the first day of the month and one to print the dates. Second, the logic to control the days of the week is simple yet efficient. In an effort to eliminate one variable (weekDay), many programmers would use the modulo statement shown below to determine the day of the week.

```
(dayCount + startDay) % 7
```

Although this logic works, it is very inefficient. Using a separate variable to control the days of the week requires simple addition, which is much more efficient. It also avoids another poor programming style: using one variable to control two processes. Although using one variable to control two processes may work initially, it often leads to subtle bugs when the program is changed.

> Never use one variable to control two processes.

while LOOPS

Example: Print Sum of the Digits

Program 6-13 accepts an integer from the keyboard and then prints the number of digits in the integer and the sum of the digits.

```
 1  /* Print the number and sum of digits in an integer.
 2         Written by:
 3         Date:
 4  */
 5  #include <stdio.h>
 6
 7  int main (void)
 8  {
 9  /* Local Definitions */
10     int number;
11     int count = 0;
12     int sum = 0;
13
14  /* Statements */
15     printf("\nEnter an integer: ");
16     scanf("%d", &number);
17     printf("Your number is:   %d\n\n", number);
18
19     while (number != 0)
20        {
21         count++;
22         sum +=  number % 10;
23         number /= 10;
24        } /* while */
25
26     printf("The number of digits is:  %3d\n", count);
27     printf("The sum of the digits is: %3d\n", sum);
28
29     return 0;
30  }  /* main*/
```

```
Results:

    Enter an integer: 12345
    Your number is:    12345

    The number of digits is:    5
    The sum of the digits is:   15
```

Program 6-13   Print sum of digits

Program 6-13 Analysis   This problem requires that we "peel" off one digit at a time
and add it to the total of the previous digits. You can solve this problems in a couple of
ways, but by far the most straightforward is to use the modulus operator (%) to extract
the rightmost digit and then to divide the number by ten to remove the right digit. For
example, given the number 123, we first extract the 3 by

```
123 % 10
```

and then eliminate it by dividing by 10 to give 12. Note that since both the dividend and the divisor are integers, the result is an integer. We loop until there is only one digit left, at which time any digit divided by ten will result in zero and the loop terminates.

Example: Print Number Backward

Now let's look at an example of a loop that prints a number backward. You can solve this problem in several ways. Perhaps the easiest is to simply use modulo division, as shown in Program 6-14.

```
 1  /* Use a loop to print a number backward.
 2         Written by:
 3         Date:
 4  */
 5  #include <stdio.h>
 6
 7  int main (void)
 8  {
 9  /* Local Definitions */
10     long num;
11     int  digit;
12
13  /* Statements */
14     printf("Enter a number and I'll print it backward: ");
15     scanf ("%d", &num);
16
17     while (num > 0)
18        {
19          digit = num % 10;
20          printf("%d", digit);
21          num   = num / 10;
22        } /* while */
23     printf("\nHave a good day.\n");
24     return 0;
25  } /* main */
```

```
Results:
   Enter a number and I'll print it backward: 12345678
   87654321
   Have a good day.
```

Program 6-14   Print number backward

do...while **LOOPS**

Example: Data Validation

Now we'll write a program that reads an integer consisting of only zeros and ones (a binary number) and converts it to its decimal equivalent. Provide a function that ensures that the number entered is a binary number. The design for this program is shown in Figure 6-19.

This design follows a classic program design: input–process–output. The input function is `getNum`; the process function is `binaryToDecimal`; and the output function is `printResults`. Study the design of `binaryToDecimal`. Note that it uses a loop and calls `firstDigit` and `powerTwo` in turn within the loop. How would you imple-

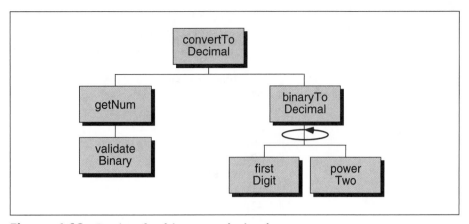

Figure 6-19 Design for binary to decimal

ment this loop? Think about it for a minute, and then look at Statement 66 in Program 6-15 to see how we did it. If you are not sure of your binary arithmetic and binary conversions, study Appendix D, "Numbering Systems."

```c
 1  /* Convert a binary number to a decimal number.
 2         Written by:
 3         Date:
 4  */
 5  #include <stdio.h>
 6
 7  /* Prototype Definitions */
 8  long getNum           (void);
 9  long binaryToDecimal (long binary);
10  long powerTwo         (long num);
11  long firstDigit       (long num);
12  int  validateBinary   (long binary);
13
14  int main (void)
15  {
16  /* Local Definitions */
17     long binary;
18     long decimal;
19
20  /* Statements */
21     binary  = getNum ();
22     decimal = binaryToDecimal (binary);
23     printf("\nThe binary number was: %ld", binary);
24     printf("\nThe decimal number is: %ld", decimal);
25     return 0;
26  }  /* main*/
27
28  /* ==================== getNum ====================
29     This function reads and validates a binary number from
```

Program 6-15 Convert binary to decimal

```
30      the keyboard.
31        Pre    nothing
32        Post   a valid binary number is returned
33   */
34   long getNum (void)
35   {
36   /* Local Definitions */
37      int   isValid;
38      long  binary;
39
40   /* Statements */
41      do
42        {
43         printf("Enter a binary number (zeros and ones): ");
44         scanf ("%ld", &binary);
45         isValid = validateBinary (binary);
46         if (!isValid)
47            printf("\a\aNot binary. Zeros/ones only.\n\n");
48        } while (!isValid);
49
50      return binary;
51   } /* getNum */
52
53   /* ================= binaryToDecimal =================
54      Change a binary number to a decimal number.
55        Pre    binary is a number consisting of only 0 and 1
56        Post   returns the decimal number
57   */
58   long binaryToDecimal (long binary)
59   {
60   /* Local Definitions */
61      int   i;
62      long  decimal;
63
64   /* Statements */
65      decimal = 0;
66      for (i = 0; binary != 0; i++)
67          {
68           decimal += firstDigit (binary) * powerTwo (i);
69           binary /= 10;
70          } /* for i */
71      return decimal;
72   } /* binaryToDecimal */
73
74   /* ================= validateBinary =================
75      Check the digits in a binary number for only 0 and 1.
76        Pre    binary is a number to be validated
77        Post   returns 1 if valid; 0 otherwise
78   */
79   int validateBinary (long binary)
```

Program 6-15 Convert binary to decimal (continued)

```
80    {
81    /* Statements */
82        while (binary != 0)
83            {
84              if (!(binary % 10 ==  0 || binary % 10 == 1))
85                  return 0;
86              binary /= 10;
87            } /* while */
88        return 1;
89    }  /* validateBinary */
90
91    /* ==================== powerTwo ====================
92       This function raises 2 to the power num
93           Pre    num is exponent
94           Post   Returns 2 to the power of num
95    */
96    long powerTwo (long num)
97    {
98    /* Local Definitions */
99        int    i;
100       long   power;
101
102   /* Statements */
103       for (power = 1, i = 1; i <= num; i++)
104           power *= 2;
105       return power;
106   }    /* powerTwo */
107   /* ================== firstDigit ==================
108      This function returns the right most digit of num
109          Pre    the integer num
110          Post   the right digit of num returned
111   */
112   long firstDigit (long num)
113   {
114   /* Statements */
115
116       return (num % 10);
117   }  /* first Digit */
118   /* ================== End of Program ================== */
```

```
    Results:
        Enter a binary number (zeros and ones): 10001
        The binary number was: 10001

        The decimal number is: 17
```

Program 6-15 Convert binary to decimal (continued)

Program 6-15 Analysis   This program has several interesting aspects. First, note the data validation that we use to ensure that the binary number that we read consists of nothing but zeros and ones. We used this series of modulus and divide statements previously in Program 6-13 and Program 6-14.

Then note how we enclosed the call to the validation function in a *do...while* that allows us to keep reading input until the user gives us a binary number. Again, note how we display an error message when the number is not valid. This is a standard data validation technique.

Next, study the `binaryToDecimal` function that converts the binary number to its decimal value. Note that when we extract a digit, it is either a zero or a one. We then multiply the extracted digit by 2 raised to the digit position we are currently evaluating, which gives us the binary value of that digit's position in the binary number. The value is then added to the decimal number. Of course, if the digit is a zero, then the product is zero and the value is unchanged. It is only when the digit is a one that we add to the decimal number.

Finally, note that throughout this program we used *long int* for the binary and decimal number. We did this because the decimal representation of a binary number can get very big very fast. On a personal computer, *int* might not be able to hold this representation of a binary number.

6-7   OTHER STATEMENTS RELATED TO LOOPING

Two other C statements are related to loops. They belong to a collection of statements known as jump statements (Figure 6-20). One jump statement, *return*, was discussed in Chapter 4; the *break* and *continue* jump statements are discussed in this section. The last of the jump statements, the *goto*, is not valid for structured programs and therefore is not discussed in this text.

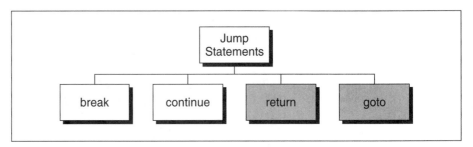

Figure 6-20   Jump statements

break

The first jump statement is **break**. We previously saw the *break* statement when we discussed **switch** in Chapter 5. In a loop, the *break* statement causes a loop to terminate. It is the same as setting the loop's limit test to false. If you are in a series of nested loops, *break* terminates only the inner loop—the one you are currently in. Figure 6-21 shows how *break* transfers control out of an inner *for* loop and continues with the next statement in the *while*. Note that *break* needs a semicolon.

The jump statement *break* can be used in any of the loop statements—*while, for,* and *do...while*—and in the selection *switch* statement. However, good structured programming limits its use to the *switch* statement. It should not be used in any of the looping statements. If you feel you must use *break,* reexamine your design. You will usually find that you have not properly structured your logic.[1]

---

[1]Although this statement is generally true, as you study advanced programming concepts, such as parsing, you will find that *break* and *continue* are used to simplify the code.

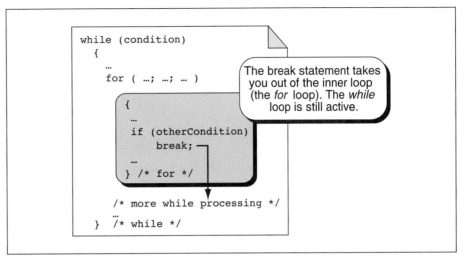

Figure 6-21   *break* and inner loops

Program 6-16 shows two examples of poor loop situations and how to restructure them so that the *break* is not needed. The *for* statement shows a never-ending loop. As coded, there is no way to terminate the loop without the *break*. Although the *break* works, better documentation and style puts the limiting condition as the second expression in the *for* statement. After all, that is the use of the limit expression in the first place.

<pre>1 /* A bad loop style */
2 for (; ;)
3   {
4   …
5   if (condition)
6   break;
7   } /* for */</pre>
	<pre>/* A good loop style */
	for (; !condition ;)
	   {
	   …
	   } /* for */</pre>

<pre>1 while (x)
2   {
3   …
4   if (condition)
5   break;
6   else
7   …
8   } /* while */</pre>
	<pre>while (x && !condition)
	   {
	   …
	   if (!condition)
	      …
	   } /* while */</pre>

Program 6-16   The *for* and *while* as perpetual loops

Even if the *break* condition is in the middle of a block, it can be removed to the limit condition, as shown in the *while* example in Program 6-16. Note that in this case, we complement the condition, which then executes the *else* logic when the limit condition has not been reached.

Sometimes the limit condition is so complex that it cannot easily be put in the limit condition. In these cases, a flag is used. A **flag** is a logical variable that tracks the presence or absence of an event. In this case, the flag is set to 1 to indicate that the end of the loop has been reached. This is shown in the *while* example in Program 6-17.

```
1   breakFlag = 0;
2   while (!breakFlag)
3      {
4      ...
5      if (x && !y || z)              /* Complex limit test */
6         breakFlag = 1;
7      else
8         ...
9      } /* while */
```

Program 6-17   Using a *break* flag

On the other hand, too many flags can make a function overly complex. The use of *break* and flags needs to be tempered with simplicity and clarity of logic. Finally, note that the flag is called `breakFlag`, which is a generic name. You should choose a more descriptive name, such as `accountFlag` or `timeLimitFlag`.

continue

The second jump statement is the ***continue***. It does not terminate the loop but simply transfers to the testing expression in *while* and *do...while* statements and transfers to the updating expression in a *for* statement. These jumps are shown in Figure 6-22. Although the transfer is to different positions in pretest and post-test loops, both can be logically thought of as a jump to the end of the loop's body.

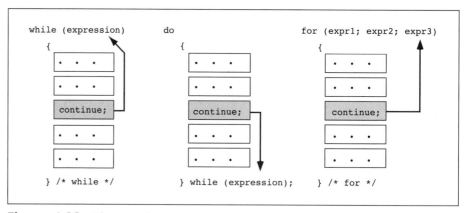

Figure 6-22   The *continue* statement

The use of the *continue* statement is also considered unstructured programming. If you think that you need a *continue,* your algorithm may not be well structured. A little study will show how to eliminate it. Program 6-18 contains a common *continue* example found in many textbooks. In this function, the assignment is to read data and return the average of nonzero numbers read. In other words, it skips zeros. Note how simply reversing the conditional test eliminates the need for the *continue*.

```
 1  float readAverage (void)          float readAverage (void)
 2  {                                 {
 3  /* Local Definitions */           /* Local Definitions */
 4  int count = 0;                    int count = 0;
 5
 6  int   n;                          int   n;
 7  float sum;                        float sum;
 8
 9  /* Statements */                  /* Statements */
10  while(scanf("%d",&n) != EOF)      while(scanf("%d",&n) != EOF)
11     {                                {
12     if (n == 0)                      if (n != 0)
13        continue;                        {
14     sum += n;                         sum += n;
15     count++;                          count++;
16     }  /* while */                    }  /* if */
17                                     } /* while */
18  return (sum / count);             return (sum / count);
19  } /* readAverage */               } /* readAverage */
```

Program 6-18   *continue* example

6-8   LOOPING APPLICATIONS

In this section, we examine four common applications for loops: summation, product, smallest or largest, and inquiries. Although the uses for loops are virtually endless, these problems illustrate many common applications. Note that a common design runs through all looping applications. With few exceptions, each loop contains initialization code, looping code, and disposition code. Disposition code handles the result of the loop, often by printing it, other times by simply returning it to the calling function.

SUMMATION

As you have seen, we can add two or three numbers very easily. But how can we add many numbers or a variable series of numbers? The solution is simple: Use the add operator in a loop. The concept of **summation** is graphically shown in Figure 6-23.

A sum function has three logical parts: (1) initialization of any necessary working variables, such as the sum accumulator; (2) the loop, which includes the summation code and any data validation code (for example, "only nonzero numbers are to be considered"); and (3) the disposition code to print or return the result. Program 6-19 is a loop function that reads a series of numbers from the keyboard and returns their sum. In each loop, we read the next number and add it to the accumulator, sum. A similar application, counting, is a special case of summation in which we add 1 to a counter instead of adding the number we read to an accumulator.

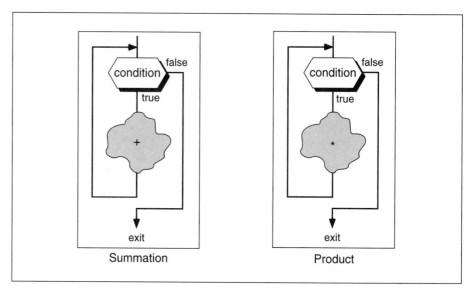

Figure 6-23   Summation and product loops

```
 1  /* Read a series of numbers, terminated by EOF, and return
 2     their sum to the calling program.
 3        Pre    nothing
 4        Post   data read from standard input and sum returned
 5  */
 6  int sumEOF (void)
 7  {
 8  /* Local Definitions */
 9     int nmbr;
10     int sum;
11
12  /* Statements */
13     sum = 0;
14     printf ("\nPlease enter an integer:    ");
15
16     while (scanf("%d", &nmbr) != EOF)
17        {
18          sum += nmbr;
19          printf("Next integer <EOF> to stop: ");
20        } /* while */
21     return sum;
22  }  /* sumEOF */
```

Program 6-19   sumEOF function

PRODUCT

Just as we can add a series of numbers in a loop, we can perform any mathematical operation. A product loop is useful for two common applications: raising a number to a power and calculating the factorial of a number. For example, Program 6-20 shows a function to return x^n. Notice that this function also includes initialization logic to validate the parameter list. If either of the parameters is invalid, we return zero as an error indicator.

```
1    /* Raise base to an integral power, exp. If the
2       exponent is zero, return 1.
3          Pre    base & exp are both positive integer values
4          Post   return either (a) the result of raising the
5                     base to the exp power
6                 or (b) zero if the parameters are invalid
7    */
8    int powers (int base ,
9                int exp)
10   {
11   /* Local Definitions */
12      int i;
13      int result;
14
15   /* Statements */
16      if (base < 1 || exp < 0)
17         /* Error Condition */
18         result = 0;
19      else
20         for  (result = 1 , i = 1; i <= exp; i++)
21               result *= base;
22
23      return result;
24   } /* powers */
```

Program 6-20 Powers function

SMALLEST AND LARGEST

You will often encounter situations in which you must determine the smallest or largest among a series of data. This is also a natural looping structure.

We can write a statement to find the smaller of two numbers. For example,

```
result = a  < b ? a : b;
```

But how can we find the smallest of several numbers? We simply put the same statement inside a loop. Each iteration then tests the current smallest to the next number. If this new number is smaller than the current smallest, we replace the smallest. In other words, we determine the smallest number by looping through a series while remembering the smallest number the loop has found. This concept is shown in Figure 6-24.

In Program 6-21, the initialization sets the initial value of smallest to INT_MAX, which is found in the limits library (<limits.h>). The loop then proceeds to read a series of numbers and tests each one against the previously stored smallest number. Since smallest starts with the maximum integer value, the first read number automatically becomes smallest. Thereafter, the result depends entirely on the data being read. The disposition simply returns the smallest value found. This function requires no data validation.

Of course, you can find the largest number by simply reversing the less than operator in the expression and making it greater than. You will also need to set the variable, renamed largest, to INT_MIN.

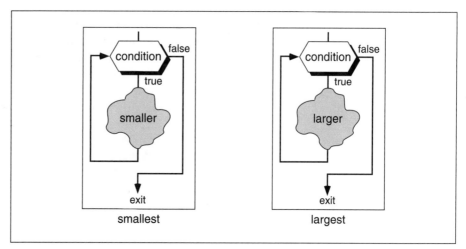

Figure 6-24   Smallest loop

```
 1  /* Read a series of numbers, terminated by EOF, and
 2     pass the smallest to the calling program.
 3          Pre    nothing
 4          Post   data read and smallest returned
 5  */
 6  int smallestEOF (void)
 7  {
 8  /* Local Definitions */
 9     int numIn;
10     int smallest;
11
12  /* Statements */
13     smallest = INT_MAX;            /* requires <limits.h> */
14
15     printf("\nPlease enter an integer: ");
16
17     while (scanf("%d", &numIn) != EOF)
18        {
19        if (numIn < smallest)
20            smallest = numIn;
21        printf("Enter next integer <EOF> to stop: ");
22        } /* while */
23     return smallest;
24  }   /* smallestEOF */
```

Program 6-21   `smallestEOF` function

INQUIRIES

An **inquiry** is simply a question asked of the computer program. In programming, we often encounter one of two basic inquiry types: **any** and **all**. We use the inquiry type *any* when we have a list of data and we want to know if *any* of them meet a given criteria. Here *any* means at least one. The answer to the inquiry is yes if one or more data meet the criteria. The answer is, of course, no if none of the data meet the criteria. We use *all* when we have a list of data and we want to make sure that *all* of them meet some specified criteria. The concept of *any* and *all* in an inquiry is shown in Figure 6-25.

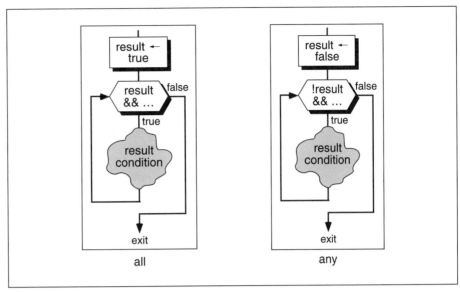

Figure 6-25 `any` and `all` inquiries

Program 6-22 is an example of an *any* inquiry. It reads a series of numbers and checks to see if any of the numbers in the list are greater than zero. The function terminates and returns TRUE as soon as a positive number is read.

```
 1   /* Read number series, and determine if any are positive.
 2      Pre    nothing
 3      Post   returns TRUE if any numbers greater than zero
 4             returns FALSE if all numbers negative or zero.
 5   */
 6   int anyPositiveEOF (void)
 7   {
 8   /* Local Definitions */
 9      int anyPositive = FALSE;
10      int numIn;
11
12   /* Statements */
13      while (!anyPositive && (scanf("%d", &numIn) != EOF))
14         {
15          anyPositive  = numIn > 0;
16         } /* while */
17      return anyPositive;
18   } /* anyPositiveEOF */
```

Program 6-22 `anyPositiveEOF` function

Program 6-22 Analysis   Note that `anyPositive` is a logical variable and is initialized to FALSE (zero). The coding in the *while* condition is also noteworthy. Since the *and* in the *while* loop stops its evaluation immediately if the first condition is false, the condition with a side effect is coded last. In this case, the *while* will stop as soon as a positive number is entered. If the *scanf* were coded first, the user would have to enter another number or EOF after the positive number before the loop stopped.

The *all* function is very similar; you just reverse the logic. For example, suppose that you want to find out if all numbers in a file are positive. In this case, you continue to read as long as all the previous numbers have been greater than zero. This function is seen in Program 6-23.

```
1   /* Read number series, and determine if all are positive.
2          Pre    nothing
3          Post   returns TRUE if all numbers greater than zero
4                 returns FALSE if any numbers zero or less.
5   */
6   int allPositiveEOF (void)
7   {
8   /* Local Definitions */
9      int allPositive = TRUE;
10     int numIn;
11
12  /* Statements */
13     while (allPositive && (scanf("%d", &numIn) != EOF))
14        {
15         allPositive =  numIn > 0;
16        } /* while */
17     return allPositive;
18  } /* allPositiveEOF */
```

Program 6-23 allPositiveEOF function

6-9 RECURSION

In general, programmers use two approaches to writing repetitive algorithms. One approach uses loops; the other uses recursion. **Recursion** is a repetitive process in which a function calls itself. Some older languages do not support recursion. One major language that does not is COBOL.

ITERATIVE DEFINITION

To study a simple example, consider the calculation of a factorial. The factorial of a number is the product of the integral values from 1 to the number. This definition is shown in Formula 1.

$$\text{factorial } (n) = \begin{bmatrix} 1 & \text{if } n = 0 \\ n * (n - 1) * (n - 2) \cdots 3 * 2 * 1 & \text{if } n > 0 \end{bmatrix}$$

Formula 1   Iterative function definition

This definition is iterative. A repetitive function is defined iteratively whenever the definition involves only the parameter(s) and not the function itself. We can calculate the value of factorial (4) using Formula 1 as follows:

```
factorial (4) = 4 * 3 * 2 * 1 = 24
```

RECURSIVE DEFINITION

A repetitive function is defined recursively whenever the function appears within the definition itself. For example, the factorial function can be defined recursively, as shown in Formula 2.

$$\text{factorial}(n) = \begin{bmatrix} 1 & \text{if } n = 0 \\ n * \text{factorial}(n - 1) & \text{if } n > 0 \end{bmatrix}$$

Formula 2   Recursive function definition

The decomposition of factorial (3), using Formula 2, is shown in Figure 6-26. Study Figure 6-26 carefully, and note that the recursive solution for a problem involves a two-way journey: First we decompose the problem from the top to the bottom, and then we solve it from the bottom to the top.

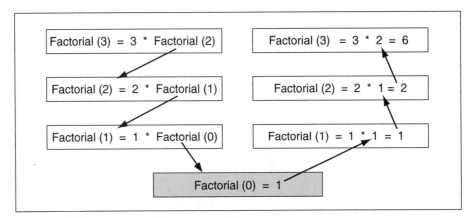

Figure 6-26   Factorial (3) recursively

Judging by the above example, the recursive calculation looks much longer and more difficult. So why would we want to use the recursive method? We use it because, although the recursive calculation looks more difficult when using paper and pencil, it is often a much easier and more elegant solution when we use computers. Additionally, it offers a conceptual simplicity to the creator and the reader.

ITERATIVE SOLUTION

Let's write a function to solve the factorial problem iteratively. This solution usually involves using a loop, as shown in Program 6-24.

```
 1  /* Calculate the factorial of a number using a loop.
 2     There is no test that the result fits in a long.
 3        Pre   n is the number to be raised factorially
 4        Post  result is returned
 5  */
 6  long factorial (int n)
 7  {
 8  /* Local Definitions */
 9     int i;
10
11     long factN;
12
```

Program 6-24   Iterative factorial function

```
13 | /* Statements */
14 |    for (i = 1, factN = 1; i <= n; i++)
15 |       factN = factN * i;
16 |
17 |    return factN;
18 | } /* factorial */
```

Program 6-24   Iterative factorial function (continued)

RECURSIVE SOLUTION

The recursive solution to factorial is shown in Program 6-25. This program does not need a loop; the concept itself involves repetition.

```
 1 | /* Calculate factorial of a number using recursion.
 2 |    There is no test that the result fits in a long.
 3 |       Pre    n is the number being raised factorially
 4 |       Post   result is returned
 5 | */
 6 | long factorial (int n)
 7 | {
 8 | /* Statements */
 9 |    if (n == 0)
10 |       return 1;
11 |    else
12 |       return (n * factorial (n - 1));
13 | } /* factorial */
```

Program 6-25   Recursive factorial

In the recursive version, we let the function `factorial` call itself, each time with a different set of parameters. Figure 6-27 shows this mechanism with the parameters for each individual call.

DESIGNING RECURSIVE FUNCTIONS

All recursive functions have two elements: Each call either solves *one* part of the problem or it *reduces* the size of the problem. In Program 6-25, Statement 10 solves a small piece of the problem—`factorial (0)` is 1. Statement 12, on the other hand, reduces the size of the problem by recursively calling the factorial with $n-1$. Once the solution to `factorial (n-1)` is known, Statement 12 provides part of the solution to the general problem by returning a value to the calling function.

As we see in Statement 12, the general part of the solution is the recursive call: Statement 12 calls its own function to solve the problem. We also see this in Figure 6-27. At each recursive call, the size of the problem is reduced from the factorial of 3, to 2, 1, and finally to factorial 0.

The statement that "solves" the problem is known as the **base case**. *Every recursive function must have a base case.* The rest of the function is known as the **general case**. In our factorial example, the base case is `factorial (0)`; the general case is n * `factorial (n-1)`. The general case contains the logic needed to reduce the size of the problem.

> Every recursive call must either solve part of the problem
> or reduce the size of the problem.

In the factorial problem, once the base case has been reached, the solution begins. The program has found one part of the answer and can return that part to the next more general

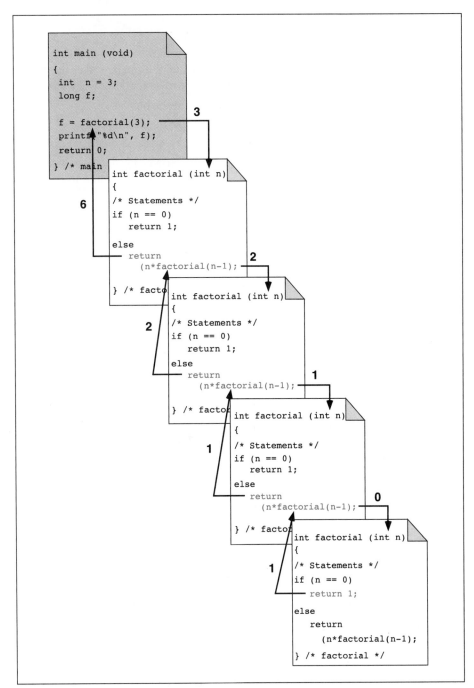

Figure 6-27   Calling a recursive function

statement. Thus, in Program 6-25, after the program has calculated that `factorial (0)` is 1, then it returns value 1. That leads to solving the next general case,

$$\text{factorial (1)} \Leftrightarrow 1 * \text{factorial (0)} \Leftrightarrow 1 * 1 \Leftrightarrow 1$$

The program now returns the value of `factorial (1)` to the more general case, `factorial (2)`, which we know to be

```
factorial (2) ⇔ 2 * factorial (1) ⇔ 2 * 1 ⇔ 2
```

As the program solves each general case in turn, the program can solve the next higher general case, until it finally solves the most general case, the original problem.

Following are the rules for designing a recursive function:

1. First determine the base case.
2. Then determine the general case.
3. Combine the base case and general case into a function.

In combining the base and general cases into a function, you must pay careful attention to the logic. Each call must reduce the size of the problem and move it toward the base case. The base case, when reached, must terminate without a call to the recursive function; that is, it must execute a *return.*

FIBONACCI NUMBERS

Another example of recursion is a function that generates Fibonacci numbers. Named after an Italian mathematician, Leonardo Fibonacci, who lived in the early thirteenth century, Fibonacci numbers are a series in which each number is the sum of the previous two numbers (Figure 6-28).

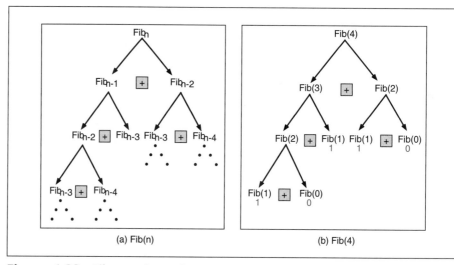

(a) Fib(n) (b) Fib(4)

Figure 6-28 Fibonacci numbers

The first few numbers in the Fibonacci series are

```
0, 1, 1, 2, 3, 5, 8, 13, 21, 34.
```

To start the series, however, we need to know the first two numbers. As you can see from the above series, they are 0 and 1. Since we are discussing recursion, you should recognize these two numbers as the base cases.

We can generalize the Fibonacci series as follows:

Given:
  $Fibonacci_0 = 0$
  $Fibonacci_1 = 1$
Then
  $Fibonacci_n = Fibonacci_{n-1} + Fibonacci_{n-2}$

The generalization of Fibonacci$_4$ is shown in Figure 6-28. Figure 6-28a shows the components of Fibonacci$_4$ using a general notation. Figure 6-28b shows the components as they would be called to generate the numbers in the series.

To determine Fibonacci$_4$, we can start at 0 and move up until we have the number, or we can start at Fibonacci$_4$ and move down to zero. The first technique is used in the iterative solution; the second is used in the recursive solution, which is shown in Program 6-26.

```
 1  /* This program prints out a Fibonacci series.
 2        Written by:
 3        Date:
 4  */
 5  #include <stdio.h>
 6
 7  /* Prototype Statements */
 8     long fib (long num);
 9
10  int main (void)
11  {
12  /* Local Definitions */
13     int looper;
14     int seriesSize;
15
16  /* Statements */
17     printf("This program prints a Fibonacci series.\n");
18     printf("How many numbers do you want? ");
19     scanf ("%d", &seriesSize);
20     if (seriesSize < 2)
21        seriesSize = 2;
22
23     printf("First %d Fibonacci numbers: \n", seriesSize);
24     for (looper = 0; looper < seriesSize; looper++)
25        {
26         if (looper % 5)
27             printf(", %8ld", fib(looper));
28         else
29             printf("\n%8ld", fib(looper));
30        }
31     printf("\n");
32     return 0;
33  }  /* main */
34
35  /* ================= fib =================
36     Calculates the nth Fibonacci number.
37         Pre    num identifies Fibonacci number
38         Post   returns nth Fibonacci number
39  */
40  long fib (long num)
```

Program 6-26 Recursive Fibonacci

```
41 | {
42 | /* Statements */
43 |    if (num == 0 || num == 1)
44 |       /* Base Case */
45 |       return num;
46 |
47 |    return (fib (num - 1) + fib (num - 2));
48 | }  /* fib */
```

```
Results:
This program prints a Fibonacci series.
How many numbers do you want? 33
First 33 Fibonacci numbers:

     0,        1,         1,        2,         3
     5,        8,        13,       21,        34
    55,       89,       144,      233,       377
   610,      987,      1597,     2584,      4181
  6765,    10946,     17711,    28657,     46368
 75025,   121393,    196418,   317811,    514229
832040,  1346269,   2178309
```

Program 6-26   Recursive Fibonacci (continued)

Program 6-26 Analysis   Compare fib in Program 6-26 with the solution in Figure 6-28. To determine the fourth number in the series, we call fib with num set to 4. To determine the answer requires that fib be called recursively eight times, as shown in Figure 6-28, which with the original call gives us a total of nine calls.

This sounds reasonable. Now, how many calls does it take to determine Fibonacci$_5$? The answer is 15 (Table 6-2). As you can see from Table 6-2, the number of calls goes up quickly as we increase the size of the Fibonacci number we are calculating.

No	Calls	Time[a]	No.	Calls	Time[a]
1	1	<1 sec.	11	287	<1 sec.
2	3	<1 sec.	12	465	<1 sec.
3	5	<1 sec.	13	753	<1 sec.
4	9	<1 sec.	14	1,219	<1 sec.
5	15	<1 sec.	15	1,973	<1 sec.
6	25	<1 sec.	20	21,891	<1 sec.
7	41	<1 sec.	25	242,785	1 sec.
8	67	<1 sec.	30	2,692,573	7 sec.
9	109	<1 sec.	35	29,860,703	1 min.
10	177	<1 sec.	40	331,160,281	13 min.

[a.] Run on a Power Macintosh 7100/66 with 32 megabytes of memory.

Table 6-2   Fibonacci run time

Table 6-2 leads us to the obvious conclusion that a recursive solution to calculate Fibonacci numbers is not realistic for more than 20 numbers.

LIMITATIONS OF RECURSION

We have introduced only the briefest explanation of recursion in this section. We have not attempted to demonstrate *how* recursion works. To understand how it works, you will need to study data structures and concepts that are beyond the scope of this text.

On the other hand, you do need to understand the two major limitations of recursion. First, recursive solutions may involve extensive overhead because they use function calls. Second, each time you make a call, you use up some of your memory allocation. If the recursion is deep—that is, if the program has a large number of recursive calls—then you may run out of memory. Both the factorial and Fibonacci numbers solutions are better developed iteratively.

Does this mean that iterative solutions are always better than recursive functions? The answer is definitely no. Many algorithms are easier to implement recursively and are efficient. When you study data structures, you will study many of them. Unfortunately, most of those algorithms require data structures beyond the scope of this text.

THE TOWERS OF HANOI

One classic recursion problem, the Towers of Hanoi, is relatively easy to follow, is efficient, and uses no complex data structures. Let's look at it.

According to legend, the monks in a remote mountain monastery knew how to predict when the world would end. They had a set of three diamond needles. Stacked on the first diamond needle were 64 gold disks of decreasing size. The monks moved one disk to another needle each hour, subject to the following rules:

1. Only one disk could be moved at a time.
2. A larger disk must never be stacked above a smaller one.
3. One and only one auxiliary needle could be used for the intermediate storage of disks.

The legend said that when all 64 disks had been transferred to the destination needle, the stars would be extinguished and the world would end. Today we know that we need to have $2^{64} - 1$ moves to do this task. Figure 6-29 shows the Towers of Hanoi with only three disks.

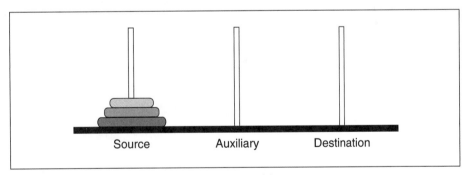

Figure 6-29   Towers of Hanoi—start position

This problem is interesting for two reasons. First, the recursive solution is much easier to code than the iterative solution would be. This is often the case with good recursive solutions. Second, its solution pattern differs from the simple examples we have been discussing. As you study the Towers solution, note that after each base case, we return to a decomposition of the general case for several steps. In other words, the problem is divided into several subproblems, each of which has a base case, moving one disk.

RECURSIVE SOLUTION OF THE TOWERS OF HANOI

To solve this problem, we must study the moves to see if we can find a pattern. We will use only three disks because we do not want the world to end! First, imagine that we have only one disk to move. This is a very simple case as shown on the next page.

> Case 1: Move one disk from source to destination needle.

Now imagine that we have to move two disks. Figure 6-30 traces the steps for two disks. First, the top disk is moved to the auxiliary needle. Then the second disk is moved to the destination. Finally, the first disk is moved to the top of the second disk on the destination. This gives us

> Case 2:   Move one disk to auxiliary needle.
>   Move one disk to destination needle.
>   Move one disk from auxiliary to destination needle.

This gives us

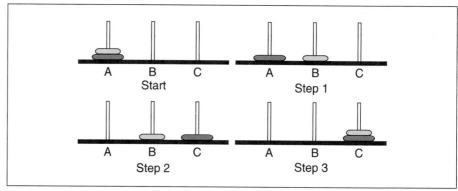

Figure 6-30   Towers solution for two disks

We are now ready to study the case for three disks. Its solution is seen in Figure 6-31. The first three steps move the top two disks from the source to the auxiliary needle. (To see how to do this, refer to Case 2.) In Step 4, we move the bottom disk to the destination. We now have one disk in place. This is an example of Case 1. It then takes three more steps to move the two disks on the auxiliary needle to the destination. These steps are summarized below.

> Case 3:   Move two disks from source to auxiliary needle.
>   Move one disk from source to destination needle.
>   Move two disks from auxiliary to destination needle.

We are now ready to generalize the problem.

> 1. Move $n - 1$ disks from source to auxiliary needle.   **General Case**
> 2. Move one disk from source to destination needle.   **Base Case**
> 3. Move $n - 1$ disks from auxiliary to destination needle.   **General Case**

Our solution will require a function with four parameters: the number of disks to be moved, the source needle, the destination needle, and the auxiliary needle. Using pseudocode, the three moves in the generalization shown above are then

```
1  Call Towers (n - 1, source, auxiliary, destination)
2  Move one disk from source to destination
3  Call Towers (n - 1, auxiliary, destination, source)
```

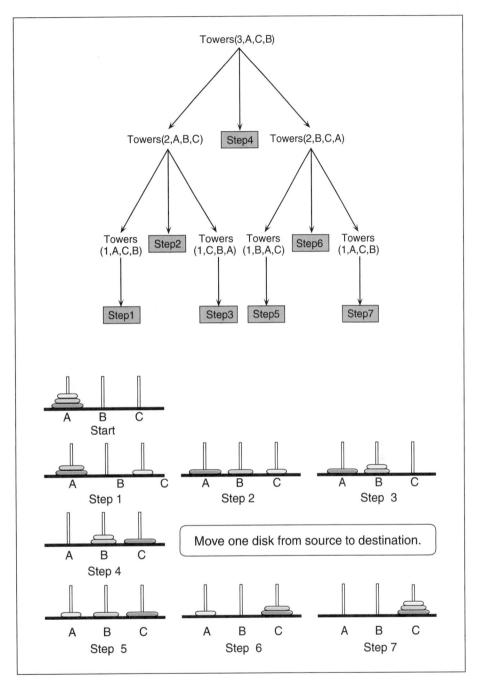

Figure 6-31 Towers solution for three disks

Study the third step carefully. After we complete the move of the first disk, the remaining disks are on the auxiliary needle. We need to move them from the auxiliary needle to the destination. In this case, the original source needle becomes the auxiliary needle. Remember that the positions of the parameters in the *called* function are source, destination, auxiliary. The calling function must remember which of the three needles is the source and which is the destination for each call.

We can now put these three calls together with the appropriate print statements to show the moves. The complete function is shown in Program 6-27. The output from the program is shown in Figure 6-32.

```
1    /* Move one disk from source to destination through
2       the use of recursion.
3          Pre    The tower consists of n disks--source,
4                 destination, & auxiliary towers given
5          Post   Steps for moves printed
6    */
7    void towers (int    n,
8                 char   source,
9                 char   dest,
10                char   auxiliary)
11   {
12   /* Local Definitions */
13      static int step = 0;
14
15   /* Statements */
16      printf("Towers (%d, %c, %c, %c)\n",
17                      n, source, dest, auxiliary);
18      if (n == 1)
19         printf("\t\t\t\tStep %3d: Move from %c to %c\n",
20                 ++step, source, dest);
21      else
22         {
23           towers (n - 1, source, auxiliary, dest);
24           printf("\t\t\t\tStep %3d: Move from %c to %c\n",
25                   ++step, source, dest);
26           towers (n - 1, auxiliary, dest, source);
27         } /* if ... else */
28      return;
29   }  /* towers */
```

Program 6-27   Towers of Hanoi

Calls:	Output:
Towers (3, A, C, B)	
Towers (2, A, B, C)	
Towers (1, A, C, B)	
	Step 1: Move from A to C
	Step 2: Move from A to B
Towers (1, C, B, A)	
	Step 3: Move from C to B
	Step 4: Move from A to C
Towers (2, B, C, A)	
Towers (1, B, A, C)	
	Step 5: Move from B to A
	Step 6: Move from B to C
Towers (1, A, C, B)	
	Step 7: Move from A to C

Figure 6-32   Tracing of Program 6-27, Towers of Hanoi

6-10   PROGRAMMING EXAMPLE—THE CALCULATOR PROGRAM

Let's look at our calculator program one more time. In Chapter 5, we gave the user the capability of selecting one of four options: add, subtract, multiply, or divide. However, if users needed to make two calculations, they had to run the program twice. We now add a loop that allows the users to make as many calculations as needed (Program 6-28). We include only two functions, main and getOption, at this point, since all of the others are the same.

```c
 1  /* This program adds, subtracts, multiplies, and divides
 2     two integers.
 3        Written by:
 4        Date:
 5  */
 6  #include <stdio.h>
 7
 8  /* Prototype Definitions */
 9  int    getOption (void);
10
11  float add2  (float num1, float num2);
12  float sub2  (float num1, float num2);
13  float mul2  (float num1, float num2);
14  float div2  (float num1, float num2);
15
16  void  printResult (float num1,   float num2,
17                        float result, int option);
18
19  int main (void)
20  {
21  /* Local Definitions */
22     int    done = 0;
23     int    option;
24     float  num1;
25     float  num2;
26     float  result;
27
28  /* Statements */
29     while (!done)
30       {
31       option = getOption();
32       if (option == 5)
33          done = 1;
34       else
35         {
36         do
37           {
38             printf("\n\nEnter two numbers: ");
39             scanf("%f %f", &num1, &num2);
40             if (option == 4 && num2 == 0)
```

Program 6-28   The complete calculator

```
41                        {
42                          printf("\a\n *** Error *** ");
43                          printf("Second number cannot be 0\n");
44                        } /* if */
45                    } while (option == 4 && num2 == 0);
46
47              switch (option)
48                {
49                  case 1: result = add2 (num1, num2);
50                          break;
51                  case 2: result = sub2 (num1, num2);
52                          break;
53                  case 3: result = mul2 (num1, num2);
54                          break;
55                  case 4: result = div2 (num1, num2);
56                } /* switch */
57
58              printResult (num1, num2, result, option);
59            } /* else option != 5 */
60          } /* while */
61     printf("\nThank you for using Calculator.\n");
62
63     return 0;
64 } /* main */
65
66 /* ==================== getOption ====================
67    This function shows a menu and reads the user option.
68       Pre    nothing
69       Post   returns a valid option
70 */
71 int getOption (void)
72 {
73 /* Local Definitions */
74    int option;
75
76 /* Statements */
77    do
78      {
79      printf("\n*******************");
80      printf("\n*      MENU       *");
81      printf("\n*                 *");
82      printf("\n*  1. ADD         *");
83      printf("\n*  2. SUBTRACT    *");
84      printf("\n*  3. MULTIPLY    *");
85      printf("\n*  4. DIVIDE      *");
86      printf("\n*  5. QUIT        *");
87      printf("\n*                 *");
88      printf("\n*******************");
89
```

Program 6-28 The complete calculator (continued)

```
90      printf("\n\n\nPlease type your choice ");
91      printf("and press the return key : ");
92      scanf("%d", &option);
93
94      if (option < 1 || option > 5)
95          printf("\nInvalid option. Please re-enter.\n");
96
97      } while (option < 1 || option > 5);
98
99      return option;
100 }   /* getOption */
```

Program 6-28   The complete calculator (continued)

Program 6-28 Analysis   As you look at the changes in this version of our program, first note the two loops in `main`. The first loop continues the calculator until the user says it's time to quit. The second loop gets and validates the numbers, making sure that the user isn't trying to divide by zero. (Your computer will get very upset if you divide by zero and will stop!)

We also modified our `getOption` function to add the quit option and to validate the options. If the user makes a mistake, we correct it in `getOption`. Extending the concept to a general principle, whenever you write a function to get data from a user, the function should handle all data validation. This makes for much simpler code in the rest of the program.

This simplification is also seen in the *switch* statement. Since we have validated the numbers before the *switch,* we no longer need to test for a valid divisor in the fourth *case* option. We also no longer need a *default,* since we know the options are valid. The result is a simpler statement, much more in line with the KISS principle.

**LOOPS IN
STRUCTURE
CHARTS**

Now that you understand how to write loops, let's look at how they are shown in a structure chart. The symbols are very simple. Loops go in circles, so the symbol we use is a circle. Programmers use two basic looping symbols. The first is a simple loop. It is represented by Figure 6-33a. The other is the conditional loop, shown in Figure 6-33b.

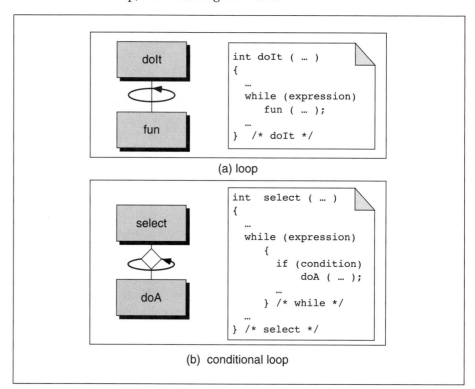

(a) loop

(b) conditional loop

Figure 6-33   Structure chart symbols for loops

When the function is called unconditionally, as in a *while* loop, the circle flows around the line above the called function. On the other hand, if the call is conditional, as in a function called in an *if...else* statement inside a loop, then the circle includes a decision diamond on the line.

Figure 6-34 shows the basic structure for a function called `process`. The circle is *below* the function that controls the loop. In this example, the looping statement is contained in `process`, and it calls three functions, A, B, and C. The exact nature of the loop cannot be determined from the structure chart. It could be any of the three basic looping constructs. To help you better visualize the process, however, let's further assume that the loop is a *while* loop that contains a *scanf* that reads until the end of file. Within the *while* loop are three calls: the first to A, the second to B, and the third, conditionally, to C.

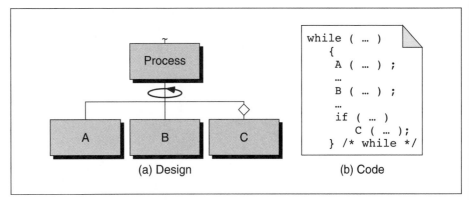

Figure 6-34 Structure chart for `process`

DETERMINING ALGORITHM EFFICIENCY

There is seldom a single algorithm for any problem. When comparing two different algorithms that solve the same problem, you will often find that one algorithm will be an order of magnitude more efficient than the other. In this case, it only makes sense that programmers have some way to recognize and choose the more efficient algorithm.

Although computer scientists have studied algorithms and algorithm efficiency extensively, the field has not been given an official name. Brassard and Bratley coined the term *algorithmics*, which they define as "the systematic study of the fundamental techniques used to design and analyse efficient algorithms."[2] We will use this term.

If a function is linear—that is, if it contains no loops—then its efficiency is a function of the number of instructions it contains. In this case, its efficiency depends on the speed of the computer and is generally not a factor in the overall efficiency in a program. On the other hand, functions that loop will vary widely in their efficiency. The study of algorithm efficiency is therefore largely devoted to the study of loops.

As we study specific examples, we will develop a formula that describes the algorithm's efficiency. We will then generalize the algorithm so that the efficiency can be stated as a function of the number of elements to be processed. The general format is

$$f(n) = \text{efficiency}$$

LINEAR LOOPS

Let's start with a simple loop. We want to know how many times the body of the loop is repeated in the following code:

```
for (i= 1; i <= 1000; i ++)
   {
   BODY;
   } /* for */
```

---

[2]Gilles Brassard and Paul Bratley, *Algorithmics Theory and Practice*, p. xiii. (Upper Saddle River, NJ: Prentice Hall, 1988).

Assuming *i* is an integer, the answer is 1000 times. But the answer is not always straightforward as it is in the above example. For example, consider the following loop. How many times is the body repeated in this loop? Here the answer is 500 times. Why?

```
for (i = 1; i <= 1000; i += 2;)
   {
    BODY;
   } /* for */
```

In both cases, however, the number of iterations is directly proportionate to a factor. The higher the factor, the higher the number of loops. If you were to plot either of these loops, you would get a straight line. Thus, they are known as linear loops.

Since the efficiency is proportionate to the number of iterations, it is

$$f(n) = n$$

LOGARITHMIC LOOPS

Now consider a loop in which the controlling variable is multiplied or divided in each loop. How many times will the body of the loops be repeated in the following program segments?

```
    Multiply Loops                Divide Loops
i  =  1;                      i = 1000;
while (i < 1000)              while (i >= 1)
    {                            {
     BODY;                        BODY;
     i *= 2;                      i /= 2;
    } /* while */                } /* while */
```

To help you understand this problem, Table 6-3 analyzes the values of *i* for each iteration.

Multiply		Divide	
Iteration	*i*	Iteration	*i*
1	1	1	1000
2	2	2	500
3	4	3	250
4	8	4	125
5	16	5	62
6	32	6	31
7	64	7	15
8	128	8	7
9	256	9	3
10	512	10	1
(exit)	1024	(exit)	0

Table 6-3   Analysis of multiply/divide loops

As you can see, the number of iterations is 10 in both cases. The reason is that in each iteration the value of *i* doubles for the multiplication and is cut in half for the division. Thus, the number of iterations is a function of the multiplier or divisor; in this case, two. That is, the loop continues while the condition shown below is true.

multiply $2^{\text{Iterations}}$ $<\ \ 1000$

divide $1000\ /\ 2^{\text{Iterations}}$ $>=\ \ \ \ 1$

Generalizing the analysis, we can say that the iterations in loops that multiply or divide are determined by the following formula:

$$f(n) = ceil\ (\log_2 n)$$

NESTED LOOPS

When we analyze loops that contain loops, we must determine how many iterations each loop completes. The total is then the product of the number of iterations for the inner loop and the number of iterations in the outer loop.

Iterations = outer loop iterations ∗ inner loop iterations

We now look at three nested loops: linear logarithmic, dependent quadratic, and quadratic.

Linear Logarithmic

The inner loop in the following code is a loop that multiplies. (To see the multiplication, look at the update expression in the inner *for* statement.)

```
for (i = 1; i < = 10; i ++)
   for (j = 1; j <= 10; j *= 2)
      {
        BODY;
      }
```

The number of iterations in the inner loop is therefore

$$ceil\ (\log_2 10)$$

However, since the inner loop is controlled by an outer loop, the above formula must be multiplied by the number of times the outer loop executes, which is 10. This gives us

$$10\ (ceil(\log_2 10))$$

which is generalized as

$$f(n) = n\ (ceil\ (\log_2 n))$$

Dependent Quadratic

Now consider the nested loop shown at the top of page 286.

```
for (i = 1; i < = 10; i ++)
  for (j = 1; j <= i; j ++)
    {
       BODY;
    } /* for j */
```

The outer loop is the same as the previous loop. However, the inner loop is executed only once in the first iteration, twice in the second iteration, three times in the third iteration, and so forth. The number of iterations in the body of the inner loop is mathematically stated as

$$1 + 2 + 3 + \ldots + 9 + 10 = 55$$

which is generalized to

$$f(n) \; = \; n\frac{n+1}{2}$$

Quadratic

In the final nested loop, each loop executes the same number of times, as seen below.

```
for (i = 1; i <= 10; i ++)
  for (j = 1; j <= 10; j ++)
    {
       BODY;
    } /* for j */
```

The outer loop—that is, the loop at the first *for* statement—is executed ten times. For each iteration, the inner loop is also executed ten times. The answer, therefore, is 100, which is 10 * 10, the square of the loops. This formula generalizes to

$$f(n) = n^2$$

BIG-O NOTATION

With the speed of computers today, we are not concerned with an exact measurement of an algorithm's efficiency as much as we are with its general magnitude. If the analysis of two algorithms shows that one executes 15 iterations while the other executes 25 iterations, they are both so fast that we can't see the difference. On the other hand, if one iterates 15 times and the other 1500 times, we should be concerned.

We have shown that the number of statements executed in the function for *n* elements of data is a function of the number of elements, expressed as *f(n)*. While the equation derived for a function may be complex, usually, a dominant factor in the equation determines the order of magnitude of the result. Therefore, we don't need to determine the complete measure of efficiency, only the factor that determines the magnitude. This factor is the big-O, as in On-the-Order-Of, and expressed as $O(n)$—that is, on-the-order-of *n*.

This simplification of efficiency is known as **big-O analysis**. For example, if an algorithm is quadratic, we would say its efficiency is

$$O(n^2)$$

or on-the-order of *n*-squared.

The big-O notation can be derived from *f(n)* using the following steps:

1. In each term, set the coefficient of the term to 1.
2. Keep the largest term in the function, and discard the others. Terms are ranked from lowest to highest, as shown below.

$$\log_2 n \qquad n \qquad n \log_2 n \qquad n^2 \qquad n^3 \qquad n^k \qquad 2^n \qquad n!$$

For example, to calculate the big-O notation for

$$f(n) = n\frac{(n+1)}{2} = \frac{1}{2}n^2 + \frac{1}{2}n$$

we first remove all coefficients. This gives us

$$n^2 + n$$

which after removing the smaller factors gives us

$$n^2$$

which in Big-O notation is stated as

$$O(f(n)) = O(n^2)$$

To consider another example, let's look at the polynomial expression

$$f(n) = a_j n^k + a_{j-1} n^{k-1} + \cdots + a_2 n^2 + a_1 n^1 + a_0$$

We first eliminate all of the coefficients, as shown below.

$$f(n) = n^k + n^{k-1} + \cdots + n^2 + n + 1$$

The largest term in this expression is the first one, so we can say that the order of a polynomial expression is

$$O(f(n)) = O(n^k)$$

STANDARD MEASURES OF EFFICIENCY

Computer scientists have defined seven categories of algorithm efficiency. We list them in Table 6-4 in order of decreasing efficiency. Any measure of efficiency presumes that a sufficiently large sample is being considered. If you are only dealing with ten elements and the time required is a fraction of a second, there will be no meaningful difference between two algorithms. On the other hand, as the number of elements processed grows, the difference between algorithms can be staggering. In Table 6-4, *n* is 10,000.

Returning to the question of why we should be concerned about efficiency, consider the situation in which you can solve a problem in three ways: One is linear, another is linear-logarithmic, and the third is quadratic. The order of their efficiency for a problem containing 10,000 elements is shown in Table 6-4, along with the other algorithmics.

Efficiency	Big-O	Iterations	Est. Time[a]
logarithmic	$O(\log_2 n)$	14	microseconds
linear	$O(n)$	10,000	.1 second
linear logarithmic	$O(n(\log_2 n))$	140,000	2 seconds
quadratic	$O(n^2)$	$10{,}000^2$	15–20 min.
polynomial	$O(n^k)$	$10{,}000^k$	hours
exponential	$O(c^n)$	$2^{10{,}000}$	intractable
factorial	$O(n!)$	10,000!	intractable

[a]. Assumes instruction speed of 1 microsecond and 10 instructions in loop.

Table 6-4   **Measures of efficiency**

Looking at the problem from the other end, if we use a computer that executes a million instructions per second and the loop contains ten instructions, then we spend .00001 second for each iteration of the loop. Table 6-4 also contains an estimate of the time to solve the problem given different efficiencies.

6-12   TIPS AND COMMON PROGRAMMING ERRORS

1. Be aware that the *while* and *for* loops are pretest loops. Their body may never be executed. If you want your loop to be executed at least once, use a *do...while*.

2. Do not use equality and inequality for the control expression in loops; use limits that include less than or greater than. You may accidentally create an infinite loop, as shown below.

```
...
i = 0;
while (i != 13)
    {
    ...
    i++;        /* sets i to 1, 3, 5, …, 13 */
    ...
    i++;        /* sets i to 2, 4, 6, …, 14 */
    ...
    }   /* while */
```

3. It is a compile error to omit the semicolon after the expression in the *do...while* statement.

4. It is most likely a logic error to place a semicolon after the expression in a *while* or *for* statement.

5. It is a compile error to code a *for* statement with commas rather than semicolons, as shown below.

```
for (i = 0, i < 10, i++)
```

6. It is a logic error to omit the update statement in the body of a *while* or *do...while* loop. Without an update statement, the loop will never terminate.

7. It is a common logic error to miscode the limit test in *for* statements. The result is usually a loop that executes one extra time or terminates one iteration short. For example, the following statement executes nine times, not ten:

```
for ( i = 1; i < 10; i++ )
```

8. It is generally a logic error to update the terminating variable in both the *for* statement and in the body of the loop, as shown below.

```
for (i = 0; i < 10; i++)
    {
    ...
    i += 1;
    } /* for */
```

9. A recursive function must have a base case. Therefore, it is most likely an error if a recursive function does not have an *if* statement that prevents the recursive call and allows the function to return. For example, the following code—based on Program 6-26, on page 273—would never terminate.

```
long fib (long num)
{
/* Statements */
    return (fib (num - 1) + fib (num - 2));
}  /* fib */
```

6-13 KEY TERMS AND CONCEPTS[3]

base case	event-controlled loop	limit-test expression
big-O analysis	flag	loop control expression
body of loop	*for*	loop update
break	general case	post-test loop
comma expression	infinite loop	pretest loop
comma operator	initialization	process-control loops
continue	inquiry	recursion
counter-controlled loop	inquiry all	summation
do...while	inquiry any	*while*
EOF	iteration	

---

[3]Note: Italic terms are C keywords or standard library functions.

6-14 SUMMARY

- The real power of computers is in their ability to repeat an operation or a series of operations many times.

- To control the loop, we need a condition to determine if more processing is needed.

- In a pretest loop, in each iteration, we check the condition first. If it is true, we iterate once more; otherwise, we exit the loop.

- In a post-test loop, in each iteration, we do the processing. Then we check the condition. If it is true, we start a new iteration; otherwise, we exit the loop.

- In a pretest loop, the processing is done zero or more times.

- In a post-test loop, the processing is done one or more times.

- In a pretest loop, if the body is executed n times, the limit test is executed $n + 1$ times.

- In a post-test loop, if the body is executed n times, the limit test is executed n times.

- The control expression in a loop must be explicitly or implicitly initialized.

- If you know exactly the number of times the body must be repeated, use a counter-controlled loop; if an event must occur to terminate a loop, use an event-controlled loop.

- C has three loop statements: *while, for,* and *do...while*.

- The *while* loop is a pretest loop. It can be used for a counter-controlled or event-controlled loop, but it is usually used only for event control.

- The *for* loop is a pretest loop. It can be used for both counter-controlled and event-controlled loops, but it is used mostly in the first case.

- The *do...while* loop is post-test loop. It is usually used when the body must be executed at least once.

- We discussed two C statements that are related to looping, *break* and *continue*. They are collectively categorized as jump statements (together with the *return* and `goto` statements).

- The *break* statement is used to terminate a loop prematurely. We strongly recommend that you use the *break* statement only within *switch* statements.

- The *continue* statement is used to skip the rest of the statements in a loop and start a new iteration without terminating the loop. We strongly recommend that you never use the *continue* statement.

- A loop in a structure chart is indicated by a circle on the line connecting it to the called functions. Only loops that call other functions are shown.

- To choose one of the three types of loops in C for a specific problem, use the following strategy:

    1. Check to see if you need a pretest or a post-test loop.

    2. If you need a post-test loop, you can use only one loop, *do...while*.

    3. If you need a pretest loop, you can use either a *for* loop or a *while* loop. Although both can be used for counter-controlled and event-controlled loops, a *for* loop is preferred for a counter-controlled loop and a *while* loop for an event-controlled loop.

- The best loop for data validation is the *do....while* loop.

- Recursion is a repetitive process in which a function calls itself.

- The statement that solves a recursive problem is known as the base case; the rest of the function is known as the general case.

6-15 PRACTICE SETS

REVIEW QUESTIONS

1. In a pretest loop, the limit test condition is tested first.
   a. True   b. False

2. The action that causes the loop limit test to change from true to false is the loop update.
   a. True   b. False

3. The value of a comma expression is the value of the first expression.
   a. True   b. False

4. Recursion is a repetitive process in which a function calls itself.
   a. True   b. False

5. Which of the following statements about pretest loops is true?

   a. If a pretest loop limit test is false, the loop executes one more time.

   b. Pretest loop initialization is done first in the loop body.

   c. Pretest loops execute a minimum of one time.

   d. Pretest loops test the limit condition after each execution of the loop body.

   e. The update for a pretest loop must be a part of the loop body.

6. Which of the following statements about loop initialization is false?

   a. Explicit initialization includes code to set the initial values of loop variables.

   b. Implicit initialization relies on preexisting values for loop variables.

   c. Initialization code is explicitly required in all loops.

   d. Initialization is preparation required for proper execution of a loop.

   e. Initialization must be done before the first execution of the loop.

7. Which of the following statements about loop updates is false?

   a. A loop update changes key variable(s) in a loop, thus allowing the loop to terminate.

   b. Loop updates may be made before or after a loop iteration.

   c. Loops may use explicit or implicit updates.

   d. In a *for* loop, updates are generally found in the *for* statement itself.

   e. The number of updates always equals the number of loop iterations.

8. Which of the following statements about counter-controlled loops is false?

   a. Counter-controlled loops are generally pretest loops.

   b. Counter-controlled loops generally increment or decrement a counter.

   c. Counter-controlled loops require a limit test.

   d. The number of times a loop iterates must be a constant.

   e. The update in a counter-controlled loop is generally explicit.

9. Which of the C loops is a pretest loop?

   a. *do...while*   d. both the *do...while* and the *for*

   b. *for*   e. both the *for* and the *while*

   c. *while*

10. Which of the following statements about the *while* statement is true?

    a. Multiple statements are allowed in a *while* loop.

    b. The limit test in a *while* loop is made before each iteration.

    c. The update in a *while* statement is contained in the *while* statement expression itself.

    d. The *while* statement is a post-test loop.

    e. The *while* statement must be terminated with a semicolon.

11. Which of the following statements about *for* and *while* statements is false?

    a. Both statements allow only one statement in the loop.

    b. Both statements are pretest loops.

    c. Both statements can be used for counter-controlled loops.

    d. Both statements include initialization within the statement.

    e. Both statements require an update statement.

12. Which of the following statements about the *do...while* loop is false?

    a. A *do...while* loop executes one or more iterations.

    b. Any statement may be used as the action in a *do...while*.

    c. The *do...while* is best suited for use as an event-controlled loop.

    d. The *do...while* is the only loop that requires a semicolon.

    e. The limit test in a *do...while* loop is executed at the beginning of each iteration.

13. The _____ is not a jump statement.

    a. *break*   c. *continue*   e. *return*

    b. *case*   d. *goto*

14. Nested loops have a _____ standard measure of efficiency.

    a. exponential

    b. linear

    c. linear logarithmic

    d. quadratic

    e. may be linear logarithmic or quadratic

15. The _____ standard measure of efficiency is considered the most efficient.

    a. exponential   c. logarithmic   e. polynomial

    b. linear   d. quadratic

EXERCISES

16. What would be printed from each of the following program segments? Compare and contrast your answers to parts a, b, and c.

    a.
    ```
    x = 12;
    while (x > 7)
         printf("%d\n", x);
    ```
    b.
    ```
    for ( x = 12; x > 7; )
         printf("%d\n", x);
    ```
    c.
    ```
    x = 12 ;
    do
         printf("%d\n", x);
    while (x > 7);
    ```

17. What would be printed from each of the following program segments? Compare and contrast your answers to parts a, b, and c.

    a.
    ```
    x = 12;
    while (x > 7)
         {
           printf("%d\n", x);
           x--;
         }
    ```
    b.
    ```
    for ( x = 12; x > 7; x--)
         printf(" %d\n", x);
    ```
    c.
    ```
    x = 12;
    do
         {
           printf( "%d\n", x);
           x--;
         } while (x > 7);
    ```

18. What would be printed from each of the following program segments? Compare and contrast your answers to parts a and b.

    a.
    ```
    x = 12;
    while (x > 7)
         {
           printf("%d\n", x);
           x -= 2;
         }
    ```
    b.
    ```
    for ( x = 12; x > 7; x -= 2)
         printf ("%d\n", x);
    ```

19. What would be printed from each of the following program segments? Compare and contrast your answers to parts a, b, and c.

    a.
    ```
    x = 12;
    while (x < 7)
         {
           printf("%d\n", x);
           x--;
         } /* while */
    ```
    b.
    ```
    for (x = 12; x < 7; x--)
         printf("%d\n", x);
    ```
    c.
    ```
    x = 12;
    do
         {
           printf( "%d\n", x);
           x--;
         }
    while (x < 7);
    ```

20. Change the following *while* loops to *for* loops.

    a.
    ```
    x = 0;
    while (x < 10)
         {
           printf("%d\n", x);
           x++;
         }
    ```
    b.
    ```
    scanf("%d", &x);
    while (x != 9999)
         {
           printf("%d\n", x);
           scanf("%d", &x);
         }
    ```

21. Change the *while* loops in Exercise 20 to *do-while* loops.

22. Change the following *for* loops to *while* loops:

    a.
    ```
    for (x = 1; x < 100; x++)
         printf("%d\n", x);
    ```
    b.
    ```
    for ( ; scanf("%d", &x) != EOF;)
         printf("%d\n", x);
    ```

23. Change the *for* loops in Exercise 22 to *do-while* loops.

24. Change the following *do-while* loops to *while* loops.

a.
```
x = 0;
do
    {
      printf("%d\n", x);
      x++;
    } while (x < 100);
```

b.
```
do
    {
      res = scanf("%d", &x);
    } while (res != EOF);
```

25. Change the *do-while* loops in Exercise 24 to *for* loops.

26. A programmer writes the following *for* loop to print the numbers 1 to 10. What is the output? If the output is incorrect, how would you correct it?
```
for (num = 0; num < 10; num++)
    printf("%d", num);
```

27. Another programmer writes the following for loop to print the numbers 1 to 10. What is the output? If the output is incorrect, how would you correct it?
```
for (num = 0; num < 10; num++)
    {
      numOut = num + 1;
      printf("%d", numOut);
    } /* for */
```

28. What will be printed from the following program segments?

a.
```
for (x = 1; x <= 20; x++)
    printf( "%d\n", x);
```

b.
```
for (x = 1; x <= 20; x++)
    {
      printf("%d\n", x);
      x++;
    }
```

29. What will be printed from the following program segments?

a.
```
for (x = 20; x >= 10 ; x--)
    printf("%d\n", x);
```

b.
```
for (x = 20; x >= 1; x--)
    {
      printf("%d\n", x);
      x--;
    }
```

30. What will be printed from the following program segments?

a.
```
for (x = 1; x <= 20; x++)
    {
      for (y = 1; y <= 5; y++)
        printf("%d", x);
      printf( "\n");
    }
```

b.
```
for (x = 20; x >= 1; x--)
    {
      for (y = x; y >= 1; y--)
        printf("%3d", x);
      printf("\n");
    }
```

31. What will be printed from the following program segments?

a.
```
for (x = 1; x <= 20; x++)
    {
      for (y = 1; y < x; y++)
        printf(" ");
      printf("%d\n", x);
    }
```

b.
```
for ( x = 20; x >= 1; x--)
    {
      for (y = x; y >=1 ; y--)
        printf (" ");
      printf ("%d\n", x);
    }
```

32. You find the statement shown below in a program you are maintaining.
```
for ( ; ; )
    {
      ...
    }
```

a. Describe the implications behind the null expressions in the *for* statement.

b. Since there is no limit condition, how can this statement be exited?

c. Is this good structured programming style? Explain your answer.

PROBLEMS

33. Write a program that uses a *for* loop to print a line of 60 asterisks.

34. Write a *for* loop that will produce each of following sequences:

    a. 6, 8, 10, 12, …, 66

    b. 7, 9, 11, 13, …, 67

    c. The sum of the numbers between 1 and 15 inclusive

    d. The sum of the odd numbers between 15 and 45 inclusive

    e. The first 50 numbers in the series 1, 4, 7, 10, … (calculate the total 1 + 4 + 7 + 10 + …)

35. Write a program that prompts the user to enter an integer, n, and then n floating-point numbers. As the numbers are read, the program will calculate the average of the positive numbers.

36. Rewrite Problem 35 to average the negative numbers.

37. Write a program that asks the user to enter a list of integers. The program is to determine the largest value entered and the number of times it was entered. For example, if the following series is entered

            5 2 15 3 7 15 8 9 5 2 15 3 7

    it would output the largest value is 15 and it was entered 3 times.

38. Write a program that creates the following pattern:

    ```
    1 2 3 4 5 6 7 8 9
    1 2 3 4 5 6 7 8
    1 2 3 4 5 6 7
    1 2 3 4 5 6
    1 2 3 4 5
    1 2 3 4
    1 2 3
    1 2
    1
    ```

39. Write a function that creates the following pattern, given the height (number of rows) and the width (asterisks per row):

    ```
    ************
    ************
    ************
    ************
    ************
    ```

40. Write a function that creates the following pattern, given the height (number of rows) and the width (print characters per line):

    ```
    ============
    *          *
    *          *
    *          *
    *          *
    *          *
    ============
    ```

41. Write a function that creates the following pattern, given the height (number of rows):

    ```
    *
    ***
    *****
    *******
    *********
    **********
    ```

42. Write a function that creates the following pattern, given the height (number of rows):

```
**********
********
*******
*****
***
*
```

43. Write a function that creates the following pattern, given the height (number of rows):

```
*
***
*****
*******
********
********
*******
*****
***
*
```

44. Modify Program 6-3 on page 239 to display the total as each number is entered. The format should be

```
Enter your numbers: <EOF> to stop.
5
Total:   5
17
Total: 22
8
Total: 30
```

45. Write a program that reads integer data from the standard input unit and prints a list of the numbers followed by the minimum integer read, maximum integer read, and the average of the list. Test your program with the data shown below.

```
{24 7 31 -5 64 0 57 -23 7 63 31 15 7 -3 2 4 6}
```

46. In "The *do...while* Loop," on page 244, we demonstrated the use of a *do...while* to validate input. The code fragment contains no message to tell the user that an invalid number has been entered. Write a function that reads only positive even numbers from the keyboard. If a negative or odd number is entered, it should print an error message and ask the user to enter another number. Each call to the function is to read only one number. The valid number read is to be returned to the calling program. If the user enters EOF, the function should return it. Then write a short program to test the function using the data shown below. The valid numbers should be printed, either in a separate function or in `main`.

```
{2 18 -18 5 7 100 1 -1}
```

47. Write a function that reads integers from the keyboard. If any of the numbers are negative, it returns a negative number. If all the numbers are positive, it returns their average. (Hint: See Program 6-22, on page 267.)

48. Program 6-19, on page 264, uses a *while* loop to read a series of numbers from the keyboard. Since you will always have at least one number in this program, rewrite it to use the *do...while*.

49. Program 6-21, on page 266, uses `INT_MAX` from the `<limits.h>` library to initialize the `smallest` variable. Another solution is to read the first number and put its value in `smallest`, then go into the loop to read the rest of the numbers. Modify Program 6-21 to make this change.

50. Euler's number, *e,* is used as the base of natural logarithms. It can be approximated using the following formula:

$$e = 1 + \frac{1}{1!} + \frac{1}{2!} + \frac{1}{3!} + \frac{1}{4!} + \frac{1}{5!} + \frac{1}{6!} + \cdots + \frac{1}{(n-1)!} + \frac{1}{n!}$$

Write a program that approximates *e* using a loop that terminates when the difference between two successive values of *e* differ by less than 0.0000001.

51. The value of pi (π) can be calculated by the following formula:

$$\pi = \sqrt{6\left(\frac{1}{1^2} + \frac{1}{2^2} + \frac{1}{3^2} + \cdots + \frac{1}{limit^2}\right)}$$

Write a function that uses this formula to calculate pi. Then write a test driver, and run it once to test your function with a limit of 5 terms and a limit of 10 terms. Display the result of each test.

52. Write a program that reads an integer from the keyboard and then calls a recursive function to print it out in reverse. For example, if the user enters 4762, it prints 2674.

53. Rewrite Program 6-26, on page 273, using an iterative solution.

PROJECTS

54. Statisticians use many different algorithms in addition to the arithmetic average. Two other averages are the geometric and the harmonic mean. The geometric mean of a set of *n* numbers, $x_1, x_2, x_3, \ldots, x_{n-1}, x_n$ is defined by the following formula:

$$\sqrt[n]{x_1 * x_2 * \ldots * x_n}$$

The harmonic mean is defined by the following formula:

$$\frac{n}{\dfrac{1}{x_1} + \dfrac{1}{x_2} + \cdots + \dfrac{1}{x_n}}$$

Write a program that reads a series of numbers and calculates the average, geometric mean, and harmonic mean.

55. Write a C program that can create four different patterns of different sizes. The size of each pattern is determined by the number of columns or rows. For example, a pattern of size 5 has 5 columns and 5 rows. Each pattern is made of character $ and a digit, which shows the size. The size must be between 2 and 9. The following shows the four patterns in size 5.

Pattern 1	Pattern 2	Pattern 3	Pattern 4
5$$$$	$$$$5	$$$$$	$$$$$
$5$$$	$$$5$	$$$$5	5$$$$
$$5$$	$$5$$	$$$55	55$$$
$$$5$	$5$$$	$$555	555$$
$$$$5	5$$$$	$5555	5555$

Your program displays a menu and asks the user to choose a pattern and size. But note that it must be robust; it must prompt the user to choose an option only between 1 and 5, and a pattern size only between 2 and 9. You are to print the menu and the user's response. The following example shows all user menu responses, including potential errors:

```
             M   E   N   U


       1.  Pattern One

       2.  Pattern Two

       3.  Pattern Three

       4.  Pattern Four

       5.  Quit


Choose an Option (between 1 and 5): 11
Your Option is incorrect. Please try again.
Choose an Option (between 1 and 5): 3
Choose a Pattern Size (between 2 and 9): 12
Your Pattern size is incorrect. Try again.
Choose a Pattern Size (between 2 and 9): 4
```

The program must consist of one `main` function and six other functions called `getOption`, `getSize`, `patternOne`, `patternTwo`, `pattern-Three`, and `patternFour`.

Run your program *once* with the following options and sizes. Note that some options and sizes are missing because either the previous option or the size is invalid.

	Option	Size
SET 1	1	2
SET 2	2	3
SET 3	3	4
SET 4	4	5
SET 5	6	
SET 5	3	6
SET 6	2	10
SET 6		7
SET 7	5	

56. Write a C program to create a calendar for a year. The program reads the year from the keyboard. It then calculates which day of the week (SUN, MON, TUE, WED, THU, FRI, SAT) is the first day of the year and prints the calendar for that year. After printing the year, it should ask if the user wants to continue. If the answer is yes, it will print the calendar for another year until the user is done.

The program prompts the user for the input, as shown below.

```
Enter the year for your calendar :    2000
```

The output is a calendar for the whole year (12 months). One month is shown below.

```
JANUARY                    2000
SUN MON TUE WED THU FRI SAT
                              1
  2   3   4   5   6   7   8
  9  10  11  12  13  14  15
 16  17  18  19  20  21  22
 23  24  25  26  27  28  29
 30  31
```

To print the correct calendar for the requested year, you must first find which day of the week is the first day of the that year. This can be done with the following formula. (For a complete explanation, see Chapter 5, Project 60, on page 227.)

$$\left(\left(\left(((\text{year}-1)*365) + \frac{\text{year}-1}{4} - \frac{\text{year}-1}{100} + \frac{\text{year}-1}{400}\right)\%7\right) + 1\right.$$

You also must calculate leap years. The formula for this calculation is also found in Chapter 5, Project 60.

Run your program once with the following sets of data[4]:

```
SET 1 ===> 1993
SET 2 ===>    0
SET 3 ===> 2000
SET 4 ===>  123
```

57. Write a C program to help a prospective borrower calculate the monthly payment for a loan. The program also prints the amortization (payoff) table to show the balance of the loan after each monthly payment.

The program prompts the user for input, as shown in the following example:

```
Amount of the loan (Principal)? 10000.00

Interest rate per year (per cent )? 12

Number of years? 10
```

The program then creates an information summary and amortization table.

Banks and financial institutions use different formulas to calculate the monthly payment of a loan. For the purpose of this assignment, we use a simple formula

```
NM      = (NY * 12)
IM      = (IY / 12) / 100
P       = (1 + IM)^NM
Q       = (P / (P - 1))
MP      = (PR * IM * Q)
```

where

---

[4]The Julian calendar was changed to our current (Gregorian) calendar in 1752. Although calendars before this date are valid Gregorian calendars, they do not represent the Julian calendar in use at that time.

NY:	Scheduled number of years to amortize the loan
NM:	Scheduled number of months for the loan
IY:	Interest rate per year (as a percentage)
IM:	Interest rate/month (decimal)
PR:	Principal (the amount of the loan)
P:	The value of $(1 + IM)^{NM}$
Q:	The value of $P / (P - 1)$
MP:	Monthly payment

The main function must call three other functions: `calculateMonthlyPay-ment`, `printInformation`, and `printAmortizationTable`. Of course, the first function may also call other functions if necessary.

Because of the approximation used in calculation, the value of the new balance at the end of the last month may become nonzero. To prevent this, the last payment must be adjusted. So we will print the information for every month except the last month. After we exit the loop, we then print the information for the last month. The monthly payment for the last month may be less or greater than the other months. It must be calculated by adding the principal paid to the interest paid for that month. The new balance at the end of the last month must be zero. The following example shows the concept. The program has been run for a loan of $5000.00 at 11% interest rate for a period of 1 year. The input was

```
Amount of the loan (Principal)? 5000.00

Interest rate / year (per cent)? 11

Number of years? 1
```

The output is shown in Figure 6-35. Note: Your answer may look a little different (a few pennies) because of different precision.

Run your program once with the following sets of data:

	Amount	Interest	Years
Set 1	10,000.00	12	1
Set 2	5,000.00	10	2
Set 3	1,000.00	8	3

58. Write a program that reads a list of integers from the keyboard and creates the following information:

a. Finds and prints the sum and the average of the integers

b. Finds and prints the largest and the smallest integer

c. Prints a Boolean (true or false) if some of them are less than 20

d. Prints a Boolean (true or false) if all of them are between 10 and 90

The input data consist of a list of integers with a sentinel. The program must prompt the user to enter the integers, one by one, and enter the sentinel when the end of the list has been reached. The prompt should look like the following:

```
Enter numbers with <return> (99999 to stop):
```

The output should be formatted as shown below.

```
The number of integers is:        xxx
The sum of the integers is:       xxxx
The average of the integers is:   xxx.xx
The smallest integer is:          xxx
The largest integer is:           xxx
```

```
The amount of the loan (principal):      5000.00
Interest rate/year (percent):            11.0
Interest rate/month (decimal):           0.009167
Number of years:                         1
Number of months:                        12
Monthly payment:                         441.91


              Old      Monthly   Interest  Principal    New
  Month     Balance    Payment     Paid      Paid     Balance
    1       5000.00    441.91     45.83     396.08    4603.92
    2       4603.92    441.91     42.20     399.71    4204.21
    3       4204.21    441.91     38.54     403.37    3800.84
    4       3800.84    441.91     34.84     407.07    3393.77
    5       3393.77    441.91     31.11     410.80    2982.97
    6       2982.97    441.91     27.34     414.57    2568.40
    7       2568.40    441.91     23.54     418.37    2150.03
    8       2150.03    441.91     19.71     422.20    1727.83
    9       1727.83    441.91     15.84     426.07    1301.76
   10       1301.76    441.91     11.93     429.98     871.78
   11        871.78    441.91      7.99     433.92     437.86
   12        437.86    441.87      4.01     437.86       0.00
Total amount paid: 5302.88
```

Figure 6-35   Sample output from Project 57

```
At least one number was < 20:      <true or false>
All numbers were (10 <= n >= 90): <true or false>
```

59. The formula for converting centigrade temperatures to Fahrenheit is

$$F = 32 + \left(C * \frac{180.0}{100.0} \right)$$

Write a program that prints out conversion tables for Celsius to Fahrenheit (0° to 100°) and Fahrenheit to Celsius (32° to 212°). Use separate functions to convert Fahrenheit to Celsius and Celsius to Fahrenheit. The output format for each table is to fit on a standard monitor display, 80 columns by 20 rows.

60. Rewrite "The Towers of Hanoi," Program 6-27, on page 278, using an iterative solution.

Text Files

7

Files existed long before computers; some of the oldest writings in history are files of trade records. In the general sense, files are organized collections of data. The type and amount of data can vary widely, from a collection of your favorite recipes to the extensive collections of data available on the Internet. Many files exist without the benefit of a computer—your favorite recipes most likely fall into this group. Other files are so vast and complex they could not exist without the use of a computer; the Internet data are in this group.

Data stored outside of the computer's primary memory are also called files. These externally stored computer files are the main topic of this chapter. We begin by defining some general principles of files, and then we look at how C supports them.

7-1 CONCEPT OF A FILE

A **file** is an external collection of related data treated as a unit. The primary purpose of a file is to keep a record of our data. Since the contents of primary memory are lost when the computer is shut down, we need files to store our data in a more permanent form. Additionally, the collection of data is often too large to reside entirely in main memory at one time. Therefore, we must have the ability to read and write portions of the data while the rest remain in the file.

> A file is an external collection of related data treated as a unit.

There are two broad classes of files: **text files** and **binary files**. In text files, all the data are stored as graphic characters, which must be converted to internal formats when they represent numeric data. Text files are also organized around lines. Each line in a text file ends with a newline character (\n). Binary files, on the other hand, store data in the internal computer formats, such as integer and floating-point numbers.[1] Such files take much less time to input and output because no format conversion is necessary.

> Two major characteristics of text files:
> - All data in a text file are human-readable graphic characters.
> - Each line of data ends with a newline character.

Files are stored in **auxiliary,** or **secondary, storage devices**. The two most common forms of secondary storage are disk and tape. Files in secondary storage can be both read and written. Files can also exist in forms that the computer can write but not read. For example, the display of information on the system monitor is a form of a file, as is data sent to a printer. In a general sense, the keyboard is also a file, although it cannot store data. Figure 7-1 shows several files in a typical personal computer environment.

When the computer reads, the data move from the external device to memory; when it writes, the data move from memory to the external device. This data movement often uses a special work area known as a buffer. A **buffer** is a temporary storage area that holds data while they are being transferred to or from memory. Its primary purpose is to synchronize the physical devices to your program needs, especially on large storage devices such as disk and tape. Because of the physical requirements of these devices, more data can be input at one time than your program can use. The buffer holds the extra data until you are ready for it. Conversely, the buffer collects output data until there are enough to write efficiently. These buffering activities are taken care of by software known as device drivers, or access methods, provided by the supplier of the operating system you are using.

---

[1]It is a misnomer to say that text data are not binary. All data in the computer are stored in binary—that's all the computer can use. The difference is that the text data are a special class of binary data with associated graphic characters.

Figure 7-1 Files in a personal computer environment

7-2 FILES AND STREAMS

A **stream** is a sequence of elements in time. Only one stream element, the current one, is available at a time. In other words, the computer looks at input and output data, whether from a physical device such as keyboard or from files resident on a secondary storage, as a stream of characters or bytes. In this way, the programmer does not have to worry about the different properties of input/output devices, since every device issues or receives time-sequenced bytes.

> All of C's file structures are byte streams.

FILE TABLE

Since files exist separately from the computer and our programs, we must have some way to connect them; we must create a linkage between the external file and its usage in our program. In C, this linkage is known as a **file table**. We define a file by using a standard **FILE** type, which has been created for us in the standard input/output header file (`<stdio.h>`). The format for the file type is shown below.

```
FILE *filename
```

You should recognize two things about this file type. First, since the identifier is all uppercase, it is some form of a predefined type. Second, since it has an asterisk as part of its type, it is an address. The filename can be any meaningful identifier that you select. Programmers often prefix the filename with **fp**, which stands for "file pointer."

The term *file table* implies that several things are stored in the table. Although you do not need to know the details, you should be aware that the file table contains all of the information necessary to locate your file wherever it is stored outside of the computer. The file table also contains information such as the name of the file, the location of its file buffer, and the current state of the file. Figure 7-2 is a symbolic representation of a file table.

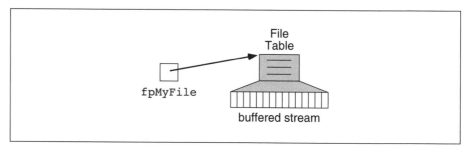

Figure 7-2 A file table

For example, suppose that we are working on a program that works with daily temperature readings. A typical day's recordings might look like Figure 7-3.

Temperature Readings for: Monday 6/2					
0000	58.6	0800	65.7	1600	81.3
0100	55.5	0900	68.9	1700	79.7
0200	55.3	1000	72.3	1800	77.1
0300	55.2	1100	75.6	1900	74.5
0400	55.1	1200	76.5	2000	73.4
0500	55.1	1300	77.7	2100	71.3
0600	58.4	1400	78.6	2200	65.1
0700	63.7	1500	80.2	2300	63.0

Figure 7-3 Temperature readings

If the data were stored in a file, we might define the file as shown below.

```
FILE *fpTempData;
```

STANDARD FILES

The C language automatically defines three **standard file streams** called **standard input**, **standard output**, and **standard error**. These three files are associated with two physical files: the keyboard and the monitor. The file tables that point to these file streams are defined in the standard input/output header file (`<stdio.h>`) and are referred to as **stdin**, **stdout**, and **stderr**, respectively (Figure 7-4). Standard input is associated with the user's primary input file, usually the keyboard. Standard output and standard error are both usually assigned to the user's monitor but can be individually directed to a printer if one is available. You may use these files without defining them as long as you include the proper header file (`<stdio.h>`).

USER FILES

Using the FILE type, you can define any external files you need. For example, suppose that you are a professor at a fully automated college. At the end of the term, you don't turn in your grades on paper, you submit them as a file over the network. The program that submits the grades requires two user files, one for the students in your class and one for the grades file sent to the registrar. These files are depicted in Figure 7-5.

Figure 7-4   Standard files

Figure 7-5   User files

FILE-STREAM ASSOCIATION

A file may be associated with one and only one stream. Similarly, a stream may be associated with only one external file. The connections from the file table to the stream and the stream to the external file are created when the file is opened. The standard files are opened automatically when your program starts. User files, on the other hand, must be explicitly opened in your program.

7-3 STANDARD LIBRARY INPUT/OUTPUT FUNCTIONS

The <stdio.h> library contains several different **input/output functions**. They are grouped into eight different categories, as shown in Figure 7-6. The first three will be discussed here. Those shown in shaded boxes will be discussed in Chapters 11 and 13.

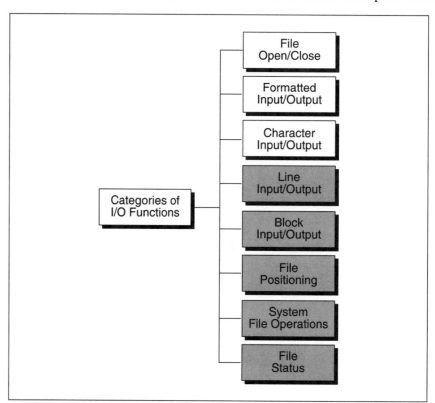

Figure 7-6 Types of standard input/output functions

FILE OPEN AND CLOSE

C separates the program from the physical devices by assigning each file a logical name. This internal logical name is related to a physical external file through the **open function** and through job control statements that are used in the operating system. By referring to files symbolically, you don't need to worry about where they are located. All you need to know is their name and their format. In other words, instead of communicating with actual input/output or auxiliary storage devices, a C program uses streams to communicate with its files. Some of this work is done in C, and some is done by the operating system.

When the program is through processing, it is necessary to disposition the file in an orderly fashion so that the file is complete. Again, a C function directs the operating system to close and, if appropriate, save the file through a **close function**.

File open (*fopen*)

The function that prepares a file for processing is *fopen*. It does two things: First, it makes the connection between the external file and the program. Second, it creates a program file table to store the information needed to process the file.

To open a file, you need to specify the filename and its mode, as shown below.

```
fopen("filename", "mode");
```

Let's examine this statement by starting on the right. The **file mode** is a string that tells C how you intend to use the file: Will you read an existing file, write a new file, or both read and write the file? The mode codes are shown in Table 7-1.

Mode	Meaning
r	Open file for reading. • If file exists, the marker is positioned at beginning. • If file doesn't exist, error returned.
w	Open text file for writing. • If file exists, it is emptied. • If file doesn't exist, it is created.
a	Open text file for append. • If file exists, the marker is positioned at end. • If file doesn't exist, it is created.

Table 7-1   Text file modes

A **filename** is a string that supplies the name of the file as it is known to the external world. For example, when you work in a DOS system, the name consists of up to eight characters with a three-character file extension. The MS/DOS filename for the temperature file described on page 304 is shown below.

```
TEMPS.DAT
```

The address of the file table that contains the file information is returned by *fopen*. The actual contents of FILE are hidden from our view because we do not need to see them. All we need to know is that we can store the address of the file table and use it to read or write the file. A complete open statement is shown below. Continuing with our temperatures example, we could open it for output (writing) with the following open statements. The first is the basic format as it might be used for the current directory in UNIX or DOS; the second is the DOS version to open a file for drive A.[2]

```
fpTempData = fopen("TEMPS.DAT", "w");
fpTempData = fopen("A:\\TEMPS.DAT", "w");
```

We see this open statement in the program in Figure 7-7.

Some explanation of the program segment in Figure 7-7 is in order. You should first note that the standard input/output library is called out at the beginning of the program.

Next, note the name we have used for the file address. The fp stands for "file pointer" and is a traditional file indicator. To the file pointer abbreviation we have added the name of the file, Temps. This combination gives a readable name that is easy to remember.

Our file variable, fpTemps, is initialized when we open the file. Note that we assign the return value from the *fopen* function to our file variable. Later in the program, when we need to read the file, we may use this file variable again.

---

[2]Note the two backslashes in the file name. Because the backslash is the escape character, to get one in the output, we must code two.

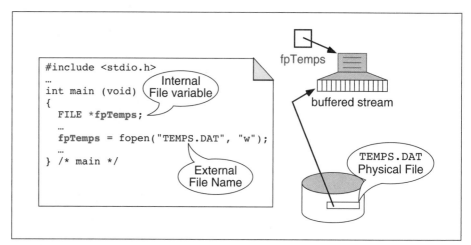

Figure 7-7   File open results

File Disposition Warning

The operating system controls what happens when you open an existing file for writing. The one consistent thing is that a new file is created. If you are in a UNIX or an MS/DOS environment, the existing file is deleted when the program completes. If you are in a VAX VMS environment, the existing file still exists, but it is no longer the current file. To read it, you would have to use special job control statements that refer to the older version. Check with the documentation for your operating system to make sure you understand what will happen.

File Mode

When we open a file, we explicitly define its mode. The mode shows how we will use the file: for reading, for writing, or for appending, which means adding new data at the end of the current file. C has six different file modes. The first three, which we discuss here, are used to read, write, or append. In Chapter 13 we will discuss the other modes, which allow both reading and writing in the same file. Table 7-1 on page 307 describes the simple open modes.

Read Mode   The **read mode**, r, is designed to open an existing file for reading. When a file is opened in this mode, the file marker is positioned at the beginning of the file (the first byte). The file must already exist: If it does not, NULL is returned as an error. Files opened for reading are shown in Figure 7-8a. If you try to write to a file opened in the read mode, you will get an error message.

Write Mode   The **write mode**, w, is designed to open a file for writing. If the file doesn't exist, it is created. If it already exists, it is opened and all its data are deleted; that is, it assumes the characteristics of an empty file. In either case, the file marker is positioned at the beginning. It is an error to try to read from a file opened in write mode. A file opened for writing is shown in Figure 7-8b.

Append Mode   The **append mode**, a, is designed to open an existing file for writing. Instead of writing from the beginning of the file, however, the writing starts after the last byte; that is, new data are added, or *appended,* at the end of the file. If the file doesn't exist, it is created and opened. In this case, the writing will start at the beginning of the file; the result will be logically the same as opening a new file for writing. Files opened

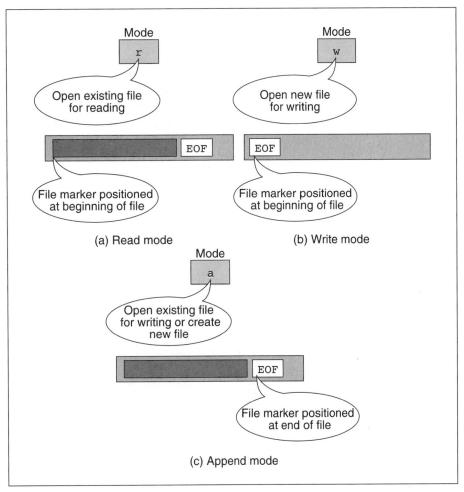

Figure 7-8 File opening modes

in append mode are shown in Figure 7-8c. If you try to read a file opened for write append, you will get an error message.

File Close (*fclose*)

When you no longer need a file, you should close it to free system resources, such as buffer space. A file is closed using the close function, *fclose,* as shown below.

```
#include <stdio.h>
...
int main (void)
{
/* Definitions */
   FILE *fpTemp;

/* Statements */
   ...
   fpTemps = fopen("TEMPS.DAT", "w");
   ...
   fclose(fpTemps);
   ...
```

Open and Close Errors

What if the open or close fails? Open and close errors occur for a number of reasons. One of the most common errors occurs when the external filename in the open function call does not match a name on the disk. When you create a new file, the open can fail if there isn't enough room on the disk.

You should always check to make sure that a file stream has opened successfully. If it has, then you have a valid address in your file variable. But if it failed for any reason, the file variable contains NULL, which is a C-defined constant for no address (see <stdio.h>). Similarly, you can test the return value from the close to make sure it succeeded. The *fclose* function returns an integer that is zero if the close succeeds and EOF if there is an error. EOF is defined in the standard input/output header file by the system programmer. Traditionally, it is –1, but the standard defines it as any noncharacter value. To ensure that the file opened or closed successfully, we use the function as an expression in an *if* statement, as shown in Program 7-1.

```
1   #include <stdio.h>
2   …
3   int main (void)
4   {
5   /* Local Definitions */
6   FILE *fpTemps;
7
8   /* Statements */
9      …
10     if ((fpTemps = fopen("TEMPS.DAT", "r")) == NULL)
11        {
12         printf("\aERROR opening TEMPS.DAT\n");
13         return (100);
14        } /* if open */
15     …
16     if (fclose(fpTemps) == EOF)
17        {
18         printf("\aERROR closing TEMPS.DAT\n");
19         return (102);
20        } /* if close */
21     …
22   }  /* main */
```

Program 7-1 Testing for open and close errors

Program 7-1 Analysis   The most common mistake in testing for a successful open is getting the parentheses wrong, as shown below.

```
    if (fpTemps = fopen("TEMPS.DAT",  "w") == NULL)
```

The above statement is syntactically correct (you will not get a compile error) but invalid. You must test the address returned by *fopen* after it has been assigned to fpTemps. In the above statement, fpTemps is assigned the logical value of the expression

```
    fopen("TEMPS.DAT", "w") == NULL
```

because the equal operator has a higher precedence than the assignment operator. Study the open in Program 7-1 carefully, and make sure you understand the difference between it and the incorrect version shown at the bottom of page 310.

The error testing for the close is much simpler; we can use a simple test for the error code, EOF. Note that we have assigned a different return code to distinguish the open failure from the close failure.

7-4 FORMATTING INPUT/OUTPUT FUNCTIONS

We first introduced the *scanf* and *printf* formatted input and output functions in Chapter 2. At that time, we introduced only their basic capabilities for the keyboard and the monitor display. It is now time to discuss them fully.

FORMAT STRINGS

Input and output functions for text files use a format string to describe how data are to be formatted when read or written. The **format string** consists of three types of data, which may be repeated: whitespace, text characters, and the most important of the three, the field specification that describes how the data are to be formatted as they are read or written.

Whitespace

Format string whitespace is handled differently for input and output. In an input function, one or more whitespaces in the format string cause zero, one, or more whitespaces in the input stream to be read and discarded. Thus, any sequence of consecutive whitespace characters in the format string will match any sequence of consecutive whitespace characters, possibly of different length, in the input stream.

> Any whitespace character in the format string will cause leading whitespace characters in the input to be discarded.

Whitespace in an output function is simply copied to the output stream. Thus, a space character is placed in the output stream for every space character in the format string. Likewise, tabs in the format string are copied to the output stream. This is not a good idea, however, because you can't see tabs in the format string. It is better to use the tab escape character (\t) so that the reader can see the tabs.

Text

Any text character other than a whitespace in an input format string must match exactly the next character of the input stream. If it does not match, a conflict occurs that causes the operation to be terminated. The conflicting input character remains in the input stream to be read by the next input operation on that stream. We therefore highly recommend that you do not use text characters in any input.

Text characters in an output format string are copied to the output stream. They are usually used to display messages to the user or to label data being output.

Field Specification

The **field specification** consists of a percent character (%), a conversion code, and other formatting instructions. With one exception, each field specification must have a matching parameter in the parameter list that follows the format string. The type in the field specification and the type of the parameter must match.

Field specifications can have up to six elements, as shown in Figure 7-9. (Note that for input there are only five; precision is not allowed.) The first element is a field specification

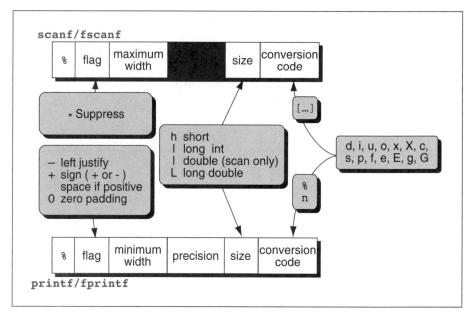

Figure 7-9 Field specification

token (%). The last element is the conversion code. Both of these elements are required; the other elements are optional. Generally, the meaning and usage of each element is the same for both input and output. The exceptions are noted in the following discussion.

> The number, order, and type of the field specifications must match the number, order, and type of the parameters in the list. Otherwise, the result will be unpredictable and may terminate the input/output function.

Conversion Codes   The **conversion code** specifies the type of data that are being formatted. For input, it specifies the type of variable into which the data are formatted. For output, it specifies the type of data in the parameter associated with the specification. *It is your responsibility to ensure that the data are of the right type.* If they are not, strange output may result.

You have already seen many conversion codes. In this section, we discuss the octal (o), hexadecimal (x), scientific formatting codes (e and g), number (n), and percent sign (%) codes. We will cover the three remaining codes, the string (s), the pointer (p), and the edit set ([   ]) in Chapters 9 and 11. Table 7-2 lists the most common codes.

Octal and Hexadecimal.   The octal (o) and hexadecimal (x or X) conversion codes perform unsigned conversion. For octal, the only valid input digits are 0...7. For hexadecimal input, the valid digits are 0...9, a...f, and A...F. For output, the number is formatted in either octal or hexadecimal, as indicated by the conversion code. The alpha hexadecimal codes are printed in lowercase if the x code is used and in uppercase for the X code. If you are not familiar with octal or hexadecimal numbers, see Appendix D, "Numbering Systems."

Scientific notation (e, E, g, G).   The C language uses two floating-point format codes for scientific notation. In scientific notation, the significand and exponent are

scanf				printf		
Flag	Size	Codes	Usage	Flag	Size	Codes
–+	h	d	*short int*	–+	h	d
			int	0		
	l		*long int*	sp	l	
–+	h	u	*unsigned short int*	–+	h	u
			unsigned int	0		
	l		*unsigned long int*	sp	l	
–+	h	o	*short*—octal	–+	h	o
			int—octal	0		
	l		*long*—octal	sp	l	
–+	h	x X	*short*—hex format	–+	h	x X
			long—hex format	0		
	l		*long*—hex format	sp	l	
		f	*float*			f
	l		*double*		l	
	L		*long double*		L	
		e, E	*float*—scientific			e, E
	l	g, G	*double*—scientific		l	g, G
	L		*long double*—scientific		L	
		c	*char*			c
		s	string			s
		p	pointer (address)			p
	h	n	*short*—I/O count			n
			int—I/O count		h	n
	l		*long*—I/O count		l	n
		[...]	edit set			
			percent sign (%)			%
				sp: space		

Table 7-2   Common input and output conversion codes

specified separately. The significand part is a floating-point number that contains as many significant digits as possible. For example, if it contains six digits, then the number is significant only to six digits; if it has twelve digits, then it is significant to twelve digits. The larger the significance, the greater the precision. Therefore, *long double* may be more precise than *double,* which may be more precise than *float.*

The exponent specifies the magnitude of the number. It may be either positive or negative. If it is positive, then the number is the significand times ten to the power of the exponent, which may be a very large number. If it is negative, then the number is the significant times the reciprocal of the base ten exponent, which may be a very small number. These forms are shown below.

$$123e03 \Rightarrow 123 \ast 10^3 \qquad 123e{-}03 \Rightarrow 123 \ast 10^{-3}$$

All of the following numbers are in scientific notation:

$$3e \qquad -1.0e{-}3 \qquad 0.1{+}e1 \qquad 2e2$$

When the e and g format codes are used for input, they work just like the floating-point (f) code. With output, the e code displays numbers using scientific notation; the g code will use either the standard floating-point format or the scientific format, depending on the specified precision; it also deletes any trailing zeros to the right of the decimal point. If there is no significant digit to the right of the decimal point, the decimal point itself is also deleted. Both E and G print the e in scientific notation as a capital letter.

Count (n)   If you need to verify the number of input or output characters, you can do so by specifying the n code. This code requires a matching variable address into which *scanf* or *printf* places the count of the characters input or output. If the code is prefaced with an h, the matching variable must be a *short;* if it is l, the variable must be *long.* Since the operation places the results in the variable, its address must be used in the parameter list. In the following example, count is a short integer that is to receive the number of characters written (note the address operator):

```
printf("%d %8.2f %d %hn", i, x, j, &count);
```

You might use this feature to control when to write a newline character. You can use it to keep track of the number of characters and when the line is full, write a newline (\n).

Percent (%)   The percent sign as a conversion code is used to output a percent sign. For example, assume that grade contains a student's score expressed as a percentage. The following statement could then be used to print the grade in the format 93.5%:

```
printf("%4.1f%%", grade);
```

If a percent sign appears in an input format, it indicates that the user is expected to enter a percent sign as a part of the input. In this case, it acts as user-supplied text.

Flag   The **flag** is the first field specification modifier. Its usage differs for input and output. For input there is only one flag (*). It means "do not store the data" and is the one exception to the rule that all field specifications must have a matching variable in the parameter list. This flag is very helpful for discarding leading material. For example, suppose that you are reading data and know that the next data in the input stream contain integer data that you don't need. Rather than reading and formatting them into a variable that you will not use, you can simply write the field specification shown below. The input function will read but not convert the data and store the results. It will stop with the next whitespace.

```
%*d
```

For output, the flag interpretation is much more extensive. The codes and their meanings are discussed next.

Justification   Normally, output is **right justified**. Therefore, if the print width (see "Field Width," below) is larger than required, the data will appear in the right side of the print area. This is fine for numeric output, but it is not what you want all the time. To reverse the justification, set the flag to minus (—). The following code fragment shows the value of k, which contains 6691, printed left justified and then right justified:

```
printf("Left Justification \t|%-10d|\n", k);
printf("Right Justification\t|%10d|\n\n", k);

Results:
    Left Justification     |6691       |
    Right Justification    |       6691|
```

Sign   Numeric data are normally **signed** only if they are negative. Some applications require that a plus sign be printed if the number is positive. Using a plus (+) for a flag causes positive numbers to print with a plus sign prefix and causes negative numbers to print with the standard minus sign prefix. Examples of signed numeric data are shown in Table 7-3.

Conversion Code	Value	Print
%d	5	5
%d	−5	−5
%+d	5	+5
%+d	−5	−5

Table 7-3   Examples of signed printing

Space   A **space flag** causes a leading space to be printed if no sign is printed. This can help alignment when you print positive numbers unsigned. (Remember, negative numbers are always signed.) The following code fragment demonstrates the use of the sign and space modifiers:

```
printf("No modifiers: %d\n", k);
printf("With plus   : %+d\n", k);
printf("With space  : % d\n\n", k);

Results:
    No modifiers: 6691
    With plus   : +6691
    With space  :  6691
```

Leading Zero Padding   If your application requires that leading zeros be printed, then you use a zero (0) flag. This is known as **leading zero padding**. Leading zero padding is shown in the printing of the Social Security number in the following code fragment:

```
printf("Enter your social security number: ");
scanf ("%3d%2d%4d", &i, &j, &k);
printf("Your Number is:    %03d-%02d-%04d\n\n",
       i, j, k);

Results:
    Enter your social security number: 012030456
    Your number is:    012-03-0456
```

Field Width   The meaning of the **field width** is conceptually the same for input and output, but in the opposite direction. For input data, the field width specifies the maximum width of the input (in characters). This allows you to break out a code that may be stored in the input without spaces. Consider what happens when you are reading a Social Security number from a file and the number has no formatting; it is just nine digits in a row, followed by a space. You could read it into three variables, thus allowing you to format it with dashes in your output, with the following format specifications:

```
scanf("%3d%2d%4d...", &ssn1, &ssn2, &ssn3, ...);
```

Note that the width is a maximum. If the amount of data is less than required, the scan terminates. What determines the end of the data depends on the type of data, but generally whitespace will terminate most scans.

For output specifications, the width provides the minimum output width. However, if the data are *wider* than the specified width, *C will print all the data.* Thus, the output width is the minimum area provided.

Precision **Precision** is specified as a period followed by an integer. Precision has meaning only for output fields, and it is an error to use it for input. Precision can control the following:

1. The minimum number of digits for integers. If the number has fewer significant digits than the precision specified, leading zeros will be printed.
2. The number of digits after the decimal point in float.
3. The number of significant digits in g and G.

Size The **size** specification is a modifier for the conversion code. Used in combination, they allow you to specify that the associated variable is, for example, a *long double* (Lf). The size codes with their associated conversion codes are explained in Table 7-2 on page 313.

The code fragment shown below demonstrates the use of the width, precision, and size codes. In this fragment, x, y, and z are defined as *double.* Note that to read them we must use the size modifier, l, but to print them we don't need the size. This is because *printf* expects a *double.* The compiler automatically converts *float* to *double,* and the conversion code for both is f. If you want to print a *long double,* then you must use a size modifier (L).

```
printf("Enter three numbers formatted as:\n");
printf("nnn.nn nnne03 nnnE-03\n");
scanf ("%lf%lf%lf", &x, &y, &z);
printf("%6.2f %6.2e %6.2G\n\n", x, y, z);

Results:
   Enter three numbers formated as:
   nnn.nn nnne03 nnnE-03
   123.45 123e03 123E-03
   123.45 1.23e+05    0.12
```

scanf AND fscanf

The *scanf* and *fscanf* functions read text data and convert the data to the types specified by a format string. The only difference between them is that *scanf* reads data from the standard input unit (the keyboard by default) and *fscanf* reads the input from a file specified by the first parameter. This file can be the standard input unit (stdin).

The name *scanf* stands for "scan formatted"; the name *fscanf* stands for "file scan formatted." These functions have the following formats:

```
scanf ("format string", address list);
fscanf(fp, "format string", address list);
```

where fp is the address of a file defined as type FILE *, "format string" is a string containing formatting instructions, and the address list specifies the address where the data are to be stored after they have been formatted. A comma must separate the format string from the variable list. If more than one variable is present, then separate the variables from each other by commas.

You must include a variable address in the address list for every field specification in the format string that requires data. If you do not, the result is "unpredictable and undefined." This is a standard ANSI/ISO disclaimer that means anything can happen. The usual result is that your program doesn't do what you expect, and often it crashes.

Input Data Formatting

The conversion operation processes input characters until

1. End-of-file is reached.
2. An inappropriate character is encountered.
3. The number of characters read is equal to an explicitly specified maximum field width.

Side Effect and Value in Scan Functions

When a scan function is called, it can create a side effect and return a value. The side effect is to read characters from a file and format them into variables supplied in the parameter list. It continues until end-of-file is reached or there is a conflict between the format string and a character read from the input stream. In either case, the value the scan returns is the *number of successfully formatted variables* before termination. If the scan detects the end-of-file before any conflict or assignment is performed, then the function returns EOF. The difference between the side effect and the value is seen in Figure 7-10.

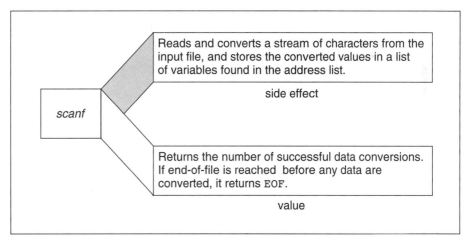

Figure 7-10   Side effect and value of *scanf*

This leads us to a common example of a **value error**. Suppose we want to read two numbers with one scan statement. If we succeed, the scan function returns a 2, indicating that both were read correctly. If the user makes a mistake with the first number, the scan function returns a 0. If there is a mistake with the second entry, *scanf* returns a 1. This allows us to validate that at least the correct amount and type of data were read. An error reading the second piece of data is shown in Figure 7-11.

When you read variables, you should verify that the data were read correctly. This is easily done by checking the return value from the scan. Program 7-2 is a program fragment that shows how the two numbers in Figure 7-11 could be checked.

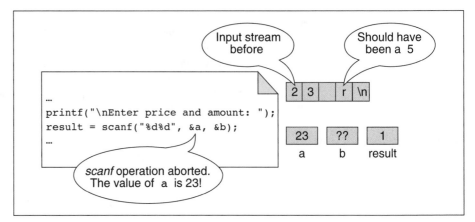

Figure 7-11 Another common error

```
1  #define FLUSH while (getchar() != '\n')
2  #define ERR1 "\aPrice incorrect. Re-enter both fields\n"
3  #define ERR2 "\aAmount incorrect. Re-enter both fields\n"
4
5  /* Read price and amount */
6     do
7       {
8         printf("\nEnter amount and price: ");
9         ioResult = scanf("%d%f", &amount, &price);
10
11        if (ioResult != 2)
12           {
13             FLUSH;
14             if (ioResult == 1)
15                 printf(ERR1);
16             else
17                 printf(ERR2);
18           } /* if */
19       } while (ioResult != 2);
```

```
Results:
   Enter amount and price: ? 15.25
   Amount incorrect. Re-enter both fields

   Enter amount and price: 100 ?
   Price incorrect. Re-enter both fields

   Enter amount and price: 100 15.25
```

Program 7-2 Checking *scanf* results

Program 7-2 Analysis   We have introduced a new define statement, FLUSH, in this program segment.

```
#define FLUSH while (getchar( ) != '\n')
```

Why is this statement necessary? Recall that when *scanf* encounters an error, it leaves the invalid data in the input stream. If we simply print the user messages and then return to the *scanf* statement, the invalid data are still there. We need to get rid of them somehow! This is the purpose of the FLUSH statement. It reads all data from the invalid input to the end of the line. For a complete discussion of the flush statement, see "Testing for Invalid User Input" on page 338.

Also note how the error messages tell the user exactly what went wrong, rather than giving a general "The numbers entered are incorrect" type of message. Whenever possible, you should tell the user exactly what went wrong.

TWO COMMON MISTAKES

There are as many mistakes to be made as there are programmers programming. Two are so common that they need to be emphasized.

Invalid Address

The first common mistake is to use a data value rather than an address for the input parameter. The scan function places the formatted input at the address specified in the parameter list. When you pass data rather than an address, C interprets the data as an address. This causes a part of memory to be destroyed. If you are lucky, your program will fail immediately. If you are unlucky, it will run until the destroyed part of your program is needed and then fail. This problem is shown in Figure 7-12.

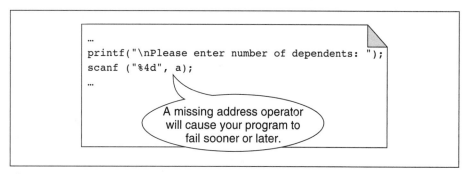

Figure 7-12 Missing address operator in *scanf*

Data Type Conflict

The second common mistake is a conflict between the format string and the input stream. This occurs, for example, when the format string calls for a numeric value and the input stream contains an alphabetic character. If any conflict occurs between the format string and the input stream, the operation will abort. The character that caused the conflict will go back to the input stream, and the rest of the input stream (including the troublemaker) remains waiting to be processed. The problem is that no warning message will be given and the input stream cannot be filled again until it has been completely processed or flushed by the programmer. The next input operation will read from the unused stream instead of reading from a new input stream. The result: Everything is a mess! In Figure 7-13, the user meant to enter the number 235 but instead entered 23r. (This is a common error. Note that the *r* is just below and to the left of the 5 on the keyboard.) When *scanf* reads the input stream, it interprets the number 23 but stops with the *r* and returns 1, indicating that one decimal number was successfully formatted. The *r* remains in the input stream, waiting for the next *scanf*. The typical result of this error is a perpetual loop looking for an integer value. Even if you detect and flush the error when the *r* is read, you still have processed the wrong data (23, not 235) in the first read!

Figure 7-14 contains three more examples that show the operation of a *fscanf* function. In the first example, the format string requests that two integers be read, and two are successfully read. The value returned by the *scanf* function is 2. In the second example, two

Figure 7-13 Data type conflict

Figure 7-14 `fscanf` examples

more numbers are requested, but only one is available in the input stream. In this case, the value of the *scanf* expression is 1. The third example shows the result if all the data have been read and the input file is at end-of-file.

scanf Examples   In this section, we present several examples of *scanf* formatting. Some of them are rarely used, but they illustrate some of the finer points of formatting. We suggest that you cover up the answer until you have tried to write the statement yourself.

1. Write the *scanf* statement that will read three values, a character, an integer, and a float, from the standard input file. The input is

     X   31416 3.1416

```
scanf("%c %d %f", &c, &i, &x);
```

2. Write the *scanf* statement that will read three values—a character, an integer, and a float—from the standard input file. All data are on different lines. The input is

    X ¬
    31416 ¬
    3.1416 ¬

```
scanf("%c %d %f", &c, &i, &x);
```

Note that this statement is the same as the first example. Since the newline is whitespace, it makes no difference if the data are separated by newlines, spaces, or tabs.

3. Write the *scanf* statement that will read two fractions from the standard input unit and place the numerators and denominators in integer variables.

14/26   25/66

```
scanf("%d/%d %d/%d", &n1, &d1, &n2, &d2);
```

4. Write the *fscanf* statement that will read a date formatted with dashes (-) into three different integer fields. The input is to be read from a file opened as `fpData`.

5-10-1936

```
fscanf(fpData, "%d-%d-%d", &month, &day, &year);
```

Note that with this statement, an error results if the user enters 5/10/1997.

5. Write the *fscanf* statement that will read three integers from a file opened as `fpData` and assign the number of successfully formatted variables to the identifier `result`.

5 10 15

```
result = fscanf(fpData, "%d %d %d", &i, &j, &k);
```

6. Given a file with four integers in each line, write a *scanf* statement to read only the first, second, and fourth integer from a line; that is, discard the third element. Read the data from the file `fpData`.

5 10 15 1

```
result = fscanf(fpData, "%d%d%*d%d", &a, &b, &d);
```

7. Write the *fscanf* statement that will read three integers from a file opened as `fpData` and assign the number of successfully formatted variables to the identifier `result`. Use a defined constant for the format string.

5 10 15

```
#define FORMAT_3D "%d %d %d"

result = fscanf(fpData, FORMAT_3D, &i, &j, &k);
```

printf* AND *fprintf

The print formatted functions display output in human readable form under the control of a format string that is very similar to the format string in *scanf*. When necessary, internal formats are converted to character formats. In other words, it is the opposite of the scan formatted functions.

These functions have the following format:

```
printf("format string", value list)
                 and
fprintf(fp, "format string", value list)
```

One of the first differences to note is that the value list is optional. Where as you always need a variable when you are reading, in many situations, such as user prompts, you display strings without a value list.

Three examples of *printf* output that might be found in a program are shown below. The first is a greeting message at the start of the program, the second displays the result of a calculation, and the last is a closing message.

```
printf ("\nWelcome to Calculator.\n");
printf ("\nThe answer is %6.2f\n", x);
printf ("Thank you for using Calculator");
```

The *fprintf* function works just like *printf* except that it specifies the file in which the data will be displayed. The file can be the standard output (`stdout`) or standard error (`stderr`) files. For example, to write the three previous lines to a report file, we use the following code:

```
fprintf (fpReport, "\nWelcome to Calculator.\n");
fprintf (fpReport, "\nThe answer is %6.2f\n", x);
fprintf (fpReport, "Thank you for using Calculator");
```

PRINT SIDE EFFECT AND VALUE

The side effect of the print functions is to write text data to the output file. The value it returns is the number of characters written. If an error occurs, EOF, which is defined in the `<stdio.h>` header file, is returned. These concepts, which are summarized in Figure 7-15, are similar to the side effects and value discussed with scan functions.

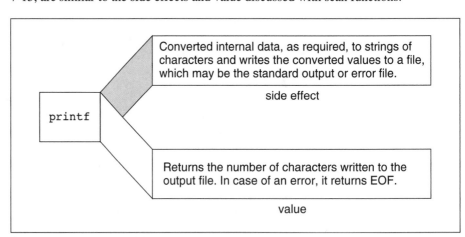

Figure 7-15 Side effect and value of `printf`

Examples

In this section we present several examples of print formatting. Although some of them are rarely used, they do illustrate some of the finer points of formatting. The sample output is shown in bold characters. You may want to cover up the answer until you have answered the question yourself.

1. Write the print statement that will print three columns of numbers. The first column contains a two-digit integer, the second column contains up to seven digits, and the third column contains a *float* with four integral numbers and three decimal places.

15   10   15.010
78 1234567 1234.123

```
printf("%2d %7ld %8.3f", i, j, x);
```

2. Write the print statement that will print the tax due as stored in a *float* named x. The output is

   The tax is: 233.12

```
printf("The tax is: %8.2f\n", x);
```

3. Modify the above example to add the words "dollars this year" after the numeric value. The output will then be

   The tax is   233.12 dollars this year.

```
printf("The tax is %8.2f dollars this year\n", x);
```

4. Write the print statement that will print three integer variables to a file opened as fpOut. Each write is to append a newline character (¬) to the output.

   100 200 300¬

```
fprintf(fpOut, "%d %d %d\n", i, j, k);
```

5. Write the print statement that will print three floating-point values. The first is a *float* with two places of precision; the second is a *double,* printed in scientific notation (G); and the third is *long double*, printed using scientific notation (E). Each value will print on a separate line.

   3.14

   200

   4.408946E+00

```
fprintf(fpOut, "%.2f\n%G\n%E\n", i, j, k);
```

6. Write the print statement that will print three integral values. The first is a *short,* printed in octal: the second is an *int,* printed using lowercase hexadecimal digits; and the third is a *long,* printed using uppercase hexadecimal digits. End the line with a newline character.

   25547 7e44 7864CB

```
fprintf(fpOut, "%ho %x %lX\n", i, j, k);
```

FILE EXAMPLES

In this section we develop four small programs that demonstrate various aspects of reading and writing files.

Read and Print File

Program 7-3 is a simple program that reads a file of integers and prints them out.

```
1  /* Read a text file of integers, and print the contents.
2        Written by:
3        Date:
4  */
5  #include <stdio.h>
6  #include <stdlib.h>
7
```

Program 7-3   Read and print text file of integers

```
 8   int main (void)
 9   {
10   /* Local Definitions */
11      FILE *fpIn;
12      int   numIn;
13
14   /* Statements */
15      fpIn = fopen("P7-03.DAT", "r");
16      if (!fpIn)
17         {
18          printf("Could not open file\a\n");
19          exit  (101);
20         } /* if open fail */
21
22      while ((fscanf(fpIn, "%d", &numIn)) == 1)
23         printf("%d ", numIn);
24
25      return 0;
26   }  /* main */
```

```
Results:
   1 2 3 4 5 6 7 8 9 10
```

Program 7-3   Read and print text file of integers (continued)

Program 7-3 Analysis   Note how we open the file in this small program. To make it easier to read the code, we split the file open and the test for successful open into two statements. This does not affect the program's efficiency and makes it much easier to code and read the statements.

Now look at the read in the *while* loop. We loop as long as the *fscanf* succeeds, as indicated by a return value of 1. When the end of file is reached, the *while* statement will be false and the program terminates. There is one slight risk to this program: If a read error is caused by a bad disk, we get the same results. In Chapter 13 we will show you how to detect this type of error.

Copy File

In Program 7-4, we copy a text file of integers to a new file.

```
 1   /* Copy a text file of integers.
 2         Written by:
 3         Date:
 4   */
 5   #include <stdio.h>
 6   #include <stdlib.h>
 7
 8   int main (void)
 9   {
10   /* Local Definitions */
11      FILE *fpIn;
12      FILE *fpOut;
13      int   numIn;
```

Program 7-4   Copy text file of integers

```
14      int    closeResult;
15
16  /* Statements */
17      printf("Running file copy\n");
18      fpIn = fopen("P7-03.DAT", "r");
19      if (!fpIn)
20         {
21          printf("Could not open input file\a\n");
22          exit  (101);
23         } /* if open fail */
24
25      fpOut = fopen("P7-04.DAT", "w");
26      if (!fpOut)
27         {
28          printf("Could not open output file\a\n");
29          exit  (102);
30         } /* if open fail */
31
32      while ((fscanf(fpIn, "%d", &numIn)) == 1)
33          fprintf(fpOut, "%d\n", numIn);
34
35      closeResult = fclose(fpOut);
36      if (closeResult == EOF)
37         {
38          printf("Could not close output file\a\n");
39          exit  (201);
40         } /* if close fail */
41
42      printf("File copy complete\n");
43      return 0;
44  }  /* main */
```

```
    Results:
       Running file copy
       File copy complete
```

Program 7-4 Copy text file of integers (continued)

Program 7-4 Analysis   Because this program has no display output, we start with a message that says we will copy a file, and we end with a message that says the copy succeeded. Users need to know that the program ran. If we don't print these messages, users will not know if the program ran. In fact, it is a good idea to print start and end messages with every program. This is a common standard in large production systems.

Now study the format string in Statement 33 carefully. Note that it requires a newline after the data have been written. It is important to use whitespace between the data in the file or it will not be readable. To verify that the data are correctly written, the file should be read and printed by Program 7-3 or a similar program.

Finally, note that we close the output file at the end of the program. While input files don't need to be closed, you should always close output files and check to make sure that they closed successfully. If the close fails, we print an error message. If it doesn't, we print the successful copy message.

Append File

Now let's append some data to the end of a file. After we wrote Program 7-5, we ran it without a file. Because append creates a file if it doesn't exist, the first run created our file. Then we ran it a second time and verified that the new data were appended to the original file.

```
 1  /* Copy a text file of integers.
 2         Written by:
 3         Date:
 4  */
 5  #include <stdio.h>
 6  #include <stdlib.h>
 7
 8  int main (void)
 9  {
10  /* Local Definitions */
11     FILE *fpAppnd;
12     int   numIn;
13     int   closeResult;
14
15  /* Statements */
16     printf("This program appends data to a file\n");
17     fpAppnd = fopen("P7-05.DAT", "a");
18     if (!fpAppnd)
19        {
20         printf("Could not open input file\a\n");
21         exit  (101);
22        } /* if open fail */
23
24     printf("Please enter first number:   ");
25     while ((scanf("%d", &numIn)) != EOF)
26        {
27         fprintf(fpAppnd, "%d\n", numIn);
28         printf("Enter next number or <EOF>: ");
29        } /* while */
30
31     closeResult = fclose(fpAppnd);
32     if (closeResult == EOF)
33        {
34         printf("Could not close output file\a\n");
35         exit  (201);
36        } /* if close fail */
37
38     printf("\nFile append complete\n");
39     return 0;
40  }  /* main */
```

```
Results:
   This program appends data to a file
   Please enter first number:  1
```

Program 7-5 Append data to file

```
        Enter next number or <EOF>: 2
        Enter next number or <EOF>: 3
        Enter next number or <EOF>:^d
        File append complete
```

Program 7-5 Append data to file (continued)

Program 7-5 Analysis   This program differs from Program 7-4 in two ways. First, this program has only one disk file. While we could have read the data to be appended from a file, it is more interesting and more flexible to get the data from the keyboard. The second change is the read loop to get the data. Because we are reading from the keyboard, we need to provide prompts for the user.

Student Grades

Programs 7-3 to 7-5 were all written in main. As our last example, let's write a program that reads and writes the student and grade files in Figure 7-5 on page 305. Recall that this figure describes a program that reads a student file and creates a grades file to be turned in at the end of the term. The code is shown in Program 7-6.

```
 1    /* Create a grades file for transmission to Registrar.
 2          Written by:
 3          Date:
 4    */
 5    #include <stdio.h>
 6
 7    /* Prototype Declarations */
 8    int getStu      (FILE  *fpStu,
 9                     int   *stuID,  int *exam1,
10                     int   *exam2,  int *final);
11    int writeStu    (FILE  *fpGrades,
12                     int    stuID,  int   avrg,  char grade);
13    void calcGrade (int     exam1,  int   exam2, int    final,
14                     int   *avrg,    char *grade);
15
16    int main (void)
17    {
18    /* Local Definitions */
19       FILE *fpStu;
20       FILE *fpGrades;
21
22       int stuID;
23       int exam1;
24       int exam2;
25       int final;
26       int avrg;
27
28       char grade;
29
30    /* Statements */
31       printf("Begin student grading\n");
```

Program 7-6 Student grades

```
32        if (!(fpStu = fopen ("CS1STU.DAT", "r")))
33           {
34            printf("\aError opening student file\n");
35            return 100;
36           } /* if open input */
37
38        if (!(fpGrades = fopen ("CS1GRADE.DAT", "w")))
39           {
40            printf("\aError opening grades file\n");
41            return 102;
42           } /* if open output */
43
44        while (getStu (fpStu, &stuID, &exam1, &exam2, &final))
45           {
46            calcGrade (exam1, exam2, final, &avrg, &grade);
47            writeStu  (fpGrades, stuID, avrg, grade);
48           } /* while */
49
50        fclose (fpStu);
51        fclose (fpGrades);
52
53        printf("End student grading\n");
54        return 0;
55    } /* main */
56
57  /* ====================== getStu ======================
58     Reads data from student file.
59        Pre   fpStu is an open file.
60              stuID, exam1, exam2, final pass by address
61        Post  reads student ID and exam scores
62              if data read   --returns 1
63              if EOF or error--returns 0
64  */
65  int getStu (FILE *fpStu,
66              int  *stuID,
67              int  *exam1,
68              int  *exam2,
69              int  *final)
70  {
71  /* Local Definitions */
72     int ioResult;
73
74  /* Statements */
75     ioResult = fscanf(fpStu, "%d%d%d%d", stuID,
76                       exam1, exam2, final);
77     if (ioResult == EOF)
78        return 0;
79     else if (ioResult != 4)
80        {
81         printf("\aError reading data\n");
```

Program 7-6 Student grades (continued)

```
 82          return 0;
 83        } /* if */
 84     else
 85        return 1;
 86  } /* getStu */
 87
 88  /* ==================== calcGrade ====================
 89     Determine student grade based on absolute scale.
 90          Pre    exam1, exam2, and final contain scores
 91                 avrg and grade are addresses of variables
 92          Post   Average and grade copied to addresses
 93  */
 94  void calcGrade (int    exam1,
 95                  int    exam2,
 96                  int    final,
 97                  int   *avrg,
 98                  char  *grade)
 99  {
100  /* Statements */
101     *avrg = (exam1 + exam2 + final) / 3;
102     if (*avrg >= 90)
103        *grade = 'A';
104     else if (*avrg >= 80)
105        *grade = 'B';
106     else if (*avrg >= 70)
107        *grade = 'C';
108     else if (*avrg >= 60)
109        *grade = 'D';
110     else
111        *grade = 'F';
112     return;
113  } /* calcGrade */
114
115  /* ==================== writeStu ====================
116     Writes student grade data to output file.
117          Pre    fpGrades is an open file
118                 stuID, avrg, and grade have values to write
119          Post   Data written to file
120  */
121  int writeStu   (FILE   *fpGrades,
122                  int     stuID,
123                  int     avrg,
124                  char    grade)
125  {
126  /* Statements */
127     fprintf(fpGrades, "%04d %d %c\n",
128                       stuID, avrg, grade);
129     return 0;
130  } /* writeStu */
```

Program 7-6 Student grades (continued)

```
Results:
    Begin student grading
    End student grading

Input--------
0090 90 90 90
0089 88 90 89
0081 80 82 81
0079 79 79 79
0070 70 70 70
0069 69 69 69
0060 60 60 60
0059 59 59 59

Output----
0090 90 A \n
0089 89 B \n
0081 81 B \n
0079 79 C \n
0070 70 C \n
0069 69 D \n
0060 60 D \n
0059 59 F \n
```

Program 7-6 Student grades (continued)

Program 7-6 Analysis   This program has several points to study. Let's start at the top. We open and close the files in `main`. Often, programmers write subfunctions for program initialization and conclusion, but in this case we decided to write them in `main`. The processing loop uses the return value from `getStu` to control the loop (see Statement 44). If data are read, then the return value is true (1); if there is an error or all data have been read, the return value is false (0). This design results in a very simple *while* loop.

Within the loop are three calls: one to read the student data (in the *while* limit test), one to calculate the grade, and one to write the grades file. Study the parameters carefully. We have used a combination of data values and addresses. Note especially the file parameters. In the function headers, the file parameters are coded as `FILE *`, which you should recognize as a file address. We do not use an address operator when we pass the files, however, because they are already addresses. (See Statements 44 and 47.)

Now study the results. The student ID is written as four digits with leading zeros because it is really a code, not a number. Note how we created the test data to verify that all of the boundaries in our multiway selection work correctly. To make it easy to verify, we made the student ID the same as the average. With these clues to the expected output, only a quick review of the results confirms that the program ran successfully.

7-5   CHARACTER INPUT/OUTPUT FUNCTIONS

Character input functions read one character at a time from a text stream. **Character output functions** write one character at the time to a text stream. We will discuss seven basic character functions: *getchar* and *putchar,* which read and write the standard input and output streams; *getc* and *fgetc,* and *putc* and *fputc,* which require that you specify the file pointer; and *ungetc,* which is available only in a file stream version.

Of course, the files must have been opened before we can use the file functions.

getchar

The *getchar* function reads the next character from the standard input stream and returns its value. The only things that stop it are the end of file or a read error. If the end of file condition results, or if an error is detected, *getchar* returns EOF. It is the programmer's responsibility to determine if some condition other than end of file has stopped the reading. The prototype statement for *getchar* is shown below.

```
int getchar (void);
```

Note that the return type is integer and not character as you might expect. The return type is integer because EOF is defined as an integer in the standard definition <stddef.h> and other header files. There is another reason for this: ANSI/ISO C guarantees that the EOF flag is not a character. This is true regardless of what character set it is using: ASCII, EBCDIC, or whatever. If you examine the control characters in ASCII, you will find none for end of file. Traditionally, EOF is defined as –1, but this is not prescribed by ANSI/ISO. An individual implementation could therefore choose a different value.

putchar

The *putchar* function writes one character to the standard output unit. If any error occurs during the write operation, it returns EOF. This may sound somewhat unusual, since EOF is normally thought of as an input file consideration, but in this case it simply means that the character couldn't be written. The prototype statement for *putchar* is shown below.

```
int putchar (int out_char);
```

Again the type is integer. An interesting result occurs with *putchar:* When `putchar` succeeds, it returns the character it wrote!

getc AND fgetc

The *getc* and *fgetc* functions read the next character from the file stream and convert it to an integer format. If the read detects an end of file, both functions return EOF. EOF is also returned if any error occurs. The prototype functions are shown below.

```
int  getc (FILE *fpIn);
int fgetc (FILE *fpIn);
```

Examples of *getc* and *fgetc* are shown below.

```
nextChar =  getc (fpMyFile);
nextChar = fgetc (fpMyFile);
```

putc AND fputc

The *putc* and *fputc* functions write the character parameter to the file stream specified. For *fputc,* the first parameter is the character to be written and the second parameter is the file. If the character is successfully written, the function returns it. If any error occurs, it returns EOF. The prototype functions are shown below.

```
int  putc (int oneChar, FILE *fpOut);
int fputc (int oneChar, FILE *fpOut);
```

Examples are shown below.

```
putc  (oneChar, fpMyFile);
fputc (oneChar, fpMyFile);
```

Note that we have discarded the return value. Although you may occasionally find a use for it, it is almost universally discarded.

You may be wondering why two different read and write functions are virtually identical. The answer lies in the history of the C language and is beyond the scope of this text.

ungetc

The *ungetc* function is the opposite of a *getc;* that is, it reverses the action by placing the specified character into the input stream. When the stream is next read, the character will be returned. The standard specifies that you will be able to "unget" at least one character. It does not state that you can "unget" multiple characters; therefore, you should not use *ungetc* more than once in succession. If the operation succeeds, the function returns the character; if it does not succeed, as with too many characters being pushed into the stream, it returns EOF.

The *ungetc* function has only one format. It requires that the first parameter be a character (as an integer value) and that the second parameter be a file. If you want to "unget" standard input, you must specify its file variable. This is seen in its prototype statement, shown below.

```
int ungetc (int oneChar, FILE *stream);
```

The intent of *ungetc* is to return a single character to the input stream for a subsequent "get." This might occur when you are reading characters that prompt action, such as in a menu system, and the wrong character is read (see below). In these situations, it is cleaner to reinsert the character into the input stream than to set a flag or otherwise pass the character through several functions.

In the following example, we want to process any option that is a character. Numeric options are processed in another function. Therefore, if we detect that an option is numeric, we put it back on the input stream and exit the function.

```
option = getc(stdin);
if (isdigit(option))
    ungetc (option, stdin);
else
    { … }
```

7-6 CHARACTER INPUT/OUTPUT EXAMPLES

This section contains several programs that use common text file applications.

CREATE TEXT FILE

Program 7-7 reads text from the standard input unit (keyboard) and creates a text file. All data are stored in text format with newlines only where input by the user.

```
 1  /* This program creates a text file.
 2        Written by:
 3        Date:
 4  */
 5  #include <stdio.h>
 6  int main (void)
 7  {
 8  /* Local Definitions */
 9     FILE *fpText;
10     int    c;
11     int    closeStatus;
12
13  /* Statements */
14     printf("This program copies your input to a file.\n");
15     printf("When you are through, enter <EOF>.\n\n");
16
17     if (!(fpText = fopen("P7-07.DAT","w")))
18        {
19         printf("Error opening FILE1.DAT for writing");
20         return (1);
21        } /* if open */
22
23     while ((c = getchar()) != EOF)
24        fputc(c, fpText);
25
26     closeStatus = fclose(fpText);
27     if (closeStatus == EOF)
28        {
29         printf("Error closing file\a\n");
30         return 100;
31        } /* if */
32
33     printf("\n\nYour file is complete\n");
34     return 0;
35  }  /* main */
```

```
Results:
    This program copies your input to a file.
    When you are through, enter <EOF>.

    Now is the time for all good students
    To come to the aid of their college.^d

    Your file is complete
```

Program 7-7 Create text file

Program 7-7 Analysis   This simple program is the beginning of a text editor. The biggest element missing is *word wrap*. Word wrap prevents a word from being split between two lines on a page.

Study the program carefully and note that we used integer for the character type (c) in Statement 10. This is an important point whenever you are checking for end of file, as we did in Statement 23. Because EOF will not be correctly represented in a character, we must use integer. But, what about when we have a character? C automatically casts the integer to a character wherever it is necessary.

COPY TEXT FILE

Program 7-8 will copy one text file to another text file. It is more generalized than Program 7-4, "Copy text file of integers," on page 324, because it will copy any file data, not just integers.

```
 1   /* This program copies one text file into another.
 2          Written by:
 3          Date:
 4   */
 5   #include <stdio.h>
 6   int   main (void)
 7   {
 8   /* Local Definitions */
 9      int    c;
10      int    closeStatus;
11      FILE *fp1;
12      FILE *fp2;
13
14   /* Statements */
15      printf("Begin file copy\n");
16
17      if (!(fp1 = fopen ("P7-07.DAT", "r")))
18         {
19          printf("Error opening P7-07.DAT for reading");
20          return (1);
21         } /* if open input */
22      if (!(fp2 = fopen ("P7-08.DAT", "w")))
23         {
24          printf("Error opening P7-08.DAT for writing");
25          return (2);
26         } /* if open output */
27
28      while ((c = fgetc(fp1)) != EOF)
29         fputc(c, fp2);
30
31      fclose(fp1);
32      closeStatus = fclose(fp2);
33      if (closeStatus == EOF)
34         {
35          printf("File close error.\a\n");
36          return 201;
37         } /* if close error */
38      printf("File successfully created\n");
39      return 0;
40   } /* main */
```

Program 7-8   Copy text file

Program 7-8 Analysis   This program contains two style points that need comments. First, we have used generic names for the files, `fp1` and `fp2`. Since this program simply copies and creates text files, we cannot give the files names that reflect their data. Better names might be `fpIn` and `fpOut`, but they are also generic.

Second, the program has two potential file open errors. We use different error codes for those operating systems whose job control can distinguish between different completion codes. We have also included the file names in the error messages so that the user knows exactly which file had the problem.

Finally, a subtle point: Note that we have arranged the local declarations in order of increasing complexity. First, we define the character and integer types: then we define the files. It is good practice to group the definitions by type and in order of increasing complexity.

COUNT CHARACTERS AND LINES

Program 7-9 counts the number of characters and lines in a program. Lines are designated by a newline. Also note that the program guards against a file that ends without a newline for the last line.

```
 1  /* This program counts characters and lines in a program.
 2        Written by:
 3        Date:
 4  */
 5  #include <stdio.h>
 6  int main (void)
 7  {
 8  /* Local Definitions */
 9     int    curCh;
10     int    preCh;
11     int    countLn = 0;
12     int    countCh = 0;
13     FILE *fp1;
14
15  /* Statements */
16     if (!(fp1 = fopen("P7-07.DAT", "r")))
17        {
18         printf("Error opening P7-07.DAT for reading");
19         return (1);
20        } /* if open error */
21
22     while ((curCh = fgetc(fp1)) != EOF)
23        {
24         if (curCh != '\n')
25             countCh++;
26         else
27             countLn++;
28         preCh = curCh;
29        } /* while */
30
31     if (preCh != '\n')
32         countLn++;
```

Program 7-9   Count characters and lines

```
33
34        printf("Number of characters: %d\n", countCh);
35        printf("Number of lines     : %d\n", countLn);
36
37        fclose(fp1);
38
39     return 0;
40  }   /* main*/
```

Program 7-9   Count characters and lines (continued)

Program 7-9 Analysis   Program 7-9 is rather straightforward. The only real problem is in making sure that the last line is counted even if there is no newline. We can check this at the end of the file by making sure that the last character we read, stored in preCh, was a newline. If it isn't, we add 1 to the line count.

Once again, we have used the integer type for our input character. Everything works correctly, even Statement 31, which compares the integer type (preCh) to a character literal.

COUNT WORDS IN FILE

Program 7-10 counts the number of words in a file. A word is defined as one or more characters separated by one or more whitespace characters—that is, by a space, a tab, or a newline.

```
1  /* Count number of words in file. Words are separated by
2     whitespace characters: space, tab, and newline.
3        Written by:
4        Date:
5  */
6  #include <stdio.h>
7
8  #define WHT_SPC (cur == ' ' || cur == '\n' || cur ==  '\t')
9
10 int main (void)
11 {
12 /*Local Definitions */
13    int    cur;
14    int    countWd = 0;
15    char   word = 'O';       /* O out of word: I in word */
16    FILE *fp1;
17
18 /* Statements */
19    if (!(fp1 = fopen("P7-07.DAT", "r")))
20       {
21        printf("Error opening P7-07.DAT for reading");
22        return (1);
23       } /* if file open error */
24    while ((cur = fgetc(fp1)) != EOF)
25       {
26        if (WHT_SPC)
```

Program 7-10   Count words

```
27              word = 'O';
28          else
29              if (word ==  'O')
30                  {
31                      countWd++;
32                      word = 'I';
33                  } /* else */
34          } /* while */
35      printf("The number of words is: %d\n", countWd);
36
37      fclose(fp1);
38      return 0;
39  }  /* main */
```

Program 7-10 Count words (continued)

Program 7-10 Analysis   The selection logic for this problem is similar to the previous program. We must determine when we are in a word and when we are between words. We are between words when we start the program and whenever we are at whitespace. To keep track of where we are, we use a flag, word. When word contains the letter I, we are in a word; when it contains the letter O, we are out of a word. We increment the counter only at the beginning of a word, when we set the word flag to I.

Note that the problem handles multiple whitespace characters by simply setting the word flag to O. Note also how we use a preprocessor *define* statement to define whitespace. This has no effect on the efficiency of the program, but it makes it easier to read.

7-7 SOFTWARE ENGINEERING AND PROGRAMMING STYLE

TESTING FILES

Testing files can be a very difficult task for two reasons. First, many errors cannot be created through normal testing. Among these types of errors are those created by bad physical media, such as disk and tapes. Often, disks and tapes become unreadable. Good programs test for these types of errors, but they are difficult to create.

Second, there are so many ways things can go wrong. Your test plan therefore needs to ensure that all possibilities have been tested. Chief among them is the case where a user enters a non-numeric character while trying to enter a number. If you don't provide for this situation, your program will not work properly. In fact, in some situations, it will not work at all.

Testing for Invalid User Input

Consider the following code to read an integer value. If the user miskeys the data, the program will go into an infinite loop.

```
printf("\nPlease enter Number of Units Sold: ");
while (scanf("%d", &unitsSold) != 1)
        /* scanf returns 1 if number read correctly */
        printf("\nInvalid number. Please re-enter.\n");
```

In this case, it looks as if the programmer has done everything correctly. The program checks for valid data being returned. A user prompt shows what data should be entered; the program checks for valid data being read; and if there were none, provides the user with a good error message and repeats the *scanf.* What is wrong?

The problem lies in what *scanf* does when it finds an invalid first digit. If the number is entirely wrong, it leaves the data pending in the input stream. This means that while the user sees the error message, the invalid data are still in the input stream waiting for a *scanf* that will properly read and process them. Remember that *scanf* thinks that these "invalid data" are the beginning of the next field. It is your job as a programmer to get rid of the "bad data." You can do this with a small piece of code that is commonly named FLUSH. Its purpose is to read through the input stream looking for the end of a line. When it finds the end of the line, it terminates. Let's first look at the code, then we will look at an easy way to implement it.

```
while (getchar( ) != '\n');
```

Examine this statement carefully. All it does is get a character and then throw it away. That is, the character it reads is not saved. Now examine the expression that is controlling the *while.* If *getchar* reads any character other than a newline, the statement is true. If it reads a newline, then the statement is false. The *while* statement will therefore read the input stream and throw away all characters until it sees a newline. When it finds the newline, it will throw it away too, but at that point, the loop will stop. In other words, it flushes the input stream to a newline character. This is exactly what we want to do when the user accidentally keys the wrong character when the program expects a digit.

Now, what's the easiest way to implement this handy statement? Well, you could simply code it everywhere you need it, but chances are that you would make some mistakes that would have to be found and debugged. A better solution is to use the preprocessor *define* declarative and code the statement only once, as shown below.

```
#define FLUSH while (getchar( ) != '\n')
```

Note that there is no semicolon at the end of the *define* declarative. We could have put one there, but it's better to put the semicolon after the FLUSH in the program. Our error code can now be changed to handle this type of error, as shown in Program 7-11.

```
1  #define FLUSH while (getchar() != '\n')
2  ...
3     printf("\nPlease enter Number of Units Sold: ");
4     while (scanf("%d", &unitsSold) != 1)
5        {
6        /* scanf returns 1 if number read corrrectly */
7        FLUSH;
8        printf("\aInvalid number. Please re-enter: ");
9        } /* while */
```

Program 7-11   Handling errors—the right way

Value Errors

In Chapter 6, we discussed some of the techniques for data validation. But the subtleties of data validation can be quite complex. Consider another type of human error, the partially correct input. In our example above, we assumed that the user erred on the first digit of the number. What if the error occurs on the second or third digit? Then the *scanf* function is happy, for the time being anyway, and returns a 1, indicating that it read one number successfully. How do you guard against this?

The best way is to echo the input to the user and ask for verification that it is correct. Although this greatly slows down the input process, for critical data it is necessary. The code for this situation is shown in Program 7-12. Here we present it as a complete function.

```
1  /* This function reads the units sold from the keyboard and
2     verifies the data with the user.
3        Pre    nothing
4        Post   units Sold read, verified, and returned
5  */
6  int getUnitsSold (void)
7  {
8     int  unitsSold;
9     int  valid;
10
11 do
12    {
```

Program 7-12   Handling errors with explanations

```
13      printf("\nPlease enter Number of Units Sold: ");
14        while (scanf("%d", &unitsSold) != 1)
15           {
16            FLUSH;
17            printf("\aInvalid number. Please re-enter: ");
18           }  /* while */
19        printf("\nVerify Units Sold: %d: ", unitsSold);
20        printf("<Y> correct: <N> not correct: \n");
21        FLUSH;
22        if (toupper(getchar ()) ==  'Y')
23            valid = TRUE;
24        else
25           {
26            FLUSH;
27            printf("\nYou responded 'no.' ");
28            printf("Please re-enter Units Sold\n");
29            valid = FALSE;
30           } /* if */
31     } while (!valid);
32   return unitsSold;
33   } /* getUnitsSold */
```

Program 7-12 Handling errors with explanations (continued)

Program 7-12 Analysis   This function merits some discussion. First, note the good user communication throughout the function. It begins with a complete prompt and provides clear error messages whenever problems are detected.

We have implemented this logic with a *do...while* statement, which always loops at least once, since we know that there will always be input. This is the standard loop for validating user input. Within the loop are two different validation steps. The first tests for totally invalid input, the second asks the user to verify the input. If either test indicates a problem, the input is flushed. Note that the user messages are different depending on the circumstances.

The function cannot end unless the *valid* flag is true. The *if* statement in the loop will set it true if the user replies positively. Otherwise, it is set false and the input is flushed. This code again demonstrates two principles of good human engineering. The *if* statement is coded in a positive manner, and the expected event, good input, is checked first.

Many other things can go wrong when you are reading a file, but these two examples cover most of them.

DATA TERMINOLOGY

Computer specialists who deal with data use a set of specific terms to describe their data. These terms deal with data that are stored in files. What we call a variable in our program, they call a *field* or a *data item*. A field is the smallest named unit of data in a file. If we were working with data about the ten western states in the continental United States, we would have data like Name, Capital, Number, Square Miles, Population, and Number of Counties. The first two fields are strings (delimited arrays of characters that we will study in Chapter 11) and the last four are integers.

These six fields grouped together make up a state record. A *record* is a collection of related data, in this case state data, treated as a unit. Each record has a *key*, one or more fields that uniquely identify the record. In our state's record, the key could be the name. Names normally do not make good keys, because they are not guaranteed to be unique. A better choice is the state number, which represents the order in which the states entered the union. This field is guaranteed to be unique.

With text files we cannot create a record. We must wait for binary files and structures to do that. But we can simulate a record by grouping these data on the same line, with each field separated from the next by whitespace. The data for the ten western states are shown in Table 7-4.

State	Capital	No.	Sq. Miles	Population	No. Counties
Arizona	Phoenix	48	113,508	3,665,228	15
California	Sacramento	31	156,299	29,760,021	58
Colorado	Denver	38	103,595	3,294,394	63
Idaho	Boise	43	82,412	1,006,451	44
Montana	Helena	41	145,388	799,065	56
Nevada	Carson City	36	109,894	1,201,833	16
New Mexico	Santa Fe	47	121,335	1,515,069	33
Oregon	Salem	33	96,184	2,842,321	36
Washington	Olympia	42	66,511	4,866,692	39
Wyoming	Cheyenne	44	96,989	453,588	23

Table 7-4   Ten western states (as of 1990)

Data can be logically organized to provide more meaning. Although computer scientists normally store this type of data using binary files, there is no reason why it can't be stored in a text file as well. We will return to the discussion again when we study strings in Chapter 11 and binary files in Chapter 13.

7-8   TIPS AND COMMON PROGRAMMING ERRORS

1. To print a percent sign, you need to use two tokens (%%).
2. After you have finished working with a file, you should close it.
3. If you open a file for writing, a new file will be created. This means that if you already have an existing file with the same name, it could be deleted.

4. If you want to write at the end of an existing text file, open the file for appending, not for writing.

5. C output is right justified when using *printf* and *fprintf* functions. If you want your data to be left justified, use the left-justify flag (–) explicitly.

6. It is a compile error to misplace the file pointer in the parameter list. The file pointer is coded last in all file functions except *fscanf* and *fprintf*, in which it is coded first.

7. An error that may cause your program run to terminate is to use a format code that does not match the variable type being read.

8. An error that will give invalid output is to use a format code that does not match the variable being printed.

9. Several common errors are created when a file operation is included in a selection statement. Three are shown below.

   a. The following code does not properly test to make sure that the file was opened correctly:

   ```
   if (fp = fopen() != NULL)        /* logic error */
   if ((fp = fopen()) != NULL)      /* good code */
   ```

   b. The following code does not store the character read in ch. It stores the logical result of the compare in ch.

   ```
   if (ch = getchar() != '\n')      /* logic error */
   if ((ch = getchar()) != '\n')    /* good code */
   ```

   c. In a similar way, the following code is invalid:

   ```
   /* logic error */
   while (ioResult = scanf(…) != EOF)

   /* good code */
   while ((ioResult = scanf(…)) != EOF)
   ```

   d. It is a logic error to define ioResult in the above statement as a character because EOF (–1) cannot be stored in a character.

10. It is a fatal logic error to code a whitespace character at the end of a *scanf* statement.

11. It is a run-time error to attempt to open a file that is already opened.

12. It is a run-time error to attempt to read a file opened in the write mode or to write a file opened in the read mode.

7-9 KEY TERMS AND CONCEPTS[3]

append mode	*fprintf*	signed
auxiliary storage devices	*fputc*	size
binary file	*fscanf*	space flag
buffer	*getc*	standard error file
character input/output	hexadecimal conversion	standard file stream
close function	input/output functions	standard input file
conversion code	leading zero padding	standard output file
fgetc	octal conversion	`stderr`
field specification	open function	`stdin`
field width	precision	`stdout`
file	*printf*	stream
`FILE`	*putc*	testing invalid input
file mode	read mode	text file
file table	right justification	*ungetc*
filename	*scanf*	value error
flag	secondary storage	write mode
format string	sign flag	

[3]Note: Italic terms are C keywords or standard library functions.

7-10 SUMMARY

■ A file is a collection of related data treated as a unit.

■ Data in a text file are stored as human-readable characters. The data in a text file are usually divided into lines separated by a newline character.

■ A stream is a sequence of elements in time.

■ A stream is associated with a file in C.

■ There are three standard file streams in C: standard input, standard output, and standard error.

■ The standard input is associated with the keyboard. The standard output and the standard error are associated with the monitor.

■ The standard file streams can be accessed respectively using `stdin`, `stdout`, and `stderr`. These are pointers (addresses) to tables (structures) containing the information about the standard streams.

■ To manipulate and access files, there are different types of input/output functions.

■ The open/close functions, *fopen* and *fclose,* are used to open and close the association between external files and internal streams.

■ A file in C can be any of the three basic modes: reading, writing, and appending.

■ When a file is opened in reading mode, the file marker is positioned at the beginning of the existing file. The file is ready to be read.

■ When a file is opened for writing, the file marker is positioned at the beginning of a newly created empty file, before the end-of-file character. The file is ready to be written.

■ When a file is opened for appending, the marker is positioned at the end of the existing file (or at the beginning of a newly created file), before the end-of-file marker. The file is then ready to be written.

■ Formatted input/output functions allow us to read data from and write data to files character by character while formatting them to the desired data types such as *char, int,* and *float.* The functions *scanf* and *fscanf* are used for reading. The functions *printf* and *fprintf* are used for writing.

■ Character input/output functions allow us to read or write files character by character. The functions *fgetc, getc,* and *getchar* can be used for reading. The functions *fputc, putc,* and *putchar* can be used for writing.

■ When we are reading data from files, we should validate the data.

7-11 PRACTICE SETS

REVIEW QUESTIONS

1. User files are created using the `FILE` type.
   a. True   b. False

2. If a file does not exist, the append mode returns an error.
   a. True   b. False

3. The field specification starts with an asterisk (*) and ends with the conversion code.
   a. True   b. False

4. The space flag is used to left-justify output in the `printf` function.
   a. True   b. False

5. One of the problems with testing files is that some errors, such as physically bad media, cannot be created so that they can be tested.
   a. True   b. False

6. Which of the following is considered auxiliary storage?
   a. disk
   b. random access memory (RAM)
   c. read only memory (ROM)
   d. tape
   e. both disk and tape

7. Which of the following is not a standard file stream?
   a. `stdin`   c. `stdfile`
   b. `stderr`   d. `stdout`

8. The C library that contains the prototype statements for file operations is
   a. `file.h`   d. `stdio.h`
   b. `proto.h`   e. `stdlib.h`
   c. `stdfile.h`

9. If a file is opened in the `r` mode, C
   a. opens the file for reading and sets the file marker at the beginning.
   b. opens the file for reading and sets the file marker at the end.
   c. opens the file for writing and sets the file marker at the beginning.
   d. opens the file for writing and sets the file marker at the end.
   e. returns a null file address indicating an error if the file exists.

10. If a file is not opened successfully, C
    a. aborts the program.
    b. continues processing with the next statement after the open.
    c. changes the file mode to write and opens a new file.
    d. displays a message and waits for an answer.
    e. returns a file address.

11. The _____ specifies the type of data that are being formatted in formatted input/output.
    a. conversion code   d. format code
    b. data code   e. pcode
    c. field code

12. The two input functions that read text data and convert the data to the types specified by a format string are
    a. *fread* and *read*   d. *read* and *readf*
    b. *fscanf* and *fprintf*   e. *scanf* and *printf*
    c. *fscanf* and *scanf*

13. Which of the following statements about the formatted input function (*scanf*) is false?
    a. *scanf* implicitly casts data to match the conversion code and its corresponding address parameter.
    b. *scanf* reads data from the keyboard and formats it according to field specifications.
    c. *scanf* returns an integer containing the number of variables successfully formatted or `EOF`.
    d. *scanf* stops formatting data when an inappropriate character for the type being formatted is encountered.
    e. To function properly, *scanf* requires at least one address.

14. The _____ function reads the next character from the standard input stream and returns its value.
    a. *fgetc*   d. *readchar*
    b. *getc*   e. *ungetc*
    c. *getchar*

15. When *scanf* finds invalid data in the input stream, it
    a. flushes the input to a newline.
    b. prints an error message and terminates the program.
    c. prints an error message and terminates the *scanf* function.
    d. skips the data and formats the next field specification, if any.
    e. terminates the *scanf* function and leaves the invalid character in the input stream.

EXERCISES

16. Given the following declaration:
    ```
    int     i1;
    int     i2;
    float   f1;
    char    c1;
    char    c2;
    char    c3;
    ```
    and the following line of data
    ```
    14   23   76   CD
    ```
    what would be the value of i1, i2, f1, c1, c2, and c3 after the following statement?
    ```
    scanf("%d %d %f %c %c %c",
          &i1, &i2, &f1, &c1, &c2, &c3);
    ```

17. Given the following declaration:
    ```
    int     i1;
    int     i2;
    float   f1;
    char    c1;
    char    c2;
    ```
    and the following line of data
    ```
    14.2   C   K   67   67.9
    ```
    what would be the value of i1, i2, f1, c1, c2, and c3 after the following statement?
    ```
    scanf("%d %c %c %i   %f ",
          &i1, &c1, &c2, &i2, &f1);
    ```

18. Given the following declaration:
    ```
    int     i1;
    int     i2;
    int     i3;
    char    c1;
    char    c2;
    char    c3;
    ```
    and the following line of data:
    ```
    c145d123 34.7
    ```
    what would be the value of i1, i2, i3, c1, c2, and c3 after the following statement?
    ```
    scanf("%c%c%d%c%d%d",
          &c1, &c2, &i1, &c3, &i2, &i3);
    ```

19. What would be printed from the following program segment?
    ```
    int     i1 = 123;
    int     i2 = - 234;
    int     i3 = -7;
    float   f1 = 23.5;
    float   f2 = 12.09;
    float   f3 = 98.34;
    ```

```
char    c1 = 65;
char    c2 = '\n';
char    c3 = 'E';


printf("%06d, %06d, %06d %c",
        i1, i2, i3, c2);
printf("%-6d, %% , \" , \\t , %-06d", i2, i1);
printf("%c %d ", c1, c2);
printf("%c %c %c ", c1 + 32, c3 + 3, c2 + 5);
```

20. What output is produced from the following program? Include in your answer the contents of any files created.

```c
#include <stdio.h>

int main (void)

{
FILE *fp;
int    i;
char  ch;
fp = fopen("TEST.DAT", "w");
for (i = 2; i < 20; i += 2)
    fprintf(fp, "%3d", i);
fclose(fp);
fp = fopen("TEST.DAT", "r");
while ((ch = fgetc(fp)) != EOF)
    if (ch == ' ')
        fputc('*', stdout);
    else if (ch != '1')
            fputc(ch, stdout);
    else
        {
        putchar('\n');
        putchar(ch);
        }
return 0;
} /* main */
```

PROBLEMS

For the problems and projects in this chapter, you need to create a test file using your text editor. End each line with a newline character; do not write in paragraph format. We suggest the "Gettysburg Address" as a suitable subject for these files:

Four score and seven years ago our fathers brought forth on this continent a new nation, conceived in liberty, and dedicated to the proposition that all men are created equal. Now we are engaged in a great civil war, testing whether that nation, or any nation so conceived and so dedicated, can long endure. We are met on a great battlefield of that war. We have come to dedicate a portion of that field as a final resting-place for those who here gave their lives that that nation might live. It is altogether fitting and proper that we should do this. But in a larger sense, we cannot dedicate, we cannot consecrate, we cannot hallow, this ground. The brave men, living and dead, who struggled here have consecrated it far above our poor power to add or detract. The world will little note, nor long remember what we say here, but it can never forget what they did here. It is for us the living, rather to be dedicated here to the unfinished work which they who fought here have thus far so nobly advanced. It is rather for us, to be here dedicated to the great task remaining before us, that from these honored dead we take increased devotion to that cause for which they gave the last full measure of devotion; that we here highly resolve that these dead shall not have died in vain; that this nation, under God, shall have a new birth of freedom, and that government of the people, by the people, for the people, shall not perish from the earth.

21. Write a function that appends one file at the end of the other.

22. Write a function that appends a file to itself.

23. Write a function that accepts a file of varying-length lines and changes it to a formatted file with 60 characters in each line.

24. Write a function that calculates the average number of characters per line in a file.

25. Write a function that deletes the last line of any file.

26. Write a function that deletes the blank lines in a file. A blank line is a line with only one single character in it: newline.

27. Write a program that prints itself.

28. Write a program that copies one text file to another and inserts blank lines between paragraphs in the new file. Paragraphs are identified by a newline character.

29. Write a program to copy only lines beginning with a user-specified character.

30. Write a program to parse words onto separate lines; that is, locate and write each word to its own line. Words are defined as one or more characters separated by whitespace.

31. When *scanf* encounters an error, the invalid data are left in the input stream, sometimes making it impossible to continue. Write a function that reads three pieces of numeric data. If an error is detected (return value not EOF but less than 3), flush the erroneous data. (See page 339 for details on how to write a flush statement.) Then test the function by entering numeric data and alphabetic data in different sequences.

32. Write a program to insert a blank line after the seventh line in a file.

33. Write a program to delete the sixth line in a file. Do not change the sixth line to a blank line; delete it completely.

34. Write a program to insert a blank line after each line in a file. In other words, double-space the text.

35. Write a program to duplicate the fourth line in a file.

36. Write a program to copy a file, deleting the first two characters of each line. (Do not replace the characters with blanks.)

37. Write a program to copy a file, inserting two space characters at the beginning of each line. In other words, each line will be shifted two characters to the right.

38. Write a program that copies the 21st character of each line in a file to a new file. All extracted characters are to be on the same line. If a line in the input file has fewer than 21 characters, write the last character. If a line is blank—that is, if it consists of only whitespace—then copy nothing. At the end of file, write a newline to the new file and close it.

39. Write a program that writes the odd-numbers between 300 and 500 to a text file.

40. Write a function that writes the multiples of num between `lowLimit` and `highLimit` to a text file. Assume that `lowLimit` < `highLimit` and that `num` is not equal to zero. Then write a test driver to validate your function.

41. Write a program to read a set of scores from a text file, count the scores over 90, copy the scores over 90 to a new file, and print the number of scores over 90 to the monitor.

42. Modify Problem 41 to count and create a file for the ranges 0 to 30, 31 to 60, 61 to 90, and over 90. Print the statistics for each range at the end of the program.

PROJECTS

43. Write a program that will read a text file and count the number of alphabetic characters (*isalpha*), digits (*isdigit*), punctuation characters (*ispunct*), and whitespace characters (*isspace*) in the file. At the end of the file, the program is to display an appropriate report. (The classifying functions are covered in Chapter 5.)

44. Write a text analyzer program that reads any text file. The program prints a menu that gives the user the options of counting lines, words, characters, or sentences (one or more words ending in a period), or all of the above. Provide a separate function for each option. At the end of the analysis, write an appropriate report.

45. Write a menu-driven text utility program. The program will have the following capabilities:

    a. Copy a user-named file to a new file.

    b. Append a user-named file to another user-named file.

    c. Change the file format to double-spaced.

    d. Remove all blank lines (change a double-spaced file to single-spaced).

    e. Display the contents of the file as a series of 60 character lines with no words split between lines.

46. Using an editor, create an inventory file using the data shown in Table 7-5 (do not include the column captions, just the data).

Part No.	Price	Quantity On Hand	Reorder Point	Minimum Order
0123	1.23	23	20	20
0234	2.34	34	50	25
3456	34.56	56	50	10
4567	45.67	7	10	5
5678	6.78	75	75	25

Table 7-5 Inventory file data for Project 46

Write a program to read the inventory file and create an inventory report. The report will contain the part number, price, quantity on hand, reorder point, minimum order, and order amount. The order amount is calculated when the quantity on hand falls below the reorder point. It is calculated as the sum of the reorder point and the minimum order less the quantity on hand. Provide a report heading, such as "Inventory Report," captions for each column, and an "End of Report" message at the end of the report. Print the part number with leading zeros.

47. Using an editor, create the employee file shown in Table 7-6.

Employee No.	Department	Pay Rate	Exempt	Hours Worked
0101	41	8.11	Y	49
0722	32	7.22	N	40
1273	23	5.43	Y	39
2584	14	6.74	N	45

Table 7-6 Employee file data for Project 47

Write a program to read the employee file and create a payroll register. The register will contain the following data:

a. Employee number (print left-justified)

b. Department

c. Pay rate

d. Exempt

e. Hours worked

f. Base pay (pay rate * hours worked)

g. Overtime pay
   Overtime pay is calculated only for nonexempt employees. An employee is exempt if Y appears in the exempt column. Overtime is paid at time and one-half for all hours worked over 40.

h. Total pay

Arrays

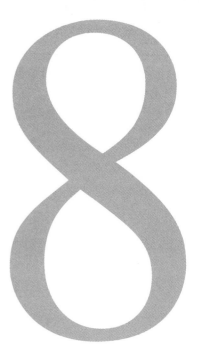

In the preceding chapters, we used only the standard data types: characters, integers, and floating-point numbers. Although these types are very useful, they can handle only limited amounts of data. In this chapter we begin presenting the derived data types with the array structure.

With the introduction of arrays, we also begin the study of **data structures.** A complete discussion of data structures is well beyond the scope of this text; however, you need to understand some of the basic concepts of data structures. Structured data are data organized to show the relationships among the individual elements. Most cases require a collecting mechanism to organize the data. One common organizing technique, the use of arrays, allows us to process the data as a group or as individual elements.

8-1   CONCEPTS

Imagine we have a problem that requires 20 integers to be processed. We need to read them, process them, and print them. We must also keep these 20 integers in memory for the duration of the program. We can declare and define 20 variables, each with a different name, as shown in Figure 8-1.

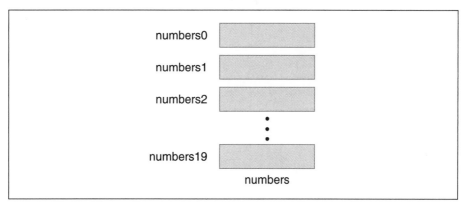

Figure 8-1   Twenty variables

But having 20 different names creates another problem. How can we read 20 integers from the keyboard and store them? To read 20 integers from the keyboard, we need 20 references, each to one variable. Furthermore, once we have them in memory, how can we print them? To print them, we need another 20 references. In other words, we need the flowchart shown in Figure 8-2 to read, process, and print these 20 integers.

Although this may be acceptable for 20 integers, it is definitely not acceptable for 200 or 2,000 or 20,000 integers. To process large amounts of data, we need a powerful data structure, such as an array. An **array** is a fixed-size, sequenced collection of elements of the same data type.

One-Dimensional Array
A fixed-size sequence of elements of the same type.

Since an array is a sequenced collection, we can refer to the elements in the array as the first element, the second element, and so forth until we get to the last element. If we were to put our 20 numbers into an array, we could designate the first element as shown below.[1]

$$numbers_0$$

In a similar fashion, we could refer to the second number as $numbers_1$ and the third number as $numbers_2$. Continuing the series, the last number would be $numbers_{19}$. We can generalize this concept in the following fashion, where the **subscripts** indicate the, ordinal number of the element counting from the beginning of the array:

$$numbers_0, numbers_1, ..., numbers_{n-1}$$

---

[1]Many areas of computer science, including C, use zero-based addressing. Thus, the first element is identified with a zero subscript.

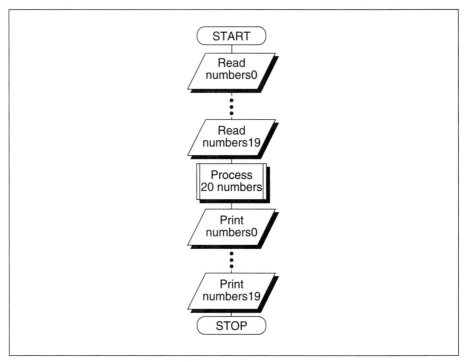

Figure 8-2   Process 20 variables

The elements of the array are individually addressed through their subscripts. This concept is graphically shown in Figure 8-3. The array as a whole has a name, numbers, but each member can be accessed individually using its subscript.

The advantages of the array would be limited if we didn't also have programming constructs that allow us to process the data more conveniently. Fortunately, a powerful set of programming constructs—loops—makes array processing easy.

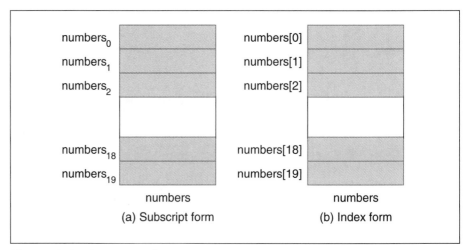

Figure 8-3   An array of numbers

We can use loops to read and write the elements in an array. We can use loops to add, subtract, multiply, and divide the elements. We can also use loops for more complex processing such as calculating averages. Now it does not matter if 2, 20, 200, 2,000, or 20,000 elements must be processed. Loops will make it easy to handle them all.

But one question still remains. How can we write an instruction so that one time it refers to the first element of an array, and the next time it refers to another element? It is really quite simple: We simply borrow from the subscript concept we have been using. Rather than using subscripts, however, we will place the subscript value in **square brackets**. Using this notation, we would refer to $numbers_0$ as

```
numbers[0]
```

Following the convention, $numbers_1$ becomes numbers[1] and $numbers_{19}$ becomes numbers[19]. This is known as **indexing**. Using a typical reference, we now refer to our array using the variable i.

```
numbers [i]
```

The flowchart to process our 20 numbers using an array and looping is shown in Figure 8-4.

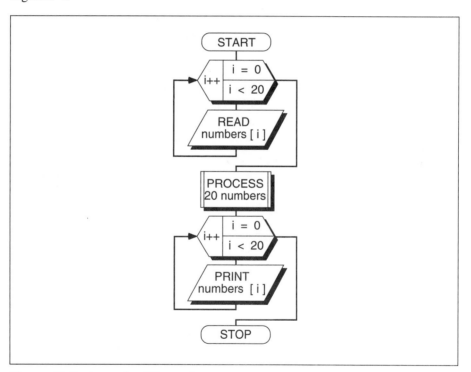

Figure 8-4   Loop for 20 numbers

8-2   USING ARRAYS IN C

In this section, we first show how to declare and define arrays. Then we present several typical applications using arrays including reading values into arrays, accessing and exchanging elements in arrays, and printing arrays. Figure 8-5 shows a typical array, named scores, and its values.

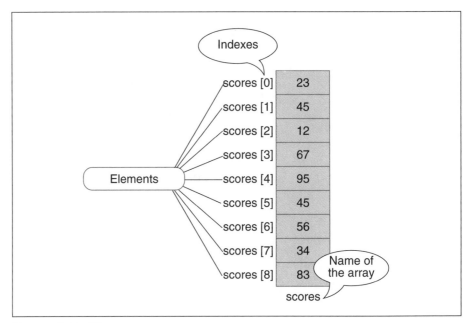

Figure 8-5 The `scores` array

DECLARATION AND DEFINITION

An array must be **declared** and **defined** before it can be used. Declaration and definition tell the compiler the name of the array, the type of each element, and the size or number of elements in the array. The size of the array is a constant and must have a value at compilation time. Figure 8-6 shows three different array declarations: one for integers, one for characters, and one for floating-point numbers.

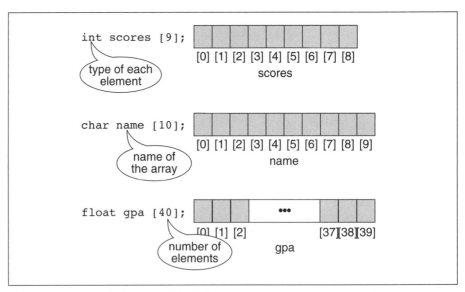

Figure 8-6 Declaring and defining arrays

ACCESSING ELEMENTS IN ARRAYS

C uses an **index** to access individual elements in an array. The index must be an integral value or an expression that evaluates to an integral value. The simplest form for accessing an element is a numeric constant. For example, given the `scores` array in Figure 8-5, we could access the first element as follows:

```
scores[0]
```

Typically, however, the index is a variable or an expression. To process all the elements in scores, a loop similar to the following code is used:

```
for (i = 0; i < 9, i++)
     scores[i] …;
```

You might be wondering how C knows where an individual element is located in memory. In scores, for example, there are nine elements. How does it find just one? The answer is simple. The array's name is a symbolic reference for the address to the first byte of the array. Whenever we use the array's name, therefore, we are actually referring to the first byte of the array. The index represents an offset from the beginning of the array to the element being referred to. With these two pieces of data, C can calculate the address of any element in the array using the following simple formula:

element address = array address + (sizeof (element) * index)

For example, assume that scores is stored in memory at location 10,000. Since scores is an integer, the size of one element is the size of an integer. Assuming an integer size of 2, the address of the element at index 3 is

```
element address = 10,000 + 2 * 3 = 10,006
```

STORING VALUES IN ARRAYS

Declaration and definition only reserve space for the elements in the array. No values will be stored. If we want to store values in the array, we must either initialize the elements, read values from the keyboard, or assign values to each individual element.

Initialization

Initialization of all elements in an array can be done at the time of declaration and definition, just as with variables. For each element in the array, we provide a value. The only difference is that the values must be enclosed in braces and, if there is more than one, separated by commas. It is a compile error to specify more values than there are elements in the array.

Figure 8-7 contains four examples of array initialization. The first example (Figure 8-7(a)) is a simple array declaration of five integers and is typical of the way array initialization is coded. When the array is completely initialized, the programmer does not need to specify the size of the array. This case is seen in Figure 8-7(b). It is a good idea, however, to define the size explicitly, because it allows the compiler to do some checking for errors and is also good documentation.

If the number of values provided is less than the number of elements in the array, the unassigned elements are filled with zeros. This case is seen in Figure 8-7(c). We can use this rule to easily initialize an array to all zeros by supplying just the first zero value, as shown in the last example in Figure 8-7(d).

Inputting Values

Another way to fill the array is to read the values from the keyboard or a file. This method of **inputting values** can be done using a loop. When the array will be completely filled, the most appropriate loop is the *for* because the number of elements is fixed and known.

```
for (i = 0; i < 9; i++)
   scanf ("%d", &scores [i]);
```

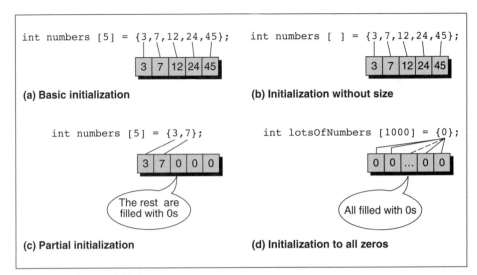

Figure 8-7 Initializing arrays

Several concepts need to be studied in this simple statement. First, we start the index, i, at 0. Since the array has 9 elements, we must load the values from index locations 0 through 8. The limit test, therefore, is set at i < 9, which conveniently is the number of elements in the array. Then, even though we are dealing with array elements, the address operator (&) is still necessary in the *scanf* call.

Finally, if all the elements might not be filled, then you should use one of the event-controlled loops (*while* or *do…while*). Which loop you use depends on the application.

Assigning Values

You can assign values to individual elements using the assignment operator. Any value that reduces to the proper type can be assigned to an individual array element. A simple assignment statement for scores is seen below.

```
scores [4] = 23;
```

On the other hand, you cannot assign one array to another array, even if they match fully in type and size. You have to copy arrays at the individual element level. For example, to copy an array of 25 integers to a second array of 25 integers, you could use a loop, as shown below.

```
for (i = 0; i < 25; i++)
    second[i] = first[i];
```

If the values of an array follow a pattern, we can use a loop to assign values. For example, the following loop assigns a value that is twice the index number to array scores:

```
for (i = 0; i < 9; i++)
    scores [i] = i * 2;
```

For another example, the following code assigns the odd numbers 1 through 17 to the elements of an array named value:

```
for (i = 0; i < 9; i++)
    value [i] = (i * 2) + 1;
```

Exchanging Values

A common application is to **exchange** the contents of two elements. We will see this operation later in the chapter when we talk about sorting arrays. When you exchange variables, you swap the values of elements without knowing what's in them.

For example, imagine we want to swap numbers[3] and numbers[1] in Figure 8-7. A common beginner's mistake would be simply to assign each element to the other, as shown below.

```
numbers [3] = numbers [1];
numbers [1] = numbers [3];
```

Although this code looks as if it will do the job, if we trace the code carefully, we find that it does only half the job. numbers[1] is moved to numbers[3], but the second half isn't done. The result is that both elements have the same value. Figure 8-8 traces the steps.

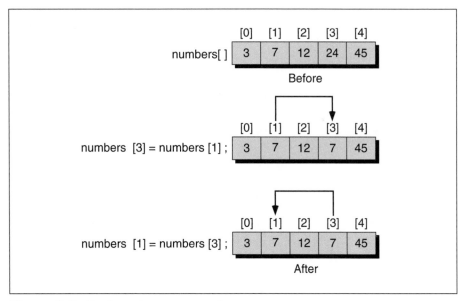

Figure 8-8 Exchanging scores—the wrong way

Figure 8-8 shows that the original value of numbers[3] is destroyed before we can move it. The solution is to use a temporary variable to store the value in numbers[3] before moving the data from numbers[1].

```
temp        = numbers[3];
numbers [3] = numbers [1];
numbers [1] = temp;
```

This technique is shown in Figure 8-9.

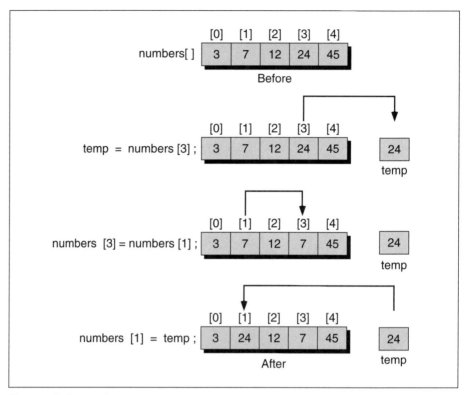

Figure 8-9 Exchanging scores with temporary variable

Outputting Values

Another common application is printing the contents of an array. This is easily done with a *for* loop, as shown below.

```
for (i = 0; i < 9; i++)
    printf ("%d ", scores [i]);
printf ("\n");
```

In this example, all the data are printed on one line. After the *for* loop completes, a final *printf* statement advances to the next line. But what if we had 100 values to be printed? In that case, we couldn't put them all on one line. Given a relatively small number width, however, we could put 10 on a line. We would then need 10 lines to print all the data. This rather common situation is easily handled by adding a counter to track the number of elements we have printed on one line. This logic is shown in Program 8-1.

```
1  /* a program fragment */
2  #define MAX_SIZE 25
3
4  /* Local Definitions */
5     int list [MAX_SIZE];
6
7  /* Statements */
8     ...
```

Program 8-1 Print ten numbers per line

```
 9    numPrinted = 0;
10    for (i = 0; i < MAX_SIZE; i++)
11       {
12        printf("%3d", list[i]);
13        if (numPrinted < 9)
14            numPrinted++;
15        else
16           {
17            printf("\n");
18            numPrinted = 0;
19           } /* else */
20       } /* for */
```

Program 8-1   Print ten numbers per line (continued)

PRECEDENCE OF INDEX OPERATORS

References to elements in arrays are postfix expressions whose precedence can be found inside the front cover. By looking at the Precedence Table, we see that array references have a priority of 17, which is very high. What is not apparent from the table, however, is that the opening and closing brackets are actually operators. They create a postfix expression from a primary expression. With a little thought, you should recognize that this is exactly as it must be: When you index an array element in an expression, the value must be determined immediately. Of course, you can override the normal precedence with parentheses, but such action is extremely rare.

Referring to the original array in Figure 8-9, what will be the result of the following code?

```
numbers[3] = numbers[4] + 15;
```

In this case, numbers[4] has a higher precedence than the addition operator (17 versus 12), so it is evaluated first. The result is then

```
numbers[3] = 45 + 15;
```

After this statement has been executed, numbers[3] has been changed from 24 to 60.

INDEX RANGE CHECKING

The C language does not check the boundary of an array. It is your job as a programmer to ensure that all references to indexed elements are valid and within the range of the array. If you use an invalid index in an expression, you will get unpredictable results. (The results are unpredictable because you have no way of knowing the value of the indexed reference.)

On the other hand, if you use an invalid index in an assignment, you will destroy some undetermined portion of your program. Usually, but not always, your program will continue to run and either produce unpredictable results or eventually abort.

An example of a common out-of-range index is seen in the code to fill an array from the keyboard. For this example, we have reproduced the code we used to fill the scores array earlier, only this time we have made a common mistake! Can you spot it?

```
for (i = 1; i <= 9; i++)                    /* Error */
    scanf ("%d", &scores [i]);
```

When dealing with array processing, be very careful at the beginning and end of the array. A careful examination of the above code discloses that we erroneously started at 1 instead of 0. So we fix it as shown below, only to find that it still doesn't work!

```
for (i = 0; i <= 9; i++)
    scanf ("%d", &scores [i]);
```

The moral of this example is to examine your logic. If you made one mistake, you may well have made two. Although we corrected the error for initialization (the beginning of the array), there is still an error at the other end. If you can't see it, check the original code on page 355.

The result of both versions of this error is that the data stored in memory after the **scores** array are erroneously destroyed. In the first version of the error, the first element of the array was not initialized.

The problems created by unmanaged indexes are among the most difficult to solve, even with today's powerful programming workbenches. So you want to plan your array logic carefully and fully test it.

Example: Print Array

Let's write a program that uses arrays. Program 8-2 uses a *for* loop to initialize each element in an array to the square of the index value and then prints the array.

```
 1  /* Initialize array with square of index and print it.
 2         Written by:
 3         Date:
 4  */
 5  #include <stdio.h>
 6  #define ARY_SIZE 5
 7
 8  int main (void)
 9  {
10  /* Local Definitions */
11     int i;
12     int sqrAry[ARY_SIZE];
13
14  /* Statements */
15     for (i = 0; i < ARY_SIZE; i++)
16        sqrAry[i] = i * i;
17
18     printf("Element\tSquare\n");
19     printf("=======\t======\n");
20     for (i = 0; i < ARY_SIZE; i++)
21        printf("%5d\t%4d\n", i, sqrAry[i]);
22
23     return 0;
24  }  /* main */
```

```
Results:
Element Square
======= ======
```

Program 8-2 Squares array

```
         0      0
         1      1
         2      4
         3      9
         4      16
```

Program 8-2   Squares array (continued)

Example: Read and Print Reversed

As another example of an array program, let's read a series of numbers from the keyboard and print them in reverse order; that is, if we read 1 2 3 4, we want to print them 4 3 2 1. With a little thought, it should be obvious that we must read all of the numbers before we can begin printing them. This definitely sounds like a problem for an array.

In Program 8-3, we read up to 50 integers and then print them reversed, 10 to a line.

```c
 1  /* Read a number series and print it reversed.
 2         Written by:
 3         Date:
 4  */
 5  #include <stdio.h>
 6
 7  int main (void)
 8  {
 9  /* Local Definitions */
10      int i;
11      int readNum;
12      int numPrinted;
13      int numbers[50];
14
15  /* Statements */
16      printf("You may enter up to 50 integers:\n");
17      printf("How many would you like to enter? ");
18      scanf ("%d", &readNum);
19
20      if (readNum > 50)
21          readNum = 50;
22
23      /* Fill the array */
24      printf("\nEnter your numbers: \n");
25      for (i = 0; i < readNum; i++)
26          scanf("%d", &numbers[i]);
27
28      /* Print the array */
29      printf("\nYour numbers reversed are: \n");
30      for (i = readNum - 1, numPrinted = 0;
31           i >= 0;
32           i--)
33        {
34         printf("%3d", numbers[i]);
```

Program 8-3   Print input reversed

```
35          if (numPrinted < 9)
36              numPrinted++;
37          else
38              {
39              printf("\n");
40              numPrinted = 0;
41              } /* else */
42      } /* for */
43
44      return 0;
45 }  /* main */
```

```
Results:
    You may enter up to 50 integers:
    How many would you like to enter? 12

    Enter your numbers:
    1 2 3 4 5 6 7 8 9 10 11 12

    Your numbers reversed are:
     12 11 10  9  8  7  6  5  4  3
      2  1
```

Program 8-3   Print input reversed (continued)

Program 8-3 Analysis   First, note how we validate the number of integers to be read. If the user requests more than 50, we simply set readNum to 50. This ensures that we will not run off the end of the array.

This is an interesting loop because we start at the end and work to the front. While many arrays are processed from the beginning, it is often necessary to process from the end. You will see more in the sorting functions later in the chapter.

Finally, note that we incorporate the logic from Program 8-1 on page 358 to print ten numbers per line. Had we made Program 8-1 a function, we could have reused the code rather than repeating it.

8-3   ARRAYS AND FUNCTIONS

To process arrays in a large program, you have to be able to pass them to functions. You can do this in two ways: pass individual elements or pass the whole array. In this section we discuss first how to pass individual elements and then how to pass the whole array.

PASSING INDIVIDUAL ELEMENTS

You can **pass individual elements** to a function like any other variable. As long as the array element type matches the function parameter type, it can be passed. Of course, it will be passed as a value parameter, which means that the function cannot change the value of the element.

For example, assume that we have a function print_square that receives an integer and prints its square on the system console. Using the array base, we can loop through the array, passing each element in turn to `print_square`. This program is shown in Figure 8-10.

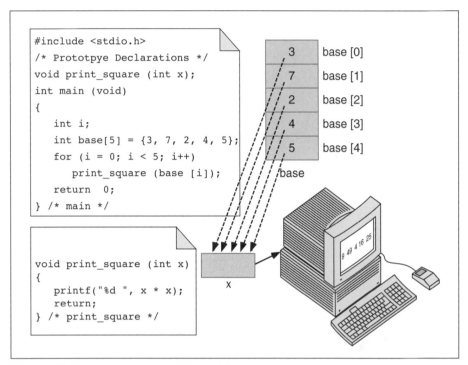

```
#include <stdio.h>
/* Prototpye Declarations */
void print_square (int x);
int main (void)
{
    int i;
    int base[5] = {3, 7, 2, 4, 5};
    for (i = 0; i < 5; i++)
        print_square (base [i]);
    return  0;
} /* main */
```

```
void print_square (int x)
{
    printf("%d ", x * x);
    return;
} /* print_square */
```

Figure 8-10   Passing individual elements

Note how only one element is passed at a time by using the indexed expression, `base[i]`. Since the value of this expression is a single integer, it matches the formal parameter type in `print_square`. As far as `print_square` is concerned, it doesn't know or care that the value it is working with came from an array.

PASSING THE WHOLE ARRAY

If we want the function to operate on the whole array, we must **pass the whole array**. Here we see the first situation in which C does not pass values to a function. The reason for this change is that a lot of memory and time would be used in passing large arrays around every time we wanted to use one in a function. For example, if an array containing 20,000 elements were passed by value to a function, another 20,000 elements would have to be allocated in the function and each element would have to be copied from one array to the other. So, instead of passing the whole array, C passes the address of the array.

In C, the name of an array is a primary expression whose value is the address of the first element in the array. Since indexed references are simply calculated addresses, all we need to refer to any of the elements in the array is the address of the array. Because the name of the array is in fact its address, passing the array name, as opposed to a single element, allows the called function to refer to the array back in the calling function.

How do you pass the whole array? In the calling function, you simply use the array name as the actual parameter. In the called function, you must declare that the corresponding formal parameter is an *array*. You do not, however, need to specify the number of elements in the array. Since the array is actually defined elsewhere, all that is important is that the compiler knows it's an array.

In summary, you must follow two rules to pass the whole array to a function:

1. The function must be called by passing only the name of the array.

2. In the function definition, the formal parameter must be an array type; the size of the array does not need to be specified.

For example, we can use a function to calculate the average of the integers in an array. In this case, we pass the name of the array to the function and it returns the average as a real number. This concept is shown in Figure 8-11.

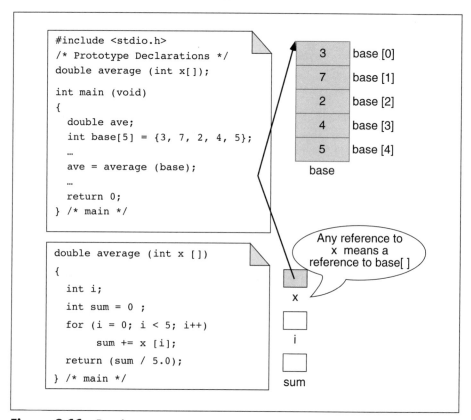

Figure 8-11   Passing arrays—average

What actually is passed in Figure 8-11 is the address of the array, **base**, as seen in the actual parameter. In the parameter list for **average**, we indicate that we are receiving an array by coding the array brackets as shown below.

```
int x []
```

The array, renamed **x**, is available in **average** and can be used in any expression or statement that supports array references. We can even let the function change the value of the array elements by passing the array name. For example, Figure 8-12 multiplies each element in **base** by 2. In this example, note that in addition to the array, a local variable in the called function is used to "walk" through the array.

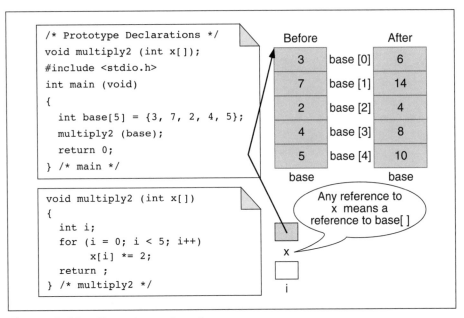

Figure 8-12 Changing values in arrays

8-4 ARRAY APPLICATIONS

In this section we study two array applications: frequency array with their graphical representation and random number permutations.

FREQUENCY ARRAYS

Two common statistical applications that use arrays are frequency distributions and histograms. A **frequency array** shows the number of elements with an identical value found in a series of numbers. For example, suppose we have taken a sample of 100 values between 0 and 19. We want to know how many of the values are 0, how many are 1, how many are 2, and so forth up through 19.

We can read these numbers into an array called numbers. Then we create an array of 20 elements that will show the frequency of each number in the series. This design is shown in Figure 8-13.

With the data structure shown in Figure 8-13 in mind, how do we write the application? Since we know that there are exactly 100 elements, we can use a *for* loop to examine each value in the array. But how can we relate the value in numbers to a location in the frequency?

One way to do it is to assign the value from the data array to an index and then use the index to access the frequency array. This technique is shown below.

```
f = numbers[i];
frequency [f]++;
```

Since an index is an expression, however, we can simply use the value from our data array to index us into the frequency array as shown below. In this example, the value of numbers[i] is determined first, and then that value is used to index into frequency.

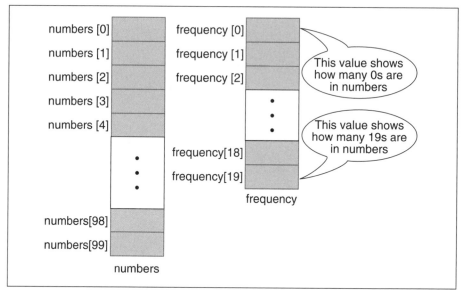

Figure 8-13   Frequency array

```
frequency [numbers [i]]++;
```

The complete function is shown in Program 8-4, on page 367, as makeFrequency. The function first initializes the frequency array and then scans the data array to count the number of occurrences of each value.

This function has a potentially serious problem. Can you see it? Remember our discussion of what happens if the index gets out of range? What if one of the numbers in our data is greater than 19? We will destroy some other part of our program! To protect against this possibility, you should test each data value to make sure that it is within the indexing range of frequency.

HISTOGRAMS

A **histogram** is a pictorial representation of a frequency array. Instead of printing the values of the elements to show the frequency of each number, we print a histogram in the form of a bar chart. For example, Figure 8-14 is a histogram for a set of numbers in the range 0…19. In this example, asterisks (*) are used to build the bar. Each asterisk represents one occurrence of the data value.

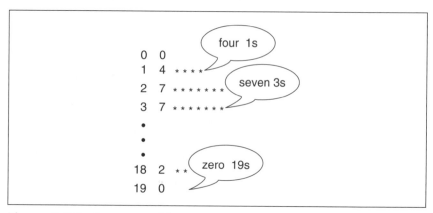

Figure 8-14   Frequency histogram

Let's write a program that builds a frequency array for data values in the range 0...19 and then prints their histogram. The data are read from a file. To provide flexibility, the getData function may only partially fill the array. The function that loads it also guards against too much data. The design for the program is shown in Figure 8-15. The code is shown in Program 8-4.

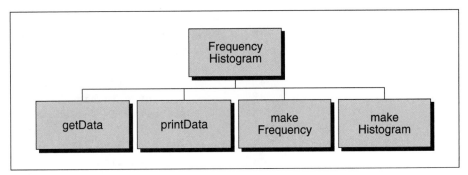

Figure 8-15   Histogram program design

```
1   /* Read data from a file into an array.
2      Build frequency array & print data in histogram.
3         Written by:
4         Data:
5   */
6   #include <stdio.h>
7   #include <stdlib.h>
8
9   #define MAX_ELMNTS 100
10  #define ANLYS_RNG 20
11
12  /* Prototype Declarations */
13     int getData (int numbers[], int size, int range);
14
15     void printData     (int numbers[],
16                            int size,        int lineSize);
17     void makeFrequency (int numbers[],   int size,
18                            int frequency[], int range);
19     void makeHistogram (int frequency[], int range);
20
21  int main (void)
22  {
23  /* Local Definitions */
24     int size;
25     int nums       [MAX_ELMNTS];
26     int frequency [ANLYS_RNG];
27
28  /* Statements */
29     size = getData (nums, MAX_ELMNTS, ANLYS_RNG);
30     printData (nums, size, 10);
```

Program 8-4   Frequency and histogram

```
31
32       makeFrequency(nums, size, frequency, ANLYS_RNG);
33       makeHistogram(frequency, ANLYS_RNG);
34       return 0;
35  }  /* main */
36
37  /* ==================== getData ====================
38     Read data from file into array. The array
39     does not have to be completely filled.
40        Pre    data is an empty array
41               size is maximum elements in array
42               range is highest value allowed
43        Post   array is filled. Return number of elements
44  */
45  int getData (int data [],
46               int size ,
47               int range)
48  {
49  /* Local Definitions */
50     int    dataIn;
51     int    loader = 0;
52     FILE *fpData;
53
54  /* Statements */
55  /* Adjust range for zero value */
56     range--;
57     if (!(fpData = fopen ("P8-04.dat", "r")))
58        printf("Error opening file\a\a\n") , exit (100);
59
60     while (loader < size
61        && fscanf(fpData, "%d", &dataIn) != EOF)
62        if (dataIn >= 0 && dataIn <= range)
63           data[loader++] = dataIn;
64        else
65           printf("\nData point %d invalid. Ignored. \n",
66                   dataIn);
67
68  /* Test to see what stopped while */
69     if (loader == size)
70        printf("\nToo much data. Process what read.\n");
71     return loader;
72  }  /* getData */
73
74  /* ==================== printData ====================
75     Prints the data as a two-dimensional array.
76        Pre    data: a filled array
77               size: number of elements in array
78               lineSize: number of elements printed/line
79        Post   the data have been printed
80  */
```

Program 8-4 Frequency and histogram (continued)

```
 81   void printData (int data[],
 82                     int size,
 83                     int lineSize)
 84   {
 85   /* Local Definitions */
 86      int i;
 87      int numPrinted = 0;
 88
 89   /* Statements */
 90      printf("\n\n");
 91      for (i = 0; i < size; i++)
 92         {
 93          numPrinted++;
 94          printf("%2d ", data[i]);
 95          if (numPrinted >= lineSize)
 96             {
 97              printf("\n");
 98              numPrinted = 0;
 99             } /* if */
100         } /* for */
101      printf("\n\n");
102      return;
103   }  /* printData */
104
105   /* ================= makeFrequency =================
106      analyze the data in nums and build their frequency
107      distribution
108         Pre    nums: array of validated data to be analyzed
109                last: number of elements in array
110                frequency: array for accumulation.
111                range: maximum index/value for frequency
112         Post   Frequency array has been built.
113   */
114   void makeFrequency (int nums[],
115                        int last,
116                        int frequency[],
117                        int range)
118   {
119   /* Local Definitions */
120      int f;
121      int i;
122
123   /* Statements */
124      /* First initialize the frequency array */
125      for (f = 0; f < range; f++)
126          frequency [f] = 0;
127
128      /* Scan numbers and build frequency array */
```

Program 8-4 Frequency and histogram (continued)

```
129        for (i = 0; i < last; i++)
130            frequency [nums [i]]++;
131        return;
132    }  /* makeFrequency */
133
134    /* ================= makeHistogram ===================
135       Print a histogram representing analyzed data.
136          Pre    freq contains times each value occurred in data
137                 size represents elements in frequency array
138          Post   histogram has been printed
139    */
140    void makeHistogram (int freq[],
141                        int range)
142    {
143    /* Local Definitions */
144       int i;
145       int j;
146
147    /* Statements */
148       for (i = 0; i < range; i++)
149           {
150            printf ("%2d %2d ", i, freq[i]);
151            for (j = 1; j <= freq[i]; j++)
152                printf ("*");
153            printf ("\n");
154           } /* for i... */
155       return;
156    }  /* makeHistogram */
157    /* ================= End of Program ================= */
```

```
Results:
Data point -1 invalid. Ignored.

Data point 20 invalid. Ignored.

    1  2  3  4  5  6  7  8  7 10
    2 12 13 13 15 16 17 18 17  7
    3  4  6  8 10  2  4  6  8 10
    4  3  5  7  1  3  7  7 11 13
    5 10 11 12 13 16 18 11 12  7
    6  1  2  2  3  3  3  4  4  4
    7  7  8  7  6  5  4  1  2  2
    8 11 11 13 13 13 17 17  7  7
   13 17 17 15 15

    0  0
    1  4 ****
    2  7 *******
    3  7 *******
    4  8 ********
```

Program 8-4 Frequency and histogram (continued)

```
 5   4 ****
 6   5 *****
 7  12 ************
 8   5 *****
 9   0
10   4 ****
11   5 *****
12   3 ***
13   8 ********
14   0
15   3 ***
16   2 **
17   6 ******
18   2 **
19   0
```

Program 8-4   Frequency and histogram   (continued)

RANDOM NUMBER PERMUTATIONS

A random number permutation is a set of random numbers in which no numbers are repeated. For example, given a random number permutation of 10 numbers, the values from 0 to 9 would all be included with no duplicates.

We saw how to generate a set of random numbers in Chapter 4. To generate a permutation, we need to eliminate the duplicates. Borrowing from the histogram concept in the previous section, we can solve the problem most efficiently by using two arrays. The first array contains the random numbers. The second array contains a logical value that indicates whether or not the number represented by its index has been placed in the random number array. This design is shown in Figure 8-16.

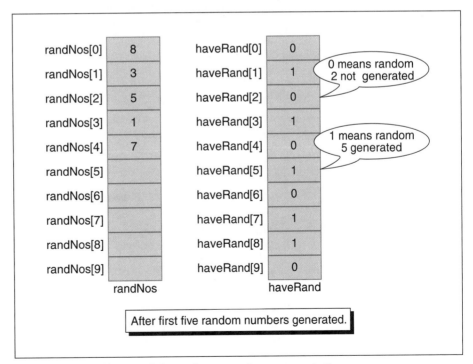

After first five random numbers generated.

Figure 8-16   Design for random number permutations

As you study Figure 8-16, note that only the first five random numbers have been placed in the permutation. For each random number in the random number array, its corresponding location in the have-random array is set to 1. Those locations representing numbers that have not yet been generated are still set to 0. The implementation of the design is shown in Program 8-5.

```
 1  /* Generate a random number permutation.
 2         Written by:
 3         Date:
 4  */
 5  #include <stdio.h>
 6  #include <stdlib.h>
 7
 8  #define  ARY_SIZE  20
 9
10  /* Prototype Declarations */
11  void bldPerm    (int randNos[]);
12  void printData (int data[],     int size, int lineSize);
13
14  int main (void)
15  {
16  /* Local Definitions */
17     int randNos [ARY_SIZE];
18
19  /* Statements */
20     printf("Begin Random Permutation Generation\n");
21
22     bldPerm    (randNos);
23     printData (randNos, ARY_SIZE, 10);
24
25     return 0;
26  }  /* main */
27
28  /* ==================== bldPerm ====================
29     Generate a random number permutation in array.
30        Pre    randNos is array to receive permutations
31        Post   randNos filled
32  */
33
34  void bldPerm (int randNos[])
35
36  {
37  /* Local Definitions */
38     int i;
39     int randNo;
40     int haveRand[ARY_SIZE] = {0};
41
42  /* Statements */
43     for (i = 0; i < ARY_SIZE; i++)
```

Program 8-5 Generate a permutation

```
44         {
45           do
46             {
47               randNo = rand() % ARY_SIZE;
48             } while (haveRand[randNo] == 1);
49           haveRand[randNo] = 1;
50           randNos[i] = randNo;
51         } /* for */
52    return;
53 } /* bldPerm */
54
55 /* ==================== printData ====================
56    Prints the data as a two-dimensional array.
57       Pre    data: a filled array
58             last: index to last element to be printed
59             lineSize: number of elements printed on a line
60       Post   the data have been printed
61 */
62 void printData (int data[],
63                 int size,
64                 int lineSize)
65 {
66 /* Local Definitions */
67    int i;
68    int numPrinted = 0;
69
70 /* Statements */
71    printf("\n");
72    for (i = 0; i < size; i++)
73       {
74        numPrinted++;
75        printf("%2d ", data[i]);
76        if (numPrinted >= lineSize)
77           {
78            printf("\n");
79            numPrinted = 0;
80           } /* if */
81       } /* for */
82    printf("\n");
83    return;
84 } /* printData */
```

```
Results:
   Begin Random Permutation Generation

   18 13 15 11  7 10 19 12  6  9
    4  0  5  3 17 14  2 16  1  8
```

Program 8-5 Generate a permutation (continued)

8-5 SORTING

One of the most common applications in computer science is sorting—the process through which data are arranged according to their values. We are surrounded by data. If the data were not ordered, we would spend hours trying to find a single piece of information. Imagine the difficulty of finding someone's telephone number in a telephone book that was not ordered!

In this chapter we introduce three sorting algorithms: the selection sort, bubble sort, and insertion sort. In each section we will first introduce the basic concept, then use the idea in an example, and finally develop the code for the algorithm.

One programming concept common to the sorting algorithms we discuss in this section is the swapping of data between two elements in a list. You might want to review our discussion of this concept on page 357.

SELECTION SORT

In the **selection sort**, the list is divided into two sublists, sorted and unsorted, which are divided by an imaginary wall. We find the smallest element from the unsorted sublist and swap it with the element at the beginning of the unsorted data. After each selection and swapping, the wall between the two sublists moves one element ahead, increasing the number of sorted elements and decreasing the number of unsorted ones. Each time we move one element from the unsorted sublist to the sorted sublist, we say that we have completed a **sort pass**. If we have a list of n elements, we need $n - 1$ passes to completely rearrange the data. The selection sort is graphically presented in Figure 8-17.

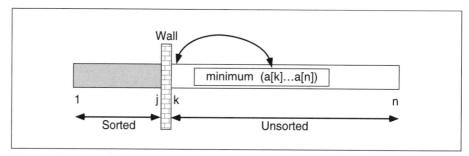

Figure 8-17 Selection sort concept

Figure 8-18 traces a set of six integers as we sort them. It shows how the wall between the sorted and unsorted sublists moves in each pass. As you study the figure, you will see that the array is sorted after five passes, which is one less than the number of elements in the array. This means that if we use a loop to control the sorting, our loop has one less iteration than the number of elements in the array.

SELECTION SORT ALGORITHM

In Program 8-6, `selectionSort` is a rather straightforward algorithm. Starting with the first item in the list, the algorithm calls `exchangeSmallest` (Program 8-7) to examine the unsorted items in the list for the smallest element. In each pass, `exchangeSmallest` "selects" the smallest element and exchanges it with the first unsorted element. It then returns to `selectionSort`, which repeats the process until the list is completely sorted.

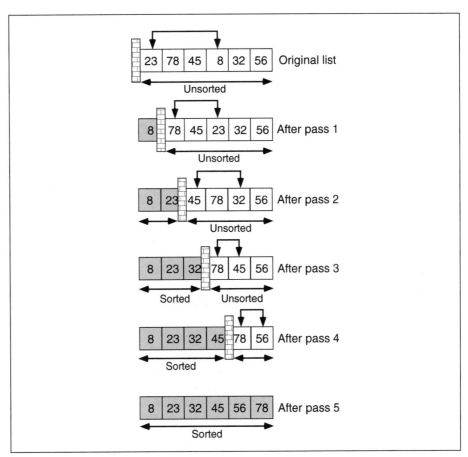

Figure 8-18 Selection sort example

```
1   /* Prototype Declarations */
2   void exchangeSmallest (int list[], int first, int last);
3
4   /* ==================== selectionSort ====================
5      Sorts by selecting smallest element in unsorted portion
6      of array and exchanging it with element at the
7      beginning of the unsorted list.
8         Pre    list must contain at least one item
9                last contains index to last element in list
10        Post   list rearranged smallest to largest
11  */
12  void selectionSort (int list[],
13                      int last)
14  {
15  /* Local Definitions */
16     int current;
17
```

Program 8-6 `selectionSort`

```
18    /* Statements */
19        for (current = 0; current < last; current++)
20            exchangeSmallest (list, current, last);
21
22        return;
23    }  /* selectionSort */
```

Program 8-6 `selectionSort` (continued)

```
 1    /* ================== exchangeSmallest ==================
 2        Given array of integers, place smallest element into
 3        position in array.
 4            Pre    list must contain at least one element
 5                   current is beginning of array (not always 0)
 6                   last element in array must be >= current
 7            Post   returns index of smallest element in array
 8    */
 9    void exchangeSmallest (int list[],
10                           int current,
11                           int last)
12    {
13    /* Local Definitions */
14        int walker;
15        int smallest;
16        int tempData;
17
18    /* Statements */
19        smallest = current;
20        for (walker = current + 1; walker <= last; walker++)
21            if (list[walker] < list[smallest])
22                smallest = walker;
23
24        /* Smallest selected: exchange with current element */
25         tempData       = list[current];
26         list[current]  = list[smallest];
27         list[smallest] = tempData;
28
29        return;
30    }  /* exchangeSmallest */
```

Program 8-7 `exchangeSmallest`

Program 8-7 Analysis   In this algorithm we see two elements that are common to all three sorts discussed in this section. First, each algorithm makes use of a subfunction either to determine the proper location of the data or to identify and exchange two elements. Each call of the subfunction is a sort pass.

Second, each time we need to move data, we must use a temporary storage area. This technique is found in every sort algorithm except those that use two sorting areas. In the selection sort, the temporary area is used to exchange the two elements.

BUBBLE SORT

In the **bubble sort**, the list is divided into two sublists: sorted and unsorted. The smallest element is *bubbled* from the unsorted sublist and moved to the sorted sublist. After moving the smallest element to the sorted list, the wall moves one element ahead, increasing the number of sorted elements and decreasing the number of unsorted ones. Each time an element moves from the unsorted sublist to the sorted sublist, one sort pass is completed. Given a list of *n* elements, the bubble sort requires up to *n* – 1 passes to sort the data. The bubble concept is seen in Figure 8-19.

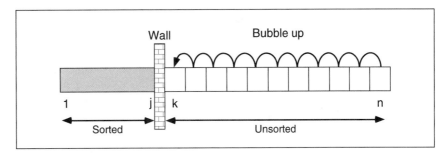

Figure 8-19   Bubble sort concept

Figure 8-20 shows how the wall moves one element in each pass. Looking at the first pass, we start with 56 and compare it to 32. Since 56 is not less than 32, it is not moved and we step down one element. No exchanges take place until we compare 45 to 8. Since 8 is less than 45, the two elements are exchanged and we step down 1 element. Because 8 was moved down, it is now compared to 78 and these two elements are exchanged. Finally, 8 is compared to 23 and exchanged. This series of exchanges places 8 in the first location and the wall is moved up one position.

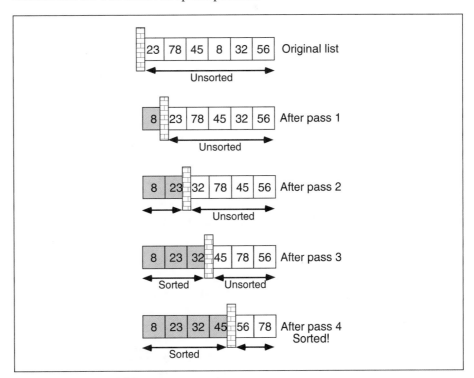

Figure 8-20   Bubble sort example

The bubble sort was originally written to "bubble up" the highest element in the list. From an efficiency point of view, it makes no difference whether the high element is bubbled or the low element is bubbled. From a consistency point of view, however, it makes comparisons between the sorts easier if all three of them work in the same manner. For that reason, we have chosen to bubble the lowest key in each pass.

BUBBLE SORT ALGORITHM

Like the selection sort, the bubble sort is quite simple. In each pass through the data, controlled by a *for* loop, the lowest element is *bubbled* to the beginning of the unsorted segment of the array. The bubbling process is actually accomplished in the called function, bubbleUp.

Each time it is called, bubbleUp makes one pass through the data. Whenever it finds two elements out of sequence, it exchanges them. It then continues with the next element. This process allows the smallest element to be bubbled to the beginning of the array, while at the same time adjacent elements along the way are rearranged. The bubble sort is shown in Program 8-8 and bubbleUp in Program 8-9.

```
 1  /* Prototype Declarations */
 2     void bubbleUp (int list[], int first, int last);
 3
 4  /* ==================== bubbleSort ====================
 5     Sort list using bubble sort. Adjacent elements are
 6     compared and exchanged until list is completely ordered.
 7        Pre   the list must contain at least one item
 8              last contains index to last element in list
 9        Post  list rearranged in sequence low to high
10  */
11  void bubbleSort (int list [],
12                   int last)
13  {
14  /*  Local Definitions */
15     int current;
16
17  /* Statements */
18     for(current = 0; current < last; current++)
19        bubbleUp (list, current, last);
20
21     return;
22  }  /* bubbleSort */
```

Program 8-8 bubbleSort

```
 1  /* ==================== bubbleUp ====================
 2     Move the lowest element in unsorted portion of an array
 3     to the current element in the unsorted portion.
 4        Pre   list must contain at least one element
 5              current identifies beginning of unsorted data
 6              last identifies the end of the unsorted data
 7        Post  array segment has been rearranged so that lowest
```

Program 8-9 bubbleUp

```
 8                        element is now at beginning of unsorted portion
 9  */
10  void bubbleUp (int list[],
11                 int current,
12                 int last)
13  {
14  /* Local Definitions */
15     int walker;
16     int temp;
17
18  /* Statements */
19     for (walker = last; walker > current; walker--)
20        if (list[walker]   < list[walker - 1])
21           {
22            temp            = list[walker];
23            list[walker]    = list[walker - 1];
24            list[walker - 1] = temp;
25           } /* if */
26     return;
27  }  /* bubbleUp */
```

Program 8-9 `bubbleUp` (continued)

Program 8-9 Analysis   If the data being sorted are already in sequence, `bubbleSort` will still go through the array element by element. One common modification is to stop the sort if there are no exchanges in `bubbleUp`. This change would require that `bubbleUp` return a "sorted" flag. We leave this modification to the practice sets at the end of the chapter.

INSERTION SORT

The **insertion sort** algorithm is one of the most common sorting techniques used by card players. As they pick up each card, they insert it into the proper sequence in their hand. (As an aside, card sorting is an example of a sort that uses two pieces of data to sort: suit and rank.)

In the insertion sort, the list is divided into two parts: sorted and unsorted. In each pass, the first element of the unsorted sublist is picked up and transferred into the sorted sublist by inserting it at the appropriate place. If we have a list of n elements, it will take at most $n - 1$ passes to sort the data (Figure 8-21).

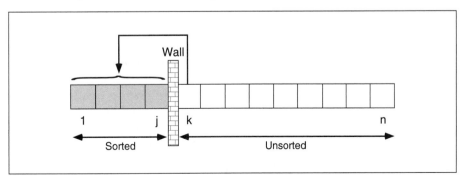

Figure 8-21   Insertion sort concept

Figure 8-22 traces the insertion sort through our list of six numbers. Each pass moves the wall as an element is removed from the unsorted sublist and inserted into the sorted sublists.

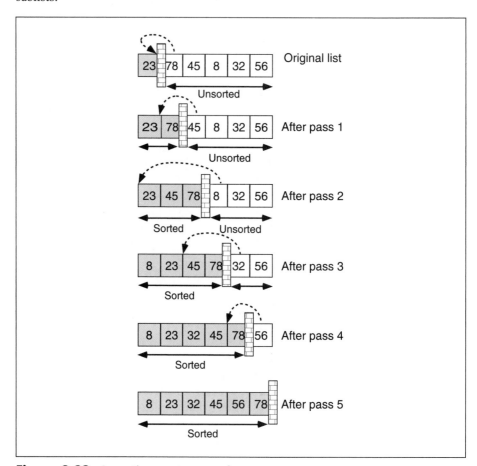

Figure 8-22   Insertion sort example

INSERTION SORT ALGORITHM

The design of the insertion sort follows the same pattern we saw in both the selection sort and the bubble sort; the sort function calls a subfunction for each sort pass. The called function then inserts the first element from the unsorted list into its proper position relative to the rest of the data in the sorted list. Program 8-10 shows the insertion sort. It uses insertOne to sort each element in turn.

```
1  /* Prototype Declarations */
2  void insertOne (int list[], int first);
3
4  /* ===================== insertionSort =====================
5     Sort list using Insertion Sort. The list is divided into
6     sorted and unsorted lists. With each pass, first element
7     in unsorted list is inserted into sorted list.
```

Program 8-10 insertionSort

```
 8        Pre   list must contain at least one element
 9              last contains index to last element in list
10        Post  list has been rearranged
11 */
12 void insertionSort (int list[],
13                     int last)
14 {
15 /* Local Definitions */
16    int current;
17
18 /* Statements */
19    for (current = 1; current <= last; current++)
20      insertOne(list, current);
21
22    return;
23 } /* insertionSort */
```

Program 8-10 insertionSort (continued)

```
 1 /* ====================== insertOne ======================
 2    Sorts current element in unsorted list into its proper
 3    location in sorted portion of the list--one sort pass.
 4        Pre   list must contain at least one element
 5              current identifies beginning of unsorted list
 6        Post  next element placed into its proper location
 7 */
 8 void insertOne (int list[],
 9                 int current)
10 {
11 /* Local Definitions */
12    int walker;
13    int located;
14    int temp;
15
16 /* Statements */
17    located = FALSE;
18    temp = list[current];
19    for  (walker = current - 1; walker >= 0 && !located;)
20      if (temp < list[walker])
21         {
22          list[walker + 1] = list[walker];
23             walker--;
24         } /* if */
25      else
26          located = TRUE;
```

Program 8-11 insertOne

```
27
28         list [walker + 1] = temp;
29         return;
30    }  /* insertOne */
```

Program 8-11 `insertOne` (continued)

Program 8-11 Analysis   Note how the exchange is worked in this sort. Before the loop starts, `insertOne` puts the data from the current element into a holding area. This is the first step in the exchange. It then looks for the correct position to place the element by starting with the largest element in the sorted list and working toward the beginning. As it searches, it spreads the sorted portion of the list by shifting each element one position higher in the list. When it locates the correct position, therefore, the data have already been moved right one position and the current location is "empty"; the sort therefore simply places the saved element in its proper location, completing the exchange.

INSERTION SORT REPROGRAMMED

In all three sorts, we have used two functions: one to control the sort phase loop and one to control the reordering of data. We did this to emphasize the sort operation; however, it is not the way you would write the sort in the field. Program 8-12 rewrites the insertion sort as it would normally be programmed.

```
1    /* Test driver for insertion sort.
2          Written by:
3          Date:
4    */
5    #include <stdio.h>
6
7    #define MAX_ARY_SIZE 15
8    #define TRUE   1
9    #define FALSE  0
10
11   /* Prototype Declarations */
12   void insertionSort  (int list[], int last);
13
14   int main (void)
15   {
16   /* Local Definitions */
17      int i;
18      int ary[MAX_ARY_SIZE] = { 89, 72,  3, 15, 21,
19                                57, 61, 44, 19, 98,
20                                 5, 77, 39, 59, 61 };
21   /* Statements */
22      printf("Unsorted: ");
23      for (i = 0; i < MAX_ARY_SIZE; i++)
24          printf("%3d", ary[i]);
25
26      insertionSort (ary, MAX_ARY_SIZE - 1);
```

Program 8-12 Reprogrammed insertion sort

```
27
28        printf("\nSorted  : ");
29        for (i = 0; i < MAX_ARY_SIZE; i++)
30            printf("%3d", ary[i]);
31        printf("\n");
32        return 0;
33     }  /* main */
34
35     /* ==================== insertionSort ====================
36        Sort list using Insertion Sort. The list is divided into
37        sorted and unsorted list. With each pass, first element
38        in unsorted list is inserted into sorted list.
39            Pre    list must contain at least one element
40                   last contains index to last element in list
41            Post   list has been rearranged
42     */
43     void insertionSort (int list[],
44                         int last)
45     {
46     /* Local Definitions */
47        int current;
48        int walker;
49        int located;
50        int temp;
51
52     /* Statements */
53        for (current = 1; current <= last; current++)
54          {
55           located = FALSE;
56           temp = list[current];
57           for  (walker = current - 1; walker >= 0 && !located;)
58              if (temp < list[walker])
59                 {
60                  list[walker + 1] = list[walker];
61                  walker--;
62                 } /* if */
63              else
64                  located = TRUE;
65
66           list [walker + 1] = temp;
67          } /* for */
68        return;
69     }  /* insertionSort */
```

```
Results:
   Unsorted:  89 72   3 15 21 57 61 44 19 98   5 77 39 59 61
   Sorted  :   3   5 15 19 21 39 44 57 59 61 61 72 77 89 98
```

Program 8-12 Reprogrammed insertion sort (continued)

Program 8-12 Analysis As you can see, we simply copied the statements from `insertOne` into the *for* loop, replacing the function call. Of greater interest is our code for the test driver. We began by creating and printing an array. Then, after calling the insertion sort function, we reprinted the array to verify that the sort worked. When you write functions that are used in other programs, you need to write a test driver to verify that they work.

SORT CONCLUSIONS

In this section, we have covered three classic sorts. With the exception of the insertion sort, you generally will not find them implemented in production systems. The insertion sort is used as a subfunction in both Quicksort and Singleton's variation, *Quickersort*, which are considered the best general-purpose sorts.[2]

Historically, however, these three sorts are the foundation of improved and faster sorting methods that you will study in a data structures course. The selection sort is the foundation of a sorting method called the heap sort; the bubble sort is the foundation for Quicksort and Quickersort; and the insertion sort is the foundation of a sorting method called Shell Sort.

8-6   SEARCHING

Another common operation in computer science is **searching**, which is the process used to find the location of a target among a list of objects. In the case of an array, searching means that given a value, we want to find the location (index) of the first element in the array that contains that value. The search concept is shown in Figure 8-23.

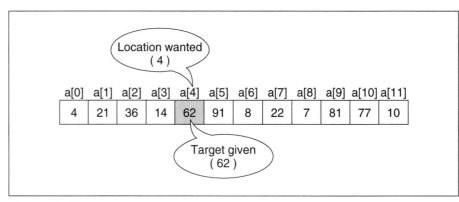

Figure 8-23   Search concept

The algorithm used to search a list depends to a large extent on the structure of the list. Since our structure is currently limited to arrays, we will study searches that work with arrays. As we study other structures, we will study different search techniques.

There are two basic searches for arrays: the sequential search and the binary search. The sequential search can be used to locate an item in any array. The binary search, on the other hand, requires the list to be sorted.

---

[2]For a discussion of Quicksort, see Richard F. Gilberg and Behrouz A. Forouzan, *Data Structures: A Pseudocode Approach With C.* Pacific Grove, CA, Brooks/Cole, 1998.

SEQUENTIAL SEARCH

The **sequential search** is used whenever the list is not ordered. Generally, you will use the technique only for small lists or lists that are not searched often. In other cases you should first sort the list and then search it using the binary search discussed later.

In the sequential search, we start searching for the target from the beginning of the list, and we continue until we find the target or until we are sure that it is not in the list. This gives us two possibilities; either we find it or we reach the end of the list. Figure 8-24 traces the steps to find the value 62. We first check the data at index 0, then 1, 2, and 3 before finding the 62 in the fifth element (index 4).

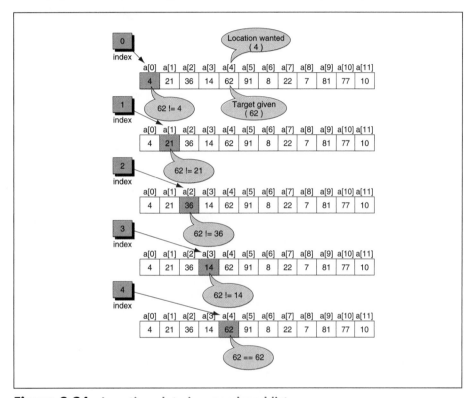

Figure 8-24   Locating data in unordered list

But what if the target is not in the list? Then we have to examine each element until we reach the end of the list. Figure 8-25 traces the search for a target of 72. When we detect the end of the list, we know that the target does not exist.

Let's write the sequential search function. A search function needs to tell the calling function two things: Did it find the data it was looking for? If it did, what is the index at which the data were found?

But a function can return only one value. For search functions, we use the return value to designate whether we found the target or not. To "return" the index location where the data were found, we will use call-by-address.

The search function requires four parameters: the list we are searching, the index to the last element in the list, the target, and the address where the found element's index location will be stored. Although we could write it without passing the index to the last element, that would mean the search would have to know how many elements are in the list. To make the function as flexible as possible, therefore, we pass the index of the last

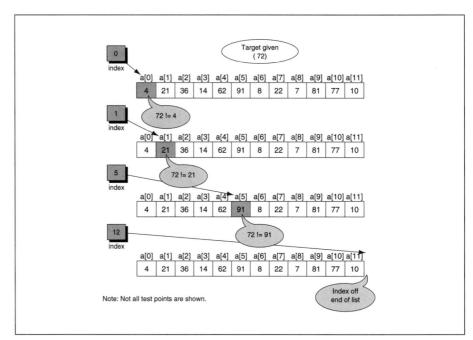

Figure 8-25 Unsuccessful search in unordered list

data value in the array. This is also a good structured design technique. With this information, we are now ready to write the algorithm (Program 8-13).

```
1  /* ===================== seqSearch =====================
2     Locate the target in an unordered list of size elements.
3        Pre    list must contain at least one item.
4               last contains index to last element in list
5               target contains the data to be located
6        Post   FOUND: matching index stored in locn address
7                      return 1 (found)
8               NOT FOUND: last stored in locn address
9                      return 0 (not found)
10 */
11 int seqSearch (int  list[],
12                int  last,
13                int  target,
14                int *locn)
15 {
16 /* Local Definitions */
17    int looker;
18
19 /* Statements */
20    looker = 0;
21    while (looker < last && target != list[looker])
```

Program 8-13 Sequential search

```
22        looker++;
23
24     *locn = looker;
25     return (target == list[looker]);
26 }  /* seqSearch */
```

Program 8-13 Sequential search (continued)

Program 8-13 Analysis   Program 8-13 is simple, but it does merit some discussion. First, why did we use a *while* statement? Even though we know the limits of the array, it is still an event-controlled loop. We search until we find what we are looking for or reach the end of the list. Finding something is an event, so we use an event loop.

Next, note that there are two tests in the limit expression of the loop. We have coded the test for the end of the array first. In this case, it doesn't make any difference which test is first from an execution point of view, but in other search loops it might. You should get in the habit of coding the limit test first because it doesn't use an indexed value and is therefore safer.

The call-by-address use for locn also merits discussion. Since we need to pass the found location back to the variable in the calling program, we need to pass its address to the function. A typical call to the search would look like the statement shown below.

```
found = seqSearch (stuAry, lastStu, stuID, &locn);
```

Notice how succinct this function is. In fact, there are more lines of documentation than there are lines of code. The entire search is contained in one *while* statement. With this short code, you might be tempted to ask, "Why write the function at all? Why not just put the one line of code wherever it is needed?" The answer lies in the structured programming concepts that each function should do only one thing and in the concept of reusability. By isolating the search process in its own function, we separate it from the process that needs the search. This is better structured programming. This also makes the code **reusable** in other parts of the program and portable to other programs that need searching.

One final point: This function assumes that the list is not ordered. If the list were ordered, we could improve the search slightly when the data we were looking for were not in the list. We will leave this improvement for a problem at the end of the chapter.

BINARY SEARCH

The sequential search algorithm is very slow. If we have an array of one million elements, we must do one million comparisons in the worst case. If the array is not sorted, this is the only solution. But if the array is sorted, we can use a more efficient algorithm called the **binary search**. Generally speaking, we should use a binary search whenever the list starts to become large. The definition of *large* is vague. We suggest that you consider binary searches whenever the list contains more than 16 elements.

The binary search starts by testing the data in the element at the middle of the array. This determines if the target is in the first half or the second half of the list. If it is in the first half, we do not need to check the second half. If it is in the second half, we don't need to test the first half. In other words, either way we eliminate half the list from further consideration. We repeat this process until we find the target or satisfy ourselves that it is not in the list.

To find the middle of the list, we need three variables, one to identify the beginning of the list, one to identify the middle of the list, and one to identify the end of the list. We will analyze two cases: the target is in the list, and the target is not in the list.

Target Found

Figure 8-26 shows how we find 22 in a sorted array. We descriptively call our three indexes `first`, `mid`, and `last`. Given `first` as 0 and `last` as 11, we can calculate `mid` as follows:[3]

```
mid = (first + last) / 2;
```

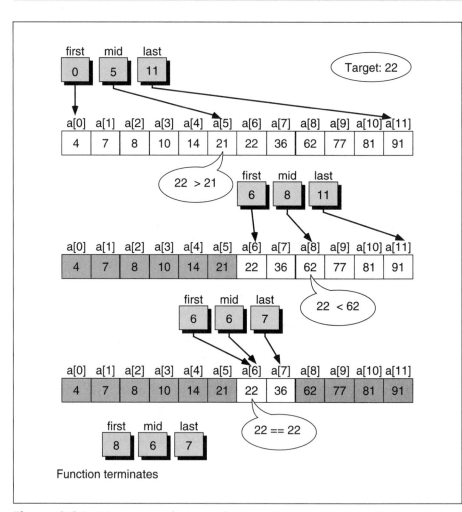

Figure 8-26   Binary search example

Since the index `mid` is an integer, the result will be the integral value of the quotient; that is, it truncates rather than rounds the calculation. Given the data in Figure 8-26, `mid` becomes 5 as a result of the first calculation.

---

[3]This formula does not work if the number of elements in the array is greater than half `MAX_INT`. In that case, the correct formula is: $mid = first + (last - first) / 2$.

```
mid = (0 + 11) / 2 = 11 / 2 = 5
```

At index location 5, we discover that the target is greater than the list value (22 > 21). We can therefore eliminate the array locations 0 through 5. (Note that mid is automatically eliminated.) To narrow our search, we assign mid + 1 to first and repeat the search.

The next loop calculates mid with the new value for first and determines that the midpoint is now 8.

```
mid = (6 + 11) / 2 = 17 / 2 = 8
```

Again we test the target to the value at mid, and this time we discover that the target is less than the list value (22 < 62). This time we adjust the ends of the list by setting last to mid − 1 and recalculate mid. This effectively eliminates elements 8 through 11 from consideration. We have now arrived at index location 6, whose value matches our target. This stops the search. Figure 8-26 traces the logic we have just described.

Target Not Found

A more interesting case is when the target is not in the list. We must construct our search algorithm so that it stops when we have checked all possible locations. This is done in the binary search by testing for first and last crossing; that is, we are done when first becomes greater than last. Thus, only two conditions terminate the binary search algorithm: Either the target is found or first becomes larger than last. For example, imagine we want to find 11 in our binary search array. This situation is shown in Figure 8-27.

In this example, the loop continues to narrow the range as we saw in the successful search, until we are examining the data at index locations 3 and 4. These settings of first and last set the mid index to 3.

```
mid = (3 + 4) / 2 = 7 / 2 = 3
```

The test at index location 3 indicates that the target is greater than the list value, so we set first to mid + 1 or 4. We now test the data at location 4 and discover that 11 < 14.

```
mid = (4 + 4) / 2 = 8/ 2 = 4
```

At this point, we have discovered that the target should be between two adjacent values; in other words, it is not in the list. We see this algorithmically because last is set to mid − 1, which makes first greater than last, the signal that the value we are looking for is not in the list.

Program 8-14 contains the implementation of the binary search algorithm we have been describing. It is constructed along the same design we saw for the sequential search. The first three parameters describe the list and the target we are looking for, and the last parameter contains the address into which we place the located index. One point worth noting: When we terminate the loop with a not-found condition, the index returned is unpredictable—it may indicate the node greater than or less than the value in target.

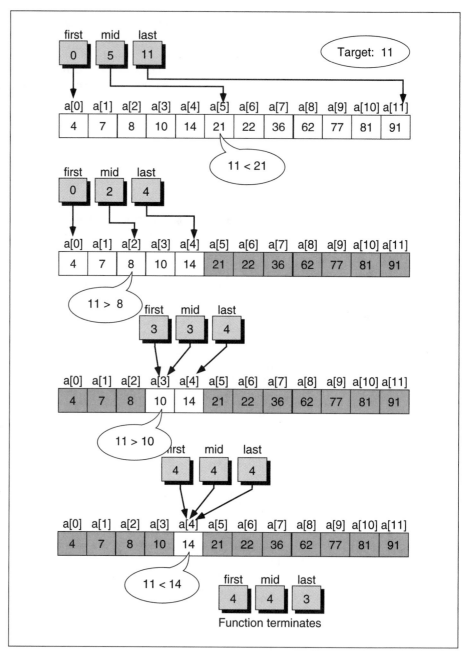

Figure 8-27 Unsuccessful binary search example

```
1   /* ==================== binarySearch ====================
2       Search an ordered list using Binary Search
3          Pre    list must contain at least one element
4                 end is index to the largest element in list
5                 target is the value of element being sought
6          Post   FOUND: locn assigned index to target element
```

Program 8-14 Binary search

```
 7                        return 1 (found)
 8           NOT FOUND: locn = element below or above target
 9                        return 0 (not found)
10  */
11  int binarySearch (int  list[],
12                     int  end,
13                     int  target,
14                     int *locn)
15  {
16  /* Local Definitions */
17     int first;
18     int mid;
19     int last;
20
21  /* Statements */
22     first = 0;
23     last = end;
24     while (first <= last)
25        {
26         mid = (first + last) / 2;
27         if (target > list[mid])
28            /* look in upper half */
29            first = mid + 1;
30         else if (target < list[mid])
31            /* look in lower half */
32            last = mid - 1;
33         else
34            /* found equal: force exit */
35            first = last + 1;
36        } /* end while */
37     *locn = mid;
38     return target == list [mid];
39  } /* binarySearch */
```

Program 8-14   Binary search (continued)

8-7   TWO-DIMENSIONAL ARRAYS

The arrays we have discussed so far are known as **one-dimensional arrays** because the data are organized linearly in only one direction. Many applications require that data be stored in more than one dimension. One common example is a table, which is an array that consists of rows and columns. Figure 8-28 shows a table, which is commonly called a **two-dimensional array**.

Although a two-dimensional array is exactly what is shown by Figure 8-28, C looks at it in a different way. It looks at the two-dimensional array as an array of arrays. In other words, a two-dimensional array in C is an array of one-dimensional arrays. This concept is shown in Figure 8-29.

Figure 8-28 Two-dimensional array

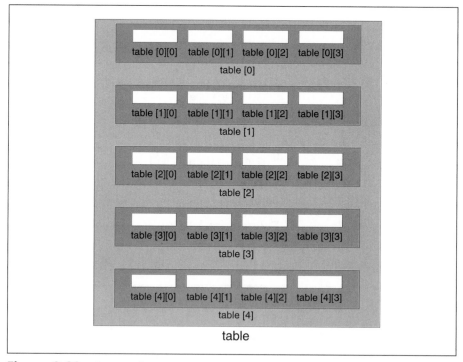

Figure 8-29 Array of arrays

DECLARING AND DEFINING TWO-DIMENSIONAL ARRAYS

Two-dimensional arrays, like one-dimensional arrays, must be declared and defined before being used. Declaration and definition tell the compiler the name of the array, the type of each element, and the size of each dimension. As we saw with the one-dimensional array, the size of the array is a constant and must have a value at compilation time. For example, the array shown in Figure 8-29 can be declared and defined as follows:

```
int table[5][4];
```

By convention, the first dimension specifies the number of **rows** in the array. The second dimension specifies the number of **columns** in each row.

Initialization

As we noted before, declaration and definition only reserve memory for the elements in the array. No values will be stored. If we don't initialize the array, the contents are unpredictable. Generally speaking, all arrays should be initialized.

Initialization of the array elements can be done when the array is defined. As we saw with one-dimensional arrays, the values must be enclosed in braces. This time, however, there is a set of data for each dimension in the array. So for `table`, we will need 20 values. One way to initialize it is shown below.

```
int table[5][4] =
    {0,1,2,3,10,11,12,13,20,21,22,23,30,31,32,33,40,41,42,43};
```

We highly recommend, however, that you nest the data in braces to show the exact nature of the array. For example, array `table` is better initialized as shown below.

```
int table [5][4] =
    {
    { 0,  1,  2,  3},
    {10, 11, 12, 13},
    {20, 21, 22, 23},
    {30, 31, 32, 33},
    {40, 41, 42, 43}
    };  /* table */
```

In this example, we define each row as a one-dimensional array of four elements enclosed in braces. The array of five rows also has its set of braces. Note that we use commas between the elements in the rows and also commas between the rows.

When we discussed one-dimensional arrays, we said that if the array is completely initialized with supplied values, you do not need to specify the size of the array. This concept carries forward to multidimensional arrays, except that only the first dimension can be omitted. All others must be specified. The format is shown below.

```
int table [][4] =
    {
    { 0,  1,  2,  3},
    {10, 11, 12, 13},
    {20, 21, 22, 23},
    {30, 31, 32, 33},
    {40, 41, 42, 43}
    };  /* table */
```

To initialize the whole array to zeros, we need only specify the first value, as shown below.

```
int table [5][4] = {0};
```

Inputting Values

Another way to fill up the values is to read them from the keyboard. For a two-dimensional array, this usually requires nested *for* loops. If the array is an *n* by *m* array, the first loop varies the row from zero to $n - 1$. The second loop varies the column from zero to $m - 1$. The code to fill the array in Figure 8-29 is shown below.

```
for (row = 0; row < 5; row++)
    for (column = 0; column < 4; column++)
        scanf ("%d", &table [row][column]);
```

When the program runs, we enter the 20 values for the elements and they are stored in the appropriate locations.

Outputting Values

We can also print the value of the elements one by one, using two nested loops. Again, the first loop controls the printing of the rows and the second loop controls the printing of the columns. To print the table in its table format, a newline is printed at the end of each row. The code to print Figure 8-29 is shown below.

```
for (row = 0; row < 5; row++)
    {
     for (column = 0; column < 4; column++)
         printf("%8d", table [row][column]);
     printf("\n");
    } /* for */
```

Accessing Values

Individual elements can be initialized using the assignment operator.

```
table[2][0] = 23;
table[0][1] = table[3][2] + 15;
```

Let's assume that we want to initialize our 5×4 array as shown below.

```
00      01      02      03
10      11      12      13
20      21      22      23
30      31      32      33
40      41      42      43
```

One way to do this would be to code the values by hand. However, it is much more interesting to examine the pattern and then assign values to the elements in the array using an algorithm. What pattern do you see? One is that the value in each element increases by one from its predecessor in the row. Another is that the first element in each row is the row index times 10. With these two patterns, we should be able to write nested loops to fill the array. The code to initialize the patterns for the array is shown in Program 8-15.

```
1  /* ==================== fillArray ====================
2     This function fills array such that each array element
3     contains a number that, when viewed as a two-digit
4     integer, the first digit is the row number and the
5     second digit is the column number.
6     Pre:   table is array in memory
7            numRows is integer for number of rows in array.
```

Program 8-15 Fill two-dimensional array

```
 8        Post: array has been initialized.
 9   */
10   void fillArray (int table[][MAX_COLS],
11                   int numRows)
12   {
13      int row;
14      int col;
15
16      for (row = 0; row < numRows; row++)
17         {
18          table [row][0] = row * 10;
19          for (col = 1; col < MAX_COLS; col++)
20              table [row][col] = table [row][col - 1] + 1;
21         } /* for */
22      return;
23   } /* fillArray */
```

Program 8-15   Fill two-dimensional array (continued)

Memory Layout

As discussed earlier, the indexes in the definition of a two-dimensional array represent rows and columns. This format maps to the way the data are laid out in memory. If we were to consider memory as a row of bytes with the lowest address on the left and the highest address on the right, then an array would be placed in memory with the first element to the left and the last element to the right. Similarly, if the array is a two-dimensional array, then the first dimension is a row of elements that are stored to the left. This is known as "row-major" storage and is seen in Figure 8-30.[4]

Figure 8-30   Memory layout

Memory Example: Map One Array to Another

To further examine how data are laid out in memory, look at Program 8-16, which converts a two-dimensional array to a one-dimensional array.

```
1   /* This program changes a two-dimensional array to the
2      corresponding one-dimensional array.
3         Written by:
```

Program 8-16   Convert table to one-dimensional array

---

[4]At least one language, FORTRAN, reverses the data values placement in memory. It stores data by columns.

```
 4        Date:
 5    */
 6    #include <stdio.h>
 7    #define ROWS 2
 8    #define COLS 5
 9
10    int main (void)
11    {
12    /* Local Definitions */
13       int table [ROWS] [COLS] =
14          {
15            {00, 01, 02, 03, 04},
16            {10, 11, 12, 13, 14}
17          }; /* table */
18       int line [ROWS * COLS];
19       int row;
20       int column;
21
22    /* Statements */
23       for (row = 0; row < ROWS; row++)
24          for (column = 0; column < COLS; column++)
25             line[row * COLS + column] = table[row][column];
26
27       for (row = 0; row < ROWS * COLS; row++)
28          printf(" %02d ", line[row]);
29
30       return 0;
31    }  /* main */
```

```
Results:
   00   01   02   03   04   10   11   12   13   14
```

Program 8-16 Convert table to one-dimensional array (continued)

Program 8-16 Analysis   In Program 8-16 we use nested *for* loops to make the conversion. The first loop controls the table rows, and the second loop controls the columns within each row. Since we know how many elements are in each row of the two-dimensional array, we can map it to the one-dimensional array by simply multiplying the row index by the number of elements in each row. When we are in row zero, we multiply the number of elements in one row (designed by the defined constant, COLS) by the row number (0) and add the result to the column. This maps the elements in the two-dimensional array to the beginning of the receiving array. When we are in row 1, we add the number of elements in one row times the row (1) to the current column, which maps the elements to the next set (in this case, 5...9). To generalize, we add the product of the row and the number of elements in a row to the column to determine the receiving location.

Study the technique we used to define the number of elements in the rows and columns. Note how they are used not only to define the arrays but also to control the loop execution. Copy this program, and then run it with different row–column sizes to help understand the differences. (You will need to change the initialization also. You might want to consider initializing the values by assignments within *for* loops.)

PASSING A TWO-DIMENSIONAL ARRAY TO A FUNCTION

With two-dimensional arrays, we have three choices for passing parts of the array to a function. (1) We can pass individual elements, as shown in "Passing Individual Elements," on page 362. (2) We can pass a row of the array. This is similar to passing an array, as we saw in "Passing the Whole Array," on page 363. (3) Finally, we can pass the whole array.

Passing a Row

Passing a row of the array is rather interesting. We pass a whole row by indexing the array name with only the row number. Referring to Figure 8-31, we see that a row is four integers. When we pass the row, therefore, the receiving function receives a one-dimensional array of four integers. The *for* loop in print_square prints the square of each of the four elements. After printing all the values, the function advances to the next line on the console and returns. The *for* loop in *main* calls print_square five times so that the final result is a table of the values squared shown on the monitor.

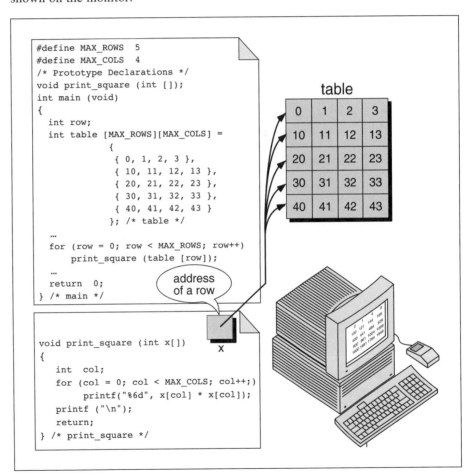

```
#define MAX_ROWS   5
#define MAX_COLS   4
/* Prototype Declarations */
void print_square (int []);
int main (void)
{
   int row;
   int table [MAX_ROWS][MAX_COLS] =
            {
              { 0, 1, 2, 3 },
              { 10, 11, 12, 13 },
              { 20, 21, 22, 23 },
              { 30, 31, 32, 33 },
              { 40, 41, 42, 43 }
            }; /* table */

   ...
   for (row = 0; row < MAX_ROWS; row++)
       print_square (table [row]);
   ...
   return  0;
} /* main */
```

```
void print_square (int x[])
{
   int  col;
   for (col = 0; col < MAX_COLS; col++;)
        printf("%6d", x[col] * x[col]);
   printf ("\n");
   return;
} /* print_square */
```

Figure 8-31   Passing a row

Note that we have declared the array dimensions as defined constants. This allows us to symbolically refer to the limits of the array in both the array definition and the *for* loops. Now, if we need to change the size of the array, all that is necessary is to change the *define* declarations, and any array initializers, and recompile the program.

Passing the Whole Array

When we pass a two-dimensional array to a function, we use the array name as the actual parameter just as we did with one-dimensional arrays. The formal parameter in the called function header, however, must indicate that the array has two dimensions. This is done by including two sets of brackets, one for each dimension, as shown below.

```
double average (int table[][MAX_COLS])
```

Note that again we do not need to specify the number of rows. It is necessary, however, to specify the size of the second dimension. Thus, we specified the number of columns in the second dimension (MAX_COLS). In summary, to pass two-dimensional arrays to functions,

1. The function must be called by passing only the array name.
2. In the function definition, the formal parameter is a two-dimensional array, with the size of the *second* dimension required.

For example, we can use a function to calculate the average of the integers in an array. In this case, we pass the name of the array to the function as seen in Figure 8-32.

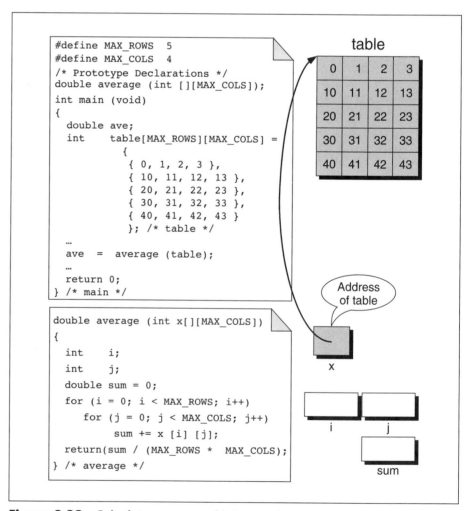

Figure 8-32   Calculate average of integers in array

ARRAY EXAMPLE

Write a program that fills the left-to-right diagonal of a square matrix (a two-dimensional array with an equal number of rows and columns) with zeros, the lower left triangle with −1s, and the upper right triangle with +1s. The output of the program, assuming a six-by-six matrix is shown in Figure 8-33. The program code is shown in Program 8-17.

Figure 8-33   Example of filled matrix

```
 1    /* This program fills the diagonal of a matrix (square
 2        array) with 0, the lower left triangle with -1, and the
 3        upper right triangle with 1.
 4           Written by:
 5           Date:
 6    */
 7    #include <stdio.h>
 8
 9    int main (void)
10    {
11    /* Local Definitions */
12       int table [6][6];
13       int row;
14       int column;
15
16    /* Statements */
17       for (row = 0; row < 6; row++)
18          for (column = 0; column < 6; column++)
19             if (row ==  column)
20                table [row][column] = 0;
21             else if (row > column)
22                table [row][column] = -1;
23             else
24                table [row][column] = 1;
25
26       for (row = 0; row < 6; row++)
27          {
28           for (column = 0; column < 6; column++)
29              printf("%3d", table[row][column]);
```

Program 8-17   Fill matrix

```
30        printf("\n");
31      } /* for row */
32    return 0;
33 }  /* main */
```

Program 8-17 Fill matrix (continued)

Program 8-17 Analysis   This is a rather simple pattern problem, similar to many we saw in Chapter 6. The only difference is that now we are creating the pattern in array elements. Since there are two dimensions, we need two loops to control the pattern. If the row equals the column, we assign 0 to the element. If the row is greater than the column, then we are in the lower half of the matrix, so we assign –1. And if the row is less than the column, then we are in the upper half of the matrix and we assign +1.

8-8   MULTIDIMENSIONAL ARRAYS

Multidimensional arrays can have three, four, or more dimensions. Figure 8-34 shows an array of three dimensions. Note the terminology used to describe the array. The first dimension is called a **plane**, which consists of rows and columns. Arrays of four or more dimensions can be created and used, but they are difficult to draw.

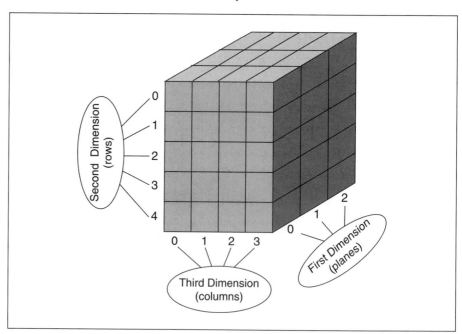

Figure 8-34   A three-dimensional array (5 × 4 × 3)

Although a three-dimensional array is exactly what is shown by Figure 8-34, the C language looks at it in a different way. It takes the three-dimensional array to be an array of two-dimensional arrays. It considers the two-dimensional array to be an array of one-dimensional arrays. In other words, a three-dimensional array in C is an array

Figure 8-35 C view of three-dimensional array

of arrays of arrays. This concept also holds true for arrays of more than three dimensions. The C view of a three-dimensional array is seen in Figure 8-35.

DECLARING AND DEFINING MULTI-DIMENSIONAL ARRAYS

Multidimensional arrays, like one-dimensional arrays, must be declared and defined before being used. Declaration and definition tell the compiler the name of the array, the type of each element, and the size of each dimension. The size of the array is a constant and must have a value at compilation time. The three-dimensional array seen in Figure 8-35 can be declared and defined as follows:

```
int table[3][5][4];
```

Initialization

As we said before, declaration and definition only reserve space for the elements in the array. No values will be stored in the array. If we want to store values, we must either initialize the elements, read values from the keyboard, or assign values to each individual element.

Once more, initialization is simply an extension of the concept we saw for initializing a two-dimensional array (see page 393). For the three-dimensional array, we nest each plane in a set of brackets. For each plane, we bracket the rows as we did for the two-dimensional array. If you group the data by plane and row as we have done in Figure 8-36, the reader will be able to visualize the array with ease. We have added comments to make it even easier to read the values.

As we saw previously, the plane's size, and only the plane's size, does not need to be specified when we use explicit initialization. The size of all dimensions after the first must be explicitly stated.

```
int table[3][5][4] =
   {
    {  /* Plane 0*/
      {0, 1, 2, 3},              /* Row 0 */
      {10, 11, 12, 13},          /* Row 1 */
      {20, 21, 22, 23},          /* Row 2 */
      {30, 31, 32, 33},          /* Row 3 */
      {40, 41, 42, 43}           /* Row 4 */
    },
    {  /* Plane 1*/
      {100, 101, 102, 103},      /* Row 0 */
      {110, 111, 112, 113},      /* Row 1 */
      {120, 121, 122, 123},      /* Row 2 */
      {130, 131, 132, 133},      /* Row 3 */
      {140, 141, 142, 143}       /* Row 4 */
    },
    {  /* Plane 2*/
      {200, 201, 202, 203},      /* Row 0 */
      {210, 211, 212, 213},      /* Row 1 */
      {220, 221, 222, 223},      /* Row 2 */
      {230, 231, 232, 233},      /* Row 3 */
      {240, 241, 242, 243}       /* Row 4 */
    }
   }; /* table */
```

Figure 8-36 Initializing a three-dimensional array

Of course, if we want to initialize all the elements to zero, we can simply initialize only the first element to zero and let the compiler generate the code to initialize the rest of the array to zeros.

```
int table [3][5][4] = {0};
```

8-9 PROGRAMMING EXAMPLE—CALCULATE AVERAGES

This programming example contains many of the programming techniques found in array problems. It contains three arrays: a two-dimensional array of integers, and two one-dimensional arrays of averages, one for rows and one for columns. When you are working with a large program with many different data structures, in this case three arrays, it often helps to draw a picture of the arrays. You can then see how the different arrays work together to solve the problem. A picture of the array structure and their relationships is shown in Figure 8-37.

The program begins by requesting the user to provide data for a two-dimensional array. Once the array has been filled, the program calculates the average of each row and places it in a parallel array of row averages. It then calculates the average for each column and places it in an array of column averages. Although we have represented the column-average array horizontally and the row-average array vertically, they are both one-dimensional arrays.

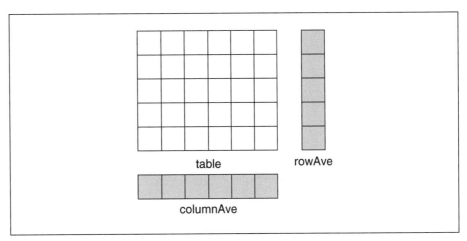

Figure 8-37 Data structures for calculate row–column averages

When all the calculations are complete, the program calls a function to print the array with the row averages at the end of each row and the column averages at the bottom of each column. The structure chart for the program is seen in Figure 8-38. Program 8-18 contains the code.

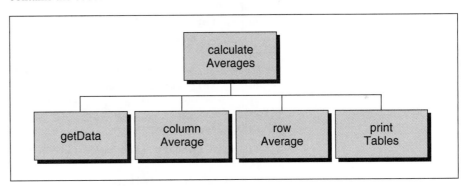

Figure 8-38 Calculate row–column average design

```
 1  /* This program reads values of a two-dimensional array
 2     from the keyboard. It then creates two one-dimensional
 3     arrays, which are the averages of rows and columns.
 4        Written by:
 5        Date:
 6  */
 7  #include <stdio.h>
 8
 9  #define MAX_ROWS 5
10  #define MAX_COLS 6
11
12  /* Prototype Declaration */
13  void getData        (int   table[][MAX_COLS]);
14  void columnAverage (int   table[][MAX_COLS],
```

Program 8-18 Calculate row and column averages

```
15                               float colAvrg []);
16  void  rowAverage       (int    table[][MAX_COLS],
17                               float rowAvrg []);
18  void  printTables      (int    table[][MAX_COLS],
19                               float rowAvrg[],
20                               float colAvrg []);
21
22  int main (void)
23  {
24  /* Local Definitions */
25     int    table      [MAX_ROWS][MAX_COLS];
26
27     float rowAve      [MAX_ROWS] = {0};
28     float columnAve [MAX_COLS] = {0};
29
30  /* Statements */
31     getData           (table);
32     columnAverage   (table, columnAve);
33     rowAverage      (table, rowAve);
34     printTables     (table, rowAve, columnAve);
35
36     return 0;
37  }  /* main */
38
39  /* ===================== getData =====================
40     This function receives data for a two-dimensional array.
41        Pre   table is empty array to be filled with integers
42        Post  the array would be filled
43  */
44  void getData (int table[][MAX_COLS])
45  {
46  /* Local Definitions */
47     int row;
48     int col;
49
50  /* Statements */
51     for (row = 0; row < MAX_ROWS; row++)
52        for (col = 0; col < MAX_COLS; col++)
53            {
54             printf("\nEnter integer and key <return>: ");
55             scanf("%d", &table[row][col]);
56            } /* for col */
57     return;
58  } /* getData */
59
60  /* ==================== columnAverage ====================
61     This function calculates the average for the columns.
62        Pre   table has been filled with integer values
63        Post  average calculated and put in the average array
```

Program 8-18   Calculate row and column averages (continued)

```
64  */
65  void columnAverage (int    table [][MAX_COLS],
66                      float  colAvrg[])
67  {
68  /* Local Definitions */
69     int row;
70     int col;
71
72  /* Statements */
73     for (col = 0; col < MAX_COLS; col++)
74        {
75         for (row = 0; row < MAX_ROWS ; row++)
76             colAvrg [col] += table [row][col];
77         colAvrg [col] /=  MAX_ROWS;
78        } /* for col */
79
80     return;
81  }  /* columnAverage */
82
83  /* ===================== rowAverage =====================
84     This function calculates the row averages for a table
85        Pre    table has been filled with values
86        Post   averages calculated & put in the average array.
87  */
88  void rowAverage (int    table[][MAX_COLS],
89                   float  rowAvrg [])
90  {
91  /* Local Definition */
92     int row;
93     int col;
94
95  /* Statements */
96  for (row = 0; row < MAX_ROWS; row++)
97        {
98         for (col = 0; col < MAX_COLS ; col++)
99             rowAvrg[row] += table [row][col];
100        rowAvrg [row] /=  MAX_COLS;
101       } /* for row */
102    return;
103 }  /* rowAverage */
104
105 /* ===================== printTables =====================
106    Print data table, with average of rows at end of each
107    row and average of columns below each column.
108       Pre    each table has been filled with its data
109       Post   the tables have been printed.
110 */
111 void printTables (int    table[][MAX_COLS],
112                   float  rowAvrg[],
```

Program 8-18 Calculate row and column averages (continued)

```
113                     float   colAvrg[])
114  {
115  /* Local Definitions */
116     int row;
117     int col;
118
119  /* Statements */
120     for (row = 0; row < MAX_ROWS; row++)
121        {
122        for (col = 0; col < MAX_COLS; col++)
123             printf("%6d", table[row][col]);
124        printf("    | %6.2f\n", rowAvrg [row]);
125        } /* for row */
126
127     printf("---------------------------------------\n");
128     for (col = 0; col < MAX_COLS; col++)
129         printf("%6.2f", colAvrg[col]);
130
131     return;
132  } /* printTables */
133  /* ================ End of Program ================ */
```

```
Results:
        10    12    14    16    18    20  |   15.00
        22    24    26    28    30    23  |   25.50
        25    27    29    31    33    35  |   30.00
        39    41    43    45    47    49  |   44.00
        51    53    55    57    59    61  |   56.00
       ---------------------------------------
        29.40 31.40 33.40 35.40 37.40 37.60
```

Program 8-18   Calculate row and column averages (continued)

8-10 SOFTWARE ENGINEERING AND PROGRAMMING STYLE

In this section, we discuss two basic concepts: testing and algorithm efficiency. To be effective, testing must be clearly thought out. We provide some concepts for testing array algorithms by studying sorting and searching. We then continue the algorithm efficiency discussion started in Chapter 6 by studying sort and search algorithms as case studies.

TESTING SORTS

As your programs become more complex, you need to spend more time creating test data that will completely validate them. In this section, we examine some techniques for testing sorts.

In general, you should conduct four tests: (1) Sort a list of random values, (2) sort a list that is already in sequence, (3) sort a list that is in reverse order, (4) sort a nearly ordered list, such as one in which every tenth item is one position out of sequence. Table 8-1 contains a summary of the tests that you should conduct and some sample test data to show the points.

Test Case	Sample Data
Random data	5 23 7 78 22 6 19 33 51 11 93 31
Nearly ordered	5 6 7 21 19 22 23 31 29 33 51 93
Ordered – ascending	5 6 7 11 19 22 23 31 33 51 78 93
Ordered – descending	93 78 51 33 31 23 22 19 11 7 6 5

Table 8-1   Recommended sort test cases

TESTING SEARCHES

When you test the sequential search, you need only four tests. Three deal with finding an element in the table—find the first, last, and any element in the middle. The last case deals with trying to find an element that is not in the list; look for any value that is not in the middle of the list. Whenever testing an array, always be sure that your test data access the first and last elements of the array. Many array processing errors occur at these locations.

> Whenever testing an array, always be sure that your test data access the first and last elements of the array.

The binary search requires the four tests discussed above, plus three more. Since it uses an ordered list, you should try to find a target lower than the first element in the list and another target greater than the last element. Finally, you should find two elements that are in adjacent array locations, such as list[0] and list[1]. The reason for this test is that the binary search includes logic that divides by two. An error could result in being able to find only even- or only odd-numbered elements. Testing for adjacent locations ensures that such an error won't happen. These test cases are seen in Table 8-2.

Expected Results	Index	Test	Search
found	0	target == list[0]	all
found	1	target == list[1]	binary only
found	$n - 1$	target == list[n]	all
found	$0 < i < n$	target == list[i]	all
not found	0	target < list[0]	binary only
not found	$n - 1$	target > list[n]	binary only
not found	$0 < i < n$	target != list[i]	all

Table 8-2   Test cases for searches

ANALYZING SORT ALGORITHMS

We have developed three sort algorithms. We examine each of them in this section.

Bubble Sort Analysis

The bubble sort essentially contains the block of code shown below. For simplicity, we have combined the first statement from `bubbleSort` with the loop from `bubbleUp`.

```
for(current = 0; current < last; current++)
    for (walker = last; walker > current; walker--)
        if (list[walker] < list[walker - 1])
            exchange (walker, walker - 1);
```

To determine the relative efficiency, we need to analyze the two *for* statements. The first *for*, the outer loop, examines each entry in the sort array. It will therefore loop $n - 1$ times.

The inner loop starts at the end of the array and works its way toward the current node as established by the outer loop. The first time it is called, it examines $n - 1$ elements; the second time, $n - 2$ elements, and so forth until it examines only one element. The average number of elements examined, therefore, is determined as shown below.

$$(n - 1) + (n - 2) + \cdots + 2 + 1 = n\frac{(n - 1)}{2}$$

This is the nested dependent loop. On the average, therefore, each iteration of the outer loop will call the inner loop $(n - 1) / 2$ times. The combination of the two loops is therefore

$$n\left(\frac{n - 1}{2}\right) = \frac{1}{2}(n^2 - n)$$

Discarding the coefficient and selecting the larger factor, we see that the dominant factor in the bubble sort is n^2, which in big-O notation would be stated as $O(n^2)$.

> The efficiency of the bubble sort is $O(n^2)$.

Selection Sort

Now let's examine the efficiency of the selection sort shown in Program 8-6 on page 375. Again, its pivotal logic is essentially shown below.

```
for (current = 0; current < last; current++)
    {
     for (walker = current + 1; walker <= last; walker++)
        if (list[walker] < list[smallest])
            smallest = walker;
    } /* for */
```

This algorithm bears a strong resemblance to the bubble sort algorithm we discussed above. Its first loop looks at every element in the array from the first element (current = 0) to the one just before the last. The inner loop moves from the current element, as determined by walker, to the end of the list. This is similar to the bubble sort, except that it works from the lower portion of the array toward the end. Using the same analysis, we see that it will test $n(n - 1) / 2$ elements, which means that the selection sort is also $O(n^2)$.

> The efficiency of the selection sort is $O(n^2)$.

Insertion Sort

The last sort we covered was the insertion sort, Program 8-10, on page 380. The nucleus of its logic is shown below.

```
for (current = 1; current <= last; current++)
    for (walker = current - 1;
         walker >= 0 && !located; )
        if (temp < list[walker])
            {
             list[walker + 1] = list[walker];
             walker--;
            }
```

Does the pattern look familiar? It should. Again we have the same basic nested *for* loop logic that we saw in the bubble sort and the selection sort. The outer loop is executed n times, and the inner loop is executed $(n - 1) / 2$ times, giving us $O(n^2)$.

> The efficiency of the insertion sort is $O(n^2)$.

As we have demonstrated, all three of these sorts are $O(n^2)$, which means that they should be used only for small lists or lists that are nearly ordered. You will eventually study sorts that are $O(n\log_2 n)$, which is much more efficient for large lists.

ANALYZING SEARCH ALGORITHMS

All of the sort algorithms involved nested loops. We now turn our attention to two algorithms that have only one loop, the sequential search and the binary search. Recall that a search is used when we need to find something in an array or other list structure. The *target* is a value obtained from some external source.

Sequential Search

The basic loop for the sequential search is shown below.

```
while (looker < last && target != list[looker])
    looker++;
```

This is a classic example of a linear algorithm. In fact, in some of the literature, this search is known as a **linear search**. Since the algorithm is linear, its efficiency is $O(n)$.

> The efficiency of the sequential search is $O(n)$.

Binary Search

The binary search locates an item by repeatedly dividing the list in half. Its loop is

```
while (first <= last)
   {
      mid = (first + last) / 2;
      if (target > list[mid])
         first = mid + 1;
      else if (target < list[mid])
         last = mid - 1;
      else
         first = last + 1;
   } /* while */
```

This is obviously a loop that divides, and it is therefore a logarithmic loop. This makes the efficiency $O(\log_2 n)$, which you should recognize as one of the more efficient of all the measures.

> The efficiency of the binary search is $O(\log_2 n)$.

Comparing the sequential search and binary search, we see that, disregarding the time required to order the list, the binary search is obviously better for a list of any significant size (see Table 8-3). We therefore recommend the binary search for all but the smallest of lists—that is, lists with less than 16 elements.

Size	Binary	Sequential (Average)	Sequential (Worst Case)
16	4	8	16
50	6	25	50
256	8	128	256
1,000	10	500	1,000
10,000	14	5,000	10,000
100,000	17	50,000	100,000
1,000,000	20	500,000	1,000,000

Table 8-3 Comparison of binary and sequential searches

The big-O concept is generally interested only in the largest factor. This tends to significantly distort the efficiency of the sequential sort, in that it is always the worst case. If the search is always successful, it turns out that the efficiency of the sequential search is $1/2n$. We include the average in Table 8-3 for comparison. (The average for the binary search is only one less than the maximum, so it is less interesting.)

8-11 TIPS AND COMMON PROGRAMMING ERRORS

1. In an array declared as `array[n]`, the index goes from 0 (not 1) to $n - 1$.
2. Three things are needed to declare and define an array: its name, type, and size.
3. The elements of arrays are not initialized automatically. You must initialize them if you want them to start with known values.
4. To initialize all elements in an array zero, all you need to do is initialize the first element to zero.
5. To exchange the value of two elements in an array, you need a temporary variable.
6. You cannot copy all elements of one array into another with an assignment statement. You need to use a loop.
7. To pass the whole array to a function, you only use the name of the array as an actual parameter.
8. The most common logic error associated with arrays is an invalid index. An invalid index used with an assignment operator either causes the program to fail immediately or destroys data or code in another part of the program and causes it to fail later.
9. Invalid indexes are often created by invalid coding in a *for* statement. For example, given an array of ten elements, the following *for* statement logic error results in an index value of ten being used. Although it loops 10 times, the indexes are 1 through 10, not zero through 9.

```
for (i = 1; i <= 10; i++)
```

10. Another cause of invalid indexes is an uninitialized index. Make sure your indexes are always properly initialized.
11. When initializing an array when it is defined, it is a compile error to provide more initializers than there are elements.
12. It is a compile error to leave out the index operators in an assignment statement, as shown below.

```
float costAry[20];
...
costAry = quantity * price;
```

13. It is most likely a logic error to leave out the index operators in a *scanf* statement, as shown below. In this case, `costAry` is the address of the array and the input will be placed in the first element of the array. Even when this is the desired result, you should code it with the index operators as shown.

```
float costAry[20];
...
scanf("%f", costAry);        /* Invalid? */
scanf("%f", &costAry[0]);    /* Clear code */
```

14. It is a compile error to omit the array size in the parameter declaration for any array dimension other than the first.

8-12 KEY TERMS AND CONCEPTS

accessing array elements
array
binary search
bubble sort
column
data structure
declaring and defining arrays
exchanging values
frequency array
histogram
index

indexing
index range checking
initialization of arrays
inputting values
insertion sort
linear search
multidimensional array
one-dimensional array
passing array rows to functions
passing the whole array
passing individual elements

plane
reusable code
row
search
selection sort
sequential search
sort pass
square brackets
subscript
two-dimensional array

8-13 SUMMARY

■ A one-dimensional array is a fixed sequence of elements of the same type.

■ We use indexes in C to show the position of the elements in an array.

■ An array must be declared and defined before being used. Declaration and definition tell the compiler the name of the array, the type of each element, and the size of the array.

■ Initialization of all elements of an array can be done at the time of the declaration and definition.

■ If a one-dimensional array is completely initialized when it is declared, it is not necessary to specify the size, but it is recommended.

■ When an array is partially initialized, the rest of the elements are set to zero.

■ We can fill the elements of an array by using a loop to read the values from the keyboard.

■ We can access the individual elements of an array using the array name and the index. Accessing is done for two purposes: inspecting the value of the element or storing a new value in the element.

■ We can output the values of an array using a loop.

■ An array reference is a postfix expression with the opening and closing brackets as operators.

■ C does not do boundary checking on the elements of an array.

■ We can pass an individual element of an array to a function. In this case, the value of the element will be passed to the function.

■ We can also pass the whole array to a function. In this case, only the address of the array will be passed. When this happens, the function can change the value of the elements in the array.

■ A frequency array is an array whose elements show the number of occurrence of data values in another array.

■ A histogram is a pictorial representation of a frequency array.

■ A two-dimensional array is a representation of a table with rows and columns.

■ We can pass either one single element, a row, or the whole array to a function.

■ A multidimensional array is an extension of a two-dimensional array to three, four, or more dimensions.

■ An array can be sorted using a sorting algorithm.

■ The selection sort divides the array into sorted and unsorted sublists. In each pass, the algorithm chooses the smallest element from the unsorted sublist and swaps it with the element at the beginning of the unsorted sublist.

■ The bubble sort divides the array into sorted and unsorted sublists. In each pass, the algorithm bubbles the smallest element from the unsorted list into the sorted sublist.

■ The insertion sort divides the array into sorted and unsorted sublists. In each pass, the algorithm inserts the first element from the unsorted list into the appropriate place in the sorted sublist.

■ Searching is the process of finding the location of a target among a list of objects.

■ The sequential search starts at the beginning of the array and searches until it finds the data or hits the end of the list. The data may be ordered or unordered.

■ A binary search is a much faster searching algorithm. In the binary search, each test removes half of the list from further analysis. The data must be ordered.

8-14 PRACTICE SETS

REVIEW QUESTIONS

1. The type of all elements in an array must be the same.
   a. True   b. False

2. Any expression that evaluates to an integral value may be used as an index.
   a. True   b. False

3. When an array is defined, C automatically sets the value of its elements to zero.
   a. True   b. False

4. When an array is passed to a function, C uses pass by address.
   a. True   b. False

5. Because of its efficiency, the binary search is the best search for any array, regardless of its size and order.
   a. True   b. False

6. The selection, insertion, and bubble sort are all $O(n^2)$ sorts.
   a. True   b. False

7. A(n) _____ is an integral value used to access an element in an array.
   a. constant   d. number
   b. element   e. variable
   c. index

8. Which of the following array initialization statements is valid?
   a. `int ary{ } = {1, 2, 3, 4};`
   b. `int ary[ ] = [1, 2, 3, 4];`
   c. `int ary[ ] = {1, 2, 3, 4};`
   d. `int ary{4} = [1, 2, 3, 4];`
   e. `int ary[4] = [1, 2, 3, 4];`

9. Which of the following statements assigns the value stored in *x* to the first element on an array, *ary*?
   a. `ary    = x;`
   b. `ary    = x[0];`
   c. `ary    = x[1];`
   d. `ary[0] = x;`
   e. `ary[1] = x;`

10. Which of the following statements concerning passing array elements is true?
    a. Arrays cannot be passed to functions, because their structure is too complex.
    b. It is not possible to pass just a row of a two-dimensional array to a function.
    c. Only the size of the first dimension is needed when a two-dimensional array is declared in a parameter list.
    d. When an array is passed to a function, it is always passed by reference (only its address is passed).
    e. When a two-dimensional array is passed to a function, the size of the second dimension must be passed as a value parameter.

11. The process through which data are arranged according to their values is known as
    a. arranging   d. searching
    b. listing   e. sorting
    c. parsing

12. The _____ sort finds the smallest element from the unsorted sublist and swaps it with the element at the beginning of the unsorted data.
    a. bubble   d. quick
    b. exchange   e. selection
    c. insertion

13. The _____ search locates the target item by starting at the beginning and moving toward the end of the list.
    a. ascending   d. selection
    b. binary   e. sequential
    c. bubble

14. Which of the following statements about a sequential search is false?
    a. Any array can be searched using the sequential search.
    b. If the target is not found, every element in the list is tested.
    c. The efficiency of the sequential search is $O(n)$.
    d. The list must be ordered.
    e. The sequential search is generally recommended only for small lists.

15. Which of the following statements about two-dimensional arrays is true?
    a. A two-dimensional array can be thought of as an array of one-dimensional arrays.
    b. Only the size of the second dimension needs to be declared when the array is used as a parameter.
    c. Two different types can be stored in a two-dimensional array.
    d. The first dimension is known as the column dimension.
    e. When passed to a function, the size of the second dimension must be passed as a value parameter.

16. What would be printed by the following program?

```
#include <stdio.h>

int main (void)

{
/* Local Definitions */
    int list [10] = {0};
    int i;

/* Statements */
    for (i = 0;  i < 5;   i++)
        list [2 *  i + 1] =  i  + 2;
    for (i = 0; i < 10;   i++)
        printf("%d\n", list [i]);
    return 0;
}   /* main */
```

17. What would be printed by the following program?

```
#include <stdio.h>

int main (void)

{
/* Local Definitions */
    int list [10] = {2, 1, 2, 1, 1, 2, 3, 2, 1, 2};
/* Statements */
    printf("%d\n", list [2]);
    printf("%d\n", list [list [2]]);
    printf("%d\n", list [list [2] + list [3]]);
    printf("%d\n", list [list [list [2]]]);
    return 0;
} /* main */
```

18. What would be printed by the following program?

```
#include <stdio.h>

int main (void)

{
/* Local Definitions */
    int list [10] = {2, 1, 2, 4, 1, 2, 0, 2, 1, 2};
    int line [10];
    int i;
/* Statements */
    for (i = 0; i < 10; i ++)
        line [i] = list [9 - i];
    for (i = 0; i < 10; i++)
        printf("%d %d\n", list [i], line [i]);
    return 0;
}   /* main */
```

19. An array contains the elements shown below. The first two elements have been sorted using a selection sort. What would be the value of the elements in the array after three more passes of the selection sort algorithm?

     7   8   26   44   13   23   98   57

20. An array contains the elements shown below. The first two elements have been sorted using a bubble sort. What would be the value of the elements in the array after three more passes of the bubble sort algorithm? Use the version of bubble sort that starts from the end and bubbles the smallest element.

     7   8   26   44   13   23   57   98

21. An array contains the elements shown below. The first two elements have been sorted using an insertion sort. What would be the value of the elements in the array after three more passes of the insertion sort algorithm?

     3   13   7   26   44   23   98   57

22. We have the following array:

     47   3   21   32   56   92

    After two passes of a sorting algorithm, the array has been rearranged as shown below.

     3   21   47   32   56   92

    Which sorting algorithm is being used (selection, bubble, insertion)? Defend your answer.

23. We have the following array:

     80   72   66   44   21   33

    After two passes of a sorting algorithm, the array has been rearranged as shown below.

     21   33   80   72   66   44

    Which sorting algorithm is being used (selection, bubble, insertion)? Defend your answer.

24. We have the following array:

     47   3   66   32   56   92

    After two passes of a sorting algorithm, the array has been rearranged as shown below.

     3   47   66   32   56   92

    Which sorting algorithm is being used (selection, bubble, insertion)? Defend your answer.

25. An array contains the elements shown below. Using the binary search algorithm, trace the steps followed to find 88. At each loop iteration, including the last, show the contents of `first`, `last`, and `mid`.

     8   13   17   26   44   56   88   97

26. An array contains the elements shown below. Using the binary search algorithm, trace the steps followed to find 20. At each loop iteration, including the last, show the contents of `first`, `last`, and `mid`.

     8   13   17   26   44   56   88   97

27. Both the selection and bubble sorts exchange elements. The insertion sort does not. Explain how the insertion sort rearranges the data without exchanges.

PROBLEMS

28. We have two arrays A and B, each of 10 integers. Write a function that tests if every element of array A is equal to its corresponding element in array B. In other words, the function must check if A[0] is equal to B[0], A[1] is equal to B[1], and so forth. The function is to return true (1) if all elements are equal and false (0) if at least one element is not equal.

29. Write a function that reverses the elements of an array so that the last element becomes the first, the second from the last becomes the second, and so forth. The function is to reverse the elements in place—that is, without using another array. (It is permissible to use a variable to hold an element temporarily.) Then write a test driver to test your function. Test it twice, once with an even number of elements in the array and once with an odd number of elements in the array.

30. The Pascal triangle can be used to compute the coefficients of the terms in the expansion of $(a + b)^n$. Write a function that creates a two-dimensional matrix representing the Pascal triangle. In a Pascal triangle, each element is the sum of the element directly above it and the element to the left of the element directly above it (if any). A Pascal triangle of size 7 is shown below.

1						
1	1					
1	2	1				
1	3	3	1			
1	4	6	4	1		
1	5	10	10	5	1	
1	6	15	20	15	6	1

In the above example, the first element of row[0] and the first two elements of row[1] are set to 1. Then each of the following rows, up to the maximum size, are set with a loop as shown in the following pseudocode:

```
1. pascal[0][0] = 1
2. pascal[1][0] = 1
3. pascal[1][1] = 1
4. prevRow      = 1
5. currRow      = 2
6. loop (currRow <= size)
     1. pascal[row][0] = 1
     2. col = 1
     3. loop (col <= currRow)
          1. pascal[row][col] =
                  pascal[row - 1][col - 1]
              + pascal[row - 1][col]
          2. col = col + 1
```

Your program must be able to create the triangle of any size.

31. An international standard book number (ISBN) is used to uniquely identify a book. It is made of 10 digits, as shown in Figure 8-39. Write a function that tests an ISBN to see if it is valid. For an ISBN number to be valid, the weighted sum of the 10 digits must be evenly divisible by 11. The tenth digit may be *x*, which indicates 10.

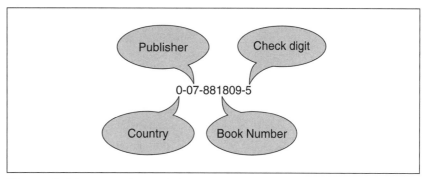

Figure 8-39   ISBN for Problem 31

To determine the weighted sum, the value of each position is multiplied by its relative position, starting from the right, and the sum of the products is determined. The calculation of the weighted sum for the ISBN shown above is

Code	Weight	Weighted Value
0	10	0
0	9	0
7	8	56
8	7	56
8	6	48
1	5	5
8	4	32
0	3	0
9	2	18
5	1	5
	Weighted Sum	220

Since the weighted sum modulus 11 is 0, the ISBN number is valid. Test your function with the above example, the ISBN number for this text (see the copyright page), and 0-08-781809-5 (an invalid ISBN—the third and fourth digits are reversed).

32. Another technique to validate the ISBN in Problem 31 is to calculate the sum of the sums modulus 11. The sum of the sums is calculated by adding each digit to the sum of the previous digits, as shown below.

Code	Sum of Digits	Sum of Sums
0	0	0
0	0	0
7	7	7
8	15	22
8	23	45
1	24	69
8	32	101
0	32	133
9	41	174
5	46	220

Rewrite the function to use the sum-of-the-sums method.

33. Write a function that copies a one-dimensional array of *n* elements into a two-dimensional array of *k* rows and *j* columns. The rows and columns must be a valid factor of the number of elements in the one-dimensional array; that is, $k * j = n$.

34. Write a program that creates an array of 100 random integers in the range 1 to 200 (see Chapter 4 for a discussion of random numbers) and then, using the sequential search, searches the array 100 times using randomly generated targets in the same range. At the end of the program, display the following statistics:

   a. The number of searches completed.

   b. The number of successful searches.

   c. The percentage of successful searches.

   d. The average number of tests per search.

   To determine the average tests per search, you will need to count the number of tests for each search. Hint: Use the comma operator to count the compares.

35. Repeat Problem 34 using the binary search.

36. The sequential search assumes that a list is unordered. If it is used when the list is in fact ordered, the search can be terminated with the target not found whenever the target is less than the current element. Modify Program 8-13, on page 386, to incorporate this logic.

37. Repeat Problem 34 with the modified search you created in Problem 36

38. Modify the bubble sort to stop as soon as the list is sorted. (See discussion in "Program 8-9 Analysis," on page 379.

39. Modify the selection sort function to count the number of exchanges needed to order an array of 50 random numbers (see Chapter 4 for a discussion of random numbers). Display the array before and after the sort. At the end of the program, display the total exchanges needed to sort the array.

40. Repeat Problem 39 using the bubble sort. Hint: Modify `bubbleUp` to return the count of the exchanges. Then, in `bubbleSort`, add the returned count to an accumulator.

41. Program 8-4, on page 367, builds a frequency array and its histogram. If there is an invalid data point in the input, it is displayed and ignored. Modify the program to make the frequency array one element larger than the data range, and use the last element of the array as a count of numbers not in the specified range.

42. Write a program that fills the right-to-left diagonal of a square matrix with zeros, the lower right triangle with –1s, and the upper left triangle with +1s. The output of the program, assuming a six-by-six matrix, is shown in Figure 8-40.

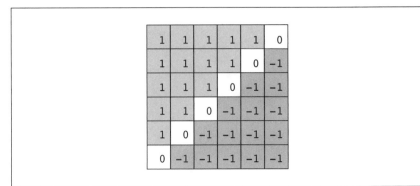

Figure 8-40 Matrix for Problem 42

43. Given an array of 100 random numbers in the range 1...999, write a function for each of the following processes. In building the array, if the random number is evenly divided by 3 or 7, store it as a negative number.

   a. Print the array ten values to a line. Make sure that the values are aligned in rows.

   b. Print the odd values, ten to a line.

   c. Print the values at the odd numbered index locations, ten to a line.

   d. Return a count of the number of even values.

   e. Return the sum of all values in the array.

   f. Return the location of the smallest value in the array.

   g. Return the location of the largest value in the array.

   h. Copy all positive values to a new array. Then use process "a" above to print the new array.

   i. Copy all negative values to a new array. Then use process "a" above to print the new array.

44. Modify the sort of your choice to sort two parallel arrays. Parallel arrays are two or more arrays that contain related data. For example, one array might contain identification numbers, and a related array might contain corresponding scores in a tournament. The sort will sort only the array containing the identifiers; however, as each element in the sorted array is moved, its corresponding element in the data array must also be moved. After the arrays have been sorted, print out the data as shown below.

ID	Score
1	72
2	89
3	98
4	105

   Write a test driver to test your sort. Use the following data—the first value is an identifier and the second value is a score: {18, 90}, {237, 47}, {35, 105}, {5,25}, {76, 739}, {103, 26}, {189, 38}, {22, 110}, {156, 31}, {49, 245}.

PROJECTS

45. Write a C program that simulates a guessing game. Each turn, you choose among nine possible guesses. As many as five guesses may be made in a turn. For each turn, the program will generate a random number between 1 and 36. Each correct guess will be rewarded with points based on how many of your current points you risked.

   A game board divides the numbers into rows and columns, as shown in Figure 8-41. This board provides the basis for your guesses.

   You can guess whether the random number is even or odd. In this case, you get 1 point for each point risked when you guess right. You can guess whether the number is low (1–12), medium (13–24), or high (25–36). In this case, you will get 2 points for each point risked. You can also guess left, center, or right, as shown in Figure 8-41. In this case, you get 2 points for each point risked when your guess is correct. Finally, you can guess a specific number between 0 and 36. In this case you get 36 points for each point risked when your guess is correct.

	LEFT	CENTER	RIGHT
LOW	01	02	03
	04	05	06
	07	08	09
	10	11	12
MEDIUM	13	14	15
	16	17	18
	19	20	21
	22	23	24
HIGH	25	26	27
	28	29	30
	31	32	33
	34	35	36
	LEFT	CENTER	RIGHT

Figure 8-41   The guessing game board

To make the game more interesting, each round allows up to five guesses. None of the five may be correct, or any number up to all five may be correct. The program stops when the player quits or when the player is out of points.

The program first asks the number of points the user wants to start with, as shown below.

```
          How many points would you like? 2000
```

The program then prints the guess menu and allows up to five guesses, as shown below.

```
          Guesses     Choices
             O           Odd
             E           Even
             L           Low
             M           Med
             H           High
             F           Left
             C           Center
             R           Right
             N           Number


How many guesses would you like?  5


       Guess 1
       Enter your choice? L
       Points at risk?      20
```

```
Guess 2   :
Enter your choice? H
Points at risk?     15


Guess 3   :
Enter your choice? N
Enter your number: 18
Points at risk?     20


Guess 4   :
Enter your choice? O
Points at risk?     120


Guess 5   :
Enter your choice? L
Points at risk?     0
```

After all guesses have been made, the program generates the random number and displays the following message:

```
My number is:   31
```

The program then prints the situation of the player:

```
Previous Points: 2000
```

Guess	Type	Number	Amount	Won/Lost
1	L		20	−20
2	H		15	+30
3	N	18	20	−20
4	O		120	+120
5	N	20	10	−10

```
You won 100 points in this turn.
Your new balance is : 2100 points
Do you want to play again (Y or N) ? Y
```

Some special rules: The minimum amount risked on a guess is 0. The maximum is the player's current balance. You need to verify that at no time are the points risked more than the player's current balance. Any combinations of guesses are allowed on a round as long as the total does not exceed the player's balance.

Some hints: You must use at least four arrays, each of five elements. The arrays hold the guess information for the *kind of guess*, *chosen number* (in case the player chooses a number), *amount of the guess*, and *points won or lost*.

Run your program twice, first with 2000 points and then with 500 points. Try different situations. Each run is to exercise each guess at least twice.

46. Write a program to keep records and perform statistical analysis for a class of students. The class may have up to 40 students. There are five quizzes during the term. Each student is identified by a four-digit student number.

The program will print the student scores and calculate and print the statistics for each quiz. The output is in the same order as the input; no sorting is needed. The input will be read from a text file. The output from the program should be similar to the following:

Student	Quiz 1	Quiz 2	Quiz 3	Quiz 4	Quiz 5
1234	78	83	87	91	86
2134	67	77	84	82	79
3124	77	89	93	87	71
High Score	78	89	93	91	86
Low Score	67	77	84	82	71
Average	73.4	83.0	88.2	86.6	78.6

Use one- and two-dimensional arrays only. Test your program with the following quiz data:

Student	Quiz 1	Quiz 2	Quiz 3	Quiz 4	Quiz 5
1234	52	7	100	78	34
2134	90	36	90	77	30
3124	100	45	20	90	70
4532	11	17	81	32	77
5678	20	12	45	78	34
6134	34	80	55	78	45
7874	60	100	56	78	78
8026	70	10	66	78	56
9893	34	9	77	78	20
1947	45	40	88	78	55
2877	55	50	99	78	80
3189	22	70	100	78	77
4602	89	50	91	78	60
5405	11	11	0	78	10
6999	0	98	89	78	20

47. Rework Project 46, creating statistics for each student. Print the students' high, low, and average scores to the right of Quiz 5. Provide appropriate column headings.

48. Program 8-4, on page 367, builds a frequency array. In the discussion of the algorithm, we noted that a potential problem occurs if any of the data are invalid.

    Write a program that uses the random number generator, *rand,* to generate 100 numbers between 1 and 22. The array is then to be passed to a modified version of Program 8-4 that will count the number of values between 0 and 19. Add a 21st element in the array to count all numbers not in the valid range (0 to 19).

    Print the input data in a 20 × 5 array—that is, 20 numbers in five rows—and then print the frequency diagram with a heading of the numbers as shown below.
    ```
    --0- --1- --2- --3- --4- --5- --6- … -18- -19- Invalid
    ```

49. Modify the program you wrote in Project 48 to include a histogram printout of the data. Its format should be similar to Figure 8-14.

50. Using the data from Project 46, build a two-dimensional array of students. Then write a search function that uses the sequential search to find a student in the array and prints the student's scores, average score, and grade based on an absolute scale (90% is A, 80% is B, 70% is C, 60% is D, less than 60% is F). After each printout, give the user the opportunity to continue or stop.

51. Modify the program you wrote in Project 50 to sort the two-dimensional array of students. Then rewrite the search function to use a binary search.

52. Write a program that sorts a 50-element array using the selection sort, the bubble sort, and the insertion sort. Each sort is to be executed twice.

   a. For the first sort, fill the array with random numbers between 1 and 1000.

   b. For the second sort, fill the array with a nearly ordered list. Create the nearly ordered list by filling the array with sequential numbers and then subtracting 5 from every 10th number in the array.

   c. Each sort (selection, bubble, insertion) is to sort the same data. For each sort, count the number of comparisons and moves necessary to order this list.

   d. After each sort execution, print the unsorted data followed by the sort data in 5 by 10 matrixes (5 rows of 10 numbers each). After the sorted data, print the number of comparisons and the number of moves required to order the data. Provide appropriate headings for each printout.

   e. To make sure your statistics are as accurate as possible, you must analyze each loop limit condition test and each selection statement in your sort functions. The best way to count them is with a comma expression, as shown below. Use similar code for the selection statements.

      ```
      while ((count++, a) && (count++, b))
      ```

   f. Analyze the heuristics you generated, and write a few lines concerning what you discovered about these sorts. Put your comments in a box (asterisks) after your program documentation at the beginning of your program.

53. Write a program to compute the arithmetic mean (average), median, and mode for up to 50 test scores. The data are contained in a text file. The program will also print a histogram of the scores.

   The program should start with a function to read the data file and fill the array. Note that there may be fewer than 50 scores. This will require that the read function return the index for the last element in the array.

   To determine the average, write a function similar to Figure 8-11 on page 364. To determine the median, you must first sort the array. The median is the score in the middle of the range. This can be determined by selecting the score at `last` / 2 if `last` is an even index and by averaging the scores at the floor and ceiling of `last` / 2 if `last` is odd. The mode is the score that occurs the most often. It can be determined as a by-product of building the histogram. After building the frequency array, use it to determine which score occurred most often. (Note that two scores can occur the same number of times.)

54. Write a menu-driven program that allows the user to fill an array of 50 integers with random numbers in the range 1...999, sort it, and then search it to determine if a given random number was generated. The menu is shown below.

MENU

Select one of the following options:

F. Fill array with a random number series

P. Print the array

S. Sort the array

Q. Query the array

Z. Terminate the program

- Each time the fill option is executed, it will fill the array with a new random number series.
- You may use any of the sorts discussed in the text.
- If the query locates the number, it will print a message that the number was located and the index location where it was found.
- If the query does not locate the number, it will print a message that the number was not in the list and then print the value and index location of the largest number less than the target and the smallest value greater than the requested number. Note that the first and last elements will not have both a smaller and larger value.
- If the array has been sorted, the query will use a binary search. If it is not sorted, it will use the sequential search.

To test the program

a. Fill (F) the array.

b. Print (P) the unsorted array.

c. Search (Q) the first, last, and a middle element.

d. Refill (F) the array.

e. Sort (S) the array.

f. Print (P) the sorted array.

g. Search (Q) the first, last, and a middle element.

h. Search (Q) for a number less than the first, greater than the last, and not found in the middle of the list.

Pointers 9

Every computer has addressable memory locations. In previous chapters, all of our data manipulations, whether for inspection or alteration, used memory location addresses symbolically. In other words, we assigned identifiers to data and then manipulated their contents through the identifiers.

For a more direct approach, we could use the data addresses directly, but we don't want to give up the ease and flexibility of symbolic names. Fortunately, C can work with addresses symbolically—using pointers. The rest of the book will emphasize, to a large extent, the use of pointers.

Pointers have many uses in C. Besides being a very efficient method of accessing data, they provide efficient techniques for manipulating data in arrays, they are used in functions as pass-by-address parameters, and they are the basis for dynamic allocations of memory.

9-1 CONCEPTS

A **pointer** is a derived data type; that is, it is a data type built from one of the standard types. Its value is any of the addresses available in the computer for storing and accessing data. Pointers are built on the basic concept of pointer constants. To understand and use pointers, you must first understand this concept.

POINTER CONSTANTS

First, we'll compare character constants and pointer constants. We know that we can have a character constant, such as any letter of the alphabet, that is drawn from a universe of all characters. In most computers, this universe is ASCII. A character constant can become a value and can be stored in a variable. Although the character constant is unnamed, the variable has a name that is declared in the program. This concept is shown in Figure 9-1.

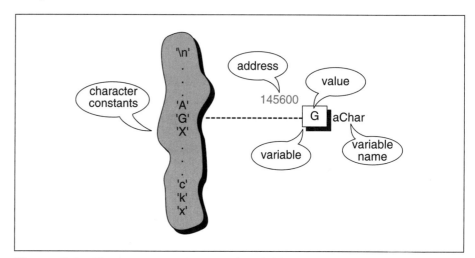

Figure 9-1   Character constants and variables

In Figure 9-1 we have a character variable, aChar. At this point, aChar contains the value 'G' that was drawn from the universe of character constants. The variable aChar has an address as well as a name. The name is created by the programmer; the address is the relative location of the variable with respect to the program's memory space. Assume, for example, that your computer has only 1 megabyte of memory (2^{20} bytes). Assume also that the computer has chosen the memory location 145600 as the byte to store this variable. This gives us the picture we see in Figure 9-1.

Like character constants, **pointer constants** cannot be changed. In Figure 9-2 we see that the address for our character variable, aChar, was drawn from the set of pointer constants for our computer.

Although the addresses within a computer cannot change, you should be aware of the fact that the address of our variable, aChar, can and will change from one run of our program to another. This is because today's modern operating systems can put a program in memory wherever it is convenient when the program is started. Thus, while aChar is stored at memory location 145600 now, which is a constant for the duration of the run, the next time the program is run, it could be located at 876050. It should be obvious, therefore, that even though addresses are constant, we cannot know what they will be. It is still necessary to refer to them symbolically.

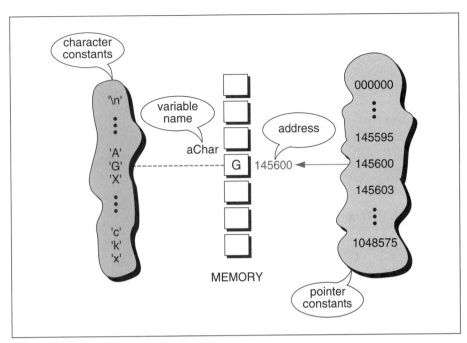

Figure 9-2 Pointer constants

> Pointer constants, drawn from the set of addresses for a computer, exist by
> themselves. We cannot change them; we can only use them.

POINTER VALUES

Having defined a pointer constant as an address in memory, we now turn our attention
to saving this address. If we have a pointer constant, we should be able to save its value
if we can somehow identify it. Not only is this possible, but you have been doing it since
you wrote your first *scanf* statement with an address operator.

The **address operator (&)** provides a pointer constant to any named location in memory. Whenever we need a pointer value, therefore, we only need to use the address operator. If you refer to the expression Precedence Table (see inside front cover), you will
find the address operator in the unary operators (Priority 15). The address operator used
with `aChar` is seen below.

```
&aChar
```

Now let's write a program that defines two character variables and prints their addresses as pointers (conversion code `%p`). Depending on the operating system, this program may print different numbers each time you run it, as we explained above. The
addresses would also be different in different computers. However, most of the time, the
computer allocates two adjacent memory locations because we defined the two variables
one after the other. If you are at your computer, take a moment to code and run the program in Figure 9-3 to demonstrate the concept of address constants.

The situation changes slightly when we talk about integers. In most computers, integers occupy either 2 or 4 bytes. Let's assume that we are working on a system with
4-byte integers. This means that each integer variable occupies four memory locations.
Which of these memory locations is used to find the address of the variable? In most
computers, the location of the first byte is used as the memory address. For characters,

```
/* Print character addresses */
#include <stdio.h>

int  main  (void)
{
/* Local Definitions */
   char   a;
   char   b;
/* Statements */
   printf ("%p %p\n", &a, &b);

   return 0;
}  /* main */
```

a [   ] 142300

b [   ] 142301

Figure 9-3   Print character addresses

there is only 1 byte, so its location is the address. For integers, the address is the first byte of 4. This is shown in Figure 9-4.

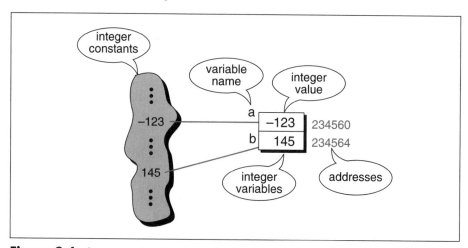

Figure 9-4   Integer constants and variables

The same system applies to floating-point and other data types. The address of a variable is the address of the first byte occupied by that variable.

> The address of a variable is
> the address of the first byte occupied by that variable.

9-2 POINTER VARIABLES

If we have a pointer constant and a pointer value, then we can have a **pointer variable**. Thus, we can store the address of a variable into another variable, which is called a pointer variable. This concept is shown in Figure 9-5.

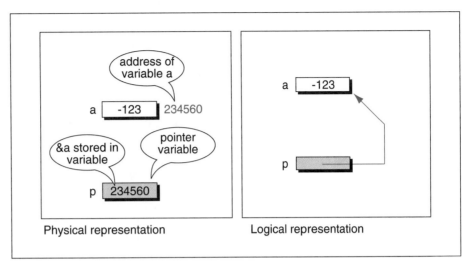

Figure 9-5 Pointer variable

We must distinguish between a variable and its value. Figure 9-5 details the differences. In this figure we see a variable, a, with its value, –123. The variable a is found at location 234560 in memory. Although the variable's name and location are constant, the value may change as the program executes. This figure also has a pointer variable, p. The pointer has a name and a location, both of which are constant. Its value at this point is the memory location 234560. This means that p is pointing to a. In Figure 9-5, the physical representation shows how the data and pointer variables exist in memory. The logical representation shows the relationship between them without the physical details.

We can go even farther and store a variable's address in two or more different pointer variables, as is also shown in Figure 9-6. This figure has a variable, a, and two pointers, p and q. The pointers each have a name and a location, both of which are constant. Their value at this point is the memory location 234560. This means that both p and q are pointing to a. There is no limit to the number of pointer variables that can point to a variable.

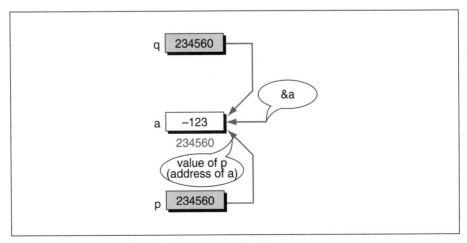

Figure 9-6 Multiple pointers to a variable

A final thought: If we have a pointer variable, but we don't want it to point anywhere, what is its value? C provides a special null pointer constant, NULL, in the standard input/output <stdio.h> library for this purpose.[1]

9-3   ACCESSING VARIABLES THROUGH POINTERS

**THE INDIRECTION
OPERATOR**

Now that we have a variable and a pointer to the variable, how can we relate the two; that is, how can we use the pointer? Once again C has provided an operator for us. Right below the address operator in the unary expressions portion of the Precedence Table (see inside front cover), you will find the **indirection operator (*)**. When you dereference a pointer, you are using its value to reference (address) another variable. The indirection operator is a unary operator whose operand must be a pointer value. The result is an expression that can be used to access the pointed variable for the purpose of inspection or alteration. To access the variable a through the pointer p, you simply code *p. The indirection operator is shown below.

```
*p
```

Let's assume that we need to add 1 to the variable a. We can do this with any of the following statements, assuming that the pointer, p, is properly initialized (p = &a).

```
a++;    a = a + 1;    *p = *p + 1;    (*p)++;
```

In the last example, (*p)++, you need the parentheses. The postfix increment has a priority of 16 in the Precedence Table while indirection, which is a unary operator, has a priority of 15. The parentheses therefore force the dereference to occur before the addition so that we add to the data variable and not to the pointer. Without the parentheses, we would add to the pointer first, which would change the address.

Figure 9-7 expands the discussion. Let's assume that the variable x is pointed to by two pointers, p and q. As you can see, the expressions x, *p, *q all are expressions that allow the variable to be either inspected or changed. When they are used in the right-hand side of the assignment operator, they can only inspect (copy or compare). When they are used in the left-hand side of the assignment operator, they change the value of x.

The indirection and address operators are the inverse of each other, and when combined in an expression, such as *&x, they cancel each other. To see this, let's break down the expression. These two unary operators are evaluated from the right. The first expression is therefore &x, the address of x, which as we have seen, is a pointer value. The second expression, *(&x), dereferences the pointer constant, giving the variable (x) itself. Therefore, the operators effectively cancel each other (Figure 9-8). Of course, we would never code the expression *&a in a program; we use it in Figure 9-7 for illustration only.

---

[1]Technically, NULL is found in the <stddef.h> library. Most systems also define it in <stdio.h>, however.

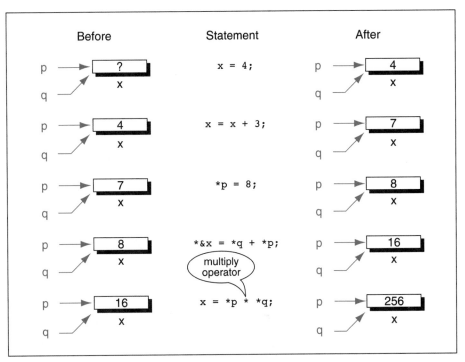

Figure 9-7   Accessing variables through pointers

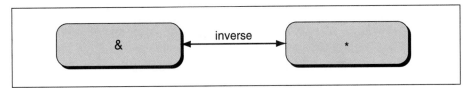

Figure 9-8   Address and indirection operators

9-4   POINTER DECLARATION AND DEFINITION

As shown in Figure 9-9, we use the indirection operator to define and declare pointer variables. When we use it in this way, it is really not an operator but rather a compiler syntactical notation. Making it the same token as the operator makes it easier to remember.

Figure 9-9   Pointer variable declaration

Figure 9-10 shows how we declare different pointer variables. Their corresponding data variables are shown for comparison. Note that in each case the pointer is declared to be of a given type. Thus, p is a pointer to characters, while q is a pointer to integers, and r is a pointer to floating-point variables.

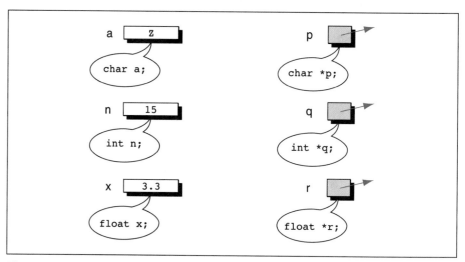

Figure 9-10   Declaring pointer variables

EXAMPLE: PRINT WITH A POINTER

Program 9-1 stores the address of a variable in a pointer and then prints the data using the variable value and a pointer.

```
1    /* Demonstrate pointer use
2           Written by:
3           Date:
4    */
5    #include <stdio.h>
6
7    int    main (void)
8    {
9    /* Local Definitions */
10      int   a;
11      int  *p;
12
13   /* Statements */
14      a = 14;
15      p = &a;
16
17      printf("%d %p\n", a, &a);
18      printf("%p %d %d\n",
19              p, *p, a);
20
21      return 0;
22   }  /* main */
```

```
 Results:
    14 00135760
    00135760 14 14
```

Program 9-1   Demonstrate use of pointers

Program 9-1 Analysis   Program 9-1 requires a little explanation. First, we have defined an integer variable, a, and a pointer to integer, to which we assign a's address. We then print twice. The first print displays the contents of the variable a and its address (note the pointer conversion code). The second print uses the pointer, p. It prints the pointer value containing the address of a, followed by the contents of a, first referenced as a pointer and then as a variable. This demonstrates two ways to access the data. We suggest that you run this program for yourself. Of course, when you do, you will get a different address. Also, some compilers display addresses as integers, and some use hexadecimal numbers.

9-5 INITIALIZATION OF POINTER VARIABLES

As we discussed above, the C language does not initialize variables. If they are initialized at all, it is done by the operating system loader. Thus, when we start our program, all of our uninitialized variables have unknown garbage in them. (The fact that an operating system clears memory when it loads a program cannot be counted on, especially with programs that run on multiple systems.)

The same thing is true for pointers. When the program starts, uninitialized pointers will have some unknown memory address in them. More precisely, they will have an unknown value that will be interpreted as a memory location. Most likely the value will not be valid for the computer you are using, or if it is, will not be valid for the memory you have been allocated. If the address does not exist, you will get an immediate run-time error. If it is a valid address, you often, but unfortunately not always, get a run-time error. (It is better to get the error when you use the invalid pointer than to have the program produce garbage.)

One of the most common causes of errors in programming, by novices and professionals alike, is uninitialized pointers. These errors can be very difficult to debug because the effect of the error is often delayed until later in the program execution. Figure 9-11 shows both an uninitialized variable and an uninitialized pointer.

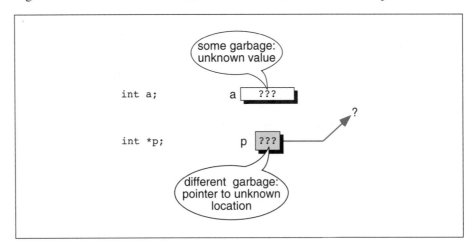

Figure 9-11   Uninitialized pointers

To correct the problem shown in Figure 9-11, we must always assign a valid memory address to the pointer, as shown on the next page.

```
int  a;              /* int variable        */
int *p = &a;         /* p has valid address */
*p = 89;             /* a assigned 89       */
```

As we saw with variables, it is also possible to initialize pointers when they are declared and defined. All that is needed is that the data variable be defined before the pointer variable. For example, if we have an integer variable, **x**, and a pointer to integer, **p**, then to set **p** to point to **x** at declaration time, we can code it as shown in Figure 9-12.

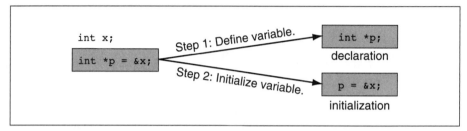

Figure 9-12 Initializing pointer variables

Note that in Figure 9-12, the initialization involves two different steps. First the variable is declared. Then the assignment statement to initialize it is generated. Some style experts suggest that you should not use an initializer in this way.[2] Their argument is that it saves no code; that is, that the initializer statement is required either as a part of the declaration and initialization or as a separately coded statement in the statement section of the function. Putting the initialization in the declaration section tends to hide it and make program maintenance more difficult. We tend to agree with them.

We can also set a pointer to NULL, either during definition or during execution. The following statement demonstrates how we could define a pointer with an initial value of NULL.

```
int *p = NULL;
```

When we dereference a null pointer, we are using address zero, which is a valid address in the computer. Depending on the operating system, this can be the physical address zero or can be the first address location in our program area. If we dereference the pointer **p** when it is NULL, we will most likely get a run-time error! NULL is not a valid address. The type of error you get will depend on the system you are using.

EXAMPLE: CHANGE VARIABLES—FUN WITH POINTERS

Now let's write a program and have some fun with pointers. Our code is shown in Program 9-2. Do not try to figure out why this program is doing what it is doing; there is no reason. Rather, just try to trace the different variables and pointers as we change them.

```
1  /* Fun with pointers
2        Written by:
3        Date:
4  */
```

Program 9-2 Fun with pointers

[2]For example, see Steve Oualline, *C Elements of Style* (Mountain View, Calif.: M&T Books, 1982).

```
 5   #include <stdio.h>
 6
 7   int main (void)
 8   {
 9   /* Local Definitions */
10      int  a;
11      int  b;
12      int  c;
13      int *p;
14      int *q;
15      int *r;
16
17   /* Statements */
18      a = 6;
19      b = 2;
20      p = &b;
21
22      q = p;
23      r = &c;
24
25      p  = &a;
26      *q = 8;
27
28      *r = *p;
29
30      *r = a + *q + *&c;
31
32      printf("%d %d %d \n",
33               a, b, c);
34      printf("%d %d %d",
35               *p, *q, *r);
36      return 0;
37   }  /* main */
```

Results:
6 8 20
6 8 20

Program 9-2 Fun with pointers (continued)

Program 9-2 Analysis   When the program starts, all the variables and their pointers are uninitialized. The variables have garbage values, and the pointers have invalid memory locations.

The first thing the program does, therefore, is to assign values to a and b, and to initialize all three pointers. After statement 23, both p and q point to b, and r points to c.

Statement 25 assigns the address of a to p. All three pointers now point to different variables. Using the indirection operator, we dereference q (*q), which assigns b the value 8.

Statement 28 demonstrates that both operands can be dereferenced when it assigns the contents of a (*p) to c (*r).

Finally, in Statement 30, we use three different formats to sum the values in the variables, a variable name, a dereferenced pointer, and a dereferenced address operator. Using the figures in the program, trace these statements carefully to assure yourself that you understand how they work.

EXAMPLE: ADD TWO NUMBERS

This example shows how we can use pointers to add two numbers. It explores the concept of using pointers to manipulate, in this case add, data. A graphic representation of the variables is shown in Figure 9-13. The code is shown in Program 9-3.

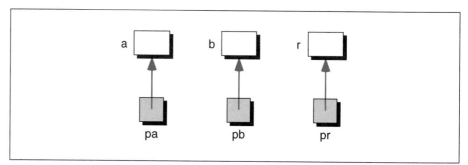

Figure 9-13 Add two numbers using pointers

```
1   /* This program adds two numbers using pointers to
2      demonstrate the concept of pointers.
3         Written by:
4         Date:
5   */
6   #include <stdio.h>
7
8   int main (void)
9   {
10  /* Local Definitions */
11     int   a;
12     int   b;
13     int   r;
14     int *pa = &a;
15     int *pb = &b;
16     int *pr = &r;
17
18  /* Statements */
19     printf("Enter the first number : ");
20     scanf("%d", pa);
21     printf("Enter the second number: ");
```

Program 9-3 Add two numbers using pointers

```
22    scanf("%d", pb);
23    *pr = *pa + *pb;
24    printf("\n%d + %d is %d", *pa, *pb, *pr);
25    return 0;
26  }   /* main */
```

```
Results:
    Enter the first number : 15
    Enter the second number: 51

    15 + 51 is 66
```

Program 9-3   Add two numbers using pointers (continued)

Program 9-3 Analysis   This program is rather straightforward except for one thing. Look at Statements 20 and 22 carefully. What is missing? When we discussed pass by address in Chapter 4, we mentioned that when input areas are passed by address, we don't use the address operator in the *scanf* statement. This is because the pointer already contains an address. It would be an error to use the address operator on the pointers in this program.

EXAMPLE: POINTER FLEXIBILITY

This example shows how we can use the same pointer to print the value of different variables. The variables and their pointer are shown in Figure 9-14, and the code is given in Program 9-4.

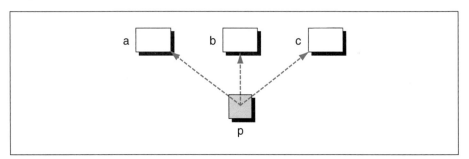

Figure 9-14   Demonstrate pointer flexibility

```
1    /* This program shows how the same pointer can point to
2        different data variables in different statements.
3            Written by:
4            Date:
5    */
6    #include <stdio.h>
7
8    int main (void)
9    {
10   /* Local Definitions */
11       int  a;
12       int  b;
13       int  c;
14       int *p;
```

Program 9-4   Using one pointer for many variables

```
15
16   /* Statements */
17      printf("Enter three numbers and key return: ");
18      scanf("%d %d %d", &a, &b, &c);
19      p = &a;
20      printf("\n%3d ", *p);
21      p = &b;
22      printf("\n%3d ", *p);
23      p = &c;
24      printf("\n%3d ", *p);
25      return 0;
26   }  /* main */
```

Program 9-4   Using one pointer for many variables (continued)

**EXAMPLE:
MULTIPLE
POINTERS FOR ONE
VARIABLE**

This example shows how we can use different pointers to print the value of the same variable. The variable and its pointers are shown in Figure 9-15. The code is shown in Program 9-5.

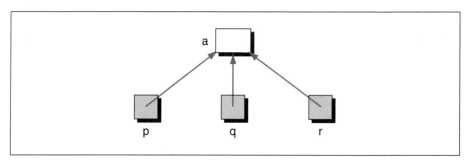

Figure 9-15   One variable with many pointers

```
1    /* This program shows how we can use different pointers
2       to point to the same data variable.
3          Written by:
4          Date:
5    */
6    #include <stdio.h>
7
8    int main (void)
9    {
10   /* Local Definitions */
11      int  a;
12      int *p = &a;
13      int *q = &a;
14      int *r = &a;
15
16   /* Statements */
17      printf("Enter a number: ");
18      scanf ("%d", &a);
19      printf("\n%d ", *p);
```

Program 9-5   Using a variable with many pointers

```
20   printf("\n%d ", *q);
21   printf("\n%d ", *r);
22
23   return 0;
24 }  /* main */
```

Program 9-5   Using a variable with many pointers (continued)

9-6   POINTERS AND FUNCTIONS

One of the most useful applications of pointers is in functions. When we discussed functions earlier, we saw that C uses the pass-by-value concept exclusively. This means that the only direct way to send something back from a function is through the *return* value. We also saw that we can simulate the concept of pass by reference by passing an address and using it to refer back to data in the calling program. We use the term *pass by address* for this concept. When we pass by address, we are actually passing a pointer to a variable. In this section, we fully develop this concept of passing addresses or pointers. We use two examples to demonstrate how pointers can be used in functions.

POINTERS AS FORMAL PARAMETERS

Figures 9-16 and 9-17 demonstrate the use of pointers. In Figure 9-16, we call the exchange function, passing it two variables whose contents are to be exchanged. When we use the pass-by-value method, the data are exchanged in the called function, but nothing changes in the calling program.

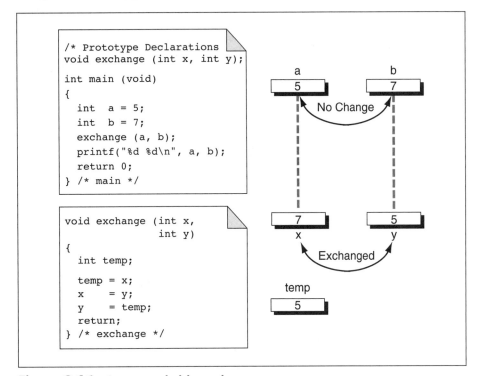

Figure 9-16   An unworkable exchange

Rather than pass the *values* of the two elements to be exchanged, we could pass pointers to the values. Once we have a pointer to a variable, it doesn't make any difference if it is local to the active function, defined in main, or even if it is a global variable; we can change it! In other words, given a pointer to a variable anywhere in our memory space, we can change the contents of the variable.

Figure 9-17 shows the exchange using pointers. To create the pointers, we use the address operator (&) in the call, as shown below. We are now passing the address of a and b rather than their values.

```
exchange (&a, &b);
```

To use pass by address, the formal parameters in the called function are defined as a pointer to variables. This definition, which is shown below, completes the connection and allows us to indirectly reference the variables in the calling program through the pointers.

```
void exchange (int *, int *);
```

To assign a value to a, all that we need to do is dereference the pointer in exchange. This allows us to access data in the calling program using call by address. It is important to understand, however, that C is still only passing a value. In this case, the value is the address of the variable we need to change. We are only simulating pass by reference.

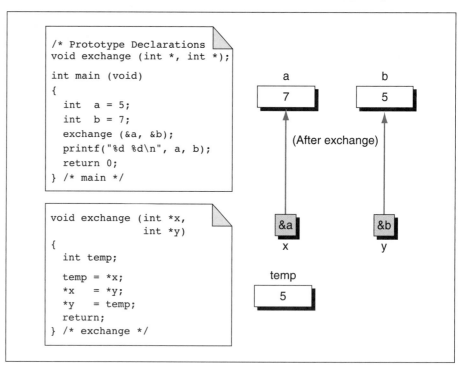

Figure 9-17   Exchange using pointers

We then call exchange using the address operator for the variables that we want to exchange. Note that exchange uses the two formal parameters, x and y, and one local variable, temp. By dereferencing the parameters, we make the exchange using the variables in main and the local variable, temp, in exchange. The working program is shown in Figure 9-17.

> Every time we want a called function to have access to a variable in the calling function, we send the address of that variable to the called function and use the indirection operator to access it.

In summary, when we need to send back more than one value from a function, we can use pointers. By passing the address of variables defined in `main`, or any other function that makes calls, we can store data directly in the calling function rather than using *return*.

FUNCTIONS RETURNING POINTERS

We have shown you many examples of functions using pointers, but so far we have shown none that return a pointer. Nothing prevents a function from returning a pointer to the calling function. In fact, as you will see, it is quite common for functions to return pointers.

As an example, let's write a rather trivial function to determine the smaller of two numbers. In this case, we need a pointer to the smaller of two variables, a and b. Since we are looking for a pointer, we pass two pointers to the function, which uses a conditional expression to determine which value is smaller. Once we know the smaller value, we can return the address of its location as a pointer. The return value is then placed in the calling function's pointer, p, so that after the call it points to either a or b, based on their values. Both the code and a diagram of the variables and pointers are seen in Figure 9-18.

Figure 9-18 Functions returning pointers

When you return a pointer, it must point to data in the calling function or a higher level function. It is an error to return a pointer to a local variable in the called function, because when the function terminates, its memory may be used by other parts of the program. Although a simple program might not notice the error, because the space was not reused, a large program would either get the wrong answer or fail when the memory being referenced by the pointer was changed.

> It is a serious error to return a pointer to a local variable.

9-7   POINTERS TO POINTERS

So far, all our pointers have been pointing directly to data. It is possible—and with advanced data structures often necessary—to use pointers that point to other pointers. For instance, we can have a pointer pointing to a pointer to an integer. This two-level indirection is seen in Figure 9-19. There is no limit as to how many levels of indirection you can use, but practically, you seldom get beyond two levels.

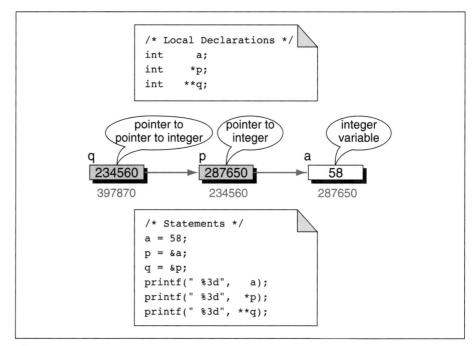

Figure 9-19   Pointers to pointers

Each level of **pointer indirection** requires a separate indirection operator when it is dereferenced. In Figure 9-19, to refer to a using the pointer p, you have to dereference it once, as shown below.

```
*p
```

To refer to a using the pointer q, you have to dereference it twice to get to the integer a because there are two levels of indirection (pointers) involved. If you dereference it only once, you are referencing p, which is a pointer to an integer. Another way to say this is that q is a pointer to a pointer to an integer. The double dereference is shown below.

```
**q
```

Let's see how we use these concepts in the C code fragment shown in Figure 9-19. All three references in the *printf* statements refer to the variable a. The first print statement prints the value of the variable a directly; the second uses the pointer p; the third uses the pointer q. The result is the value 58 printed three times, as shown below.

```
58    58    58
```

POINTER-TO-POINTER EXAMPLE

The last example in this section shows how we can use different pointers with pointers to pointers and pointers to pointers to pointers to read the value of the same variable. A graphic representation of the variables is shown in Figure 9-20. The code is shown in Program 9-6.

Figure 9-20 Using pointers to pointers

```
1   /* Show how pointers to pointers can be used by different
2      scanf functions to read data to the same variable.
3         Written by:
4         Date:
5   */
6   #include <stdio.h>
7
8   int main (void)
9   {
10  /* Local Definitions */
11     int    a;
12     int   *p;
13     int  **q;
14     int ***r;
15
16  /* Statements */
17     p = &a;
18     q = &p;
19     r = &q;
20
21     printf("Enter a number: ");
22     scanf ("%d", &a);
23     printf("The number is : %d\n", a);
24
25     printf("\nEnter a number: ");
26     scanf ("%d", p);
27     printf("The number is : %d\n", a);
28
29     printf("\nEnter a number: ");
30     scanf ("%d", *q);
31     printf("The number is : %d\n", a);
32
33     printf("\nEnter a number: ");
34     scanf ("%d", **r);
35     printf("The number is : %d\n", a);
36
37     return 0;
38  }  /* main */
```

Program 9-6 Using pointers to pointers

```
Results:
   Enter a number: 1
   The number is : 1

   Enter a number: 2
   The number is : 2

   Enter a number: 3
   The number is : 3

   Enter a number: 4
   The number is : 4
```

Program 9-6   Using pointers to pointers (continued)

Program 9-6 Analysis   In each successive read, we use a higher level of indirection. In the print statements, however, we always use the integer variable, a, to prove that the reads were successful.

9-8   COMPATIBILITY

It is important to recognize that pointers have a type associated with them. They are not just pointer types, but rather are pointers to a *specific* type, such as integer. Each pointer therefore takes on the attributes of the type to which it refers in addition to its own attributes. This is demonstrated by Program 9-7, which prints the size of a pointer and what it refers to.

```
 1  /* Demonstrate size of pointers.
 2        Written by:
 3        Date:
 4  */
 5  #include <stdio.h>
 6
 7  int main (void)
 8  {
 9  /* Local Definitions */
10     char   c;
11     char   *pc;
12     int    sizeofc      = sizeof(c);
13     int    sizeofpc     = sizeof(pc);
14     int    sizeofStarpc = sizeof(*pc);
15
```

Program 9-7   Demonstrate size of pointers

```
16      int   a;
17      int  *pa;
18      int   sizeofa        = sizeof(a);
19      int   sizeofpa       = sizeof(pa);
20      int   sizeofStarpa   = sizeof(*pa);
21
22      double  x;
23      double *px;
24      intsizeofx        = sizeof(x);
25      intsizeofpx       = sizeof(px);
26      intsizeofStarpx = sizeof(*px);
27
28  /* Statements */
29      printf("sizeof(c): %3d | ",  sizeofc);
30      printf("sizeof(pc): %3d | ", sizeofpc);
31      printf("sizeof(*pc): %3d\n", sizeofStarpc);
32
33      printf("sizeof(a): %3d | ",  sizeofa);
34      printf("sizeof(pa): %3d | ", sizeofpa);
35      printf("sizeof(*pa): %3d\n", sizeofStarpa);
36
37      printf("sizeof(x): %3d | ",  sizeofx);
38      printf("sizeof(px): %3d | ", sizeofpx);
39      printf("sizeof(*px): %3d\n", sizeofStarpx);
40
41      return 0;
42  }   /* main */
```

```
Results:
    sizeof(c):    1 | sizeof(pc):    4 | sizeof(*pc):    1
    sizeof(a):    2 | sizeof(pa):    4 | sizeof(*pa):    2
    sizeof(x):   12 | sizeof(px):    4 | sizeof(*px):   12
```

Program 9-7 Demonstrate size of pointers (continued)

Program 9-7 Analysis   What is this code telling us? First, note that the variables a, c, and x are never assigned values. This means that the sizes are independent of whatever value may be in a variable. In other words, the sizes are dependent on the type and not its values. Now look at the size of the pointers. It is 4 in all cases, which is the size of an address in the computer on which this program was run. This makes sense: All computers today have over 32,767 bytes, which is the maximum address that could be stored in two bytes. But note what happens when we print the size of the type that the pointer is referring to: The size is the same as the data size! This means that in addition to the size of the pointer, the system also knows the size of whatever the pointer is pointing to. To confirm this, look at the size of the pointer, px, and what it is pointing to when dereferenced (*px).

COMPATIBILITY AND THE *VOID* POINTER

With one exception, it is invalid to assign a pointer of one type to a pointer of another type, even though the values in both cases are memory addresses and would therefore seem to be fully compatible. Although the addresses may be compatible because they are drawn from the same set, what is not compatible is the underlying data type of the referenced object. In C, we can't use the assignment operator with pointers to different types; if we try to, we get a compile error.

The exception to the rule is the void pointer. The void pointer is known as the universal or generic pointer. It can be used with any pointer, and any pointer can be assigned to a void pointer. However, since a void pointer has no object type, it cannot be dereferenced. A void pointer is created as shown below.

```
void *pVoid;
```

CASTING POINTERS

You can make an explicit assignment between incompatible pointer types by using a cast, just as you can cast an *int* to a *float*. For example, if for some unfathomable reason we decided that we needed to use the character pointer, p, to point to an integer (a), we could cast it as shown below.

```
int    a;
char  *p;

p = (char *)&a;
```

But in this case, *user beware!* Unless you cast all operations that use p, you have a great chance of creating mounds of garbage. In fact, with the exception of the void pointer, you should never cast a pointer. The following assignments are all valid, but they are extremely dangerous and must be used with a very carefully thought-out design.

```
/* Local Definitions */
   void *pVoid;
   char *pChar;
   int  *pInt;
/* Statements */
   pVoid = pChar;
   pInt  = pVoid;
   pInt  = (int *) pChar;
```

Let's construct an example in which we have two variables: one integer and one character. The character has one pointer associated with it; the integer has two, one a second-level pointer. These variables and their pointers are shown in Figure 9-21.

Without casting the assignment, we cannot make the character pointer point to the integer value. For example, it is invalid and will result in a compiler error to store the address of the integer variable a in the character pointer pc.

Even when the pointers are associated with the same type, as shown in the integer pointers and examples in Figure 9-21, any assignment must be at the correct level. It is an error to assign the address of a, even though it is an integer, to the pointer to pointer ppa. This is because ppa is a pointer to a pointer to an integer; its type is pointer to pointer, not pointer to integer. Therefore, it can only be assigned the address of a pointer to an integer. As shown in Figure 9-22, pointer types must match.

Figure 9-21 Pointer compatibility

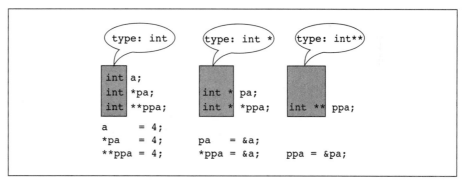

Figure 9-22 Pointer types must match

9-9 LVALUE AND RVALUE

In C, an expression is either an lvalue or an rvalue. As you know, every expression has a value. But the value in an expression (after evaluation) can be used in two different ways.

1. An **lvalue** expression must be used whenever the object is receiving a value; that is, it is being modified.

2. An **rvalue** expression can be used to supply a value for further use; that is, to examine or copy its value.

But how do you know when an expression is an lvalue and when it is an rvalue? Fortunately, only seven types of expressions are lvalue expressions. They are shown in Table 9-1.

	Expression Type[a]	Comments
1.	identifier	Variable identifier
2.	expression[…]	Array indexing
3.	(expression)	Expression must already be lvalue
4.	*expression	Dereferenced expression
5.	expression.name	Structure selection
6.	expression->name	Structure indirect selection
7.	function call	If function uses *return* by address

[a] The shaded expressions have not yet been covered.

Table 9-1　lvalue expressions

For example, the following are lvalue expressions:

```
a = …     a[5] = …     (a) = …     *p = …
```

All expressions that are not lvalue expressions are rvalues. The following show some rvalue expressions:

```
5     a + 2     a * 6     a[2] + 3     a++
```

Note that even if an expression is an lvalue, if it is used as part of a larger expression in which the operators create only rvalue expressions, then the whole expression is an rvalue. For example, a[2] is an lvalue. But when it is used in the expression a[2] + 3, the whole expression is an rvalue, not an lvalue. Similarly, in the expression a++, the variable a is an lvalue while the whole expression (a++) is an rvalue.

You may ask, "Why worry so much about lvalues and rvalues?" The reason is that some operators need an lvalue as their operand. If we use one of these operators and use an rvalue in place of the operand, we will get a compile error. Fortunately, only a few operators need an lvalue expression as an operand. They are shown in Table 9-2.

Type of Expression	Examples	
Address operator	`&score`	
Postfix increment/decrement	`x++`	`y--`
Prefix increment/decrement	`++x`	`--y`
Assignment (left operand)	`x = 1`	`y += 3`

Table 9-2　Operators that require lvalue expressions

Table 9-3 contains several examples of invalid expressions that will create syntax errors because an rvalue is used when an lvalue is needed.

One final thought. A variable name can assume the role of either an lvalue or an rvalue depending on how it is used in an expression. In the following expression, a is an

Expression	Problem
`a + 2 = 6;`	a + 2 is an rvalue and cannot be the left operand in an assignment; it is a temporary value that does not have an address; no place to store 6.
`&(a + 2);`	a + 2 is an rvalue, and the address operator needs an lvalue; rvalues are temporary values and do not have addresses.
`&4;`	Same as above (4 is an rvalue).
`(a+2)++;` `++(a +2);`	Postfix and prefix operators require lvalues; (a + 2) is an rvalue.

Table 9-3   Invalid rvalue expressions

lvalue because it is on the left of the assignment and b is an rvalue because it is on the right of the assignment.

$$a = b$$

9-10   POINTER APPLICATIONS

In this section we demonstrate two ways we can use pointers when calling functions.

CONVERT SECONDS TO HOURS

We begin with a simple function that converts time in seconds to hours, minutes, and seconds. While the function is simple, it does require three address parameters to return the values. The code is shown in Program 9-8.

```
 1  /* ================== secToHours ==================
 2     Given time in seconds, convert it to hours, minutes,
 3     and seconds.
 4        Pre    time in seconds
 5               addresses of hours, minutes, seconds
 6        Post   hours, minutes, seconds calculated
 7        Return error indicator--1 success, 0 bad time
 8  */
 9  int secToHours (long   time,
10                  int   *hours,
11                  int   *minutes,
12                  int   *seconds)
13  {
14  /* Local Definitions */
15     long localTime;
16
17  /* Statements */
18     localTime = time;
19     *seconds  = localTime % 60;
20     localTime = localTime / 60;
```

Program 9-8   Convert seconds to hours, minutes, and seconds

```
21
22      *minutes  = localTime % 60;
23
24      *hours    = localTime / 60;
25
26      if (*hours > 24)
27          return 0;
28      else
29          return 1;
30  }  /* secToHours */
```

Program 9-8 Convert seconds to hours, minutes, and seconds (continued)

Program 9-8 Analysis The first question you might ask when reading this simple function is "Why define a local variable for the time?" In this short function, it really wasn't necessary. However, a good programmer does not change a value parameter within the function, because its original value maybe needed later. We have seen times when "later" turned out to be a maintenance change and hours were spent debugging the error when the wrong value was computed.

> Create local variables when a value parameter will be changed within a function so that the original value will always be available for processing.

Another important design point: If you need to send back two values from a called function, *do not pass one back through a pointer and return the other.* Either use the return for some other reason, such as a status flag, or make the return *void*. Keeping your design consistent—in this case by using a consistent method of returning the values—makes your programs easier to understand and is an example of the KISS principle.

> When several values need to be sent back to the calling function, use address parameters for all of them. Do not return one value and use address parameters for the others.

QUADRATIC EQUATIONS

Let's look at a typical program design that reads, processes, and prints data. This is a processing cycle that is common to many, many programs. Figure 9-23 shows its structure chart.

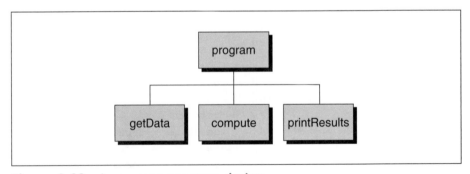

Figure 9-23 A common program design

To demonstrate the universality of this design, let's compute the real roots for a quadratic equation. Recall that a quadratic equation has the form

$$ax^2 + bx + c = 0$$

Four possible situations can occur when you solve for the roots in a quadratic equation. First, it is an error if both a and b are 0: There is no solution. Second, if a is 0 and b is not 0, there is only one root:

$$x = \frac{-c}{b}$$

Third, if $b^2 - 4ac$ is 0 or positive, there are two, possibly equal, roots derived from the following equation:

$$x = \frac{-b \pm (\sqrt{b^2 - 4ac})}{2a}$$

Finally, if $b^2 - 4ac$ is negative, the roots are imaginary.

Figure 9-24 diagrams the interaction of the variables and pointers for Program 9-9. In this short program, we use pointers to pass data from a read function, pass both values and pointers to a compute function, and finally pass the values to a print function.

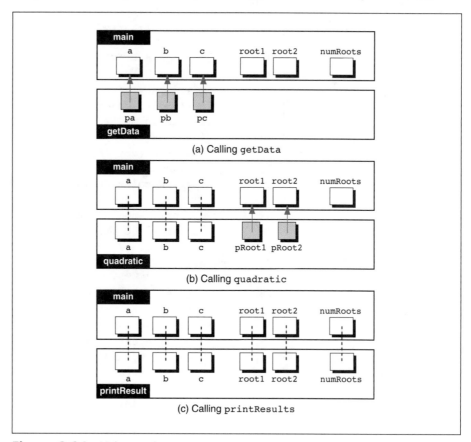

(a) Calling getData

(b) Calling quadratic

(c) Calling printResults

Figure 9-24 Using pointers as parameters

```
 1  /* Test driver for quadratic function.
 2        Written by:
 3        Date:
 4  */
 5  #include <stdio.h>
 6  #include <math.h>
 7
 8  /* Prototype Statements */
 9  void getData       (int    *a,     int *b, int *c);
10  int  quadratic     (int     a,     int  b, int  c,
11                      double *pRoot1, double *pRoot2);
12  void printResults (int     numRoots,
13                      int     a,     int  b, int  c,
14                      double root1, double root2);
15
16  int main (void)
17  {
18  /* Local Definitions */
19     int     a;
20     int     b;
21     int     c;
22     int     numRoots;
23     double root1;
24     double root2;
25     char    again = 'Y';
26
27     /* Statements */
28     printf("Solve quadratic equations.\n\n");
29     while (again == 'Y' || again == 'y')
30        {
31         getData (&a, &b, &c);
32         numRoots = quadratic (a, b, c, &root1, &root2);
33         printResults (numRoots, a, b, c, root1, root2);
34
35         printf("\nDo you have another equation (Y/N): ");
36         scanf (" %c", &again);
37        } /* while */
38     printf("\nThank you.\n");
39     return 0;
40  }  /* main */
41
42  /* ================== getData ==================
43     Read coefficients for quadratic equation.
44        Pre    a, b, and c contains addresses
45        Post   data read into addresses in main
46  */
47  void getData    (int *a,
48                   int *b,
49                   int *c)
```

Program 9-9 Quadratic roots

```
50  {
51  /* Statements */
52     printf("Please enter coefficients a, b, & c: ");
53     scanf ("%d%d%d", a, b, c);
54
55     return;
56  }  /* getData */
57
58  /* ================= quadratic =================
59     Compute the roots for a quadratic equation.
60        Pre    a, b, & c are the coefficients
61               pRoot1 & pRoot2 are variable pointers
62        Post   roots computed, stored in calling function
63        Return 2 two roots,
64               1 one root,
65               0 imaginary roots
66               -1 not quadratic coefficients.
67  */
68  int quadratic (int      a,
69                 int      b,
70                 int      c,
71                 double *pRoot1,
72                 double *pRoot2)
73  {
74  /* Local Definitions */
75     int result;
76
77     double discriminant;
78     double root;
79
80  /* Statements */
81     if (a == 0 && b == 0)
82        result = -1;
83     else
84        if (a == 0)
85           {
86            *pRoot1 = -c / (double) b;
87            result = 1;
88           } /* a == 0 */
89        else
90           {
91            discriminant =  b * b  - (4 * a * c);
92            if (discriminant >= 0)
93               {
94                root    = sqrt(discriminant);
95                *pRoot1 = (-b + root) / (2 * a);
96                *pRoot2 = (-b - root) / (2 * a);
97                result  = 2;
```

Program 9-9 Quadratic roots (continued)

```
 98            } /* if >= 0 */
 99          else
100               result = 0;
101          } /* else */
102    return result;
103  }   /* quadratic */
104
105  /* ================= printResults =================
106     Prints the factors for the quadratic equation.
107         Pre   numRoots contains 0, 1, 2
108               a, b, c contains original coefficients
109               root1 and root2 contains roots
110         Post  roots have been printed
111  */
112  void printResults   (int    numRoots,
113                       int    a,
114                       int    b,
115                       int    c,
116                       double root1,
117                       double root2)
118  {
119  /* Statements */
120     printf("Your equation: %dx**2 + %dx + %d\n",
121          a, b, c);
122     switch (numRoots)
123        {
124         case 2:  printf("Roots are: %6.3f & %6.3f\n",
125                  root1, root2);
126                  break;
127         case 1:  printf("Only one root: %6.3f\n",
128                  root1);
129                  break;
130         case 0:  printf("Roots are imaginary.\n");
131                  break;
132         default: printf("Invalid coefficients\n");
133                  break;
134        } /* switch */
135     return;
136  }  /* printResults */
137  /* ==================== End of Program ==================== */
```

```
Results:
   Solve quadratic equations.

   Please enter the coefficients a, b, & c: 2 4 2
   Your equation: 2x**2 + 4x + 2
   Roots are: -1.000 & -1.000
```

Program 9-9 Quadratic roots (continued)

```
Do you have another equation (Y/N): y
Please enter the coefficients a, b, & c: 0 4 2
Your equation: 0x**2 + 4x + 2
Only one root: -0.500

Do you have another equation (Y/N): y
Please enter the coefficients a, b, & c: 2 2 2
Your equation: 2x**2 + 2x + 2
Roots are imaginary.

Do you have another equation (Y/N): y
Please enter the coefficients a, b, & c: 0 0 2
Your equation: 0x**2 + 0x + 2
Invalid coefficients

Do you have another equation (Y/N): y
Please enter coefficients a, b, & c: 1 -5 6
Your equation: 1x**2 + -5x + 6
Roots are:  3.000 &  2.000

Do you have another equation (Y/N): n

Thank you.
```

Program 9-9   Quadratic roots (continued)

Program 9-9 Analysis   This problem has many interesting points. The function `main` is a test driver—that is, code that will not be put into production. Therefore, we code much of the test logic in `main` rather than providing separate functions for it.

The *scanf* function used in `getData` does not have the usual address operator (&) in front of variables a, b, and c. Why? Because they are already pointer values pointing to variables in `main` and therefore are already addresses.

The variables in these examples are either integers or pointers to integers. Parameters that receive something from `main` are integers whose values will be filled when the call is made. Those that send data back to `main` are pointers to integer that will be filled with the addresses of the corresponding variables in `main`. As a general rule, if a value will be changed, it must be passed as a pointer. If it will not be changed, it should be passed as a value. This protects data from accidental destruction.

In `quadratic`, note the extensive testing to make sure that the coefficients are valid. To ensure valid code, they are all necessary. Look at how we calculated the square root of the discriminant separately (Statement 94). Since square root is a complex function, it is more efficient to call it just once and save the value for later use. Note also that the function has only one *return* statement. This is proper structured code, although many professional programmers would simply return at Statements 82, 87, 97, and 100.

Study our test data carefully. Note that this set of test data executes every line of code in the program. Designing test data that completely validates a function is not an easy task. Ensuring that all code has been executed is even more difficult and tedious. One way to make sure that all code has been tested is to use your debugger to set a break point at every statement and then clear them as the program executes. When all break points have been cleared, you know every instruction has been executed.

Executing every line of code does not ensure that the function has no bugs, however. With large programs, it is virtually impossible to test every possible combination of data. One of the advantages of structured programming is that by breaking the program down into separate functions we can test it better.

This program has a potential problem. Do you see it? Hint: What if the user enters invalid data? There is no error checking in `getData`. If this were a production program, it would contain code to check for errors. It would then return a status flag to indicate if `getData` was successful or not.

9-11 SOFTWARE ENGINEERING AND PROGRAMMING STYLE

In the previous chapters, software engineering has always been related to the material in the chapter. This chapter is an exception. In this chapter, we discuss a general software engineering topic, quality, which can be applied to any topic, including pointers.

You will find no one who would even consider minimizing software quality, at least publicly. Everyone wants the best software available, and to listen to the creators of systems on the market, their systems are all perfect. Yet, as a user of software, we often feel that quality software is a contradiction in terms. We all have our favorite software products, but not one of them is without a wart or two.

Since you are now moving into the world to be one of those software creators, you need to be aware of the basic concepts of software quality. In this chapter, we discuss some of the attributes of a quality product and how you go about achieving quality.

QUALITY DEFINED

Quality software is defined as

> Software that satisfies the user's explicit and implicit requirements, is well documented, meets the operating standards of the organization, and runs efficiently on the hardware for which it was developed.

Every one of these attributes of good software falls squarely on you, the system designer and programmer. Note that we place on you the burden of satisfying not only the users' explicit requirements, but also their implicit needs. Often, users don't fully know what they need. When this happens, it is your job to determine their implicit requirements, which are hidden in the background. This is a formidable task indeed.

Of course, it is also your job to document the software. If you are lucky, you will have a technical writer to help, but even if you do, the final product is still your responsibility. And as an analyst and programmer, you are expected to know the standards of your organization and to implement them properly.

Finally, it is your program, so you are responsible for its efficiency. This means that you are expected to use appropriate and efficient algorithms. This was the focus of our discussion in Chapters 6 and 8 when we talked about analyzing algorithms and the big-O theory.

But quality software is not just a vague concept. If we want to attain it, we have to be able to measure it. Whenever possible, these measurements should be quantitative; that is, they should be numerically measurable. For example, if an organization is serious about quality, it should be able to tell you the number of errors (bugs) per thousand lines of code and the mean time between failures for every software system it maintains. These are measurable statistics.

On the other hand, some of the measurements may be qualitative, meaning that they cannot be numerically measured. Flexibility and testability are examples of qualitative software measurements. This does not mean that they can't be measured, but rather that they rely on someone's judgment in assessing the quality of a system.

QUALITY FACTORS Software quality can be divided into three broad measures: operability, maintainability, and transferability. Each of these measures can be further broken down as shown in Figure 9-25.

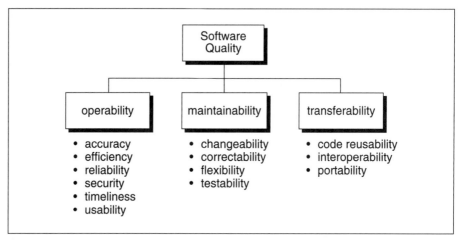

Figure 9-25 Software quality

Operability *Operability* refers to the basic operation of a system. The first thing a user notices about a system is its "look and feel." This means, especially for an online, interactive system, how easy and intuitive it is to use. Does it fit well into the operating system it is running under? For example, if it is running in a windows environment, its pull-down and pop-up menus should work the same way the operating system's menus do. In short, operability answers the question, "How does it drive?"

But these factors are subjective; they are not measurable. So let's look at the factors that comprise operability. They are listed alphabetically.

Accuracy A system that is not accurate is worse than no system at all. Most workers would rather rely on intuition and experience than on a system that they know gives false and misleading information.

Any system that you develop, therefore, must be thoroughly tested, both by you (whitebox) and by a systems test engineer and the user (blackbox). If you get the opportunity, take a course on software testing.

Accuracy can be measured by such metrics as mean time between failures, number of bugs per thousand lines of code, and number of user requests for change.

Efficiency Efficiency is, by and large, a subjective term. In some cases the user will specify a performance standard, such as that a realtime response must be received within 1 second, 95% of the time. This is certainly measurable.

Reliability Reliability is really the sum of the other factors. If users count on the system to get their job done and are confident in it, then it is most likely reliable. On the other hand, some measures speak directly to a system's reliability, most notably, mean time between failures.

Security The security of a system refers to how easy it is for unauthorized persons to get at the system's data. Although this is a subjective area, there are checklists that assist in assessing the system's security. For example, does the system have and require passwords to identify users?

Timeliness   Does the system deliver its output in a timely fashion? For online systems, does the response time satisfy the users' requirements? For batch systems, are the reports delivered in a timely fashion? It is also possible, if the system has good auditability, to determine if the data in the system are timely; that is, are data recorded within a reasonable time after the activity that creates them takes place?

Usability   Usability is also highly subjective. The best measure of usability is to watch the users and see if they are using the system. User interviews will often reveal problems with the usability of a system.

Maintainability   *Maintainability* refers to keeping a system running correctly and up to date. Many systems require regular changes, not because they were poorly implemented but because of changes in external factors. For example, the payroll system for a company must be changed yearly, if not more often, to meet changes in government laws and regulations.

Changeability   The ease of changing a system is a subjective factor. Experienced project leaders, however, can estimate how long a requested change will take. If it takes too long, it may well be because the system is difficult to change. This is especially true of older systems.

Current software measurement tools will estimate a program's complexity and structure. These tools should be used regularly, and if a program's complexity is high, you should consider rewriting the program. Programs that have been changed many times over the years have often lost their structured focus and are difficult to change. They also should be rewritten.

Correctability   One measure of correctability is mean time to recovery—how long it takes to get a program back in operation when it fails. Although this is a reactive definition, there are currently no predictors of how long it will take to correct a program before it fails.

Flexibility   Users are constantly requesting changes in systems. This qualitative attribute attempts to measure how easy it is to make these changes. If a program needs to be completely rewritten to effect a change, it is not flexible. Fortunately, this factor became less of a problem with the advent of structured programming.

Testability   You might think that testability is a highly subjective area, but a test engineer has a checklist of factors that can be used to assess a program's testability.

Transferability   *Transferability* refers to the ability to move data and/or a system from one platform to another and to reuse code. In many situations, it is not an important factor. On the other hand, if you are writing generalized software, it can be critical.

Code Reusability   If functions are written so that they can be reused in different programs and on different projects, then they are highly reusable. Good programmers build libraries of reusable functions that they can use when they need to solve a similar problem.

459

Interoperability   Interoperability addresses the capability of sending data to other systems. In today's highly integrated systems, interoperability is a desirable attribute. In fact, it has become so important that operating systems now support the ability to move data between systems, such as between a word processor and a spreadsheet.

Portability   Portability addresses the ability to move software from one hardware platform to another; for example, from a Macintosh to a Windows environment or from an IBM mainframe to a VAX environment.

THE QUALITY CIRCLE

The first and most important point to recognize is that quality must be designed into a system. It can't be added as an afterthought. It begins at Step 1, determining the user requirements, and continues throughout the life of the system. Since quality is a continuous concept that, like a circle, never ends, we refer to it as the quality circle.

There are six steps to developing quality software: quality tools, technical reviews, formal testing, change control, standards, and measurement and reporting. These steps are shown in Figure 9-26.

Figure 9-26   The quality circle

While no one can deny that quality begins with the software engineers assigned to the team, they need quality tools to develop a quality product. Fortunately, today's development tools are excellent. A whole suite of quality tools known as computer-assisted software engineering (CASE) guides software development through requirements, design, programming and testing, and into production. Programmers can use workstations that not only assist in writing the program but also in testing and debugging. For example, some CASE tools track tests through a program and then determine which statements were executed and which were not. Tools such as these are invaluable for whitebox testing.

Another major step in quality software is the technical review. These reviews should be conducted at every step in the development process including requirements, design, programming, and testing. A typical program review begins after the programmer has designed the data structures and structure chart for a program. A design review board consisting of the systems analyst, test engineer, user representative, and one or two peers is then convened. Note that no one from management is allowed to attend a technical review. During the review, the programmer explains the approach and discusses interfaces to other programs while the reviewers ask questions and make suggestions.

Quality also requires formal testing. Formal testing ensures that the programs work together as a system and meet the defined requirements. After the programmer has completed unit testing, the program is turned over to another software engineer for integration and system testing. On a small project, this is most likely the systems analyst and/or the user. A large project will have a separate testing team.

Large systems take months and sometimes years to develop. It is only natural that over extended periods of time changes to the requirements and design will be necessary. To ensure quality, each change should be reviewed and approved by a change control board. The impact of a requested change on each program needs to be assessed and properly planned. Uncontrolled change causes schedule and budget overruns and poor-quality products.

Finally, a good-quality environment measures all aspects of quality and regularly reports the results. Without measurement, you cannot tell if quality is good or bad, improving or deteriorating. At the same time, published standards provide the yardstick for many of the quality measurements.

CONCLUSION

In this short discussion, we have only introduced the concept of software quality. Consider these points as you design and program systems in the future. For a more complete discussion of the subject, we recommend Chapter 12 in Roger Pressman's *Software Engineering, A Practitioner's Approach*.[3]

9-12 TIPS AND COMMON PROGRAMMING ERRORS

1. The address of a memory location is a pointer constant and cannot be changed.
2. Only an address (pointer constant) can be stored in a pointer variable.
3. Remember compatibility. Do not store the address of a data variable of one type into a pointer variable of another type. In other words, a variable of pointer to *int* can only store the address of an *int* variable, and a variable of pointer to *char* can only store the address of a *char* variable.
4. The value of a data variable cannot be assigned to a pointer variable. In other words, the following code creates an error:

---

[3]Roger Pressman, *Software Engineering, A Practitioner's Approach.* Second Edition (N.Y., N.Y., McGraw-Hill Book Company, 1987).

461

```
int *p;
int a;
p = a;                          /* ERROR */
```

5. You must not use a pointer variable before it is assigned the address of a variable. In other words, the following lines create an error unless p is assigned an address:

```
int *p;
x   = *p;                       /* ERROR */
*p  = x;                        /* ERROR */
```

6. A pointer variable cannot be used to refer to a nonexistent pointed variable. For example, the following lines create a run-time error because p exists, but *p does not exist until it is assigned a value.

```
int  *p;
*p = ...
```

7. You cannot dereference a pointer variable of type *void *.

8. Remember that the definition for a pointer variable allocates memory only for the pointer variable, not for the variable to which it is pointing.

9. The address operator (&) must be used only with an lvalue.

10. A function that uses addresses as parameters needs a pointer to data as a formal parameter; the actual parameter in the function call must be a pointer value (address).

11. If you want a called function to change the value of a variable in the calling function, you must pass the address of that variable to the called function.

12. When using multiple definitions in one statement—a practice we do not recommend—the pointer token is recognized only with one variable. Therefore, in the following definition, only the first variable is a pointer to an integer; the rest are integers.

```
int *ptrA, ptrB, ptrC;
```

13. It is a compile error to initialize a pointer to a numeric constant.

```
int *ptr = 59;
```

14. Similarly, it is a compile error to assign an address to any variable other than a pointer.

```
int x = &y;                     /* ERROR */
```

15. It is a compile error to assign a pointer of one type to a pointer of another type without a cast. (Exception: If one pointer is a void pointer, it is permitted.)

16. It is a common compile error to pass values when addresses are required in actual parameters. Remember to use the address operator when passing identifiers to pointers to simulate pass by reference.

17. It is a logic error to use a pointer before it has been initialized.

18. It is a logic error to dereference a pointer whose value is NULL.

9-13   KEY TERMS AND CONCEPTS

address operator (&)   pointer   pointer variable
indirection operator (*)   pointer constant   rvalue
lvalue   pointer indirection

9-14   SUMMARY

- Every computer has addressable memory locations.
- A pointer is a derived data type consisting of addresses available in the computer.
- A pointer constant is an address that exists by itself. We cannot change it. We can only use it.
- The address operator (&) makes a pointer value from a pointer constant. To get the address of a variable, we simply use this operator in front of the variable name.
- The address operator can only be used in front of an lvalue. The result is an rvalue.
- A pointer variable is a variable that can store an address.
- The indirection operator (*) accesses a variable through a pointer containing its address.
- The indirection operator can only be used in front of a pointer value.
- Pointer variables can be initialized just like data variables. The initializer must be the address of a previously defined variable or another pointer variable.
- A pointer can be defined to point to other pointer variables (pointers to pointers).
- The value of a pointer variable can be stored in another variable if they are compatible—that is, if they are of the same type.

- One of the most useful applications of pointers is in functions.
- We can simulate the process of call by reference in a function using pointers.
- If we want a called function to access a variable in the calling function, we pass the address of that variable to the called function and use the indirection operator to access the variable.
- When we need to return more than one value from a function, we must use pointers.
- If a data item is not to be changed, it is passed to the called function by value. If a data item is to be changed, its address is passed to let the called function change its value.
- A function can also return a pointer value.
- In software engineering, *quality factors* refer to characteristics that a piece of software must have to become quality software.
- Quality factors are defined as operability, maintainability, and transferability.
- One of the most important points about the quality of a piece of software is that quality must be designed into the system. It cannot be added as an afterthought. To design quality into a system, we can use a tool called the quality circle.

9-15   PRACTICE SETS

REVIEW QUESTIONS

1. Pointer constants are drawn from the set of addresses for a computer.
   a. True   b. False

2. Pointers are declared using the address operator as a token.
   a. True   b. False

3. The underlying type of a pointer is address.
    a. True   b. False

4. An rvalue expression can be used only to supply a value.
    a. True   b. False

5. Which of the following statements about pointers is false?
    a. Pointers are built on the standard type, address.
    b. Pointers are machine addresses.
    c. Pointers are derived data types.
    d. Pointers can be defined variables.
    e. Pointers can be constants.

6. The _____ operator is used with a pointer to dereference the address contained in the pointer.
    a. address (&)
    b. assignment (=)
    c. indirection (*)
    d. pointer (^)
    e. selection (->)

7. Which of the following statements will not add 1 to a variable?
    a. a++;
    b. a += 1;
    c. a = a + 1;
    d. *p = *p + 1;
    e. *p++;

8. Which of the following defines a pointer variable to an integer?
    a. int &ptr;
    b. int &&ptr;
    c. int *ptr;
    d. int **ptr;
    e. int ^ptr;

9. Which of the following defines and initializes a pointer to the address of x?
    a. int *ptr = *x;
    b. int *ptr = ^x;
    c. int *ptr = &x;
    d. int &ptr = *x;
    e. int &ptr = ^x;

10. *Pointers to pointers* is a term used to describe
    a. any pointer that points to a variable.
    b. any two pointers that point to the same variable.
    c. any two pointers that point to variables of the same type.
    d. pointers used as formal parameters in a function header.
    e. pointers whose contents are the address of another pointer.

11. Given the following definitions, which answer points to the value stored in **x**?
    ```
    int    x;
    int   *p = &x;
    int **pp = &p;
    ```
    a. p
    b. pp
    c. &p
    d. *pp
    e. **pp

12. Given the definitions shown below, which answer is not valid?
    ```
    int    i;
    float  f;
    int   *pd;
    float *pf;
    ```
    a. i = 5;
    b. f = 5;
    c. pd = &i;
    d. pf = &f;
    e. pd = pf;

13. Which of the following statements about pointer compatibility is true?
    a. Because all pointers are addresses, pointers of different types can be assigned without a cast.
    b. If pointers of different types are assigned, C uses an implicit cast.
    c. It is possible to cast a pointer to integer as a pointer to float.
    d. When a pointer is cast, C automatically reformats the data to reflect the correct type.
    e. When a void pointer is dereferenced, it must be cast.

14. Which of the following operators does not require an lvalue as its operand?
    a. address operator (&total)
    b. assignment (x = …)
    c. indirection (*ptr)
    d. postfix increment (x++)
    e. prefix increment (++x)

15. Which of the following is not an attribute of quality software?
    a. Meets operating standards of organization.
    b. Runs efficiently on any hardware.
    c. Satisfies the user's explicit requirements.
    d. Satisfies the user's implicit requirements.
    e. Well documented.

EXERCISES

16. Declare and define the following:

    a. A pointer variable `pi` pointing to an integer

    b. A pointer variable `ppi` pointing to a pointer to an integer

    c. A pointer variable `pf` pointing to a float

    d. A pointer variable `ppc` pointing to a pointer to a char

17. If `a` is declared as integer, which of the following statements is true and which is false?

    a. The expression `*&a` and `a` are the same.

    b. The expression `*&a` and `&*a` are the same.

18. Given the following declarations:

    ```
    int     x;
    double  d;
    int     *p;
    double *q;
    ```

    Which of the following expressions are not allowed?

    a. `p = &x;`

    b. `p = &d;`

    c. `q = &x;`

    d. `q = &d;`

    e. `p = x;`

19. Given the following declarations:

    ```
    int    a = 5;
    int    b = 7;
    int   *p = &a;
    int   *q = &b;
    ```

    What is the value of each of the following expressions?

    a. `++a`

    b. `++(*p)`

    c. `—(*q)`

    d. `—b`

20. What is the error (if any) in each of the following expressions?

    a. `int a = 5;`

    b. `int *p = 5;`

    c. `int a;`
       `int *p = &a;`

    d. `int a;`
       `int **q = &a;`

21. Which of the following program segments is valid? Describe each error in the invalid statements.

    a. `int *p;`
       `scanf("%d", &p);`
    b. `int *p;`
       `scanf("%d", &*p);`
    c. `int *p;`
       `scanf("%d", *p);`
    d. `int a;`
       `int *p = &a;`
       `scanf("%d", p);`

22. Which of the following program segments has a logical error in it?

    a. `int **p;`
       `int *q;`
       `q = &p;`
    b. `int **p;`
       `int *q;`
       `p = &q;`
    c. `int **p;`
       `int **q;`
       `p = &q;`
    d. `char    c = 'A';`
       `char    **p;`
       `char    *q;`
       `q = & c;`
       `printf("%c", *p);`

23. Given the following declaration:
    `int ***p;`

    What is the type of each of the following expressions?

    a. `p`
    b. `*p`
    c. `**p`
    d. `***p`

24. If `p` is a name of a variable, which of the following expressions is an lvalue and which one is an rvalue? Explain.

    a. `p`
    b. `*p`
    c. `&p`
    d. `*p + 2`

25. If `p` and `q` are variable names and `a` is an array, which of the following expressions are not syntactically correct, because they violate the rules concerning lvalues and rvalues?

    a. `*p = *p + 2;`
    b. `&p = &a[0];`
    c. `q = &(p + 2);`
    d. `a[5] = 5;`

26. Write a function prototype statement for a function named `calc` that returns *void* and contains a reference parameter to an integer, `x`, and a reference parameter to a long double, `y`.

27. Write a function prototype statement for a function named `spin` that returns a pointer to an integer and contains a reference parameter to an integer, `x`, and a pointer parameter to the address of a long double, `py`.

28. Assuming all variables are integer, and all pointers are typed appropriately, show the final values of the variables in Figure 9-27after the following assignments.

```
a   = ***p;
s   = **p;
t   = *p;
b   = **r;
**q = b;
```

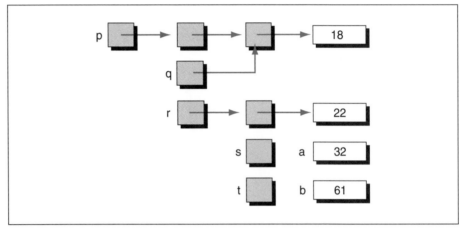

Figure 9-27   Exercise 28

29. Assuming all variables are integer, and all pointers are typed appropriately, show the final values of the variables in Figure 9-28 after the following assignments.

```
t   = **p;
b   = ***q;
*t  = c;
v   = r;
w   = *s;
a   = **v
*u  = *w
```

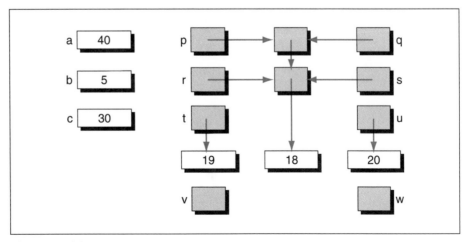

Figure 9-28   Exercise 29

30. In the following program, show the configuration of all the variables and the output.

```
#include <stdio.h>
int main (void)
{
/* Local Definitions */
    int a;
    int *p;
    int **q;
/* Statements */
    a = 14;
    p = &a;
    q = &p;
    printf("%d\n" ,    a);
    printf("%d\n ", *p);
    printf("%d\n ", **q);
    printf("%p", p);
    printf("%p", q);
    return 0;
}   /* main */
```

PROBLEMS

31. Write a function that converts a Julian date to a month and day. A Julian date consists of a year and the day of the year relative to January 1. For example, day 41 is February 10. The month and day are to be stored in integer variables whose addresses are passed as parameters. The function is to handle leap years. (For a discussion of the calculation of a leap year, see Chapter 5, Project 60, page 227.) If there is an error in a parameter, such as a day greater than 366, the function will return zero. Otherwise, it returns a positive number.

32. Modify Program 9-3 on page 436 to include subtraction, multiplication, division, and remainder.

33. Write a function that receives a floating-point number representing the change from a purchase. The function will pass back the breakdown of the change in dollar bills, half-dollars, quarters, dimes, nickels, and pennies.

34. Write a function that receives a floating-point number and sends back the integer and fraction parts.

35. Write a function that receives two integers and passes back the greatest common divisor and the least common multiplier. The calculation of the greatest common divisor can be done using Euclid's method of repetitively dividing one number by the other and using the remainder (modulo). When the remainder is zero, the divisor has been found. For example, the greatest common divisor of 247 and 39 is 13, as in Table 9-4.

num1	num2	Remainder
247	39	13
39	13	0

Table 9-4   Greatest common divisors

Once you know the greatest common divisor (gcd), the least common multiplier (lcm) is determined as shown below.

$$lcm = \frac{(\text{factor1} * \text{factor2})}{gcd}$$

PROJECTS

36. Write a program that creates the structure shown in Figure 9-29 and then reads an integer into variable a and prints it using each pointer in turn. That is, the program must read an integer into variable a and print it using p, q, r, s, t, u, and v.

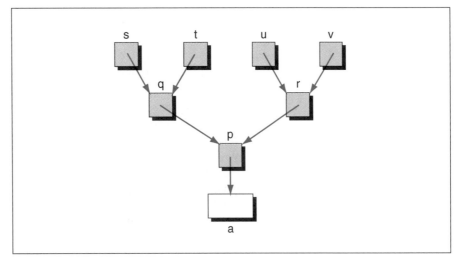

Figure 9-29   Structure for Project 36

37. Write a program that creates the structure shown in Figure 9-30. It then reads data into a, b, and c using the pointers p, q, and r.

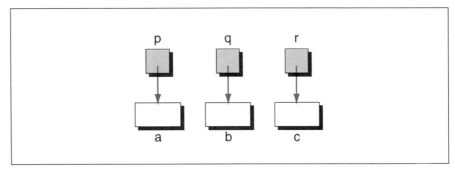

Figure 9-30   Data structure for Project 37

After the data have been read, the program reassigns the pointers so that p points to c, q points to a, and r points to b. After making the reassignments, the program prints the variables using the pointers. For each variable, print both its contents and its address.

38. Write a program that creates the structure shown in Figure 9-31 and reads data into a and b using the pointers x and y.

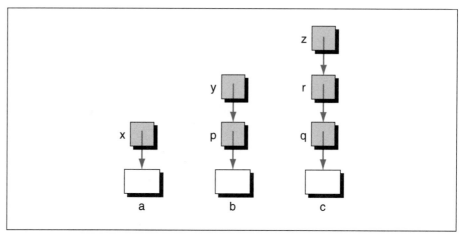

Figure 9-31   Data structure for Project 38

The program then multiplies the value of a by b and stores the result in c using the pointers x, y, and z. Finally, it prints all three variables using the pointers x, y, and z.

39. Write an exploratory program to study pointers. In this program, prompt the user to enter a character, an integer, a long integer, and a floating-point number. The program then calls a print function that accepts a void pointer as its only parameter and prints the address of the pointer followed by the data, first as a character, then as an integer, a long integer, and a floating-point number. Since void pointers have no type, you will need to cast the pointer appropriately in each of your print statements.

A proposed output format is shown below. It is the result of calling the print function with a pointer to integer. You will most likely get different results. Call the print function for each of the user inputs, each time printing the results shown below. (The first line may be printed before calling the print function.)

```
Printing int 123

Printing data at location: 01D70C44

Data as char :

Data as int  :      123

Data as long :  8069185

Data as float:     0.00
```

Using the addresses that you printed, build a memory map of the variables as they existed in your program. Then, by analyzing the results of the printout, write a short explanation of what happened when your program ran. To fully understand the results, you may have to refer to your system documentation to determine the physical memory sizes of the various types.

40. Assume an environment in which transactions and responses are being sent across a network. When a transaction is sent, a time stamp is created and attached to the transaction. When the response is received, the time is noted. Using an integral time stamp, as shown in Program 9-8, on page 449, write a function to determine the elapsed time in hours, minutes, and seconds between the transaction submittal and its response. Assume that no transaction takes longer than 24 hours. Create a test driver to validate your function. Test the function with at least five test cases, including one that spans midnight and one that is longer than 24 hours.

Pointer Applications

10

In this chapter we explore two basic uses of pointers: with arrays and in dynamic memory. We will show the natural affinity between pointers and arrays that stems at least in part from the fact that an array name is a pointer constant. After discussing the use of pointers with arrays, we will examine one of the most powerful aspects of most modern computer languages, dynamic memory, which uses pointers exclusively to access data.

10-1   ARRAYS AND POINTERS

Arrays and pointers have a very close relationship. The name of an array is a pointer constant to the first element. Because the array's name is a pointer constant, its value cannot be changed. Figure 10-1 shows an array with the array name as a pointer constant.

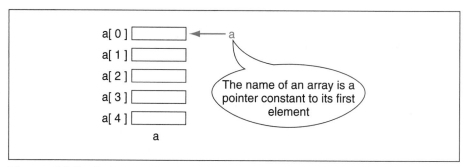

Figure 10-1   Pointers to arrays

Since the array name is a pointer constant to the first element, the address of the first element and the name of the array both represent the same location in memory. We can, therefore, use the array name anywhere we can use a pointer, as long as it is being used as an rvalue. Specifically, this means that we can use it with the indirection operator. When we dereference an array name, we are dereferencing the first element of the array; that is, we are referring to `array[0]`. However, when the array name is dereferenced, it refers only to the first element, not the whole array.

a ←——— same ———→ &a[0]

a is a pointer only to the first element—not the whole array.

Prove this to yourself by writing a program with the code shown below. The code prints the address of the first element of the array (`&a[0]`) and the array name, which is a pointer constant. Note that we have typed the conversion code for the print as a pointer (`%p`).

```
/* Demonstrate that array name is pointer constant */
    int a [5];
    printf("%p %p", &a[0], a);
```

We cannot tell you the values that this code will print, but they will be addresses in your computer. Furthermore, the first printed address (the first element in the array) and the second printed address (the array pointer) will be the same, proving our point.

A simple variation on this code is to print the value in the first element of the array using both a pointer and an index. This code is demonstrated in Figure 10-2. Note that the same value, 2, is printed in both cases, again proving our point that the array name is a pointer constant to the beginning of the array.

Let's investigate another point. If the name of an array is really a pointer, let's see if we can store this pointer in a pointer variable and use it in the same way we use the name of the array. The program that demonstrates this is shown in Figure 10-3.

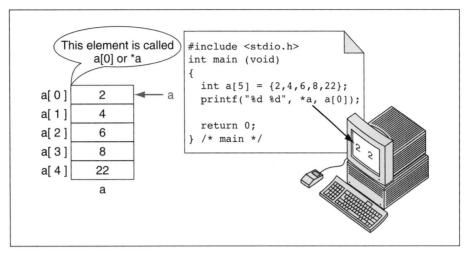

Figure 10-2 Dereference of array name

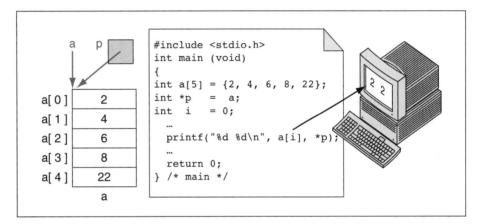

Figure 10-3 Array names as pointers

Right after we define and initialize the array, we define a pointer and initialize it to point to the first element of the array by assigning the array name. Note especially that the array name is unqualified; that is, there is no address operator or index specification. We then print the first element in the array, first using an index notation and then pointer notation.

Let's look at another example that explores the close relationship between an array and a pointer. We store the address of the second element of the array in a pointer variable. Now we can use two different names to access each element. This does not mean that we have two arrays; rather, it shows that a single array can be accessed through different pointers.

Figure 10-4 demonstrates the use of multiple names for an array to reference different locations at the same time. First, we have the array name. We then create a pointer to integer and set it to the second element of the array (a[1]). Now, even though it is a pointer, we can use it as an array name and index it to point to different elements in the array. We demonstrate this by printing the first two elements using first the array name and then the pointer. Note especially that, when a pointer is not referencing the first element of an array, the index can be negative [−1]. This is shown in the reference to p[−1].

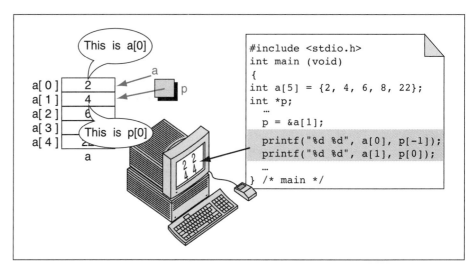

Figure 10-4   Multiple array pointers

> To access an array, any pointer to the first element can be used instead of the name of the array.

10-2   POINTER ARITHMETIC AND ARRAYS

Besides indexing, programmers use another powerful method of moving through an array: **pointer arithmetic**. Pointer arithmetic offers a restricted set of arithmetic operators for manipulating the addresses in pointers. It is especially powerful when we need to move through an array from element to element, such as when we are searching an array sequentially.

POINTERS AND ONE-DIMENSIONAL ARRAYS

If we have an array, a, then a is a constant pointing to the first element and a + 1 is a constant to the second element. Again, if we have a pointer, p, pointing to the second element of an array (see Figure 10-4), then p − 1 is a pointer to the previous (first) element and p + 1 is a pointer to the next (third) element. Furthermore, given a, a + 2 is the address two elements from a, and a + 3 is the address three elements from a. We can generalize the notation as follows:

> Given pointer, p, p ± n is a pointer to the value *n* elements away.

It does not matter how a and p are defined or initialized; as long as they are pointing to one of the elements of the array, we can add or subtract to get the address of the other elements of the array. This concept is portrayed in Figure 10-5.

But the meaning of adding or subtracting here is different from normal arithmetic. When you add an integer *n* to a pointer value, you will get a value that corresponds to another index location, *n elements away*. In other words, *n* is an **offset** from the original pointer. To determine the new value, C must know the size of one element. The size of

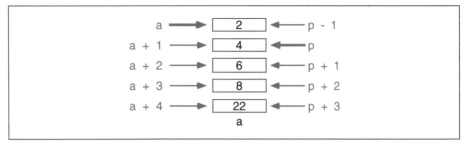

Figure 10-5   Pointer arithmetic

the element is determined by the type of the pointer. This is one of the prime reasons that pointers of different types cannot be assigned to each other.

If the offset is 1, then C can simply add or subtract one element size from the current pointer value. This may make the access more efficient than the corresponding index notation. If it is more than 1, then C must compute the offset by multiplying the offset by the size of one array element and adding it to the pointer value. This calculation is shown below.

```
address = pointer + (offset * size of element)
```

Depending on the hardware, the multiplication in this formula can make it less efficient than simply adding 1, and the efficiency advantage of pointer arithmetic over indexing may be lost.

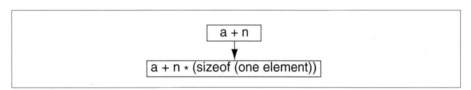

We see the result of pointer arithmetic on different-sized elements in Figure 10-6. For *char,* which is usually implemented as 1 byte, adding 1 moves us to the next memory address (101). Assuming that integers are 4 bytes, adding 1 to the array pointer b moves

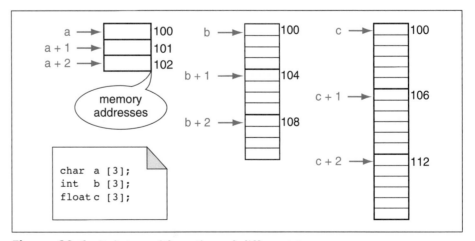

Figure 10-6   Pointer arithmetic and different types

us 4 bytes in memory (104). Finally, assuming the size of float is 6 bytes, adding 1 to array pointer c moves us 6 bytes in memory (106). In other words, a + 1 means different things in different situations.

We've seen how to get the address of an array element using a pointer and an offset, now let's see how we can use that value. We have two choices: First, we can assign it to another pointer. This is a rather elementary operation that uses the assignment operator as shown below.

```
p = aryName + 5;
```

Second, we can use it with the indirection operator to access or change the value of the element we are pointing to. This possibility is seen in Figure 10-7.

```
a[0]   or   *(a + 0)    2   ◄──── a
a[1]   or   *(a + 1)    4   ◄──── a + 1
a[2]   or   *(a + 2)    6   ◄──── a + 2
a[3]   or   *(a + 3)    8   ◄──── a + 3
a[4]   or   *(a + 4)   22   ◄──── a + 4

                        a
```

Figure 10-7   Dereferencing array pointers

For practice, let's use pointers to find the smallest number among five integers stored in an array. Figure 10-8 tracks the code as it works its way through the array.

> The two following expressions are exactly the same when a is the name of an array and *n* is an integer.
>
> $*(a + n)$ is identical to a[n]

We start with the smallest pointer (pSm) set to the first element of the array. The function's job is to see if any of the remaining elements are smaller. Since we know that the first element is not smaller than itself, we set the working pointer (pWalk) to the second element. The working pointer then advances through the remaining elements, each time checking the element it is currently looking at against the smallest to that point, (pSm). If the current element is smaller, its location is assigned to pSm.

POINTERS AND OTHER OPERATORS

Arithmetic operations involving pointers are very limited. Addition can be used when one operand is a pointer and the other is an integer. Subtraction can be used only when both operands are pointers or when the first operand is a pointer and the second operand is an index integer. You can also manipulate a pointer with the postfix and unary increment and decrement operators. All of the following pointer arithmetic operations are valid:

```
p + 5    5 + p    p - 5    p1 - p2    p++    --p
```

When one pointer is subtracted from another, the result is an index representing the number of elements between the two pointers. Note, however, that the result is meaningful only if the two pointers are associated with the same array structure.

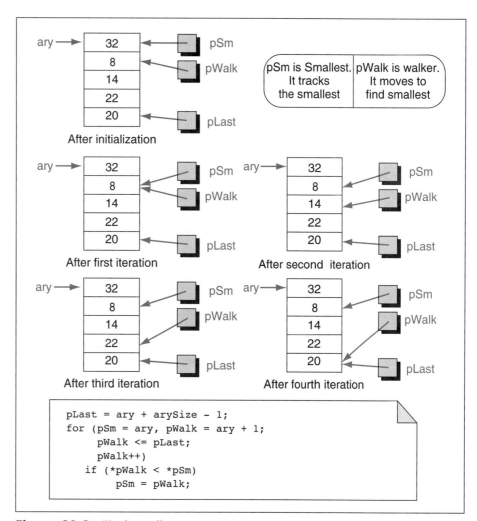

Figure 10-8   Find smallest

The relational operators (such as less than and equal) are allowed only if both operands are pointers of the same type. Two pointer relational expressions are shown below.

```
p1 >= p2        p1 != p2
```

The most common comparison is a pointer and the NULL constant, as shown in Table 10-1.

Long Form	Short Form
if (ptr == NULL)	if (!ptr)
if (ptr != NULL)	if (ptr)

Table 10-1   Pointers and relational operators

USING POINTER ARITHMETIC

In this section, we write two small programs that demonstrate moving through arrays using pointers.

Printing an Array

Program 10-1 prints an array, first by adding 1 to advance through the array and then subtracting 1 to print it backward.

```
 1   /* Print an array forward by adding 1 to a pointer. Then
 2      print it backward by subtracting one.
 3         Written by:
 4         Date:
 5   */
 6   #include <stdio.h>
 7
 8   #define MAX_SIZE 10
 9
10   int main (void)
11   {
12   /* Local Definitions */
13      int  ary[] = {1, 2, 3, 4, 5, 6, 7, 8, 9, 10};
14      int *pWalk;
15      int *pEnd;
16
17   /* Statements */
18      /* Print array forward */
19      printf("Array forward : ");
20      for (pWalk = ary, pEnd = ary + MAX_SIZE;
21           pWalk <  pEnd;
22           pWalk++)
23        printf ("%3d", *pWalk);
24      printf ("\n");
25
26      /* Print array backward */
27      printf("Array backward: ");
28      for (pWalk = pEnd - 1; pWalk >= ary; pWalk--)
29        printf ("%3d", *pWalk);
30      printf ("\n");
31
32      return 0;
33   } /* main */
```

```
Results:
   Array forward :   1  2  3  4  5  6  7  8  9 10
   Array backward:  10  9  8  7  6  5  4  3  2  1
```

Program 10-1 Print array with pointers

Program 10-1 Analysis   While this program is quite simple, it does demonstrate one efficiency point. Note that before we printed the forward loop, we set pEnd. Many programmers would use the following test in the limit condition:

pWalk < ary + MAX_SIZE

While this logic works, some compilers will calculate the end address in each loop, an obvious inefficiency. We recommend, therefore, that whenever possible you calculate the end pointer in the loop initialization.

Searching with Pointers

The logic seen in Program 10-1 works well for the sequential search but not for the binary search.[1] Recall that the binary search requires the calculation of the index or the address of the entry in the middle of a table. When we wrote the program using indexes, the calculation of the midpoint was done with the statement shown below.

```
mid = (first + last) / 2;
```

Since we cannot use addition with two pointers, this formula will not work. We need to come up with the pointer arithmetic equivalent. Another formula determines the midpoint in an array by calculating the number of elements from the beginning of the array. This method, known as the offset method, is shown below.

```
mid = first + (last - first) / 2;
```

The offset calculation works with pointers also. The subtraction of the first pointer from the last pointer will give us the number of elements in the array. The offset from the beginning of the array is determined by dividing the number of elements in the array by 2. We can then add the offset to the pointer for the beginning of the list to arrive at the midpoint. The pointer code is shown below.

```
midPtr = firstPtr + (lastPtr - firstPtr) / 2;
```

The pointer implementation of the binary search is shown in Program 10-2.

```
 1  /* ==================== binary Search ====================
 2     Search an ordered list using Binary Search
 3        Pre    list must contain at least one element
 4               endPtr is pointer to largest element in list
 5               target is value of element being sought
 6        Post   FOUND: locnPtr pointer to target element
 7                      return 1 (found)
 8               !FOUND: locnPtr = element below or above target
 9                      return 0 (not found)
10  */
11  int binarySearch (int    list[],
12                    int   *endPtr,
13                    int    target,
14                    int **locnPtr)
15  {
16  /* Local Definitions */
17     int *firstPtr;
18     int *midPtr;
19     int *lastPtr;
20
21  /* Statements */
22     firstPtr = list;
23     lastPtr  = endPtr;
24     while (firstPtr <= lastPtr)
```

Program 10-2   Pointers and the binary search

---

[1]We discussed the binary search in Program 8-14, on page 390.

```
25          {
26            midPtr = firstPtr + (lastPtr - firstPtr) / 2;
27            if (target > *midPtr)
28               /* look in upper half */
29               firstPtr = midPtr + 1;
30            else if (target < *midPtr)
31               /* look in lower half */
32               lastPtr = midPtr - 1;
33            else
34               /* found equal: force exit */
35               firstPtr = lastPtr + 1;
36          } /* end while */
37       *locnPtr = midPtr;
38       return (target == *midPtr);
39  }   /* binarySearch */
```

Program 10-2 Pointers and the binary search (continued)

Program 10-2 Analysis Although the code in this function is relatively simple, the coding for `locnPtr` merits some discussion. In the calling function, `locnPtr` is a pointer to the found location. To store the pointer in `locnPtr`, therefore, we need to pass a pointer to a pointer to an integer (see Statement 14). To create a pointer to pointer, the calling function must pass the address of its location pointer.

In addition to demonstrating the subtraction of two pointers, we also see the use of a relational operator with two pointers in Statement 24.

POINTERS AND TWO-DIMENSIONAL ARRAYS

The first thing to notice about two-dimensional arrays is that, just as in a one-dimensional array, the name of the array is a pointer constant to the first element of the array. In this case, however, the first element *is another array!* Assume that we have a two-dimensional array of integers. When we dereference the array name, we don't get one integer, we get an array of integers. In other words, the dereference of the array name of a two-dimensional array is a pointer to a one-dimensional array. Figure 10-9 contains a two-dimensional array and a code fragment to print the array.

Each element in the figure is shown in both index and pointer notation. Note that `table[0]` refers to an array of four integer values. The equivalent pointer notation is the dereference of the array name plus 0, `*(table + 0)`, which also refers to an array of four integers.

```
table[0] is identical to *(table + 0)
```

To demonstrate pointer manipulation with a two-dimensional array, let's print the table in Figure 10-9. To print the array requires nested *for* loops. When dealing with multidimensional arrays, however, there is no simple pointer notation. To refer to a row, we dereference the array pointer, which gives us a pointer to a row. Given a pointer to a row, to refer to an individual element, we dereference the row pointer. This double dereference is shown below.

```
*(*(table))
```

But the above expression refers only to the first element of the first row. To step through all the elements, we need to add two offsets, one for the row and one for the el-

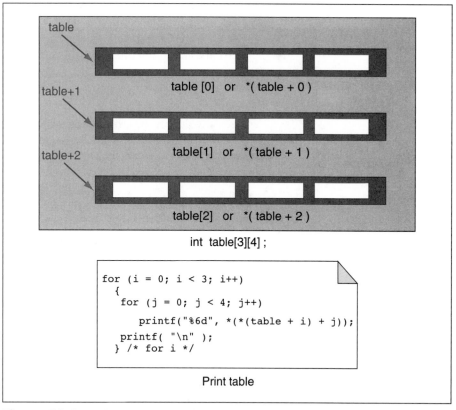

int table[3][4] ;

```
for (i = 0; i < 3; i++)
  {
   for (j = 0; j < 4; j++)
      printf("%6d", *(*(table + i) + j));
   printf( "\n" );
  } /* for i */
```

Print table

Figure 10-9   Pointers to two-dimensional arrays

ement within the row. We use loop counters, i and j, as the offsets. This is the same
logic we saw when we printed a two-dimensional array using indexes. To print an element, we use the array name, table, and adjust it with the loop indexes. This gives us
the relatively complex expression shown below.

```
*(*(table + i) + j)
```

This pointer notation is equivalent to the index syntax, table[i][j]. With multidimensional arrays, the pointer arithmetic has no efficiency advantage over indexing. Because the pointer notation for multidimensional arrays is so complex and there is no
efficiency advantage, most programmers find it easier to use the index notation.

10-3   PASSING AN ARRAY TO A FUNCTION

Now that we have discovered that the name of an array is actually a pointer to the first
element, we can send the array name to a function for processing. When we pass the array, we do not use the address operator. Remember, the array name is a pointer constant,
so the name is already the address of the first element in the array. A typical call would
look like the following:

```
doIt (aryName);
```

The called program can declare the array in one of two ways. First, it can use the traditional array notation. This format has the advantage of telling the user very clearly that we are dealing with an array rather than a single pointer. This is an advantage from a structured programming and human engineering point of view.

```
int doIt (int ary[])
```

You can also declare the array in the function header as a simple pointer. The disadvantage to this format is that, while it is technically correct, it actually masks the data structure (array). For one-dimensional arrays, it is the code of choice among professional programmers.

```
int doIt (int *arySalary)
```

If you choose to code this way, use a good descriptive name for the parameter to minimize any reader confusion. The function documentation should also indicate clearly that an array is being passed.

Note, however, that if you are passing a multidimensional array, you must use the array syntax in the header declaration and definition. The compiler needs to know the size of the dimensions after the first to calculate the offset for pointer arithmetic. Thus, to receive a three-dimensional array, you would use the following declaration in the function's header:

```
float doIt (int bigAry[][12][5])
```

To see how passing array pointers works, let's write a program that calls a function to multiply each element of a one-dimensional array by 2. The program's variables are shown in Figure 10-10, and the code is shown in Program 10-3.

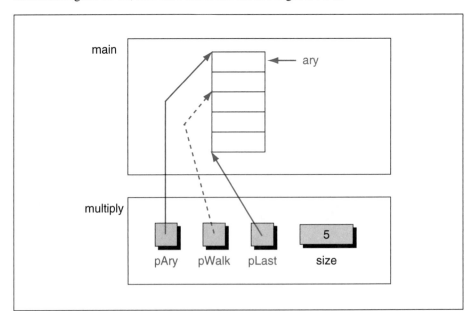

Figure 10-10   Variables for multiply array elements by 2

```
 1   /* Read integers from keyboard & print them multiplied by 2.
 2          Written by:
 3          Date:
 4   */
 5   #include <stdio.h>
 6   #define SIZE   5
 7
 8   /*  Prototype Declarations */
 9   void multiply (int *pAry, int size);
10
11   int main (void)
12   {
13   /* Local Definitions */
14      int ary [SIZE];
15      int *pLast;
16      int *pWalk;
17
18   /* Statements */
19      pLast = ary + SIZE - 1;
20      for (pWalk = ary; pWalk <= pLast; pWalk++)
21         {
22          printf("Please enter an integer: ");
23          scanf("%d", pWalk);
24         } /* for */
25
26      multiply (ary, SIZE);
27
28      printf ("Doubled value is: \n");
29      for (pWalk = ary; pWalk <= pLast; pWalk++)
30          printf (" %3d", *pWalk);
31
32      return 0;
33   } /* main */
34
35   /* ==================== multiply ====================
36      Multiply elements in an array by 2
37         Pre    array has been filled
38                size indicates number of elements in array
39         Post   values in array doubled
40   */
41   void multiply (int *pAry,
42                  int  size)
43   {
44   /* Local Definitions */
45      int *pWalk;
46      int *pLast;
47
48   /* Statements */
```

Program 10-3   Multiply array elements by 2

```
49    pLast = pAry + size - 1;
50    for (pWalk = pAry; pWalk <= pLast; pWalk++)
51        *pWalk = *pWalk * 2;
52    return;
53 }  /* multiply */
54 /* ================= End of Program ================= */
```

```
Results:
Please enter an integer: 1
Please enter an integer: 2
Please enter an integer: 3
Please enter an integer: 4
Please enter an integer: 5
Doubled value is:
    2   4   6   8  10
```

Program 10-3 Multiply array elements by 2 (continued)

Program 10-3 Analysis   This program contains several points of interest. First, we have declared the array in the prototype using the more common pointer notation, but we have given it a name that indicates it is a pointer to an array (pAry).

In the multiply function, we use a separate pointer (pWalk) to walk through the list. We could have used pAry, since it was not being used other than to identify the beginning of the array. All too often, however, this type of "shortcut" saves a line or two of code only to create hours of debugging when the program is changed later. As we have pointed out before, do not use formal parameters as variables unless their intent is to change a value in the calling program. This rule is especially important when the parameter is a pointer, as in this case.

Finally, note that we have passed the size of the array to the multiply function. We still need to know how much data we need to process, and we use the size to calculate the address of the last element in the list. As a variation on the limit test, however, we could have passed a pointer to the last element of the array, &ary[SIZE — 1]. This would save the calculation of pLast. From a style and efficiency point of view, neither method has an advantage over the other. The structure and needs of other parts of the program usually dictate which method is used.

10-4 UNDERSTANDING COMPLEX DECLARATIONS

The declarations have become increasingly more complicated throughout this text. Sometimes the declarations are difficult to interpret, even for someone well experienced in the C language.

To help you read and understand complicated declarations, we provide a rule that we call the **right–left rule**. Using this rule to interpret a declaration, you start with the identifier in the center of a declaration and read the declaration by alternatively going right and then left until you have read all entities. Figure 10-11 is a representation of the basic concept.

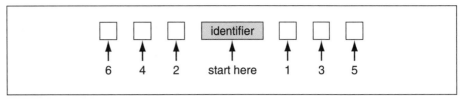

Figure 10-11 Right–left rule concept

We will begin with some simple examples and proceed to the more complicated.

1. Consider the simple declaration

```
    int x
```

This is read as "x is # an integer."[2]

```
    int        x        #
     ↑         ↑        ↑
     2         0        1
```

Since there is nothing on the right, we simply go left.

2. Now consider the example of a pointer declaration. This example is read as "p is # a pointer # to integer."

```
    int        *        p        #        #
     ↑         ↑        ↑        ↑        ↑
     4         2        0        1        3
```

Note that we keep going right even when there is nothing there until all the entities on the left have been exhausted.

3. In the next example, we have an equal number of entities on the right and the left.

```
    int      table      [4]
     ↑         ↑         ↑
     2         0         1
```

This declaration is read as "table is an array of 4 integers."

4. Regardless of how many dimensions are in an array, it is considered as one element in the rule. Therefore, given the following declaration of a multidimensional array,

```
    int      table     [4][5]
     ↑         ↑         ↑
     2         0         1
```

it is read as "table is a [4][5] array of integers."

---

[2]The pound sign (#) is just a place holder to show that there is no entity to be considered. It is ignored when read.

5. The next example is quite difficult and is often misread. In this declaration, we have an array of pointers to integers. The structure is seen in Figure 10-12a.

```
int  *  aryOfPtrs [5] #
 ↑   ↑     ↑      ↑  ↑
 4   2     0      1  3
```

It is read as "aryOfPtrs is an array of 5 pointers to # integer."

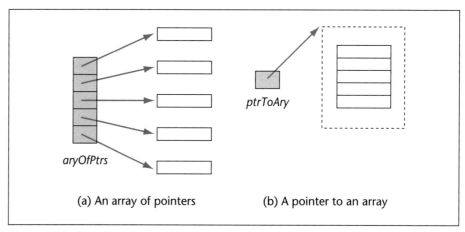

(a) An array of pointers   (b) A pointer to an array

Figure 10-12 Array of pointers versus pointer to array

6. By using parentheses, we change the previous example to a pointer to an array of five integers. In this case, the pointer is to the whole array, not just one element in it. (See Figure 10-12.)

```
int (*ptrToAry #) [5]
 ↑   ↑    ↑     ↑   ↑
 4   2    0     1   3
```

This declaration is read "ptrToAry is # a pointer to an array of 5 integers."

7. This example deals with function declarations. Here, we see a simple prototype for a function that returns an integer.

```
int doIt  (…)
 ↑    ↑    ↑
 2    0    1
```

This declaration is read as "doIt is a function returning an integer."

8. The final example shows a function returning a pointer to an integer.

```
int * doIt (int) #
 ↑  ↑  ↑    ↑   ↑
 4  2  0    1   3
```

This example is read "doIt is a function returning a pointer to # an integer."

10-5 MEMORY ALLOCATION FUNCTIONS

One of the most serious limitations of the first high-level programming languages, FORTRAN and COBOL, is that their data structures are always fully defined at compile time. If they use an array that can vary greatly in size, the programmer must guess what will be the largest array ever needed. Of course, in keeping with Murphy's law that "what can go wrong, will!" their best guess is never big enough. Modern languages, such as C, do not have this limitation because they can allocate memory at execution. This feature is known as *dynamic memory allocation*.

This gives us two choices when we want to reserve memory locations for an object: static allocation and dynamic allocation. **Static memory allocation** requires that the declaration and definition of memory be fully specified in the source program. The number of bytes reserved cannot be changed during run time. This is the technique we have used to this point. Static allocation works fine as long as you know exactly what your data requirements are.

Dynamic memory allocation uses predefined functions to allocate and release memory for data while the program is running. This effectively postpones the data definition to run time. To use dynamic memory allocation, the programmer must use either standard data types or already must have declared any derived types. Figure 10-13 shows the characteristics of memory allocation.

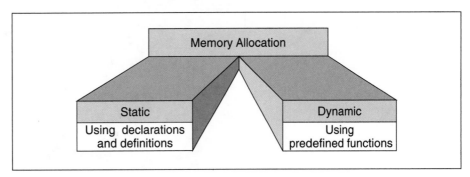

Figure 10-13 Memory allocation

MEMORY USAGE

Four memory management functions are used with dynamic memory. Three of them, *malloc*, *calloc*, and *realloc*, are used for memory allocation. The fourth, *free*, is used to return memory when it is no longer needed. All the memory management functions are found in the standard library header file (<stdlib.h>). The collection of memory functions is shown in Figure 10-14.

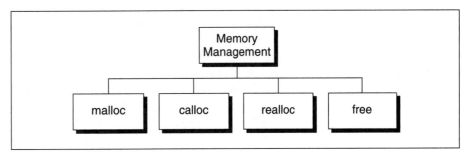

Figure 10-14 Memory management functions

To understand how dynamic memory allocation works, you must study how memory is used. Conceptually, memory is divided into program memory and data memory. Program memory consists of the memory used for main and all called functions. Data memory consists of permanent definitions, such as global data and constants, local definitions, and dynamic data memory. Exactly how C handles these different needs is a function of the operating system and the compiler writer's skills. We can, however, generalize the concepts.

Obviously, main must be in memory at all times. Beyond main, each called function must be in memory only while it or any of its called functions are active. As a practical matter, most systems keep all functions in memory while the program is running.

Although the program code for a function may be in memory at all times, the local variables for the function are available only when it is active. Furthermore, more than one version of the function can be active at a time. (See the discussion of recursion in Chapter 6.) In this case, multiple copies of the local variables are allocated, although only one copy of the function is present. The memory facility for these capabilities is known as the **stack**.

In addition to the stack, a memory allocation known as the heap is available. The **heap** is unused memory allocated to the program and available to be assigned during its execution. It is the memory pool from which memory is allocated when requested by the memory allocation functions. This conceptual view of memory is shown in Figure 10-15.

Figure 10-15   A conceptual view of memory

It is important to recognize that this is a conceptual view of memory. As we said before, implementation of memory is up to the software engineers who design the system. For example, nothing prevents the stack and the heap from sharing the same pool of memory. In fact, it would be a good design concept.

MEMORY ALLOCATION (*MALLOC*)

The *malloc* function allocates a block of memory that contains the number of bytes specified in its parameter. It returns a *void* pointer to the first byte of the allocated memory. The allocated memory is not initialized. You should therefore assume that it will contain garbage and initialize it as required by your program.

The *malloc* prototype is shown below.

```
void *malloc (size_t size);
```

The type, *size_t,* is defined in several header files including <stdio.h>. The type is usually an unsigned integer, and by the standard it is guaranteed to be large enough to hold the maximum address of the computer.

To provide portability, the size specification in *malloc*'s actual parameter is generally computed using the *sizeof* operator. For example, if we want to allocate an integer in the heap, we code the call as shown below.

```
pInt = (int *)malloc (sizeof (int));
```

Note that the pointer being returned by *malloc* has been cast as an integer. Although this is not required in ANSI/ISO C, we recommend it, because many compilers are not yet fully compliant with the standard.

As mentioned above, *malloc* returns the address of the first byte in the memory space allocated. However, if it is not successful, *malloc* returns a NULL pointer. An attempt to allocate memory from the heap when memory is insufficient is known as **overflow**. It is up to the program to check for memory overflow. If it doesn't, the program produces invalid results or aborts with an invalid address the first time the pointer is used.

> You can refer to memory allocated in the heap only through a pointer.
> It does not have its own identifier.

Exactly what action should be taken when memory overflow is encountered is application dependent. If memory might be released by another portion of the program, the memory request can be held. Generally, however, the programmer must terminate the program and allocate more memory to the heap.

The *malloc* function has one more potential error. If you call *malloc* with a zero size, the results are unpredictable. It may return a NULL pointer, or it may return some other implementation-dependent value. *You should never call* malloc *with a zero size.*

Figure 10-16 shows a typical *malloc* call. In this example, we are allocating one integer object. If the memory is allocated successfully, ptr contains a value. If it doesn't, there is no memory and we exit the program with error code 100.

```
                  ┌─┐
                  │▪│ ptr      if (!(ptr = (int *)malloc(sizeof(int))))
                  └┬┘              /* No memory available */
                   │               exit (100) ;
                  ┌─────┐       /* Memory available */
                  │     │       ...
                  └─────┘
                one integer
```

Figure 10-16   *malloc*

CONTIGUOUS MEMORY ALLOCATION (*CALLOC*)

The second memory allocation function, ***calloc***, is primarily used to allocate memory for arrays. It differs from *malloc* in three ways.

First, it allocates a contiguous block of memory large enough to contain an array of elements of a specified size. It therefore requires two parameters, the first for the number of elements to be allocated and the second for the size of each element.

Second, *calloc* returns a pointer to the first element of the allocated array. Since it is a pointer to an array, the size associated with its pointer is the size of one element, *not the entire array.*

Finally *calloc* clears memory. That is, the memory it allocates is set to zero. Note, however, that the zero value is not guaranteed to be the null value for types other than integer; specifically, the proper null for characters is space and the null for *float* may have a different format.

The *calloc* prototype is shown below.

```
void *calloc (size_t element-count,
              size_t element_size);
```

The result is the same for both *malloc* and *calloc* when overflow occurs and when a zero size is given.

A sample *calloc* call is shown in Figure 10-17. In this example, we allocate memory for an array of 200 integers.

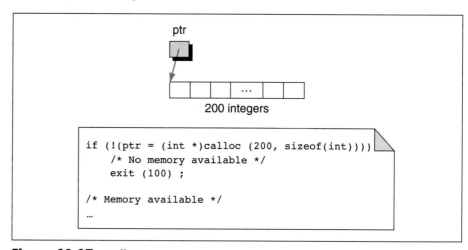

Figure 10-17   *calloc*

REALLOCATION OF MEMORY (*REALLOC*)

The ***realloc*** function can be highly inefficient and therefore should be used advisedly. When given a pointer to a previously allocated block of memory, *realloc* changes the size of the block by deleting or extending the memory at the end of the block. If the memory cannot be extended because of other allocations, *realloc* allocates a completely new block, copies the existing memory allocation to the new allocation, and deletes the old allocation. The programmer must ensure that any other pointers to the data are correctly changed. The operation of *realloc* is shown in Figure 10-18.

```
void *realloc (void *ptr, size_t newSize);
```

RELEASING MEMORY (*FREE*)

When memory locations allocated by *malloc, calloc,* or *realloc* are no longer needed, they should be freed using the predefined function *free*. It is potentially an error to *free* memory with a null pointer, a pointer to other than the first element of an allocated block, or to refer to memory after it has been released. The prototype statement for *free* is shown below.

```
void free (void *ptr);
```

Figure 10-19 shows two examples. The first one releases a single element, allocated with *malloc,* back to the heap. In the second example, the 200 elements were allocated with *calloc.* When we *free* the pointer in this case, all 200 elements are returned to the heap. You should note two things in this figure. First, it is not the pointers that are being

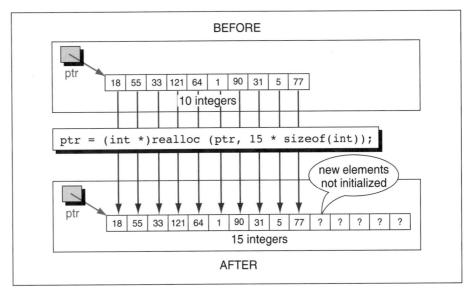

Figure 10-18   *realloc* operation

released but rather what they point to. Second, to release an array of memory that was allocated by *calloc,* you need only release the pointer once. It is an error to attempt to release each element individually.

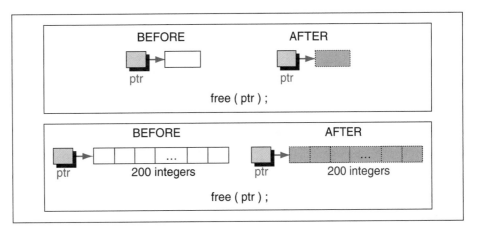

Figure 10-19   Freeing memory

Releasing memory does not change the value in a pointer. It still contains the address in the heap. It is a *logic* error to use the pointer after memory has been released. Your program may continue to run, but the data may be destroyed if the memory area is allocated for another use. This logic error is very difficult to trace in your program. We suggest that immediately after you free memory you also clear the pointer by setting it to NULL.

One final thought: You should free memory whenever it is no longer needed. It is not necessary, however, to clear memory at the end of the program. The operating system will release all memory when your program terminates.

> Using a pointer after its memory has been released is a common programming error. Guard against it by clearing the pointer.

10-6   ARRAY OF POINTERS

Another useful structure that uses arrays and pointers is an **array of pointers**. This structure is especially helpful when the size of the data in the array is variable.

To look at an example, Table 10-2 is a two-dimensional array in which only one row (1) is full. The rest of the rows contain from one to four elements. This array is also known as a *ragged array* because the right elements in each row may be empty, giving it an uneven (ragged) right border.

32	18	12	24			
13	11	16	12	42	19	14
22						
13	13	14				
11	18					

Table 10-2   A ragged table

If we use a two-dimensional array for storing these numbers, we are wasting a lot of memory. The solution in this case is to create five one-dimensional arrays that are joined through an array of pointers. One implementation of this concept is seen in Figure 10-20 along with the statements needed to allocate the arrays in the heap. Note that `table` is a pointer to a pointer to an integer and must be declared as shown below, not as an array.

```
int **table
```

Program 10-6 on page 498 demonstrates the concept in a complete program. We will show other variations on this data structure in the next few chapters.

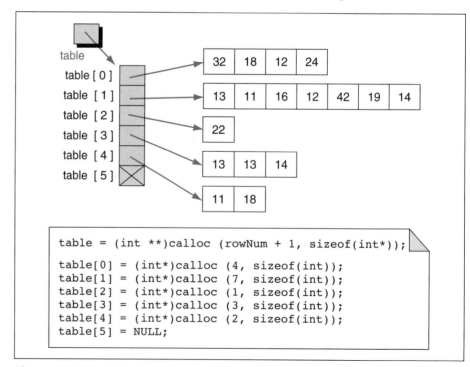

```
table = (int **)calloc (rowNum + 1, sizeof(int*));

table[0] = (int*)calloc (4, sizeof(int));
table[1] = (int*)calloc (7, sizeof(int));
table[2] = (int*)calloc (1, sizeof(int));
table[3] = (int*)calloc (3, sizeof(int));
table[4] = (int*)calloc (2, sizeof(int));
table[5] = NULL;
```

Figure 10-20   A ragged array

10-7   PROGRAMMING APPLICATIONS

This section contains two applications. The first is a rewrite of the selection sort, this time using pointers. The second uses dynamic arrays.

SELECTION SORT REVISITED

Let's revisit the selection sort we developed in Chapter 8. Now that we know how to use pointers, we can improve it in several ways. First, and perhaps most important, it is structured. The structure chart is shown in Figure 10-21. Note that main contains no detailed code. It simply calls the three functions that will get the job done. First, getData reads data from the keyboard and puts it into an array. Then selectSort calls two functions to sort the data. Finally, printData displays the result. The complete algorithm is shown in Program 10-4.

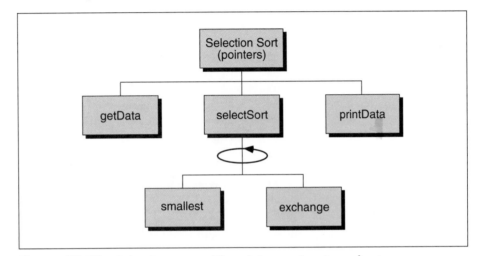

Figure 10-21   Selection sort with pointers—structure chart

```
1  /* Demonstrate pointers with Selection Sort
2         Written by:
3         Date written:
4  */
5  #include <stdio.h>
6  #define SIZE 25
7
8  /* Prototype Declarations */
9  int   *getData    (int *pAry,   int  arySize);
10 void   selectSort (int *pAry,   int *last);
11 void   printData  (int *pAry,   int *last);
12 int   *smallest   (int *pAry,   int *pLast);
13 void   exchange   (int *current, int *smallest);
14
15 int main (void)
16 {
17 /* Local Definitions */
18    int  ary[SIZE];
```

Program 10-4   Selection sort revisited

```
19        int *pLast;
20
21   /* Statements */
22        pLast = getData (ary, SIZE);
23        selectSort      (ary, pLast);
24        printData       (ary, pLast);
25
26        return 0;
27   }  /* main */
28
29   /* ==================== getData ====================
30      Reads data from keyboard and places in array for sorting.
31          Pre    pAry is pointer to array to be filled
32                 arySize is integer with maximum array size
33          Post   array filled. Returns address of last element
34   */
35   int *getData (int *pAry,
36                 int  arySize)
37   {
38   /* Local Definitions */
39        int  ioResult;
40        int  readCnt = 0;
41        int *pFill   = pAry;
42
43   /* Statements */
44        do
45          {
46           printf("Please enter number or <EOF>: ");
47           ioResult = scanf("%d", pFill);
48           if (ioResult == 1)
49              {
50               pFill++;
51               readCnt++;
52              } /* if */
53          } while (ioResult == 1 && readCnt < arySize);
54
55        printf("\n\n%d numbers read.", readCnt);
56        return (--pFill);
57   }  /* getData */
58
59   /* ==================== selectSort ====================
60      Sorts by selecting smallest element in unsorted portion
61      of the array and exchanging it with element at the
62      beginning of the unsorted list.
63          Pre    array must contain at least one item
64                 pLast is pointer to last element in array
65          Post   array rearranged smallest to largest
66   */
67   void selectSort (int *pAry,
68                    int *pLast)
```

Program 10-4   Selection sort revisited (continued)

```
 69  {
 70  /* Local Definitions */
 71     int *pWalker;
 72     int *pSmallest;
 73
 74  /* Statements */
 75     for (pWalker = pAry; pWalker < pLast; pWalker++)
 76         {
 77          pSmallest = smallest (pWalker, pLast);
 78          exchange (pWalker, pSmallest);
 79         } /* for */
 80     return;
 81  }  /* selectSort */
 82
 83  /* ==================== smallest ====================
 84     Find smallest element starting at current pointer.
 85         Pre    pAry points to first unsorted element in array
 86         Post   smallest element identified and returned
 87  */
 88  int *smallest (int *pAry,
 89                 int *pLast)
 90     {
 91  /* Local Definitions */
 92     int *pLooker;
 93     int *pSmallest;
 94
 95  /* Statements */
 96     for (pSmallest = pAry, pLooker = pAry + 1;
 97          pLooker <= pLast;
 98          pLooker++)
 99        if (*pLooker < *pSmallest)
100            pSmallest = pLooker;
101     return pSmallest;
102  }  /* smallest */
103
104  /* ==================== exchange ====================
105     Given pointers to two array elements, exchange them
106         Pre    p1 & p2 are pointers to values to be exchanged
107         Post   exchange is completed
108  */
109  void exchange (int *p1,
110                 int *p2)
111     {
112     /* Local Definitions */
113     int temp;
114
115     /* Statements */
116     temp = *p1;
117     *p1  = *p2;
118     *p2  = temp;
```

Program 10-4 Selection sort revisited (continued)

```
119
120     return;
121 }  /* exchange */
122
123 /* ================== printData ===================
124    Given a pointer to an array, print the data.
125       Pre    pAry points to array to be filled
126              pLast identifies last element in the array
127       Post   data have been printed
128 */
129 void  printData (int *pAry,
130                  int *pLast)
131 {
132 /* Local Definitions */
133    int  nmbrPrt;
134    int *pPrint;
135
136 /* Statements */
137    printf("\n\nYour data sorted are: \n");
138    for (pPrint = pAry, nmbrPrt = 0;
139         pPrint <= pLast;
140         nmbrPrt++, pPrint++)
141       printf ("\n#%02d %4d", nmbrPrt, *pPrint);
142    printf("\n\nEnd of List ");
143    return;
144 }  /* PrintData */
145 /* ================== End of Program =================== */
```

Program 10-4   Selection sort revisited (continued)

Program 10-4 Analysis   Here are a few points you should note as you study this algorithm.

1. Note that we have used pointers and pointer arithmetic in all functions.

2. getData fills the array. Since the pointer, pFill, is always one ahead of the read, when we reach the end of file, it is pointing to an empty element. Therefore, when we return it we subtract 1.

3. selectSort advances through the array using a *for* statement. For each iteration, it selects the smallest element in the unsorted portion of the array and exchanges it with the first element in the unsorted portion of the array. Each loop, therefore, examines a smaller number of unordered elements. We stop at the element just before the last one because smallest always tests the first element and at least one element after the first one. When we are at the element just before the last, therefore, we are also testing the last element.

4. Finally, note the style used to code the *for* statement in both smallest and printData. Long *for* statements are more readable if you put each expression on a separate line.

DYNAMIC ARRAY   This program creates a dynamic table that can store a ragged array. The column and the width of the **dynamic array** are tailored to the needs of the user. The program starts by asking the user for the number of rows that must be stored. After allocating the row pointers (using *calloc*), the program asks for the number of entries in each row. The table is then filled with data supplied by the user from the keyboard. To demonstrate the applications that could be used with this type of structure, we then determine the minimum, maximum, and average of each row of data. The design is shown in Figure 10-22.

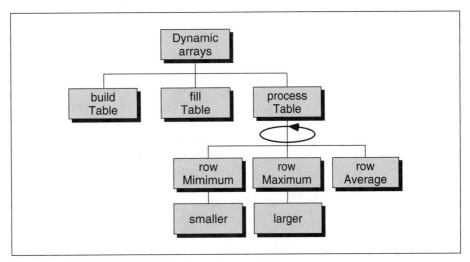

Figure 10-22   Dynamic array structure chart

The data structure is shown in Figure 10-23. The table pointer points to the first pointer in an array of pointers. Each array pointer points to a second array of integers, the first element of which is the number of elements in the list. All arrays are allocated out of the heap, giving us a structure that is limited only by the computer's memory.

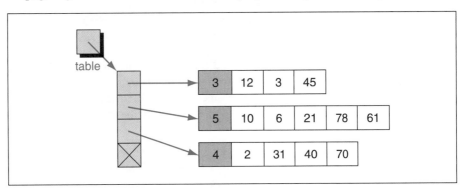

Figure 10-23   Ragged array structure

The complete set of programs to build and fill the table and some sample applications are shown in Programs 10-5 through 10-13.

```
1   /* Demonstrate concept of storing arrays in the heap. This
2      program builds and manipulates a variable number of ragged
3      arrays. It then calculates the minimum, maximum, and
4      average of the numbers in the arrays.
```

Program 10-5   Dynamic arrays: *main*

```
 5          Written by:
 6          Date:
 7     */
 8     #include <stdio.h>
 9     #include <stdlib.h>
10     #include <limits.h>
11
12     /* Prototype Declarations */
13     int **buildTable    (void);
14     void  fillTable     (int **table);
15     void  processTable  (int **table);
16     int   smaller       (int first, int second);
17     int   larger        (int first, int second);
18     int   rowMinimum    (int *rowPtr);
19     int   rowMaximum    (int *rowPtr);
20     float rowAverage    (int *rowPtr);
21
22     int main (void)
23     {
24     /* Local Definitions */
25        int **table;
26
27     /* Statements */
28        table = buildTable();
29        fillTable     (table);
30        processTable  (table);
31        return 0;
32     }  /* main */
```

Program 10-5   Dynamic arrays: *main* (continued)

Program 10-5 Analysis   The main function in Program 10-5 is a classic example of a well-designed program. It contains only one variable, the pointer to the array. There are only three functions calls in main: The first returns the address of the array; the other two use the array, and only the array. All detail processing is done in subfunctions.

```
 1     /* ==================== buildTable ====================
 2        Create backbone of the table by creating an array of
 3        pointers, each pointing to an array of integers.
 4           Pre    nothing
 5           Post   returns pointer to the table
 6     */
 7     int **buildTable (void)
 8     {
 9     /* Local Definitions */
10        int    rowNum;
11        int    colNum;
12        int  **table;
```

Program 10-6   Dynamic arrays: buildTable

```
13      int    row;
14
15   /* Statements */
16      printf("\nEnter the number of rows in the table: ");
17      scanf("%d", &rowNum);
18      table = (int **) calloc(rowNum + 1, sizeof(int*));
19      for (row = 0; row < rowNum; row++)
20          {
21            printf("Enter number of integers in row %d: ",
22                     row + 1);
23            scanf("%d", &colNum);
24            table[row] = (int*)calloc(colNum + 1, sizeof(int));
25            table[row] [0] = colNum;
26          } /* for */
27      table[row] = NULL;
28      return table;
29   }   /* buildTable */
```

Program 10-6   Dynamic arrays: `buildTable` (continued)

Program 10-6 Analysis   We begin Program 10-6 by asking the user how many rows of data must be entered. Using the *calloc* function, we then allocate the memory for an array of pointers plus one extra pointer at the end. Each entry in the allocated table is used to point to an array of integers, also stored in the heap.

```
 1   /* ==================== fillTable ====================
 2      This function fills the array rows with data.
 3          Pre    array of pointers
 4          Post   array filled
 5   */
 6   void fillTable (int **table)
 7   {
 8   /* Local Definitions */
 9      int row = 0;
10      int column;
11
12   /* Statements */
13      printf("\n ============================");
14      printf("\n Now we fill the table.\n");
15      printf("\n For each row enter the data");
16      printf("\n and press return: ");
17      printf("\n ============================\n");
18
19      while (table[row] != NULL)
20         {
21           printf("\n row %d (%d integers) =====> ",
22                    row + 1, table[row][0]);
23           for (column = 1; column <= *table[row]; column++)
```

Program 10-7   Dynamic arrays: `fillTable`

```
24          scanf("%d", table[row] + column);
25       row++;
26      } /* while */
27    return;
28  }  /* fillTable */
```

Program 10-7   Dynamic arrays: `fillTable` (continued)

Program 10-7 Analysis   Filling the rows, Program 10-7 requires a *while* statement to loop through the array pointers and a *for* statement to enter the data. We use the *while* statement because the pointer array is designed with a null pointer at the end, and we use it to tell we are at the end of the array. We use the *for* statement for filling the row because the user has already told us how many elements are in each row.

```
 1  /* ==================== processTable ====================
 2     Process the table to create the statistics.
 3        Pre    table
 4        Post   statistics (min, max, and average) for each row.
 5  */
 6  void processTable (int **table)
 7  {
 8  /* Local Definitions */
 9  int    row = 0;
10  int    rowMin;
11  int    rowMax;
12  float rowAve;
13
14  /* Statements */
15     while (table[row] != NULL)
16        {
17         rowMin = rowMinimum (table[row]);
18         rowMax = rowMaximum (table[row]);
19         rowAve = rowAverage (table[row]);
20         printf("\n\nThe statistics for row %d ", row + 1);
21         printf("\nThe minimum: %5d",    rowMin);
22         printf("\nThe maximum: %5d",    rowMax);
23         printf("\nThe average: %8.2f ", rowAve);
24         row++;
25        } /* while */
26     return;
27  }  /* processTable */
```

Program 10-8   Dynamic arrays: `processTable`

Program 10-8 Analysis   Processing the table in Program 10-8 calls three functions to show how you could use a dynamic structure such as this. Obviously, many more applications could be used. Remember the structure of this example. You will be able to use this structure in future applications. Programs 10-9 through 10-13 continue the code for the functions.

```
 1  /* ================== rowMinimum ==================
 2     This function determines the minimum of the data in a row.
 3        Pre    given pointer to the row
 4        Post   returns the minimum for that row
 5  */
 6  int rowMinimum (int *rowPtr)
 7  {
 8
 9  /* Local Definitions */
10     int rowMin = INT_MAX;
11     int column;
12
13  /* Statements */
14     for (column = 1; column <= *rowPtr; column++)
15         rowMin = smaller (rowMin, *(rowPtr + column));
16     return rowMin;
17  }  /*rowMinimum */
```

Program 10-9   Dynamic arrays: find row minimum

```
 1  /* ================== rowMaximum ==================
 2     This function calculates the maximum of the data in a row.
 3        Pre    given pointer to the row
 4        Post   returns the maximum for that row
 5  */
 6  int rowMaximum (int *rowPtr)
 7  {
 8  /* Local Definitions */
 9     int rowMax = INT_MIN;
10     int column;
11
12  /* Statements */
13     for (column = 1; column <= *rowPtr; column++)
14         rowMax = larger  (rowMax, *(rowPtr + column));
15     return rowMax;
16  }  /*rowMaximum */
```

Program 10-10   Dynamic arrays: find row maximum

```
 1  /* ================== rowAverage ==================
 2     This function calculates the average of the data in a row.
 3        Pre    pointer to the row
 4        Post   returns the average for that row
 5  */
 6  float  rowAverage (int *rowPtr)
 7  {
 8  /* Local Definitions */
```

Program 10-11   Dynamic arrays: find row average

```
 9      float   total = 0;
10      float   rowAve;
11      int     column;
12
13  /* Statements */
14      for (column = 1; column <= *rowPtr; column++)
15          total += (float)*(rowPtr + column);
16      rowAve = total / *rowPtr;
17      return rowAve;
18  }   /*rowAverage */
```

Program 10-11   Dynamic arrays: find row average (continued)

```
 1  /* ==================== smaller ====================
 2      This function returns the smaller of two numbers.
 3          Pre    two numbers
 4          Post   returns the smaller
 5  */
 6  int   smaller (int first,
 7                 int second)
 8  {
 9  /* Local Definitions */
10      int result;
11
12  /* Statements */
13      result = first < second ? first : second;
14      return result;
15  }   /* smaller */
```

Program 10-12   Dynamic arrays: find smaller

```
 1  /* ==================== larger ====================
 2      This function returns the larger of two numbers.
 3          Pre    two numbers
 4          Post   returns the larger
 5  */
 6  int   larger  (int first,
 7                 int second)
 8  {
 9  /* Local Definitions */
10      int result;
11
12  /* Statements */
13      result = first > second ? first : second;
14      return result;
15  }   /* larger */
```

Program 10-13   Dynamic arrays: find larger

10-8 SOFTWARE ENGINEERING AND PROGRAMMING STYLE

Pointer applications need careful design to ensure that they work correctly and efficiently. The programmer not only must take great care in the program design but also must carefully consider the data structures that are inherent with pointer applications. The design of the data structures is beyond the scope of this text, but we can discuss the design of the pointers.

Before we discuss specific aspects of pointer applications, a word of caution: Remember the KISS principle. The complexity of pointers grows exponentially as you move from single references to double references to triple references. In other words, the complexity of a statement that uses a double dereference is twice as complex as a single dereference, and a triple dereference is eight times more complex than a single dereference. Keep it short and simple!

POINTERS AND FUNCTION CALLS

You should always pass by value when possible. If you have to use a pointer to pass back a value, however, whenever possible, pass a pointer to the ultimate object to be referenced. When the pointer refers to the data variable, it is a single dereference. Despite your best efforts, at times you will have to pass a pointer to a pointer. When a function opens a file whose file pointer is in the calling function, you must pass a pointer to the pointer to the file table. In Figure 10-17, on page 490, we allocated a dynamic array of 200 integers. If the allocation is performed in a subfunction, then it must receive a pointer to the pointer to the array in memory so that it can store the address of the array.

> Whenever possible, use value parameters.

POINTERS AND ARRAYS

When you combine pointers and arrays, the complexity again becomes difficult very fast. This is especially true when the array is multidimensional. Whenever possible, therefore, rather than passing a multidimensional array, pass just one row. This reduces the complexity significantly, because the function is now dealing with a one-dimensional array. Not only are the references easier to work with, but it allows simple pointer arithmetic, which is usually more efficient.

When you must work with a two-dimensional array, use index rather than pointer notation. Index notation is much simpler to work with, and there is no difference in efficiency. If you are not sure of this recommendation, consider the following equivalent expressions. Which one would you rather find in a strange program?

```
*(*(ary + i) + j)     or     a[i][j]
```

ARRAY INDEX COMMUTATIVITY

Commutativity is a principle in mathematics that says the results of an expression do not depend on the order in which the factors are evaluated. For example, a + b is identical to b + a. Pointer addition is commutative; subtraction is not. Thus, the following two expressions are identical.

```
a + i     i + a
```

But we also know that `a + i` is identical to `a[i]`. Similarly, `i + a` would be equivalent to `i[a]`. Therefore, using the principle of commutativity, we see that

`a[i]` is identical to `i[a]`

A word of caution. Commutavity works in C because of the pointer concept and pointer arithmetic. Do not try this in another language.

DYNAMIC MEMORY: THEORY VERSUS PRACTICE

Do not get carried away with dynamic memory. The programming complexity of dynamically managing memory is very high. What you will often find, therefore, is that memory is not fully reused. To test your system, run Program 10-14.

```
 1  /* This program tests the reusability of dynamic memory.
 2         Written by:
 3         Date:
 4  */
 5  #include <stdio.h>
 6  #include <stdlib.h>
 7
 8  int main (void)
 9  {
10  /* Local Definitions */
11     int  looper;
12     int *ptr;
13
14  /* Statements */
15     for (looper = 0; looper < 5; looper++)
16        {
17         ptr = malloc(16);
18         printf("Memory allocated at: %p\n", ptr);
19
20         free (ptr);
21        } /* for */
22     return 0;
23  }  /* main */
```

```
    Results in Personal Computer:
        Memory allocated at: 00E7FC32
        Memory allocated at: 00E8024A
        Memory allocated at: 00E8025C
        Memory allocated at: 00E8026E
        Memory allocated at: 00E80280

    Results in UNIX system:
        Memory allocated at: 10001010
        Memory allocated at: 10001010
        Memory allocated at: 10001010
        Memory allocated at: 10001010
        Memory allocated at: 10001010
```

Program 10-14 Testing memory reuse

Program 10-14 Analysis   First look at the logic of this simple program. It loops five times, each time allocating 16 bytes and immediately freeing them. The program was run on two different systems, a personal computer and a UNIX network.

If the memory management was doing its job, the same 16 bytes should be allocated each time. What we see, however, is that for the personal computer, each address is different. It is also interesting to note that the difference between all the allocations except the first was 18 bytes, not 16. For some unknown reason, the difference between the first and second allocations was 24 bytes (18 hexadecimal). The larger UNIX network system is more sophisticated, and it appears to reuse dynamic memory efficiently.

10-9 TIPS AND COMMON PROGRAMMING ERRORS

1. If `ary` is an array, then

   ```
   ary       is the same as       &ary[0]
   ```

2. If `ary` is the name of an array, then

   ```
   ary[i]   is the same as   *(ary + i)
   ```

3. Remember that we usually pass the name of an array as a pointer value to a function that needs to access the elements of the array.

4. Remember that

   ```
   int *a[5];     is different from     int (*a)[5];
   ```

5. Similar to array indexes, the most common pointer error is referencing a nonexistent element in an array. This is especially easy to do with pointer arithmetic.

6. It is a compile error to use pointer arithmetic with a pointer that does not reference an array.

7. It is a logic error to subtract two pointers that are referencing different arrays.

8. It is a compile error to subtract a pointer from an index.

9. It is a compile error to attempt to modify the name of an array using pointer arithmetic, such as

   ```
   table++;              /* Error: table is constant */
   table = ...;          /* Error: table is constant */
   ```

10. The header file `<stdlib.h>` is required when using memory allocation functions.

11. It is a compile error to assign the return value from *malloc* or *calloc* to anything other than a pointer.

505

12. It is a logic error to set a pointer to the heap to `NULL` before the memory has been released.

13. It is a compile error to use pointer arithmetic with multiply, divide, or modulo operators.

10-10   KEY TERMS AND CONCEPTS[3]

array of pointers	heap memory	*realloc*
calloc	*malloc*	right–left rule
dynamic array	offset	stack memory
dynamic memory allocation	overflow	static memory allocation
free	pointer arithmetic	

---

[3]Note: Italic terms are C keywords or standard function names.

10-11   SUMMARY

- Arrays and pointers have a close relationship. The name of an array is a pointer constant to the first element of the array.

- The name of an array and the address of the first element in the array represent the same thing: an rvalue pointer.

- The name of an array is a pointer only to the first element, not the whole array.

- A pointer variable to the first element of an array can be used anywhere the name of the array is permitted, such as with an index.

- In pointer arithmetic, if `ptr` is pointing to a specific element in an array, `ptr + n` is the pointer value *n* elements away.

- The following two expressions are exactly the same when `ary` is the name of an array and *n* is an integer:

      *(ary + n)   ary[n]

- The name of a two-dimensional array is a pointer to a one-dimensional array—the first row.

- In a multidimensional array, the following two expressions are equivalent.

      ((a + i) + j)   a[i][j]

- We can pass an array to a function in many ways. One way is to pass the name of the array as a pointer.

- A ragged array—that is, an array of pointers—can be used to save space when not all rows of the array are full.

- The memory in a computer can be divided into program memory and data memory. Data memory can be partitioned into global area, heap, and stack.

- Static allocation of memory requires that the declaration and definition of memory be fully specified at compilation time.

- Dynamic allocation of memory is done during run time through the use of predefined functions.

- C has four predefined memory allocation functions: *malloc, calloc, realloc,* and *free.*

- To read and interpret a complex declaration, we can use the right–left rule.

10-12 PRACTICE SETS

REVIEW QUESTIONS

1. Given a pointer to an array element, ptr, ptr − 5 is a pointer to the value 5 elements toward the beginning of the array.
   - a. True
   - b. False

2. Adding 1 to a pointer increases the address stored in it by 1 byte.
   - a. True
   - b. False

3. The parameter declaration int *a can be used to declare an array of integers passed to a function.
   - a. True
   - b. False

4. Dynamically allocated memory can only be referred to through pointers.
   - a. True
   - b. False

5. Which of the following statements about pointers and arrays is true?
   - a. The following expressions are identical when ary is an array: *ary and &ary[0].
   - b. The following expressions are identical when ary is an array: *ary and *ary[0].
   - c. The name of an array can be used with the indirection operator to reference data.
   - d. The name of the array is a pointer variable.
   - e. The only way to reference data in an array is with the index operator.

6. Which of the following statements about pointer arithmetic is true?
   - a. Any arithmetic operator can be used to change the value of a pointer.
   - b. Given a pointer ptr, ptr + n is a pointer to the value n elements away.
   - c. Pointer arithmetic is a short-hand notation that changes the value that a pointer is referencing.
   - d. Pointer arithmetic is valid only with pointers to arithmetic variables, such as pointer to integer.
   - e. Pointer arithmetic is valid only with the name of the array.

7. Which of the following parameters is a two-dimensional array of integers?
   - a. int ary
   - b. int ary[ ][SIZE2]
   - c. int *ary
   - d. int *ary[ ][SIZE2]
   - e. int *ary[SIZE2]

8. Which of the following is not a C memory allocation function?
   - a. *alloc( )*
   - c. *free( )*
   - e. *realloc( )*
   - b. *calloc( )*
   - d. *malloc( )*

9. Which of the following statements about memory allocation is true?
   - a. Allocated memory can be referred to only through pointers; it does not have its own identifier.
   - b. *calloc* (change allocation) is used to change the allocation to memory previously allocated through *malloc*.
   - c. *malloc* (memory allocation) is used to allocate blocks of memory for arrays.
   - d. *realloc* (release allocation) is used to release memory when it is no longer needed.
   - e. Underflow can occur only with calloc and malloc.

10. The C function that allocates an array is:
    - a. *alloc( )*
    - c. *free( )*
    - e. *realloc( )*
    - b. *calloc( )*
    - d. *malloc( )*

11. Which of the following statements about releasing memory allocation is false?
    - a. It is an error to dereference a pointer to allocated memory after the memory has been released.
    - b. It is an error to free memory with a pointer to other than the first element of an allocated array.
    - c. Memory should be freed as soon as it is no longer needed.
    - d. Only one call to *free* is necessary to release an entire array allocated with *calloc*.
    - e. To ensure that it is released, allocated memory should be freed before the program ends.

12. Which of the following statements about ragged arrays is false?
    - a. Ragged arrays are two-dimensional arrays in which the right elements of a row may be empty.
    - b. Ragged arrays can be implemented using an array of pointers to one-dimensional arrays.
    - c. Ragged arrays can only be used with arrays of integers.
    - d. Ragged arrays implemented as an array of pointers save memory.
    - e. Ragged arrays implemented as an array of pointers can be created in dynamic memory.

EXERCISES

13. Rewrite each of the following expressions by replacing the index operator ([...]) with the indirection operator (*).

    a. `tax[6]`   c. `num[4]`

    b. `score[7]`   d. `prices[9]`

14. Rewrite each of the following expressions by replacing the indirection operator (*) with the index operator ([...]). Each identifier refers to an array.

    a. `*(tax + 4)`   c. `*(number + 0)`

    b. `*(score + 2)`   d. `*prices`

15. Imagine we have the following declarations:

    ```
    int ary[10];
    int *p = &ary[3];
    ```

    Show how you can access the sixth element of `ary` using the pointer p.

16. Given the following declarations:

    ```
    float ary[200];
    ```

    Write the prototype declaration for a function named `fun` that can manipulate a one-dimensional array of floating-point numbers, `ary`. Provide an additional parameter, a pointer to the last element in the array. Code a call to the function.

17. Show what would be printed from the following block:

    ```
    {
      int num[5] = { 3, 4, 6, 2, 1 };
      int *p = num;
      int *q = num +2;
      int *r  = &num[1];
      printf("\n%d %d", num[2], *(num + 2));
      printf("\n%d %d", *p, *(p + 1));
      printf("\n%d %d", *q, *(q + 1));
      printf("\n%d %d", *r, *(r + 1));
      return 0;
    }
    ```

18. Show what would be printed from the following block.

    ```
    {
    /* Prototype Declaration */
       void printOne (int *);
       void printTwo (int *);
       void printThree (int *);
    /* Local Definitions */
       int num [5] = {3 , 4 , 6 , 2 , 1};
    /* Statements */
       printOne (num);
       printTwo (num + 2);
       printThree (&num [2]);
       return 0;
    }
    void printOne (int *x)
    {
    ```

```
        printf("\n%d", x[2]);
        return;
    }
    void printTwo (int *x)
    {
        printf("\n%d", x[2]);
        return;
    }
    void printThree (int *x)
    {
        printf("\n%d", *x);
        return;
    }
```

19. Given the following definition:

    ```
    int table [4][5];
    ```

    write the prototype declaration for a function named fun that can accept the whole array using a pointer. Write the statement that calls this function.

20. Given the following definition:

    ```
    int table [4][5];
    ```

    write the prototype declaration for a function named torture that accepts one row of an array at a time.

21. Draw pictures to show the memory configuration for each of the following declarations.

    a. int *x [5];   b. int (*x) [5];

22. Show what would be printed from the following block:

    ```
    {
    /* Local Definitions */
        int x [2][3] =
          {
           { 4 , 5 , 2 } ,
           { 7 , 6 , 9 }
          };
        int (*p) [3]  = &x [1];
        int (*q) [3]  =  x;
    /* Statements */
        printf("\n%d %d %d", (*p)[0],(*p)[1],(*p)[2]);
         printf("\n%d %d",    *q[0],  *q[1]);
    }
    ```

23. Show what would be printed from the following block:

    ```
    {
    /* Local Definitions */
        int x [2][3] = {
                        { 4 , 5 , 2 } ,
                        { 7 , 6 , 9 }
                  };
    ```

```
/*   Statements */
    fun (x);
    fun (x + 1);
    return 0;
}
void fun (int  (*p)[3])
{
    printf("\n%d %d %d", (*p)[0],(*p)[1],(*p)[2]);
    return;
}
```

24. Given the following definitions:
    ```
    int num[26] = {23, 3, 5, 7, 4, -1, 6};
    int *n = num;
    int i  = 2;
    int j  = 4;
    ```
    show the value of the following expressions:

    a. n   d. *(n + 1)
    b. *n   e. *n + j
    c. *n + 1   f. *&i

25. Given the following definitions:
    ```
    char a[20] = {'z', 'x', 'm', 's', 'e', 'h'};
    char *pa = a;
    int i = 2;
    int j = 4;
    int *pi = &i;
    ```

    show the value of the following expressions:

    a. *(pa + j)   b. *(pa + *pi)

26. Given the following definitions:
    ```
    int data[15] = {5,2,3,4,1,3,7,2,4,3,2,9,12};
    ```
    show the value of the following expressions:

    a. data + 4   c. *data + 4
    b. *(data + 4)   d. *(data + (*data + 2))

27. Given the following definitions:
    ```
    int i = 2;
    int j = 4;
    int *pi = &i;
    int *pj = &j;
    ```

    show the value of the following expressions:

    a. *&j   d. **&pj
    b. *&*&j   e. &**&pi
    c. *&pi   f. &i + 8

28. Given the following definitions:
    ```
    char a[20] = {'z', 'x', 'm', 's', 'e', 'h'};
    int i = 2;
    int j = 4;
    ```

write pointer expressions that evaluate to the same value as each of the following:

a. a[0]

b. a[5]

c. The address of the element just before a[0].

d. The address of the last element in a.

e. The address of the element just after the last element in a.

f. The next element after a[3].

g. The next element after a[12].

h. The next element after a[j].

29. Given the following definitions:

```
int num[10] = {23,3,5,7,4,-1,6,12,10,-23};

int i = 2;

int j = 4;
```

write index expressions that evaluate to the same value as each of the following:

a. *(num + 2)   d. *(num + j)

b. *(num + i + j)   e. *(num + i) + *(num + j)

c. *(num + *(num + 1))

30. Given the following definition:

```
int num[2000] = {23, 3, 5, 7, 4, -1, 6};
```

write two pointer expressions for the address of num[0].

31. Given the following definitions:

```
int  num[26] = {23, 3, 5, 7, 4, -1, 6};

int  i = 2;

int  j = 4;

int *n = num;
```

write the equivalent expressions in index notation.

a. n   d. *(n + 1)

b. *n   e. *(n + j)

c. *n + 1

32. Given the following definitions:

```
int  num[26] = {23, 3, 5, 7, 4, -1, 6};

int *pn;
```

write a test to check whether pn points beyond the end of num.

33. Given the following prototype for mushem and the definitions shown below

```
int mushem (int *, int *);

int  i = 2;

int  j = 4;

int *pi = &i;

int *pj = &j;
```

indicate whether each of the following calls to mushem is valid:

a. i = mushem (2, 10);   d. j = mushem (i, j);

b. j = mushem (&i, &j);   e. mushem (pi, pj);

c. i = mushem (pi, &j);

34. What is the output from the following program?

```c
#include <stdio.h>

int fun (int *, int, int *);

int main (void)
{
/*  Local Definitions */
    int a = 4;
    int b = 17;
    int c[5] = {9, 14, 3, 15, 6};
/*  Statements */
    a = fun(&a, b, c);
    printf("2. %d %d %d %d %d %d %d\n",
            a, b, c[0], c[1], c[2], c[3], c[4]);
    return 0;
}   /* main */

int fun (int *px,
         int y,
         int *pz)
{
/*  Local Definitions */
    int a = 5;
    int *p;
/*  Statements */
    printf("1. %d %d %d\n", *px, y, *pz);
    for (p = pz; p < pz + 5; ++p)
        *p = a + *p;
    return (*px + *pz + y);
}   /* fun */
```

35. What is the output from the following program?

```c
#include <stdio.h>

int sun (int *, int, int *);

int main (void)
{
/*  Local Definitions */
    int a = 4;
    int b = 17;
    int c[5] = {9, 14, 3, 15, 6};
    int *pc = c;
/*  Statements */
    a = sun(pc, a, &b);
    printf("2. %d %d %d %d %d %d %d\n",
            a, b, c[0], c[1], c[2], c[3], c[4]);
    return 0;
}
```

```
int sun (int *px,
         int y,
         int *pz)
{
/* Local Definitions */
   int i = 5;
   int *p;
/* Statements */
   printf("1. %d %d %d\n", *px, y, *pz);
   for (p = px; p < px + 5; p++)
       *p = y + *p;
   *px = 2 * i;
   return (*pz + *px + y);
} /* sun */
```

PROBLEMS

36. We have two arrays A and B, each containing 10 integers. Write a function that checks if every element of array A is equal to its corresponding element in array B. In other words, the function must check if A[0] is equal to B[0], A[1] is equal to B[1], and so on. The function must accept only two pointer values and return an integer, zero for equal and not zero for unequal.

37. Generalize the function in Problem 36 to include the number of elements to be compared as a parameter.

38. Write a function that reverses the elements of an array in place. In other words, the last element must become the first, the second from last must become the second, and so on. The function must accept only one pointer value and return *void*.

39. The Pascal triangle can be used to compute the coefficients of the terms in the expansion of $(a + b)^n$. Write a function that creates a ragged array representing the Pascal triangle. In a Pascal triangle, each element is the sum of the element directly above it and the element to the left of the element directly above it (if any). A Pascal triangle of size 7 is shown below.

1						
1	1					
1	2	1				
1	3	3	1			
1	4	6	4	1		
1	5	10	10	5	1	
1	6	15	20	15	6	1

Your function must be able to create the triangle of any size. The function should accept an integer representing the size of the triangle and return a pointer to the array it created.

40. Write a function that tests an International Standard Book Number (ISBN) to see if it is valid. The ISBN is used to define a book uniquely. It is made of 10 digits, as shown below. For an ISBN number to be valid, the weighted sum of the ten digits must be evenly divisible by 11. The tenth digit may be *X,* which indicates 10. (If you are not familiar with the algorithm for the weighted sum, it is explained in Chapter 8, Problem 31 on page 416.) The ISBN format is shown in Figure 10-24.

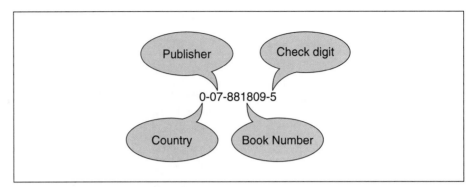

Figure 10-24   Project 40 structure

The function must accept a pointer value (the name of the array) and return an integer, zero for invalid and nonzero for valid.

41. Write a function that copies a one-dimensional array of *n* elements into a two-dimensional array of *j* rows and *k* columns. The resulting array will be placed in the heap. The data will be inserted into the array in row order; that is, the first *k* items will be placed in row 0, the second *k* items in row 1, and so forth until all rows have been filled.

   If *j* and *k* are not factors of *n*—that is, if $n \neq j * k$—the function returns a null pointer. Otherwise, it returns the pointer to the two-dimensional array. The input array and *j*, *k*, and *n* will be passed as parameters.

42. Given the following definition:

```
int num[20];
```

   and using only pointer notation, write a *for* loop to read integer values from the keyboard to fill the array.

43. Given the following definition

```
char a[40];
```

   and using only pointer notation, write a *for* loop to read characters from the keyboard to fill the array.

44. Given the following declaration and definition:

```
char a[6] = {'z', 'x', 'm', 's', 'e', 'h'};
```

   and using only pointer notation, write a loop to rotate all values in a to the right (toward the end) by one element.

45. Repeat Problem 44, with the rotation one element to the left.

46. Write a function named addem with two call-by-address integer parameters. The function will add 2 to the first parameter and 5 to the second parameter. Test the function by calling it with the values of 17 and 25.

PROJECTS

47. Write a program that will read ten integers from the keyboard and place them in an array. The program then will sort the array into ascending and descending order and print the sorted lists. The program must not change the original array or create any other integer arrays.

   The solution to this problem requires two pointer arrays as shown in Figure 10-25. The first pointer array is rearranged so that it points to the data in ascending sequence. The second pointer array is rearranged so that it points to the data in descending sequence.

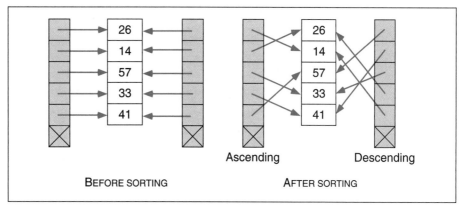

Figure 10-25 Structure for Project 47

Your output should be formatted with the three arrays printed as a vertical list next to each other, as shown in Figure 10-26.

Ascending	Original	Descending
14	26	57
26	14	41
33	57	33
41	33	26
57	41	14

Figure 10-26 Format for Project 47

48. Write a program that creates a two-dimensional array in the heap and then analyzes it to determine the minimum, maximum, and average of each column.

   The data are to be read from a file. The first two elements are the number of rows in the array and the number of columns in each row. The file data for a 12×8 array are shown in Table 10-3.

12	8						
838	758	113	515	51	627	10	419
212	86	749	767	84	60	225	543
89	183	137	566	966	978	495	311
367	54	31	145	882	736	524	505
394	102	851	67	754	653	561	96
628	188	85	143	967	406	165	403
562	834	353	920	444	803	962	318
422	327	457	945	479	983	751	894
670	259	248	757	629	306	606	990
738	516	414	262	116	825	181	134
343	22	233	536	760	979	71	201
336	61	160	5	729	644	475	993

Table 10-3 Data for Project 48

49. Rewrite the straight insertion sort from Chapter 8 using pointer arithmetic. The data to be sorted are to be read from a file. The array is to be dynamically allocated in the heap after reading the file to determine the number of elements. While reading the data to determine the size of array you will require, print them ten integers to a line. Use the test data in Table 10-4.

838	758	113	515	51	627	10	419	212	86
749	767	84	60	225	543	89	183	137	566
966	978	495	311	367	54	31	145	882	736
524	505	394	102	851	67	754	653	561	96
628	188	85	143	967	406	165	403	562	834
353	920	444	803	962	318	422	327	457	945
479	983	751	894	670	259	248	757	629	306
606	990	738	516	414	262	116	825	181	134
343	22	233	536	760	979	71	201	336	61

Table 10-4 Data for Project 49

The data will be sorted as they are read into the array. *Do not fill the array and then sort the data.* After the array has been sorted, print the data again using the same format you used for the unsorted data.

50. Write a program to answer inquiries about student data. Using a menu-driven user interface, provide the capability to print out the scores, average, or grade for a student. A fourth menu option is to provide all information about a given student. All array functions are to receive the array as a pointer and use pointer arithmetic.

The data in Table 10-5 will be stored in a two-dimensional array.

Student	Quiz 1	Quiz 2	Quiz 3	Quiz 4	Quiz 5
1234	52	7	100	78	34
1947	45	40	88	78	55
2134	90	36	90	77	30
2877	55	50	99	78	80
3124	100	45	20	90	70
3189	22	70	100	78	77
4532	11	17	81	32	77
4602	89	50	91	78	60
5405	11	11	0	78	10
5678	20	12	45	78	34
6134	34	80	55	78	45
6999	0	98	89	78	20
7874	60	100	56	78	78
8026	70	10	66	78	56
9893	34	9	77	78	20

Table 10-5 Student data for Project 50

51. Contract bridge is a popular card game played by millions of people throughout the world. It began in the 1920s as a variation of an old English card game, whist. In bridge, the entire deck is dealt to four players named North, South, East, and West. In tournament bridge, teams of players (North-South versus East-West) compete with other players using the same hands (sets of 13 cards). Today it is common for large tournaments to use computer-generated hands. Write a program to shuffle and deal the hands for one game.

To simulate the bridge deck, use an array of 52 integers initialized from 1 to 52. To shuffle the deck, loop through the array, exchanging the current card element with a random element (use the random number generator discussed in Chapter 4). After the deck has been shuffled, print the hands in four columns using the player's position as a heading. Use the following interpretation for the cards' suits:

1 to 13	Clubs
14 to 26	Diamonds
27 to 39	Hearts
40 to 52	Spades

To determine the rank of the card, use its number (modulo 13) + 1. The interpretation of the rank follows: 1 is an ace, 2 through 10 have their value, 11 is a jack, 12 is a queen, and 13 is a king.

52. Modify Project 51 to sort each hand by suit (clubs lowest and spades highest) and within suit, by rank after the shuffle. Hint: After shuffling the deck, consider the first 13 cards the hand for North, the next 13 cards the hand for East, and so forth. Then use a function to sort each hand in turn.

Strings

It is impossible to write a well-structured and human-engineered program without using strings. Although you probably weren't aware of it, you have been using strings ever since you wrote your first C program.

Some languages, such as Pascal and Ada, provide intrinsic string types, but C does not. In C, the programmer implements strings. Because strings are so important, however, functions to manipulate them have been defined in an ad hoc standard library.

In this chapter we first consider how strings are defined and stored, and then we explore the standard string functions that are available in C.

11-1   STRING CONCEPTS

In general, a string is a series of characters treated as a unit. Computer science has long recognized the importance of strings, but it has not adapted a standard for their implementation. We find, therefore, that a string created in Pascal differs from a string created in C.

Virtually all string implementations treat a string as a variable-length piece of data. Consider, for example, one of the most common of all strings, a name. Names, by their very nature, vary in length. It makes no difference if we are looking at the name of a person, a textbook, or an automobile.

Given that we have data that can vary in size, how do we accommodate them in our programs? We can store them in fixed-length objects, or we can store them in variable-length objects. This breakdown of strings is seen in Figure 11-1.

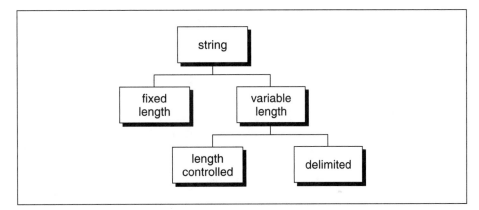

Figure 11-1   String taxonomy

FIXED-LENGTH STRINGS

When implementing a **fixed-length string** format, the first decision is the size of the variable. Make it too small, and you can't store all the data. Make it too big, and you waste memory.

Another problem associated with storing variable data in a fixed-length data structure is how to tell the data from the nondata. A common solution is to add nondata characters, such as spaces, at the end of the data. Of course, this means that the character selected to represent the nondata value cannot be used as data.

VARIABLE-LENGTH STRINGS

A much preferred solution is to create a structure that can expand and contract to accommodate the data. Thus, to store a person's name that consists of only one letter, you would provide only enough storage for one character.[1] To store a person's name that consists of 30 characters, the structure would be expanded to provide storage for 30 characters.

This flexibility does not come without a cost, however. There must be some way to tell when you get to the end of the data. Two common techniques are to use length-controlled strings and delimited strings.

---

[1]The shortest name that we are aware of is O. To accommodate the computers of credit card and other companies, however, Mr. O was forced to legally change his name to Oh.

Length-Controlled Strings

Length-controlled strings add a count that specifies the number of characters in the string. Generally, the count will be a single byte, which provides for strings of up to 255 characters. This count is then used by the string manipulation functions to determine the actual length of the data.

Delimited Strings

Another technique used to identify the end of the string is the **delimiter**. You are already familiar with the concept of delimiters, although you probably don't recognize them as such. In English, each sentence, which is a variable-length string, ends with a delimiter, the period. Commas, semicolons, colons, and dashes are other common delimiters found in English.

The major disadvantage of the delimiter is that it eliminates one character from being used for data. Since this leaves us with 127 different characters (255 if we use Extended ASCII or EBCDIC), this is not a major problem. The most common delimiter is the ASCII null character, which is the first character in the ASCII character sequence (\0). This is the technique used by C.

Figure 11-2 shows fixed-length, length-controlled, and **delimited strings** in memory.

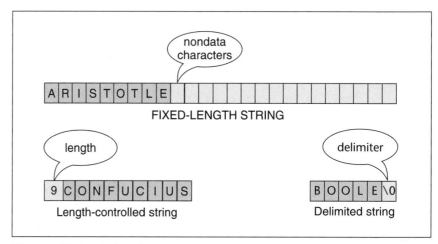

Figure 11-2   String formats

11-2   C STRINGS

A C **string** is a variable-length array of characters that is delimited by the null character. Generally, string characters are selected only from the printable ASCII character set. Nothing in C, however, prevents any ASCII character, other than the null delimiter, from being used in a string. In fact, it is quite common to use formatting characters, such as tabs, in strings.

STORING STRINGS

A string is stored in an array of characters. It is terminated by the null character (' \0 '). Figure 11-3 shows how a string is stored in memory. What precedes the string and what follows it is not important. What is important is that the string is stored in an array of characters that ends with a null delimiter.

Figure 11-4 shows the difference between a character stored in memory and a one-character string stored in memory. The character requires only one memory location. The one-character string requires two memory locations: one for the data and one for the

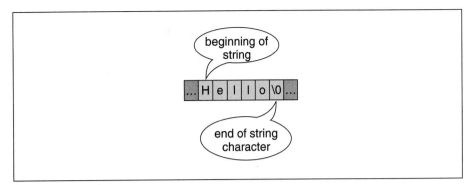

Figure 11-3   Storing strings

delimiter. The figure also shows how an empty string is stored. Empty strings require only the end-of-string marker.

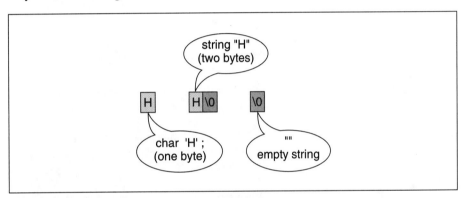

Figure 11-4   Storing strings and characters

THE STRING DELIMITER

At this point, you may be wondering, "Why do we need a null character at the end of a string?" The answer is that a string is not a data type but a data structure. This means that its implementation is logical, not physical. The physical structure is the array in which the string is stored. Since the string, by its definition, is a variable-length structure, we need to identify the logical end of the data within the physical structure.

Looking at it another way, if the data are not variable in length, then we don't need the string data structure to store them. They are easily stored in an array, and the end of the data is always the last element in the array. But, if the data length is variable, then we need some other way to determine the end of the data.

The null character is used as an end-of-string marker. It is the sentinel used by the standard string functions. In other words, the null character at the end lets us treat the string as a sequence of objects (characters) with a defined object at the end that can be used as a sentinel. Figure 11-5 shows the difference between an array of characters and a string.

Because strings are variable-length structures, you must provide enough room for the maximum-length string you will have to store, plus one for the delimiter. It is possible that the structure will not be filled, so we can have an array with the null character in the middle. In this case, we treat the part of the array from the beginning to the null character as the string and ignore the rest. In other words, any part of an array of characters can be treated as a string as long as the string ends in a null character. This is shown in Figure 11-6.

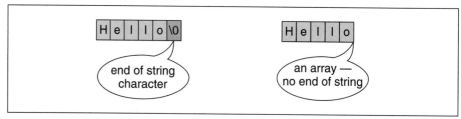

Figure 11-5 Differences between strings and character arrays

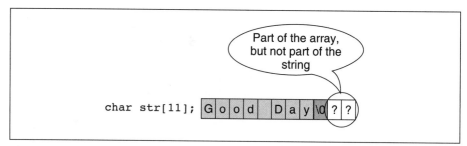

Figure 11-6 Strings in arrays

STRING LITERALS

A string literal—or as it is also known, string constant—is a sequence of characters enclosed in double quotes. For example, each of the following is a string literal:

```
"C is a high-level language."
"Hello"
"abcd"
```

When string literals are used in a program, C automatically creates an array of characters, initializes it to a null-delimited string, and stores it, remembering its address. It does all this because we use the double quotes that immediately identify the data as a string value.

> A string literal is enclosed in double quotes.

STRINGS AND CHARACTERS

When all we need to store is a single character, we have two options: We can store the data as a character literal or as a string literal. To store it as a character literal, we use *single quote marks*. To store it as a string literal, we use *double quote marks*. Although the difference when we code the literal is only a shift-key operation on most keyboards, the difference in memory is great. The character occupies a single memory location, usually a byte. The data portion of the string also occupies a single memory location, but there is an extra memory location required for the delimiter.

The differences in the ways we manipulate the data are even greater. For example, moving a character from one location to another requires only an assignment. Moving a string requires a function call. It is important, therefore, that you clearly understand the differences. Figure 11-7 shows examples of both character literals and string literals.

Another important difference between a string and a character is how we represent the absence of data. Technically, there is no such thing as an empty character. Logically, we often specify that a space (' ') or a null character (' \0 ') represents the absence of data. Since the character exists in all cases, however, both of these concepts require that you program for the interpretation of no data.

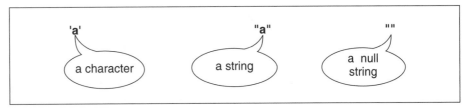

Figure 11-7 Character literals and string literals

A string, on the other hand, can be empty. That is, since it is a variable-length structure, a string can exist with no data in it. A string that contains no data consists of only a delimiter. This concept is specified in the definition of a string and is programmed into all the string-handling functions. We can, therefore, move or compare an empty string without knowing that we are dealing with no data. An example of a null string is also shown in Figure 11-7.

Referencing String Literals

A string literal is stored in memory. Just like any object stored in memory, it has an address. Thus, you can refer to a string literal by using pointers.

Let's first examine addressing a string literal. The literal, since it is an array of characters, is itself a pointer constant to the first element of the string. Generally, when you use it, you are referring to the entire string. It is possible, however, to refer to only one of the characters in the string, as shown in Figure 11-8.

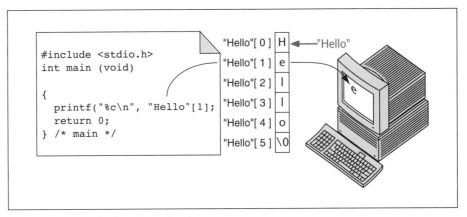

Figure 11-8 String literal references

STRINGS AS VARIABLES

As we said, C has no string type. To provide for string variables, therefore, you must use one of the other available structures. Since strings are a sequence of characters, it is only natural that the structure used to store string variables is the character array.

In defining the array to store a string, you must provide enough room for the data and the delimiter. The storage structure, therefore, must be 1 byte larger than the maximum data size. A string declaration for a ten-character string, including its delimiter, is shown below.

```
char str[11];
```

Initializing Strings

You can initialize a string the same way that you initialize any storage structure by assigning a value to it when it is defined. In this case, the value is a string literal. For example, to assign "Good Day" to a string, we would code

```
char str[11] = "Good Day";
```

In this example, we create an 11-byte array and fill the first 9 positions with the string value and its delimiter. This definition corresponds to Figure 11-6, on page 522. Note that the last two positions in the array are not part of the string. Since the string is initialized as part of the definition, however, the value of the last 2 bytes is known. Do you remember what it is? (Hint: What is the value of any array element when only a portion of the array is specified by initialization?)

Since a string is stored in an array of characters, we do not need to indicate the size of the array if we initialize it when it is defined. For instance, we could define a string to store the month January, as shown below.

```
char month[] = "January";
```

In this case, the compiler will create an array of 8 bytes and initialize it with January and a null character. We must be careful, however, because month is an array. If we now tried to store "December" in it, we would overrun the array and destroy whatever came after the array. This example points out one of the dangers of strings: You must make them large enough to hold the longest value you will place in the variable.

C provides two more ways to initialize strings. A common method is to assign a string literal to a character pointer, as shown below. This creates a string for the literal and then stores its address in the string pointer variable, pStr. To clearly see the structure, refer to Figure 11-9.

```
char *pStr = "Good Day!";
```

We can also initialize a string as an array of characters. You will not see this method used too often, because it is so tedious to code. Note that in this example, the programmer must ensure that the null character is at the end of the string.

```
char str[10] =
    {'G','o','o','d',' ','D','a','y','!','\0'};
```

The structures created by these three examples are shown in Figure 11-9.

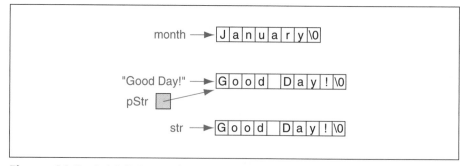

Figure 11-9 Initializing strings

Strings and the Assignment Operator

Since the string is an array, the name of the string is a pointer constant. As a pointer constant, it is an rvalue and therefore cannot be used as the left operand of the assignment operator. This is one of the most common errors in writing a C program; fortunately, it is a compile error, so it cannot affect your program.

```
char str1[11] = "Hello";
char str2[11];
str2 = str1;                          /* Compile error */
```

Although you could write a loop to assign characters individually, there is a better way. C provides a rich library of functions to manipulate strings, including moving one string to another. You will see this library in the section "String Manipulation Functions," on page 538.

Reading a String

A string can be read from a file. Several string input/output functions are supplied for just this purpose. We will discuss them in the section "String Input/Output Functions" later in the chapter.

STRINGS AND POINTERS

As you know, the name of an array is actually a pointer constant to the first element of the array. So you would think that this must also be true about strings. It is! The string name itself is a pointer constant to the first element (character) in the string. This is demonstrated in Figure 11-10. Note that we have used the character conversion code (%c) and pointer arithmetic to print one character at a time. (There is another conversion code, *s*, which you will see in the section "String Input/Output Functions." It prints the whole string with one function call.)

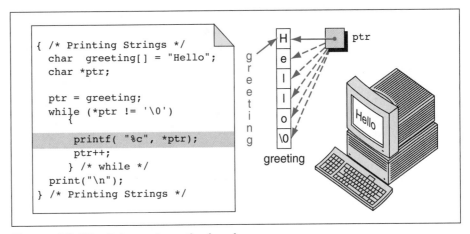

```
{ /* Printing Strings */
char  greeting[] = "Hello";
char *ptr;

ptr = greeting;
while (*ptr != '\0')
     {
     printf( "%c", *ptr);
     ptr++;
     } /* while */
print("\n");
} /* Printing Strings */
```

Figure 11-10   Print strings the hard way

11-3   STRING INPUT/OUTPUT FUNCTIONS

C provides two basic ways to read and write strings. First, you can read and write strings with the formatted input/output functions, *scanf* and *printf*. Then you can use a special set of string-only functions, get string (*gets/fgets*) and put string (*puts/fputs*).

FORMATTED STRING INPUT/OUTPUT

In this section, we cover the string-related portions of the formatted input and output functions.

Formatted String Input: *scanf*

We have already discussed the basic operations of the format input functions (see Chapter 7). However, two conversion codes pertain uniquely to strings, and we discuss them here.

The String Conversion Code (%s) Reading strings in some languages, such as Pascal, require that you read each character individually and assign it to the next position in the array. In C, it is much easier. You simply tell the read function (*scanf*) that you want the data read as a string. The conversion code for a string is "s." The *scanf* function then does all the work for you. First, it skips any leading whitespace. Once it finds a character, it reads until it finds whitespace, putting each character in the array in order. When it finds a trailing whitespace character, it ends the string with a null character. The whitespace character is left in the input stream. To delete the whitespace from the input stream, use a space in the format string before the next conversion code or FLUSH the input stream, whichever is more appropriate.

For example, to read a string, such as month, from the keyboard, you could simply write the statement shown below.

```
scanf("%s", month);
```

An address operator is not required for month, since it is already a pointer constant. In fact, it would be an error to use one. The only thing you need to worry about is to make sure that the array is large enough to store all the data. If it isn't, then you will destroy whatever follows the array in memory. Therefore, make sure you don't exceed the length of the data. Assuming that month has been defined as

```
char month[10];
```

you can protect against the user entering too much data by using a width in the field specification. (Recall that the width specifies the *maximum* number of characters to be read.) The modified *scanf* statement is shown below.

```
scanf("%9s", month);
```

Note that we set the maximum number of characters at nine while the array size is ten. This is because *scanf* will read up to nine characters and then insert the null character. Now, if the user accidentally enters more than nine characters, the extra characters will be left in the input stream. But this can cause a problem. Assuming that the data are being entered as a separate line—that is, that there is only one piece of data on the line—we use the preprocessor-defined statement, FLUSH, to eliminate any extra characters that were entered. This function also flushes the newline that is left in the input stream by *scanf* when the user correctly enters data. The complete block of code to read a month is shown in Program 11-1.

```
1  {  /* Read Month */
2     #define FLUSH while (getchar() != '\n')
3     char month[10];
4
5     printf("Please enter a month. ");
6     scanf("%9s", month);
7     FLUSH;
8  }  /* Read Month*/
```

Program 11-1 Reading strings

The Edit Set Conversion Code (`%[...]`)   The **edit set** conversion specification consists of the open bracket (`[`), followed by the edit characters, and terminated by the close bracket (`]`). The characters in the edit set identify the valid characters, known as the **scanset**, that are to be allowed in the string. All characters except the close bracket can be included in the set.

Edited conversion reads the input stream as a string. Each character read by *scanf* is compared against the edit set. If the character just read is in the edit set, it is placed in the string and the scan continues. The first character that does not match the scan set stops the read. The nonmatching character remains in the input stream for the next read operation. If the first character read is not in the edit set, the *scanf* terminates and a null string is returned.

A major difference between the edit set and the string conversion code (`%s`) is that the edit set does not skip leading whitespace. Leading whitespace is either put into the string being read when the edit set contains the corresponding whitespace character, or stops the conversion when it is not.

In addition to reading a character that is not in the edit set, there are two other terminating conditions. First, the read will stop if an end-of-file is detected. Second, the read will stop if a field width specification is included and the maximum number of characters has been read.

Always use a width in the field specification when reading strings.

For example, let's assume we have an application that requires we read a string containing only digits, commas, periods, the minus sign, and a dollar sign; in other words, we want to read a dollar value as a string. No other characters are allowed. Let's also assume that the maximum number of characters in the resulting string is ten. The format string for this operation would be[2]

```
scanf("%10[0123456789.,-$]", str);
```

Sometimes it is easier to specify what is not to be included in the edit set rather than what is valid. For instance, suppose that we want to read a whole line. You can do this by stating that all characters except the newline (`\n`) are valid. To specify invalid characters, you start the edit set with the caret (`^`) symbol. The caret is the negation symbol and in effect says that the following characters are not allowed in the string. (If you know UNIX, this should sound familiar.) To read a line, we would code the *scanf* as shown below.

```
scanf("%81[^\n]", line);
```

In this example, *scanf* reads until it finds the newline and then stops. Note that we have again set the width of the data to prevent our string, `line`, from being overrun. You would never use this code, however. As you will see in the next section, an intrinsic string function does it for you.

For the last example, let's read a 15-character string that can have any character except the special characters on the top of the keyboard. In this case, we again specify what is not valid. This conversion code is shown in the following example.

---

[2]UNIX users note that the dash (−) does not have the same meaning in the scanset that it does in UNIX.

```
scanf("%15[^~!@#$%^&*()_+]", str);
```

Note that the caret can be included in the edit set, as long as it is not the first character.

Read Part of Line   When data are stored in secondary files, the data you need are often only a part of a file. Program 11-2 demonstrates how to use the edit set to read part of a line and discard the rest. In the following example, the input contains numeric data, with each line containing two integers and a float. We are interested only in the second integer; the rest of each line will be discarded. As we wrote the program, it could contain any type or amount of data after the second integer. It is important to note, however, that if there are not two integers at the beginning of the line, the program fails.

```
 1 | /* Read and print second integer from each line.
 2 |       Written by:
 3 |       Date:
 4 | */
 5 | #include <stdio.h>
 6 |
 7 | int main (void)
 8 | {
 9 | /* Local Definitions */
10 |    int amount;
11 |
12 | /* Statements */
13 |    printf("Enter <integer> <integer> <float>: ");
14 |    while (fscanf(stdin, "%*d%d%*[^\n]", &amount) != EOF)
15 |       {
16 |        printf("Second integer: %d\n", amount);
17 |        printf("Enter <integer> <integer> <float>: ");
18 |       } /* while */
19 |
20 |    printf("\nThank you\n");
21 |
22 |    return 0;
23 | }  /* main */
```

```
Results:
   Enter <integer> <integer> <float>: 123 456 7.89
   Second integer: 456
   Enter <integer> <integer> <float>: 987 654 3.21
   Second integer: 654
   Enter <integer> <integer> <float>: ^d
   Thank you
```

Program 11-2   Demonstrate string edit set

Program 11-2 Analysis   As long as the user enters two numbers at the beginning of each line, this program works just fine. It skips the first number, reads the number into `amount`, and then discards the rest of the line. Study the format string in Statement 14 carefully. It consists of only three field specifications. The first one reads and discards an integer. The second one reads `amount`. The third one considers the rest of the line as a long string; *scanf* reads until it finds a newline. Because we are not interested in these data for the first and third parts of the line, we used the suppress flag to discard them.

Delete Leading Whitespace From Line   A similar problem occurs when a file contains leading whitespace at the beginning of a line. In program Program 11-3, we first determine if there is a whitespace character at the beginning of the line. If there is, we delete all leading spaces using the edit set and then read the rest of the line. Its only limitation is that the nonspace portion of the line cannot be longer than 80 characters.

```
1   /* Delete leading spaces at beginning of line.
2          Written by:
3          Date:
4   */
5   #include <stdio.h>
6   #include <ctype.h>
7
8   int main (void)
9   {
10  /* Local Definitions */
11     char line[80];
12
13  /* Statements */
14     printf("Enter data:   ");
15     while ((*line = fgetc(stdin)) != EOF)
16        {
17         if (isspace (*line))
18            {
19             /* Put whitespace back in case only one */
20             ungetc(*line, stdin);
21             fscanf(stdin, "%*[\t\v\f ]%79[^\n]", line);
22            } /* if */
23         else
24             fscanf(stdin, "%79[^\n]", line + 1);
25
26         printf ("You entered: %s\n", line);
27
28         /* Discard newline and set line to null string*/
29         fgetc (stdin);
30         *(line + 1) = '\0';
31         printf("Enter data:   ");
32        } /* while */
33
34     printf("\nThank you\n");
35     return 0;
36  }  /* main */
```

```
Results:
   Enter data:  No whitespace here.
   You entered: No whitespace here.
```

Program 11-3 Delete leading whitespace

```
Enter data:    Only one whitespace character.
You entered: Only one whitespace character.
Enter data:            Tabs and spaces here.
You entered: Tabs and spaces here.
Enter data:    Next line is only one space.
You entered: Next line is only one space.
Enter data:
You entered:
Enter data:    ^d
Thank you
```

Program 11-3 Delete leading whitespace (continued)

Program 11-3 Analysis   When writing a program, one of the most difficult challenges is finding all the things that could go wrong. The first version of this program handled everything except a single whitespace character at the beginning of the line. In that case, it lost the first character on the line, because *scanf* had to read at least one character for the first field specification (remember, the edit set does not skip leading whitespace). We therefore had to use the *ungetc* to put the first whitespace character back into the input stream so that the program would work correctly. This shows why it is so important to think of all the possible test cases the program might encounter.

Formatted String Output: *printf*

Formatted string output is provided in the *printf* function. It uses the same string conversion code (s) that we used for string input.

C has three options of interest when you write strings using *printf*: the left-justify flag, width, and precision. The left-justify flag (—) and the width are almost always used together. The width sets the *minimum* span of the string in the output. If it is used without a flag, the string is printed right justified as shown below.

```
    printf("|%30s|\n", "This is the string");
Output:
    |            This is the string|
```

The justification flag (—) is used to left justify the output. It has meaning only when a width is also specified, and then only if the length of the string is less than the format width. Using the justification flag results in the output being left justified, as shown below.

```
    printf("|%-30s|\n", "This is the string");
Output:
    |This is the string            |
```

Strings can get quite long. Because the width is the minimum number of characters that can be printed, a long string can easily exceed the width specified, which destroys column formatting. Therefore, C also uses the precision option to set the maximum number of characters that will be written. In the following typical example, we set the maximum characters to one less than the width to ensure a space between the string and the next column.

```
        printf("|%-15.14s|", "12345678901234567890");
Output:
             |12345678901234 |
```

STRING INPUT/ OUTPUT

In addition to the formatted string functions, C has two sets of string functions that read and write strings without reformatting any data. These functions convert text file lines to strings and strings to text file lines. A line consists of a string of characters terminated by a newline character.

Line to String (*gets*/*fgets*)

The *gets* and *fgets* functions take a line (terminated by a newline) from the input stream and make a null-terminated string out of it. They are therefore sometimes called line-to-string input functions.

The prototype statements for get string are shown below.

```
char *gets  (char *strPtr);
char *fgets (char *strPtr, int size, FILE *fp);
```

Figure 11-11 shows the concept. As you can see, they do not work the same. The *gets* function converts the return (newline character) to the end-of-string character (\0), while the *fgets* puts it in the string and appends an end-of-string delimiter.

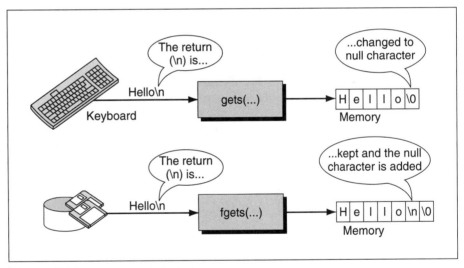

Figure 11-11 *gets* and *fgets* functions

The *gets* function reads from the standard input file stream; *fgets* reads the file stream specified by the file pointer (fp). Both accept a string pointer and return the same pointer if the input is successful. If any input problems occur, such as detecting end-of-file before reading any data, they return NULL. If no data were read, the input area is unchanged. If an error occurs after some data have been read, the contents of the read-in area cannot be determined. The current string may or may not have a valid null character.

Note that since no size is specified in *gets,* the *gets* function will read data until it finds a newline or until the end of file. If a newline is read, it is discarded and replaced with a null character.

The *fgets* function requires two additional parameters: one specifying the array size that is available to receive the data, and the other a file pointer (**fp**) that identifies the input file. It can be used with the keyboard by specifying the *stdin* file pointer. In addition to newline and end of file, the reading will stop when **size − 1** characters have been read.

Since no length checking is possible with *gets,* we recommend that you never use it. Should a user enter too much data, you will destroy the data after the string input area, and your program will not run correctly. Rather, use *fgets,* and specify the standard input file pointer (*stdin*).

> Always make sure you have defined enough memory for *gets.*

Now let us write a simple program that uses *fgets.* In Program 11-4, we use *fgets* to read a string and then print it.

```
 1  /* Demonstrate the use of fgets in a program
 2         Written by:
 3         Date:
 4  */
 5  #include <stdio.h>
 6
 7  int main (void)
 8  {
 9  /* Local Definitions */
10     char str[81];
11
12  /* Statements */
13     printf("Please enter a string: ");
14     fgets (str, sizeof (str), stdin);
15     printf("Here is your string: \n\t%s", str);
16     return 0;
17  }  /* main */
```

```
Results:
    Please enter a string: Now is the time for all students
    Here is your string:
        Now is the time for all students
```

Program 11-4   Demonstrate *fgets* operation

String-to-Line Output (*puts*/*fputs*)

The ***puts*** and ***fputs*** functions take a null-terminated string from memory and write it to a file as a line. Thus, they are sometimes called string-to-line output functions.

Figure 11-12 shows how *puts* and *fputs* work. Both functions change the string to a line. The null character is replaced with a newline in *puts*; it is dropped in *fputs.* When you consider that *puts* is writing to the standard output unit, usually a display, this is entirely logical. On the other hand, *fputs* is assumed to be writing to a file where newlines are not necessarily required. It is the programmer's responsibility to make sure the newline is present at the appropriate place. Note how the newline is handled in these two functions. Then compare their use of the newline to the *gets* and *fgets* functions. While the output functions treat the newline the opposite of the input functions, they are compatible. As long as you are reading from a file and writing to a file, the newlines will be handled automatically. Care must be taken, however, if you read from the keyboard and write to a file.

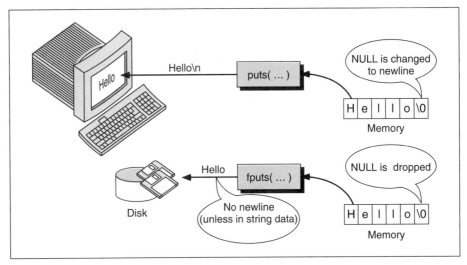

Figure 11-12 *puts* and *fputs* operations

The prototypes for these functions are shown below.

```
int puts   (const char *strPtr);
int fputs  (const char *strPtr, FILE *fp);
```

The string pointed to by `strPtr` is written to the indicated file as explained above. If the write is successful, it returns a non-negative integer; if any transmission errors occur, it returns `EOF`. Note that the absence of a null character to terminate the string is not an error; however, it will most likely cause your program to fail.

The next program contains a block of code that calls *puts* two times. The first time, we pass a pointer to the beginning of an array. The second time, we pass a pointer that is at the middle of the array. If you were to run this code, you would see that it does not matter where a string pointer starts. The function starts at the address in the pointer and writes until it finds a null character. The output is shown in Program 11-5.[3]

```
1  {
2      char str[] = "Necessity Is the Mother of Invention.";
3      char *pStr = str;
4
5      puts(pStr);
6      puts(pStr + 13);
7  }
```

```
Results:
    Necessity Is the Mother of Invention
    the Mother of Invention.
```

Program 11-5 Demonstration of *puts* string

---

[3]The quote in Program 11-5 is attributed to the American economist Thorstein Veblen.

EXAMPLES

This section contains examples to demonstrate the use of these string functions.

Typewriter Program

Program 11-6 plays the role of a line-at-a-time typewriter. In other words, it accepts text, line by line, from the keyboard and writes it to a text file. The program stops when it detects an end of file.

```
 1  /* This program creates a text file from keyboard input.
 2         Written by:
 3         Date:
 4  */
 5  #include <stdio.h>
 6
 7  int main (void)
 8  {
 9  /* Local Definitions */
10     char   str[100];
11     FILE  *fpOut;
12
13  /* Statements */
14     if (!(fpOut = fopen ("P11-06.TXT", "w")))
15        {
16         printf("\aCould not open output file.\n");
17         exit (100);
18        } /* (if) */
19     while (fgets(str, sizeof (str), stdin))
20        fputs(str,   fpOut);
21
22     fclose (fpOut);
23     return 0;
24  }  /* main */
```

Program 11-6   Typewriter program

Program 11-6 Analysis   Note that we are reading the keyboard (*stdin*) using *fgets* (see Statement 19). This requires that we specify the file name, even though we do not have to declare it or open it. By using *fgets* we are able to ensure that the user will not overrun our string variable area (`str`). But even if the user enters too much data, nothing is lost. The data are left in the input stream buffer and are read in the next loop iteration.

This little program has two problems, one stylistic and one technical. The style problem is that it contains no instructions to the user, who must therefore guess what is to be done. This leads directly to the second problem. Some systems have a problem if the user should end the program with an end of file but no return. Depending on the system, the last line is lost or the system may just wait for an end of file at the beginning of the line. This problem can be prevented by adding good user instructions and a prompt.

Print Selected Lines

Program 11-7 reads text from the keyboard, line by line, and prints only the lines that start with uppercase letters. In this case we will write to the standard output (*stdout*) file. This will allow us to direct the output to the printer by assigning standard output to a printer. If standard output is assigned to the monitor, then the input and output will be interleaved, as shown in the results.

```
 1  /* Echo keyboard input that begins with a capital letter.
 2         Written by:
 3         Date written:
 4  */
 5  #include <ctype.h>
 6  #include <stdio.h>
 7
 8  int main (void)
 9  {
10  /* Local Definitions */
11     char strng[81];
12
13  /* Statements */
14     while (fgets (strng, sizeof(strng), stdin))
15         if (isupper(*strng))
16             fputs(strng, stdout);
17     return 0;
18  }   /* main */
```

```
Results:
   Now is the time
   Now is the time
   for all good students
   to come to the aid
   of their school.
   Amen
   Amen
```

Program 11-7   Print selected sentences

Program 11-7 Analysis   In this program, we use the character function, *isupper*, to determine which lines we want to write. The output lines are printed in color. Although we are guarding against excessive input, we do not flush the line. If the user enters very long lines, they will be obvious when the program runs.

If you use this program or any variation of it to write to your printer, you will need to assign the printer to the standard error file. Refer to the documentation for your system to determine how to do this.

Print File Double Spaced

Program 11-8 reads a single-spaced text from a file and prints the text double-spaced. In other words, it inserts a blank line after each line. In this program we direct the output to the standard output file, *stdout,* which is usually the monitor. To get the output to a printer, you need to redirect the output or assign *stdout* to the printer.

```
 1  /* Write file double spaced.
 2         Written by:
 3         Date:
 4  */
 5  #include <stdio.h>
 6
```

Program 11-8   Print file double-spaced

```
 7   int main (void)
 8   {
 9   /* Local Definitions */
10       char   strng[81];
11       FILE *textIn;
12
13   /* Statements */
14       if (!(textIn = fopen("P11-06.TXT", "r")))
15          {
16           printf("\aCan't open textdata\n");
17           exit (100);
18          } /* if */
19       while (fgets(strng, sizeof(strng), textIn))
20          {
21           fputs(strng, stdout);
22           putchar ('\n');
23          } /* while */
24
25       return 0;
26   } /* main */
```

Program 11-8   Print file double-spaced (continued)

Program 11-8 Analysis   Because we are reading data from a text file, we use the *fgets*
function. This function guarantees that we will not overrun our input string variable.
Note how we used the *sizeof* operator to set the maximum number of characters to be
read. Since *fgets* adds a newline character at the end of the data being read, we don't
need to worry about adding one when we write. After writing the data string, we use a
putchar to write the blank line.

11-4   ARRAYS OF STRINGS

When we discussed arrays of pointers in Chapter 10, we introduced the concept of a
ragged array. Ragged arrays are very common with strings. Consider, for example,
the need to store the days of the week in their textual format. We could create a two-
dimensional array of seven days by ten characters (Wednesday requires nine characters), but this wastes space.

It is much easier and more efficient to create a ragged array using an array of string
pointers. Each pointer points to a day of the week. In this way each string is independent,
but at the same time, they are grouped together through the array. In other words, although each string is independent, we can pass them as a group to a function by passing
only the name of the array of pointers. Program 11-9 demonstrates this structure.

```
1   /* This program demonstrates an array of pointers to strings.
2        Written by:
3        Date written:
4   */
```

Program 11-9   Print days of the week

```
 5   #include <stdio.h>
 6
 7   int main (void)
 8   {
 9      /* Local Definitions */
10      char   *pDays[7];
11      char   **pLast;
12      char   **pWalker;
13
14      /* Statements */
15      pDays[0] = "Sunday";
16      pDays[1] = "Monday";
17      pDays[2] = "Tuesday";
18      pDays[3] = "Wednesday";
19      pDays[4] = "Thursday";
20      pDays[5] = "Friday";
21      pDays[6] = "Saturday";
22
23      printf("The days of the week\n");
24      pLast = pDays + 6;
25      for (pWalker = pDays; pWalker <= pLast; pWalker++)
26           printf("%s\n", *pWalker);
27
28      return 0;
29   } /* main*/
```

Program 11-9   Print days of the week (continued)

Program 11-9 Analysis   To print the days of the week, we use a *for* loop. Since pDays is a pointer constant, we also need a pointer variable to use pointer arithmetic. The pointer variable must point to the strings through pDays, which means that it will be a pointer to a pointer, as seen in Statement 12.

A point of efficiency is the way we handled the limit test in the *for* loop. We could have simply coded it as

```
pWalker <= pDays + 6
```

This would require, however, that the ending address be recalculated for each limit test. (A good optimizing compiler should recognize that pDays is a pointer constant and that the calculation needs to be done only once, but we can't be sure that such efficient code would in fact be generated.) Therefore, we calculate the ending address just once, before the *while* loop, and then we can be sure that the limit test will be efficient.

Study this code carefully. Note first that pWalker is a pointer to a pointer to a character. Then notice how it is used in the *for* statement. It is initialized to the first element in pDays, then it is incremented until it is no longer less than or equal to pLast. Finally, note how it is used in the *printf* statement. The *printf* syntax requires that the variable list contain the address of the string to be printed. But pWalker is a pointer to an address that in turn points to the string (a pointer to a pointer). Therefore, when we dereference pWalker, we get the pointer to the string, which is what *printf* requires. This example is diagrammed in Figure 11-13.

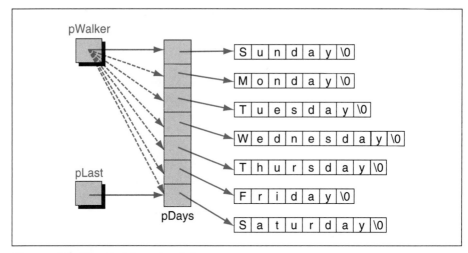

Figure 11-13 Pointers to strings

11-5   STRING MANIPULATION FUNCTIONS

Since a string is not a standard type, you cannot use it directly with most C operators. For example, to move one string to another, you must move the individual elements of the sending string to the receiving string. You cannot simply assign one string to another. If we were to write the move, we would have to put it in a loop.

C has provided a rich set of string functions. Besides making it easier for us to write programs, putting the string operations in functions provides the opportunity to make them more efficient when the operation is supported by hardware instructions. For example, computers often have a machine instruction that moves characters until a token, such as a null character, is reached. When this instruction is available, it allows a string to be moved in one instruction rather than in a loop.

All of the string functions, which are found in the string library (`<string.h>`), have the prefix `str` as shown below.

```
str… (parameters)
```

STRING LENGTH
(*strlen*)

The *strlen* function returns the length of a string, specified as the number of characters in the string excluding the null character. If the string is empty, it returns zero. The prototype statement is shown below.

```
int strlen (const char *string);
```

To demonstrate the use of *strlen,* let's write a program that reads text from the keyboard, line by line, and adds two blanks (spaces) at the beginning of each line before writing it to a file. In other words, it shifts each line two characters to the right. The code is shown in Program 11-10.

```
1  /* Typewriter program: adds two spaces to the left margin &
2     writes line to file
3        Written by:
```

Program 11-10 Add left margin

```
 4        Date:
 5   */
 6   #include  <stdio.h>
 7   #include  <string.h>
 8
 9   int main (void)
10   {
11   /* Local Definitions */
12      FILE *outFile;
13      char  strng[81];
14
15   /* Statements */
16      if (!(outFile = fopen("P11-07.TXT", "w")))
17         {
18          printf("\aCould not open output file.\n");
19          exit (100);
20         } /* (if) */
21
22      while (fgets(strng, sizeof(strng), stdin))
23         {
24          fputc(' ', outFile);
25          fputc(' ', outFile);
26          fputs(strng, outFile);
27          if (strng[strlen(strng) - 1] != '\n')
28              fputs("\n", outFile);
29         } /* while */
30      fclose (outFile);
31      return 0;
32   } /* main */
```

Program 11-10   Add left margin (continued)

Program 11-10 Analysis   To ensure that the user doesn't overrun the input area, we use the *fgets* function to read the keyboard. Some data may be left in the buffer, but we don't flush the buffer, because we want to write them to the file on the next line. Also, since *fputs* does not add a newline when it writes the file, we need to ensure that there will be a new line at the end of each line. Therefore, in Statement 27 we test the last character of the input string and if it isn't a newline, we write one.

   Because we want to add characters to the beginning of the line, we must use a character operation. The function *fputc* writes one character to a designated file. To insert two characters, therefore, we use it twice, and then use *fputs* to write the line read by *fgets*.

STRING COPY

C has two string copy functions. The first, **strcpy**, copies the contents of one string to another string. The second, **strncpy**, also copies the contents of one string to another, but it sets a maximum number of characters that can be moved. Therefore, *strncpy*, is a safer function.

strcpy

The *strcpy* function is a basic copy function that copies the contents of the from-string, including the null character, to the to-string. Its prototype is shown on the next page.

```
char *strcpy (char *to_strng, const char *from_strng);
```

If the from-string is longer than the to-string, the data in memory after the to-string are destroyed. It is your responsibility to ensure that the destination string array is large enough to hold the sending string. This should not be a problem, since you control the definition of both string variables. The address of the to-string is returned, which allows string functions to be used as arguments inside other string functions. We will demonstrate the use of these returned pointers later in the chapter.

Figure 11-14 shows two examples of string copy. In the first example, the source string is shorter than the destination variable. The result is that, after the string has been copied, the contents of the last three bytes of s1 are still unknown; s1 is a valid string, however.

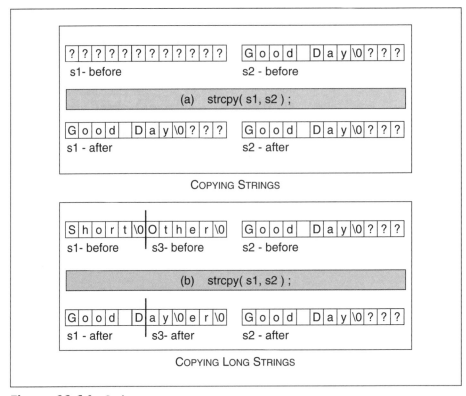

Figure 11-14 String copy

In the second example in Figure 11-14, the destination variable, s1, is only 6 bytes, which is too small to hold all the data being copied from s2 (8 bytes plus the delimiter). Furthermore, s1 is immediately followed by another string, s3. Even though s1 is too small, the entire string from s2 is copied, partially destroying the data in s3. Although s1 is a valid string, any attempt to access the data in s3 will result in a string containing only ay.

If the source and destination strings overlap—that is, if they share common memory locations, then the results of the copy are unpredictable. In Figure 11-14, this would occur if we tried to execute the following statement:

```
strcpy((s2 + 2), s2);          /* Invalid copy—overlap */
```

strncpy

Many of the problems associated with unequal string-array sizes can be controlled with *strncpy*, string-number copy. This function contains a parameter that specifies the *maximum* number of characters that can be moved at a time, as shown in its prototype statement below.

```
char *strncpy (char  *to_string,
               const  char *from_string,
               int    size);
```

In this function, `size` specifies the maximum number of characters that can be moved. Actually, the operation is a little more complex. If the source string is smaller than `size`, the entire string is copied and then null characters are placed in the destination string until exactly `size` characters have been filled. Thus, it is more correct to think of `size` as the destination characters that must be filled.

If the sending string is longer than `size`, the copy stops after `size` bytes have been copied. In this case, the destination variable will not be a valid string; it will not have a delimiter. On the other hand, the data following the destination variable will be intact, assuming the `size` was properly specified. Figure 11-15 shows the operation of *strncpy* under these two conditions.

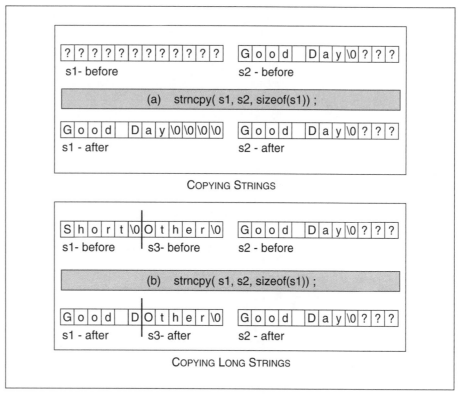

Figure 11-15 String-number copy

In the first example in Figure 11-15, the source string is smaller than the destination-string array. (Note how we coded the `size` using the *sizeof* operator. This is the preferred method to ensure that the destination variable is not overrun.) A close examination of the figure reveals that the last 3 bytes of the destination field have been set to null characters.

The second example in Figure 11-15 shows the problem that develops when the receiving-string array is too small. In this case, only six characters are copied, and s1 is an invalid string, because it does not have a delimiter. Any attempt to access s1 as a string will result in Good DOther as data. If this is a concern, you can easily test for a short copy and repair the string with the following statements:

```
if (*(s1 + (sizeof (s1) - 1)))          /* if not null */
    *(s1 + (sizeof (s1) - 1)) = '\0';
```

An even simpler solution is to move one less character than the maximum and then automatically place a null character in the last position. The code for this solution is shown below.

```
strncpy(s1, s2, sizeof(s1) -1);
*(s1 + (sizeof (s1) - 1)) = '\0';
```

Since the *strncpy* places null characters in all unfilled characters, you are guaranteed that the last character in the string array is a null character. If it is not, then the copy was short. By executing the above statements, you are assured that s1 will be a valid string, even if it doesn't have the desired contents. A closing note: If size is zero or negative, nothing is copied. The destination string is unchanged.

Let's write a small program that uses the *strcpy* function. Program 11-11 builds an array of strings in dynamic memory using the *calloc* function (see Chapter 10). It then fills the array from strings entered at the keyboard. When the array is full, it displays the strings to show that they were entered and stored correctly.

```
1   /* Build a dynamic array of names.
2          Written by:
3          Date:
4   */
5   #include <stdio.h>
6   #include <stdlib.h>
7   #include <string.h>
8
9   #define FLUSH while (getchar() != '\n')
10
11  int main (void)
12  {
13  /* Local Definitions */
14     char  input[81];
15     char **pNames;          /* array of pointers to char */
16
17     int size;
18     int namesIndex;
19
20  /* Statements */
21     printf("How many names do you plan to input? ");
22     scanf ("%d", &size);
```

Program 11-11 Build name array in heap

```
23    FLUSH;
24
25    /* Allocate array in heap.
26       One extra element added for loop control */
27    pNames = (char **) calloc (size + 1, sizeof (char *));
28    printf("Enter names. <EOF> to stop\n");
29
30    namesIndex = 0;
31    while (namesIndex < size
32        && fgets(input, sizeof(input), stdin))
33        {
34         *(pNames + namesIndex)  = (char *)
35              calloc (strlen(input) + 1, sizeof(char));
36         strcpy (*(pNames + namesIndex), input);
37         namesIndex++;
38        } /* while */
39
40    *(pNames + namesIndex) = NULL;
41    printf("\nYour names are: \n");
42    namesIndex = 0;
43    while (*(pNames + namesIndex))
44        {
45         printf("%3d: %s",
46              namesIndex, *(pNames + namesIndex) );
47         namesIndex++;
48        } /* while */
49
50    return 0;
51 } /* main */
```

```
Results:
How many names do you plan to input? 3
Enter names. <EOF> to stop
Tom
Rico
Huang

Your names are:
  0: Tom
  1: Rico
  2: Huang
```

Program 11-11   Build name array in heap (continued)

Program 11-11 Analysis   This little 51-line program contains some rather difficult code. To understand it better, let's look at the array structure, shown in Figure 11-16.

The identifier, pNames, is a pointer to an array of pointers to a character that is dynamically allocated from the heap. Then, as each name is read, space is allocated from the heap, and its pointer is placed in the next location in the pNames array. The only way to refer to the names is by dereferencing pNames. To access an individual element,

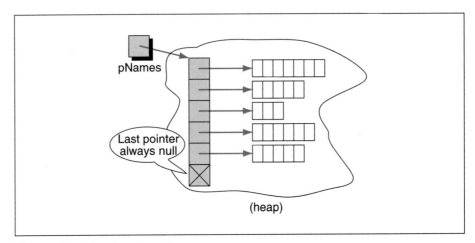

Figure 11-16 Structure for names array

we use `pNames` and index it to get to an individual string pointer in the array. This code is shown below. Since the first parameter in the string copy is a pointer to a string, only one dereference is required.

```
strcpy (*(pNames + namesIndex), input);
```

To build the pointer array, we use a *while* loop with two limit tests: end of file and a full array. Either condition will stop the loading of the array. To print the array, however, we only need to test for a null pointer, since the pointer array is allocated with one extra element. This is a common programming technique that makes processing arrays of pointers easier and more efficient.

STRING COMPARE
As with the string copy functions, C has two string compare functions. The first, *strcmp*, compares two strings until unequal characters are found or until the end of the strings is reached. The second, *strncmp*, compares until unequal characters are found, a specified number of characters have been tested, or until the end of a string is reached.

Both functions return an integer to indicate the results of the compare. Unfortunately, the results returned do not map well to the true–false logical values that we see in the *if...else* statement (see Chapter 5), so you will need to memorize a new set of rules:

1. If the two strings are equal, the return value is *zero*. Two strings are considered equal if they are the same length and all characters in the same relative positions are identical.
2. If the first parameter is less than the second parameter, the return value is *less than zero*. A string, `s1`, is less than another string, `s2`, if when comparing character by character the `s1` character is less than the `s2` character, or if the end of `s1` is reached and `s2` is not at its end.
3. If the first parameter is greater than the second parameter, the return value is *greater than zero*. A string, `s1`, is greater than another string, `s2`, if when comparing character by character the `s1` character is greater than the `s2` character, or if `s1` is not at its end and the end of `s2` is reached.

Note that the not-equal values are specified as a range. If the first parameter is less than the second parameter, the value can be any negative value. Likewise, if the first parameter is greater than the second parameter, the value can be any positive number. This differs from other situations, such as EOF, where we can count on one given value being returned.

Generally, the ANSI/ISO standard does not specify how a compiler is to be implemented; rather, it simply states what is to be accomplished. For the string compare functions, however, the standard recognizes the common implementations in effect when the standard was formulated. Most compilers—*but not all*—implement the string compare by scanning for a nonequal pair of characters up to the end of the first string and then subtracting the character in string2 from the character in string1. In addition to properly setting the return value for the function, this logic also has the effect of returning the binary difference between the two unequal characters.

The string compare operation is shown in Figure 11-17.

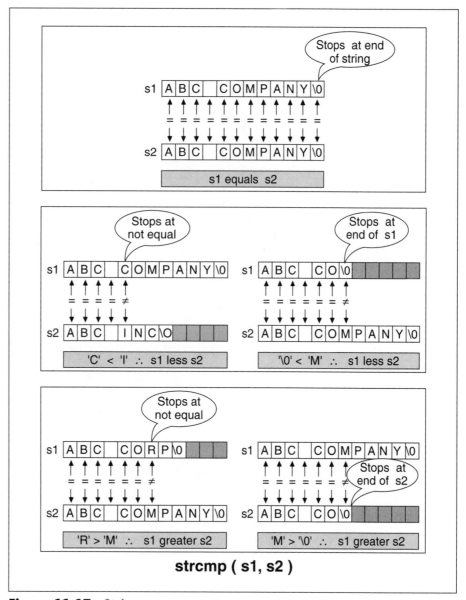

Figure 11-17   String compares

strcmp

The prototype statement for string compare is shown below.

```
int strcmp (const char *string1, const char *string2);
```

Since the equal return value is zero, to test for equality in a selection statement, we must negate the value returned by the string compare function. This is because zero is false in the selection statements and true in the string compare functions. For example, to compare two strings for equal, we must write the statement as shown below.

```
if (strcmp(str1, str2) == 0)
    /* strings are equal */
else
    /* strings are not equal */
```

The following statement tests whether the first string is less than the second string.

```
if (strcmp (string1, string2) < 0)
    /* string1 is less than string2 */
```

To test for `string1` greater than `string2`, use the following statement:

```
if (strcmp (string1, string2) > 0)
    /* string1 is greater than string2 */
```

You can also test for greater than or equal to with the following statement:

```
if (strcmp (string1, string2) >= 0)
    /* string1 is greater than or equal to string2 */
```

Alternatively, the same condition could be coded as shown below. This style has the disadvantage of being negative logic, which is often confusing to the reader (but never to the compiler).

```
if (!(strcmp (string1, string2) < 0))
    /* string1 is greater than or equal to string2 */
```

strncmp

The string number compare function—*strncmp*—tests two strings for a specified maximum number of characters (`size`). The prototype for *strncmp* is shown below.

```
int strncmp (const char *string1,
             const char *string2,
                   int    size);
```

In this function, `size` specifies the maximum number of characters to be compared in the first string. The *strncmp* compare logic is the same as seen in *strcmp,* except for the length limit.

Table 11-1 shows the results of comparing two strings using the *strncmp* function for various sizes..

string1	string2	Size	Results	Returns
`"ABC123"`	`"ABC123"`	8	equal	0
`"ABC123"`	`"ABC456"`	3	equal	0
`"ABC123"`	`"ABC456"`	4	string1 < string2	< 0
`"ABC123"`	`"ABC"`	3	equal	0
`"ABC123"`	`"ABC"`	4	string1 > string2	> 0
`"ABC"`	`"ABC123"`	3	equal	0
`"ABC123"`	`"123ABC"`	−1	equal	0

Table 11-1   Results for *strncmp*

STRING CONCATENATE

The string concatenate functions, called *strcat* and *strncat*, append one string to the end of a second string. Both functions return the address pointer to the destination string. The size of the destination string array is assumed to be large enough to hold the resulting string. If it isn't, the data at the end of the string array will be destroyed. As we saw with string copy, the results are unpredictable if the strings overlap

strcat

The prototype statement for string concatenation is shown below.

```
char *strcat (char *string1, const char *string2);
```

The function copies `string2` to the end of `string1`, beginning with `string1`'s delimiter. That is, the delimiter is replaced with the first character of `string2`. The delimiter from `string2` is copied to the resulting string to ensure that a valid string results. The length of the resulting string is the sum of the length of `string1` plus the length of `string2`. Figure 11-18a shows the operation of *strcat*.

strncat

The prototype statement for *strncat* is shown below.

```
char *strncat (          char   *string1,
               const     char   *string2,
                         int     size);
```

Figure 11-18b demonstrates the operation of the `strncat` function. If the length of `string2` is less than `size`, then the call works the same as the basic string concatenation described above. However, if the length of `string2` is greater than `size`, then only the number of characters specified by `size` are copied, and a null character is appended at the end.

If the value of `size` is zero or less than zero, then both strings are treated as null, and no characters are moved. The variable `string1` is unchanged.

CHARACTER IN STRING

Sometimes you need to know if a given character is contained in a string. If it is, you also want to know where it is; that is, you want a pointer to the located character. Two functions will search for a character in a string. The first function is called string character— *strchr*—and it searches for the first occurrence from the beginning of the string. The second, string rear character called, ***strrchr***, searches for the first occurrence beginning at the end and working toward the beginning.

Figure 11-18   String concatenation

In either case, if the character is located, the function returns a pointer to it. If the character is not in the string, the function returns a null pointer. The prototypes for these two functions are shown below.

```
char *strchr  (const char *string, int ch);
char *strrchr (const char *string, int ch);
```

Note that, as often is the case in the library functions, the character is typed as an integer. You don't need to worry about this. The compiler will implicitly cast any character types to integer types before the call. Figure 11-19 shows three examples of character-in-string calls.

In the first example, we locate the first *N* at the third position in the string (s1[2]). The pointer is then assigned to p1. In the second example, we locate the last *N* in the string at s1[12]. In the third example, we want to locate the second *N*. To do this, we need to start the search after the first *N*. Since we saved the location of the first *N*, this is easily done with a pointer and pointer arithmetic as shown.

STRING IN STRING   If we can locate a character in a string, we should be able to locate a string in a string. We can, but only from the beginning of the string. There is no function to locate a substring starting at the rear.

As you might expect, the function is named ***strstr***. Its prototype statement is shown below.

```
char *strstr (const char *string,
              const char *sub_string);
```

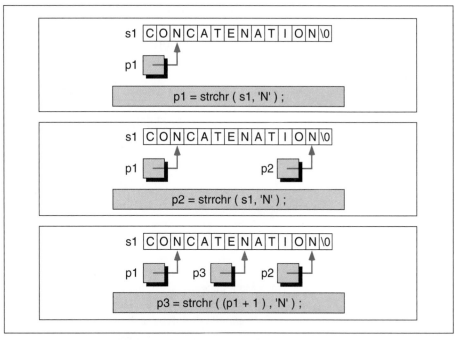

Figure 11-19   Character in string (*strchr*)

As you can see from the prototype, this function also returns a pointer to a character. This pointer identifies the beginning of the substring in the string. If the substring does not exist, then *strstr* returns a null pointer. Figure 11-20 demonstrates the operation of string in string.

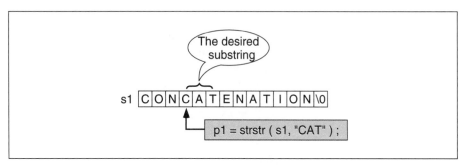

Figure 11-20   String in string

STRING SPAN

Very often, you need to locate one of a set of characters in a string. C provides two functions to do this. The first, ***strspn,*** locates the first character that does *not* match the string set. The second, ***strcspn,*** locates the first character that is in the set.

strspn

String span—*strspn*—searches the string, spanning characters that are in the set and stopping at the first character that is not in the set. It returns the number of characters that matched those in the set. If no characters match those in the set, it returns zero. The prototype statement is seen below.

```
int strspn(const char *string1, const char *set);
```

An example of *strspn* is shown in Figure 11-21. We use *strspn* to determine the number of characters that match the characters in the string set. In this example, len is set to five, since the first five characters match the set.

Figure 11-21   String span

strcspn

The second function is string complement span—*strcspn*—and it stops at the first character that matches one of the characters in the set. If none of the characters in the string match the set, it returns the length of the string. Figure 11-21 also contains an example of *strcspn*. Its prototype is shown below.

```
int strcspn(const char *string1, const char *set);
```

strpbrk

Similar to *strcspn*, the **strpbrk** function returns a pointer to the first character found in the set. Its prototype statement is shown below.[4]

```
char *strpbrk (const char *string1, const char *set);
```

strtok

The string token function, **strtok,** is used to locate substrings, called tokens, in a string. Its most common use is to parse a string into tokens, much as a compiler parses lines of code. Depending on how it is called, it either locates the first or the next token in a string. Its prototype statement is shown below.

```
char *strtok (char *string, const char *delimiters);
```

The first parameter is the string that is being parsed; the second parameter is a set of delimiters that will be used to parse the first string. If the first parameter contains an address, then *strtok* starts at that address, which is assumed to be the beginning of the string. It first skips over all leading delimiter characters. If all the characters in the string are delimiters, then it terminates and returns a null pointer. When it finds a nondelimiter character, it changes its search and skips over all characters that are not in the set; that is, it searches until it finds a delimiter. When a delimiter is found, it is changed to a null character ('\0'), which turns the token just parsed into a string.

If the first parameter is not a string, *strtok* assumes that it has already parsed part of the string and begins looking at the end of the previous string token for the next delimiter. When a delimiter is located, it again changes the delimiter to a null character, marking the end of the token, and returns a pointer to the new token string.

---

[4]Traditional C has a function called *strrpbrk* that returns a pointer to the last character found in the set. This function is not part of the ANSI/ISO C function library.

STRING TO NUMBER

The string library provides several functions that convert a string to a number. The two most important are string to long and string to double.

strtol

The string-to-long function, **strtol,** converts a string to a long integer.[5] It skips leading whitespace characters and stops with the first non-numeric character, which is considered to be the start of a trailing string. The address of the trailing string is stored in the second parameter, unless it is a null pointer. A third parameter determines the base of the string number. The function prototype statement is shown below.

```
long strtol (char *str, char **ptr, int base);
```

The base is determined by the following rules:

1. The base may be 0 or 2...35.
2. The letters a...z or A...Z represent the values 10...35. Only the numeric and alphabetic characters less than the base are permitted in any string.
3. If the base is 0, the format is determined by the string as follows:
   a. If the number begins 0x or 0X, the number is a hexadecimal constant.
   b. If the first digit is 0 and the second digit is not x or X, the number is an octal constant.
   c. If the first digit is a nonzero, the number is a decimal constant.

If the string does not begin with a valid number, zero is returned and the trailing string pointer is set to the beginning of the string. Program 11-12 demonstrates the use of *strtol*.

```
 1  /* Demonstrate string to long function.
 2         Written by:
 3         Date:
 4  */
 5  #include <stdio.h>
 6  #include <string.h>
 7
 8  int main (void)
 9  {
10  /* Local Definitions */
11      long    num;
12      char    *ptr;
13
14  /* Statements */
15      num = strtol ("12345 Decimal constant: ", &ptr, 0);
16      printf("%s %ld\n", ptr, num);
17
18      num = strtol ("11001 Binary constant : ", &ptr, 2);
19      printf("%s %ld\n", ptr, num);
20
21      num = strtol ("13572 Octal constant  : ", &ptr, 8);
```

Program 11-12   Demonstrate *strtol*

---

[5]To convert a string to an unsigned long integer, use *strtoul*, which is identical except for the type returned.

```
22      printf("%s %ld\n", ptr, num);
23
24      num = strtol (" 7AbC Hex constant     : ", &ptr, 16);
25      printf("%s %ld\n", ptr, num);
26
27      num = strtol ("11001 Base 0-Decimal  : ", &ptr, 0);
28      printf("%s %ld\n", ptr, num);
29
30      num = strtol ("01101 Base 0-Octal    : ", &ptr, 0);
31      printf("%s %ld\n", ptr, num);
32
33      num = strtol ("0x7AbC Base 0-Hex     : ", &ptr, 0);
34      printf("%s %ld\n", ptr, num);
35
36      num = strtol ("Invalid input    : ", &ptr, 0);
37      printf("%s %ld\n", ptr, num);
38
39      return 0;
40  }   /* main */
```

```
Results:
    Decimal constant:  12345
    Binary constant :  25
    Octal constant  :  6010
    Hex constant    :  31420
    Base 0-Decimal  :  11001
    Base 0-Octal    :  577
    Base 0-Hex      :  31420
    Invalid input   :  0
```

Program 11-12 Demonstrate *strtol* (continued)

Program 11-12 Analysis   The first thing to note in this program is that the address of the character pointer must be passed to *strtol*. If this surprises you, go back and look at the prototype statement again. Note that the declaration of `ptr` has two asterisks.

Observe that the pointer is set to the first character after the last valid digit. In our example, this character was always a space. If there were no characters after the last digit, the pointer would point to the string delimiter, resulting in a null string.

strtod

The string-to-double function is similar to the string-to-long function, except that it does not have a base. Its prototype statement is seen below.

```
double strtod (char *str, char **ptr);
```

The numeric string must be a floating-point in either decimal or scientific notation. The valid numeric values in the string are the digits, the plus and minus signs, and the letter *e* or *E* in the exponent. After using the longest possible sequence of digits and characters to convert the string to a number, *strtod* sets the pointer to the address of the next character in the string. If no characters are present, the pointer is set to the string delimiter. As with string-to-long, if the number is invalid, zero is returned and the pointer is set to the beginning of the string.

STRING EXAMPLES

In this section, we discuss two functions that use string functions. The first uses *strtok* to parse an algebraic expression. The second uses string input/output functions and several string manipulation functions to compare strings.

Parsing Tokens

Assume we want to parse a string containing a simple algebraic expression as shown below.

```
sum = sum + 10;
```

Each token in this simple expression is separated by whitespace. Our program will identify each token and print it out. The step-by-step parsing is shown in Figure 11-22. The code is shown in Program 11-13.

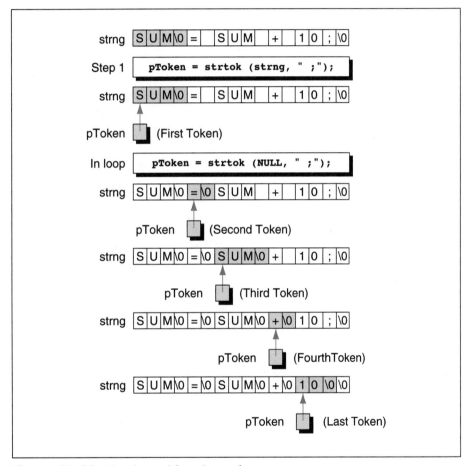

Figure 11-22 Parsing with string token

```
1  /* Sample program to parse a simple algebraic expression.
2        Written by:
3        Date:
4  */
5  #include <stdio.h>
6  #include <string.h>
```

Program 11-13 Parsing a string with *strtok*

```
 7
 8   int main (void)
 9   {
10   /* Local Definitions */
11       char *strng = "sum = sum + 10;";
12       char *pToken;
13       int   tokenCount;
14
15   /* Statements */
16       tokenCount = 0;
17       pToken = strtok (strng, " ;");
18
19       while (pToken)
20          {
21           tokenCount++;
22           printf("Token %2d contains %s\n",
23                   tokenCount, pToken);
24           pToken = strtok (NULL, " ;");
25          } /* while */
26
27       printf("\nEnd of tokens\n");
28       return 0;
29   }  /* main */
```

```
    Results:
        Token  1 contains sum
        Token  2 contains =
        Token  3 contains sum
        Token  4 contains +
        Token  5 contains 10

        End of tokens
```

Program 11-13   Parsing a string with *strtok* (continued)

Program 11-13 Analysis   Since the first call to *strtok* must contain the address of the string, it is coded *before* the loop. If the string contains at least one token, the first call will return a valid address and the *while* loop will print it and parse out the remaining tokens. Note that the delimiter set includes the semicolon as well as the blank between tokens. The semicolon serves as the last token in the string.

Compare Packed Strings

When working with strings, you will often find that two strings are logically the same but physically different to the computer. For example, consider a program that generates mailing labels. Often a name is put into a mailing list with an extra space or other character that prevents it from being matched to an existing name. One way to eliminate such errors is to compare only the letters of the names by removing everything except alphabetic characters. Program 11-14 shows a function that compares two strings after packing the data so that only letters are left.

```
 1   /* This program tests the string packed compare function.
 2          Written by:
 3          Date:
 4   */
 5   #include <stdio.h>
 6   #include <string.h>
 7
 8   #define ALPHA \
 9       "ABCDEFGHIJKLMNOPQRSTUVWXYZabcdefghijklmnopqrstuvwxyz"
10
11   /* Prototype Declarations */
12   int  strCmpPk (char *S1, char *S2);
13   void strPk    (char *s1, char *s2);
14
15   int main (void)
16   {
17   /* Local Definitions */
18      int  cmpResult;
19      char s1[80];
20      char s2[80];
21
22   /* Statements */
23      printf("Please enter first string:\n");
24      fgets (s1, 80, stdin);
25      s1[strlen(s1) - 1] = '\0';
26
27      printf("Please enter second string:\n");
28      fgets (s2, 80, stdin);
29      s2[strlen(s2) - 1] = '\0';
30
31      cmpResult = strCmpPk (s1, s2);
32      if (cmpResult < 0)
33         printf("string1 < string2\n");
34      else if (cmpResult > 0)
35         printf("string1 > string2\n");
36      else
37         printf("string1 == string2\n");
38
39      return 0;
40   }  /* main */
41
42   /* ================== strCmpPk ==================
43      Packs two strings and then compares them.
44         Pre    s1 and s2 contain strings
45         Post   returns result of strcmp of packed strings
46   */
47   int strCmpPk (char *s1,
48                 char *s2)
49   {
50   /* Local Definitions */
```

Program 11-14 Compare packed string function

```
51        char s1In [80];
52        char s1Out[81];
53        char s2In [80];
54        char s2Out[81];
55
56   /* Statements */
57        strncpy (s1In, s1, sizeof(s1In) - 1);
58        strncpy (s2In, s2, sizeof(s2In) - 1);
59        strPk (s1In, s1Out);
60        strPk (s2In, s2Out);
61        return (strcmp (s1Out, s2Out));
62   }   /* strCmpPk */
63
64   /* ================== strPk ==================
65      Deletes all non-alpha characters from s1 and
66      copies to s2.
67          Pre    s1 is a string
68          Post   packed string in s2
69                 s1 destroyed
70   */
71   void strPk (char *s1,
72               char *s2)
73   {
74   /* Local Definitions */
75        int strSize;
76
77   /* Statements */
78        *s2 = '\0';
79        while (*s1 != '\0')
80            {
81            /* Find non-alpha character & replace */
82            strSize = strspn(s1, ALPHA);
83            s1[strSize] = '\0';
84            strncat (s2, s1, 79 - strlen(s2));
85            s1 += strSize + 1;
86            } /* while */
87        return;
88   }   /* strPk */
```

```
Results:
   Please enter first string:
   a b!c 234d
   Please enter second string:
   abcd
   string1 == string2

   Please enter first string:
   abcd
   Please enter second string:
   aabb
   string1 > string2
```

Program 11-14 Compare packed string function (continued)

Program 11-14 Analysis   To test the string compare, we need to write a test driver. Since the test driver is throwaway code, we have coded the test logic in `main`.

Statement 8 contains a C language construct that we have not used before, the *statement continuation*. When a statement does not fit on a line, it can be continued by putting an escape character (\) immediately before the end of the line. This is consistent with the meaning of the escape character; in this case, it means escape the end of line that follows; it is not really an end of line. This allows us to continue the *define* statement on the next line.

Since we are passing addresses to strings, we need to be careful that we don't destroy the original data. The first thing we do in `strCmpPk`, therefore, is to use *strncpy* to copy the input string to a work area. Once we have protected the original data, we pack the two strings to be compared and then use the *strcmp* function to determine if the reformatted data are equal.

The `strPk` function merits a little discussion. It uses a *while* loop to process the input string. Each iteration of the loop scans the valid characters, as defined in `ALPHA`, looking for invalid data. When `strPk` finds an invalid character—and there will always be at least one, the input string delimiter—it (1) replaces that character with a string delimiter, (2) concatenates the input string to the output string, and then (3) adjusts the input string pointer to one past the last scanned character. This is necessary to point it to the data beyond the string just copied.

But what if the pointer adjustment puts it beyond the end of the input data? In that case, we will have a delimiter, because we used *strncpy* to copy the data from the original input, and it pads the output string with delimiters. Therefore, the character after the original string delimiter is another delimiter. Note that we made the output area one character larger than the input area to provide for this extra delimiter even with a full string.

At least three test cases are required to test the program. We show two of them in the result. In addition to an equal and greater-than result, you should conduct at least one less-than test case.

11-6   MEMORY FORMATTING

Two string functions are closely related to the *scanf* and *printf* functions but do not read or write files. Rather, they read and write strings in memory. They are often used with the *gets* and *puts* functions to give the programmer more control over the formatting. Additionally, if a string is completely read in its character format and then the data are converted to their internal formats, the input function is more efficient. Similarly, if the data are converted to text format and then written with the put-string function, the output is more efficient.

SCAN MEMORY STRING (*sscanf*)

The string scan format function is called ***sscanf***. The *sscanf* function scans a string as though the data were coming from the keyboard. Just like *scanf*, it requires a format string. All format codes valid for *scanf* are usable. The *sscanf* function also returns the number of variables successfully formatted. If *sscanf* reaches the end of a string before all the format string conversion codes have been used—that is, if it attempts to "read" beyond the end of string—it operates as though an end-of-file were reached.

The prototype statement for *sscanf* is shown below.

```
int sscanf (char *str, const char *format_string, …);
```

The first parameter specifies the string holding the data to be scanned. The ellipsis (...) indicates that a variable number of pointers identify the fields into which the formatted data will be placed.

Let's demonstrate the use of *sscanf* with an example. Assume that we have a text file that contains a name terminated with a semicolon, a four-digit student number, an exam score, and a character grade. Each field is separated from the rest by at least one blank or tab, and each line represents a different student. We will read each line using the *fgets* function and then parse it using *sscanf.* This situation is seen in Figure 11-23. A data sample is shown below.

```
Einstein, Albert; 1234 67 D
```

Figure 11-23   *sscanf* operation

In this problem, we want to treat the name and student number as strings, the score as an integer, and the grade as a character. We therefore construct the following format string:

```
"%25[^;]%*c%4s%d%*[^ABCDF]%c"
```

Let's examine each format code individually. First, we are expecting a string of up to 25 characters terminated by a semicolon. Note that we used the edit set with a terminating token of a semicolon. If there is no semicolon, our program will abort, but since the data come from a file, we can assume that they have been properly formatted.

Following the edit set that reads to a semicolon is a format code that will read and discard one character. The asterisk is a flag indicating that the character is not to be stored. This code is necessary because the terminating semicolon from the string remains in the input string. We need to read and discard it.

The third format code is a simple four-character string. Any leading whitespace will be discarded with the string token(s). Likewise, the third field, the score, will be converted to an integer format after the leading whitespace is discarded.

Parsing the grade is a little more difficult. We can have one or more whitespaces between the numeric grade and the alphabetic grade, but we must dispose of them ourselves, because the character token (c) does not discard whitespace. Our solution is to use an edit set with the suppress flag (`*`) to discard all characters up to the grade. Again, we use the negation to set the terminating character. Having discarded all the leading whitespace, we can now format the grade with a character token.

Using our example above, we can code the *sscanf* call as shown below.

```
sscanf(strIn, "%25[^;]%*c%4s%d%*[^ABCDF]%c",
       name, stuNo, &score, &grade);
```

Note that this code has six format codes but only four variables because the second and fifth fields have their formatting suppressed.

---

sscanf is a one-to-many function.
It splits one string into many variables.

Using *sscanf* for Data Validation

The primary purpose of *sscanf* is to give the programmer more control over the formatting of data from a text file. Consider the situation where a user at a keyboard is entering several pieces of data. Rather than receiving a report that some unknown error occurred, it would be much better to receive a report about specific errors with a meaningful error message. To demonstrate this concept, let's write a program that uses *sscanf* to read and validate name input. The program reads the name as a string and then uses two functions to format the name into last name and first name variables. Of course, in a large program, they would be just two of several functions to validate and reformat the input. The code is seen in Program 11-15.

```
 1  /* Demonstrate memory formatting function: sscanf.
 2         Written by:
 3         Date:
 4  */
 5  #include <stdio.h>
 6  #include <string.h>
 7  #define NAME_SIZE 26
 8
 9  /* Prototype Statements */
10  char *getLast  (char *pInput, char *pLast);
11  char *getFirst (char *pInput, char *pFirst);
12
13  int main (void)
14  {
15  /* Local Definitions */
16     char   input[81];
17     char  *pInput;
18
19     char   last [NAME_SIZE];
20     char   first[NAME_SIZE];
21
22  /* Statements */
23     printf("Enter: last-name, first-name;\n");
24     fgets (input, sizeof(input), stdin);
```

Program 11-15 Memory formatting

```
25
26       pInput = input;
27       pInput = getLast (pInput, last);
28
29       if (pInput)
30          {
31           printf("Last Name : %s\n", last);
32           pInput = getFirst (pInput, first);
33           if (pInput)
34               printf("First Name: %s\n", first);
35          } /* if */
36       return 0;
37  }   /* main */
38
39  /* ==================== getLast ====================
40     Verify format of name, and parse into variables.
41         Pre    pInput is pointer to string to be checked
42                pLast is pointer to last name variable
43         Post   last name validated and formatted
44                If no errors, returns pointer to first name
45                If errors, returns null pointer
46  */
47  char *getLast (char *pInput,
48                 char *pLast)
49  {
50  /* Local Definitions */
51     char *pEndLast;
52
53  /* Statements */
54     /* Get last name */
55     pEndLast = strchr(pInput, ',');
56     if (!pEndLast)
57        {
58         printf("\aNo comma in name.\n");
59         return NULL;
60        } /* if */
61     else
62        if (pEndLast - pInput > NAME_SIZE - 1)
63           {
64            printf("\aLast Name too big\n");
65            return NULL;
66           } /* if */
67        else
68           sscanf(pInput, "%[^,]", pLast);
69
70     return pEndLast + 1;
71  }   /* getLast */
72
73  /* ==================== getFirst ==================
```

Program 11-15 Memory formatting (continued)

```
74        Verify format of name, and parse into variables.
75            Pre    pInput is pointer to string with input
76                   pFirst is pointer to first name variable
77            Post   first name validated and formatted
78                   If no errors, returns pointer to first name
79                   If errors, returns null pointer
80  */
81  char *getFirst (char *pInput,
82                  char *pFirst)
83  {
84  /* Local Definitions */
85     char *pEndFirst;
86
87  /* Statements */
88     /* Get first name - Eliminate leading spaces */
89     while (*pInput == ' ')
90        pInput++;
91
92     pEndFirst = strchr(pInput, ';');
93     if (!pEndFirst)
94        {
95         printf("\aNo semicolon in name.\n");
96         return NULL;
97        } /* if */
98     else
99        if (pEndFirst - pInput > NAME_SIZE - 1)
100           {
101            printf("\aFirst Name too big\n");
102            return NULL;
103           } /* if */
104        else
105           sscanf(pInput, "%[^;]", pFirst);
106
107     return pEndFirst + 1;
108  }  /* getFirst */
```

```
    Results:
       Enter: last-name, first-name;
       Washington, George;
       Last Name : Washington
       First Name: George

    Results with error:
       Enter: last-name, first-name;
       Arnold,Benedict
       Last Name : Arnold
       No semicolon in name.
```

Program 11-15 Memory formatting (continued)

Program 11-15 Analysis   Program 11-15 contains four highly descriptive error messages. Note that each error message starts with an audible alert (\a) to get the user's attention. A production program would undoubtedly have many more data validation tests. For example, you could check to make sure the names start with an uppercase character. But even this short program demonstrates how much more control the programmer has over the input by using the *fgets* and *sscanf* functions together.

FORMAT MEMORY STRING (*sprintf*)

The string print format function—called ***sprintf***—follows the rules of *printf*. Rather than sending the data to a file, however, it simply "writes" them to a string. When all data have been formatted to the string, a terminating null character is added to make the result a valid string. If an error is detected, *sprintf* returns any negative value, traditionally EOF. If the formatting is successful, it returns the number of characters formatted, not counting the terminating null character. The *sprintf* operation is shown in Figure 11-24.

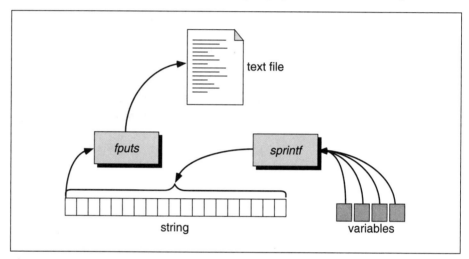

Figure 11-24   *sprintf* operation

The prototype statement for *sprintf* is shown below.

```
int sprintf (      char *out_string,
                const char *format_string, …);
```

The first parameter is a pointer to a string that will contain the formatted output. The format string is the same as *printf* and follows all of the same rules. The ellipse (...) contains the fields that correspond to the format codes in the format string.

> *sprintf* is a many-to-one function.
> It joins many pieces of data into one string.

sprintf Example

Let's look at a useful function that formats dollar output. Given a floating-point value, format it for text output using a dollar sign and commas. Since the logic is somewhat complex, we include pseudocode for it in Program 11-16.

You can write this function in several ways. For our solution, we use the *sprintf* and several string functions. Three function parameters are required: the number to be formatted, the address of a format area, and the maximum width of the output area. The function is shown in Program 11-17.

```
1 Copy "$" to output area.
2 Separate number into dollars string and cents string
3 Calculate number of commas needed
4 If number of digits + commas > width
  1 return error
5 else
  1 format number
6 return no error
```

Program 11-16   Pseudocode for format dollars

```c
 1 | /* Test driver for formatDlr.
 2 |        Date written:
 3 |        Written by:
 4 | */
 5 | #include <stdio.h>
 6 | #include <string.h>
 7 | #include <stdlib.h>
 8 | #include <math.h>
 9 |
10 | #define COMMA ","
11 |
12 | /* Prototype Declarations */
13 | int formatDlr (double num, char *out, int width);
14 |
15 | int main (void)
16 | {
17 | /* Local Definitions */
18 |    double amt;
19 |    char   outArea[36];
20 |
21 | /* Statements */
22 |    printf("Enter a floating-point number: ");
23 |    scanf ("%lf", &amt);
24 |
25 |    if (formatDlr (amt, outArea, 36))
26 |        printf("Your number is: %s\n", outArea);
27 |    else
28 |        printf("\a\nNumber could not be formatted.\n");
29 |
30 |    return 0;
31 | }  /* main */
32 |
33 | /* ==================== formatDlr ====================
34 |    Format float as dollar amount with $ and commas.
35 |       Pre   num is a floating point number
36 |             out is address of a string output area
37 |             width is maximum size of the output
38 |       Post  num has been formatted and one returned
```

Program 11-17   Format dollars

```
39                   or if errors detected, zero returned and
40                            out is undefined.
41  */
42  int formatDlr (double num,
43                 char  *out,
44                 int    wdth)
45  {
46  /* Local Definitions */
47     char *dlrs;                          /* Dollars string */
48     char *pDlrs;
49     char *pCents;
50     int   numCommas;
51     int   result;
52     int   size;
53
54  /* Statements */
55     dlrs = (char *)malloc (wdth + 1);
56     strcpy (out, "$");
57     sprintf(dlrs, "%.2f", num);
58     pDlrs     = dlrs;
59     strtok (dlrs, ".");
60     pCents    = strtok (NULL, ".");
61     numCommas = (ceil (strlen (dlrs) / 3.0) - 1);
62
63     if ((strlen (dlrs) + numCommas + 4) > wdth)
64        result = 0;
65     else
66        {
67         switch (numCommas)
68            {
69             case 5:        /* ddd,ddd,ddd,ddd,ddd,ddd.dd */
70                    size    = strlen (pDlrs) - 15;
71                    strncat (out, pDlrs, size);
72                    strcat  (out, COMMA);
73                    pDlrs   = pDlrs + size;
74             case 4:            /* ddd,ddd,ddd,ddd,ddd.dd */
75                    size    = strlen (pDlrs) - 12;
76                    strncat (out, pDlrs, size);
77                    strcat  (out, COMMA);
78                    pDlrs   = pDlrs + size;
79             case 3:                /* ddd,ddd,ddd,ddd.dd */
80                    size    = strlen (pDlrs) - 9;
81                    strncat (out, pDlrs, size);
82                    strcat  (out, COMMA);
83                    pDlrs   = pDlrs + size;
84             case 2:                    /* ddd,ddd,ddd.dd */
85                    size    = strlen (pDlrs) - 6;
86                    strncat (out, pDlrs, size);
87                    strcat  (out, COMMA);
```

Program 11-17 Format dollars (continued)

```
 88                          pDlrs   = pDlrs + size;
 89            case 1:                              /* ddd,ddd.dd */
 90                          size = strlen (pDlrs) - 3;
 91                          strncat (out, pDlrs, size);
 92                          strcat  (out, COMMA);
 93                          pDlrs = pDlrs + size;
 94            default:                             /*ddd.dd */
 95                          size = strlen (pDlrs) ;
 96                          strncat (out, pDlrs, size);
 97                          strcat  (out, ".");
 98                          strcat  (out, pCents);
 99              } /* switch */
100          } /* else */
101      free (dlrs);
102      return 1;
103  }  /* formatDlr */
```

```
    Results:
        Enter a floating-point number: 123456789012.987
        Your number is: $123,456,789,012.99

        Enter a floating-point number: 12345678.91
        Your number is: $12,345,678.91

        Enter a floating-point number: 1.23333
        Your number is: $1.23
```

Program 11-17 Format dollars (continued)

Program 11-17 Analysis   This useful function has several noteworthy points. At the beginning of the function, we use *sprintf* to format the number into a work area (`dlrs`) and then use *strtok* to format the work area into a dollars string and a cents string. Once we know how many digits are in the dollars string, we can calculate the number of commas that will be needed and make sure the output width is large enough to hold all the output.

Once the preliminary calculations have been verified, we use a switch to format the data. Note that the program has no *break* statements; each entry point flows into the next.

The logic in each of the *case* statements is similar. We determine how many digits are to be printed and concatenate them to the output area along with a comma. We then adjust the formatted input pointer by the number of characters copied to the output area.

Finally, note how we used comments to indicate the formatting in each of the *case* statements. They make it easy to see exactly what is being formatted as we fall through the formatting code.

We show three test cases. The complete set of test cases formats all possibilities from zero dollars to a number too large to be formatted. By studying the code, can you tell what will be printed if the value of the number is zero dollars and ten cents?[6]

---

[6]The answer is $0.10.

11-7 A PROGRAMMING EXAMPLE—MORSE CODE

Morse code, patented by Samuel F. B. Morse in 1837, is the language that was used to send messages by telegraph from the middle of the nineteenth century until the advent of the modern telephone and today's computer-controlled communications systems. In Morse code, each letter in the alphabet is represented by a series of dots and dashes, as shown in Table 11-2.

Letter	Code	Letter	Code	Letter	Code	Letter	Code
A	.-	H	....	O	---	V	...-
B	-...	I	..	P	.--.	W	.--
C	-.-.	J	.---	Q	--.-	X	-..-
D	-..	K	-.-	R	.-.	Y	-.--
E	.	L	.-..	S	...	Z	--..
F	..-.	M	--	T	-		
G	--.	N	-.	U	..-		

Table 11-2 Morse code

Program 11-18 encodes (converts) a line of text to Morse code and decodes (converts) Morse code to a line of text. We use a two-dimensional array of pointers in which each row has two string pointers, one to a string containing English characters and one to a string containing the corresponding Morse code. Note that the pointers are stored in the program's memory, while the strings are stored in the heap. The array structure is shown in Figure 11-25.

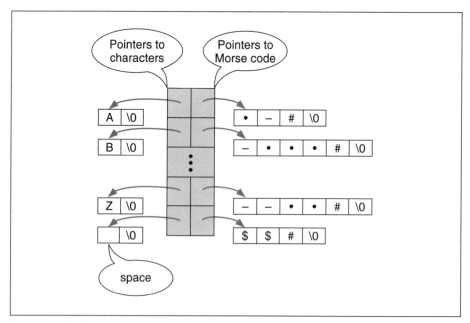

Figure 11-25 Character to Morse code structure

Each column has 27 pointers. Each pointer in the first column points to a string of length one, which contains one English letter (uppercase). Each pointer in the second column points to a string of varying size, a ragged array, which contains the corresponding Morse code for the English letter.

The program is menu driven. The menu, which is shown in Figure 11-26, has three options: encode English to Morse code, decode Morse code to English, and quit.

Figure 11-26   Morse code menu

The program begins by initializing the conversion table. It then displays the menu and loops until the user quits. Each loop either encodes a line of English text or decodes a line of Morse code. The only allowable characters are the alphabetic characters and spaces. When Morse code is entered, each coded character is terminated by a pound sign (#). Morse code space is represented by two dollar signs ($$). The complete design is shown in Figure 11-27.

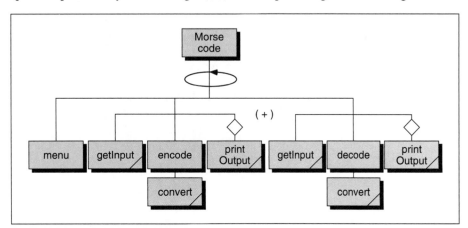

Figure 11-27   Morse code program design

If the encode or decode function detects an error—such as an invalid character or an invalid Morse code sequence—it returns an error code, and the calling program prints an error message.

The solution, as shown in Program 11-18, uses three arrays. The first is the encode/decode (encDec) array. As seen in Figure 11-25, this is a two-dimensional array of pointers to English and Morse code values. The second array is an array of 81 characters to hold the input line. The third is an array of 81 characters to hold the output line. To ensure that we do not overrun the output line, we limit the input string to 16 characters when we are reading English text. When appropriate, we provide some analysis to points in the individual functions.

```
 1  /* Convert English to Morse code and Morse code to English.
 2        Written by:
 3        Date Written:
 4  */
 5  #include <stdio.h>
 6  #include <stdlib.h>
 7  #include <string.h>
 8  #include <ctype.h>
 9
10  #define FLUSH while(getchar() != '\n')
11  #define STR_LEN 81
12
13  /* Prototype Declarations */
14  char menu            (void);
15  void getInput        (char *inStr);
16  void printOutput     (char *inStr, char *outSt);
17  int  encode          (char *(*encDec)[2],
18                        char *inStr,
19                        char *outStr);
20  int  decode          (char *(*encDec)[2],
21                        char *inStr,
22                        char *outStr);
23  int  convert         (char *(*encDec)[2],
24                        char *s1,
25                        int   col,
26                        char *s2);
27
28  int main (void)
29  {
30  /* Local Definitions */
31     char *encDec [27][2] =
32        {
33         { "A", ".-#" },
34         { "B", "-...#" },
35         { "C", "-.-.#" },
36         { "D", "-..#" },
37         { "E", ".#" },
38         { "F", "..-.#" },
39         { "G", "--.#" },
40         { "H", "....#" },
41         { "I", "..#" },
42         { "J", ".---#" },
43         { "K", "-.-#" },
44         { "L", ".-..#" },
45         { "M", "--#" },
46         { "N", "-.#" },
47         { "O", "---#" },
48         { "P", ".--.#" },
49         { "Q", "--.-#" },
```

Program 11-18 Morse code: *main*

```
50        { "R", ".-.#" },
51        { "S", "...#" },
52        { "T", "-#" },
53        { "U", "..-#" },
54        { "V", "...-#" },
55        { "W", ".--#" },
56        { "X", "-..-#" },
57        { "Y", "-.--#" },
58        { "Z", "--..#" },
59        { " ", "$$#" },
60     }; /* Encode / Decode array */
61  char inStr  [STR_LEN];
62  char outStr [STR_LEN];
63  char option;
64  int  done = 0;
65
66 /* Statements */
67  while (!done)
68     {
69      option = menu ();
70      switch (option)
71         {
72          case 'E' :
73                 getInput (inStr);
74                 if (!encode (encDec, inStr, outStr))
75                     {
76                      printf ("Error! Try again");
77                      break;
78                     } /* if */
79                 printOutput (inStr, outStr);
80                 break;
81          case 'D' : getInput (inStr);
82                 if (!decode (encDec, inStr, outStr))
83                     {
84                      printf ("Error! Try again");
85                      break;
86                     } /* if */
87                 printOutput (inStr, outStr);
88                 break;
89          default :
90                 done = 1;
91                 printf("\nEnd of Morse Code.\n");
92                 break;
93         } /* switch */
94     } /* while */
95  return 0;
96 }  /* main */
```

Program 11-18   Morse code: *main* (continued)

Program 11-18 Analysis   The function main is rather straightforward. Although it could be argued that the *switch* statements should be in a subfunction, we place it here because it controls the entire program. One noteworthy point is the default condition. We test for only two options, encode and decode. If it is neither, then we assume quit. We can do this because we validate the option in menu (see Program 11-19). At this point in the program, therefore, option can be one of only three values. We test for two and default the third.

```
 1  /* ==================== menu ====================
 2     Display menu of choices; return selected character.
 3        Pre    nothing
 4        Post   returns validated option code
 5  */
 6  char menu (void)
 7  {
 8  /* Local Definitions */
 9     char   option;
10     int    validData;
11
12  /* Statements */
13     printf("\t\t\tM E N U \n");
14     printf("\t\tE)   encode \n");
15     printf("\t\tD)   decode \n");
16     printf("\t\tQ)   quit \n");
17
18     do
19       {
20        printf ("\nEnter option: press return key: ");
21        option = toupper (getchar());
22        FLUSH;
23        if (option == 'E' || option == 'D' || option == 'Q')
24           validData = 1;
25        else
26           {
27            validData = 0;
28            printf("\aEnter only one option\n");
29            printf(" \tE, D, or Q\n ");
30           } /* else */
31       } while (!validData);
32     return option;
33  } /* menu */
```

Program 11-19   Morse Code: *menu*

Program 11-19 Analysis   The menu function in Program 11-19 displays the options and reads the user's choice. It then validates the choice and if invalid, displays an error message and asks for the option again. Although it is always good design to validate the user input, it must be validated in the correct place. Since menu is communicating with the user, this is the logical place to do the validation. One more point: As the option is read, it is converted to uppercase. Not only does this make the validation simpler, but it also simplifies the *switch* statement in *main*. Whenever you have a single character code, convert it to uppercase or lowercase for processing in the program.

The input string is read in Program 11-20.

```
 1  /* ================== getInput ==================
 2     Reads input string to be encoded or decoded.
 3        Pre    inStr is a pointer to the input area
 4        Post   string read into input area
 5  */
 6  void getInput (char *inStr)
 7  {
 8  /* Local Statements */
 9     printf ("\nPlease enter line of text to be coded: \n");
10     fgets  (inStr, STR_LEN, stdin);
11
12     /* Eliminate newline in input string */
13     *(inStr-1 + strlen(inStr)) = '\0';
14
15     if (isalpha(*inStr) && strlen(inStr) > 16)
16        {
17         /* Exceeds English input length */
18         printf("\n***WARNING: Input length exceeded: ");
19         printf("Only 16 chars will be encoded.\a\a\n");
20         *(inStr + 16) = '\0';
21        } /* if */
22     return;
23  } /* getInput */
```

Program 11-20 Morse code: get input

Program 11-20 Analysis   Note that to prevent a runaway string in `getInput` we use the *fgets* function and specify the maximum number of characters in the string area. This function creates a minor problem, however; it places the newline in the input string. We must therefore overlay it with a null character.

The code to print the output of this program is shown in Program 11-21.

```
 1  /* ================= printOutput =================
 2     Print the input and the transformed output
 3        Pre    inStr contains the input data
 4               outStr contains the transformed string
 5        Post   output printed
 6  */
 7  void printOutput (char *inStr,
 8                    char *outStr)
 9  {
10  /* Statements */
11     printf("\nThe information entered was: \n");
12     puts(inStr);
```

Program 11-21 Morse code: print output

```
13 ||    printf("\nThe transformed information is: \n");
14 ||    puts(outStr);
15 ||    return;
16 || }  /* printOutput */
```

Program 11-21   Morse code: print output (continued)

Program 11-22 transforms character data to Morse Code.

```
 1 || /* ==================== encode ====================
 2 ||    Transforms character data to Morse Code
 3 ||       Pre     encDec is the conversion table
 4 ||               inStr contains data to be put into Morse
 5 ||       Post    data have been encoded in outStr
 6 ||       Return  TRUE  if all valid characters;
 7 ||               FALSE if invalid character found
 8 || */
 9 || int encode (char *(*encDec)[2],
10 ||             char *inStr,
11 ||             char *outStr)
12 || {
13 || /* Local Definitions */
14 ||    char s1[2];
15 ||    char s2[6];
16 ||    int  error = 0;
17 ||
18 || /* Statements */
19 ||    outStr[0] = '\0';
20 ||    while (*inStr != '\0' && !error)
21 ||       {
22 ||         s1[0] = toupper(*inStr);
23 ||         s1[1] = '\0';
24 ||         error = !convert (encDec, s1, 0, s2);
25 ||         strcat (outStr, s2);
26 ||         inStr++;
27 ||       } /* while */
28 ||    return (!error);
29 || }  /* encode */
```

Program 11-22   Morse code: encode to Morse

Program 11-22 Analysis   Note how the encode/decode table is declared in the formal parameter list in Statement 9. It uses a complex type. To understand it, let's use right–left analysis (see Chapter 10).

```
char *  (  *  encDec #)  [2] #
  ↑  ↑   ↑  ↑      ↑    ↑  ↑
  6  4   2  0      1    3  5
```

Reading this declaration, at 0 we have `encDec`. Moving to the right, we find the 1, which is ignored. Moving left, at 2 we find a pointer. We therefore have `encDec` as a pointer. Moving right to 3, we see that it is a pointer to an array of two. Moving to the left to 4, we see that it is an array of pointers.

At this point, we see that `encDec` is a pointer to an array of two pointers. Now, moving back to the right, we see that 5 is empty, so we go to the left and find *char* at 6. The final type is therefore a pointer to an array of two pointers to *char*. Referring back to Figure 11-25 on page 566, we see that this is exactly what we have.

The code to decode Morse code to English is shown in Program 11-23.

```
 1  /* ==================== decode ====================
 2     Transforms Morse Code data to character string
 3          Pre     encDec is the conversion table
 4                  inStr contains data to transform to string
 5          Post    data encoded and placed in outStr
 6          Return TRUE  if all valid characters;
 7                  FALSE if invalid character found
 8  */
 9  int decode (char *(*encDec)[2],
10              char *inStr,
11              char *outStr)
12  {
13  /* Local Definitions */
14     char   s1[6];
15     char   s2[2];
16     int    error = 0;
17     int    i;
18
19  /* Statements */
20     outStr[0] ='\0';
21     while (*inStr != '\0' && !error)
22        {
23         for (i = 0; i < 5 && *inStr != '#'; i++, inStr++)
24             s1[i] = *inStr;
25
26         s1[i]   = *inStr;
27         s1[++i] = '\0';
28
29         error = !convert (encDec, s1, 1, s2);
30         strcat (outStr, s2);
31         inStr++;
32        } /* while */
33     return (!error);
34  } /* decode */
```

Program 11-23 Morse code: decode to English

Program 11-24 converts characters to Morse Code and Morse Code to characters.

```
1   /* ==================== convert ====================
2       Looks up code in table and converts to opposite format
3           Pre    encDec is a pointer decoding table
4                  s1 is string being converted
5                  s2 is output string
6                    col is code: 0 for character to Morse
7                                 1 for Morse to character
8           Post   converted output s2
9   */
10  int convert (char *(*encDec)[2],
11                char *s1,
12                int   col,
13                char *s2)
14  {
15  /* Statements */
16      int found = 0;
17      int i;
18
19      for (i = 0; i < 27 && !found; i++)
20          found = !strcmp(s1, encDec[i][col]);
21
22      if (found)
23          strcpy (s2, encDec [i - 1][(col + 1) % 2]);
24      else
25          *s2 = '\0';
26
27      return found;
28  }  /* convert */
29  /* ================= End of Program ================ */
```

Program 11-24 Morse code: convert codes

Program 11-24 Analysis   The `convert` function does the actual conversion. Note, however, how it is designed to handle the conversion both from English to Morse and Morse to English. The only difference between the two conversions is which pointer we want to use. We pass the column to be used for the search as a parameter. Once we have located the correct string, we use the formula shown below to pick up the matching string (see Statement 23).

```
(col + 1) % 2
```

If we are searching on the English letters in column 0, then the modulus of the column $(0 + 1)$ is column 1, which contains the pointer to the matching Morse code string. Conversely, if we are searching Morse code using the pointers in column 1, then the modulus of the column $(1 + 1)$ is column 0, which contains the pointer to the English letter.

11-8 SOFTWARE ENGINEERING AND PROGRAMMING STYLE

In this section, we've formalized some of the principles of good programming that we've discussed throughout the text. Although you will find little in this discussion of software engineering that relates directly to the subject of strings, all of the string functions have been written using the principles discussed on the following pages.

PROGRAM DESIGN CONCEPTS

You will study many different analysis and design tools as you advance in computer science. Since this text deals primarily with program analysis and design, we will discuss the primary tool we have used throughout the text, the structure chart.

The overriding premise of good design is that the program is modular; that is, it is well structured. This is the *sine qua non* of good programming. A program's degree of good design can be measured by two principles: Its modules are independent—that is, their implementation is hidden from the user—and they have a single purpose.

INFORMATION HIDING

Information hiding is the principle of program design in which the data structure and functional implementation are screened from the user. Modules are independent when their communication is only through well-defined parameters and their implementation is hidden from the user. The purpose of the function should be defined in its inputs and outputs, and the user should not need to know how it is implemented or how its data are structured. Pressman states it well when he says:

> Hiding implies that effective modularity can be achieved by defining a set of independent modules that communicate with one another only that information necessary to achieve software function. … Hiding defines and enforces access constraints to both procedural detail within a module and any local data structure used by the module. [7]

The concept of information hiding is the basis of the object-oriented design, programming, and database movements gaining popularity today. When you study data structures, you will see another technique used for information hiding, the abstract data type.

COHESION

The most common weakness of function design is combining related processes into one primitive function. In Chapter 4 we discussed the concept that each module (function) should do only one thing. This principle of structured programming is known as cohesion. **Cohesion**, first discussed by Larry Constantine in the 1960s[8], is a measure of how closely the processes in a function are related.

We are concerned with cohesion for three primary reasons. The first and most important is *accuracy*. The more cohesive a function is, the simpler it is. The simpler it is, the easier it is to write, and the fewer errors it will have.

---

[7]Roger S. Pressman, *Software Engineering: A Practitioner's Approach,* 2nd ed, McGraw-Hill Series in Software Engineering and Technology (New York: McGraw-Hill, 1982), p. 228.

[8] E. N. Yourdon and L. L. Constantine, *Structured Design* (Upper Saddle River, N.J.: Prentice Hall, 1978).

This is closely related to the second reason for high cohesion, *maintainability*. If a function is easy to understand, it is easy to change. This means that we will get the job done faster and with fewer errors.

Finally, cohesive modules are more *reusable*. Reusability is also closely related to the concepts of accuracy and ease of use. Existing functions have stood the test of time and have been tempered in the heat of use. They are more likely to be error free, and they certainly are easier and faster to develop.

Cohesion is most applicable to the primitive functions in a program, those that are at the bottom of the structure chart and least applicable to the controlling functions that appear above the lowest level. This does not mean, however, that cohesion can be ignored at the higher levels. To make the point with an absurd example, you wouldn't write a program to manage your checkbook and maintain your daily calendar. Even though both of these processes are related to things you do, they are so unrelated that you wouldn't put them in the same program. The same concept applies in a program. For example, at the lower levels of your program, you shouldn't combine functions that read data with functions that print a report.

The seven levels of cohesion are shown in Figure 11-28.

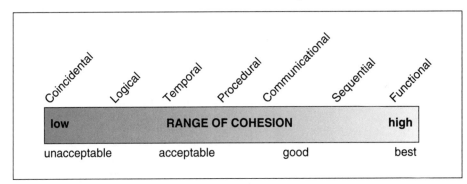

Figure 11-28 Types of cohesion

Functional Cohesion

Functional modules that contain only one process demonstrate **functional cohesion**. This is the highest level of cohesion and the level that we should hold up as a model. Using the example of printing a report, the report function should call three lower-level functions, one to get the data, one to format and print the report header, and one to format and print the data. This design is shown in Figure 11-29. The print report heading function is optional because it is called only when a page is full.

Sequential Cohesion

A sequential module contains two or more related tasks that are closely tied together, usually with the output of one flowing as input to the other. An example of **sequential cohesion** is shown in the calculations for a sale. The design for this function might well be

1. Extend item prices
2. Sum items
3. Calculate sales tax
4. Calculate total

Figure 11-29 Example of functional cohesion

In this example, the first process multiplies the quantity purchased by the price. The extended prices are used by the process that calculates the sum of the purchased items. This sum is then used to calculate the sales tax, which is finally added to the sum to get the sale total. In each case, the output of one process was used as the input of the next process.

Although it is quite common to find the detail code for these processes combined into a single function, it does make the function more complex and less reusable. On the other hand, reusability would be a concern if the same or similar calculations were being made in different parts of one program.

Communicational Cohesion

Communicational cohesion combines processes that work on the same data. It is natural to have communicational cohesion in the higher modules in a program, but you should never find it at the primitive level. For example, consider a function that reads an inventory file, prints the current status of the parts, and then checks to see if any parts need to be ordered. The pseudocode for this process is shown in Program 11-25.

```
1 While not end of file
  1 read a record
  2 print report
  3 check reorder point
```

Program 11-25 Process inventory pseudocode

All three of these processes use the same data. If they are calls to lower-level functions, they are acceptable. If the detail code is found in the function, however, the design is unacceptable.

The first three levels of cohesion are all considered to be good structured programming principles. Beyond this point, however, ease of understanding and implementation, maintainability, and accuracy begin to drop off rapidly. The next two levels should be used only at the higher levels of a structure chart, and then only rarely.

Well-structured programs are highly cohesive and loosely coupled.

Procedural Cohesion

The fourth level of cohesion, **procedural cohesion**, combines unrelated processes that are linked by a control flow. (This differs from sequential cohesion, where data flows from one process to the next.) As an example, consider the high level logic main line of a program that builds and processes a list. A procedural flow could look like Program 11-26.

```
1 Open files.
2 Initialize work areas.
3 Create list.
4 Print menu.
5 while not stop
   1 get users response
   2 if locate …
   3 if insert …
   4 if delete …
   5 print menu
6 clean up
7 Close files
```

Program 11-26 Process list pseudocode

A much better approach would be to have only three function calls in main, initialize, process, and end. Not only is this easier to understand, but it also simplifies the communication.

Temporal Cohesion

The fifth level, **temporal cohesion**, is acceptable only over a limited range of processes. It combines unrelated processes that always occur together. Two temporally cohesive functions are initialization and end of job. They are acceptable because they are used only once in the program and because they are never portable. Recognize, however, that they should still contain calls to functionally cohesive primitive functions whenever practical.

Logical and Coincidental Cohesion

The last two levels are seldom found in programs today. **Logical cohesion** combines processes that are related only by the entity that controls them. A function that conditionally opened different sets of files based on a flag passed as a parameter would be logically cohesive. Finally, **coincidental cohesion** combines processes that are unrelated. Coincidental cohesion exists only in theory. We have never seen a productional program that contained coincidental cohesion.

SUMMARY

We have discussed two design concepts in this chapter: information hiding and cohesion. Cohesion describes the relationship among processes within a function. Keep functions as highly cohesive as possible. When designing a program, pay attention to the levels of cohesion. It is much easier to design high cohesion into a program than it is to program it in. For more information about these concepts, refer to *The Practical Guide to Structured Systems Design* by Meilir Page-Jones.[9]

---

[9]Meilir Page-Jones, *The Practical Guide to Structured Systems Design*, Yourdon Press Computing Series (Upper Saddle River, N.J.: Prentice-Hall, 1988).

11-9   TIPS AND COMMON PROGRAMMING ERRORS

1. Do not confuse characters and string constants: The character constant is enclosed in single quotes, and the string constant is enclosed in double quotes.

2. Remember to allocate memory space for the string delimiter when declaring and defining an array of *char* to hold a string.

3. Strings are manipulated with string functions, not operators.

4. The header file <string.h> is required when using string functions.

5. The standard string functions require a delimited string. You cannot use them on an array of *char* that is not terminated with a delimiter.

6. Do not confuse string arrays and string pointers. In the following example, the first definition is a string (array of characters), and the second is a pointer to a character (string). Each is shown with a typical initialization statement.

```
char str[20];
strcpy (str, "Now is the time");

char *str;
str = "Now is the time";
```

7. Passing a character to a function when a string is required is another common error. This is most likely to occur with the formatted input/output functions, in which case, it is a logic error. Passing a character in place of a string when a prototype header is declared is a compile error.

8. Using the address operator for a parameter in the *scanf* function with a string is a coding error. The following is an invalid call and will most likely cause the program to fail:

```
scanf("%s", &string);        /* Coding Error */
```

9. It is a compile error to assign a string to a character, even when the character is a part of a string.

10. Using the assignment operator with strings instead of a function call is a compile error.

```
char string [20];

string = "This is an error";   /* Compile Error */
```

11. Since strings are built in an array structure, they may be accessed with indexes and pointers. When accessing individual bytes, it is a logic error to access beyond the end of the data structure (array).

11-10 KEY TERMS AND CONCEPTS[10]

cohesion	information hiding	*strcmp/strncmp*
coincidental cohesion	length-controlled string	*strcpy/strncpy*
communicational cohesion	logical cohesion	string
delimited string	procedural cohesion	*strlen*
delimiter	*puts*	*strpbrk*
edit set	scanset	*strspn/strcspn*
fgets	sequential cohesion	*strstr*
fixed-length string	*sprintf*	*strtod*
fputs	*sscanf*	*strtok*
functional cohesion	*strcat/strncat*	*strtol*
gets	*strchr/strrchr*	temporal cohesion

---

[10]Note: Italic terms are functions found in the standard C libraries.

11-11 SUMMARY

- Strings can be fixed length or variable length.

- A variable-length string can be controlled by a length or a delimiter.

- The C language uses a null-terminated (delimited) variable-length string.

- A string constant in C is a sequence of characters enclosed in double quotes. A character constant is enclosed in single quotes.

- When string constants are used in a program, C automatically creates an array of characters, initializes it to a null-terminated string, and stores it remembering its address.

- To store a string, we need an array of characters whose size is one more than the length of the string.

- There is a difference between an array of characters and a string. An array of characters is a derived data type (built on the type character) and is an intrinsic structure in C. A string is a data structure that uses the array as its basic type. It requires a delimiter for all of its operations.

- We can initialize a string:
  1. With an initializer when we define it.
  2. By using *strcpy*.
  3. By reading characters into it.

- A string identifier is a pointer constant to the first element in the string.

- An array of strings is a very efficient way of storing strings of different sizes.

- The *scanf* and *printf* functions can be used to read and write strings using the %s format.

- The edit set format, %[...], can also be used in the *scanf* function to read a string.

- The functions *gets, fgets, puts,* and *fputs* are used for reading and writing strings. They transform a line to a string or a string to a line.

- The functions *sscanf* and *sprintf* are used for reading and writing strings from memory—that is, memory-to-memory formatting.

- The functions *strcpy* and *strncpy* are used to copy one string into another.

- The functions *strcmp* and *strncmp* are used to compare two strings.

- The function *strlen* is used to determine the length of a string.

- The functions *strcat* and *strncat* are used to concatenate one string to the end of the other.

- The functions *strchr* and *strrchr* are used to look for a character in a string.

- The function *strstr* is used to look for a substring in a string.

- The functions *strspn* and *strcspn* are used to locate the position of a set of characters in a string.

■ Information hiding is the principle of programming in which the data structure and function's implementation are screened from the user.

■ The cohesion principle dictates that each module must do only a single job.

■ The *sine qua non* of good programming is modularity.

■ Program design has seven layers of cohesion; only the first three (functional, sequential, and communicational) should be used for lower-level functions. The last two (logical and coincidental) should never be used.

11-12 PRACTICE SETS

REVIEW QUESTIONS

1. The two basic techniques for storing variable-length data are fixed-length strings and delimiters.
   a. True   b. False

2. To initialize a string when it is defined, it is necessary to put the delimiter character before the terminating double quote, as in `"hello\0"`.
   a. True   b. False

3. Both the *gets* and *fgets* functions change the newline to a delimiter.
   a. True   b. False

4. The function that can be used to format several variables into one string in memory is string token (*strtok*).
   a. True   b. False

5. A(n) _____ is a series of characters treated as a unit.
   a. array   d. record
   b. character   e. string
   c. field

6. The delimiter in a C string is
   a. a newline   d. defined by the programmer
   b. a null character e. not specified in ANSI C
   c. a del character

7. Which of the following statements about string variables is false?
   a. String variables cannot be used with the assignment operator.
   b. The array bracket operator is not needed if a string is initialized when it is defined.
   c. The string name is a pointer.
   d. When a string is initialized at definition time, C automatically inserts the delimiter.
   e. When a string is read with *scanf*, it automatically inserts the delimiter.

8. Which of the following *printf* statements will not print a string? (Assume that name is properly defined and formatted.)
   a. `printf("%s", name);`
   b. `printf("%30s", name);`
   c. `printf("%-30s", name);`
   d. `printf("%30[^\0]", name);`

9. The _____ function reads a string from the standard input device.
   a. *fgets*   d. *getstr*
   b. *fputs*   e. *puts*
   c. *gets*

10. The _____ string manipulation function returns the number of characters in the string excluding the null character.
    a. *strcmp*   d. *strsize*
    b. *strcpy*   e. *strtok*
    c. *strlen*

11. Which of the following statements will determine if the contents of `string1` are the same as the contents of `string2`? Assume that `string1` and `string2` are properly defined and formatted strings.
    a. `if (string1 == string2)`
    b. `if (strcmp (string1, string2))`
    c. `if (strcmp (string1, string2) == 0)`
    d. `if (strcmp (string1, string2) < 0)`
    e. `if (strcmp (string1, string2) > 0)`

12. The _____ string manipulation function adds a string to the end of another string.
    a. *stradd*   d. *strcpy*
    b. *strcat*   e. *strtok*
    c. *strcmp*

13. The _____ string manipulation function determines if a character is contained in a string.
    a. *strchr*   d. *strcpy*
    b. *strchar*   e. *strtok*
    c. *strcmp*

14. The _____ function is used to format a string into variables in memory.
    a. *scanf*
    b. *sscanf*
    c. *strfrmt*
    d. *strscan*
    e. *strtok*

15. The best level of cohesion is
    a. coincidental
    b. communicational
    c. procedural
    d. sequential
    e. functional

EXERCISES

16. Find the value of *x, *(x + 1), and *(x + 4) for the following declaration:
    ```
    char *x = "The life is beautiful";
    ```

17. Find the value of *y, *(y + 1), and *(y + 4) for the following program segment:
    ```
    char x [] = "Life is beautiful";
    char *y = &x [3];
    ```

18. What is the error in the following program block?
    ```
    {
      char *x;
      scanf("%s", x);
    }
    ```

19. What would be printed from the following program block?
    ```
    {
      char   s1[50] = "xyzt";
      char   *s2      = "xyAt";
      int    dif;
      dif = strcmp (s1, s2);
      printf("\n%d", dif);
    }
    ```

20. What would be printed from the following program block?
    ```
    {
      char  s1[50] = "xyzt";
      char *s2 = "uabefgnpanm";
      char *s3;
      char *s4;
      char *s5;
      char *s6;
      s3 = s1;
      s4 = s2;
      strcat (s1, s2);
      s5 = strchr(s1, 'y');
      s6 = strrchr(s2, 'n');
      printf ("\n%s", s3);
      printf ("\n%s", s4);
      printf ("\n%s", s5);
      printf ("\n%s", s6);
    }
    ```

21. What would be printed from the following program block?
    ```
    {
      char  s1[50] = "uabefgnpanm";
      char *s2 =   "ab";
      char *s3  =    "pan";
      char *s4  =    "bef";
      char *s5  =    "panam";
    ```

```
char *s6;
char *s7;
char *s8;
char *s9;
s6 = strstr (s1, s2);
s7 = strstr (s1, s3);
s8 = strstr (s1, s4);
s9 = strstr (s1, s5);
printf ("\n%s",  s6);
printf ("\n%s",  s7);
printf ("\n%s",  s8);
printf ("\n%s",  s9);
}
```

22. What would be printed from the following program block?

```
{
char *s1 = "abefgnpanm";
char *s2 = "ab";
char *s3 = "pan";
char *s4 = "bef";
char *s5 = "panam";
int d1;
int d2;
int d3;
int d4;
d1 = strspn (s1, s2);
d2 = strspn (s1, s3);
d3 = strcspn (s1, s4);
d4 = strcspn (s1, s5);
printf ("\n%d",  d1);
printf ("\n%d",  d2);
printf ("\n%d",  d3);
printf ("\n%d",  d4);
}
```

23. What would be printed from the following program block?

```
{
char *w  = "BOOBOO";
printf ("%s\n", "DOO");
printf ("%s\n", "DICK" + 2);
printf ("%s\n", "DOOBOO" +3);
printf ("%c\n", w[4]);
printf ("%s\n", w+4);
w++;
w++;
printf ("%s\n",w);
printf ("%c\n", *(w+1));
}
```

24. What would be printed from the following program block?

```
{
char *a[5]  = {"GOOD", "BAD", "UGLY", "WICKED", "NICE"};
printf ("%s\n",  a[0]);
printf ("%s\n", *(a + 2));
printf ("%c\n", *(a[2] + 2));
printf ("%s\n",  a[3]);
printf ("%s\n",  a[2]);
```

```
    printf ("%s\n",   a[4]);
    printf ("%c\n", *(a[3] +2));
    printf ("%c\n", *(*(a+4)+3));
}
```

25. What would be printed from the following program block?

```
{
    char  c[] = "programming";
    char *p;
    int   i;
    for (p = &c[5]; p >= &c [0];  p--)
        printf("%c", *p);
    printf ("\n");
    for (p = c+5, i=0; p >= c; p--,i++)
        printf("%c", *(p - i));
}
```

PROBLEMS

26. Write a function that accepts a string (a pointer to a character) and deletes the last character by moving the null character one position to the left.

27. Write a function that accepts a string (a pointer to a character) and deletes the first character.

28. Write a function that accepts a string (a pointer to a character) and deletes all the trailing spaces at the end of the string.

29. Write a function that accepts a string (a pointer to a character) and deletes all the leading spaces.

30. Write a function that returns the number of times the character is found in a string. The function has two parameters. The first parameter is a pointer to a string. The second parameter is the character to be counted.

31. Write a function that inserts a string into another string at a specified position. It returns a positive number if it is successful or zero if it has any problems, such as an insertion location greater than the length of the receiving string. The first parameter is the receiving string, the second parameter is the string to be inserted, and the third parameter is the insertion (index) position in the first string.

32. Write a function that, given a string, a width, and an empty string for output, centers the string in the output area. The function is to return 1 if the formatting is successful and 0 if any errors, such as string length greater than width, are found.

33. Write a function called `newStrCpy` that does the same job as *strcpy* without using any library functions. The prototype for your function is to be the same as the library function.

34. Write a function called `newStrCat` that does the same job as *strcat* without using any library functions. The prototype for your function is to be the same as the library function.

35. Write a function called `newStrCmp` that does the same job as *strcmp* without using any library functions. The prototype for your function is to be the same as the library function.

36. A string is a palindrome if it can be read forward and backward with the same meaning. Capitalization and spacing are ignored. For example, *anna* and *go dog* are palindromes. Write a function that accepts a string and returns true (nonzero value) if the string is a palindrome and false (zero value) if it is not. Test your function with the following two palindromes and at least one case that is not a palindrome:

    Madam, I'm Adam
    Able was I ere I saw Elba

37. Today's spelling checkers do much more than simply test for correctly spelled words. They also verify common punctuation. For example, a period must be followed by only one space. Write a program that reads a text file and removes any extra spaces after a period, comma, semicolon, or colon. Write the corrected text to a new file.

Your program is to read the data using *fgets* and parse the strings using *strtok*. Print your test data before and after they are run through your program.

PROJECTS

38. Write a C program that converts a string representing a number in Roman numeral form to decimal form. The symbols used in the Roman numeral system and their equivalents are given below.

I	1
V	5
X	10
L	50
C	100
D	500
M	1000

For example, the following are Roman numbers: XII (12) CII (102); XL (40). The rules for converting a Roman number to a decimal number are as follows:

a. Set the value of the decimal number to zero.

b. Scan the string containing the Roman character from left to right. If the character is not one of the symbols in the numeral symbol set, the program must print an error message and terminate. Otherwise, continue with the following steps. (Note that there is no equivalent to zero in the Roman numerals.)

   • If the next character is a null character (if the current character is the last character), add the value of the current character to the decimal value.

   • If the value of the current character is greater than or equal to the value of the next character, add the value of the current character to the decimal value.

   • If the value of the current character is less than the next character, subtract the value of the current character from the decimal value.

   Solve this project using parallel arrays. Do not solve it using a *switch* statement.

39. Rework Project 38 to convert a decimal number to a Roman numeral.

40. Write a program that simulates the search and replace operation in a text editor. The program is to have only three function calls in `main`. The first function prompts the user to type a string of less than 80 characters. It then prompts the user to type the search substring of 10 or fewer characters. Finally, it prompts the user to type the replace substring of 10 or fewer characters.

The second call is the search and replace function, which replaces all occurrences of the search substring with the replace substring and creates a new string. If no occurrences are found, it returns the original string. Theoretically, the new string could be 800 characters long (80 identical characters replaced by ten characters each). Your function must be able to handle overflow by using the *realloc* function to extend the new string when necessary. (Start with an output string of 80 characters and extend by 80 as necessary.) The search and replace function returns the address of the new string.

After the search and replace function returns, a print function prints the resulting string as a series of 80 character lines. It performs word-wrap. That is, a line can end only at a space. If there is no space in 80 characters, then print 79 characters and a hyphen, and continue on the next line.

Write each called function using good structured programming techniques. It is expected to call subfunctions as necessary.

Run the program at least three times:

a. First, run it with no substitutions in the original input.

b. Second, run it with two or more substitutions.

c. Finally, run it with substitutions that cause the output to be at least three lines, one of which requires a hyphen.

41. Write a program that "speaks" pig-latin. Words in pig-latin are taken from English. To form a word in pig-latin, the first letter of the English word beginning with a consonant is removed and added at the end of the word, adding the letters *ay* after the moved consonant. Words that begin with a vowel are simply appended with *ay*. Thus, in pig-latin, *pig-latin* is *igpay-atinlay*.

Your program will read a sentence at a time using *fgets*. It is to parse the words into strings. As words are parsed, they are to be converted to pig-latin and printed.

42. Write a program that provides antonyms to common words. An antonym is a word with the opposite meaning. For example, the antonym of *happy* is *sad*.

The data structure is to be patterned after the Morse code problem on page 566. Given a word, the program is to look for the word on both sides of the structure and, if found, report the antonym. If the word is not found, the program is to display an appropriate message.

The program is to use an interactive user interface. The words are to be read from a dictionary file. Use your dictionary to provide at least 30 antonyms, including at least one from each letter in the alphabet.

Test your program by finding the antonyms for the first word, last word, and a word somewhere in the middle on both sides of the structure. Include in your test data at least three words that are not found, one less than the first word on the left side, one in the middle somewhere, and one greater than the last word on the right side.

43. The Morse code program in this chapter is a public example of a cryptographic system. We can apply the same techniques to encoding and decoding any message. For example, we can substitute the letter *Z* for the letter *A*, the letter *Y* for the letter *B*, and so forth, to create the following simple encoded message:

```
NZWZN, R ZN ZWZN
MADAM, I AM ADAM
```

Write a program that encodes and decodes messages using any user-supplied code. To make it more difficult to read, include spaces and the common punctuation characters in the code. The code is to be read from a text file to build the encode/decode array. The user is then given a menu of choices to encode, decode, or enter a new code from the keyboard.

Test your program with the following code and message and with the complete alphabet entered in its encoded sequence so that it prints out in alphabetical order:

```
ABCDEFGHIJKLMNOPQRSTUVWXYZ .,?!;
?Q.W,EMRNTBXYUV!ICO PZA;SDLFKGJH
```

Message

```
WNWLSVPLM, LN A
```

44. Write a program that parses a text file into words and counts the number of occurrences of each word. Allow for up to 100 different words. After the list has been built, sort and print it.

45. Modify the program you wrote in Project 44 to eliminate common words such as *the*, *a*, *an*, *and*, *for*, and *of*. You may add other common words to the list.

Derived Types—Enumerated, Structure, and Union

We have already discussed two of the five derived types, arrays in Chapter 8 and pointers in Chapter 9. In this chapter, we discuss the three remaining derived types: enumerated, structure, and union. We also discuss a very useful typing construct, the type definition. The derived types are shown in Figure 12-1.

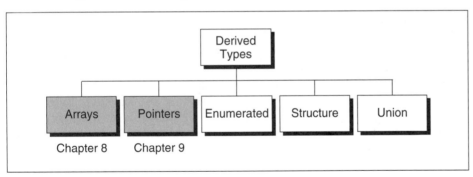

Figure 12-1 Derived types

12-1 THE TYPE DEFINITION (*typedef*)

Before discussing the derived types, let's discuss a C construct that applies to all of them—the type definition.

A type definition, ***typedef*,** gives a name to a data type by creating a new type that can then be used anywhere a type is permitted. The primary advantage of the type definition is that it allows you to replace a complex name, such as a pointer declaration, with a mnemonic that makes the program easier to read and follow. The format for the type definition is shown in Figure 12-2.

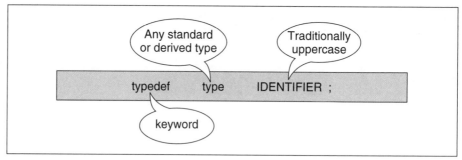

Figure 12-2 Typed definition format

You can use the type definition with any type. For example, you can redefine *int* to `INTEGER` with the statement shown below, although we would never recommend this.

```
typedef int INTEGER;
```

Note that the *typedef* identifier is traditionally coded in uppercase. This alerts the reader that there is something unusual about the type. You saw this previously with defined constants in Chapter 2. Simple style standards such as this make it much easier to follow the program.

One of the more common uses of the type definition is with complex declarations. To demonstrate the concept, let's see how we can declare a rather simple construct, an array of pointers to strings (a ragged array). Without a type definition, we must define the array as shown below.

```
char *stringPtrAry[20];
```

We can simplify the declaration by using a type definition to create a string type and then defining the array using the new type as shown below.

```
typedef  char *STRING;
STRING   stringPtrAry[20];
```

12-2 ENUMERATED TYPES

The enumerated type, *enum,* is built on the integer type. In an enumerated type, each integer value is given an identifier called an **enumeration constant**. This allows us to use symbolic names rather than numbers, which makes our programs much more readable.

For example, with enumeration it is possible to give symbolic names to the *case* identifiers in a *switch* statement, thereby making the switch cases more readable.

Once we have defined the enumerated types, we can create variables from them, just as we can create variables from the standard types. In fact, C allows the enumerated constants, or variables that hold enumerated constants, to be used anywhere that integers can be used.

A word of caution is in order here. The ANSI/ISO C standard is somewhat loose in this area. We find, therefore, that some versions of C allow you to mix integer variables and enumerated constants while others do not. We consider mixing them to be poor programming practice and highly recommend that, even if your compiler allows it, you do not do it. Keep the enumerated types separate from integer types. Use them primarily as a way to improve the readability of your program.

As shown in Figure 12-3, C has two basic formats for the enumerated type. Both definitions start with the keyword *enum*. In the first format, *enum* is followed by a list of the enumerated identifiers. It ends with a variable identifier. This format declares a single variable; it is not a reusable type. Therefore, if you need more than one variable, do not use this format. Instead, use Format 2.

```
enum {enumeration constants} variable_identifier ;
```
Format 1: enumerated variable

```
enum tag {enumeration constants} ;

enum tag variable_identifier ;
```
Format 2: enumerated tag

Figure 12-3 Enumerated type

To use multiple enumerated types in a program, you need to create an enumerated type. This is the purpose of the second format. Note that it includes a tag after the keyword *enum;* the tag is an *enum* identifier. This format creates an enumerated type that can be used wherever needed in the program.

An enumerated type for the months of the year is shown below. Note that it is a type. No variable is created, just the type, `enum months`.

```
enum months
{jan,feb,mar,apr,may,jun,jul,aug,sep,oct,nov,dec};
```

The list of constant identifiers provides the symbolic names we can use in our programs. The first thing you should notice is that the list is contained within braces. This is a standard technique whenever C needs to define a group of anything. For example, you also saw braces used in this way when we used initializers for an array in Chapter 8.

Next we see that the enumeration constants are nothing more than a list of one or more identifiers separated by commas. Look at the list for our enumerated types, `enum months`. It consists of the standard three-character abbreviations for the months of the year. (We've written them in C style, with the first character in lowercase. If you preferred, you could use a leading uppercase letter.)

Since the purpose of an enumerated type is to assign names to integers, the question is, What integers are we assigning these names to? When you don't tell C what values you want to use, it simply starts at zero and then equates each enumerated constant to the next higher integral number. In this case, therefore, `jan` equates to 0, `feb` equates to 1, and so forth until we get to `dec`, which equates to 11.

There's nothing wrong with the way we set up our months, unless we are asking users to give us a month. In that case, it's not a good idea to ask users to have to manipulate the data they give us. Often this leads to errors. What we should do, therefore, is to equate each month to its normal value, such as 1 for January. This is done with an assignment operator as shown below.

```
enum months {jan =  1, feb =  2, mar =  3,
              apr =  4, may =  5, jun =  6,
              jul =  7, aug =  8, sep =  9,
              oct = 10, nov = 11, dec = 12};
```

This is perfectly good code. However, we can shorten it a little by using the compiler. Because C assigns the next larger integer to each enumeration constant, all we need to do is tell it the starting point and let it do all of the work. Here's `months` properly coded.

```
enum months {jan = 1,  feb, mar, apr,
              may, jun, jul, aug,
              sep, oct, nov, dec};
```

Now `jan` will start with 1 rather than 0, and all the other months will fall in line just as we want them to.

To define a variable that can hold our months, we need to show the keyword *enum* and the tag. The following statements define two different enumerated month variables. Note that in both of them, the type is `enum months`.

```
enum months  birthMonth;
enum months  startMonth;
```

If you have cable TV, you know that the cable supplier is always changing the channels around. To help us keep track of our favorite channels, therefore, we wrote a program that prints out the cable television channels for Sunnyvale, California. Since the channels are changing continually, using their names in an enumerated type makes it easy to change them and to follow the code. The implementation is seen in Program 12-1.

```
 1  /* Print selected TV stations for Cable TV in Sunnyvale, CA
 2         Written by:
 3         Date:
 4  */
 5  #include <stdio.h>
 6
 7  int main (void)
 8  {
 9  /* Local Definitions */
10     enum TV {fox = 2, nbc  =  4, cbs  =  5,
```

Program 12-1 Print cable TV stations

```
11          abc = 11, hbo  = 15, show = 17,
12          max = 31, espn = 39, cnn  = 51};
13
14  /* Statements */
15     printf("Here are my favorite cable stations:\n");
16     printf("  ABC: \t%2d\n", abc);
17     printf("  CBS: \t%2d\n", cbs);
18     printf("  CNN: \t%2d\n", cnn);
19     printf("  ESPN:\t%2d\n", espn);
20     printf("  Fox: \t%2d\n", fox);
21     printf("  HBO: \t%2d\n", hbo);
22     printf("  Max: \t%2d\n", max);
23     printf("  NBC: \t%2d\n", nbc);
24     printf("  Show:\t%2d\n", show);
25     printf("End of my favorite stations. \n");
26     return 0;
27  }  /* main */
```

```
Results:
   Here are my favorite cable stations:
      ABC:      11
      CBS:       5
      CNN:      51
      ESPN:     39
      Fox:       2
      HBO:      15
      Max:      31
      NBC:       4
      Show:     17
   End of my favorite stations.
```

Program 12-1   Print cable TV stations (continued)

Two final thoughts about enumerated types: C allows you to assign the same integer to multiple enumeration constants in the same definition. For example, we could have assigned nbc and kron both to the integer 4 in Program 12-1. However, this is not recommended practice.

Second, since the underlying type for enumeration is integer, C treats it like an integer. However, there is no range checking. This means that you can assign an enumerated variable a value for which there is no assigned constant identifier. It is your responsibility as a programmer, therefore, to ensure that data being assigned to an enumerated type are valid.

ENUMERATED TYPE DEFINITION

Type definition is often used to define enumerated types. Consider the enumeration of colors as shown in Figure 12-4. In the first example, the type must be coded as enum colors whenever it is used.

This code can be simplified with a type definition as shown in the second example in Figure 12-4. By creating a typed definition, we can now refer to it by a single type identifier, in this case COLORS. Note that in this format, the tag is not used.

```
enum colors{red, white, blue, green, yellow};

enum colors aColor ;
```
Enumerated tag

```
typedef enum {red, white, blue, green, yellow} COLORS ;

COLORS aColor ;
```
Enumerated typedef

Figure 12-4   Typed definition example

12-3   STRUCTURE

Today's modern applications require complex data structures to support them. For example, the structures needed to support the graphical user interface found in computer workstation windows obvioulsy are very complex. So complex, in fact, that they could not be built using the relatively primitive data types we have seen so far. A much more powerful capability is needed. This is the role of the structure.

A **structure** is a collection of related elements, possibly of different types, having a single name. For example, consider the file table you have been using ever since you wrote your first program that used files. The file table is a type-defined structure, `FILE`. The symbolic figure shown in Figure 12-5 represents the structure.

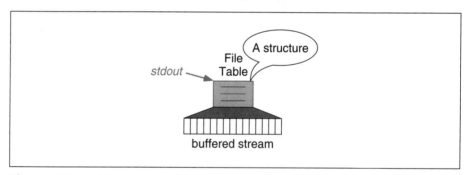

Figure 12-5   A file structure

Even relatively simple structures like file tables have many different objects to track. A file pointer needs to know where the physical device is located, the file's logical name, the current state of the file, and many other things. To track all of these data with separate variables would be very difficult. The programmers who built the file-handling functions, therefore, put these data in a structure.

Each element in a structure is called a field. A **field** is the smallest element of named data that has meaning. It has many of the characteristics of the variables you have been using in your programs. It has a type, and it exists in memory. It can be assigned values, which in turn can be accessed for selection or manipulation. A field differs from a variable primarily in that it is part of a structure.

We have studied another derived data type that can hold multiple pieces of data, the array. The difference between an array and a structure is that all elements in an array must be of the same type, while the elements in a structure can be of the *same or different types*.

Figure 12-6 contains two examples of structures. The first example, `fraction`, has two fields, both of which are integers. The second example, `student`, has three fields, made up of two different types..

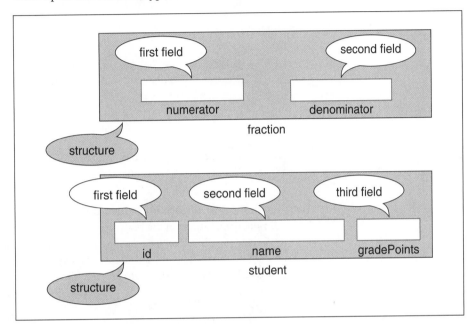

Figure 12-6 Structure examples

Another way to look at a structure is as a template. A template is a pattern or outline that can be applied to data to extract individual parts. It allows us to refer to a collection of data using a single name and, at the same time, to refer to the individual components through their names. By collecting all the attributes of an object in one structure, we simplify our programs and make them more readable.

> The elements in a structure can be of the same or different types. But all elements in the structure must be related.

One design caution, however. The data in a structure should all be related to one object. In Figure 12-6, the integers in the fraction both belong to the same fraction, and the data in the second example all relate to one student. Do not combine unrelated data for programming expediency. It would not be good structured programming.

STRUCTURE DECLARATION AND DEFINITION

Like all data types, structures must be declared and defined. C has three different ways to declare and/or define a structure: variable structures, tagged structures, and type-defined structures.

Structure Variable

The **structure variable** definition consists of the keyword *struct* followed by a field list and an identifier, as shown in Figure 12-7. The keyword *struct* alerts the compiler that what follows is a collection of related data. However, it creates a structure that can be used for *only one variable definition*. Since it does not have a structure identifier (tag), it cannot be shared; it is not really a type. This is such a major limitation that we recommend you never use it. It offers no advantages over the other declaration formats, the tagged structure and the typed definition structure.

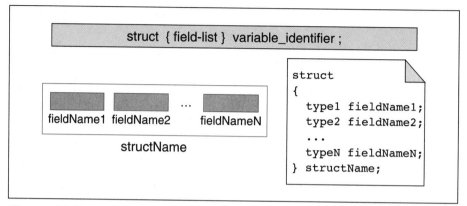

Figure 12-7 Structure variable

Following *struct* is a field-list body as indicated by the opening and closing braces. All field declarations in the body are part of the structure. You can include any standard or derived type in a structure, as long as it has already been declared. A structure variable containing three fields for a student is shown below. The name of the whole structure is student. Within the structure are id, name, and gradePoints.

```
struct
    {
    char  id[10];
    char  name[26];
    int   gradePoints;
    } student;
```

Tagged Structure

The second way to define a structure is to use a **tagged structure**. By giving the structure a tag, we can use it to define variables, parameters, and return types. Let's examine the components of a structure declaration by looking at Figure 12-8.

A tagged structure also starts with the keyword *struct*. The second element in the declaration is the *tag*. The tag is the identifier for the structure, and it allows you to use it for other purposes, such as variables and parameters.

If you conclude the structure with a semicolon after the closing brace, no variables are defined. In this case, the structure is simply a type template with no associated storage.

To define variables at the same time you declare the structure, you simply list the variables, separated by commas, after the closing brace. We do not recommend that you do so, however, for two reasons. First, the proper place for structure declarations is in the global area of the program before main. This puts them within the scope of the entire program and is mandatory if the structure is to be shared by functions. In fact, on large projects, you will usually find the structures declared in a header file that is shared by all members of the project. The second reason is that it breaks the rule of putting mul-

Figure 12-8 Tagged structure

tiple definitions in one statement. If you do define a variable when you declare the structure, therefore, we strongly suggest that you define only one.

Once you have declared a tagged structure type, you can then use it to define variables. Remember, however, that the structure type name includes the keyword *struct*. Thus, to declare and use the student structure shown in Figure 12-6, you code it as shown below.

```
struct student
    {
     char   id[10];
     char   name[26];
     int    gradePoints;
    };

struct student aStudent;
...
void   printStudent (struct student Stu);
```

Type-Defined Structure

The most powerful way to declare a structure is to use a type definition, ***typedef***, as we do in Figure 12-9. The type-defined structure differs from the tagged declaration in two ways. First, the keyword, *typedef,* is added to the beginning of the definition. Second, the identifier at the end of the block is the type definition name, not a variable. You cannot define a variable with the *typedef* declaration. Otherwise, all the syntax rules for both variable structure and tagged structure declarations are allowed.

Figure 12-9 also shows an example of a *typedef* declaration and its use to define a variable, `strName`. Note that the *typedef* name is all uppercase. To make it readable, the

Figure 12-9 Type-defined structure

words are separated with an underscore. Our student example is repeated once more, this time as a type definition.

```
typedef struct
    {
     char    id[10];
     char    name[26];
     int     gradePoints;
    } STUDENT;

STUDENT aStudent;
...
void    printStudent (STUDENT Stu);
```

You can combine the tagged structure and the typed definition in a tagged typed definition. The only difference between this structure and a simple typed definition is that the structure has a tag name.

Figure 12-10 summarizes the three different structure formats.

INITIALIZATION

We can initialize a structure. The rules for structure initialization are similar to the rules for array initialization. The initializers are enclosed in braces and separated by commas. They must match their corresponding types in the structure definition. Finally, if you use a nested structure (see "Nested Structures" on page 606), the nested initializers must be enclosed in their own set of braces.

Figure 12-11 shows two examples of structure initialization. The first example shows an initializer for each field. Note how they are mapped to the structure in sequence. The second example demonstrates what happens when not all fields are initialized. As we saw with arrays, when one or more initializers are missing, the structure elements will be assigned null values, zero for integers and floating-point numbers, and ' \ 0 ' for characters and strings.

struct {
      ...
      } variable_identifier ;

structure variable

struct tag
      {
      ...
      } variable_identifier ;

struct tag variable_identifier ;

tagged structure

typedef struct
      {
      ...
      } TYPE_ID ;

TYPE_ID variable_identifier ;

type-defined structure

Figure 12-10 *struct* **format variations**

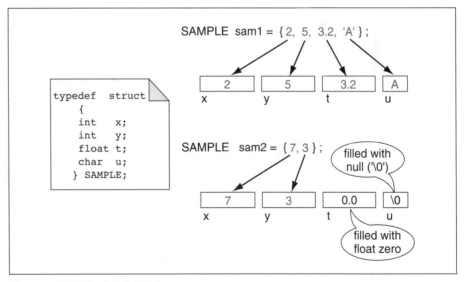

Figure 12-11 Initializing structures

12-4 ACCESSING STRUCTURES

Now that you know how to declare and initialize structures, it's time to see how you can use them in your programs. We will first describe how to access individual components of a structure and then examine the assignment of whole structures. After looking at how pointers are used with structures, we conclude with a program that uses structures.

**REFERENCING
INDIVIDUAL FIELDS**

Each field in a structure can be accessed and manipulated using expressions and operators. Anything you can do with an individual variable can be done with a structure field. The only problem is to identify the individual fields you are interested in.

Since each field in a structure has a name, we could simply use the name. The problem with such a simple approach is that if we wanted to compare a student's `id` in one structure to a student's `id` in another structure, the statement would end up being

```
if (id == id)
```

which is an ambiguous expression. We therefore need some way to identify the structures that contain the field identifiers, in this case, `id`. C uses an operator that is common to many other languages, the member operator, which is simply a period (.). If you refer to the Precedence Table (see inside front cover), you will find the member operator at Priority 17 among the postfix expressions.

Using the structure `student` on page 594, we would refer to the individual components as shown below.

```
aStudent.id
aStudent.name
aStudent.gradePoints
```

Figure 12-12 contains another example using the structure `SAMPLE`, defined in Figure 12-11. With this structure, we can use a selection statement to evaluate the char-

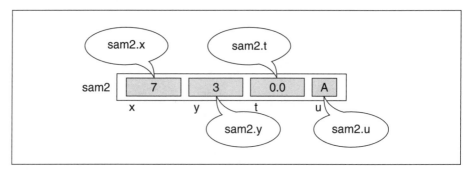

Figure 12-12 Structure member operator

acter member, u, and if it is an *A*, add the two integer elements and store the result in the first. This code is shown below.

```
if (sam2.u == 'A')
    sam2.x += sam2.y;
```

We can also read data into and write data from structure members just as we can from individual variables. For example, the value for the fields of the sample structure can be read from the keyboard and placed in `sam1` using the following *scanf* statement. Note that the address operator is at the beginning of the variable structure identifier.

```
scanf("%d %d %f %c",
       &sam1.x, &sam1.y, &sam1.t, &sam1.u);
```

PRECEDENCE OF MEMBER OPERATOR

As we saw above, references to the elements in a structure are postfix expressions that have a priority of 17, which is very high. What may not be apparent, however, is that the dot is actually an operator, just as the bracket is an operator for array reference. The dot operator creates a postfix expression from a primary expression. When you are using the dot operator, the value must be determined immediately. For example, consider the following statements:

```
sam2.x++;          ++sam2.x;
```

The precedence of the member operator (17) is higher than the precedence of the postfix increment (16) and the unary increment (15). Therefore, no parentheses are required, which makes it much easier to code these statements.

Example: Multiply Fractions

Let's look at a program that multiplies two fractions and prints the result. The structure for this example was shown in Figure 12-6 on page 593. The code is shown in Program 2-2.

```
 1  /* This program uses structures to simulate the
 2     multiplication of fractions.
 3        Written by:
 4        Date:
 5  */
 6  #include <stdio.h>
 7  /* Global Declarations */
 8     typedef  struct
 9        {
10         int numerator;
11         int denominator;
12        } FRACTION;
13
14  int main (void)
15  {
16  /*Local Definitions */
17     FRACTION   fr1;
18     FRACTION   fr2;
19     FRACTION   res;
20
21  /* Statements */
22     printf("Write the first fraction in the form of x/y: ");
23     scanf ("%d /%d", &fr1.numerator, &fr1.denominator);
24     printf("Write second fraction in the form of x/y:    ");
25     scanf ("%d /%d", &fr2.numerator, &fr2.denominator);
26
27     res.numerator   = fr1.numerator   * fr2.numerator;
28     res.denominator = fr1.denominator * fr2.denominator;
29
```

Program 12-2 Multiply fractions

```
30      printf("\nThe result of %d/%d * %d/%d is %d/%d",
31              fr1.numerator, fr1.denominator,
32              fr2.numerator, fr2.denominator,
33              res.numerator, res.denominator);
34
35  return 0;
36  }  /* main */
```

```
Results:
   Write the first fraction in the form of x/y: 2/6
   Write second fraction in the form of x/y:    7/4

   The result of 2/6 * 7/4 is 14/24
```

Program 12-2 Multiply fractions (continued)

Program 12-2 Analysis   Although this is a very simple program, several points are of interest.

1. Note that we have coded the *typedef* in the global area before main. This is the first time that we have included statements here other than preprocessor directives. Even though this program has no subfunction, it is customary to put the typed definition statements there so that they are in scope for the entire compilation unit.

2. Note that the name of the typed definition is all UPPERCASE. This is another C style tradition. It warns the reader that there is something special about this type, in this case that it is a typed definition.

3. Now examine the *scanf* statements. Since we need a pointer for *scanf,* we must use the address operator as well as the member operator. As you can see, we have not used the parentheses around the field name. The reason is that the dot operator has a higher priority (17) than the address operator (15). In other words, the expression

```
&fr1.numerator
```

is interpreted by the compiler as

```
&(fr.numerator)
```

which is exactly what we need.

STRUCTURE OPERATIONS

The structure is an entity that can be treated as a whole. However, only one operation, assignment, is allowed on the structure itself. That is, a structure can only be copied to another structure of the same type using the assignment operator.

Rather than assign individual members when we want to copy one structure to another, as we did earlier, we can simply assign one to the other. Figure 12-13 copies sam1 to sam2 as you might want to do after you had read data from the keyboard into sam1.

Slack Bytes

It is interesting to examine why we cannot compare two structures. Sometimes hardware requires that certain data, such as integers and floating-point numbers, be aligned on a word boundary in memory. When you group data in a structure, the arrangement of the data may require that **slack bytes** be inserted to maintain these boundary requirements. For example, consider the structure shown below. In this structure we assume that a floating-point number is stored in a word that requires 6 bytes and must be on an address evenly divisible by 6, such as 24 or 30. We also assume that integers are stored in 2-byte words that require an address evenly divisible by 2. The 25-byte string at the beginning of the structure forces 5 slack bytes between the string and the float. Then the character after the float forces a slack byte to align the integer at the end of the structure.

Since these extra bytes are beyond the control of the program, you cannot guarantee what their values will be. Therefore, if you wanted to compare two structures and their first components were equal, the inserted slack bytes could cause an erroneous compare result, either high or low, if they weren't equal. C prevents this problem by not allowing selection statements with structures. Of course, if you really need to compare structures, you can simply write a structure compare function of your own that would compare the individual fields in the structure.

Figure 12-13   Copying a structure

POINTER TO STRUCTURES

Structures, like other types, can also be accessed through pointers. In fact, this is one of the most common methods used to reference structures. For example, let's use our SAMPLE structure with pointers (Figure 12-14).

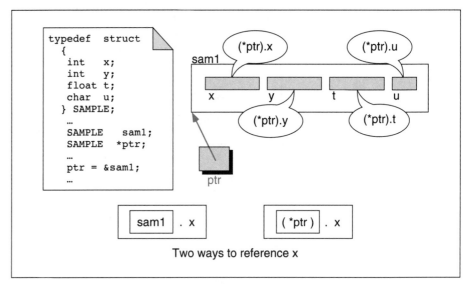

Figure 12-14 Pointers to structures

The first thing we need to do is define a pointer for the structure as shown below.

```
SAMPLE *ptr;
```

We now assign the address of sam1 to the pointer using the address operator (&) as we would with any other pointer.

```
ptr = &sam1;
```

Now we can access the structure itself and all the members using the pointer, ptr. The structure itself can be accessed like any object using the indirection operator (*).

```
*ptr                    /* Refers to whole structure */
```

Since the pointer contains the address of the beginning of the structure, we no longer need to use the structure name with the member operator. The pointer takes its place. The reference to each of the sample members is shown below and in Figure 12-14.

```
(*ptr).x    (*ptr).y    (*ptr).t    (*ptr).u
```

Note the parentheses in the above expressions. *They are absolutely necessary,* and to omit them is a very common mistake. The reason they are needed is that the precedence priority of the member operator (17) is higher than the indirection operator (15). If you forget to put the parentheses, C applies the dot operator first and the asterisk operator next. In other words,

```
*ptr.x is interpreted as *(ptr.x)
```

which is wrong. The expression `*(ptr.x)` means that we have a completely different (and undefined) structure called `ptr` that contains a member, `x`, which must be a pointer. Since this is not the case, you will get a compile error. Figure 12-15 shows how this error is interpreted.

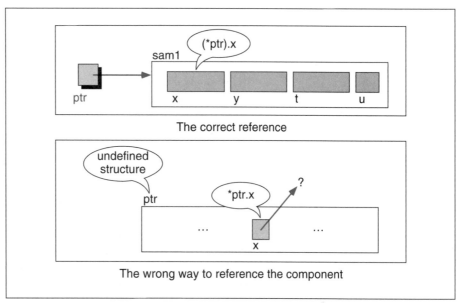

Figure 12-15   Interpretation of invalid pointer use

The correct notation, `(*ptr).x`, first resolves the primary expression `(*ptr)` and then uses the pointer value to access the member, `x`.

SELECTION OPERATOR

Fortunately, another operator eliminates the problems with pointers to structures—the selection operator. The selection operator is at the same level in the Precedence Table (see inside front cover) as the member operator.

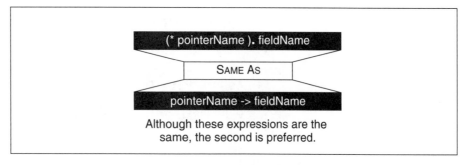

The token for the selection operator is an arrow formed by the minus sign and the greater than symbol (—>). It is placed immediately after the pointer identifier and before the member to be referenced. We use this operator to refer to the members of our previously defined structure, `sam1`, in Figure 12-16.

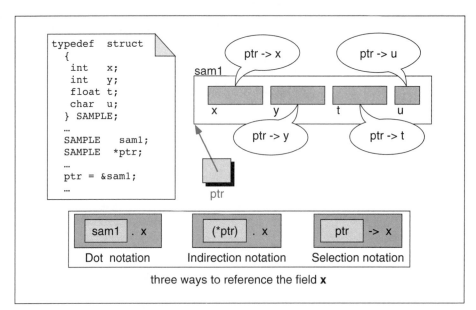

Figure 12-16   Pointer selection operator

Example: Clock Structure

Program 12-3 simulates a digital clock that shows time. A structure is defined to represent the three components of time: hour, minute, and second. Two functions are used. The first function, called `increment`, simulates the passage of the time. The second function, called `show`, shows the time at any moment.

```
1  /* This program uses a structure to simulate the time.
2       Written by:
3       Date:
4  */
5  #include <stdio.h>
6
7  typedef struct
8    {
9      int hr;
10     int min;
11     int sec;
12    } CLOCK;
13
14 /* Prototype Declaration */
15 void increment (CLOCK *clock);
16 void show       (CLOCK *clock);
17
18 int main (void)
19 {
20 /* Local Definition */
21    CLOCK clock = {14, 38, 56};
22    int   i;
23
```

Program 12-3   Clock simulation with pointers

```
24  /* Statements */
25     for(i = 0; i < 6; ++i)
26        {
27         increment (&clock);
28         show (&clock);
29        }
30
31     return 0;
32  }  /* main */
33
34  /* ==================== increment ====================
35     This function accepts a pointer to clock and increments
36     the time by one second.
37        Pre    previous clock setting
38        Post   clock incremented by one second.
39  */
40  void increment (CLOCK *clock)
41  {
42  /* Statements */
43     (clock->sec)++;
44     if (clock->sec == 60)
45        {
46         clock->sec = 0;
47         (clock->min)++;
48         if (clock->min == 60)
49            {
50             clock->min = 0;
51             (clock->hr)++;
52             if (clock->hr == 24)
53                clock->hr = 0;
54            } /* if 60 min*/
55        } /* if 60 sec */
56     return ;
57  }  /* increment */
58
59  /* ==================== show ====================
60     This function shows the current time in military form.
61        Pre    clock time
62        Post   clock time displayed
63  */
64  void show (CLOCK *clock)
65  {
66  /* Statements */
67     printf("%02d:%02d:%02d\n",
68             clock->hr, clock->min, clock->sec);
69     return;
70  }  /* show */
```

Program 12-3 Clock simulation with pointers (continued)

```
Results:
   14:38:57
   14:38:58
   14:38:59
   14:39:00
   14:39:01
   14:39:02
```

Program 12-3   Clock simulation with pointers (continued)

12-5   COMPLEX STRUCTURES

As mentioned earlier, structures were designed to deal with complex problems. The limitations on structures are not on the structures themselves but on the imagination of the software engineers who solve the problems. Structures within structures (nested structures), arrays within structures, and arrays of structures are all common. We deal with the first two here and arrays of structures in the next section.

NESTED STRUCTURES

We can have structures as members of a structure. When a structure includes another structure, it is a **nested structure**. There is no limit to the number of structures that can be nested, but you will seldom go beyond three.

For example, we can have a structure called `stamp` that stores the date and the time. The date is in turn a structure that stores the month, day, and year. The time is also a structure that stores the hour, minute, and second. This structure design is shown in Figure 12-17.

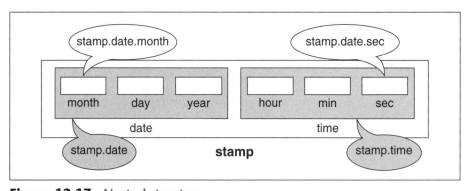

Figure 12-17   Nested structure

There are two concerns with nested structures: defining them and referencing them.

Declaring Nested Structures

Although it is possible to declare a nested structure with one declaration, it is not recommended. It is far simpler and much easier to follow the structure if each structure is declared separately and then grouped in the high-level structure.

When you declare the structures separately, the most important point you must remember is that nesting must be done from inside out—that is, from the lowest level to the most inclusive level. In other words, you must declare the innermost structure first, then the next level, working upward toward the outer, most inclusive structure.

Consider the time stamp structure seen in Figure 12-17. The inner two structures, `date` and `time`, must be declared before the outside structure, `stamp`, is declared. We show the declaration of `stamp` and a variable that uses it in the following example.

```
            Preferred                        Not Recommended
typedef  struct                     typedef  struct
    {                                   {
     int month;                         struct
     int day;                             {
     int year;                            int month;
    } DATE;                               int day;
typedef struct                            int year;
    {                                     } date;
     int hour;                         struct
     int min;                             {
     int sec;                             int hour;
    } TIME;                               int min;
typedef struct                            int sec;
    {                                     } time;
     DATE  date;                      } STAMP;
     TIME  time;
    } STAMP;

STAMP stamp;                        STAMP stamp;
```

It is possible to nest the same structure type more than once in a declaration. For example, consider a structure that contains start and end times for a job. Using the STAMP structure, we create a new declaration as shown below.

```
typedef struct
    {
     ...
     STAMP startTime;
     STAMP endTime;
    } JOB;
JOB job;
```

Regardless of how we declared the structure, using it will be the same. The major advantage of declaring each of the structures separately is that it allows much more flexibility in working with them. For example, with DATE declared as a separate type definition, it is possible to pass the date structure to a function without having to pass the rest of the stamp structure.

Referencing Nested Structures

When you access a nested structure, you must include each level from the highest (stamp) to the component being referenced. The complete set of references for stamp is shown below. The last two references are to job.

```
stamp
stamp.date
stamp.date.month
stamp.date.day
stamp.date.year
stamp.time
stamp.time.hour
stamp.time.min
stamp.time.sec

job.startTime.time.hour
job.endTime.time.hour
```

Nested Structure Initialization

Initialization follows the rules mentioned for a simple structure. Each structure must be initialized completely before proceeding to the next member. Each structure is enclosed in a set of braces. For example, to initialize stamp, first we initialize date, then time, separated by a comma. To initialize date, we provide values for month, day, and year, each separated by commas. We can then initialize the members of time. A definition and initialization for stamp are shown below.

```
STAMP stamp = {{05, 10, 1936}, {23, 45, 00}};
```

STRUCTURES CONTAINING ARRAYS

Structures can have one or more arrays as members. The arrays can be accessed either through indexing or through pointers, as long as they are properly qualified with the member operator.

Defining Arrays for Structures

As with nested structures, an array may be included within the structure or may be declared separately and then included. If it is declared separately, the declaration must be complete before it can be used in the structure. For example, consider the structure that contains the student name, three midterm scores, and the final exam score, as shown in Figure 12-18.

Referencing Arrays in Structures

Regardless of how we declared the structure, each element will have the same reference. First we refer to the structure, then to the array component. When we refer to the array, we can use either index or pointer notation. Let us look at each in turn.

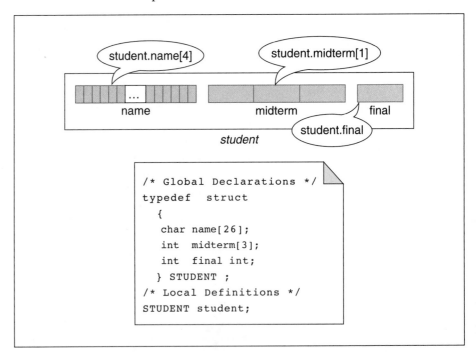

Figure 12-18 Arrays in structures

The index applies only to elements within an array. Therefore, it must follow the identifier of an array. Our student example has two arrays, one of characters (a string) and the other of midterm scores. Each of these arrays can be referenced with an index as shown on the next page.

```
student
student.name
student.name[i]
student.midterm
student.midterm[j]
student.final
```

We have already seen how to refer to fields in a structure using the selection operator (–>). When one structure contains an array, we can use a pointer to refer directly to the array elements. For example, given a pointer to integer, pScores, we could refer to the scores in student as shown below.

```
pScores     = student.midterm;
totalScores = *pScores + *(pScores + 1) + *(pScores + 2);
```

Array Initialization in Structures

The initialization of a structure containing an array is simply an extension of the rules for structure initialization to include the initialization of the array. Since the array is a separate member, its values must be included in a separate set of braces. For example, the student structure can be initialized as shown below.

```
STUDENT student = {"John Marcus", {92, 80, 70}, 87}
```

Note that the name is initialized as a string and the midterm scores are simply enclosed in a set of braces.

STRUCTURE CONTAINING POINTERS

It should not be surprising that a structure can have pointers as members. In fact, we will see that pointers are very common in structures.

The use of pointers can save memory. For example, suppose that we wanted to use the alphabetic month in our stamp structure rather than an integer month. We could add an array of nine characters to each structure element, but it would be much more memory efficient to use a 4-byte pointer if we had to store a lot of these structures. Given the months of the year defined as strings, as shown below, we could then use a pointer to the correct month.

```
char jan[] = "January";
char feb[] = "February";
...
char dec[] = "December";
```

To assign the month May to the structure, you would use the following statement. Note that we are copying a pointer to a string, not the string itself.

```
stamp.date.month = may;
```

The modified structure is shown in Figure 12-19.
The structure code for the date structure is shown below.

```
typedef  struct
    {
    char *month;
    int  day;
    int  year;
    } DATE;
```

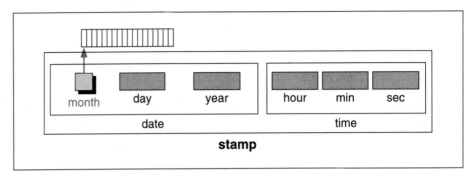

Figure 12-19   Pointers in structures

12-6 ARRAY OF STRUCTURES

In many situations, you will need to create an array of structures. To name just one example, you would use an array of students when you are working with a group of students and the data are stored in a structure. By putting the data in an array, you can quickly and easily work with the data, to calculate averages, for instance.

Let's create an array to handle the scores for up to 50 students in a class. Figure 12-20 shows how such an array might look.

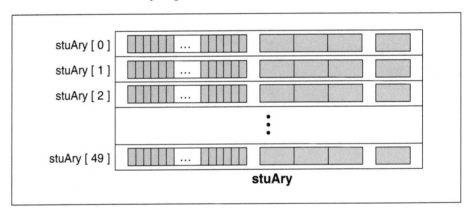

Figure 12-20   Array of structures

Since a structure is a type, you can create the array just as you would create an array of integers. The code is shown below.

```
STUDENT stuAry[50];
```

Study this array carefully. Note that it is an array that contains two other arrays, name and midterm. This is not a multidimensional array. To be a multidimensional array, each level must have the same data type. In this case, each type is different: the styAry is STUDENT, while name is character, and midterm is integer.

To access the data for one student, you need to refer only to the structure name with an index or a pointer as shown below.

```
stuAry[i]                *pStu
```

For example, let's write a short segment of code to compute the average for the final exam. We use a *for* loop since we know the number of students in the array.

```
int       totScore = 0;
float     average;
STUDENT  *pStu;
STUDENT  *pLastStu;
...
pLastStu  = stuAry + 49;
for (pStu = stuAry; pStu <= pLastStu; pStu++)
   totScore += pStu->final;
average = totScore / 50.0;
```

However, to access an individual element in one of the student's arrays, such as the second midterm for the fifth student, you need to use an index or pointer for each field as shown below.

```
stuAry[4].midterm[1]
```

To access students' midterms with pointers, you need one index or pointer for the array. You also need a second index or pointer for the midterms. The code to compute the average for each midterm is shown below. We use a separate array, `midTermAvrg`, to store the average for the midterms. In this example, we use indexes to access the midterms and pointers to access the students.

```
float     midTermAvrg[3];
int       sum;
STUDENT *pStu;
STUDENT *pLastStu;
...
pLastStu   = stuAry + 49;
for (i = 0; i < 3; i++)
    {
     sum = 0;
     for (pStu = stuAry; pStu <= pLastStu; pStu++)
         sum += pStu->midterm[i];
     midTermAvrg[i] = sum / 50.0;
    } /* for i */
```

The Precedence Table (see inside front cover) shows that the index operator, the member operator, and the selection operator all have the same precedence and that the associativity is from left to right. So we do not need parentheses to total the scores for a midterm.

INSERTION SORT REVISITED

To demonstrate using structures in arrays, let's sort an array of students. We will use the `student` structure seen in Figure 12-18. Whenever you sort a structure, you need to define the field that controls the sort. This control field is usually called a key. In our `student` structure, the key field is the name. Program 12-4 shows the code.

```
1   /* This program sorts an array of student structures
2         Written by:
3         Date:
```

Program 12-4 Sort array of student structures

```
 4  */
 5
 6  #include <stdio.h>
 7  #include <string.h>
 8
 9  #define NUM_STU 5
10
11  /* Global Structures */
12     typedef struct
13        {
14         char   name[26];
15         int    midterm[3];
16         int    final;
17        } STUDENT;
18
19  /* Prototype Declarations */
20  void insertionSort (STUDENT list[], int last);
21
22  int main (void)
23  {
24  /* Local Definitions */
25     STUDENT *pStuPtr;
26     STUDENT  stuAry[NUM_STU] =
27        {
28         {"Charles, George", {85, 94, 79}, 93},
29         {"Adams, Karin",    {75, 91, 89}, 89},
30         {"Nguyen, Tuan",    {87, 88, 89}, 90},
31         {"Oh, Bill",        {78, 96, 88}, 91},
32         {"Chavez, Maria",   {83, 79, 93}, 91}
33        } /* stuAry */;
34
35  /* Statements */
36     printf("Unsorted data:\n");
37     for (pStuPtr = stuAry;
38          pStuPtr < stuAry + NUM_STU;
39          pStuPtr++)
40       printf("%-26s %4d %4d %4d %4d\n",
41               pStuPtr->name,
42               pStuPtr->midterm[0],
43               pStuPtr->midterm[1],
44               pStuPtr->midterm[2],
45               pStuPtr->final);
46     printf("\n");
47
48     insertionSort (stuAry, NUM_STU - 1);
49
```

Program 12-4 Sort array of student structures (continued)

```
50    printf("Sorted data:\n");
51    for (pStuPtr = stuAry;
52         pStuPtr < stuAry + NUM_STU;
53         pStuPtr++)
54      printf("%-26s %4d %4d %4d %4d\n",
55              pStuPtr->name,
56              pStuPtr->midterm[0],
57              pStuPtr->midterm[1],
58              pStuPtr->midterm[2],
59              pStuPtr->final);
60    return 0;
61 }  /* main */
62
63 /* ================= insertionSort =================
64    Sort list using Insertion Sort. The list is divided into
65    sorted and unsorted list. With each pass, first element
66    in unsorted list is inserted into sorted list.
67       Pre    list must contain at least one element
68              last is index to last element in list
69       Post   list has been rearranged.
70 */
71 void insertionSort (STUDENT  list[],
72                     int      last)
73 {
74 /* Local Definitions */
75    int      located;
76    STUDENT  temp;
77    STUDENT *pCurrent;
78    STUDENT *pWalker;
79    STUDENT *pLast;
80
81 /* Statements */
82    for (pCurrent = list + 1, pLast = list + last;
83         pCurrent <= pLast;
84         pCurrent++)
85      {
86      located =  0;                        /* False */
87      temp    = *pCurrent;
88
89      for  (pWalker  = pCurrent - 1;
90            pWalker >= list && !located;
91           )
92        if (strcmp(temp.name, pWalker->name) < 0)
93          {
94            *(pWalker + 1) = *pWalker;
95            pWalker--;
```

Program 12-4 Sort array of student structures (continued)

```
 96              } /* if */
 97            else
 98              located = 1;                       /* True */
 99          *(pWalker + 1)  = temp;
100          } /* for pCurrent */
101      return;
102  }  /* insertionSort */
103  /* ================= End of Program ================= */
```

```
Results:
  Unsorted data:
  Charles, George          85   94   79   93
  Adams, Karin             75   91   89   89
  Nguyen, Tuan             87   88   89   90
  Oh, Bill                 78   96   88   91
  Chavez, Maria            83   79   93   91

  Sorted data:
  Adams, Karin             75   91   89   89
  Charles, George          85   94   79   93
  Chavez, Maria            83   79   93   91
  Nguyen, Tuan             87   88   89   90
  Oh, Bill                 78   96   88   91
```

Program 12-4   Sort array of student structures (continued)

Program 12-4 Analysis   To write this program, we started with the original insertion sort we studied back in Chapter 8. We then combined the insertOne function as a nested loop in insertionSort. This is the way the sort would be written in a production environment. Aside from combining the sort into one function, there are only two significant changes: First, all the array handling is done with pointers, and second, the compare logic was changed to use the *strcmp* function.

To test the sort, we wrote a small driver that uses an initialized array for its data. To verify that the sort works, we printed the data before and after the sort process.

12-7   STRUCTURES AND FUNCTIONS

For structures to be fully useful, we must be able to pass them to functions and return them. A function can access the members of a structure in three ways:

1. Individual members can be passed to the function.

2. The whole structure can be passed and the function can access the members using pass by value.

3. The address of a structure or member can be passed, and the function can access the members through indirection and selection operators (pass by address).

SENDING INDIVIDUAL MEMBERS

Sending individual members to a function is no different from what we have done since Chapter 4. To demonstrate the calling sequence, we will use a simple example to multiply two fractions. The flow is shown in Figure 12-21.

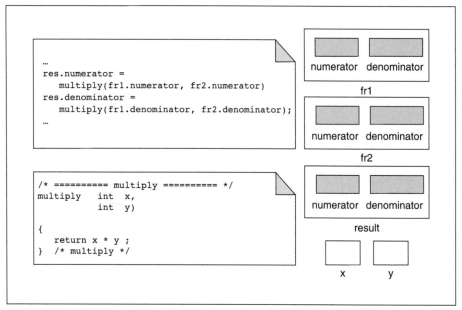

Figure 12-21 Passing structure members to functions

As you can see from Figure 12-21, the only difference is that you must use the member operator to refer to the individual members for the actual parameters. The called program doesn't know if the two integers are simple variables or structure members.

SENDING THE WHOLE STRUCTURE

The problem with the above solution is that the multiplication logic is split between the calling and called programs. This is not considered good structured programming. A much better solution is to pass the entire structure and let `multiply` complete its job in one call.

Passing a structure is really no different from passing individual elements. Since the structure is a type, we simply specify the type in the formal parameters of the called function. Similarly, the function can return a structure. Again, all that is necessary is to specify the structure as the return type in the called function. Note, however, that not all compilers have implemented returning structures.

The same pass-by-value rules apply, however; when we pass a structure to a function, C will copy the values to the local structure just as it does for variables. This may lead to some inefficiencies when large structures are used. We address this problem in the next section.

Let us rework the multiply fractions program to pass structures. In this case, we have written the complete program. The design is shown in Figure 12-22, and the code is shown in Program 12-5.

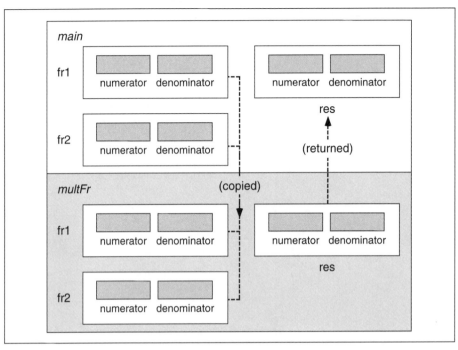

Figure 12-22   Passing and returning structures

```
1   /* This program uses structures to multiply fractions.
2          Written by:
3          Date:
4   */
5   #include <stdio.h>
6
7   /* Global Declarations */
8   typedef   struct
9        {
10        int numerator;
11        int denominator;
12        } FRACTION;
13
14  /* Prototype Declarations */
15  FRACTION getFr    (void);
16  FRACTION multFr   (FRACTION fr1, FRACTION fr2);
17  void printFr      (FRACTION fr1,
18                        FRACTION fr2,
19                        FRACTION result);
20
21  int main (void)
22  {
23  /* Local Definitions */
24     FRACTION fr1;
```

Program 12-5   Passing and returning structures

```
25      FRACTION fr2;
26      FRACTION res;
27
28  /* Statements */
29      fr1 = getFr ();
30      fr2 = getFr ();
31      res = multFr (fr1, fr2);
32      printFr (fr1, fr2, res);
33
34      return 0;
35  }  /* main */
36
37  /* ==================== getFr ====================
38     Get two integers from the keyboard, make & return
39     a fraction to the main program.
40        Pre    nothing
41        Post   returns a fraction
42  */
43  FRACTION getFr (void)
44  {
45  /* Local Definitions */
46      FRACTION fr;
47
48  /* Statements */
49      printf("Write a fraction in the form of x/y: ");
50      scanf ("%d/%d", &fr.numerator, &fr.denominator);
51      return fr;
52  }  /* getFraction */
53
54  /* ==================== multFr ====================
55     Multiply two fractions and return the result.
56        Pre    fr1 and fr2 are fractions
57        Post   returns the product
58  */
59  FRACTION multFr (FRACTION fr1,
60                   FRACTION fr2)
61  {
62  /* Local Definition */
63      FRACTION res;
64
65  /* Statements */
66      res.numerator   = fr1.numerator   * fr2.numerator;
67      res.denominator = fr1.denominator * fr2.denominator;
68      return res;
69  }  /* multFr */
70
```

Program 12-5 Passing and returning structures (continued)

```
71  /* ==================== printFr ====================
72      Prints the value of the fields in three fractions.
73         Pre    two original fractions and the product
74         Post   fractions printed
75  */
76  void  printFr  (FRACTION fr1,
77                  FRACTION fr2,
78                  FRACTION res)
79  {
80  /* Statements */
81      printf("\nThe result of %d/%d * %d/%d is %d/%d\n",
82                 fr1.numerator, fr1.denominator,
83                 fr2.numerator, fr2.denominator,
84                 res.numerator, res.denominator);
85      return;
86  }  /* printFractions */
87  /* ==================== End of Program ==================== */
```

```
Results:
    Write a fraction in the form of x/y: 4/3
    Write a fraction in the form of x/y: 6/7

    The result of 4/3 * 6/7 is 24/21
```

Program 12-5 Passing and returning structures (continued)

Program 12-5 Analysis   There are five points you should study in this program.

1. The fraction structure is declared in global memory before `main`. This makes it visible to all the functions.

2. In `getFr`, the data are read by using the address operator and the member operator. Since the structure member operator (.) has a higher priority, they can be coded without parentheses.

3. In `getFr` we pass back two values in the structure without using pointers. This is another advantage of structures: You can return more than one piece of data when you put the data in a structure.

4. The structure type is passed using the `FRACTION` type definition.

5. The references to the data in `multFr` and `printFr` must use the member operator to get to the individual members.

PASSING STRUCTURES THROUGH POINTERS

As mentioned, passing structures is still pass by value. For the multiply fractions program, this is the correct way to write the program. It provides the necessary data protection and data encapsulation for good structured programming while at the same time being efficient (see "Software Engineering and Programming Style" at the end of the chapter).

When the structure is very large, however, efficiency can suffer, especially with a heavily used function. Therefore, you will often find that structures are passed through pointers. It is also common to pass structures through pointers when the structure is in dynamic memory. In these cases, all you have to pass is the pointer.

We modify the multiply fractions program once more to pass the structures using pointers. The memory flow is shown in Figure 12-23 and the coding in Program 12-6.

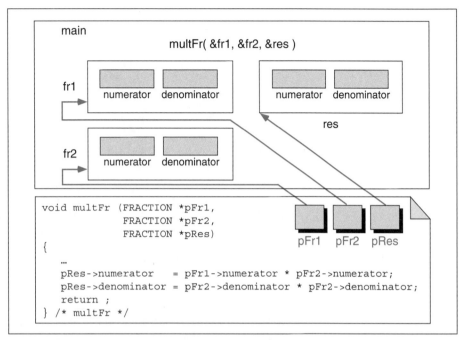

Figure 12-23 Passing structures through pointers

```
1   /* This program uses structures to multiply fractions.
2          Written by:
3          Date:
4   */
5   #include <stdio.h>
6
7   /* Global Declarations */
8   typedef   struct
9           {
10            int numerator;
11            int denominator;
12          } FRACTION;
13
14  /* Prototype Declarations */
15  void getFr   (FRACTION *pFr);
16  void multFr  (FRACTION *pFr1,
17                FRACTION *pFr2,
18                FRACTION *pRes2);
19  void printFr (FRACTION *pFr1,
20                FRACTION *pFfr2,
21                FRACTION *pRes);
22
23  int   main (void)
24  {
25  /* Local Definitions */
26     FRACTION fr1;
27     FRACTION fr2;
28     FRACTION res;
```

Program 12-6 Passing structures through pointers

```
29
30   /* Statements */
31      getFr    (&fr1);
32      getFr    (&fr2);
33      multFr   (&fr1, &fr2, &res);
34      printFr  (&fr1, &fr2, &res);
35
36   return 0;
37   }  /* main */
38
39   /* ==================== getFr ====================
40      Get two integers from the keyboard, make & return a
41      fraction to the main program.
42          Pre   pFr is pointer to fraction structure
43          Post  fraction stored at pFr.
44   */
45   void getFr (FRACTION *pFr)
46   {
47   /* Statements */
48      printf("Write a fraction in the form of x/y: ");
49      scanf ("%d/%d", &pFr->numerator, &(*pFr).denominator);
50      return;
51   }  /* getFr */
52
53   /* ==================== multFr ====================
54      Multiply two fractions and return the result.
55          Pre   fr1, fr2, pRes are pointers to fractions
56          Post  product stored at pRes
57   */
58   void multFr   (FRACTION *pFr1,
59                  FRACTION *pFr2,
60                  FRACTION *pRes)
61   {
62   /* Statements */
63      pRes->numerator    = pFr1->numerator * pFr2->numerator;
64      pRes->denominator =
65          pFr1->denominator * pFr2->denominator;
66      return;
67   }  /* multFr */
68
69   /* ==================== printFr ====================
70      Prints the value of the fields in three fractions.
71          Pre   pointers to two fractions and their product
72          Post  fractions printed
73   */
74   void  printFr (FRACTION *pFr1 ,
75                  FRACTION *pFr2 ,
76                  FRACTION *pRes)
77   {
78   /* Statements */
```

Program 12-6 Passing structures through pointers (continued)

```
79      printf("\nThe result of %d/%d * %d/%d is %d/%d\n",
80              pFr1->numerator, pFr1->denominator,
81              pFr2->numerator, pFr2->denominator,
82              pRes->numerator, pRes->denominator);
83
84      return;
85  }  /* printFr */
86  /* ================= End of Program ================= */
```

Program 12-6 Passing structures through pointers (continued)

Program 12-6 Analysis   In this version of the program, the structure is passed and returned as a pointer. Note the syntactical notation for reading the data in the `getData` function. We reproduce it below for your convenience.

```
scanf("%d/%d", &pFr->numerator, &(*pFr).denominator);
```

Even though we are using pointers, we still need to pass *scanf* addresses. We have used two different notations in this example. (This is not good coding style, but it demonstrates both techniques in one statement.) In both cases, since we are reading a field within the structure, we need to pass the address of the individual field, not the structure. In the first example, we use the selection operator (->). Since it has a higher precedence than the address operator (&), it can be coded without parentheses.

In the second example, we use the member operator (.). In this case we need parentheses because the member operator has a higher precedence than the indirection operator (*) and the address operator. However, since the address and member operator are at the same level, we need to use the parentheses only around the pointer dereference.

12-8   UNIONS

The **union** is a construct that allows memory to be shared by different types of data. This redefinition can be as simple as redeclaring an integer as four characters or as complex as redeclaring an entire structure. For example, we know that a short integer is 2 bytes and that each byte is a character. If we wanted, therefore, we could process a short integer as a number or as two characters.

The union follows the same format syntax as the structure. In fact, with the exception of the keywords *struct* and *union,* the formats are the same. Figure 12-24 shows how we declare a union that can be used as either a short integer or as two characters.

Figure 12-24 Unions

Program 12-7 uses SH_CH2 to print a variable, first as a number and then as two characters.

```
1  /* Demonstrate union of short integer and two characters.
2        Written by:
3        Date:
4  */
5  #include <stdio.h>
6
7  /* Global Declarations */
8     typedef union
9        {
10        short   num;
11        char    chAry[2];
12        } SH_CH2;
13
14 int main (void)
15 {
16 /* Local Definitions */
17    SH_CH2 data;
18
19 /* Statements */
20    data.num = 16706;
21
22    printf("Short: %hd\n", data.num);
23    printf("Ch[0]: %c\n",  data.chAry[0]);
24    printf("Ch[1]: %c\n",  data.chAry[1]);
25
26    return 0;
27 }  /* main */
```

```
Results:
   Short: 16706
   Ch[0]: A
   Ch[1]: B
```

Program 12-7   Demonstrate effect of union

Program 12-7 Analysis   Note that we initialize data using characters to make it easier to verify the results. To prove to yourself that A and B are in fact 16706, however, you will need to either analyze the bit pattern of the two values or run the program assigning data.num to 16706. Don't be surprised, however, if you get a different number on your computer. If you do, it means that you have a "little-endian" computer (see the box "Big and Little Endian," on page 625).

REFERENCING UNIONS

The rules for referencing a union are identical to those for structures. To reference individual fields within the union, we use the member (dot) operator. Each reference must be fully qualified from the beginning of the structure to the element being referenced. This includes the name of the union itself. When a union is being referenced through a pointer, the selection operator (arrow) is used. The following are all valid references to the unions shown in Figures 12-24 and 12-25.

Figure 12-24	Figure 12-25
data.num	data.un.company
data.chAry[0]	data.un.person.last

unions IN STRUCTURES

In a _union_, each piece of data starts at the same memory location and occupies at least a part of the same memory. Thus, when a _union_ is shared by two or more different data types, only one piece of data can be in memory at one time.

Consider, for example, an address book that contains both company and individual names. When we store a company name, the name has only one field. On the other hand, when we store an individual's name, the name has at least three parts—first name, middle initial, and last name. If we want to have only one name field in our address book, we need to use a _union_ to store the name. This design is shown in Figure 12-25.

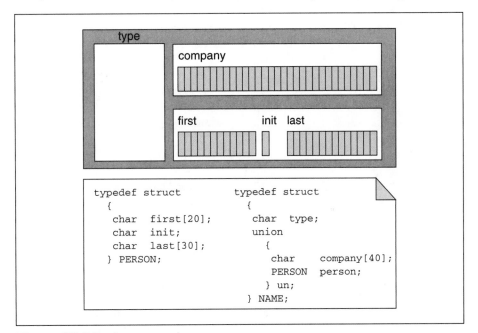

Figure 12-25   A name union

Because two different types of data can be stored in the same _union_, we need to know which type currently is stored. This is done with a type flag that is created when the data are stored. If the name is in the company format, the flag is _C,_ and if it is in the person format it is a _P._

When a _union_ is defined, C reserves enough room to store the _largest_ data object in the construct. In Figure 12-25, the size of the company name is 40 bytes and the size of the person name is 51 bytes. The size of the union structure is therefore 52 bytes (the size of the person name plus the type) regardless of what type of data are being stored. When a company name is stored, the last 11 bytes are present but unused.

Program 12-8 demonstrates the use of a _union_ in a structure by printing each format.

```
1  /* Demonstrate use of unions in structures.
2     Written by:
3     Date:
```

Program 12-8   Demonstrate unions in structures

```
 4  */
 5  #include <stdio.h>
 6  #include <string.h>
 7
 8  /* Global Structures */
 9  typedef struct
10    {
11     char   first[20];
12     char   init;
13     char   last[30];
14    } PERSON;
15
16  typedef struct
17    {
18     char   type;                /* C--company: P--person */
19     union
20       {
21        char      company[40];
22        PERSON    person;
23       } un;
24    } NAME;
25
26  int main (void)
27  {
28  /* Local Definitions */
29     int  i;
30     NAME business = {'C', "ABC Company"};
31     NAME friend;
32     NAME names[2];
33
34  /* Statements */
35     friend.type = 'P';
36     strcpy (friend.un.person.first, "Martha");
37     strcpy (friend.un.person.last,"Washington");
38     friend.un.person.init  = 'C';
39
40     names[0] = business;
41     names[1] = friend;
42
43     for (i = 0; i < 2; i++)
44         switch (names[i].type)
45             {
46               case 'C': printf("Company: %s\n",
47                         names[i].un.company);
48                      break;
49               case 'P': printf("Friend:  %s %c %s\n",
50                         names[i].un.person.first,
51                         names[i].un.person.init,
52                         names[i].un.person.last);
53                      break;
```

Program 12-8 Demonstrate unions in structures (continued)

```
54              default:  printf("Error in type\a\n");
55                      break;
56          } /* switch */
57      return 0;
58 } /* main */
```

```
Results:
Company: ABC Company
Friend:  Martha C Washington
```

Program 12-8 Demonstrate unions in structures (continued)

Program 12-8 Analysis   We begin by creating two union structures, one for a business and one for a friend. To initialize the business *union*, we used initializers (see below). To initialize the friend *union*, we used string copy and assignment. Once the unions were created, we copied them to an array to demonstrate one common processing concept.

Unions are often processed with a *switch* statement that uses the type to determine what data format is currently being processed. Note that it is the programmer's responsibility to process the data correctly. If a business identifier is used while person data are present, the program will run but garbage will be produced.

Once the correct union type has been determined, the rest of the processing is routine. We simply print the data in the union using the appropriate identifiers for its content. Note that we provide a *break* statement even though there is no possibility of an error in this simple program.

INITIALIZERS

While ANSI/ISO C permits unions to be initialized, only the first type declared in the *union* may be initialized when the variable is defined. The other types can only be initialized by assigning values or reading values into the *union*.

Program 12-8 contains an example of an initializer for the company name. When initializing a *union*, you must enclose the values in a set of braces, even if there is only one value.

Big and Little Endian

Computer hardware can be physically designed to store the most significant byte of a number at either the left end of the number (big-endian) or at the right end of the number (little-endian), as shown below.

Big-Endian   **Little-Endian**

If we consider memory as an array of bytes, then a computer that uses big endian stores the most significant byte—that is, the larger portion of the number (16,000 in the above example—at the beginning of the array. This is shown in the example on the left. Note that data[0] is 'A' and data[1] is 'B'.

In a little-endian computer, the most significant byte is stored on the right. This example is seen on the right in the above example. This time, data[0] contains 'B' and data[1] contains 'A'. If you want to know if your computer is big- or little-endian, then run Program 12-7 and check out the results.

INTERNET ADDRESSES

As a final example of *union* processing, let's consider how Internet addresses are formatted and processed. We are most familiar with the Internet domain names such as www.deanza.edu. These names are easy to remember and use. The real Internet Protocol (IP) address, however, is formatted in decimal–dot format, as shown below.

```
153.18.8.105
```

The decimal–dot format is used primarily by system administrators. To conserve transmission time and facilitate processing, however, the IP address must be converted to a 4-byte integer for transmission down the internet.

Each portion of the IP address has a maximum value of 255. This means that it can be stored in 1 byte. To store the address in an integer, we simply convert each portion of the address to 1 byte and store it in the appropriate portion of the integer. Thus, in our example, we convert 153 to its corresponding (extended) ASCII character and store it in the first byte of the integer. Then we convert the 18 and store it in the second byte, 8 into the third byte, and finally 105 into the fourth byte. To process the integer address as both an integer and an array of four characters requires a union.

Given that the IP address is a string, we use the string token operator and a loop for the conversion. The code is shown in Program 12-9.

```
 1  /* Reformat IP string address to long integer.
 2         Written by:
 3         Date:
 4  */
 5  #include <stdio.h>
 6  #include <string.h>
 7  #include <stdlib.h>
 8
 9  /* Global Structures */
10     typedef union
11        {
12         unsigned char chAddr[4];
13         unsigned long numAddr;
14        } IP_ADDR;
15
16  int main (void)
17  {
18  /* Local Definitions */
19     int       i;
20     IP_ADDR   addr;
21     char      *parser;
22     char      *strAddr = "153.18.8.105";
23
24  /* Statements */
25     /* Convert first address segment */
26     parser = strtok (strAddr, ".");
27     addr.chAddr[0] = strtol (parser, (char **)NULL, 10);
28
29     for (i = 1; i < 4; i++)
```

Program 12-9 Convert IP address to *long*

```
30        {
31            /* Convert decimal dot positions 2, 3, 4 */
32            parser = strtok (NULL, ".");
33            addr.chAddr[i] = strtol (parser, (char **)NULL, 10);
34        } /* for */
35
36        /* Now print results */
37        printf ("IP decimal dot    : %d.%d.%d.%d\n",
38                addr.chAddr[0], addr.chAddr[1],
39                addr.chAddr[2], addr.chAddr[3]);
40        printf ("IP binary address: %lu\n", addr.numAddr);
41
42        return 0;
43  } /* main */
```

Results: (Big Endian only — see page 625.)
IP decimal dot   : 153.18.8.105
IP binary address: 2568095849

Program 12-9 Convert IP address to *long* (continued)

Program 12-9 Analysis   Before you study this program, you may want to review the parsing concepts discussed in Chapter 11 (see *strtok* in Chapter 11, on page 550). They are used extensively in this program.

In Statement 22, we set up an IP address using the decimal–dot notation. It is constructed so that each portion is a graphical character (A.B.y.z). We then parse the first number and place it in the first byte of the binary address. This is necessary because the first string token format differs from the one that parses the rest of the string (see Statements 26 and 33).

Within the loop, we parse the rest of the string, convert it to a decimal value, and store the address elements in the second, third, and fourth positions of the binary address. After the loop, we print converted address, first in its character format and then as a long integer.

12-9   PROGRAMMING APPLICATION

In this section, we develop a program that simulates the operation of an elevator. The elevator serves floors from zero (the basement) to the top floor. The elevator is very old and is not fully automatic. When people enter the elevator, they enter their desired floor number. Several numbers can be requested at a time. After all numbers have been entered, the passengers close the door by pressing the close door button (the return key).

Each time the door closes, the elevator checks to see if any floors in the current direction (up or down) need to be serviced. If there are, then it services these floors first, starting with the closest one to the current floor. If no floors in the current direction need service, it checks the opposite direction, again servicing the one closest to the current floor.

Each time the elevator arrives at a floor, new passengers can get on and request their floor. The new requests are added to the ones still pending, and the elevator again evaluates which floor will be processed next.

The structure for this program is portrayed in Figure 12-26. The elevator is represented as a structure with two fields, the current floor and a pointer to an array of buttons. The button values are IN, meaning the floor has been requested, and OUT, meaning the floor has not been requested. After a floor has been serviced, the button is reset.

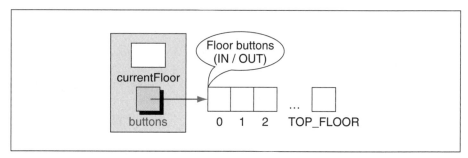

Figure 12-26 Elevator structure

The elevator design is shown two different ways. Figure 12-27 is a structure chart for the program. Figure 12-28 is a state diagram for the elevator. A state diagram is a design technique that is often used with realtime systems to show how a system moves from one state to another. For an elevator, it can be in one of three states: moving up, moving down, or stopped. Each of these states is represented by a circle in the diagram. To move from one state to another, a change must occur in the elevator environment. For example, to change from the stop state to the up state, a button must be pressed. This is reflected on the line between stop and up as anyUp.

The main function for the elevator program is seen in Program 12-10.

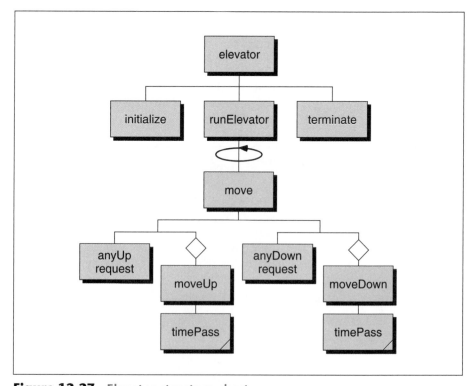

Figure 12-27 Elevator structure chart

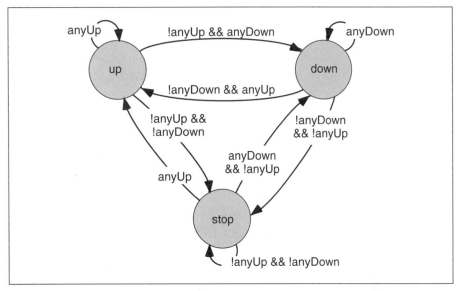

Figure 12-28   Elevator state diagram

```
 1   /* This program simulates the operation of an elevator.
 2         Written by:
 3         Date:
 4   */
 5   #include <stdio.h>
 6   #include <stdlib.h>
 7   #include <ctype.h>
 8
 9   #define TOP_FLOOR 10
10   #define DELAY_FACTOR 10000
11
12   typedef enum {OUT, IN} BUTTON_STATUS;
13   typedef enum {DOWN, STOP, UP} DIRECTION_STATUS;
14   typedef struct
15      {
16       int              currentFloor;
17       BUTTON_STATUS    *buttons;
18      } ELEVATOR;
19
20   /* Prototype Declaration */
21   void initialize       (ELEVATOR *elev);
22   void runElevator      (ELEVATOR *elev);
23   void terminate        (ELEVATOR *elev);
24   void move             (ELEVATOR *elev);
25   int  anyUpRequest     (ELEVATOR *elev);
26   int  anyDownRequest   (ELEVATOR *elev);
27   void moveUp           (ELEVATOR *elev);
28   void moveDown         (ELEVATOR *elev);
29   void timePass         (int m);
```

Program 12-10   Elevator: `main`

```
30
31  int main (void)
32  {
33  /* Local Definitions */
34  ELEVATOR elevator;
35
36  /* Statements */
37     initialize   (&elevator);
38     runElevator  (&elevator);
39     terminate    (&elevator);
40
41     return 0;
42  }  /* main */
```

Program 12-10 Elevator: `main` (continued)

Program 12-10 Analysis   Elevator's `main` simply calls three functions: `initialize` (Program 12-11), `runElevator` (Program 12-12), and `terminate` (Program 12-17). Of the three, `runElevator` is obviously the function of interest. It simulates the actual running of the elevator.

```
1   /* ================= initialize =================
2      This function dynamically allocates memory locations for
3      the buttons and initializes the current floor to 1 to show
4      that the elevator is parked in the first floor.
5         Pre    nothing
6         Post   elevator created, all buttons reset, and
7                parked at first floor (not basement)
8   */
9   void initialize (ELEVATOR *elev)
10  {
11  /* Local Definitions */
12     int i;
13
14  /* Statements */
15     elev->buttons =
16        (BUTTON_STATUS *) calloc(TOP_FLOOR + 1,
17            sizeof (BUTTON_STATUS));
18
19     for (i = 0; i <= TOP_FLOOR; i++)
20        elev->buttons [i] = OUT;
21     elev->currentFloor = 1;
22
23     return;
24  }  /* initialize */
```

Program 12-11 Elevator: `initialize`

Program 12-12 simulates the operation of the elevator.

```
1   /* ================= runElevator ==================
2      Simulate the operation of the elevator.
3          Pre    elevator structure has been initialized
4          Post   simulation is complete
5   */
6   void runElevator (ELEVATOR *elev)
7   {
8   /* Local Definitions */
9      char  buffer [81];
10     int   floor;
11     char *pStrIn;
12
13  /* Statements */
14     printf("\n\nThis elevator goes from basement (0) ");
15     printf("to floor %d", TOP_FLOOR);
16     printf( "\n\nType floors & press return key to start");
17     printf( "\nIf no new floors, just press return key.");
18     printf("\nTo quit, key EOF");
19     printf("\n\nPlease enter floors: ");
20
21     while (fgets(buffer, 81, stdin))
22        {
23         pStrIn = buffer;
24         while (*pStrIn != '\n')
25            {
26              /* Locate next floor digit & convert to int */
27             while (*pStrIn == ' ')
28                pStrIn++;
29             if (!isdigit (*pStrIn))
30                {
31                 printf("\aInvalid floor %c\n", *pStrIn);
32                 pStrIn++;
33                } /* if */
34             else
35                {
36                 sscanf (pStrIn, "%d", &floor);
37                 if (floor  == elev->currentFloor)
38                     printf("\n\aAlready on floor %d.",
39                             elev->currentFloor);
40                 else
41                    if (floor < 0 || floor > TOP_FLOOR)
42                        printf("\n\a%d is not a valid floor",
43                                floor);
44                    else
45                        elev->buttons [floor] = IN;
46
47                 /* Synchronize sscanf & *pStrIn */
```

Program 12-12 Elevator: runElevator

```
48              while (isdigit (*pStrIn))
49                  pStrIn++;
50          } /* else */
51        } /* while */
52
53      move (elev);
54      printf("\n\nPlease enter floors: ");
55    } /* while */
56    return ;
57 }  /* runElevator */
```

Program 12-12   Elevator: `runElevator` (continued)

Program 12-12 Analysis   The simulation is controlled by `runElevator`. The technique we use to prevent invalid user input is interesting. After reading the input stream, we use a pointer to parse the string after skipping whitespace. If the current character is a digit, we use *sscanf* to format the digit(s) as an integer. If it is not a digit, print an error message and skip it. (Of course, in a real elevator, it is impossible to get an invalid floor.) Then, after converting the digit string to an integer, we synchronize the buffer and our pointer with a small *while* loop.

As we parse out the integers in the input stream, we "push" their corresponding buttons in our data structure. This code is shown at Statement 45 in Program 12-12.

Program 12-13 moves the elevator to a requested floor.

```
 1 /* ================= move =================
 2    Moves the elevator to a requested floor. It stops
 3    the elevator after responding to one request.
 4        Pre    given elevator
 5        Post   elevator has been moved--while it is
 6               moving, the floors are called out
 7 */
 8 void move (ELEVATOR *elev)
 9 {
10 /* Local Definitions */
11    static DIRECTION_STATUS direction = STOP;
12
13    int anyUp;
14    int anyDown;
15
16 /* Statements */
17    anyUp    = anyUpRequest   (elev);
18    anyDown  = anyDownRequest (elev);
19
20    if (direction == UP)
21       {
22        if (!anyUp && anyDown)
```

Program 12-13   Elevator: move

```
23          direction = DOWN;
24      else
25          if (!anyUp && !anyDown)
26              direction = STOP;
27      } /* UP */
28
29  else if (direction == DOWN)
30      {
31      if (!anyDown && anyUp)
32          direction = UP;
33      else
34          if (!anyDown && !anyUp)
35              direction = STOP;
36      } /* DOWN */
37
38  else if (direction == STOP)
39      {
40      if (anyUp)
41          direction = UP;
42      else
43          if (anyDown)
44              direction = DOWN;
45      } /* else if stop */
46
47  if (direction == UP)
48      moveUp (elev);
49  else
50      if (direction == DOWN)
51          moveDown (elev);
52      else
53          printf("\n***** NO BUTTON PRESSED ***** ");
54  return;
55  } /* move */
```

Program 12-13   Elevator: move (continued)

Program 12-13 Analysis   The move function is one of the more interesting functions in the simulation. At any given point in the operation, the elevator can be in one of three states: moving up, moving down, or stopped. We use an enumerated type to track the state.

If the elevator is moving up, we will continue up as long as there are requests for higher floors. If there are none, we test for down requests. If there are any down requests, we change the state to down and proceed. If there are no up requests and no down requests, we change the state to stopped. This logic is seen in Statements 20 through 45 of Program 12-13. Note the use of the blocks to ensure that the *if* and *else* statements are properly paired.

Program 12-14 simulates the elevator movement as it moves up and down.

```
1    /* ================== moveUp ==================
2       This function simulates the movement of the elevator when
3       it is going up.
4          Pre    given moving up elevator
5          Post   up simulation is displayed on the screen
6    */
7    void  moveUp (ELEVATOR *elev)
8    {
9    /* Statements */
10       printf ("\nThe door is being closed …");
11       printf ("\nWe are going up.");
12       (elev->currentFloor)++;
13       while (elev->buttons[elev->currentFloor] != IN)
14          {
15            printf("\n");
16            timePass (2);
17            printf("\nPassing floor %d", elev->currentFloor);
18            printf("\n ");
19            timePass (2);
20            (elev->currentFloor)++;
21          } /* while */
22
23       elev->buttons [elev->currentFloor] = OUT;
24       printf("\nThe door is  being opened …");
25       printf("\n");
26       printf("\n ***** FLOOR %d ***** ", elev->currentFloor);
27       printf("\n");
28       timePass(4);
29       return;
30   }  /* moveUp */
31
32   /* ================== moveDown ==================
33      This function simulates the movement of the elevator when
34      it is going down.
35         Pre    given moving down elevator
36         Post   down simulation is displayed on the screen
37   */
38   void moveDown (ELEVATOR *elev)
39   {
40   /* Statements */
41      printf("\nThe door is being closed …");
42      printf("\nWe are going down");
43      (elev->currentFloor)--;
44      while (elev->buttons [elev ->currentFloor] != IN)
45         {
46           printf("\n");
47           timePass (2);
```

Program 12-14 Elevator: moveUp

```
48        printf("\nPassing floor %d", elev->currentFloor);
49        printf("\n");
50        timePass (2);
51        (elev->currentFloor)--;
52      } /* while */
53    elev->buttons [elev->currentFloor] = OUT;
54    printf("\nThe door is being opened ...");
55    printf("\n ");
56    printf("\n ***** FLOOR %d ***** ", elev->currentFloor);
57    printf("\n");
58    timePass (4);
59
60    return;
61 }  /* moveDown */
```

Program 12-14 Elevator: moveUp (continued)

Program 12-14 Analysis Both moveUp and moveDown operate similarly. They move past the current floor in the correct direction and "call out" the floor as we pass them. A timing loop is included to simulate the time it takes the elevator to reach the next floor.

Program 12-15 contains two functions: anyUpRequest checks for floors above the current position; anyDownRequest checks for floors below the current position.

```
 1 /* ================ anyUpRequest ==================
 2    This function checks to see if any request is for a floor
 3    above the current floor.
 4        Pre    given elevator
 5        Post   return 1 if button above current floor pushed
 6               return 0 otherwise.
 7 */
 8 int anyUpRequest (ELEVATOR *elev)
 9 {
10 /* Local Definitions */
11    int   check;
12    int   isAny = 0;
13
14 /* Statements */
15    for (check = elev->currentFloor;
16         check <= TOP_FLOOR && !isAny;
17         check++)
18      isAny = (elev->buttons[check] == IN);
19
20    return isAny;
21 }  /* anyUpRequest */
22
23 /* ================ anyDownRequest ==================
24    This function checks to see if any request is for a floor
25    below the current floor.
26        Pre    given elevator
```

Program 12-15 Elevator: anyUpRequest

```
27              Post   return 1 if button below current floor pushed
28                     return 0 otherwise
29  */
30  int anyDownRequest (ELEVATOR *elev)
31  {
32  /* Local Definitions */
33     int   check;
34     int   isAny = 0;
35
36  /* Statements */
37     for (check = elev->currentFloor; check >=  0; check--)
38        isAny = isAny || (elev->buttons[check] == IN);
39
40     return isAny;
41  }   /* anyDownRequest */
```

Program 12-15   Elevator: `anyUpRequest` (continued)

Program 12-15 Analysis   Compare the *for* loops in `anyDownRequest` and `anyUpRequest`. One is much more efficient than the other. Do you see why? In `anyUpRequest`, we stop when we find the first request for a floor above the current one. In `anyDownRequest`, we check all floors below the current one, even if the first one has been requested. This means we always examine all lower floors.

Note the logic to set `isAny` at Statement 38 in Program 12-15. The current setting is or'd with a button. If either are true, the result is true. Thus, once we find a floor has been requested, `isAny` will remain set regardless of the settings of the other buttons. This is a common technique to analyze a series of logical values.

Program 12-16 contains a loop to simulate time passing. We use a simple *for* loop.

```
1   /* ================== timePass ==================
2      This function simulates the concept of passing time by
3      executing an empty for-loop.
4         Pre   time to be passed (number of moments)
5         Post  time has passed
6   */
7   void timePass   (int time)
8    {
9   /* Local Definitions */
10     long  i;
11
12  /* Statements */
13     for (i = 0; i < (time * DELAY_FACTOR); i++)
14        ;
15     return;
16  }  /* timePass */
```

Program 12-16   Elevator: `timePass`

Program 12-16 Analysis   The factor in the timing loop depends on the speed of your computer. In this case, we use 10,000. On a faster computer, you need to make the factor larger. On a slower computer, you need to make it smaller.

Note how we code the null statement in the *for* loop. Putting the null statement on a line by itself makes the function more readable. If the null statement were put at the end of the *for* statement, it would be too easy to think that the next statement, the *return* in this function, were part of the *for* loop.

The termination code is shown in Program 12-17.

```
 1  /* ================= terminate =================
 2      Release the memory occupied by buttons.
 3          Pre    given elevator
 4          Post   elevator memory is released
 5  */
 6  void terminate (ELEVATOR *elev)
 7  {
 8  /* Statements */
 9      free (elev->buttons);
10      return ;
11  }   /* terminate */
12  /* ================= End of Program ================= */
```

Program 12-17   Elevator: terminate

Program 12-17 Analysis   Although we do not need to release memory when terminating a program, we include the logic to do so for completeness.

In this section we discuss two important aspects of program design: function coupling and data hiding.

COUPLING

In Chapter 11, we discussed a concept known as functional cohesion, a measure of how closely related the processes are within a function. A related topic, coupling, is a measure of how tightly two functions are bound to each other. The more tightly coupled they are, the less independent they are. Since our objective is to make the modules as independent as possible, we want them to be loosely coupled.

Loose coupling is desirable for several reasons:

1. Independent—that is, loosely coupled—functions are more likely to be reusable.
2. Loosely coupled functions are less likely to create errors in related functions; conversely, the tighter the coupling, the higher the probability that an error in one function will generate an error in a related function.
3. Maintenance modifications—that is, modifications required to implement new user requirements—are easier and less apt to create errors with loosely coupled functions.

In his book on designing structured systems, Page-Jones describes five types of coupling. We review them here. For an in-depth discussion of the concept, refer to Chapter 5 in Page-Jones's book, *The Practical Guide to Structured Systems Design.*[1]

Data Coupling

Data coupling passes only the minimum required data from the calling function to the called function. All required data are passed as parameters, and no extra data are passed. This is the best form of coupling and should be used whenever possible.

When you write simple functions that work on only one task, the coupling naturally tends to be data coupling. Consider, for example, the function `exchange` in the selection sort in Program 10-4 on page 493. This function exchanges two integers. It receives pointers to the two integers that it will exchange and nothing else. It makes no references to any data outside the function, except through the parameter pointers. This function uses data coupling and is highly reusable.

> Functions in well-structured programs are
> highly cohesive and loosely coupled.

We could have fallen into the trap of passing extra parameters by passing the function the array and the index locations of the two integers to be exchanged. The function would have worked just as well, but the coupling would not have been as loose. Now it requires an array of integers instead of

[1]Meilir Page-Jones, *The Practical Guide to Structured Systems Design*, Yourdon Press Computing Series (Upper Saddle River, N.J.: Prentice Hall, 1988).

just integers. Furthermore, we could have made the coupling even tighter had we referred to the maximum size of the array using the precompiler declaration `SIZE`. At this point, it is highly questionable whether the function could be used in another program.

Stamp Coupling

Functions are **stamp coupled** if the parameters are composite objects such as arrays or structures. Most of the functions in the selection sort in Chapter 10 use stamp coupling because they pass the array. (Although it could be argued that we are passing only a pointer to the array, the intent is to modify the array. We are, therefore, passing the array for the purposes of this discussion.)

You should now be arguing, "But we have to pass the array!" Yes, that is true. Stamp coupling is not bad and is often necessary. The danger with stamp coupling is that often it is just too easy to send a structure when all the data in the structure are not required. When extra data are sent, we begin to open the door for errors and undesired side effects.

Consider the time stamp described in Figure 12-19 on page 610. This structure contains two nested structures, `date` and `time`. If we were to use these data, for example, to print the date in a report heading, and passed the whole structure, we would send too much data! In addition, if we were to pass the structure by address rather than by value, we risk the possibility of an error in one function accidentally changing the data in the structure and causing a second error. The correct solution is to pass only the data that are needed and then only by value when possible.

> Stamp coupling should pass only the data needed.

A common practice to reduce the number of parameters required for a function is to create a structure that contains all the data the function needs and pass it. Page-Jones refers to this as *bundling*.[2] It is a common practice, but it is not a good practice for three reasons.

1. Maintenance is made more difficult because it is more difficult to trace data through a program.
2. Extra data can be passed. For example, a bundled structure is created for a series of related functions, but not all of them use all the data. The temptation is just too great to pass the structure even though only one or two of the members are needed.
3. The semantics of the structure are often artificial, making the program more difficult to read and understand.

> Avoid bundling unrelated data just to reduce the number of parameters being passed between functions.

Control Coupling

Control coupling is the passing of flags that may be used to direct the logic flow of a function. It closely resembles data coupling except that a flag is being passed rather than data.

---

[2]Meilir Page-Jones, *The Practical Guide to Structured Systems Design*.

In C, flags are often returned from a function rather than being passed as parameters, but the intent and usage are the same. For example, consider the return values from *scanf*. It returns either EOF, a definite flag, or the number of values successfully read, which can also be used as a flag for success. An example of a flag being passed in a function you might write is the user-selected option in the menu function of an interactive program. This flag directs the entire flow of the program. The option is a special type of flag known as a data flag. It is data entered by the user and at the same time it is a flag intended to direct the flow of the program.

Properly used, control coupling is a necessary and valid method of communicating between two functions. Like stamp coupling, however, it can be misused. Properly used, it communicates status: The end of the file has been reached. The search value was found.

Poor flag usage is usually an indication of poor program design, for example, when a process is divided between two or more independent functions. Flags used to communicate horizontally across several functions in the structure chart are often an indication of poor design. Action flags, as opposed to status flags, that require the receiving function to perform some special processing are also highly suspect. An example of an action flag is a flag that directs a customer's purchase not be approved rather than simply reporting that the credit limit has been exceeded or that no payment was received last month.

> Control coupling should be used only to pass status.

Global Coupling

Global coupling uses global variables to communicate between two, or usually more, functions. Page-Jones calls it *common coupling*. With all that we have said about not using global variables, it should not come as a surprise that this is not a good coupling technique. In fact, it should *never* be used.

You should never use global coupling for several reasons. We cite only the big three.

1. Global coupling makes it virtually impossible to determine which modules are communicating with each other. When a change needs to be made to a program, therefore, it is not possible to evaluate and isolate the impact of the change. This often causes functions that were not changed to suddenly fail.
2. Global coupling tightly binds a function to the program. This means that it cannot be easily transported to another program.
3. Global coupling leads to multiple flag meanings. This problem is often made worse by using generic flag names, such as f1, f2, …, f21. (Finding 21 flags in a single program is not an exaggeration. We know of one assembly program that had more flags. In fact, it had one flag that was used solely to indicate that another flag had been set but was now turned off; in other words, a flag that returned the status of a flag!)

   The danger here should be obvious. If a flag can be used globally to communicate between two functions, it is highly probable that at some point this flag could be erroneously changed by a third function that used it for another purpose.

Content Coupling

The last type of coupling is very difficult, but not impossible, to use in C. **Content coupling** occurs when one function refers directly to the data or statements in another function. Obviously, this concept breaks all the tenets of structured programming.

Referring to the data in another function requires that the data be made externally visible outside the function. This is impossible in C. The only thing that comes even remotely close is global variables. Since we have stressed the dangers of global variables before, we will simply state here that they should not be used for communication within one compile unit.

DATA HIDING

We have previously discussed the concept of global and local variables. In the discussion, we pointed out that anything placed before main was said to be in the global part of the program. With the exception of data that need to be visible to functions in other compile units, no data need to be placed in this section.

One of the principles of structured programming states that the internal data structure should be hidden from the user's view. The two terms you usually hear are *data hiding* and *data encapsulation*. Both of these principles have as their objective protecting data from accidental destruction by parts of your program that don't need access to the data. In other words, if a part of your program doesn't need data to do its job, it shouldn't be able to *see* the data.

Any variables placed in the global area of your program—that is, before main—can be used and changed by every part of your program. This is in direct conflict with the structured programming principles of data hiding and data encapsulation.

SUMMARY

We have described five different ways that two functions can communicate. The first three are all valid and useful, although not without some dangers. These communication techniques also provide data hiding. Data coupling is universally accepted and provides the loosest communication between two functions. Stamp and control coupling present some dangers that must be recognized. When using stamp coupling, do not pass more data than are required. Keep control coupling narrow—that is, between only two functions. You should always avoid the last two, global and content coupling. They do not protect the data.

12-11 TIPS AND COMMON PROGRAMMING ERRORS

1. Don't forget the semicolon at the end of the declaration of structures and unions. This is one of the locations where you see a semicolon after a closing brace (}) in C.

2. Because the member operator has a higher precedence than the indirection operator, parentheses are required to reference a member with a pointer.

   ```
   (*ptr).mem
   ```

3. The selection operator (−>) is one token. Do not put a space between its symbols (between − and >).

4. To access a member in an array structure, you need the index operator. For example, the correct expression to access a member named mem in an array of structure named ary is

   ```
   ary[i].mem
   ```

5. The type name in a *typedef* comes after the closing brackets and before the semicolon:

   ```
   typedef   struct
        {
        ...;
        ...;
        } TYPE_NAME;
   ```

6. You cannot define a variable at the same time that you declare a type definition. In other words, you are *not* allowed to do the following:

   ```
   typedef   struct
        {
        ...
        ...;
        } TYPE_NAME variable_name;          /* ERROR */
   ```

7. You may not use the same structure name with a tag inside a structure. The following declaration is not valid:

   ```
   typedef   struct   TAG_NAME
        {
        ...;
        ...;
        struct TAG_NAME field_name;          /* ERROR */
        } ID;
   ```

8. A union can store only one of its members at a time. You must always keep track of the available member. In other words, storing one data type in a union and accessing another data type is a logic error and maybe a serious run-time error.

9. Although structures can be assigned to each other, it is a compile error to assign a structure of one type to a structure of a different type.

10. It is a compile error to use a structure type with only its tag; that is, without the keyword *struct,* as shown below.

```
struct stu
    {...};
stu aStudent;              /* Compile Error */
struct stu aStudent;       /* Correct Code  */
```

11. It is a compile error to compare two structures or unions, even if they are of the same type.

12. It is a compile error to refer to a structure member without qualification, such as id rather than `student.id`.

13. It is a compile error to omit a level of qualification when structures are nested. For example, in Figure 12-17 on page 606, it is an error to omit the time qualifier in the following reference.

```
stamp.time.min
```

14. It is a compile error to forget the address operator with *scanf* when referring to a nonstring member. The pointer is the address of the structure, not the address of the member.

15. Referencing an identifier in a union when a different type is active is a logic error and may cause the program to fail.

16. It is a compile error to initialize a union with data that do not match the type of the first member.

12-12   KEY TERMS AND CONCEPTS[3]

content coupling
control coupling
data coupling
enumeration constant
field

global coupling
nested structures
slack bytes
stamp coupling
struct

structure
structure variable
tagged structure
typedef
union

[3]Note: Italic terms are keywords.

12-13   SUMMARY

- C has five different derived types: array, pointer, enumerated, structure, and union.

- An enumerated type is built on the standard type, integer.

- In an enumerated type, each identifier is given an integer value.

- A structure is a collection of related elements, possibly of different types, having a single name.

- Each element in a structure is called a field.

- One difference between an array and a structure is that all elements in an array must be of the same type while the elements in a structure can be of the same or different types.

- C has three different ways to declare and/or define a structure: variable structure, tagged structure, and type-defined structure.

- A structure can be initialized when it is defined. The rule for structure initialization is the same as for array initialization.

- We can access the members of a structure using the member operator (**.**).

- Structures can be accessed through a pointer. The best way to do this is to use the selection operator (—>).

- The following two expressions are the same if `ptr` is a pointer to a structure:

```
(*p).x              p->x
```

- One of the applications of structures is in a construct called array of structures.

- The information in a structure can be sent to a function using one of the following methods:
  1. Sending individual members
  2. Sending the whole structure
  3. Sending a pointer to the structure

- A union is a construct that allows a portion of memory to be used by different types of data.

- In software engineering, coupling is the measure of how tightly two functions are bound to each other.

- Computer science has identified five types of coupling: data, stamp, control, global, and content.

- Functions in a well-structured program are loosely coupled.

- Data coupling means passing only the data needed.

- Stamp coupling means passing data in a structure.

- Control coupling means passing only control status.

- Avoid global coupling.

- Never use content coupling.

- Good program design can be measured by three principles: Modules must be independent, modules must be loosely coupled, and each module must do a single job.

12-14   PRACTICE SETS

REVIEW QUESTIONS

1. Variables are created with a type definition (*typedef*).
   a. True   b. False

2. An integer value can be assigned to only one enumeration constant in an enumerated type.
   a. True   b. False

3. A structure variable is used to declare a type containing multiple fields.
   a. True   b. False

4. The selection operator is used with a pointer to access individual fields in a structure.
   a. True   b. False

5. The structured programming concept known as coupling describes how data are passed to functions.
   a. True   b. False

6. Which of the following is not a derived type?
   a. Arrays   c. Float   e. Union
   b. Enumerated   d. Pointers

7. The _____ can be used to create a new type that can be used anywhere a type is permitted.
   a. array
   b. record type
   c. structure (*struct*)
   d. type definition
   e. both a structure and a type definition

8. The enumerated type (*enum*) is derived from the _____ type.
   a. character
   b. boolean
   c. floating-point
   d. integer
   e. structured

9. Which of the following statements about enumerated types is true?
   a. Declaring an enumerated type automatically creates a variable.
   b. Declaring an enumerated variable without a tag creates an enumerated type.
   c. Enumerated types cannot be used in a type definition.
   d. The enumerated values are automatically assigned constant values unless otherwise directed.
   e. The identifiers in an enumerated type are enumeration variables.

10. A(n) _____ is the smallest element of named data that has meaning.
    a. array
    b. field
    c. record type
    d. structure (*struct*)
    e. type

11. Which of the following statements about structures (*struct*) is true?
    a. A structure without a tag can be used as a derived type.
    b. Structures are derived types based on the integer standard type.
    c. The fields in a structure must be of the same type.
    d. The variable structure is coded with a tag.
    e. C has three different structure declarations: variable, tagged, and type-defined structures.

12. The _____ structure creates a type that can be used later to define variables. Variables cannot be created at the same time.
    a. array
    b. record-typed
    c. tagged
    d. type-defined
    e. variable

13. Given a structure variable named `stu`, whose type is `STU`, which contains a field named `major`, which of the following statements correctly refers to `major`?
    a. `major`
    b. `stu-major`
    c. `stu.major`
    d. `STU-major`
    e. `STU.major`

14. Given a pointer, `ptr`, to a structure `stu` containing a field `name`, which of the following statements correctly references `name`?
    a. `ptr.name`
    b. `ptr->name`
    c. `ptr.stu.name`
    d. `ptr->stu->name`
    e. `ptr->stu.name`

15. A(n) _____ is a construct that allows a portion of memory to be shared by different types of data.
    a. array
    b. field
    c. *struct*
    d. *union*
    e. variable

16. Determine which of the following statements are true and which are false:
    a. A structure cannot have two fields with the same name.
    b. A structure cannot have two fields of the same type.
    c. A structure must have at least one field.
    d. A field in a structure can itself be a structure.

17. Determine which of the following statements are true and which are false:
    a. A *union* can have another *union* as one of the fields.
    b. A structure cannot have a *union* as one of its fields.
    c. A structure cannot have an array as one of its elements.
    d. When accessing the fields of a structure through a pointer p, the following two expressions are the same:
       `(*p).field_name`   `p >field_name`

EXERCISES

18. Declare a tagged structure for a student record consisting of five fields: student ID (integer), first name (a dynamically allocated string), last name (a dynamically allocated string), total credits completed (integer), and accumulated grade point average (floating-point). A graphic representation of the structure is shown in Figure 12-29.

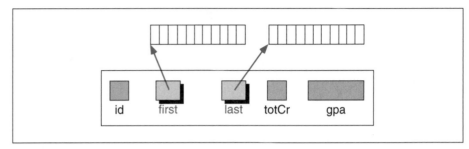

Figure 12-29   Data for Exercise 18

19. Declare a type-defined structure for an inventory item consisting of six fields: part number (integer), part description (a dynamically allocated string), reorder point (integer), number of items currently on hand (integer), unit measure (a string, maximum size 8), and unit price (floating-point). A graphic representation of the structure is shown in Figure 12-30.

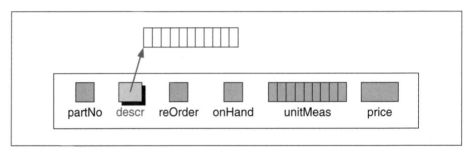

Figure 12-30   Data for Exercise 19

20. Declare an array of 12 elements. Each element is a structure with three fields. The first field shows the month in numeric form (1 to 12). The second field shows the name of the month (a dynamically allocated string). The third field shows the number of days in the month. Initialize the array. A graphic representation of the structure is shown in Figure 12-31.

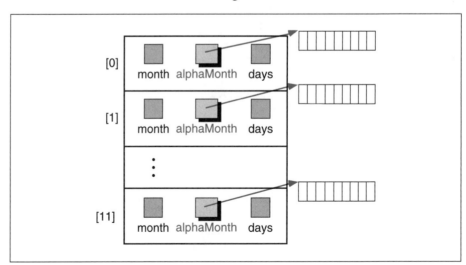

Figure 12-31   Data for Exercise 20

21. Declare a calendar as an array of 366 elements. Each element of the array is a structure having three fields. The first field is the name of the month (a dynamically allocated string). The second field is the day in the month (an integer). The third field is the description of activities for a particular day (a dynamically allocated string). A graphic representation of the structure is shown in Figure 12-32.

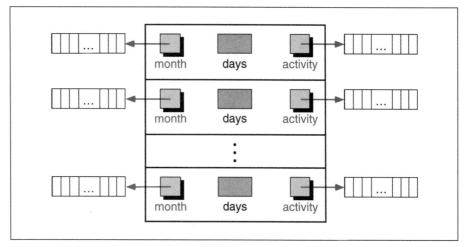

Figure 12-32 Data for Exercise 21

22. Imagine we have declared the following structure:

```
typedef struct FUN
    {
     char    x;
     char    *y;
     int     z[20];
    } FUNNY;
```

Determine which of the following definitions are valid and which are invalid. If invalid, explain the error.

a. `struct FUN f1;`

b. `struct FUN f5 [23];`

c. `struct FUNNY f2;`

d. `FUNNY f3;`

e. `FUNNY f4 [20];`

23. Imagine we have the following declaration and definitions:

```
typedef  struct   FUN
    {
     char  x;
     char *y;
     int   z[20];
    } FUNNY;

struct FUN fn1;
FUNNY  fn2;
struct FUN fn3 [10];
FUNNY  fn4 [50];
```

Determine which of the following assignment statements are valid and which are invalid. If invalid, explain the error.

a. `fn1.x = 'b';`

b. `fn2.y = 'b';`

c. `fn3[4].z[5] = 234;`

d. `fn4[23].y = "1234";`

e. `fn4[23] = fn3[5];`

24. Imagine we have the following declaration:

```
typedef enum {ONE = 1, TWO = 2} CHOICE;
typedef union
    {
      char  choice1;
      int   choice2;
    } U_TYPE;

  typedef struct
    {
      float    fixedBefore;
      CHOICE   choice;
      U_TYPE   flexible;
      float    fixedAfter;
    } S_TYPE;
```

Draw a schematic diagram for `S_TYPE`.

25. Using the declaration of `S_TYPE` (declared in Exercise 24), show what will be printed from the following program segment. (Assume that the `S_TYPE` declaration is global.)

```
#include <stdio.h>
int main (void)
{
 S_TYPE  s;
 S_TYPE  *ps;

 s.fixedBefore = 23.34;
 s.choice = ONE;
 s.flexible.choice1 = 'B';
 s.fixedAfter = 12.45;
 ps = & s;
 printf ("\n%f", ps->fixedAfter);
 printf ("\n%d", ps->flexible.choice1);
 printf ("\n%d", s.fixedBefore);
 return 0;
}
```

PROBLEMS

26. Write a function called `elapsedTime` with two parameters, the start time and the end time. Each parameter is a structure with three fields showing the hours, minutes, and seconds of a specific time (see Figure 12-17 on page 606). The function is to return a time structure containing the time elapsed between the two parameters. You must handle the situation when the start time is in the previous day.

27. Write a function called `increment` that accepts a date structure with three fields. The first field contains the month (a pointer to a string). The second field is an integer showing the day in the month. The third field is an integer showing the year. The function increments the date by 1 day and returns the new date. If the date is the last day in the month, the month field must also be changed. If the month is December, the value of the year field must also be changed when the day is 31. A year is a leap year if

    a. It is evenly divisible by 4 but not by 100, or

    b. It is evenly divisible by 400.

28. Write a function called `futureDate`. The function is to use two parameters. The first parameter is a structure containing today's date (as defined in Problem 27). The second parameter is an integer showing the number of days after today. The function returns a structure showing the next date, which may be in a future year.

29. Write a function called `later` that receives two date parameters, compares the two dates, and returns true (1) if the first date is earlier than the second date and false (0) if the first date is later. Each parameter is a structure containing a date (as defined in Problem 27).

30. Write a function that accepts an integer representing money in dollars (no fraction) and returns a structure with 6 fields. The fields represent, respectively, the minimum number of $100, $50, $20, $10, $5, and $1 bills needed to total the money in the parameter.

31. Write a function that compares two fraction structures (see Figure 12-6 on page 593). If the fractions are equal, it returns zero. If the fraction in the first parameter is less than the fraction in the second parameter, it returns a negative number. Otherwise, it returns a positive number. Hint: Convert the fraction to a floating-point number.

32. A point in a plane can be represented by its two coordinates, x and y. Therefore, we can represent a point in a plane by a structure having two fields as shown below.

    ```
    typedef   struct
       {
       int  x;
       int  y;
       } POINT;
    ```

    Write a function that accepts the structure representing a point and returns an integer (1, 2, 3, or 4) that indicates in which quadrant the point is located, as shown in Figure 12-33.

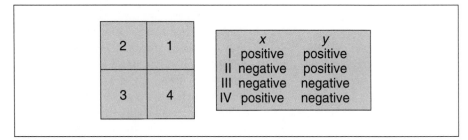

Figure 12-33   Problem 7 quartile coordinates for Problem 32

33. A straight line is an object connecting two points. Therefore, a line can be represented by a nested structure having two structures of the type POINT, as defined in Problem 32.

```
typedef    struct
          {
          POINT   beg;
          POINT   end;
          } LINE;
```

Write a function that accepts two parameters of type POINT and returns a structure of type LINE representing the line connecting the two points.

34. Write a function that accepts a structure of type LINE (see Problem 33) and returns an integer (1, 2, 3), where 1 means vertical, 2 means horizontal, and 3 means oblique. A vertical line is a line whose x coordinates are the same. A horizontal line is a line whose y coordinates are the same. An oblique line is a line that is not vertical or horizontal.

35. Write a function that shuffles a deck of cards. The deck of cards is represented by an array of 52 elements. Each element in the array is a structure for one card, as shown below.

```
typedef    struct
          {
          char *suit;    /*Clubs, Diamonds, Hearts, Spades*/
          int   value;   /*Ace, 2..9, Jack, Queen, King*/
          } CARD;

typedef CARD DECK [52];
```

The function must use a random number (see Chapter 4) to ensure that each shuffle results in a different card sequence). Hint: Generate a random number in the range 0...51, and then exchange the current card with the card in the random position.

36. Program 12-8 on page 623 creates a union of company and person names. Write a program that reads names from the keyboard and places them into an array of names. For each entry, prompt the user to enter a code that indicates if the name is a company or person name. After all names have been entered, print the array. Your program is to contain separate functions for reading names and printing the array.

37. Modify the program in Problem 36 to add a function to sort the names after they have entered. Person names is to be sorted on last name, first name, and initial.

PROJECTS

38. Write a program to keep records and perform statistical analysis for a class of students. For each student, we need a name of up to 20 characters, an ID for four digits, four quizzes, and one examination. The student data will be stored in an array of student structures. Provide for up to 50 students.

The input is read from a text file. Each line in the file contains a student's name, four quiz scores, and one examination score in order. If a quiz or examination was not taken, the score is zero. The student's name, the quiz scores, and the examination score are all separated from each other by one or more spaces. A newline ends the data for one student. The number of lines in this file is the same as the number of students.

The output consists of a listing of the students in the order they are read from the file; no sorting is required. Print each student on a separate line with an appropriate caption for each column. After the last student, print the highest, lowest, and average score for each quiz and the examination. In determining the lowest score, do not consider zero scores. A suggested report layout is shown in Table 12-1.

DATA						
Name	ID	Quiz 1	Quiz 2	Quiz 3	Quiz 4	Exam
Student 1	1234	23	19	22	23	89
Student 2	4321	0	23	21	18	76
…						
Student n	1717	21	22	18	19	91
STATISTICS						
Highest scores		23	25	23	25	96
Lowest scores		17	15	12	18	53
Average scores		21.3	20.1	19.8	21.1	81.3

Table 12-1   Sample output for Project 38

The data for the project are shown in Table 12-2.

Name	ID	Quiz 1	Quiz 2	Quiz 3	Quiz 4	Exam
Julie Adams	1234	52	7	100	78	34
Harry Smith	2134	90	36	90	77	30
Tuan Nguyen	3124	100	45	20	90	70
Jorge Gonzales	4532	11	17	81	32	77
Amanda Trapp	5678	20	12	45	78	34
Lou Mason	6134	34	80	55	78	45
Sarah Black	7874	60	100	56	78	78
Bryan Devaux	8026	70	10	66	78	56
Ling Wong	9893	34	09	77	78	20
Bud Johnson	1947	45	40	88	78	55
Joe Giles	2877	55	50	99	78	80
Jim Nelson	3189	82	80	100	78	77
Paula Hung	4602	89	50	91	78	60
Ted Turner	5405	11	11	0	78	10
Evelyn Gilley	6999	0	98	89	78	20

Table 12-2   Data for Project 38

39. Rework Project 38 to report the average quiz score, total quizzes score, and total score for each student. Then assign a grade based on an absolute scale of 90% for A, 80% for B, 70% for C, and 60% for D. Any score below 60% is an F.

A total of 500 points are available. Print the student data to the right of the input data. At the end of the report, print the number of students who earned each grade, A to F.

40. Write a program that uses an array of student structures to answer inquiries. Using a menu-driven user interface, provide inquiries that report a student's scores, average, or grade based on an absolute scale (90% A, 80% B, etc.). A fourth menu option provides all data for a requested student, and a fifth prints a list of student IDs and names. To create the array, load the data from Project 38.

41. Using a sort of your choice, modify Project 40 to sort the data on student ID.

42. A standard deck of playing cards consists of 52 cards as shown in Table 12-3. Create an array of 52 structures to match a new deck of cards. Then simulate shuffling the deck using the following algorithm.

Suit	Rank
Clubs	Ace...King
Diamonds	Ace...King
Hearts	Ace...King
Spades	Ace...King

Table 12-3 The order of a new deck of playing cards

```
1. For each card in the deck
   1.1 Get a random number in range 0...51
   1.2 Swap current card with card at random position
   After the cards have been shuffled, print them in a 13 × 4 matrix.
```

43. Write a function that calculates the area of one of the geometric figures shown in Figure 12-34. The function receives one parameter, a structure that contains the type of figure and the size of the components needed for the calculation structured as a union. The format of the structure is shown in Figure 12-34. Use an enumerated type for the figure type.

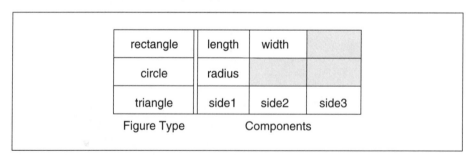

Figure 12-34 Structure for Project 43

The formulas for the figures are shown below.

$$AreaofRectangle = length * width$$

$$AreaofCircle = \pi r^2$$

$$AreaofTriangle = \sqrt{t(t - side1)(t - side2)(t - side3)}$$

$$\text{where } t \;=\; \frac{1}{2}(side1 + side2 + side3)$$

Then write an interactive test driver that prompts the user for the type of figure to be entered and the appropriate components. It then calls the area function and prints the area before looping for the next input. Hint: Use a *switch* statement to process the different codes.

44. Modify Program 12-5, on page 616, to include functions to add, subtract, divide, and compare fractions. Also change the print function to print the fraction in its simplified format—that is, to reduce the numerator and denominator by the largest common factor. Thus, the fraction

$$\frac{20}{8}$$

would be printed as

$$\frac{5}{2}$$

The compare function is to compare the functions algebraically. Thus, if the following two fractions were compared, it would return equal:

$$\frac{20}{8} \text{ and } \frac{5}{2}$$

Then modify *main* to include a loop that allows the user to enter two fractions and an option to add, subtract, multiply, divide, or compare the fractions.

Binary Files

There are two broad categories of files, text files and binary files. Chapter 7 was devoted to text files. In this chapter, we explore the concepts behind binary files. We first describe their general concepts, and then we discuss their operations.

13-1 CLASSIFICATION OF FILES

In a general sense, a file is a collection of data. This definition is too broad, however, and is not in concert with the usage of the term in computer science. For one thing, this definition includes files stored outside the computer.

We need to narrow the definition by including two additional attributes of files: The data in a file must be somehow related, and files are usually stored on auxiliary storage devices. This gives us the definition we use:

> A **file** is a collection of related data stored in an auxiliary storage device.

Application programmers are not usually concerned with the way the file is stored or with the details of the actual device on which it is stored. These details are handled by the operating system. Programmers deal only with the logical structure of the file. This means that they are concerned only with the relationship among the data items stored in the file and how to process them.

One way to classify a file is by the interpretation of each byte (8 bits) in the file. All computer-usable data are recorded in 0s and 1s. An auxiliary storage device—such as a disk or a tape— stores data in the form of a stream of 0s and 1s without assigning any relationship between bits. Figure 13-1 portrays data as bits in a file.

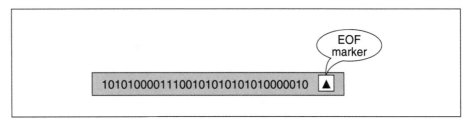

Figure 13-1   Data on auxiliary storage device

When the data are read into a program, however, they must be organized in a way that can be interpreted by the program for analysis and presentation to the user. At this time, the sequence of 0s and 1s is interpreted as either a text file or a binary file. These file types are shown in Figure 13-2.

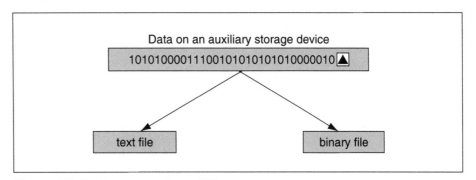

Figure 13-2   Interpretation of files

In other words, we can store a sequence of 0s and 1s on a disk and interpret them later as a text or binary file. But of course, the result will be meaningful only if the data were stored in the format that we expect when we read them. That is, you cannot read binary data using text data types or vice versa.

TEXT FILES

A **text file** is a file of characters. Because its structure is the character, it cannot contain integers, floating-point numbers, or any other data structures in their internal memory format. To store these data types, they must be converted to their character-equivalent formats.

Some files can only use character data types. Most notable are file streams for keyboards, monitors, and printers. This is why we need special formatting input and output functions (*scanf* and *printf*) to read data from or write data to these devices.

Let's look at an example. When data (a file stream) are sent to the printer, the printer takes 8 bits, interprets them as 1 byte, and decodes them into the encoding system of the printer (ASCII or EBCDIC). If the character belongs to the printable category, it will be printed; otherwise, some other activities take place, usually printing a space. After finishing 8 bits, the printer takes the next 8 bits and repeats the process. This is done until the file stream is exhausted.

Figure 13-3 traces five characters from the keyboard to a file stream format and then to a monitor or printer. The ¬ symbol represents the return key, and the ▲ symbol represents the end of file.

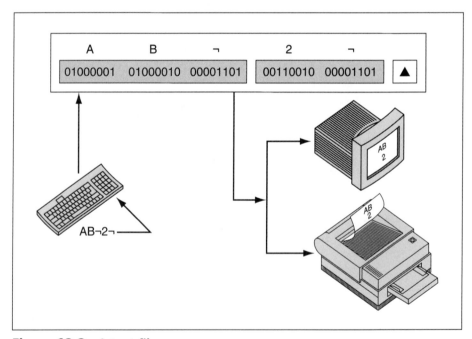

Figure 13-3   A text file

BINARY FILES

A **binary file** is a collection of data stored in the internal format of the computer. In this definition, data can be an integer, a floating-point number, a character, an array, or any other structured data (except a file).

Unlike text files, binary files contain data that are meaningful only if they are properly interpreted by a program. If the data are textual, 1 byte represents one character. But if the data are numeric, 2 or more bytes are considered as a data item. For example, assume we are using a personal computer that uses 2 bytes to store an integer. In this case, when we read or write an integer, 2 bytes are interpreted as one integer.

Another difference between text and binary files is found in the concept of records. A record is a collection of related data (fields). In C, we use a *struct* to define a record (see Chapter 12). Many binary files are logically organized around records.

When the data are written to the file, no conversion takes place. They are transferred exactly as they are stored in the program. Likewise, when we read the data from the file into memory, no conversion takes place. The data are simply taken from the file and placed in memory as they are.

This unformatted transfer takes place regardless of the data type. We can even write complex structures, such as arrays and records, to a binary file. The computer simply transfers the data from memory as they are stored without any interpretation. The only thing the computer needs to know is how much data are to be read or written. Figure 13-4 shows an integer being written to a binary file.

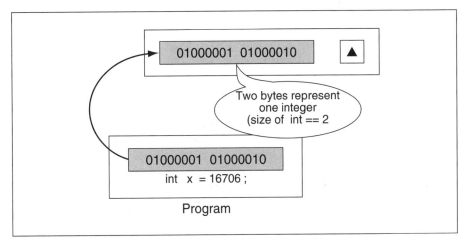

Figure 13-4 A binary file

This uninterpreted input and output results in much faster and more flexible file handling. But these advantages come with a cost: File transportability across different hardware platforms is reduced when the data are stored in their binary formats. If the internal structure of the receiving computer is not identical to the computer that created the file, you may not be able to read the file.

Look at Figure 13-4 again. Now consider the following two points.

1. If the file is interpreted as a text file, the first 2 bytes are read as two characters (A and B in ASCII). This leads to the conclusion that the program logic that interprets the data is as important as the data themselves.

2. If we store the integer 16706 using a text file, we need 5 bytes, 1 byte for each digit. Therefore, binary files usually take less space.

The term *binary file* is misleading, however. All computer memory, including files, is binary. Therefore all data, even text files, are stored in files as binary data. What distinguishes the different types of files is how we interpret the binary data stored on them. But years ago, some computer scientist decided to call structured files binary files and we are now stuck with the term.

Binary files store data using the internal format of the computer.

13-2   USING BINARY FILES

Given that binary files are most commonly used with structures, Figure 13-5 shows a binary file of structures (records). Each rectangle represents a record structure. At the end of the file (after the last record), there is a marker (▲) known as the **end of file (EOF) marker**.

Figure 13-5   A binary file of structures (records)

STATE OF A FILE

An opened file is either in a read state, a write state, or an error state. The **error state** results when an error occurs during the open or during either a read or a write operation. When a file is in an error state, you cannot read from it or write to it.

If we want to read from a file, it must be in the **read state**. If we want to write to a file, it must be in the **write state**. If we try to read from a file in the write state, an error occurs. Likewise, if we try to write to a file in the read state, an error occurs.

When a file is opened in the write state, it can be in one of two modes: write (w) or append (a). In write mode, the writing starts at the beginning of the file. If the file already exists, its data are lost. In append mode, the data are added at the end of the file. If the file exists, the writing begins after the existing data. If the file does not exist, a new file is created.

As you will see below, it is possible to open a file for both reading and writing. This is sometimes referred to as opening a file in **update mode**. Even when the file is opened for updating, however, it can still be in only one file state at a time. If it is opened for read and update, then it is initially in the read state. If it is opened for write or append and update, then it is initially in the write state. These states and their potential error conditions are shown in Figure 13-6.

Study this figure carefully. If a state is shaded gray, then that state is not available for the indicated file mode. If you study the read mode (rb), you will see that only two states are possible, read and error. The file will stay in the read state as long as you use only read functions. That is the meaning of the looping arrow in the read-state circle. However, if you try to write when the file is in the read state, the state changes to the error state. Once the file is in an error state, any subsequent attempt to read it will result in an error.

Now look at the update mode, r+b. In this mode, the file can be in either the read or the write state. To move from one to the other, you must use one of the positioning functions. That is the meaning of the arrows between the read state and write state. If you try to write after a read without repositioning, the file will be in the error state. The error can be cleared by *clearerr,* which is discussed on page 667, in "File Status Functions."

OPENING BINARY FILES

The basic open operation is unchanged for binary files—only the mode changes. The prototype for *fopen* is repeated here for convenience.

```
FILE *fopen (const char *filename, const char *mode);
```

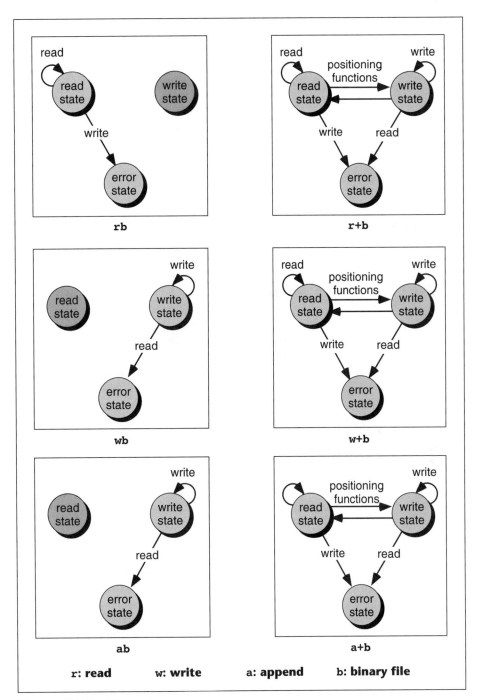

Figure 13-6 File states

You will recall that the file name is the name used for the file by the operating system. The name you use internally in your program is a file pointer whose address is filled by the *fopen* return value. Here, we are most interested in the mode, which is a string that contains a code defining how the file is to be opened—for reading, writing, or both—and its format—text or binary. The basic mode codes summarized in Table 13-1 are the same as for the text files with the addition of the token b, which stands for binary.

Mode	Meaning
rb	Open file for reading • Read starting at beginning • If file doesn't exist, error is returned
wb	Open file for writing • If file exists, it is emptied • If file doesn't exist, it is created
ab	Open file for append • New records inserted at end • If file doesn't exist, it is created

Table 13-1 Basic file modes

UPDATE MODE

In many situations in data processing, we need to both read and write the same file. Perhaps the most common is when permanent files, such as student records, need to be changed. The data are first read, then changed, and finally written back to the file. Physically, this can be done only on a randomly accessible file, such as a disk. It is not possible to both read and write a tape.

The **file mode** determines the initial state when the file is opened. To change between read and write mode, you must call one of the file positioning functions discussed in "Positioning Functions," on page 668. If you issue a write without repositioning while the file is in the read state, an error results. Conversely, if you issue a read without repositioning while the file is in a write state, an error results.

All three of the processing modes—read, write, and append—provide the capability of both reading and writing. To indicate both read and write, simply add a plus in the file mode. Thus rb becomes r+b, wb becomes w+b, and ab becomes a+b. The update modes are shown in Table 13-2.

Mode	Meaning
r+b	Open file for both read and write • Initial state: read • Read starts at beginning • If file doesn't exist, error is returned
w+b	Open file for both read and write • Initial state: write • If file exists, it is emptied • If file doesn't exist, it is created
a+b	Open file for both read and write • Initial state: write • Write starts at end • If file doesn't exist, it is created

Table 13-2 Update file modes

For each mode, the basic operation is the same. Thus, if a file is opened in the read plus mode (r+b), the reading and writing will be positioned at the beginning of an existing file, with the initial file state set to read. If the file doesn't exist, the null error indicator is returned.

Similarly, the write plus mode will open a new file for writing and reading. In this case, even though you indicate that you want to read, any data in an existing file will be discarded when the file is opened. Since the file will then be empty, you must write something before you can do a read operation.

Finally, the append plus mode opens an existing file or creates a new one and positions the file for writing at the end.

The update flag (+) may be before or after the binary flag, but it may not be first. For the update modes, therefore, you can have any of the following codes:

```
rb+, r+b, wb+, w+b, ab+, a+b
```

Figure 13-7 shows the basic file modes and the file state they create.

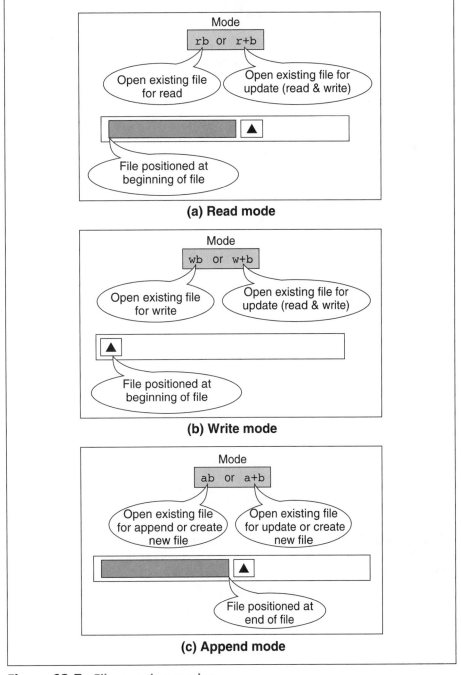

Figure 13-7 File-opening modes

CLOSING BINARY FILES

Just like text files, binary files must be closed when they are not needed any more. Closing destroys the file table and erases the logical file name. The close function was covered in Chapter 7. Its prototype statement is repeated here for your convenience.

```
int fclose (FILE *fp);
```

13-3 STANDARD LIBRARY FUNCTIONS FOR FILES

C has eight categories of standard file library functions (see Figure 13-8). We have already discussed the first four; open and close, character input and output, formatted input and output, and line input and output. We discuss the other four functional categories, which are more related to binary files, in this section.

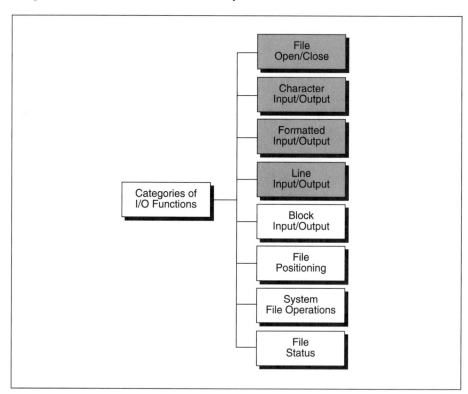

Figure 13-8 Types of standard input/output functions

BLOCK INPUT/ OUTPUT FUNCTIONS

The C language uses the block input and output functions to read and write data to binary files. As we discussed previously, when we read and write binary files, the data are transferred just as they are found in memory. There are no format conversions. This means that, with the exception of character data, you cannot "see" the data in a binary file; it looks like hieroglyphics. If you have ever accidentally opened a binary file in a text editor, you have seen these strange results.

The block read function is file read (*fread*). The block write function is file write (*fwrite*).

File Read (*fread*)

The function *fread,* whose prototype is shown below, reads a specified number of bytes from a binary file and places them into memory at the specified location.

```
int fread (void *pInArea,
           int   elementSize,
           int   count,
           FILE *fp);
```

The first parameter, `pInArea`, is a pointer to the input area in memory. Note that a generic (void) pointer is used. This allows any pointer type to be passed to the function.

File read expects a pointer to the input area, which is usually a structure. This is because binary files are most often used to store structured records. However, C gives us the flexibility to read any type of data, from a character to a complex record structure or even a multidimensional array.

The next two elements, `elementSize` and `count`, are multiplied to determine how much data are to be transferred. The size is normally specified using the *sizeof* operator and the count is normally one when writing structures.

The last parameter is the file pointer of an open file. Figure 13-9 is an example of a file read that reads data into an array of integers. When *fread* is called, it transfers the next three integers from the file to the array, `inArea`. The code to read the file is shown in Program 13-1.

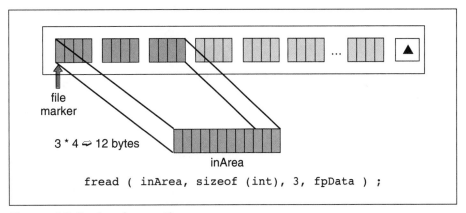

Figure 13-9 *fread* operation

```
 1  /* Read a file of integers, three integers at a time. */
 2  ...
 3  /* Local Definitions */
 4     FILE *intFile;
 5     int   i;
 6     int   itemsRead;
 7     int   intAry[3];
 8
 9  /* Statements */
10     intFile = fopen("int_file.dat", "rb");
11     ...
12     while ((itemsRead = fread(intAry,
```

Program 13-1 Read file of integers

```
13              sizeof(int), 3, intFile)) != 0)
14      {
15       /* process array */
16       for (i = 0; i < itemsRead ; i++)
17           ...
18       } /* while */
19     ...
20 }  /* function */
```

Program 13-1   Read file of integers (continued)

File read returns the number of items read. In Figure 13-9, it will range between 0 and 3 because we are reading three integers at a time. For example, assume that when we try to read the file, only two integers are left to be read. In this case, *fread* will return 2. If we return and try to read the file again, *fread* will then return 0.

Note that *fread* does not return end of file—it returns the number of elements read. End of file is detected in the above situation when we called *fread* with less than three integers left in the file. The question is, how can we tell that we are at the end of file? C provides another input/output function, *feof,* to test for end of file. We discuss this function in "File Status Functions" on page 667.

Now let's look at a more common use of *fread,* reading structures (records). Assume that we have defined a structure that stores data about students. Given the type of data that will be stored, we would expect the structure to contain some string data and other data, such as integers or floating-point numbers. One advantage of block input/output functions is that they can transfer these data a structure (record) at a time. A second advantage is that the data do not need to be formatted. Figure 13-10 shows the operation of *fread* when a structure is being read. We can use the code shown in Program 13-2 to read the file.

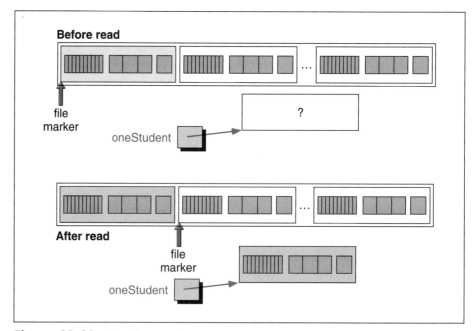

Figure 13-10   Reading a structure

```
 1  /* Reads one student's data from a file
 2         Pre    stuFile is opened for reading
 3         Post   stu data structure filled
 4                ioResults returned
 5  */
 6  int readStudent (STU  *oneStudent,
 7                    FILE *stuFile)
 8  {
 9  /* Local Definitions */
10     int ioResults;
11
12  /* Statements */
13     ioResults = fread(oneStudent,
14                        sizeof(STU), 1, stuFile);
15     return ioResults;
16  } /* readStudent */
```

Program 13-2   Read student file

Program 13-2 Analysis   Different companies have different standards. One company with which we are familiar has a standard that programs shall have only one read and one write statement for each file. The standard was created to make it easier to make changes to the programs. Program 13-2 is a typical implementation of this standard. One difficulty with this type of function, however, is that it is impossible to generalize the steps that are to be taken for various input results, such as error handling and end of file. Therefore, we pass the input/output result back to the calling function for analysis and action.

File Write (*fwrite*)

The function *fwrite,* whose prototype is shown below, writes a specified number of items to a binary file.

```
int fwrite (void  *pOutArea,
            int    elementSize,
            int    count,
            FILE  *fp);
```

The parameters for file write correspond exactly to the parameters for the file read function.

Functionally, *fwrite* copies elementSize * count bytes from the address specified by pOutArea to the file. It returns the number of items written. For example, if it writes three integers, it returns 3. You can use the return value, therefore, to test the write operation. If the number of items written is less than count, then an error has occurred. Depending on the device you are working with, it may be possible to repeat the write, but generally the program should be aborted when you get a write error. Figure 13-11 shows the write operation that parallels the read in Figure 13-9.

Assuming that we are writing a file of student structures, Figure 13-12 shows the write operation. Program 13-3 contains the code for the function that writes the data.

Figure 13-11 *fwrite* operation

Figure 13-12 Writing a structure

```
1  /* Writes one student's record to a binary file.
2         Pre   aStudent has been filled
3               fileOut is open for writing
4         Post  aStudent written to fileOut
5  */
6  void writeStudent   (STU  *aStudent,
7                       FILE *fileOut)
8  {
9  /* Local Definitions */
10    int ioResult;
11
```

Program 13-3 Write structured data

```
12   /* Statements */
13      ioResult = fwrite(aStudent,
14                         sizeof(STU), 1, fileOut);
15      if (ioResult != 1)
16         {
17          printf("\a Error writing student file \a\n");
18          exit (100);
19         } /* if */
20      return;
21   } /* writeStudent */
```

Program 13-3 Write structured data (continued)

Program 13-3 Analysis   Contrast this write structured data function with the one that
we wrote to read data. Although it is not possible to generalize on the action to be taken
if data are not read, it is possible to do so with write errors. If the program cannot write
data, it must be aborted. Therefore, we put the error checking and action in the write
function itself.

FILE STATUS FUNCTIONS

C provides three functions to handle file status questions: test end of file (*feof*), test error (*ferror*), and clear error (*clearerr*).

Test EOF (*feof*)

The ***feof*** function is used to check if the end of file has been reached. If the file is at the
end—that is, if all data have been read— the function returns true (nonzero). If end of file
has not been reached, false (zero) is returned. The prototype declaration is shown below.

```
int feof (FILE *stream);
```

In general, two different techniques can be used to detect end of file. Some languages
have a look-ahead function. When look-ahead logic is being used, the system transfers the
current data to your program and then reads the next data. Under this design, you can detect
the end of file at the same time that you read (transfer data back to your work area) the last
data from the file. The second technique, the one used by C, detects end of file when you
attempt to read and there is nothing left on the file. Even if all the data have been read from
the file, *feof* does not return true until you attempt to read beyond the last data.

Test Error (*ferror*)

Test error (***ferror***) is used to check the error status of the file. Errors can be created for
many reasons, ranging from bad physical media (disk or tape) to illogical operations,
such as trying to read a file in the write state. The *ferror* function returns true (nonzero)
if an error has occurred. It returns false (zero) if no error has occurred. The prototype is
shown below.

```
int ferror (FILE *stream);
```

Note, however, that testing for an error does not reset the error condition. Once a file
enters the error state (see Figure 13-6, on page 659) it can only return to a read or write
state by calling clear error (see below).

Clear Error (*clearerr*)

When an error occurs, the subsequent calls to *ferror* return nonzero, until the error status
of the file is reset. The function ***clearerr*** is used for this purpose. Its prototype is on the
next page.

```
void clearerr (FILE *stream);
```

Note, however, that even though you have cleared the error, you have not necessarily cured the problem. You may find that the next read or write returns you to the error state.

POSITIONING FUNCTIONS

Positioning functions have two uses. First, for randomly processing data in disk files (you cannot process tape files randomly), you need to position the file to read the desired data. Second, you can use the positioning functions to change a file's state. Thus, if you have been writing a file, you can change to a read state after you use one of the positioning functions. It is not necessary to change states after positioning a file, but it is allowed.

We will discuss three file position functions: rewind, tell location, and file seek.

Rewind File (*rewind*)

Although the ***rewind*** function is most commonly used with tape files, it can be used with disk as well. It simply sets the file position indicator to the beginning of the file (Figure 13-13). The prototype declaration is shown below.

```
void rewind(FILE *fp);
```

A common use of the rewind is to change a work file from a write state to a read state. Often it is necessary to place data in a file temporarily for later processing. When all the data have been written and you are ready to begin reading, you rewind the file and simply start reading. Remember, however, that to read and write a file with only one open, you must open it in update mode, in this case, w+ or w+b.

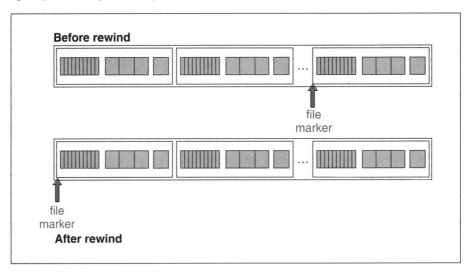

Figure 13-13   *rewind* file

The same effect can be accomplished by closing the output file and opening it as input. However, the rewind is a faster operation.

Current Location (*ftell*)

The *ftell* function tells you the current position of the file marker in the file, relative to the beginning of the file. Recall that C considers files as streams of data. It measures the position in the file by the number of bytes, relative to zero, from the beginning of the file. Thus, when the file position indicator is at the beginning of the file, *ftell* returns zero. If the file position indicator is at the second byte of the file, *ftell* returns 1, representing the position 1 byte offset from the beginning of the file. The prototype declaration for *ftell* is shown below.

```
long int ftell(FILE *stream);
```

Note that *ftell* returns a long integer. This is necessary because many files have more than 32,767 bytes, which is the maximum integer value on many computers. The operation of *ftell* is graphically shown in Figure 13-14.

Figure 13-14   *ftell* operation

Another important factor that you must consider if you use *ftell* is that it returns the number of bytes from the beginning of the file. This is true even when you are reading or writing structures. If you want to know the structure number relative to the first structure, then you must calculate it. This can be done by dividing the *ftell* return value by the size of the structure, as shown below.

```
numberCharacter = ftell (fp);
numberStructure = numberCharacter / sizeof (STRUCTURE_TYPE);
```

In Figure 13-14, *ftell* returns 16. Since each structure is 4 bytes, the result of the calculation shown above is 4, which means that there are four structures before the current location. Another way to look at it is that the file is positioned at the fourth integer relative to zero.

If *ftell* encounters an error, it returns −1. We know of only two conditions that can cause an error. The first, using *ftell* with a device that cannot store data, such as the keyboard, is a program logic or design error. The second error occurs when the position is larger than can be represented in a long integer. Obviously, this could occur only with very large files, but files of over a million records are common in industry.

The primary purpose of *ftell* is to provide a data address (offset) that can be used in a file seek. It is especially useful when you are dealing with text files in which you cannot calculate the position of data.

Set Position (*fseek*)

The *fseek* function positions the file location indicator to a specified byte position in a file. It gets its name from the disk-positioning operation, seek. Seek moves the access arm on a disk to a position in the file for reading or writing. Since this is exactly the purpose of file seek, it is an appropriate name. Its prototype declaration is shown below.

```
int fseek(FILE *stream, long offset, int wherefrom);
```

The first parameter is a pointer to an open file. Since the seek is used with both reading and writing files, the file state can be either read or write. The second parameter is a signed integer that specifies the number of bytes the position indicator must move absolutely or relatively. To understand what we mean by absolutely or relatively, we must first discuss the third parameter, *wherefrom*.

C provides three named constants that can be used to specify the starting point (*wherefrom*) of the seek. They are shown below.

```
#define SEEK_SET 0
#define SEEK_CUR 1
#define SEEK_END 2
```

When *wherefrom* is SEEK_SET(0), then the offset is measured absolutely from the beginning of the file. This is the most common use of file seek. Thus, to set the file indicator to byte 100 on a file, you would code the following statement:

```
fseek(fp, 99L, SEEK_SET);
```

You can use zero in place of SEEK_SET. If you are puzzling over the second parameter in the above statement, remember that the file position is relative to zero and must be a long integer. Actually, the compiler is smart enough to convert an integer value to long integer, but it is more efficient if you specify the correct type, especially with literals.

Now let's look at the *wherefrom* option, **SEEK_CUR.** If *wherefrom* is **SEEK_CUR(1)**, then the displacement is calculated relatively from the current file position. If the displacement is negative, you move back toward the beginning of the file. If it is positive, you move forward toward the end of the file. It is an error to move beyond the beginning of the file. If you move beyond the end of the file, the file is extended, but the contents of the extended bytes are unknown. Whenever you extend the file, there is always the possibility of running out of space, which is an error. To position yourself to the next record in a structured file, you execute the following statement:

```
fseek(fp, sizeof(STRUCTURE_TYPE), SEEK_CUR);
```

To position the student file described earlier at the structure indicated by the integer variable stuLoc, you execute the following statement:

```
fseek(stuFile, (stuLoc - 1)* sizeof(STU), SEEK_SET);
```

It is necessary to adjust the integer location, stuLoc, by subtracting 1 to convert the ordinal structure number to a zero base. That is, if stuLoc contains 55, indicating you want to read the 55th student in the file, you must position the file to the location of the 54th student relative to zero.

Finally, if *wherefrom* is **SEEK_END**, you will position the file location indicator relative to the end of the file. If the offset is negative, you will move backward toward the beginning of the file; if it is positive, you will extend the file. This technique can be used to write a new record at the end of the file. Simply position the file at the end with a SEEK_END and a displacement of zero as shown below and then write the new record.

```
fseek(stuFile, 0L, SEEK_END);
```

The seek function returns zero if the positioning is successful. It returns nonzero if the positioning is not successful. Figure 13-15 shows the effect of *fseek* in different situations.

Figure 13-15 *fseek* operation

The file seek is intended primarily for binary files. It does, however, have limited functionality with text files. You can position a text file to the beginning using *fseek* with a zero offset from the beginning of the file (SEEK_SET). However, *rewind* provides the same functionality and is more appropriate for text files. To position a text file at the end, you can use *fseek* with a zero offset and a *wherefrom* SEEK_END, as discussed earlier.

You cannot use file seek to position yourself in the middle of a text file unless you have used *ftell* to record the location. The reasons for this have to do with control codes, newlines, vertical tabs and other nuisances of text files. However, if you have recorded a location using *ftell* and you want to go back to that position, you can use *fseek*, as shown below.

```
fseek(fp, ftell_location, SEEK_SET);
```

Note that since *ftell* returns a position relative to the beginning of the file, you must use SEEK_SET when you reposition the file.

**BLOCK INPUT/
OUTPUT EXAMPLE:
APPEND FILES**

Let's look at a program that reads and writes binary files. Suppose, for example, that we had two copies of files with integer data. Perhaps one file represents data from one week and the other file represents data for a second week. We want to combine both files into a single file. The most efficient way to do this is to append the data from one file to the end of the other file. This logic is shown in Program 13-4.

```
 1  /* This program appends two binary files of integers.
 2        Written by:
 3        Date:
 4  */
 5  #include <stdio.h>
 6
 7  int main (void)
 8  {
 9  /* Local Definitions */
10  FILE   *fp1;
11  FILE   *fp2;
12  int     data;
13  long    dataCount;
14  char    fileID[13];
15
16  /* Statements */
17     printf("\nThis program appends two files.\n");
18     printf("Please enter the file ID of the primary file: ");
19     scanf("%12s", fileID);
20     if (!(fp1 = fopen (fileID, "ab")))
21        printf("\aCan't open %s\n", fileID), exit (100);
22     fseek (fp1, 0, 2);
23     if (!(dataCount = (ftell (fp1))))
24        printf("\a%s has no data\n", fileID), exit (101);
25     dataCount /= sizeof(int);
26
27     printf("Please enter the file ID of the second file: ");
28     scanf("%12s", fileID);
29     if (!(fp2 = fopen (fileID, "rb")))
30        printf("\aCan't open %s\n", fileID), exit (110);
31
32     while (fread (&data, sizeof(int), 1, fp2) == 1)
33        {
34         fwrite (&data, sizeof(int), 1, fp1);
35         dataCount++;
36        } /* while */
37
38     if (! feof(fp2))
39        printf("\aRead Error. No output.\n"), exit (120);
40
41     fclose (fp1);
42     fclose (fp2);
43
44     printf("Append complete: %ld records in file\n",
45            dataCount);
46     return 0;
47  }  /* main */
```

Program 13-4   Append two binary files

Program 13-4 Analysis   First, note the way the files are opened in Program 13-4. Since it appends the data from the second file to the end of the first file, the first file is opened in append mode and the second file is opened in read mode. Both files are opened as binary.

Opening the first file in append mode presents a minor problem: The open is successful even if the file doesn't exist. Recall that the append mode places the file marker at the end of an existing file or, if there is no existing file, at the beginning of a new file. To ensure that an existing file was opened successfully, therefore, we use the *ftell* function in Statement 23. If an existing file was opened, `dataCount` will be nonzero.

Now look at the way the external file names are handled. Under the assumption that this program will be used to append different files at different times, we asked the user to enter the file names. This technique provides maximum flexibility for generalized programs.

Statement 21 contains one of the few valid uses of multiple statements on one line—in this case, multiple expressions separated by the comma operator. Why is this statement considered valid when we have so strongly emphasized one statement per line? The answer is that we are handling an error situation that should never occur. In good human engineering style, we want to deemphasize the error logic so that it doesn't distract the reader. Therefore, we place the print error message and exit in one expression.

The heart of the program is contained in Statements 32 through 36. As long as the read is successful, we keep going. When we reach end of file, *fread* returns zero and the loop terminates. We now have another problem, however. We don't know if the read terminated at end of file or because of a read error. We therefore use the *feof* function to make sure we read to the end of the file.

The program concludes with a printed message that contains the number of records on the appended file. Since we didn't read all the data on the first file, however, we must calculate the number of integers in it. To do this, we used the result of the *ftell* that verified that the first file existed. Recall that *ftell* returns the number of bytes to the current location in the file—in this case, the end of the file. To get the number of integers, we simply divide by the size of one integer. (See Statement 25.) Then, each time we write, we add 1 to the record count. This gives us the number of integers in the combined file.

SYSTEM FILE OPERATIONS

A few functions operate on the whole file instead of the contents. These functions generally use operating system calls to perform operations such as remove a file, rename a file, or create a temporary binary file.

Remove (*remove*)

The *remove* function removes or deletes the file using its external name. The parameter is a pointer to the name of the file. Its prototype is shown below.

```
int remove (char *filename);
```

It returns zero if the deletion is successful. It returns nonzero if there is an error, such as the file can't be found.

For example, if we want to delete a file named `file1.dat`, we execute the statement shown below.

```
if (remove ("file1.dat"))
    printf("Error, file cannot be deleted");
```

Any attempt to access a file after it has been removed will result in an error.

Rename (*rename*)

When you create a new version of a file and you want to keep the same name, you need to rename the old version of the file. The *rename* prototype statement is shown below.

```
int rename  (const char *oldFilename,
                 const char *newFilename);
```

Both the old name and the new name must be given as parameters. The rename function returns zero if renaming is successful; it returns nonzero if there is an error.

For example, in a DOS system, if you want to rename a student file and designate it a backup, you could use the rename function as shown below.

```
if (rename ("STUFILE.DAT", "STUFILE.BAK"))
    printf("Error, the file cannot be renamed");
```

Create Temporary File (*tmpfile*)

The *tmpfile* function creates a new temporary output file. Although you could do the same thing with an *fopen* in the w+b mode, the difference is that the file is available only while the program is running. It will be closed and erased when the execution of the program is finished. It is a temporary file, not a permanent one. Its prototype is

```
FILE * tmpfile (void);
```

To create a temporary file, you must first define a file pointer and then open it, as shown below.

```
FILE * fp;

fp = tmpfile ();
```

Now you can write to the file as you would to any file. Because the file is opened in the w+b mode, if you want to read from the file, you must reposition it using one of the repositioning functions such as *rewind* or *fseek*.

13-4   CONVERTING FILE TYPE

A rather common but somewhat trivial problem is to convert a text file to a binary file and vice versa. C has no standard functions for these tasks. You must write a program to make the conversion. We describe the file conversion logic in this section.

CREATING A BINARY FILE FROM A TEXT FILE

To create a binary file, you usually start with data provided by the user. Since the user is providing the data, it will be in human readable form—that is, in text form. If only a small amount of initial data are required, they are often read from a keyboard. With a lot of data, however, it is easier for the user to enter the data with a text editor and then read the text file and create the binary file.

When you read the text file, you can use either the *fscanf* function to convert the data as they are being read or the *fgets* and *sscanf* functions to read the data a line at a time and then convert the data to the proper internal format. As the data are being converted, they are placed in a structure. At the end of each line, the structure is written to the binary file. This process is repeated until the text file has been completely converted to the binary structure. The structure chart for this program is shown in Figure 13-16.

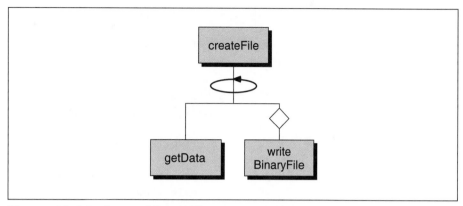

Figure 13-16   Create binary file structure chart

Let's assume that we want to convert student data to a binary file. The data consist of a student's name, ID, three exams, eight problems, and a final grade. In the text file version, each separate field is separated by one or more whitespace characters and each student's data are stored on a separate line. The create file program is shown in Program 13-5.

```
1   /* Reads text file of student data, and creates a binary file.
2         Written by:
3         Date:
4   */
5   #include <stdio.h>
6
7   /* Global Declarations */
8   typedef struct stuData
9      {
10      char   name[26];
11      char   id[5];
12      int    exams[3];
13      int    problems[8];
14      char   grade;
15      } STU_DATA;
16
17  /* Prototype Declarations */
18  char *getData          (FILE      *textFile,
19                          STU_DATA *aStudent);
20  void  writeBinaryFile (STU_DATA *aStudent, FILE *binFile);
21
22  int main (void)
23  {
24  /* Local Definitions */
25     char *textFileID = "students.txt";
26     char *binFileID  = "students.bin";
27
```

Program 13-5   Text to binary student file

```
28      STU_DATA aStudent;
29
30      FILE *textFile;
31      FILE *binFile;
32
33   /* Statements */
34      printf("\nBegin Student Binary File Creation\n ");
35
36      if (!(textFile = fopen(textFileID, "r")))
37         {
38          printf("\nCannot open %s\n", textFileID);
39          exit (100);
40         } /* if textFile*/
41      if(!(binFile = fopen(binFileID, "wb")))
42         {
43          printf("\nCannot open %s\n", binFileID);
44          exit (200);
45         } /* if binFile */
46
47      while (getData (textFile, &aStudent))
48         writeBinaryFile (&aStudent, binFile);
49
50      fclose(textFile);
51      fclose(binFile);
52
53      printf("\n\nFile creation complete\n");
54
55      return 0;
56   }  /* main */
57
58   /* ==================== getData ====================
59      This function reads the text file.
60         Pre    textFile is opened for reading
61         Post   data read and returned
62   */
63   char *getData   (FILE      *textFile,
64                    STU_DATA *aStu)
65   {
66   /* Local Definitions */
67      char *ioResult;
68      char  buffer[100];
69
70   /* Statements */
71      ioResult = fgets(buffer, sizeof(buffer), textFile);
72      if (ioResult)
73         sscanf(buffer, "%s %s %d%d%d%d%d%d%d%d%d%d %c",
74           aStu->name, aStu->id,
75           &aStu->exams[0], &aStu->exams[1],&aStu->exams[2],
```

Program 13-5 Text to binary student file (continued)

```
 76              &aStu->problems[0], &aStu->problems[1],
 77              &aStu->problems[2], &aStu->problems[3],
 78              &aStu->problems[4], &aStu->problems[5],
 79              &aStu->problems[6], &aStu->problems[7] ,
 80              &aStu->grade);
 81       return ioResult;
 82  } /* getData */
 83
 84  /* ================= writeBinaryFile =================
 85     This function writes the student data to a binary file.
 86          Pre    binFile is opened as a binary output file
 87                 aStudent is complete
 88          Post   Record written
 89  */
 90  void writeBinaryFile (STU_DATA   *aStudent,
 91                        FILE        *binFile)
 92  {
 93  /* Local Definitions */
 94      int amtWritten;
 95
 96  /* Statements */
 97      amtWritten = fwrite (aStudent,
 98                  sizeof(STU_DATA), 1, binFile);
 99      if (amtWritten != 1)
100         {
101          printf("Can't write student file. Exiting\n");
102          exit (201);
103         } /* if */
104      return;
105  } /* writeBinaryFile */
```

Program 13-5   Text to binary student file (continued)

Program 13-5 Analysis   Note how we specified the external file names as strings. This makes it easy to change the file names if and when necessary. It also allows us to identify the file by name if the open fails.

The program starts and ends with a message that identifies what program is running and that it has successfully completed. This is a good programming technique and a standard in many organizations.

The *while* loop is controlled by the results of the getData function call. To understand how it works, therefore, we first look at getData. When you need to read a lot of text data, especially if it is coming from a file, the preferred technique is to use the get string (*fgets*) function and then use the string scan (*sscanf*) function to convert it into internal binary formats. The get string function reads text data until it finds a newline character, an end of file, or the maximum number of characters has been read. It returns the address of the input string, in this case buffer. When end of file is detected, it returns a null pointer.

To make this function robust, we would break the *sscanf* into several calls, one for the first two strings, one for the exams, one for the problems, and one for the grade at the end. This would allow us to easily verify that the correct data were read by examining the returned value from *sscanf*.

Now that we understand that the `getData` function returns either an address or NULL, we understand how the *while* at Statement 47 works. It simply loops until an end of file is detected—that is, until NULL is returned.

CREATING A TEXT FILE FROM A BINARY FILE

Programmers convert a binary file to a text file in two situations. The first is when we need to display the data for people to read; we discuss this below. The second is when it is necessary to export the data to another system, which can't read the binary file. This occurs, for example, if the word sizes for integers and floats are different on the two different hardware systems. As long as all lines are formatted the same and they use the same ASCII code, text files are portable.

An interesting problem is to create a report of the data in the binary file. Obviously, you need to read the binary file and write the data as a text file, but there is much more to it than that. First, the report needs a name, so each page must have a title. The title should include the report date and a page number. To make the report meaningful, each column should have a column caption. Finally, the report should have an end of report message as the last line of the report so that the user knows that all data have been reported.

Since we will put a title on the top of each page, we need to know when a page is full. This is generally done by counting the number of lines on a page and when the count exceeds the maximum, skipping to the next page. Good structured programming requires that the heading logic be in a separate function. The design for printing the student data is shown in Figure 13-17.

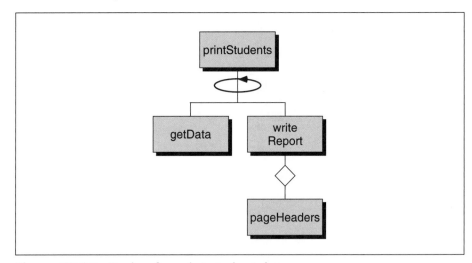

Figure 13-17   Design for print student data

We will write the data to a file so that it can be sent to the printer when we want a hard copy.

You should be aware of one final point before looking at the program. In the print functions, we use a type modifier known as the *static* storage class (see Statements 99 and 129). We discuss the concept of storage classes in Appendix K. For now, you only need to know that *static* keeps the contents of a variable available between calls. The first time you call a function with a static variable, the variable is initialized. After that, its value is retained between calls. This is a great C feature that reduces the need to pass parameters just to retain a local variable. The program is shown in Program 13-6.

```
 1 | /* Reads a binary file of student data, and prints it.
 2 |      Written by:
 3 |      Date:
 4 | */
 5 | #include <stdio.h>
 6 |
 7 | #define MAX_LINES_PER_PAGE  50
 8 | #define BUFFER_SIZE        133
 9 | #define FORM_FEED          '\f'
10 |
11 | /* Global Structures */
12 | typedef struct stuData
13 |    {
14 |     char  name[26];
15 |     char  id[5];
16 |     int   exams[3];
17 |     int   problems[8];
18 |     char  grade;
19 |    } STU_DATA;
20 |
21 | /* Prototype Declarations */
22 | STU_DATA getData       (FILE *binFile);
23 | void     writeReport  (STU_DATA aStudent, FILE *prtFile);
24 | void     pageHeaders   (FILE *prtFile);
25 |
26 | int main (void)
27 | {
28 | /* Local Definitions */
29 |    char       stuFileID[] = "P13-stu.bin";
30 |    char       prtFileID[] = "P13-stu.prt";
31 |    STU_DATA  aStudent;
32 |    FILE      *stuFile;
33 |    FILE      *prtFile;
34 |
35 | /* Statements */
36 |    printf("\nBegin Student Report Creation\n ");
37 |
38 |    if(!(stuFile = fopen(stuFileID, "rb")))
39 |       {
40 |        printf("\nCannot open %s\n", stuFileID);
41 |        exit (100);
42 |       } /* if stuFile */
43 |    if (!(prtFile = fopen(prtFileID, "w")))
44 |       {
45 |        printf("\nCannot open %s\n", prtFileID);
46 |        exit (200);
47 |       } /* if prtFile */
48 |
49 |    aStudent = getData (stuFile);
```

Program 13-6 Print student data

```
50      while (!feof(stuFile))
51         {
52          writeReport (aStudent, prtFile);
53          aStudent = getData (stuFile);
54         } /* while */
55
56      fprintf(prtFile, "\nEnd of Report\n");
57
58      fclose(stuFile);
59      fclose(prtFile);
60
61      printf("\n\nEnd Student Report Creation\n");
62
63      return 0;
64  } /* main */
65
66  /* ==================== getData ====================
67     This function reads the student binary file.
68        Pre    stuFile is opened for reading
69        Post   one student record read and returned
70  */
71  STU_DATA getData (FILE *stuFile)
72  {
73  /* Local Definitions */
74     int        ioResult;
75     STU_DATA   aStu;
76
77  /* Statements */
78     ioResult = fread(&aStu, sizeof(STU_DATA), 1, stuFile);
79     if (!ioResult)
80        if (!feof(stuFile))
81           {
82            printf("\n\nError reading student file\n");
83            exit (100);
84           } /* if !feof */
85
86     return aStu;
87  } /* getData */
88
89  /* ==================== writeReport ====================
90     This function writes the student report to a text file.
91        Pre    prtFile is opened as a text output file
92               aStudent is complete
93        Post   Report line written w/ page header if necessary.
94  */
95  void writeReport  (STU_DATA  aStu,
96                     FILE      *prtFile)
97  {
98  /* Local Definitions */
```

Program 13-6 Print student data (continued)

```
 99      static int lineCount = MAX_LINES_PER_PAGE + 1;
100      char    buffer[BUFFER_SIZE];
101
102  /* Statements */
103      if (++lineCount > MAX_LINES_PER_PAGE)
104         {
105          pageHeaders  (prtFile);
106          lineCount = 1;
107         } /* if */
108
109      sprintf (buffer,
110         "%-25s %4s %4d%4d%4d%4d%4d%4d%4d%4d%4d%4d%4d %c\n",
111         aStu.name, aStu.id,
112         aStu.exams[0],    aStu.exams[1],    aStu.exams[2],
113         aStu.problems[0], aStu.problems[1], aStu.problems[2],
114         aStu.problems[3], aStu.problems[4], aStu.problems[5],
115         aStu.problems[6], aStu.problems[7],
116         aStu.grade);
117      fputs (buffer, prtFile);
118      return;
119  } /* writeReport */
120
121  /* ================== pageHeaders ==================
122     Writes the page headers for the student report.
123         Pre    prtFile is opened as a text output file
124         Post   Report headers and captions written
125  */
126  void pageHeaders (FILE *prtFile)
127  {
128  /* Local Definitions */
129      static int pageNo = 0;
130
131  /* Statements */
132      pageNo++;
133      fprintf(prtFile, "%c", FORM_FEED);
134      fprintf(prtFile, "%-66s  Page %4d\n",
135              "Student Report ", pageNo);
136      fprintf(prtFile, "%-25s %-6s %-10s %-27s Grade\n\n",
137              "Student Name", "ID", "Exams", "Problems");
138      return;
139  }  /* pageHeaders */
140  /* ================== End of Program ================== */
```

Program 13-6 Print student data (continued)

Program 13-6 Analysis   Even though this program is rather simple, you should note the following points:

First, we have declared the maximum number of lines per page and the print buffer size as preprocessor-defined constants. This makes it easy to change them should it be necessary. It also makes it easy to set the print logic so that it will print the header the first time through the function. This leads us to the second thing you should note. The logic for `pageHeaders` will cause the first page to be blank. That is, we issue a page form feed before any data have been written. This is standard in production programs, but you may want to change it so that the first page is not wasted. In this case, you will have to call the `pageHeaders` function before you start the file reading to write the first headings and move the form feed write to just before Statement 105.

The file is read using look-ahead logic. At Statement 49, we read the first record of the file. This allows us to use the *feof* function to control the *while* loop. At the end of the loop, we read the file again. Although this loop closely resembles a posttest loop, there is one difference. If the file is empty, a post-test loop would fail. By reading the first record from the file before the loop, we ensure that we can process any file condition using the simplest possible logic.

Note the way we handle the report title and line captions in `pageHeaders`. Many programmers simply try to code them in the format string. This works, but it takes a lot of hit and miss to get it right. Our technique simply adds the widths from the data write and uses them for the widths in the caption prints. The program may still need a little manual adjustment, but it is a much simpler approach.

Finally, note how we formatted the student output. We used *sprintf* to format a line of output. There is no significant advantage to using the string format function rather than the print function, but we wanted to demonstrate its use. After the data have been formatted, we use *fputs* to write them. Note also the way we aligned the data for readability. Since it takes several lines, we group the common data on lines by themselves. This makes it much easier to read the code. We could have used *for* statements to print the array data, but that would have been less efficient.

13-5 FILE PROGRAM EXAMPLES

This section contains two common file applications. The first uses the file positioning functions to randomly process the data in a file. The second merges two files.

RANDOM FILE ACCESSING

Program 13-7 demonstrates the concept of randomly accessing data in a file. We begin by creating a binary file of integers. Each integer is the square of the data's position in the file, relative to 1. After the file has been created, we print it in sequence, starting at the beginning of the file. We then print it in a random sequence using *fseek* and a random number generator.

```
 1  /* Shows some of the application of functions we have learned
 2     in this chapter. The program first creates a binary file
 3     of integers. It then prints the file, first sequentially
 4     and then randomly using rand().
 5        Written by:
 6        Date:
 7  */
 8  #include <stdio.h>
 9  #include <stdlib.h>
10  /* Prototype Statements */
11  void buildFile   (FILE **fp);
12  void printFile   (FILE  *fp);
```

Program 13-7 Random file application

```
13  void randomPrint (FILE   *fp);
14
15  int main (void)
16  {
17  /* Local Definitions */
18     FILE *fpData;
19
20  /* Statements */
21
22     buildFile    (&fpData);
23     printFile    (fpData);
24     randomPrint  (fpData);
25
26     return 0;
27  }  /* main */
```

Program 13-7 Random file application (continued)

Program 13-7 Analysis   The main function simply calls three functions in order. The first function receives a pointer to the file pointer, which is the only variable declared in main. It is necessary to use double dereferencing here because buildFile needs to pass back the file pointer to main. The other two calls do not change the file pointer, they just use it. Therefore, it can be passed to them by value.

Program 13-8 builds a binary file.

```
1  /* =================== buildFile ===================
2     Creates a disk file that we can process randomly.
3        Pre    nothing
4        Post   file has been built
5  */
6  void buildFile (FILE **fpData)
7  {
8  /* Local Definitions */
9     int  i;
10    int  data;
11
12 /* Statements */
13    if (!(*fpData = fopen("SAMPLE.DAT", "w+b")))
14       {
15        printf("\aError opening file.\n");
16        exit (100);
17       } /* if open */
18    for (i = 1; i <= 10; i++)
19       {
20         data = i * i;
21         fwrite(&data, sizeof(int), 1, *fpData);
22       } /* for */
23    return;
24 }  /* buildFile */
```

Program 13-8 Random file: buildFile

Program 13-8 Analysis   The buildFile function in Program 13-8 simply creates a file with ten records. Each record consists of a single integer, which is the square of the ordinal record number relative to 1 (not 0). The file is opened with write plus so that we can first write to it and then later in the program read it. Note that all references to the file use the dereference operator to update the file pointer, which exists in main.

Program 13-9 prints the file sequentially.

```
 1  /* =================== printFile ===================
 2     Prints the file starting at the first record.
 3        Pre    fp is an open file
 4        Post   file has been printed
 5  */
 6  void printFile (FILE *fpData)
 7  {
 8  /* Local Definitions */
 9     int data;
10     int recNum;
11
12  /* Statements */
13     recNum = 0;
14     rewind(fpData);
15     fread(&data , sizeof(int), 1, fpData);
16     while (!feof(fpData))
17        {
18          printf("Record %2d: %3d\n", recNum++, data);
19          fread(&data, sizeof(int), 1, fpData);
20        } /* while */
21     return;
22  }  /* printFile */
```

```
Results:
    Record 0:    1
    Record 1:    4
    Record 2:    9
    Record 3:   16
    Record 4:   25
    Record 5:   36
    Record 6:   49
    Record 7:   64
    Record 8:   81
    Record 9:  100
```

Program 13-9   Random file sequential print

Program 13-9 Analysis   The printFile function in Program 13-9 simply reads the file sequentially starting at the beginning (Record 0). Study the *while* loop. Note that we have coded it with the first read before the loop. We use this technique so that we can detect end of file in the *while* statement. The *while* loop prints the current record and then reads the next record. When all records have been processed, the read will detect end of file, and the loop will terminate with all records processed.

Program 13-10 prints the file randomly.

```
 1   /* ==================== randomPrint ====================
 2      This function randomly prints the file. Some data may
 3      be printed twice, depending on the random numbers
 4      generated.
 5         Pre  fp is an open file
 6         Post Ten records have been printed
 7   */
 8   void randomPrint (FILE *fpData)
 9   {
10   /* Local Definitions */
11      int data;
12      int i;
13      int randomSeek;
14
15   /* Statements */
16      printf("\n\nFile contents in random sequence.\n");
17      for (i = 0; i < 10; i++)
18         {
19          randomSeek =  (rand () % 10);
20          fseek(fpData, sizeof(int) * randomSeek, SEEK_SET);
21          fread(&data, sizeof(int), 1, fpData);
22          printf("Record %3d ==> %3d\n", randomSeek, data);
23         } /* for */
24      return;
25   }  /* randomPrint */
```

```
Results:
   File contents in random sequence.
   Record  8 ==>  81
   Record  8 ==>  81
   Record  3 ==>  16
   Record  5 ==>  36
   Record  1 ==>   4
   Record  7 ==>  64
   Record  0 ==>   1
   Record  9 ==> 100
   Record  2 ==>   9
   Record  6 ==>  49
```

Program 13-10   Random file `randomPrint`

Program 13-10 Analysis   The `randomPrint` function is the most interesting. We use a *for* loop to print ten records. Within the loop, we use a random number generator to determine which record we will read next. Since there are ten records in the file, we set the random number to modulo ten, which gives us potential record numbers from zero to nine. This corresponds exactly with the file on disk, which occupies record positions zero to nine. The function output created using our computer is shown in Program 13-10. Note that it starts by printing Record 8 twice and then prints all other records other than Record 4. Compare the output to the file print in Program 13-9.

MERGE FILES

In "Block Input/Output Example: Append Files," on page 671, we discussed the concept of combining two files by appending the data. In this section, we discuss another way to combine data, the file merge. When you **merge** data from two files, the result is one file with the data ordered in key sequence. This requires that we completely read two input files and create a new output file. This concept is shown in Figure 13-18.

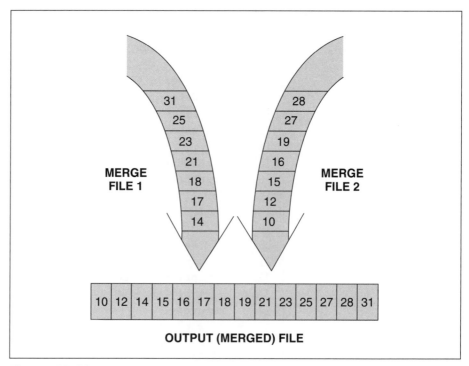

Figure 13-18 File merge concept

The merge files pseudocode is shown in Program 13-11. The design is rather simple. We start by reading data from each merge file. We then (1) compare the data in the two files, (2) write the smaller to the merge output file, (3) read the next record from the file whose record was written, and (4) continue the loop.

The difficult part of the merge design is the end of file logic. One of the merge files will end first, but you never know which one. To simplify the end of file processing, this design introduces a concept known as a sentinel. A sentinel is a guard; in our merge algorithm, the sentinel guards the end of file. The sentinel has the property that its value is larger than any possible key. For the sentinel value, we use `MAX_INT`, which is found in the `<limits.h>` header file. The merge code is shown in Program 13-12.

```
This program merges two files
1 input (File1, Rec1)
2 input (File2, Rec2)
3 HighSentinel = high-value
4 while (not eof(File1)) OR (not eof(File2))
   1  if  Rec1.Key  <=  Rec2.Key  then
      1   output (File3, Rec1)
      2   input  (File1, Rec1)
```

Program 13-11 Pseudocode for merging two files

```
     3   if eof(File1)
         1   Rec1.Key = HighSentinel
   2   else
       1   output (File3, Rec2)
       2   input  (File2, Rec2)
       3   if eof(File2)
           1   Rec2.Key = HighSentinel
END Merge
```

Program 13-11   Pseudocode for merging two files (continued)

```c
 1  /* This program merges two files
 2          Written by:
 3          Date:
 4  */
 5  #include <stdio.h>
 6  #include <limits.h>
 7
 8  #define READ_MODE   "rb"
 9  #define WRITE_MODE  "wb"
10
11  int main (void)
12  {
13  /* Local Definitions */
14     FILE *fpM1;
15     FILE *fpM2;
16     FILE *fpOut;
17
18     int recM1;
19     int recM2;
20
21     char file1ID[]   = "P13Mrg1.bin";
22     char file2ID[]   = "P13Mrg2.bin";
23     char fileOutID[] = "P13Mrg3.bin";
24     int  sentinel    = INT_MAX;
25     int  mergeCnt    = 0;
26
27  /* Statements */
28     printf("Begin File Merge:\n");
29     if (!(fpM1 = fopen (file1ID, READ_MODE)))
30         printf("\aError on %s\n", file1ID), exit (100);
31
32     if (!(fpM2 = fopen (file2ID, READ_MODE)))
33         printf("\aError on %s\n", file2ID), exit (200);
34
35     if (!(fpOut = fopen (fileOutID, WRITE_MODE)))
36         printf("\aError on %s\n", fileOutID), exit (300);
37
38     fread (&recM1, sizeof(int), 1, fpM1);
39     if (feof(fpM1))
40         recM1 = sentinel;
```

Program 13-12   Merge two files

```
41    fread (&recM2, sizeof(int), 1, fpM2);
42    if (feof(fpM2))
43        recM2 = sentinel;
44
45    while (!feof(fpM1) || !feof(fpM2))
46       {
47        if (recM1 <=  recM2)
48           {
49            fwrite (&recM1, sizeof(int), 1, fpOut);
50            mergeCnt++;
51            fread  (&recM1, sizeof(int), 1, fpM1);
52            if (feof(fpM1))
53                recM1 = sentinel;
54           } /* if */
55        else
56           {
57            fwrite (&recM2, sizeof(int), 1, fpOut);
58            mergeCnt++;
59            fread  (&recM2, sizeof(int), 1, fpM2);
60            if (feof(fpM2))
61                recM2 = sentinel;
62           } /* else */
63       } /* while */
64    fclose (fpM1);
65    fclose (fpM2);
66    fclose (fpOut);
67    printf("End File Merge. %d items merged.\n", mergeCnt);
68    return 0;
69 } /* main */
```

Program 13-12 Merge two files (continued)

Program 13-12 Analysis   We have written this simple program without any subfunctions. Once again we have used the multiple-statement error message format for the error message and exit after each open statement.

Programs that involve the comparison of data from two files require that the first record from both files be read before any comparisons can be made. This is sometimes called "priming the files." The reads that prime the files are coded before the main *while* loop. Since duplicate read statements are required in the loop, you might wonder why we didn't use a *do...while*. The reason is that the program would fail if both files were empty. As we coded it, the program works if either or both merge files are empty.

Study the logic at Statements 53 and 61 carefully. These statements implement the sentinel concept. When a file reaches its end, we set the key in the record area for the file to the sentinel value. This ensures that all the data on the other file will compare low and be written to the output file.

The most difficult statement in this simple program is the *while* statement. We need to keep looping as long as either of the files is not at the end of file. The most straightforward code is as we coded it in Statement 45. Another common way to code it is shown below.

```
(!(feof(fpM1) && feof(fpM2)))
```

Use De Morgan's (see Chapter 5) rule to prove to yourself that these two statements are identical.

Any file environment requires some means of keeping the file current. Data are not static; they are constantly changing, and these changes need to be reflected in their files. The function that keeps files current is known as **updating**. To complete our discussion of files, we discuss some of the software engineering design considerations for file updating. For this discussion, we assume a student binary file similar to the ones we have discussed in the chapter.

UPDATE FILES

Three specific files are associated with an update program. First is the permanent data file, called the master file. The **master file** contains the most current computer data for an application.

The second file is the **transaction file**. It contains changes to be applied to the master file. Three basic types of changes occur in all file updates; others may also occur, depending on the application. *Add transactions* contain data about a new student to be added in the master file. *Delete transactions* identify students who will be deleted from the file. And *change transactions* contain revisions to specific student records in the file.

To process any of these transactions, we need a key. A **key** is one or more fields that uniquely identify the data in the file. For example, in the student file, the key would be student ID. In an employee file, the key would be Social Security number.

The third file needed in an update program is an **error report file**. An update process is very rarely error free. When an error occurs, we need to report it to the user. The *error report* contains a listing of all errors discovered during the update process and is presented to the user for corrective action.

File updates are of two types: batch and online. In a **batch update**, changes are collected over time and then all changes are applied to the file at once. In an **online update**, the user is directly connected to the computer and the changes are processed one at a time—often, as the change occurs.

SEQUENTIAL FILE UPDATE

For our discussion, we will assume a batch, sequential file environment. A **sequential file** is a file that must be processed serially starting at the beginning. It does not have any random processing capabilities. The sequential master file has the additional attribute that it is ordered on the key.

A sequential file update actually has two copies of the master file, the old master and the new master. This is because whenever a sequential file is changed, it must be entirely re-created—even if only one student's score on one exam is changed.

Figure 13-19 contains an environment chart for a sequential file update. In this chart, we see the four files we discussed above. We use the tape symbol for the files because it is the classic symbol for sequential files. Sequential files could just as easily be stored on a disk. Note that after the update program completes, the new master file is sent to off-line storage, where it is kept until it is needed again. When the file is to be updated, the master file is retrieved from the off-line storage and used as the old master.

Generally, at least three copies of a master file are retained in off-line storage, in case it becomes necessary to regenerate an unreadable file. This retention cycle is known as the grandparent system because three generations of the file are always available: the grandparent, the parent, and the child.

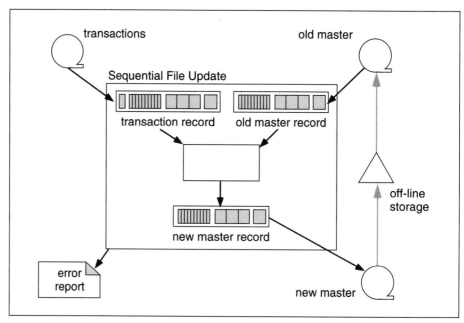

Figure 13-19 Sequential file update environment

THE UPDATE PROGRAM DESIGN

Nearly two decades ago, a computer scientist named Barry Dwyer published an update algorithm in the *Communications of the ACM* that was so elegant that it has become a classic.[1] We have adapted his algorithm for our discussion.

Since a sequential master file is ordered on a key and since it must be processed serially, the transaction file must also be ordered on the same key. The update process requires that we match the keys on the transaction and master file and, assuming that there are no errors, take one of the following three actions:

1. If the transaction file key is less than the master file key, add the transaction to the new master.
2. If the transaction file key is equal to the master file key, either
   a. Change the contents of the master file data if the transaction is a revise transaction, or
   b. Remove the data from the master file if the transaction is a delete.
3. If the transaction file key is greater than the master file key, write the old master file record to the new master file.

This updating process is shown in Figure 13-20. In the transaction file, the transaction codes are A for add, D for delete, and R for revise. The process begins by matching the keys for the first record on each file, in this case,

```
14 > 10
```

---

[1]Barry Dwyer, "One More Time—How to Update a Master File," *Communications of the ACM*, 24, no. 1 (January 1981): 3–8.

Figure 13-20 File updating example

Thus, Rule 3 is used, and we write the master record to the new master record. We then match 14 and 13, which results in 13 being written to the new master. In the next match, we have

```
14 == 14
```

Thus, according to Rule 2a, we use the data in the transaction file to change the data in the master file. However, we do not write the new master file at this time. More transactions may match the master file, and we need to process them too.

After writing 16 to the new master, we have the following situation:

```
17 < 20
```

According to Rule 1, we must add 17 to the new master file. We do this by copying the transaction to the new master file, but again, we don't write it yet. This newly added record may have some revision transactions, and we need to be able to process them. For example, this capability is needed when a new student registers and adds classes on the same day. The computer has to be able to add the new student and then process the class registrations in the same batch run. We will write the new master for 17 when we read transaction 18.

The processing continues until we read the delete transaction, at which time we have the following situation:

```
21 == 21
```

and since the transaction is a delete, according to Rule 2b, we need to drop 21 from the new master file. To do this, we simply read the next master record and transaction record without writing the new master. The processing continues in a similar fashion until all records on both files have been processed.

UPDATE ERRORS

Two general classes of errors can occur in an update program. The user can submit bad data, such as a grade that is not A, B, C, D, or F. For our discussion, we will assume that no data errors are present. Detecting data errors is the subject of data validation and has been discussed.

The second class of errors is file errors. File errors occur when the data on the transaction file are not in synchronization with the data on the master file. Three different situations can occur:

1. An add transaction matches a record with the same key on the master file. Master files do not allow duplicate data to be present. When the key on an add transaction matches a key on the master file, therefore, we reject the transaction as invalid and report it on the error report.
2. A revise transaction's key does not match a record on the master file. In this case, we are trying to change data that do not exist. This is also a file error and must be reported on the error report.
3. A delete transaction's key does not match a record on the master file. In this case, we are trying to delete data that do not exist, and this must also be reported as an error.

UPDATE STRUCTURE CHART

The structure chart for the sequential file update is shown in Figure 13-21. In this structure chart, `process` contains the updating function.

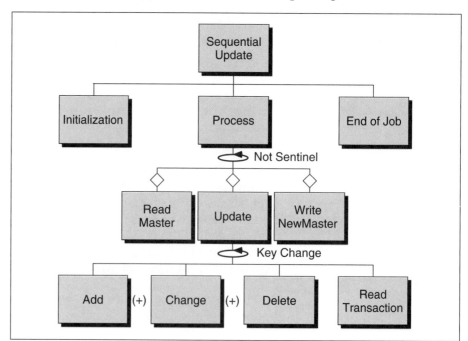

Figure 13-21 Update structure chart

UPDATE LOGIC

`Initialization` is a function that opens the files and otherwise prepares the environment for processing. `EndofJob` is a function that closes the files and displays any end of job messages. The mainline processing is done in `Process`.

Although it is beyond our scope to develop the complete set of update functions, it is important that you at least understand the mainline logic found in `Process`. Its pseudocode is shown in Program 13-13.

```
Sequential File Update Process
1 read first record from transaction file
2 read first record from old master file
3 select next entity to be processed
4 while current entity not sentinel
    1   if current entity = old master entity
        1   copy old master to new master work area
        2   read old master file
    2   if current entity = transaction entity
        1   update new master work area
    3   if current entity = new master entity
        1   write new master file
    4   select next entity to be processed
```

Program 13-13   Pseudocode for file update

Let's look at the update logic in a little more detail. The first three statements contain initialization logic for `Process`. The driving force behind the update logic is that in each *while* loop, we process all the data for one student (entity). To determine which student we need to process next, we compare the key of the transaction file with the key of the master file and select the smaller as the current entity to be processed. This logic is seen in Statement 3.

Before we can compare the keys, however, we must read the first record in each file. This is known as "priming the files" and is seen in Statements 1 and 2.

The *while* statement in Program 13-13 contains the driving logic for the entire program. It is built on a very simple principle: As long as data are present in either the transaction file or the master file, we continue to loop. When a file has been completely read, we set its key to a sentinel value. When both files are at their end, therefore, both of their keys will be sentinels. Then, when we select the next student to be processed, it will be a sentinel, which is the event that terminates the *while* loop.

Three major processing functions take place in the *while* loop. First, we determine if the student on the old master file needs to be processed. If it does, we move it to the new master output area and read the next student from the old master file. The key on the old master can match the current key in two situations: a change or delete transaction exists for the current student. This logic is seen in Statement 4.1.

The second major process handles transactions that match the current student. It calls a function that determines the type of transaction being processed (add, change, or delete) and handles it accordingly. If it is an add, it moves the new student's data to the new master area. If it is a change, it updates the data in the new master area. And if it is a delete, it clears the key in the new master area so that the record will not be written. To handle multiple transactions in the update function, it reads the next transaction and continues if its key matches the current student.

The last major process writes the new master when appropriate. If the current student matches the key in the new master file area, then the record needs to be written to the file. This will be the case unless a delete transaction was processed.

SUMMARY

In this section we looked at a very important algorithm, the classic sequential file update, and discussed its mainline logic flow.

The elegance of Dwyer's algorithm, as seen in Program 13-13, lies in the determination of the current student and the separation of the update process into three distinct functions: read the old master, update the current student, and write the new master. Study the concept of the current student carefully, and make sure you understand how it controls the three major processes in the loop. Then, with a little thought, you should be able to develop the other functions in the update program.

Also note that Program 13-13 contains only one read transaction function. Its function is to read a valid transaction. Therefore, it contains all of the simple data validation logic to determine if the data are correct. It does not perform any file errors; they are handled in the update function. If any errors are found, the read transaction function writes the transaction to an error report and reads the next transaction. When it returns to the calling function, it has either read a valid transaction or has found the end of the file.

13-7 TIPS AND COMMON PROGRAMMING ERRORS

Refer to the "Tips and Common Programming Errors" section in Chapter 7. Many of those tips apply to binary files as well.

1. EOF is type integer, and its value is normally –1. Therefore, if you want to test the value of a variable to EOF, use an integer variable, not a character. In most systems, a character variable cannot store a negative number (–1 here).

2. Remember to open a file before using it.

3. You can create a file for writing; but to read a file, it must exist.

4. When you open a file for writing using w mode, you must close it and open it for reading (r mode) if you want to read from it. To avoid this problem, you can open it in w+ mode.

5. An open file can be in one of the three states: read, write, or error. If you want to switch from read to write or from write to read, you must use one of the file-positioning functions.

6. Do not open a file in w mode when you want to preserve the contents of the file. Opening a file in w mode erases the contents of the file.

7. Remember that in general you cannot print the contents of a binary file. It must be converted to a text file first.

8. Unlike other input/output functions, the first parameter of the *fread* and *fwrite* functions is a pointer to the input area, not a file pointer. The file parameter is the last (fourth) parameter.

9. The second parameter of the *fread* and *fwrite* functions is the size of the element, and the third parameter is the count of elements.

10. The *fread* and *fwrite* functions return the number of elements read or written, not the number of bytes read or written.

11. Remember that *feof* does not look ahead. It returns true only if an attempt is made to read the end of file.

12. The second parameter in the *fseek* function is the number of bytes, not the number of elements.

13. When the third parameter in the *fseek* function is SEEK_END (2), the middle parameter should normally be a negative long integer to access a byte in the file. If it is positive, it is referring to a byte after the end of file.

14. To add an element at the end of the file, you use the *fseek* function with the second parameter set to zero and the third parameter to the value of SEEK_END.

15. Remember that every time you use the *fread* or *fwrite* function, it automatically advances the file position indicator toward the end of the file the number of bytes equal to the size of the element.

16. It is good practice to close all files before terminating a program.

17. It is a compile error to refer to a file with its external file name rather than its file pointer.

18. It is a compile error to omit the file pointer when using a file function. This error most often occurs when using the file versions of the file format functions, such as *fprintf*.

19. It is a logic error to refer to a file before it is opened.

20. It is a logic error to open a file for reading when it doesn't exist. This is usually an error in the external file name in the open statement.

21. It is a logic error to attempt to read from a file in the write state and vice versa. This is true even when the file has been opened in the update mode.

22. Opening an output disk file will fail if the disk is full.

23. Opening an existing file in write mode deletes the file. If your input file disappears, check your open modes.

24. It is a logic error to use *fseek* to place the file marker before the first byte of a file.

13-8   KEY TERMS AND CONCEPTS[2]

batch update	*fseek*	SEEK_CUR
binary file	*ftell*	SEEK_END
clearerr	*fwrite*	SEEK_SET
end of file (EOF) marker	key	sequential file
error report file	master file	text file
error state	merge	*tmpfile*
feof	online update	transaction file
ferror	read state	update mode
file	*remove*	updating
file mode	*rename*	write state
fread	*rewind*	

[2]Note: Italic terms are standard function names.

13-9 SUMMARY

■ A file is a collection of related data stored in an auxiliary storage device.

■ A stored stream of 0s and 1s can be interpreted as either a text or a binary file.

■ A text file is a file of characters.

■ A binary file is a collection of related data stored in the internal format of the computer.

■ A file is always in one of the following states: read, write, or error.

■ A binary file can be opened in one of the following modes: rb, r+b, wb, w+b, ab, and a+b.

■ The *fread* function reads a specified number of bytes from a binary file.

■ The *fwrite* function writes a specified number of bytes into a binary file.

■ The *feof* function checks for end of file.

■ The *ferror* function is used to check the error status of a file.

■ The *clearerr* function is used to clear an error.

■ The *rewind* function sets the file position indicator to the beginning of the file.

■ The *ftell* function tells you the current position of the file position indicator.

■ The *fseek* function positions the file position indicator to the beginning of a specified byte.

■ The *remove* function removes or deletes a file from the disk.

■ The *rename* function renames a file on the disk.

■ The *tmpfile* function creates a new temporary file.

13-10 PRACTICE SETS

REVIEW QUESTIONS

1. A file can be read only if it is opened in the read state.
   a. True   b. False

2. A file opened in the r+b mode is a binary file opened in the read state and update mode.
   a. True   b. False

3. Binary files are read using the block input/output function *fread*.
   a. True   b. False

4. Using *fseek* to position a file beyond the current end of file places the file in an error state.
   a. True   b. False

5. To merge two files, you can use the merge function found in the standard input/output library.
   a. True   b. False

6. Which of the following statements about files is true?
   a. All files must be opened before they can be used.
   b. Binary files are more portable than text files.
   c. Binary files are slower than text files.
   d. Files must be closed.
   e. Text files contain data stored in the internal format of the computer.

7. Which of the following statements about files is false?
   a. Because they are more flexible, binary files are more portable.
   b. Binary files contain data stored in the internal format of the computer.
   c. Binary files usually contain records in the form of structured data.
   d. Text files store only character data.
   e. Some text file data need to be converted to internal storage formats for processing.

8. The _____ results when a failure occurs during an open or during either a read or write operation.
   a. Error state   d. Update state
   b. Fail state   e. Write state
   c. Read state

9. If a file in the read state is written to, then the following occurs:
   a. The file is placed in an error state regardless of the file mode.
   b. The file is placed in an error state unless it was opened in the update write mode (w+b).
   c. The file state is automatically switched if the file is opened for updating.
   d. The program is aborted regardless of how the file was opened.
   e. The program is aborted unless the file was opened for updating.

10. Which of the following file modes opens a file in the write state for updating?
   a. ab
   b. a+b
   c. rb
   d. r+b
   e. wb

11. Which of the following C functions is used to output data to a binary file?
   a. *fwrite*
   b. output
   c. write
   d. *writef*
   e. *fprintf*

12. Which of the following is a file status function?
   a. *feof*
   b. *freport*
   c. *frewind*
   d. *fseek*
   e. *ftell*

13. The _____ function may be used to position a file at the beginning.
   a. *fclose*
   b. *feof*
   c. *freport*
   d. *fseek*
   e. *ftell*

14. A _____ is one or more fields that uniquely identify the data in a file.
   a. field
   b. identifier
   c. key
   d. structure
   e. transaction

15. Which of the following statements about sequential file updating is false?
   a. Add, change, and delete transactions are used to update the file.
   b. Sequential files are often updated in an online environment.
   c. Sequential files contain structures (records) with a key to identify the data.
   d. The file must be processed starting at the beginning.
   e. The file must be entirely re-created when it is updated.

EXERCISES

16. Explain the difference between the following pairs of modes:
   ```
   rb and r+b
   wb and w+b
   ab and a+b
   ```

17. Find the error(s) in the following code. (Assume the PAY_REC type has been properly defined.)
   ```
   char *m = "wb";
   char *str = "Payroll";
   PAY_REC payRec;
   FILE  *fp;
   fp = fopen (str, m);
   fread(payRec, sizeof(payRec), 1, fp);
   ```

18. Given the following declarations:
   ```
   FILE  *fp;
   char s[20];
   ```
   Find any errors in each of the following statements:
   a. `fread(s, 20, fp);`
   b. `fread(s, 20, 1, fp);`
   c. `fread(s, 1, 20, fp);`
   d. `fread(fp, 1, 20, s);`
   e. `fread(fp, 20, 1, s);`

19. Given the following declarations:
   ```
   FILE  *fp;
   char s[20];
   ```

Find any errors in each of the following lines:

a. `ftell(fp);`

b. `ftell(1, fp);`

c. `fseek(0, 20L, fp);`

d. `fseek(fp, 20L, 0);`

e. `fseek(fp, 20L, 1);`

20. What would be printed from the following program? Draw a picture of the file with the file marker to explain your answer.

```
#include <stdio.h>

int main (void)
{
 char c;
 long int pos;
 FILE *fp;

 fp = fopen("SAMPLE.DAT", "w+b");
 for (c = 'A'; c <= 'E'; c++)
    fwrite(&c , sizeof (char), 1, fp);
 pos = ftell (fp);
 printf("The position of the file marker is : %ld", pos);
 return 0;
}
```

21. What would be printed from the following program? Draw a picture of the file with the file marker to explain your answer.

```
#include <stdio.h>

int main (void)
{
 char c;
 FILE *fp;

 fp = fopen("SAMPLE.DAT", "w+b");
 for (c = 'A'; c<= 'E'; c++)
    fwrite(&c, sizeof (char), 1, fp);
 fseek(fp, 2, 0);
 fread(&c, 1, 1, fp);
 printf("\n\n%c", c);
 return 0;
}
```

22. What would be printed from the following program? Draw a picture of the file with the file marker to explain your answer.

```
#include <stdio.h>

int main (void)
{
```

```
char c;
FILE *fp;


fp = fopen("SAMPLE.DAT", "w+b");
for (c = 'A'; c <= 'E'; c++)
    fwrite(&c , sizeof (char), 1, fp);
rewind(fp);
fread(&c, 1, 1, fp);
printf("\n\n%c", c);
return 0;
}
```

23. What would be printed from the following program? Draw a picture of the file with the file marker to explain your answer.

```
#include <stdio.h>

int main (void)

{
char c;
long int pos;
FILE *fp;


fp = fopen("SAMPLE.DAT", "w+b");
for (c = 'A'; c <= 'E'; c++)
    fwrite(&c, sizeof (char), 1, fp);
pos = ftell (fp);
pos--;
pos--;
fseek(fp, pos, 0);
fread(&c, 1, 1, fp);
printf("\n\n%c", c);
return 0;
}
```

24. What would be printed from the following program? Draw a picture of the file with the file marker to explain your answer.

```
#include <stdio.h>

int main (void)

{
char c;
long int pos;
FILE *fp;


fp = fopen("SAMPLE.DAT", "w+b");
for (c = 'A'; c <= 'E'; c++)
```

```
        fwrite(&c , sizeof (char), 1, fp);
    pos = ftell(fp);
    pos--;
    pos--;
    fseek(fp, -pos, 1);
    fread(&c, 1, 1, fp);
    printf("\n\n%c", c);
    return 0;
}
```

25. What would be printed from the following program? Draw a picture of the file with the file marker to explain your answer.

```
#include <stdio.h>

int main (void)
{
 char c;
 long int pos;
 FILE *fp;

 fp = fopen("SAMPLE.DAT", "w+b");
 for (c = 'A'; c <= 'E'; c++)
     fwrite(&c , sizeof (char), 1, fp);
 pos = ftell(fp);
 pos--;
 pos--;
 fseek(fp, 2, 2);
 fseek(fp, 1, 1);
 fread(&c, 1, 1, fp);
 printf("\n\n%c", c);
 return 0;
}
```

26. What would be printed from the following program? Draw a picture of the file with the file marker to explain your answer.

```
#include <stdio.h>

int main (void)
{
 int i;
 long int pos;
 FILE *fp;

 fp = fopen("SAMPLE.DAT", "w+b");
 for (i = 1; i <= 5; i++)
     fwrite(&i , sizeof (int), 1, fp);
```

```
pos = ftell(fp);
printf("The position of the file marker is : %ld", pos);
return 0;
}
```

27. What would be printed from the following program? Draw a picture of the file with the file marker to explain your answer.

```
#include <stdio.h>
int main (void)
{
int i;
FILE *fp;

fp = fopen("SAMPLE.DAT", "w+b");
for (i = 1; i <= 5; i++)
    fwrite(&i , sizeof (int), 1, fp);
fseek(fp, sizeof (int) * 2, 0);
fread(&i, sizeof (int), 1, fp);
printf("%d\n", i),
return 0;
}
```

28. What would be printed from the following program? Draw a picture of the file with the file marker to explain your answer.

```
#include <stdio.h>
int main (void)
{
  int i;
  FILE *fp;

fp = fopen ("SAMPLE.DAT", "w+b");
for (i = 1; i <= 5; i++)
    fwrite(&i, sizeof (int), 1, fp);
fseek(fp, -sizeof (int) * 2, 1);
fread(&i, sizeof (int), 1, fp);
printf("%d", i);
fclose (fp);
return 0;
}
```

29. What would be printed from the following program? Draw a picture of the file with the file marker to explain your answer. Is the answer strange? Why?

```
#include <stdio.h>
int main (void)
{
  int i;
```

```
FILE *fp;

fp = fopen("SAMPLE.DAT", "w+b");
for (i = 1; i <= 5; i++)
    fwrite(&i , sizeof (int), 1, fp);
fseek(fp, 7, 0);
fread(&i, sizeof (int), 1, fp);
printf("%d", i);
fclose (fp);
return 0;
}
```

30. What would be printed from the following program? Draw a picture of the file with the file marker to explain your answer.

```
#include <stdio.h>
int main (void)
{
int i;
long int pos;
FILE *fp;

fp = fopen("SAMPLE.DAT", "w+b");
for (i = 1; i <= 5; i++)
    fwrite(&i, sizeof (int), 1, fp);
pos = ftell(fp);
pos -= 2 * sizeof (int);
fseek(fp, pos, 0);
fread(&i, sizeof (int), 1, fp);
printf("%d", i);
fclose (fp);
return 0;
}
```

PROBLEMS

31. Write a function that copies the contents of a binary file of integers to a second file. The function must accept two file pointers and return an integer (zero representing a processing error and nonzero indicating successful completion).

32. Write a function that prints a specified number of records from the beginning of a file. The function is to accept two parameters. The first is a pointer to a binary file of structure type STR. The second is an integer that specifies the number of records to be printed (inclusive). The structure type is shown below:

```
typedef struct
    {
      int   i;
```

```
    float f;
   } STR;
```

If any errors occur, such as fewer records in the file than specified, it should return zero. Otherwise, it returns nonzero.

33. Write a function that compares two files and returns 0 (equal) or 1 (not equal) based on the result of the comparison. The functions should receive file pointers to two opened files and compare them byte by byte.

34. Write a function that returns the number of items in a binary file.

35. Write a function that prints the last integer in a binary file of integers.

36. Write a function that physically removes all items with a specified value (`data`) from a binary file of structure `STR`. You may use a temporary file. The file may contain more than one record with the delete value. The key value removed is to be entered from the keyboard.

```
   typedef struct
      {
      int    data;
      char   c;
      } STR;
```

37. Write a function that appends one binary file at the end of another.

38. Write a function that, given a binary file, copies the odd items (items 1, 3, 5, ..., *n*) to a second binary file and the even items (items 2, 4, 6, ..., *n*) to a third binary file.

39. Write a function that reads items from a binary file and copies them to a dynamically allocated array. The function must first find the size of the binary file to allocate the array.

40. Write a function that takes a binary file of long integers and appends a new long integer at the end that is the sum of all integers in the original file.

PROJECTS

41. A company has two small warehouses. The list of the products in each warehouse is kept in a text file (`InvFile1` and `InvFile2`), with each line representing information about one product. The manager wants to have only one list showing information about all products in both warehouses. Therefore, the two text files must be combined into one single text file (`OutFile`).

Write a program that will copy information from the two text files (`InvFile1` and `InvFile2`) to two binary files (`BinFile1` and `BinFile2`). After creating the binary files, the program is to merge the two binary files to produce a combined binary file. After the combined binary file has been created, create a report file that can be printed. The report file is to contain page headers with an appropriate title and page numbers. The structure for the files is shown below.

```
   typedef struct inv_rec
      {
      char   partNo[5];
      char   partName[15];
      int    qtyOnHand;
      } INV_REC;
```

42. A company keeps a list of parts that it purchases, with a line of information for each part that gives the part's unique code, name, and three codes for three suppliers that supply that particular part. This list is kept in a binary file and is sorted in ascending order according to the supplier's code.

    The company also keeps a list of its suppliers, with a line of information for each supplier, that gives the supplier's unique code, name, and address. This list is also kept in a binary file, which is sorted in ascending order according to the supplier's code.

    Write a program that enables the user to enter a part's unique code and to receive a list of three suppliers. If the code is found, the program prints the names and addresses of the three suppliers. If the code is not found, it prints a message to tell the user that the code is not in the file. After each inquiry, the program gives the user the option to quit.

    Each record in the part file is made up of a part's code, name, and the codes for three suppliers. The part's code is an integer; the name is a string with a maximum length of ten characters; and each supplier's code is an integer. Note that not all parts have three suppliers. For parts with less than three suppliers, a special supplier code of 0000 is used to indicate no supplier.

    Each record in the supplier file is made up of a supplier's code, name, and address. The supplier's code is an integer, the name is a string with a maximum length of ten characters, and the address has a maximum length of 20 characters.

    The output is to be formatted with the first line showing the data for the part and the following lines showing data for the suppliers, indented one tab.

    Sample data for the files are shown in Tables 13-3 and 13-4. You will first need to write a file conversion program to create the binary files. We suggest that you create a text file version of each file with your text editor and then read it to create the binary version.

Part Code	Part Name	Supplier 1	Supplier 2	Supplier 3
1000	Pen	5010	5007	5012
1001	Pencil	5006	5008	0000
1002	Paper	5001	5000	5003
1003	Ball Pen	5013	5009	5014
1004	Folder	5009	5007	5002
1005	Pointer	5012	5006	5005
1006	Mouse	5012	0000	0000
1007	Monitor	5000	5002	5007

Table 13-3 Project 2 part file

Supplier Code	Supplier Name	Supplier Address
5000	John Marcus	2322 Glen Place
5001	Steve Chu	1435 Main Ave.
5002	David White	2345 Steve Drive
5003	Bryan Walljasper	780 Rose Mary Street

Table 13-4 Project 2 supplier file

Supplier Code	Supplier Name	Supplier Address
5004	Andrew Tse	P. O. Box 7600
5005	Joanne Brown	1411 Donnybrook Square
5006	Lucy Nguyen	2345 Saint Mary Road
5007	Fred West	11 Duarte Rd.
5008	Dennis Andrews	14 California Ave.
5009	Leo Washington	134234 San Rosa Place
5010	Frankie South	12234 North Justin St.
5011	Amanda Trapp	1345 South Bush Circle
5012	Dave Lightfoot	222 George Territory Drive
5013	Danna Mayor	11 George Bush Street
5014	Robert Hurley	14 Republican Alley

Table 13-4 Project 2 supplier file (continued)

To read a record on the files, you will need to determine its position on the file. This is easily done by subtracting 1000 from the `PartCode` for the part file and 5000 from the `SupplierCode` for the supplier file. Then use *fseek* to position the file for reading.

43. Write a program that builds a histogram (see Chapter 8) using a randomly accessed disk file. The program is to begin by creating a new file of 20 integers. Each integer will represent the accumulator for its relative position; the first for the number 0, the second for the number 1, and so forth until the last for the number 19. The program is to then use the random number generator to create 100 random numbers in the range 0…19. As each random number is generated, it will be displayed in a 10 × 10 matrix (10 lines of 10 numbers each) and 1 added to its accumulator on the disk using the *fseek* function. After the random numbers have been generated, the file is to be read sequentially and a histogram displayed.

44. Your stockbroker has an online inquiry system that allows you to check the price of stocks using your personal computer. Simulate this system as described below.

Each stock is assigned a unique integral number in the range 1000…5000. They are stored on the disk so that stock 1000 is stored in location 0, stock 1001 in location 1, stock 2010 in location 1010, and so forth. To calculate the disk address for a requested stock, your program subtracts 1000 from the stock number and uses the result as the address in the file. (This is actually a simplified version of a concept known as "hashing," which you will learn when you study data structures.)

The data for each stock are described as follows:

```
structure
    stock key              short integer
    stock name             string[21]
    stock symbol           string[6]
    current price          floating-point number
    YTD High               floating-point number
```

YTD Low	**floating-point number**
Price-Earning Ratio	**short integer**

(YTD: Year to Date)

Using data from your local newspaper, create a binary file of at least 20 stocks. Then write a menu-driven system that allows the user to request data on any individual stock.

In addition, provide a capability to get a report of up to 20 stocks at one time. When this option is requested, open a temporary work file, and write the requested stocks to the file. After the last stock has been entered, read the file (without closing it), and prepare the report.

Linked Lists

14

Aside from some advanced C concepts and functions that we leave for your future studies, we have covered the basics of the C language. In this chapter, we turn our attention to a concept that is so pervasive in computer science that it should be studied by all programming students: the linked list.

14-1 LINKED LIST STRUCTURE

A **linked list** is an ordered collection of data in which each element contains the location of the next element; that is, each element contains two parts: **data** and **link**. The data part holds the useful information, the data to be processed. The link is used to **chain** the data together. It contains a pointer that identifies the next node in the list. A pointer variable points to the first node in the list. The name of the list is the same as the name of this pointer variable.

Figure 14-1 shows a linked list, named `pList`, containing four nodes. The link in each node, except the last, points to its successor. The link in the last node contains `NULL`, indicating the end of the list. We define an **empty linked list** as a single pointer having the value of `NULL`. Figure 14-1 also contains an example of an empty linked list.

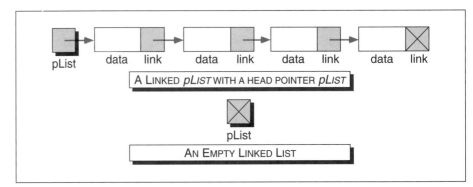

Figure 14-1 A linked list

NODES

A **node** in a linked list is a structure that has at least two fields. One of the fields is a data field; the other is a pointer that contains the address of the next node in the sequence. Figure 14-2 shows three nodes. The first node contains a single field, `number`, and a link. The second node is more typical. It contains a structure with three data fields, a name, `id`, and grade points (`grdPts`), and a link. The third example is the one we recommend. The fields are defined in their own structure, which is then put into the definition of a node structure. The one common element in all examples is a link field.

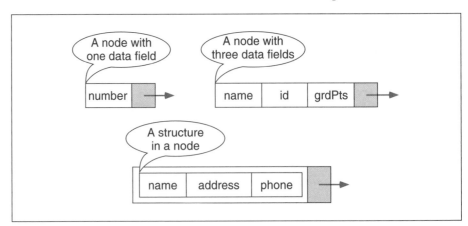

Figure 14-2 Nodes

When you study data structures, you will see that the node structure can become quite complex and can contain several pointers. We will limit our discussion in this text to nodes that contain data and only one link field.

TYPE DEFINITION FOR A LINKED LIST

The nodes in a linked list are called **self-referential structures**. Each instance of the structure contains a pointer to another instance of the same type. Let's code a generic model of the type definition for a linked list. The sections shown with an ellipsis (...) must be filled in for the particular application being created.

```
/* Global Declarations */
   typedef int KEY_TYPE;          /* Application Dependent */

   typedef struct
      {
       KEY_TYPE   key;
       ...                        /* Other Data Fields    */
      } DATA;

   typedef struct nodeTag
      {
       DATA              data;
       struct nodeTag *link;
      } NODE;
```

The DATA structure can be any structure that satisfies the application. We include a key field for those functions that require searching by key. A **key** is one or more fields that identify a node or otherwise control its use. The key type defined above is a generic type. In your program, you have to use either one of the standard types or create a type definition for it. To test the programs in this chapter, we have used a structure with only an integer key; no data have been included.

The NODE structure is the one that we need to study in detail. First, note that it contains DATA. Now study the link structure carefully. Note that link is a pointer to a struct nodeTag; that is, it is a pointer to another structure of its own type. This gives us the ability to create our linked list structure in which one instance of a node structure points to another instance of the node structure.

POINTERS TO LINKED LISTS

One of the attributes of a linked list is that its data are not stored with physical adjacency—that is, next to each other. When data are stored in an array, we know from the array structure where the list begins. The successor to each element is simply the next element in the array. But in a linked list, there is no physical relationship between the nodes.

Without a physical relationship between the nodes, we need some way to distinguish the beginning of the list—that is, to identify the first logical node in the list. This pointer is known as a **head pointer** because it points to the node at the head of the list. We name it pList, for pointer to list (see Figure 14-1).

A linked list must therefore always have a head pointer. Depending on how you will use the linked list, you may have several other pointers as well. For example, if you will search a linked list, you will undoubtedly have a pointer (pLoc) to the location where you found the data you were looking for. In many structures, efficiency will result if the structure has a pointer to the last node in the list as well as a head pointer. This last pointer is often called either pLast, for pointer to last, or pRear, for pointer to rear.

LINK LIST ORDER

Because a linked list is a linear structure, it always has an order. The order may be chronological or key sequence.

Chronological Linked Lists

Chronological linked lists are ordered by time. There are two basic chronological lists: the first-in, first-out (FIFO) list and the last-in, first-out (LIFO) list. FIFO lists place the new data at the end of the list; LIFO lists place the new data at the beginning of the list.

Key-Sequence Linked Lists

Most lists are key sequenced. In a key-sequenced list, the key in each node in the list is equal to or greater than its predecessor. New data added to the list must therefore be placed at the correct location relative to the data already in the list.

14-2   PRIMITIVE LINKED LIST FUNCTIONS

To work with a linked list, we need some basic operations that manipulate the nodes. For example, we need functions to insert a node at the beginning or end of the list, or anywhere in the middle of the list. We also need a function to delete a node from the list. Finally, we need a function to find a requested node in the list. Given these primitive functions, we can build functions that will process any linked list.

FUNCTIONAL DESIGN APPROACH

Before discussing these operations, however, we need to discuss our design approach. Functions that change the contents of the list, such as insert a node and delete a node, return the list head pointer. This design allows us to maintain the list easily by assigning the function's return value to the head as shown below.

```
pList = insertNode (…);
```

If the head of the list changes, it is automatically updated. If it doesn't change, then the list head is simply reset to its original address.

Functions that do not change the contents of the list return values consistent with their purpose. For example, a function to locate a node will return an integer to indicate found or not found. A function to determine the number of nodes in the list will return an integer count. Finally, functions that process the entire list, such as print the list, usually return void.

INSERT A NODE

Use the following four steps to **insert a node** to a linked list:

1. Allocate memory for the new node.
2. Determine the insertion point—that is, the position within the list where the new data will be placed. To identify the insertion position, we need to know only the new node's logical predecessor (pPre).
3. Point the new node to its successor.
4. Point the predecessor to the new node.

As seen in step 2 above, to insert a node into a list, we need to know the location of the node that precedes the new node (pPre). This pointer can be in one of two states: It can contain the address of a node, or it can be null. A linked list and its pointers are shown in Figure 14-3.

If the predecessor is null, then you are inserting either to an empty list or at the beginning of the list. If it is not null, then you are inserting somewhere after the first

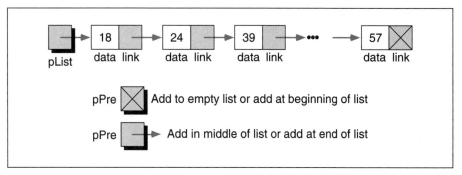

Figure 14-3 Pointer combinations for insert

node—that is, in the middle of the list—or you are inserting at the end of the list. Let's discuss each of these situations in turn.

Insert into Empty List   When the head of the list is null, then the list is empty. This situation is shown in Figure 14-4. All that is necessary to insert a node to an empty list is to point the list head pointer to the address of the new node and make sure that its link field is null. We could use a constant null to set the link field of the new node, but we will use the null contained in the list head pointer. The reason for this will become apparent in the next section.

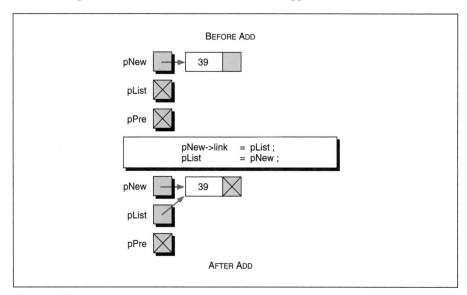

Figure 14-4 Insert node to empty list

The statements to insert a node into an empty list are shown below.

```
pNew->link = pList;          /* set link to NULL        */
pList      = pNew;           /* point list to first node */
```

Note the order of these two statements. You must first point the new node to NULL, then you can change the head pointer. If you reverse these statements, you will end up with the new node pointing to itself, which would put your program into a never-ending loop when you process the list.

Insert at Beginning

We insert a node at the beginning of the list whenever it must be placed before the first node of the list. We determine that we are inserting at the beginning of the list by testing the predecessor pointer (`pPre`). If it is null, then there is no predecessor, so we are at the beginning of the list.

To insert a node at the beginning of the list, we simply point the new node to the first node of the list and then set the head pointer (`pList`) to point to the new first node. We know the address of the new node. How can we find the address of the first node currently in the list so we can point the new node to it? The answer is simple: The first node's address is stored in the head pointer (`pList`). The statements to insert at the beginning of the list are shown below.

```
pNew->link  = pList;
pList       = pNew;
```

If you compare these two statements to the statements to insert into an empty list, you will see that they are the same. This is because, logically, inserting into an empty list is the same as inserting at the beginning of a list. We can therefore use the same logic to cover both situations. Inserting at the beginning of the list is shown in Figure 14-5.

Figure 14-5 Insert node at beginning

Insert in Middle

When we insert a node anywhere in the middle of the list, the predecessor (`pPre`) is not null. This case is shown in Figure 14-6.

To insert a node between two nodes, we must point the new node to its successor and then point the predecessor to the new node. Again, the address of the new node's successor can be found in the predecessor's link field. The statements to insert a node in the middle of the list are shown below.

```
pNew->link  = pPre->link;
pPre->link  = pNew;
```

Insert at End

When you insert at the end of the list, you only need to point the predecessor to the new node. There is no successor to point to. It is necessary, however, to set the new node's link field to `NULL`. The statements to insert a node at the end of a list are shown below.

```
pNew->link  = NULL;
pPre->link  = pNew;
```

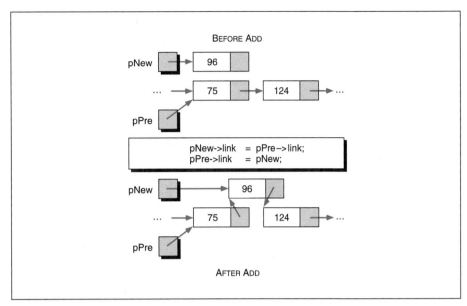

Figure 14-6 Insert node in middle

Rather than have special logic in the function for inserting at the end, however, we can take advantage of the existing linked list structure. We know that the last node in the list will have a `link` pointer of NULL. If we use this pointer rather than a constant, then the code becomes exactly the same as the code for inserting in the middle of the list. The revised code is shown below. Compare it to the code for "Insert in Middle," above.

```
pNew->link   = pPre->link;
pPre->link   = pNew;
```

Figure 14-7 shows the logic for inserting at the end of a linked list.

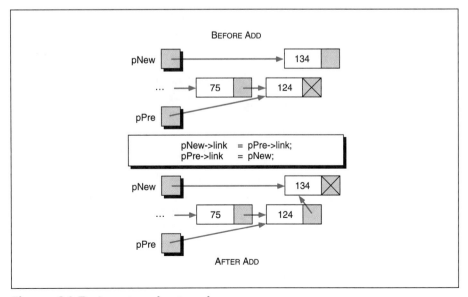

Figure 14-7 Insert node at end

Insert Node Function

Now let's write the function that puts it all together and inserts a node into the list. We are given the head pointer (pList), the predecessor (pPre), and the data to be inserted (item). We must allocate memory for the new node (*malloc*) and adjust the link pointers appropriately. Since we might insert a node before the beginning of the list, we also need to be able to change the contents of the head pointer. We ensure that the head pointer is always correct by returning it. The prototype declaration for insertNode is shown below.

```
NODE *insertNode (NODE *pList,
                  NODE *pPre,
                  DATA item);
```

The complete function is shown in Program 14-1.

```
1  /* ==================== insertNode ====================
2     This function inserts a single node into a linked list.
3        Pre    pList is pointer to the list; may be null
4               pPre points to new node's logical predecessor
5               item contains data to be inserted
6        Post   returns the head pointer
7  */
8  NODE *insertNode (NODE *pList,
9                    NODE *pPre,
10                   DATA  item)
11 {
12 /* Local Definitions */
13    NODE *pNew;
14
15 /* Statements */
16    if (!(pNew  = (NODE *)malloc(sizeof(NODE))))
17        printf("\aMemory overflow in insert\n"), exit (100);
18
19    pNew->data = item;
20    if (pPre == NULL)
21       {
22        /* Inserting before first node or to empty list */
23        pNew->link  = pList;
24        pList       = pNew;
25       } /* if pPre */
26    else
27       {
28        /* Inserting in middle or at end*/
29        pNew->link = pPre->link;
30        pPre->link = pNew;
31       } /* else */
32    return pList;
33 }  /* insertNode */
```

Program 14-1   Insert a node

Program 14-1 Analysis   We have discussed all the logic in this function except the memory allocation. Recall that *malloc* returns either an address in the heap or null when there is no more room in the heap. Therefore, we need to test to see if memory is available.

When memory is exhausted, we have an **overflow** condition. The action taken depends on the application being programmed; however, the general course of action is to abort the program. We assume the general case in the algorithm; if null is returned from *malloc,* we print a message to the user and exit the program.

With the idea in mind that all code needs to be tested, how can we test the overflow logic? We could use the brute-force method—insert data until the list overflows—but that could take a long time. We tested it by inserting an array of 10,000 long double variables to the data structure. On our system, we got an overflow on the fifth node and the logic was tested.

The technique used to call `insertNode` is important, since it returns the head of the list under all circumstances. The call should assign the return value to the list head pointer. This ensures that when the head of the list changes, the change will be reflected in the calling function. A typical call to insert data into a student list is coded below. Note that the head pointer (`stuList`) is found both in the assignment and as an actual parameter.

```
stuList = insertNode (stuList, pPre, stuData);
```

DELETE A NODE

Deleting a node requires that we logically remove the node from the linked list by changing various link pointers and then physically deleting it from the heap. The delete situations parallel those for insert. We can delete the first node, any node in the middle, or the end node of a list. As you will see below, these three situations reduce to only two combinations: Delete the first node, and delete any other node.

To logically delete a node, we must first locate the node itself (identified by `pCur`) and its predecessor (identified by `pPre`). We will discuss location concepts shortly. After we locate the node that we want to delete, we can simply change its predecessor's link field to point to the deleted node's successor. We then recycle the node using *free.* We need to be concerned, however, about deleting the only node in a list. Deleting the only node results in an empty list, so we must be careful that in this case the head pointer is set to `NULL`.

Delete First Node

When we delete the first node, we must reset the head pointer to point to the first node's successor and then recycle (*free*) the deleted note. We can tell we are deleting the first node by testing the predecessor (`pPre`). If the predecessor is null, we are deleting the first node. This situation is diagrammed in Figure 14-8.

The statements to delete the first node are shown below.

```
pList = pCur->link;
free(pCur);
```

If you examine this logic carefully, you will note that it also handles the situation when we are deleting the only node in the list. If the first node is the only node, then its link field is null. Since we move its link field (a null) to the head pointer, the result is by definition an empty list.

General Delete Case

We call deleting any node other than the first a general case, since the same logic handles deleting a node in the middle of the list and deleting a node at the end of the list. For both of these cases, we simply point the predecessor node, identified by `pPre`, to the successor of the node being deleted. The node being deleted is identified by the current node pointer, pCur. Its successor is therefore pCur−>link.

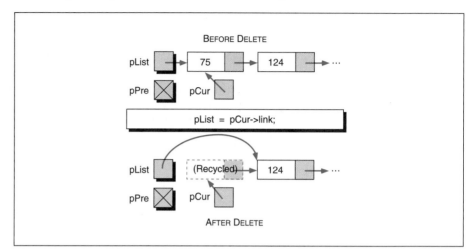

Figure 14-8 Delete first node

Deleting the last node is handled automatically. When the node being deleted is the last node of the list, its null pointer is moved to the predecessor's link field, making the predecessor the new logical end of the list. After the pointers have been adjusted, the current node is recycled. The general case is shown in Figure 14-9.

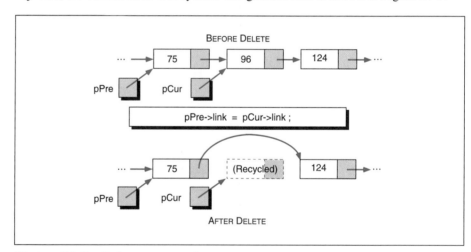

Figure 14-9 Delete—general case

The delete general case statements are shown below.

```
pPre->link =  pCur->link;
free (pCur);
```

Function to Delete a Node

The complete logic to delete a node is shown in Program 14-2. It is given a pointer to the head of the list, the node to be deleted, and the delete node's predecessor. After deleting and recycling the node, it returns the pointer to the beginning of the list.

```
 1  /* ===================== deleteNode =====================
 2     This function deletes a single node from the link list.
 3        Pre    pList is a pointer to the head of the list
 4               pPre points to node before the delete node
 5               pCur points to the node to be deleted
 6        Post   deletes and recycles pCur
 7               returns the head pointer
 8  */
 9  NODE *deleteNode (NODE *pList,
10                    NODE *pPre,
11                    NODE *pCur)
12  {
13  /* Statements */
14     if (pPre == NULL)
15        /* Deleting first node */
16        pList = pCur->link;
17     else
18        /* Deleting other nodes */
19        pPre->link = pCur->link;
20
21     free  (pCur);
22     return pList;
23  }  /* deleteNode */
```

Program 14-2 Delete a node

Program 14-2 Analysis   Three points in this function merit discussion. The first and most important is that the node to be deleted must be identified before this function is called. It assumes that the predecessor and current pointers are properly set. If they aren't, then the program will most likely fail. Even if it doesn't fail, the data will be wrong. (It is better that the program fail than report invalid results.)

Second, when we discussed the individual logic cases, we placed the recycle statement (*free*) after each delete. In the implementation, we moved it to the end of the function. When the same statements appear in both the true and false blocks of a selection statement, they should be moved out of the selection logic. This is the same concept as factoring common expressions in algebra. The result is a program that is smaller and easier to maintain.

Finally, we return the list. This is necessary because it is possible for the first node of the list to be deleted, which results in a new node being the head of the list.

LOCATING DATA IN LINKED LISTS

When we insert and delete data in a linked list, we must first search the list. To insert a node, we search to identify the logical predecessor of the new node in its key sequence. To delete a node, we search to identify the location of the node to be deleted and its logical predecessor. Just how we locate these positions depends on the structure of the list. For a chronological list, we use a seek function to place the predecessor pointer at the beginning or end of the list. For key-sequenced lists, we use a search function.

Seek Node Position

We designed the seek node position function after the binary file seek function. Given a pointer to the beginning of the linked list and an offset, we return the predecessor to the requested node. If the offset is 1, we return the beginning of the list (the list pointer itself).

If it is greater than 1, then we scan down the list and return the predecessor to the node at the position indicated by the offset. Thus, an offset of 3 returns the predecessor to the node in the third position in the list, and an offset of 5 returns the predecessor of the node in the fifth position in the list. To set the predecessor to the last node in the list, the offset is set to –1 (EOF). The seek node function is shown in Program 14-3.

```
 1  /* ==================== seekNode ====================
 2     This function locates the predecessor to a requested
 3     node in the link list.
 4        Pre    pList points to a head node
 5               pPre points to variable to receive predecessor
 6               pCur points variable to receive current node
 7               offset is ordinal position of node in list
 8                  -1 requests last node in list
 9        Post   pCur points to requested node
10               -or- null if offset > size of list
11               pPre points to offset - 1
12               -or- null if offset is 1
13               function returns 1 if located, 0 if not
14               -or- exits program if invalid offset
15  */
16  int seekNode (NODE    *pList,
17                NODE    **pPre,
18                NODE    **pCur,
19                int      offset)
20  {
21  /* Local Definitions */
22     int   nodeCnt;
23     int   rtnCode;
24
25  /* Statements */
26     if (offset < 1 && offset != -1)
27        {
28         /* Invalid offset--exit program */
29         printf("Invalid offset in seekNode\n");
30         exit (100);
31        } /* else */
32
33     *pPre = NULL;
34     *pCur = pList;
35
36     if (offset == -1)
37        {
38         /* find end of list */
39         while (*pCur)
40            {
```

Program 14-3 Locate node predecessor

```
41          *pPre = *pCur;
42          *pCur = (*pCur)->link;
43       } /* while */
44     rtnCode = 1;
45   } /* if */
46   else
47   {
48     /* Locate requested node */
49     nodeCnt = offset;
50     while (nodeCnt > 1 && *pCur)
51       {
52          *pPre = *pCur;
53          *pCur = (*pCur)->link;
54          nodeCnt--;
55       } /* while */
56     if (*pCur)
57         rtnCode = 1;
58     else
59         rtnCode = 0;
60   } /* else */
61   return rtnCode;
62 } /* seekNode */
```

Program 14-3   Locate node predecessor (continued)

Program 14-3 Analysis   To be valid, the offset must be -1 or a number greater than 0. Any other value, and we exit the program after printing an appropriate message.

Given a valid offset, we first determine if the request is for the end of the list (-1) or another location. For the end of list, we simply loop until we get to the end of the list, identified by a null pointer. At this point, the predecessor pointer is pointing to the last node in the list.

While the search for other locations is relatively simple, we must guard against the possibility that the offset is greater than the number of nodes in the list. Therefore, in Statement 50, we loop until we reach the requested node or we run out of nodes. If pCur is null, then we have run out of nodes and return with the predecessor set to the last node in the list and the location pointer set to null (not located).

One efficiency concern about this function. If it is used to simply find the end of list for a FIFO chronological list, then it is highly inefficient. It would be much better to use a rear pointer. Of course, adding a rear pointer would require that the insert and delete function be modified to maintain it.

Search Linked List

Both the insert and delete for key-sequenced lists require that we search the list. For inserts, we need to know the predecessor to the node to be inserted; for deletes, we need to know the predecessor to the node to be deleted. Also, to locate a node for processing, such as adding to a count or printing its contents, we need to know its location. Although we could write separate search functions for all three cases, the traditional solution is to write one search that will satisfy all requirements. This means that our search must return both the predecessor and the current (found) locations.

To search a list on a key, we need a key field. For simple lists, the key and the data can be the same field. More complex structures require a separate key field. We reproduce the node structure we introduced on page 709 for your convenience.

```
/* Global Declarations */
    typedef int KEY_TYPE;            /* Application Dependent */

    typedef struct
        {
        KEY_TYPE  key;
        ...                          /* Other Data Fields     */
        } DATA;

    typedef struct nodeTag
        {
        DATA            data;
        struct nodeTag *link;
        } NODE;
```

Given a target key, the search attempts to locate the requested node in the linked list. If a node in the list matches the target value, the search returns true (1); if no key matches, it returns false (0). The predecessor and current pointers are set according to the rules in Table 14-1. Each of these conditions is also shown in Figure 14-10.

Condition	pPre	pCur	return
target < first node	NULL	first node	0
target == first node	NULL	first node	1
first < target < last	largest node < target	first node > target	0
target == middle node	node's predecessor	equal node	1
target == last node	last's predecessor	last node	1
target > last node	last node	NULL	0

Table 14-1   Linear list search results

Since the list is in key sequence, we use a modified version of the sequential search. Knuth[1] calls this search "sequential search in ordered table." We simply call it an ordered sequential search.

We start at the beginning and search the list sequentially until the target value is no longer greater than the current node's key. At this point, the target value is either less than or equal to the current node's key while the predecessor is pointing to the node immediately before the current node. We now use the current node pointer (pCur) to test for equal and set the return value to 1 (TRUE) if the target value is equal to the list value or 0 if it is less (it cannot be greater) and terminate the search. The code for this search is shown in Program 14-4.

---

[1]Donald E. Knuth, *The Art of Computer Programming, Volume 3 Sorting and Searching.* (Reading, Mass.: Addison-Wesley, 1973), Algorithm T, p. 396.

Figure 14-10   Search results

```
1   /* ===================== searchList =====================
2      Given key value, finds the location of a node
3         Pre    pList points to a head node
4                pPre points to variable to receive predecessor
5                pCur points variable to receive current node
6                target is key being sought
7         Post   pCur points to first node with equal/greater key
8                -or- null if target > key of last node
9                pPre points to largest node smaller than key
10               -or- null if target < key of first node
11               function returns 1 if found, 0 if not found
12  */
13  int searchList (NODE       *pList,
14                  NODE       **pPre,
15                  NODE       **pCur,
16                  KEY_TYPE   target)
17  {
18  /* Local Definitions */
19     int found = 0;
20
21  /* Statements */
22     *pPre = NULL;
23     *pCur = pList;
24
```

Program 14-4   Search linked list

```
25    /* start the search from beginning */
26    while (*pCur != NULL && target > (*pCur)->data.key)
27        {
28         *pPre = *pCur;
29         *pCur = (*pCur)->link;
30        } /* while */
31    if (*pCur && target == (*pCur)->data.key)
32        found = 1;
33
34    return found ;
35  } /* searchList */
```

Program 14-4 Search linked list (continued)

Program 14-4 Analysis   Examine the *while* statement at Statement 26 carefully. Note that there are two tests. The first test protects us from running off the end of the list; the second test stops the loop when we find the target or, if the target doesn't exist, when we find a node larger than the target. It is important to make the null list test first. If the function is at the end of the list, then pCur is no longer valid. Testing the key first gives unpredictable results.

You can make the search slightly more efficient if you have a rear pointer. In that case, you can test the last node before the loop to make sure that the target isn't larger than its key value. If the target is larger, you simply exit the search function after setting the predecessor pointer to the last node and the current pointer to null. Once you know that the target is not greater than the last node, the loop doesn't need to test for running off the end of the list.

14-3   TRAVERSING LINKED LISTS

Algorithms that traverse a list start at the first node and examine each node in succession until the last node has been processed. Several different types of functions use **list traversal** logic. Some examples are printing the list, counting the number of nodes in the list, totalling a numeric field in the node, or calculating the average of a field. In fact, any application that requires processing the entire list uses a traversal. Figure 14-11 is a graphic representation of a linked list traversal.

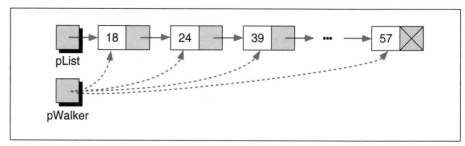

Figure 14-11 Linked list traversal

The basic logic to traverse a linked list is found in the pseudocode shown on the next page. It incorporates two concepts. First, an event loop is used to guard against overrunning the end of the list. Second, after processing the current node, the looping pointer is advanced to the next element.

```
traverse (list)
1 Set pointer to the first node in list
2 while (not end of the list)
  1   process (current node)
  2   set pointer to next node
end traverse
```

PRINT LINKED LIST

Program 14-5 uses the traversal logic to print a linked list. Since we are printing only integer keys, we print them ten in a line.

```
 1  /* Traverse and print a linked list.
 2        Pre    pList is a valid linked list
 3        Post   List has been printed
 4  */
 5  void printList (NODE *pList)
 6  {
 7  /* Local Definitions */
 8     NODE *pWalker;
 9     int    lineCount = 0;
10
11  /* Statements */
12     pWalker = pList;
13     printf("\nList contains:\n");
14
15     while (pWalker)
16        {
17         if (++lineCount > 10)
18            {
19              lineCount = 1;
20              printf("\n");
21            } /* if */
22
23          printf("%3d ", pWalker->data.key);
24          pWalker = pWalker->link;
25        } /* while */
26     printf("\n");
27     return;
28  } /* printList */
```

Program 14-5   Print linked list

Study the code in Statement 15 carefully. This is the most common form of pointer evaluation for a linked list. ANSI/ISO C guarantees that the evaluation of a null pointer will be false, and all other pointer values will evaluate to true. This expression is therefore equivalent to

```
while (pWalker != NULL)
```

where pWalker is a pointer to current node.

The other important piece of code in the traversal is in Statement 24.

```
pWalker = pWalker->link;
```

This statement advances us through the list. If you forget it, you will be in a permanent loop. Since pWalker points to the current node, we need to change it to advance to the next node. This is done by simply assigning the link field to pWalker. When we finally arrive at the end of the list, link is NULL, which when assigned to pWalker terminates the *while* loop.

LINKED LIST AVERAGE

Let's do one more linked list traversal algorithm, one that will average the values in a linked list. To pass a linked list to a function, you only need to pass the value of the head pointer. Look at Program 14-6. The actual data structure is not shown, but the function assumes that data.key is an integer field.

```
1   /* This function averages the values in a linked list.
2          Pre    pList is a pointer to a linked list
3          Post   list average is returned
4   */
5   double averageList (NODE *pList)
6   {
7   /* Local Definitions */
8      NODE *pWalker;
9      int    total;
10     int    count;
11
12  /* Statements */
13     total   = count = 0;
14     pWalker = pList;
15     while (pWalker)
16        {
17          total += pWalker->data.key;
18          count++;
19          pWalker = pWalker->link;
20        } /* while */
21     return (double)total / count;
22  } /* averageList */
```

Program 14-6 Average linked list

Program 14-6 Analysis   To traverse the list, we used the descriptive pointer, pWalker, that "walks" us through the list. Although we could have used pList, we advise against ever using the list pointer for any function logic. Keep it in its original state. Then, if you need to modify the function, you will still know its starting point. This is a small point, but it's the small points that make a program easy to maintain.

14-4   BUILDING A LINKED LIST

In the previous sections, we wrote three low-level functions for a linked list—insert, delete, and search—and two applications—print the list and average. It's time to put them all together in a program.

Regardless of how the list is ordered, the basic insert logic is the same. We need to get the data, create the node, determine the insertion position in the list, and then insert the new node. The design is shown in Figure 14-12. For the chronological list, we name the function `buildChron`. For the key-sequenced list, we name it `buildSeq`.

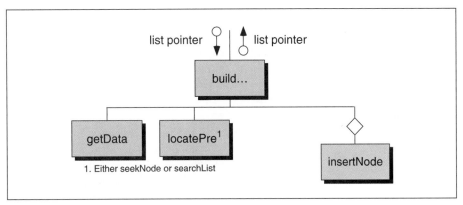

Figure 14-12   Design for inserting a node in a list

BUILD CHRONOLOGICAL LIST

We develop two programs: one for a chronological list (`buildChron`) and one for a key-sequenced list (`buildSeq`). Both programs use the same design—only the locate function differs. The chronological implementation is shown in Program 14-7.

```
 1  /* =================== buildChron ===================
 2     This function builds a chronological linked list.
 3        Pre   fileID is file that contains data for list
 4        Post  list built
 5              returns pointer to head of list
 6  */
 7  NODE *buildChron (char *fileID)
 8  {
 9  /* Local Definitions */
10     DATA   data;
11     NODE   *pList;
12     NODE   *pPre;
13     NODE   *pCur;
14     FILE   *fpData;
15
16  /* Statements */
17     pList  = NULL;
18     fpData = fopen(fileID, "r");
```

Program 14-7   Build chronological linked list

```
19      if (!fpData)
20         {
21          printf("Error opening file %s\a\n", fileID);
22          exit (200);
23         } /* if open fail */
24
25      while (getData (fpData, &data))
26         {
27          /* Determine insert position */
28          seekNode  (pList, &pPre, &pCur, -1);
29          pList = insertNode(pList, pPre, data);
30         } /* while */
31
32      return pList;
33  } /* buildChron */
```

Program 14-7   Build chronological linked list (continued)

Program 14-7 Analysis   This program uses the functions developed in the previous sections. The major point to note is that before the first call to insert a node, we create a null list by assigning a null pointer to pList (Statement 17).

As discussed when we developed the seek next function, however, this is a very inefficient way to insert data into a FIFO list. Every insert requires that we traverse the growing list to the end. It would be much better to use a rear pointer so that the list did not have to be traversed to insert a node at the end.

We do not include the get data function in the listing. It simply reads the data and returns a success or failure flag.

BUILD KEY-SEQUENCED LIST

Building the key-sequenced list is identical to building the chronological list except that it uses the search function rather than the seek function to determine the insertion position. As we said above, it uses the design shown in Figure 14-12 on page 725. The implementation is shown in Program 14-8.

```
 1  /* ==================== buildSeq ====================
 2     This program builds a key-sequenced linked list.
 3        Pre    fileID is file that contains data for list
 4        Post   list built
 5               returns pointer to head of list
 6  */
 7  NODE *buildSeq (char *fileID)
 8  {
 9  /* Local Definitions */
10     DATA    data;
11     NODE    *pList;
12     NODE    *pPre;
13     NODE    *pCur;
14     FILE    *fpData;
15
```

Program 14-8   Build key-sequenced linked list

```
16  /* Statements */
17     pList = NULL;
18
19     fpData = fopen(fileID, "r");
20     if (!fpData)
21        {
22         printf("Error opening file %s\a\n", fileID);
23         exit (210);
24        } /* if open fail */
25
26     while (getData (fpData, &data))
27        {
28         /* Determine insert position */
29         searchList (pList, &pPre, &pCur, data.key);
30         pList = insertNode(pList, pPre, data);
31        } /* while */
32     return pList;
33  } /* buildSeq */
```

Program 14-8   Build key-sequenced linked list (continued)

Program 14-8 Analysis   Note that we used the same data sequence in this program as when we built the chronological list. This time, however, the data are stored in key sequence.

Note that in Statement 29, we do not test for duplicate keys when search list returns. If we want to prevent duplicates, we would test the return value and print an error message rather than insert the data when a duplicate key is detected.

REMOVE A NODE

The design to remove a node is also simple. After reading the location of a node in a chronological list, or the key in a key-sequenced list, we determine its location and its predecessor and then call `deleteNode` to do the physical deletion. The design is shown in Figure 14-13.

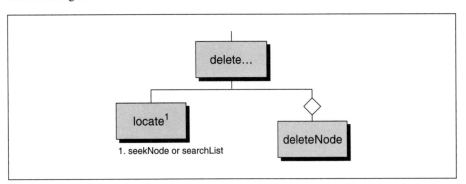

Figure 14-13   Design for removeNode

We call the chronological delete function `deleteChron` and the key-sequenced list function `deleteSeq`. Only the chronological list is developed here. It is shown in Program 14-9. The implementation for the key-sequenced list is left for a project at the end of the chapter.

```
 1  /* ==================== deleteChron ====================
 2     Delete node from a chronologically linked list.
 3         Pre    list is a pointer to the head of the list
 4         Post   node has been deleted
 5                -or- a warning message printed if not found
 6                returns pointer to first node (pList)
 7  */
 8  NODE *deleteChron (NODE *pList)
 9  {
10  /* Local Definitions */
11     int    locn;
12     int    valid;
13     NODE *pHead;
14     NODE *pCur;
15     NODE *pPre;
16
17  /* Statements */
18     if (!pList)
19         {
20          printf("List is empty...Can't delete.\n");
21          return pList;
22         } /* if */
23
24     printf("Enter position of node to be deleted: ");
25     scanf ("%d", &locn);
26
27     if (locn < 1)
28         printf("%d is an invalid location\a\n", locn);
29     else if (locn == 1)
30         pHead = deleteNode (pList, NULL, pList);
31     else
32         {
33          /* seek locations for delete node */
34          valid = seekNode (pList, &pPre, &pCur, locn);
35          if (valid)
36              pHead = deleteNode (pList, pPre, pCur);
37          else
38              {
39               printf("%d is an invalid location\a\n", locn);
40               pHead = pList;
41              } /* else locn not valid*/
42         } /* else delete after 1 */
43
44     return pHead;
45  } /* deleteChron */
```

Program 14-9 Remove nodes

Program 14-9 Analysis   While this function is somewhat academic, it contains some interesting code. We begin by checking to make sure that the list contains data. If it doesn't, we simply return the list pointer (which is NULL). We then verify that the location is valid by testing to make sure that it is not less than 1. We use the negative statement here because the action to handle a bad location is very short, and we dispose of it immediately.

Given that data are in the list and we have a valid location, we then determine if the first node is being deleted. While we could have skipped this logic; it is shorter and more efficient to handle it at the beginning.

Having established that the request is for a node after the first, we use `seekNode` to locate the node being deleted and its predecessor. If the location is valid but doesn't exist, `seekNode` returns an error flag, and we report that the node doesn't exist. In this case, we must also set `pHead` to the beginning of the list so that when we return it, we don't destroy the list pointer.

LINKED LIST TEST DRIVER

Now we need to test our functions. To test them, we write a test driver that builds a chronological list, then prints it, inserts more data into it, computes its average, and finally deletes data from it. The design of our test driver is shown in Figure 14-14.

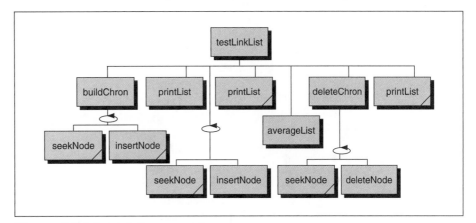

Figure 14-14   Link list test driver

The code for the test driver is shown in Program 14-10.

```
1   /* Test driver for chronological list functions.
2         Written by:
3         Date:
4   */
5   #include <stdio.h>
6   #include <stdlib.h>
7
8   /* Global Structures */
9   typedef int KEY_TYPE;
10  typedef struct
11     {
12      KEY_TYPE key;
13     } DATA;
14  typedef struct nodeTag
15     {
16      DATA            data;
```

Program 14-10   Test driver for link list

```
17       struct nodeTag    *link;
18       } NODE;
19
20  /* Prototype Declarations */
21  NODE  *insertNode  (NODE   *pList,  NODE   *pPre, DATA  item);
22  NODE  *deleteNode  (NODE   *pList,  NODE   *pPre, NODE *pCur);
23  int    seekNode    (NODE   *pList,  NODE  **pPre,
24                      NODE  **pCur,   int     offset);
25  void   printList   (NODE   *pList);
26  double averageList (NODE   *pList);
27  NODE  *buildChron  (char   *fileID);
28  NODE  *deleteChron (NODE   *pList);
29  int    getData     (FILE   *fpData, DATA  *pData);
30
31  int main (void)
32  {
33  /* Local Definitions */
34     NODE   *pList;
35     NODE   *pPre;
36     NODE   *pCur;
37     DATA    data;
38     double  avrg;
39     int     locn;
40     int     success;
41     char    more;
42
43  /* Statements */
44     printf("Begin chronological list functions\n\n");
45
46     /* Build List */
47     pList = buildChron("P14CHRON.DAT");
48     if (!pList)
49        {
50         printf("Error building chron file\a\n");
51         exit  (100);
52        } /* if */
53
54     printf("List Built\nContents: ");
55     printList (pList);
56
57     printf("\nInsert data tests.\n");
58     printf("Enter first integer          : ");
59     scanf ("%d", &data.key);
60     do
61        {
62         printf("Enter location for data:        ");
```

Program 14-10 Test driver for link list (continued)

```
63          scanf ("%d", &locn);
64
65          /* Determine insert position */
66          success = seekNode (pList, &pPre, &pCur, locn);
67          if (success)
68              pList = insertNode(pList, pPre, data);
69          else
70              printf("Invalid location.\a\n");
71
72          printf("Enter an integer <-1> to stop: ");
73          scanf ("%d", &data.key);
74        } while (data.key != -1);
75
76     printf("\nData Inserted\nContents: ");
77     printList (pList);
78
79     avrg = averageList(pList);
80     printf("\nData average: %.1f\n", avrg);
81
82     printf("\nDelete data tests.\n");
83     do
84        {
85         pList = deleteChron (pList);
86         printf("Delete another <Y/N>: ");
87         scanf (" %c", &more);
88        } while (more == 'Y' || more == 'y');
89
90     printList (pList);
91     printf("\nChronological tests complete.\n");
92     return 0;
93  } /* main */
```

```
Results:
Begin chronological list functions

List Built
Contents:
List contains:
111 222 333 444 555 666 777

Enter first integer          : 3333
Enter location for data:        33
Invalid location.
Enter an integer <-1> to stop: 999
Enter location for data:        -1
Enter an integer <-1> to stop: 400
Enter location for data:         4
Enter an integer <-1> to stop: 100
```

Program 14-10 Test driver for link list (continued)

```
Enter location for data:        1
Enter an integer <-1> to stop: -1

Data Inserted
Contents:
List contains:
100 111 222 333 400 444 555 666 777 999

Data average: 460.7

Delete data tests.
Enter position of node to be deleted: 33
33 is an invalid location
Enter position of node to be deleted: 10
Delete another <Y/N>: Y
Enter position of node to be deleted: 5
Delete another <Y/N>: y
Enter position of node to be deleted: 1
Delete another <Y/N>: n

List contains:
111 222 333 444 555 666 777

Chronological tests complete.
```

Program 14-10   Test driver for link list (continued)

Program 14-10 Analysis   While the code is rather lengthy, if you have studied each of the functions carefully, you will find this program straightforward. Of greater interest are the test cases. Note that for the inserts, we insert at the end, at the beginning, and in the middle. Likewise, for the deletes, we delete the last node, the first node, and one in the middle. We also try to delete a node that doesn't exist.

14-5   PROGRAMMING EXAMPLES

We include two short programs using linked lists that use the functions developed in this chapter. They have been placed in a header file, which we call P14-LINK.H. This file is included in the application program and serves as the prototype statements for the functions. (See Statement 9 in Program 14-11.) We also create a header file, P14-DATA.H, for the data structure, which we include in the programs. This is a common practice that ensures that everyone on a project is using the same data structures.

APPEND LISTS

In this program, we build two linked lists and then append the second one to the end of the first one. The data structure is shown in Figure 14-15. The implementation is shown in Programs 14-11 and 14-12.

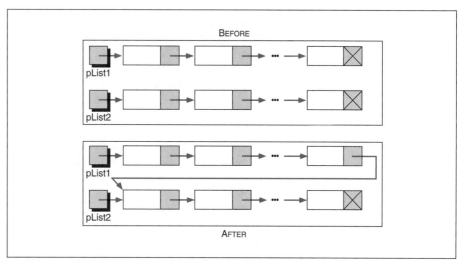

Figure 14-15   Append linked lists

```
1   /* This program appends two linked lists.
2         Written by:
3         Data:
4   */
5
6   #include <stdio.h>
7   #include <stdlib.h>
8   #include "P14-DATA.H"
9   #include "P14-LINK.H"
10
11  int main (void)
12  {
13  /* Local Definitions */
14     NODE *pList1;
15     NODE *pList2;
16
17  /* Statements */
18     pList1 = buildChron ("P14FILE1.DAT");
19     printList (pList1);
20     pList2 = buildChron ("P14FILE2.DAT");
21     printList (pList2);
22
23     append (pList2, pList1);
24
25     /* The lists are now appended. Print to prove success */
26     printList (pList1);
27
28     return 0;
29  }  /* main */
```

Program 14-11   Append two linked lists

```
Results:
  List contains:
  101 111 121 131 141 151 161 171 181 191

  List contains:
  202 212 222 232 242 252 252 272 282 292

  List contains:
  101 111 121 131 141 151 161 171 181 191
  202 212 222 232 242 252 252 272 282 292
```

Program 14-11 Append two linked lists (continued)

Program 14-11 Analysis   Note the *include* files in Program 14-11. We have included two application header files, P14-DATA.H and P14-LINK.H. You can tell that they are application header files because they are enclosed in double quotes rather than pointed brackets. The first one contains a structure that describes the user's data. It must contain a type definition with the name DATA. The data structure is the same one we developed in "Type Definition for a Linked List" on page 709.

The second header file contains all the linked list functions we described in the chapter. In main, we use only three of them, buildChron, append, and printList. If you study main carefully, you will note that these functions have no prototype statements. This is because the *include* places these functions above main. Since they have already been defined, we do not need prototype statements for them.

Once the lists were built, we used the printList function in the library to print both lists. This allows us to verify that the lists have been properly appended.

The function to append the lists is shown in Program 14-12.

```
 1  /* ==================== append ====================
 2     This function appends the first list to the end
 3     of the second list.
 4         Pre    lists have been created
 5         Post   first list appended to the second list
 6  */
 7  void append (NODE *list1,
 8               NODE *list2)
 9  {
10  /* Local Definitions */
11     NODE *pCur;
12
13  /* Statements */
14     pCur = seekNode(list2, -1);
15     pCur->link = list1;
16
17     return;
18  }  /* append */
19  /* ==================== End of Program ==================== */
```

Program 14-12 Append lists

Program 14-12 Analysis   Given the functions in our linked list application library, the append function is quite simple. We simply use seekNode to find the last node in the second list and then change its link pointer to point to the beginning of the first list.

ARRAY OF LINKED LISTS

In building an array of linked lists, the data for each linked list are read from a set of existing files and inserted into the list. After the lists have been built, they are printed to verify that they are complete. The data structure is shown in Figure 14-16. The code to build the array of linked lists is shown in Program 14-13. For simplicity, the array contains only two lists (see Statement 13).

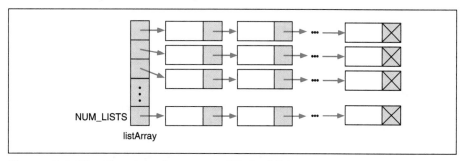

Figure 14-16   Structure for array of linked lists

```
 1 | /* Creates an array of linked lists. Each list is read from
 2 |    a file. After the lists have been created, they are
 3 |    printed to verify that they were built properly.
 4 |       Written by:
 5 |       Data:
 6 | */
 7 | #include <stdio.h>
 8 | #include <stdlib.h>
 9 | #include <string.h>
10 | #include "P14-DATA.H"
11 | #include "P14-LINK.H"
12 |
13 | #define NUM_LISTS 2
14 |
15 | /* Prototype Declarations */
16 | void buildAry (NODE **listArray, int numLists);
17 | void printAry (NODE **listArray, int numLists);
18 |
19 | int main (void)
20 | {
21 | /* Local Definitions */
22 |    NODE *listArray [NUM_LISTS];
23 |
24 | /* Statements */
25 |    buildAry (listArray, NUM_LISTS);
26 |    printAry (listArray, NUM_LISTS);
27 |
28 |    return 0;
29 | }  /* main */
```

Program 14-13   Build lists

Program 14-13 Analysis   The code in *main* is very simple. It contains one structure, the array of pointers to the linked lists, and two calls. The first call creates the linked lists, the second one prints them.

Program 14-14 contains the code to build the linked lists from files.

```
1  /* ==================== buildAry ====================
      Read files with a sequential name of FILEn.DAT
      and put the contents of the file into linked lists pointed
      to by an array of pointers.
         Pre    nothing
         Post   array of linked lists built
   */
2  void buildAry (NODE **listArray,
3                      int    numLists)
4  {
5  /* Local Definitions */
6     int     row ;
7     char    fileNum [3];
8     char    filename[20];
9
10 /* Statements */
11    for (row = 0; row < numLists; row++)
12       {
13       /* Convert row to text number - open file */
14       strcpy (filename, "P14FILE");
15       sprintf(fileNum,  "%d", row + 1);
16       strcat (filename, fileNum);
17       strcat (filename, ".DAT");
18
19       listArray[row] = buildSeq (filename);
20       } /* for */
21    return;
22 }  /* buildAry */
```

Program 14-14   Build array of linked lists

Program 14-14 Analysis   This function has several interesting points. First, note how we build the names of the files. The names have been constructed as a sequential series, P14FILE1.DAT, P14FILE2.DAT, ..., P14FILEn.DAT. We use the control variable in the *for* loop, row, as the source for the sequential number at the end of the file name. To convert it to a string, we use *sprintf* and append it to the file name. We then call buildSeq, passing it the file name, and let it build the list. When it returns, the head pointer is automatically stored in the array at the current row location.

Now consider the structure carefully. What we have is the linked list version of a two-dimensional array. Each linked list represents one row in the array. The nodes in the linked list represent the columns. This interesting and flexible structure can be used to solve many different problems. For testing, we set the number of files (rows) to 2.

To prove that the array of linked lists was built successfully, we print it using printAry, as shown in Program 14-15.

```
 1  /* ==================== printAry ====================
 2     This function prints contents of lists in listArray.
 3        Pre    listArray has been filled
 4               numLists is number of list pointers in array
 5        Post   lists printed, one after the other
 6  */
 7  void printAry (NODE **listArray,
 8                 int    numLists)
 9  {
10  /* Local Definitions */
11     int row;
12
13  /* Statements */
14
15     for (row = 0; row < numLists; row++)
16       printList (listArray [row]);
17     return;
18  }  /* printAry */
19  /* ==================== End of Program ==================== */
```

```
Results:
   List contains:
   101 111 121 131 141 151 161 171 181 191

   List contains:
   202 212 222 232 242 252 252 272 282 292
```

Program 14-15   Print array of linked lists

Because linked lists are useful structures, programmers use them in many applications. Rather than rewrite their functions each time we need them, we can write functions once and put them in a library. Then when we need to use a linked list, we simply include the library. The name given to a complete set of functions built like this is *abstract data type* (ADT). To present the concept, we need to define a few new terms.

ATOMIC AND COMPOSITE DATA

Atomic data are data that we choose to consider as a single, nondecomposable, entity. For example, the integer 4562 may be considered as a single integer value. Of course, you can decompose it into digits, but the decomposed digits will not have the same characteristics of the original integer; they will be four one-digit integers in the range 0 to 9.

An **atomic data type** is a set of atomic data having identical properties. These properties distinguish one atomic data type from another. Atomic data types are defined by a set of values and a set of operations that act on the values.

ATOMIC DATA TYPE
1. A set of values.
2. A set of operations on values.

For example, we can define the following atomic data types:

```
int
    VALUES:       -∞, …, -2, -1, 0, 1, 2, …, ∞
    OPERATIONS:   *, +, -, %, /, ++, --, <, >, …
float
    VALUES:       -∞, …, 0.0, …. ∞
    OPERATIONS:   *, +, -, /, <, >, …
char
    VALUES:       \0, …, 'A', 'B', …, 'a', 'b', …, \127
    OPERATIONS:   <, >, …
```

The opposite of atomic data is **composite data**. Composite data can be broken into subfields that have meaning. As an example of a composite data item, consider your telephone number. A telephone number actually has three different parts. First is the area code. Then, what you consider to be your phone number is actually two different data items, a prefix consisting of three digits and the number within the prefix, consisting of four digits. Years ago, these prefixes were names such as DAvenport and CYpress.

DATA STRUCTURE

A **data structure** is a collection of elements and the relationships among them. Data structures can be nested. That is, we can have a data structure that consists of other data structures.

1. A combination of elements, each of which is either a data type or another data structure.
2. A set of associations or relationships (structure) involving the combined elements.

For example, we can define the two structures *array* and *struct*, as shown in Table 14-2.

array	struct
A homogeneous combination of data structures.	A heterogeneous combination of data structures.
Position association.	No association.

Table 14-2   Two structures

Most programming languages support several data structures. In addition, modern programming languages allow programmers to create new data structures that are not available in the language they are using. In C, this is done with *struct* (see Chapter 12).

ABSTRACT DATA TYPE

Generally speaking, programmers' capabilities are determined by the tools in their tool kits. These tools are acquired by education and experience. Your knowledge of C is one of your tools. As you continue to study subjects such as data structures, file management, and systems analysis, your tools will increase. ADTs are another tool to add to your tool kit.

The first computer programming languages had no ADTs. To read a file, programmers wrote the code to read the file device. It did not take long to realize that programmers were writing the same code over and over again. So they created what is known today as an ADT. A programmer wrote the code to read a file and placed it in a library for all programmers to use.

This concept is found in C today. For example, the standard input/output library is an ADT. It has data structures and a set of operations that can be used to read and write data.

With an ADT, the user is not concerned with *how* the task is done but rather with *what* it can do. In other words, the ADT consists of a set of prototype definitions that allow the programmer to use the functions while hiding the implementation. This generalization of operations with unspecified implementations is known as abstraction. We abstract the essence of the process and leave the implementation details hidden.

The concept of abstraction means
• We know *what* a data type can do.
• *How* it is done is hidden.

Consider the concept of a list. At least three data structures will support a list. We can use an array, a linked list, or a file. If we place the list in an abstract data type, the user should not be aware of the structure we use. As long as data can be inserted and retrieved, it should make no difference how we store the data. Figure 14-17 shows several structures that might be used to hold a list.

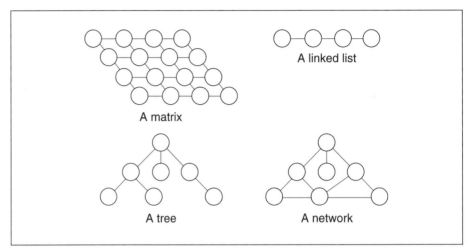

Figure 14-17   Structures for holding a list

An **abstract data type (ADT)** is formally defined as a data declaration packaged together with the operations that are allowed on the data type. In other words, we *encapsulate* the data and the operations on data, and we *hide* their implementation from the user.

> Abstract Data Type
> 1. Declaration of data.
> 2. Declaration of operations.

The ADT definition implies two attributes for ADTs:

1. *The structures are opaque.* We can use them without knowing how they are implemented.
2. *The operations are opaque.* We know what they will do; we don't know how they will do it.

We cannot stress the importance of hiding the implementation too much. For example, the programmer should not have to know the data structure to use the ADT. This is a common fault in many implementations that keep the ADT from being fully portable to other applications. Fortunately, C's rich library capability gives us the tools to fully implement any ADT.

A MODEL FOR AN ABSTRACT DATA TYPE

The ADT model is shown in Figure 14-18. The model is represented by the dark shaded area with an irregular outline. Inside the model are two different aspects of the model: the data structure and the operational functions. Both are entirely contained in the model and are not within the user's scope. However, the data structure is available to all the ADT's operations as needed, and an operation may call on other functions to accomplish its task. In other words, the data structure and the functions are within scope of each other.

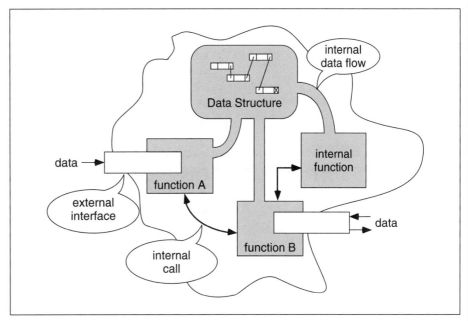

Figure 14-18 Abstract data type model

Data flows in and out of the ADT through the operation headers drawn as rectangles partially in and partially out of the structure. Each operation header is a function. For instance, a linked list ADT would have operations that we saw in this chapter, such as insert, remove, and search. A linked list ADT might also have an operation to return the number of nodes in the linked list or perhaps the data in the last node in the list. In C, these operations are defined as prototype header declarations that are visible to the user. They are the only thing the user needs to know to use the ADT.

To use the ADT in your program, you need to create a user header file. When you create a header file for a linked list ADT, you give its header file a name, such as `linklist.h`. To include it in your program, you use the following preprocessor directive:

```
#include "linklist.h"
```

ADT DATA STRUCTURE

When the list is controlled entirely by the program, it is often implemented using simple structures such as those shown in this chapter. Since the ADT must hide the implementation from the user, however, all data about the structure must be maintained inside the ADT. But just encapsulating the structure in the ADT is not sufficient. In addition, multiple versions of the structure must be able to coexist. This means that we must hide the implementation from the user while storing data about the structure in the user's program.

You have seen this concept before. When you create a file, you use the predefined structure `FILE`. Defining a file in your program creates a file structure that becomes a part of your program. We can do the same thing with the ADT. Each ADT must have a defined type that the users can define in their programs. Just like the file type, the ADT type will be a pointer to a structure that contains attributes about the structure. When the ADT attribute structure is created, it is stored in the heap. The only structural element in the user's program is a pointer to the structure.

This short description of ADTs just begins to introduce the topic. When you take data structures class, you may have the opportunity to create and use some in your programs.

14-7   TIPS AND COMMON PROGRAMMING ERRORS

1. The link field in the last node of a linked list must always have a null value.
2. Memory must be allocated for a node before you add the node to a linked list.
3. Be sure to free memory after you delete a node.
4. You must create an empty linked list (by assigning NULL to the header pointer) before using the functions introduced in this chapter.
5. Remember that a null link means there is no pointer; therefore, you cannot use it to dereference another node (or any other object). For example, the following code creates a run-time error because when the loop terminates, the value of pCur is NULL.

```
while (pCur != NULL)
   {
   ...
   pCur = pCur->link;
   }
printf("%d", pCur->data.member_name);    /* ERROR */
```

6. It is a compile error to declare a self-referential structure without a structure tag.
7. It is a logic error to allocate a node in the heap and not test for overflow.
8. It is a logic error to refer to a node after its memory has been released with *free*.
9. It is a logic error to set a pointer to null before the node has been freed. The node is irretrievably lost.
10. It is a logic error to individually release the elements of an array allocated with *calloc*.
11. It is a logic error to delete a node from a linked list without verifying that the node contains the target of the delete.
12. It is a logic error to fail to set the head pointer to the new node when a node is added before the first node in a linked list. The new node is irretrievably lost.
13. It is a logic error to update the link field in the predecessor to a new node before pointing the new node to its logical successor. This error will result in a never-ending loop next time the list is traversed.
14. It is a logic error to fail to set the link field in the last node to null. This causes the next traversal to run off the end of the list.

15. It is a potential logic error to use the node pointer in a linked list search before testing for a null pointer. In the following statement, the compares need to be reversed to prevent an invalid memory access.

```
while ((*pCur)->data.key < target
    &&   *pCur != NULL)
```

14-8   KEY TERMS AND CONCEPTS

abstract data type (ADT)	data structure	linked list
atomic data	delete node	list traversal
atomic data type	empty linked list	node
chain	head pointer	overflow
composite data	insert node	self-referential structure
data	link	

14-9   SUMMARY

- A linked list is a collection of nodes in which each element contains the address of the next node.

- The link in each node, except the last, points to its successor.

- An empty linked list can be defined as a single pointer having the value of NULL.

- A node in a linked list is a structure with at least two fields: one data field and one link field.

- A node in a linked list is self-referential because it contains a pointer to another structure of its type.

- To add a node to a linked list, we must allocate memory for the new node, determine the insertion location, point the new node to its successor, and point the predecessor to the new node.

- To process the nodes in a linked list, we use three variable pointers: pPre, pCur, and pWalker.

- Traversing a linked list means going through a linked list node by node and processing each node. For example, counting the number of nodes, printing the contents of nodes, and summing the values of some fields are examples of traversing a linked list.

- Traversing a linked list can be in full or in part. For example, we can print the value of the nth node in a linked list if we traverse the first $n - 1$ nodes.

- There are four different cases when we add a node: add to an empty list, add at the beginning, add at the middle, and add at the end of the list.

- Deleting a node means removing a node from the list. There are two general cases when we delete a node: Delete the first node, or delete any other node.

- Before using functions to add or delete a node, we need to use another primitive function to find the location of the action.

14-10   PRACTICE SETS

REVIEW QUESTIONS

1. Each element in a linked list must contain data and a link field.
   - a. True
   - b. False

2. All linked lists require a head pointer to identify the beginning of the list.
   - a. True
   - b. False

3. The first step in adding a node to a linked list is to allocate memory for the new node.
   a. True
   b. False

4. For efficiency, searching a linked list should use the binary search.
   a. True
   b. False

5. Composite data are stored in standard types.
   a. True
   b. False

6. A(n) _____ is an ordered collection of data in which each element contains the location of the next element.
   a. array
   d. node
   b. file
   e. structure
   c. linked list

7. Which of the following statements about linked lists is false?
   a. A linked list is an ordered collection of data.
   b. Each node in a linked list must contain at least one pointer.
   c. Nodes in a linked list must be structures.
   d. The link field in a linked list always points to a successor.
   e. The sequence of a link list is controlled by the link fields.

8. A(n) _____ identifies the first logical node in a linked list.
   a. array identifier
   b. head pointer
   c. list identifier
   d. structure variable identifier
   e. structure tag

9. Which of the following is not a step in adding a node to a linked list?
   a. Allocate memory for the new node.
   b. Determine the insertion point.
   c. Point the new node to the successor.
   d. Point the predecessor to the new node.
   e. Traverse the list.

10. Which of the following statements about linked list deletes is false?
    a. Deletion of a node from the middle of the list requires that its predecessor be changed.
    b. Deletion of the first node requires that the head pointer be changed.
    c. Deletion of the rear node requires a separate test to set the predecessor's link to null.
    d. Deletion physically removes a node from the list.
    e. The deleted node must be recycled.

11. Data that consist of a single, nondecomposable entity are known as
    a. atomic data
    d. standard data
    b. composite data
    e. structured data
    c. derived data

12. A(n) _____ is a collection of elements and the relationship among them.
    a. abstract data type
    d. standard type
    b. array
    e. type definition
    c. data structure

EXERCISES

13. Imagine we have the linked list shown in Figure 14-19. Show what will happen if we apply the following statement to this linked list:

$$pList = pList \rightarrow link;$$

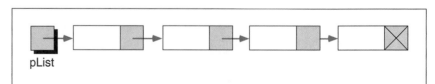

Figure 14-19   Linked list for Exercise 13

What is the problem with using this kind of statement? Does it justify the need for two walking pointers (`pPre` and `pCur`) that we introduced in the text?

14. Imagine we have the linked list shown in Figure 14-20. As discussed in "Search Linked List" on page 719, `search` we need to be able to pass back both the location of the predecessor (`pPre`) and the location of the current (`pCur`) node based on search criteria. A typical search design is shown in Figure 14-20.

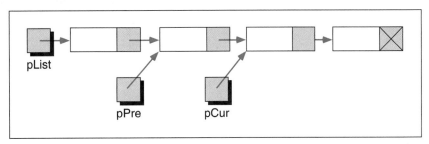

Figure 14-20 Linked list for Exercise 14

The following code to set `pPre` and `pCur` contains a common error. What is it, and how should it be corrected? (Hint: What are the contents of these pointers at the beginning of the search?)

```
pCur = pCur->link;
pPre = pPre->link;
```

15. Imagine we have a dummy node at the beginning of a linked list. The dummy node does not carry any data. It is not the first data node; it is an empty node. Figure 14-21 shows a linked list with a dummy node. Write the code to delete the first node (the node after the dummy node) in the linked list.

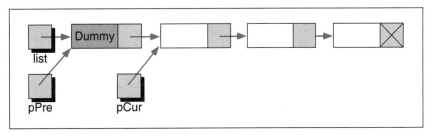

Figure 14-21 Linked list for Exercise 15

16. Write the code to delete a node in the middle of a linked list with the dummy node (see Exercise 15). Compare your answer with the answer to Exercise 15. Are they the same? What do you conclude? Does the dummy node simplify the operation on a linked list? How?

17. Figure 14-22 shows an empty linked list with a dummy node. Write the code to add a node to this empty linked list.

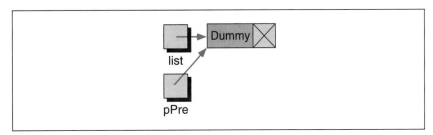

Figure 14-22 Linked list for Exercise 17

18. Write the statements to add a node in the middle of a linked list with the dummy node (see Exercise 15). Compare your answer with the answer to Exercise 17. Are they the same? What do you conclude? Does the dummy node simplify the operation on a linked list? How?

19. Imagine we have the two linked lists shown in Figure 14-23. What would happen if we apply the following statement to these two lists?

$$\text{list1 = list2;}$$

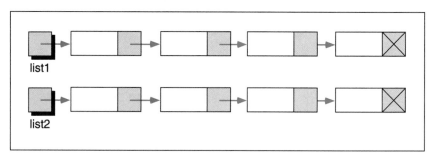

Figure 14-23   Linked lists for Exercise 19

20. What would happen if we apply the following statements to the two lists in Exercise 19?

```
temp = list1;
while (temp -> link != NULL)
    temp = temp -> link;
temp->link = list2;
```

21. Imagine we have the linked list shown in Figure 14-24. What would happen if we apply the following statements to this list?

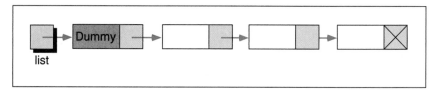

Figure 14-24   Linked list for Exercise 21

```
temp = list;
while (temp -> link != NULL)
    temp = temp -> link;
temp->link =  list;
```

PROBLEMS

22. Write a program that reads a list of integers from the keyboard, creates a linked list from them, and prints the result.

23. Write a function that accepts a linked list, traverses it, and returns the data in the node with the minimum key value.

24. Write a function that traverses a linked list and deletes all nodes whose keys are negative.

25. Write a function that traverses a linked list and deletes all nodes that are after a node with a negative key.

26. Write a function that traverses a linked list and deletes all nodes that are before a node with a negative key.

27. Modify Program 14-11, on pages 733–734, to count the number of nodes in the appended list. Display the count after the complete list has been printed.

28. Write a program that creates a two-dimensional linked list. The nodes in the first column contain only two pointers, as shown in Figure 14-25. The left pointer points to the next row. The right pointer points to the data in the row.

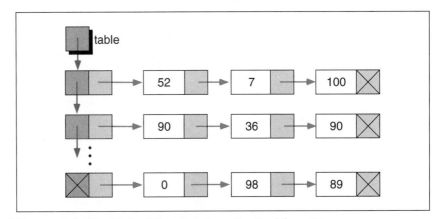

Figure 14-25 Linked list structure for Problem 28

29. Modify Program 14-9, on page 728, to delete data from a key-sequenced list. Include the modified function in a test driver such as Program 14-10, on page 729.

30. We can simplify most of the algorithms in the text using a linked list with a dummy node at the beginning, as shown in Figure 14-26.

Figure 14-26 Linked list for Problem 30

Rewrite the function, "Insert a node," Program 14-1, on page 714, using a linked list with a dummy node.

31. Rewrite the function `deleteNode` (see Program 14-2, on page 717) using a linked list with a dummy node.

32. Rewrite the function `searchList` (see Program 14-4, on page 721) using a linked list with a dummy node.

33. Write a function that returns a pointer to the last node in a linked list.

34. Write a function that appends two linked lists together.

35. Write a function that appends a linked list to itself.

36. Write a function that swaps (exchanges) two nodes in a linked list. The nodes are identified by number and are passed as parameters. If the exchange is successful, the function is to return 1. If it encounters an error, such as an invalid node number, it returns 0.

PROJECTS

37. Write a program that builds a linked list of 100 random numbers. It then sorts the list using one of the sorts found in Chapter 8. (You will need to modify the sort to use the linked list and pointers. You may find "Selection Sort Revisited," on page 493, helpful.) Display the list before and after it is sorted.

38. Modify Program 14-7, "Build chronological linked list," on page 725, to use rear pointers rather than seek next. (You will need to modify the insert function to set the rear pointer when a new node is being inserted at the end.)

39. Write a program that reads a file and builds a key-sequenced linked list. After the list is built, display it on the monitor. You may use any appropriate data structure, but it must have a key field and data. Two possibilities are a list of your favorite CDs or your friends' telephone numbers.

40. Modify the program you wrote in Project 39. After the file has been created, the program is to present the user with a menu to insert new data, remove existing data, or print a list of all data.

41. Write a program to read a list of students from a file and create a linked list. Each entry in the linked list is to have the student's name, a pointer to the next student, and a pointer to a linked list of scores. You may have up to four scores for each student. A picture of the structure is shown in Figure 14-27.

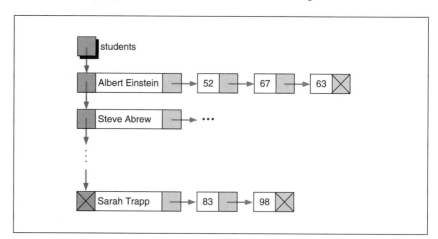

Figure 14-27 Data structure for Project 41

The program initializes the student list by reading the students' names from the text file and creating null scores lists. After building the student list, it loops through the list, prompting the user to enter the scores for each student. The scores prompt is to include the name of the student.

After all scores have been entered, the program prints the scores for each student along with the score total and average score. The average includes only the entered scores.

The data for each student are shown in Table 14-3.

STUDENT NAME	Score 1	Score 2	Score 3	Score 4
Albert Einstein	52	67	63	
Steve Abrew	90	86	90	93
David Nagasake	100	85	93	89
Mike Black	81	87	81	85
Andrew Dijkstra	90	82	95	87
Joanne Nguyen	84	80	95	91
Chris Walljasper	86	100	96	89
Fred Albert	70	68		
Dennis Dudley	74	79	77	81
Leo Rice	95			
Fred Flintstone	73	81	78	74
Frances Dupre	82	76	79	
Dave Light	89	76	91	83
Hua Tran	91	81	87	94
Sarah Trapp	83	98		

Table 14-3   Data for Project 41

42. Modify Project 41 to insert the data into the student list in key sequence. Since the data are entered in a first name–last name format, you will need to write a special `compare` function that reformats the name into last name–first name format and then does a string compare. All other functions should work as previously described.

43. Write a program that adds and subtracts polynomials. Use a linked list to store each polynomial. The first node in the list represents the first term in the polynomial, the second node represents the second term, and so forth.

   Each node contains three fields. The first field is the term's coefficient. The second field is the term's power, and the third field is a pointer to the next term. For example, consider the polynomials shown in Figure 14-28. The first term in the first polynomial has a coefficient of 5 and an exponent of 4, which then is interpreted as $5x^4$.

   The rules for the addition of polynomials are

   a. If the powers are equal, the coefficients are algebraically added.

   b. If the powers are unequal, the term with the higher power is inserted in the new polynomial.

   c. If the exponent is 0, it represents x^0, which is 1. The value of the term is therefore the value of the coefficient.

   d. If the result of adding the coefficients is 0, the term is dropped. (Zero times anything is zero.)

   A polynomial is represented by a series of lines, each of which has two integers. The first integer represents the coefficient; the second integer represents the exponent. Thus, the first polynomial in Figure 14-28 would be

   $$
   \begin{array}{cc}
   5 & 4 \\
   6 & 3 \\
   7 & 0
   \end{array}
   $$

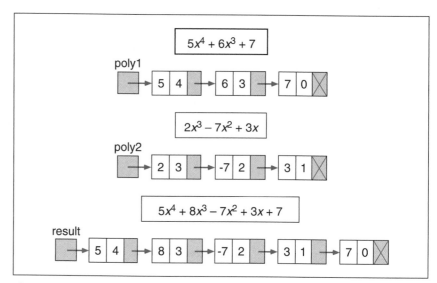

Figure 14-28   Linked list polynomials for Project 43

To add two polynomials, the program reads the coefficients and exponents for each polynomial and places them into a linked list. The input can be read from separate files or entered from the keyboard with appropriate user prompts. After the polynomials have been stored, they are added and the results placed in a third linked list.

The polynomials are added using an operational merge process. An operational merge combines the two lists while performing one or more operations—in our case, addition. To add, we take one term from each of the polynomials and compare the exponents. If the two exponents are equal, the coefficients are added to create a new coefficient. If the coefficient is zero, then the term is dropped; if it is not zero, it is appended to the linked list for the resulting polynomial. If one of the exponents is larger than the other, the corresponding term is immediately placed into the new linked list, and the term with the smaller exponent is held to be compared with the next term from the other list. If one list ends before the other, the longer list is simply appended to the list for the new polynomial.

After the polynomials have been added, delete any node whose coefficient is zero. Then print the two input polynomials and their sum by traversing the linked lists and displaying them as sets of numbers. Be sure to label each polynomial.

Test your program with the two polynomials shown in Table 14-4.

Polynomial 1		Polynomial 2	
Coefficient	Exponent	Coefficient	Exponent
7	9	−7	9
2	6	2	8
3	5	−5	7
4	4	2	4
2	3	2	3
6	2	9	2
6	0	−7	1

Table 14-4   Test data for Project 43

Bitwise Operators

15

While the preceding chapters contain the material required for a traditional first course in programming, we have not discussed all the basic capabilities of the C language. This chapter discusses the C bitwise operators.

The C language is well suited to system programming because it contains operators that can manipulate data at the bit level. For example, the Internet requires that bits be manipulated to create addresses for subnets and supernets.

C has two categories of **bitwise operators** that let you operate on data at the bit level: logical bitwise operators and shift bitwise operators.

15-1 LOGICAL BITWISE OPERATORS

The logical operators look at data as individual bits to be manipulated. Four operators are provided to manipulate bits: bitwise *and* (&), bitwise *inclusive or* (|), bitwise *exclusive or* (^), and *one's complement* (~). The first three are binary expressions; the one's complement is a unary expression.

Bitwise *and* Operator

The **bitwise *and*** is a binary operator (&—priority 8) that requires two integral operands (character or integer). It does a bit-by-bit comparison between the two operands. The result of the comparison is 1 only when both bits are 1; it is 0 otherwise. Table 15-1 shows the result of bit-by-bit comparison.

First Operand Bit	Second Operand Bit	Result
0	0	0
0	1	0
1	0	0
1	1	1

Table 15-1 *and* truth table

Program 15-1 demonstrates the bitwise *and* operator. Since C does not provide a binary conversion code to display data in binary, we have written one called `makeBin16`. The results of the program execution are seen at the end of the program.

```
 1  /* Demonstrate bitwise AND operator
 2         Written by:
 3         Date:
 4  */
 5  #include <stdio.h>
 6  #include <string.h>
 7
 8  /* Prototype Declarations */
 9  char *makeBin16 (unsigned int dec, char *strNum);
10
11  int main (void)
12  {
13  /* Local Definitions */
14     char strNum[17];
15     int  num1 = 0257;      /* Octal 0257-Binary 010101111 */
16     int  num2 = 0463;      /* Octal 0463-Binary 100110011 */
17     int  res;
18
19  /* Statements */
20     res = num1 & num2;
21
22     printf("First Number : %s\n", makeBin16(num1, strNum));
23     printf("Second Number: %s\n", makeBin16(num2, strNum));
24     printf ("AND Result   : %s\n", makeBin16(res,  strNum));
```

Program 15-1 Simple bitwise *and* demonstration

```
25
26   return 0;
27   }  /*main */
28   /* ==================== makeBin16 ====================
29      Convert a decimal to binary.
30         Pre   dec is a positive decimal number
31         Post  returns 17-byte string in binary format
32   */
33   char *makeBin16 (unsigned  int   dec,
34                                char *strNum)
35   {
36   /* Local Definitions */
37      char str[17] = "0000000000000000";
38
39      int bitLocn;
40
41   /* Statements */
42      bitLocn = sizeof(str) - 2;
43      while (dec > 0)
44         {
45          if (dec % 2)
46             *(str + bitLocn--) = '1';
47          else
48             *(str + bitLocn--) = '0';
49          dec /= 2;
50         } /* while */
51      strcpy (strNum, str);
52      return strNum;
53
54   }  /* makeBin16 */
```

```
Run results:

First Number : 0000000010101111
Second Number: 0000000100110011
AND Result   : 0000000000100011
```

Program 15-1   Simple bitwise *and* demonstration (continued)

Program 15-1 Analysis   Study the results closely. If you are not familiar with binary numbers, see Appendix D, "Numbering Systems." Note that the result is one only when both the first and second bits are both one. If either or both of them contain a zero, the result is zero.

The function, `makeBin16,` requires some discussion. The algorithm uses modulo two arithmetic with remainder as the bit. We describe the parameter `dec` as *unsigned*. This is necessary because C is not standard in its handling of signed integer values when they are being manipulated by bitwise operators. If the number is received as a signed integer, it will not be converted correctly.

Bitwise *Inclusive or* Operator

The **bitwise *inclusive or*** is a binary operator (| —priority 6) that requires two integral operands (character or integer). It does a bit-by-bit comparison between the two operands. The result of the comparison is 0 if both operands are 0; it is 1 otherwise. Table 15-2 shows the result of bit-by-bit comparison.

First Bit	Second Bit	Result
0	0	0
0	1	1
1	0	1
1	1	1

Table 15-2   *Inclusive or* truth table

Program 15-2 demonstrates the basic operation of the *inclusive or*. It uses the same function to convert the integers to bit strings that we used in Program 15-1, on page 752.

```
1   /* Demonstrate the inclusive OR operator
2         Written by:
3         Date:
4   */
5   #include <stdio.h>
6
7   /* Prototype Declarations */
8   char *makeBin16 (unsigned int dec, char *strNum);
9
10  int main (void)
11  {
12  /* Local Definitions */
13     char strNum[17];
14     int num1 = 0257;      /* Octal 0257--Binary 010101111 */
15     int num2 = 0463;      /* Octal 0463--Binary 100110011 */
16     int res;
17
18  /* Statements */
19     res = num1 | num2;
20
21     printf("First Number : %s\n", makeBin16(num1, strNum));
22     printf("Second Number: %s\n", makeBin16(num2, strNum));
23     printf("OR Result    : %s\n", makeBin16(res,  strNum));
24
25     return 0;
26  }  /* main */
```

```
Run results:

First Number : 0000000010101111
Second Number: 0000000100110011
OR Result    : 0000000110111111
```

Program 15-2   Simple *inclusive or* demonstration

Program 15-2 Analysis   With the exception of the leading zeros, only bit 6 is zero. This is because, except for bit 6, either the first number or the second number has a one bit.

Bitwise *Exclusive or* Operator

The **bitwise *exclusive or*** is a binary operator (^—priority 7) that requires two integral operands (character or integer). It does a bit-by-bit comparison between the two operands. The result of the comparison is 1 only if one of the operands is 1 and the other is 0; it is 0 if both operands' bits are 0 or 1—that is, if they are both the same. Table 15-3 shows the result of bit-by-bit comparison.

First Bit	Second Bit	Result
0	0	0
0	1	1
1	0	1
1	1	0

Table 15-3 *Exclusive or* truth table

Program 15-3 demonstrates the basic operation of the bitwise *exclusive or*. It uses the same function to convert the integers to bit strings that we used in Program 15-1, on page 752.

```
 1   /* This program demonstrates the use of the exclusive OR
 2          Written by:
 3          Date:
 4   */
 5   #include <stdio.h>
 6
 7   /* Prototype Declarations */
 8   char *makeBin16 (unsigned int dec, char *strNum);
 9
10   int main (void)
11   {
12   /* Local Definitions */
13      char strNum[17];
14      int num1 = 0257;        /* Octal 0257--Binary 010101111 */
15      int num2 = 0463;        /* Octal 0463--Binary 100110011 */
16      int res;
17
18   /* Statements */
19      res = num1 ^ num2;
20
21      printf("First Number : %s\n", makeBin16(num1, strNum));
22      printf("Second Number: %s\n", makeBin16(num2, strNum));
23      printf("XOR Result   : %s\n", makeBin16(res,  strNum));
24
25      return 0;
26   }  /* main */
```
```
Run Results

First Number : 0000000010101111
Second Number: 0000000100110011
XOR Result   : 0000000110011100
```

Program 15-3 Simple *exclusive or* demonstration

One's Complement Operator

The **one's complement** is a unary operator (~—priority 15) applied to an integral value (character or integer). It complements the bits in the operand; that is, it reverses the bit value. The result is 1 when the original bit is 0; it is 0 when the original bit is 1. Table 15-4 shows the result of the *one's complement*.

Original Bit	Result
0	1
1	0

Table 15-4 *One's complement* truth table

Program 15-4 demonstrates the basic operation of the *one's complement*. It uses the same function to convert the integers to bit strings that we used in Program 15-1, on page 752.

```
 1  /* Demonstrate use of one's complement
 2         Written by:
 3         Date:
 4  */
 5  #include <stdio.h>
 6
 7  /* Prototype Declarations */
 8  char *makeBin16 (unsigned int dec, char *strNum);
 9
10  int main (void)
11  {
12  /* Local Definitions */
13     char str[17];
14     int  num = 0257;        /* Octal 0257--Binary 010101111 */
15     int  res;
16
17  /* Statements */
18     printf("Original Num     : %s\n", makeBin16(num, str));
19     res = ~num;
20
21     printf("Complemented Num: %s\n", makeBin16(res, str));
22
23     return 0;
24  } /* main */
```
```
    Results:
       Original Num     : 0000000010101111
       Complemented Num: 1111111101010000
```

Program 15-4 *One's complement*

15-2 SHIFT OPERATORS

The shift operators move bits to the left or the right. When applied to unsigned numbers, these operators are implementation independent. When used with signed numbers, however, the implementation is left to the discretion of the software engineer who designs the system. It is often predicated on the hardware for which the compiler is being written. Therefore, they must be used with caution with signed numbers. Because ANSI/ISO C leaves the implementation up to the compiler writer (there is no standard) *code that shifts signed numbers may not be portable to other platforms.*

Bitwise *Shift-Left* Operator

The bitwise ***shift left*** is a binary operator (<<—priority 11) that requires two integral operands (character or integer). The first operand is the value to be shifted. The second operand specifies the number of bits to be shifted.

Shifting binary numbers is just like shifting decimal numbers. If we have an eight-digit decimal number, and we shift it three places to the left, then the leftmost three digits are lost and three zero digits are added on the right. The binary shift operation is shown in Figure 15-1.

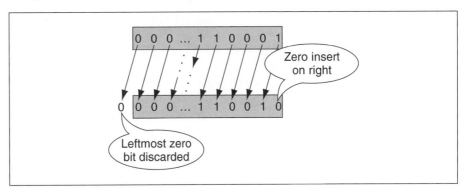

Figure 15-1 *Shift-left* operation

Program 15-5 demonstrates the basic operation of the *shift-left* operator.

```
 1  /* Demonstrate the bitwise shift-left operator.
 2         Written by:
 3         Date:
 4  */
 5  #include <stdio.h>
 6
 7  int main (void)
 8  {
 9  /* Local Definitions */
10  int num  = 49U;
11  int res;
12
```

Program 15-5 Simple *shift-left* demonstration

```
13    /* Statements */
14    res =  num << 1;
15
16    printf("Original value: %3d\n", num);
17    printf("Shifted 1 left: %3d\n", res);
18
19    res =  num << 2;
20    printf ("Shifted 2 left: %3d \n", res);
21
22    res = num << 4;
23    printf ("Shifted 4 left: %3d \n", res);
24
25    return 0;
26    } /* main */
```

```
Results:

Original value:  49
Shifted 1 left:  98        (times   2)
Shifted 2 left: 196        (times   4)
Shifted 4 left: 784        (times  16)
```

Program 15-5   Simple *shift-left* demonstration (continued)

Multiplying by 2

Let's start with something we know, decimal numbers. When we shift a decimal number one position to the left and insert a 0 on the right, we are in effect multiplying by 10. If we shift it two places, we are multiplying by 100. If we shift it three places, we are multiplying by 1000. But actually, we are multiplying by a power of 10—in our examples, 10^1, 10^2, and 10^3.

Applying the same principle to binary numbers, the left-shift operator multiplies by a power of 2. If we shift a binary number two places to the left, we are multiplying by 4 (2^2). If we shift it three places, we are multiplying by 8 (2^3). Table 15-5 shows the multiplication pattern used with bit shifting.

$2^{\text{shift value}}$	Multiplies by	Shift Operator
1	2	$<< 1$
2	4	$<< 2$
3	8	$<< 3$
4	16	$<< 4$
...	...	...
n	2^n	$<< n$

Table 15-5   Multiply by shift

Bitwise *Shift-Right* Operator

The bitwise *shift right* is a binary operator (>>—priority 11 in the Precedence Table; see inside front cover) that requires two integral operands (character or integer). The first operand is the value to be shifted. The second operand specifies the number of bits to be shifted.

When bits are shifted right, the bits at the rightmost end are deleted. What is shifted in on the left, however, depends on the type and the implementation. If the type is unsigned, then the standard calls for zero bits to be shifted in. If the type is signed, however, the implementation may either shift in zeros or copies of the leftmost bit. Since the implementation is the system programmer's responsibility, any function that shifts signed values may not be portable. The shift-right operation is diagrammed in Figure 15-2.

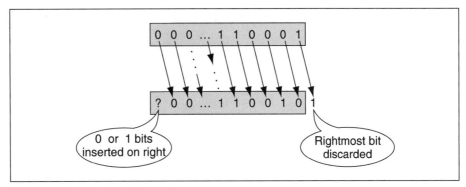

Figure 15-2 *Shift-right* operation

Program 15-6 demonstrates the *shift-right* operation.

```
1   /* Demonstrate the bitwise shift-right operator.
2         Written by:
3         Date:
4   */
5   #include <stdio.h>
6
7   int main (void)
8   {
9   /* Local Definitions */
10      int num  = 64;
11      int res;
12
13  /* Statements */
14      res =  num >> 1;
15
16      printf("Original value: %3d\n", num);
17      printf("Shifted right 1:%3d\n", res);
18
19      res =  num >> 2;
20      printf("Shifted right 2:%3d\n", res);
21
22      res =  num >> 4;
23      printf("Shifted right 4:%3d\n", res);
24
25      return 0;
26  }  /* main */
```
```
Results:
   Original value:   64
   Shifted 1 right:  32    (divide by  2)
   Shifted 2 right:  16    (divide by  4)
   Shifted 4 right:   4    (divide by 16)
```

Program 15-6 Simple *shift-right* demonstration

Dividing by 2

Shift right is the opposite of *shift left*; divide is the opposite of multiply. It is reasonable to assume, therefore, that shifting right has the effect of dividing by a power of 2. If you examine the results of Program 15-6 closely, you will note that is exactly what happens. Table 15-6 shows the shift operator values for division.

2^{shift}	Divides by	Shift Operator
1	2	>> 1
2	4	>> 2
3	8	>> 3
4	16	>> 4
...	...	...
n	2^n	>> n

Table 15-6   Divide by shift

15-3   BITWISE USE

In many programs, bits are used as binary flags: 0 is off, and 1 is on. To set and test the flags, we use a bit mask. A **mask** is a variable or constant, usually stored in a byte or short integer, that contains a bit configuration used to control the setting or testing of bits in a bitwise operation. The bits are numbered from the least significant bit (rightmost), starting at 0, as shown in Figure 15-3.

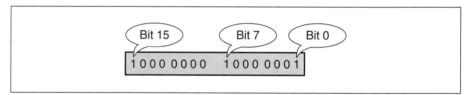

Figure 15-3   Bit mask in a short integer

CREATING MASKS

Masks can be created statically or dynamically. Static masks are generally literals. For example, to create the mask in Figure 15-3, we could code the constant `0x8081`. Dynamic flags are created using the bit manipulation operators: *shift, and, or.* In this section, we examine the basic techniques for creating dynamic masks that may change as the program executes.

One-Bit Masks

Given a byte flag in which bit 5 is an error flag, we need to create a mask to test it. To test bit 5, the mask must have bit 5 set to 1 and the rest of the bits to 0. This is easily done, as shown below.

```
char mask;

mask = 1 << 5;
```

$$00000001 << 5 \rightleftharpoons 00100000$$

We start with a constant binary 1. This places a one bit in the rightmost position. We then shift the one bit to the left five positions. The result is shown in the previous example.

An easier way to control the location of the bit flags is to name them. This is easily done with a defined constant, as shown in the next example.

```
#define FLAG1    0
#define FLAG2    1
...
#define FLAG5    5

mask = 1 << FLAG5;
```

By using named flag positions, we free ourselves from remembering their locations and at the same time make the code more readable. Of course, in an application, we would use meaningful names, such as OVERFLOW_FLAG, not FLAG1.

Two-Bit Masks

Creating a mask with two flags requires that we set 2 bits on. The easiest way to do this is to set two individual flags and then *or* them.

```
char FLAG1;
char FLAG5;
char mask;

mask1 = 1 << FLAG1;
mask5 = 1 << FLAG5;
mask  = mask1 | mask5;
```

The result of the above code would set the mask as shown below.

```
00100010
```

Setting Bit Range Masks

To set a range of bits requires a loop. The following example sets bits 3 through 6 to 1.

```
mask = '\0';

for (i = 3; i <= 6; i++)            /* 01111000 */
    {
     temp = 1 << i;
     mask = mask | temp;
    } /* for */
```

Complement Masks

To create a mask that turns off a specific bit—that is, that complements it—we must set the bit to 0 while setting the rest of the bits in the mask to 1. This requires two statements. In the first statement, we set only the desired bit on. In the second step, we complement the mask, changing all zero bits to 1 and all one bits to 0. The code is shown below.

```
mask = 1 << FLAG1;
mask = ~mask;
```

USING MASKS

Now that we've seen how to create masks with various bit flags set, let's look at some examples that use them.

Turning Bits Off

One of the applications of the bitwise *and* operator is turning bits off—that is, forcing selected bits to zero. We **force to zero** by building a mask for the second operand. Any bit location that is to be 0 in the result is set to 0 in the mask; any bit location that is to be unchanged in the results is set to 1 in the mask. Therefore, the rules for constructing an *and* mask are shown below. To refresh your memory on how these rules work, refer to Table 15-1 on page 752.

1. To force a location to 0, use a zero bit.
2. To leave a location unchanged, use a one bit.

For example, assume that we want to turn off the 5 leftmost bits (bits 3 through 7) of a number stored as an 8-bit byte. The mask should start with 5 zero bits to turn off the first 5 bits and then contain 3 one bits to leave the last three unchanged. The *and* mask is seen in the following example:

```
operator &    number  XXXXXXXX
              mask    00000111
                      --------
              result  00000XXX
```

The mask bit is the second bit. Note how when it is a 0, the result is always 0. When it is a 1, the result is always the same as the first bit. In other words, any bit *and* 0 is 0, any bit *and* 1 is unchanged. As you can see from the example, the job of forcing bits to zero (turning them off) is done by the 0s in the mask operand. The power to force a 0 is in the 0s in the second operand.

As an example, we know that in ASCII code, uppercase and lowercase differ by only 1 bit, bit 5. The lowercase letters have a 1 in bit 5, the uppercase letters have a 0. So it is very easy to change a lowercase letter to uppercase by using an appropriate mask to turn off bit 5. The mask should have one bits in all positions but bit 5, which should be 0, as shown in the following example.

```
char    'a'    01100001
mask           11011111
               --------
Result  'A'    01000001
```

Program 15-7 converts lowercase characters to uppercase.

```
 1  /* Changes lowercase characters in words to uppercase.
 2         Written by:
 3         Date:
 4  */
 5  #include <stdio.h>
 6
 7  #define CASE 5
 8
 9  int main (void)
10  {
11  /* Local Definitions */
12     char  word[81];
13     char *pStr = word;
```

Program 15-7 Convert words to uppercase

```
14      char   mask;
15
16  /* Statements */
17      printf("Please enter a word (alpha characters only)\n");
18      fgets (word, sizeof(word) - 1, stdin);
19      printf("\nOriginal string: %s\n", word);
20
21      mask = 1 << CASE;
22      mask = ~mask;                              /* mask 11011111 */
23
24      while (*pStr != '\n')
25         {
26          *pStr =  *pStr & mask;
27          pStr++;
28         } /* while */
29
30      printf("Modified string: %s\n", word);
31      return 0;
32  }  /*main */
```

```
Results
    Please enter a word (alpha characters only)
    computers

    Original string: computers

    Modified string: COMPUTERS
```

Program 15-7   Convert words to uppercase (continued)

Program 15-7 Analysis   Note that the *while* loop stops when it finds a newline character. This is because the *fgets* function transfers the newline to the string. We use *fgets* because it is safer than *gets,* which has no length limit and can overrun the input field.

To create the mask, we start with 1 and shift it to the left (Statement 21). We then complement the mask to set bit 5 to 0 with the rest of the bits set to 1 (Statement 22). Note that we have used a comment to show the bit configuration. This helps the reader because mentally converting hexadecimal to binary is not an easy task.

This little program is not the same as the standard library function, *toupper.* Do you see why? To show just one problem, let's see what happens if we apply the mask in the program to a space character.

```
Space   00100000
mask    11011111
        --------
Result  00000000
```

As you can see, the result is a null character, and the loop stops. If the first operand is not an alphabetic character, the result is unpredictable.

Turning Bits On   One common application of bit *inclusive or* is turning bits on—that is, forcing selected bits in a field to one. To **force to one**, all that we need to do is to construct a mask with the desired one bit set on. This guarantees that the result will have a one bit in that location. The rules for constructing an *or* mask are

1. To force a location to 1, use a one bit.
2. To leave a location unchanged, use a zero bit.

For example, assume that we need to turn on the 5 leftmost bits in a field stored as an 8-bit integer. We must set the leftmost bits of the mask to 1 and the remaining bits to 0. The mask is shown below.

```
operator |    number   XXXXXXXX
              mask      11111000
                        --------
              result    11111XXX
```

As you can see from this example, the job of forcing a bit to 1 (on) is done by the 1s in the mask operand.

Let's look at our alphabetic conversion program again. This time, we want to change all uppercase characters to lowercase. To do this, our mask must have a one bit in the fifth position. This guarantees that the letter will be lowercase. An example using the uppercase A is shown below.

```
char    'A'    01000001
mask           00100000
               --------
result  'a'    01100001
```

The implementation is shown in Program 15-8.

```
1   /* Change uppercase to lowercase without
2      affecting any lowercase letters.
3         Written by:
4         Date:
5   */
6   #include <stdio.h>
7
8   #define CASE 5
9
10  int main (void)
11  {
12  /* Local Definitions */
13     char string [81];
14     char *pStr = string;
15     char mask;
16
17  /* Statements */
18     printf("Please enter a word with upper & lower case: ");
19     fgets (string, sizeof(string) - 1, stdin);
20     printf("Original string: %s\n", string);
21
22     mask = 1 << CASE;                        /* mask 00100000 */
```

Program 15-8 Convert words to lowercase

```
23 │    while (*pStr != '\n')
24 │      {
25 │       *pStr  =  *pStr | mask;
26 │       pStr++;
27 │      } /* while */
28 │
29 │    printf("Revised string:  %s\n", string);
30 │
31 │    return 0;
32 │ } /* main */
```

```
Results
   Please enter a word with upper & lower case: cOmPuTErs

   Original string: cOmPuTErs

   Revised string:   computers
```

Program 15-8   Convert words to lowercase (continued)

Program 15-8 Analysis   Like Program 15-7, this simple program works only on alphabetic characters. It is not the equivalent of the standard library function, *tolower*.

Flipping Bits

One of the applications of bitwise *exclusive or* is flipping bits—that is, forcing 0s to 1s and 1s to 0s, called **force to change**. The resulting bit is 1 when 1 bit is a 0 and the other is a 1; if both bits are 0 or both are 1, the result is 0. To force a bit to change: therefore, the forcing bit in the mask is set to 1; bits that are to be unchanged are set to 0. The rules for constructing an *exclusive or* mask are

1. To force a location to change, use a one bit.
2. To leave a location unchanged, use a zero bit.

For example, assume that we want to change the 5 leftmost bits of a number stored as an 8-bit integer. We create the mask with 5 one bits and 3 zero bits, as shown below. (Y indicates a changed bit.)

```
operator ^   number    XXXXXXXX
             mask      11111000
                       --------
             result    YYYYYXXX
```

As you can see from this example, the job of forcing a bit to change is done by the 1s in the masking operand.

Returning once again to our program that changes the case of the letters in a word, we know that in ASCII code, the lowercase characters have a 1 in the fifth bit, while the uppercase characters have a 0. So it is very easy to change an uppercase letter to a lowercase letter and vice versa using the *exclusive or* operator, as shown below.

```
char    'A' 01000001    char    'a' 01100001
mask        00100000    mask        00100000
            --------                --------
Result  'a' 01100001    result  'A' 01000001
```

Program 15-9 reverses the case in a word.

```
1   /* This program reverses the case, that is,
2      changes upper to lower and lower to upper
3         Written by:
4         Date:
5   */
6   #include <stdio.h>
7
8   #define CASE 5
9
10  int main (void)
11  {
12  /* Local Definitions */
13     char  word [81];
14     char *pStr = word;
15     char  mask;
16
17  /* Statements */
18     printf("Please enter a word: ");
19     fgets (word, sizeof(word) - 1, stdin);
20     printf("\nOriginal word: %s\n", word);
21
22     mask = 1 << CASE;                        /* mask: 00100000 */
23     while (*pStr != '\n')
24        {
25          *pStr = *pStr ^ mask;
26          pStr++;
27        } /* while */
28     printf("Revised word : %s\n", word);
29
30     return 0;
31  }  /* main */
```

```
Results:
   Please enter a word: Computers

   Original word: Computers

   Revised word : cOMPUTERS
```

Program 15-9   Reverse case of words

ROTATING BITS

Rotation requires that bits be taken off one end of a value and moved to the other end. When we rotate bits right, we shift them off the right end of the value and insert them on the left. When we rotate left, we shift off the left end and insert them on the right. An example of shifting 3 bits to the right is shown below with the shifted bits in bold.

0100 0000 0010 **1100** ⇔ **100**0 1000 0000 0101

Rotation requires three steps. Assume that the previous example's value is stored in a short integer named `data`. We begin by creating a mask that contains `data`'s three rightmost bits shifted to the leftmost positions. Note that after the shift, all of the bits on the right are 0.

```
mask = data << 13;                  /* sizeof short - 3 */

      0100 0000 0010 1100 ⮥ 1000 0000 0000 0000
```

Next, we shift the 3 bits to be rotated off the right end of `data`. The shift right inserts 3 zero bits at the left end of `data`.

```
data = data >> 3;

      0100 0000 0010 1100 ⮥ 0000 1000 0000 0101
```

We are now ready to *or* the mask to insert the three positions that started on the right on the left.

```
data = data | mask;

data:   0000 1000 0000 0101
mask:   1000 0000 0000 0000
result: 1000 1000 0000 0101
```

15-4 BITWISE APPLICATIONS

Let's write two functions to demonstrate the use of bitwise operators in a program. The first program revisits our function to print a number as a binary number, this time using bitwise operators. The second example is a rotation function that uses *sizeof* to determine how many bits need to be rotated.

PRINT BINARY REVISITED

In Program 15-1, we printed a binary number by using string manipulation. In Program 15-10, we print using the bitwise operators.

```
1  /* Test driver for printBin.
2         Written by:
3         Date:
4  */
5  #include <stdio.h>
6
7  /* Prototype Declarations */
8  void printBin (int num);
9
10 int main (void)
11 {
```

Program 15-10 Print binary number revisited

```
12  /* Statements */
13      printBin(  8);
14      printBin( 66);
15      printBin(234);
16
17      return 0;
18  }  /* main */
19
20  /* ==================== printBin ====================
21      Print an integer as a binary number.
22          Pre    num contains a value
23          Post   num printed
24  */
25  void printBin (int num)
26  {
27  /* Local Definitions */
28      int    temp;
29      int    i;
30      int    spaceCnt;
31
32  /* Statements */
33      for (i  = sizeof(int) * 8 - 1, spaceCnt = 0;
34           i >= 0;
35           i--, spaceCnt++)
36        {
37         temp  = num >> i;
38         temp &= 1;
39         if (spaceCnt == 4)
40            {
41             /* insert space */
42             printf(" %d", temp);
43             spaceCnt = 0;
44            } /* if */
45         else
46             printf("%d", temp);
47        } /* for */
48      printf("\n");
49
50      return;
51  }  /* printBin */
```

```
Results:
   0000 0000 0000 1000
   0000 0000 0100 0010
   0000 0000 1110 1010
```

Program 15-10 Print binary number revisited (continued)

Program 15-10 Analysis   While the code is relatively straightforward, two points are worth mentioning. First, note how we specify the initialization in the *for* loop. The results indicate that the program was run on a computer whose integers are 16 bits. Other computers have 32-bit integers. By using the *sizeof* operator, we do not need to be concerned about how large an integer is.

Second, notice how we printed the binary number in groups of 4 bits. This makes it much easier to read the number and is a de facto standard in hexadecimal systems.

BIT ROTATION

In Program 15-11, we write a function to rotate bits to the right. Again, it is generalized to the point that the size of an integer is not a concern.

```c
 1  /* Test driver for rotateRight.
 2         Written by:
 3         Date:
 4  */
 5  #include <stdio.h>
 6
 7  /* Prototype Declarations */
 8  void rotateRight (int numIn, int *numOut, int numBits);
 9  void printBin    (int num);
10
11  int main (void)
12  {
13  /* Local Definitions */
14     int num;
15
16  /* Statements */
17     printf     ("Before rotation: ");
18     printBin   (234);
19     rotateRight (234, &num, 4);
20
21     printf     ("After rotation : ");
22     printBin   (num);
23
24     return 0;
25  }  /* main */
26
27  /* ==================== rotateRight ====================
28     Rotate integer numBits to the right.
29        Pre    numIn contains value to be rotated
30               numOut is address to received new num
31               numBits is number of bits to be rotated
32        Post   numOut contains rotated value
33               -or- if numBits invalid, zero
34  */
35  void rotateRight (int  numIn,
36                    int *numOut,
37                    int  numBits)
38  {
39  /* Local Definitions */
40     int    temp;
41
```

Program 15-11   Rotate right function

```
42    /* Statements */
43       if (numBits > sizeof(int) * 8)
44          *numOut = 0;
45       else
46          {
47           temp    = numIn << sizeof(int) * 8 - numBits;
48          *numOut = numIn >> numBits;
49          *numOut = *numOut | temp;
50          } /* else */
51
52       return;
53    }  /* rotateRight */
```

```
Results:
   Before rotation: 0000 0000 0000 0000 0000 0000 1110 1010
   After rotation : 1010 0000 0000 0000 0000 0000 0000 1110
```

Program 15-11   Rotate right function (continued)

Program 15-11 Analysis   This program was obviously run on a computer that uses 32-bit integer values. This demonstrates the value of writing generalized code. In Program 15-10, `printBin` printed 16-bit integers. In Program 15-11, it printed 32-bit integers. Likewise, `rotateRight` can handle either size integer.

Note also that we tested the number of bits to be rotated and set the result to 0 if the number was greater than the number of bits in an integer. What would happen if the number of bits was equal to an integer?[1]

---

[1]No change—the shifted result would be the same as the input!

15-5 SOFTWARE ENGINEERING AND PROGRAMMING STYLE

In Chapter 12, we looked at what makes a good function. In this section, we look at how you design good programs.

PAYROLL CASE STUDY

To provide a discussion focus, we will use a payroll program. Although our example is rather simple, it does contain all the elements involved in designing a program. The description of the payroll program is shown in Figure 15-4.

Payroll Case Study

1. Requirements:

   Given employees and their hours worked, compute net pay and record all payroll data for subsequent processing, such as W2 statements. Prepare paychecks and a payroll ledger.

   Maintain data on a sequential payroll file.

2. Provide for the following nonstatutory deductions:

   a. Health plan

   b. United Way

   c. Union dues

3. The payroll data are

   a. Employee number

   b. Pay rate

   c. Union member flag

   d. United Way contribution

4. Maintain the following year-to-date totals

   a. Earnings

   b. FICA taxes

   c. SDI taxes

   d. Federal withholding

   e. State withholding

   f. Health plan fees

   g. United Way donations

   h. Union dues

5. Algorithms

   a. Gross Pay = (Reg Hrs * Rate) + (OT Hours * Rate * 1.5)

   b. FICA Taxes = (Gross Pay*FICA Rate) if less than Max FICA

   c. SDI Taxes = (Gross Pay * SDI Rate) if less than Max SDI

   d. Taxable Earnings = (Gross Pay –
      (Exemptions * Exemption Rate))

   e. Federal Taxes = (Taxable Earnings * Federal TaxRate)

   f. State Taxes = (Taxable Earnings * State Tax Rate)

   g. Net Pay = (Gross Pay – (FICA Taxes + SDI Taxes + Taxable Earnings + Federal Taxes + State Taxes + Health Fee + United Way Donation + Union Dues))

Figure 15-4 Requirements for payroll case study

PROGRAM DESIGN STEPS

As you know by now, a program is developed in seven steps:

1. Determine requirements.
2. Determine data structures.
3. Build structure charts.
4. Create test cases.
5. Write and unit test programs.
6. Test system.
7. Implement system in production.

Our interest here is only in the third step: Build the structure charts. A few general comments are in order, however. The second and third steps are often reversed or done concurrently. Which one is done first is not of major consequence, as long as they are done before the fourth step.

Many programmers think that test cases should be built after the program is written. Good programmers know better. By creating test cases based on the requirements (Step 1) and your design (Steps 2 and 3), you will understand the problem better. You will even find occasions when you change your design based on what you learned creating test cases.

This does not mean that you will be done with creating test cases at Step 4; you just start there. You will develop more test cases *while you are writing the program,* and you will create still more as you conduct unit testing.

STRUCTURE CHART DESIGN

A good program starts with a good design, as reflected in the structure chart. By now, you should have progressed to the point where you are designing your programs before you start coding; that is, you are creating your structure chart first.

One tool to design the structure chart is known as **transform analysis**. Transform analysis is a design technique that identifies the processes in a program as input, process, and output and then organizes them around one or more processes that convert inputs to outputs. These conversion processes are known as the **central transforms**. Having determined the first-cut design, you repeat the process, decomposing the identified modules into subtasks using transform analysis.

This is a good design technique whenever a program reads, processes, and writes data, which covers the majority of programs. Although it is usually used in conjunction with another tool known as a data flow diagram, you can use it independently.

> Good programs start with a good structure chart design.

Recognize, however, that transform analysis is an approach to the design of a program. It is not a cookbook that leads to the same results every time. Different programmers using the same steps will arrive at different designs.

Programmers use six steps in designing a structure chart:

1. Determine program modules.
2. Classify modules.
3. Construct preliminary structure chart.
4. Decompose modules.

5. Complete structure chart.
6. Validate design.

Determine Modules

The first step in program design is to identify the processes that the program will use. This is usually done by reviewing the program specification and identifying the tasks it needs to accomplish. A review of our payroll case identifies the following tasks. (The references are to the case study description in Figure 15-4, on page 771.)

1. Read hours worked (1).
2. Compute pay (1).
3. Maintain payroll master file (1).
4. Prepare paychecks (1).
5. Prepare payroll ledger (1).
6. Calculate nonstatutory deductions (2).
7. Calculate year-to-date totals (4).
8. Calculate gross pay (5).
9. Calculate taxes (5).

Remember the rule that each module should do only one thing. You might be tempted to start with a module to prepare output instead of prepare paychecks and prepare payroll ledger. And in fact, you may well end up with an intermediate module that combines the preparation of all reports. But at this point, we want to keep different things separate as much as possible. On the other hand, experience indicates that to have separate modules for calculating FICA taxes, SDI taxes, federal taxes, and state taxes is unnecessary.

Classify Modules

In transform analysis, we look for the central transforms—that is, the module(s) that turns inputs into outputs. To identify these transforms, we classify each identified task, which now represents a module in the structure chart, as afferent, efferent, or transform. A module is an **afferent module** if its processing is directed toward the central transform. Another way of looking at this concept is to say that the module is a gatherer of data. **Efferent modules** direct data away from the central processing or toward the outputs of the program. (Remember that input comes before output and *a* comes before *e*; therefore, afferent is input and efferent is output.) A **transform module** is balanced; that is, it has data flowing both in and out. The concepts of afferent, efferent, and transform are shown in Figure 15-5.

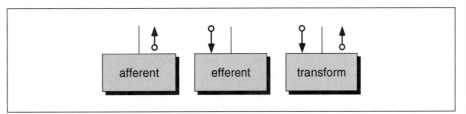

Figure 15-5 Afferent, efferent, and transform modules

Table 15-7 classifies each of the modules identified above as afferent, efferent, or transform.

773

Module	Afferent	Efferent	Transform
Read hours worked	✓		
Compute pay			✓
Maintain payroll master file	✓	✓	
Prepare paychecks		✓	
Prepare payroll ledger		✓	
Calculate nonstatutory deductions			✓
Calculate year-to-date totals			✓
Calculate gross pay			✓
Calculate taxes			✓

Table 15-7 Classified payroll modules

We have two comments about this classification. Note that "maintain master file" is classified as both input and output. This is because it is a master file. We will need to read it to get the employee personnel and history data, and we will need to write the updated data after they have been calculated. Therefore, it is really two modules: one to read the master and one to write the master.

Second, there are many transform modules. This will result in a large fan out, which is not desirable. **Fan out** is the number of submodules emanating from a module. We will need to reduce the fan out later.

Construct Structure Chart

At this point, you are ready to construct the first-cut structure chart. Transform analysis structure charts are organized with inputs on the left, transforms in the center, and outputs on the right. This organization is shown in Figure 15-6.

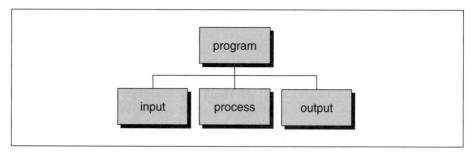

Figure 15-6 Basic structure chart organization

For the first-cut structure chart, place all afferent modules below the input block, all transform modules below the process block, and all efferent modules below the output block. In this process, analyze each module to determine if it needs to be called before or after the other processes at the same level. Those that need to be called first are placed on the left, and those that need to be called last are placed on the right. The resulting structure chart is shown in Figure 15-7.

Up to this point, we have been almost algorithmic; that is, we have exercised little judgment. We now need to analyze the preliminary struc-

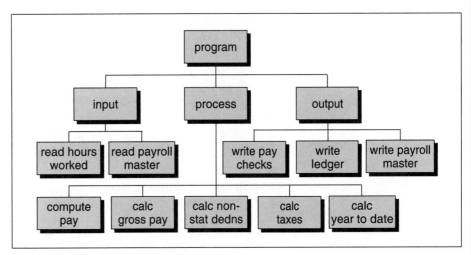

Figure 15-7   First-cut structure chart

ture chart to see if it makes sense. This is done by asking a simple question, "What do we mean by . . .?" For example, "What do we mean by compute pay?" The answer is that we must take hours worked and multiply them by the pay rate, also considering overtime and so forth. Or, to put it another way, we compute gross pay. But this is already a module in the structure chart, so these two modules are the same. We will therefore delete compute pay since it is a less specific description than calculate gross pay.

Decompose Modules

To decompose modules, we look at the cohesion of each module. For example, when we ask what we mean by calculate taxes, the answer is calculate federal taxes and calculate state taxes. Since we are dealing with two different entities (things), the cohesion of this module is communicational; it uses the gross pay and payroll data to calculate the different taxes.

When we find that a module is doing more than one thing, or that it is so complex that it is difficult to understand, then we need to consider breaking the module into submodules. This refinement of the modules was named **stepwise refinement** by Niklaus Wirth, the creator of Pascal.[2] It refines the processes in a module until each module is at its most basic, primitive meaning.

Decomposition continues until the lowest levels in our structure chart are all functionally cohesive and easily understood.

Complete Structure Chart

At this point we have the nucleus of the structure chart complete, and all we have to do is add the finishing touches. These steps are almost mechanical.

1. Identify any common processes with a cross-hatch in the lower right corner. In our payroll case, there are none.
2. Consider adding intermediate (middle-level) modules if necessary to reduce fan out. This step should not be done arbitrarily, however. If the modules next to each other have a common entity, then they can

[2]Niklaus Wirth, "Program Development by Stepwise Refinement," *Communications of the ACM*, 14, no. 4 (April 1971).

be combined. If they don't, they should be left separate. For example, in the payroll case, we have combined calculate nonstatutory deductions and calculate taxes into one module called calculate deductions. We would not combine calculate gross pay with calculate nonstatutory deductions, and we would not combine calculate taxes with calculate year-to-date deductions.

3. Verify that the names are descriptive and meaningful for their processes.
4. Add loops, conditional calls, and *exclusive or* designators.
5. Add input/output modules, if not already present.
6. Add initialization and end of job modules.
7. Add error routines (if necessary).
8. Add data flows and flags as required.

The completed design for the payroll case study is shown in Figure 15-8.

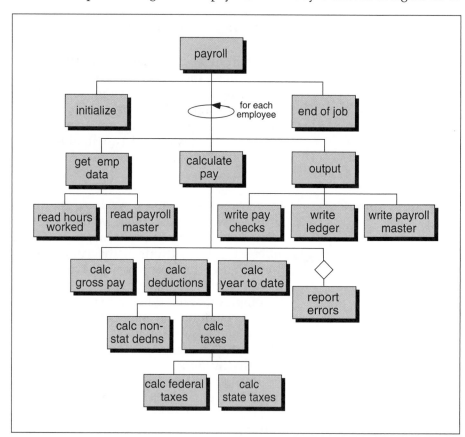

Figure 15-8 Final payroll structure chart

Validate the Design

At this point, you are ready to validate the design with a structured walkthrough. Before you convene the review board, however, you should review your design once more by repeating all the design steps, especially the functional decomposition step.

15-6   TIPS AND COMMON PROGRAMMING ERRORS

1. The bitwise *and* operator is only one ampersand (&), not two.

2. The bitwise *inclusive or* operator is only one bar (|), not two.

3. The bitwise *exclusive or* operator (^) will flip only bits specified in the mask.

4. The bitwise *complement* operator (~) flips all the bits in a variable.

5. There are two differences between the *logical and* operator (&&) and the bitwise *and* operator (&).

    a. The result of && is always 0 or 1. The result of & can be any number.

    b. The evaluation of an expression that uses && terminates if the first operand is false (zero). Expressions with the & operator are always completely evaluated.

6. There are two differences between the logical *or* operator (||) and the bitwise *inclusive or* operator (|).

    a. The result of the || is always 0 or 1. The result of | can be any number.

    b. The evaluation of an expression that uses the || operator terminates if the first operant is true (1). Expressions with the | operator are always completely evaluated.

7. There is a difference between the *not* operator (!) and the *one's complement operator* (~). The result of ! is always true (1) or false (0). The result of ~ depends how the number is stored in the machine.

8. The difference between bitwise *exclusive or* (^) and the *one's complement* (~) is that the ~ operator complements all the bits; the ^ operator complements only the specific bits in the mask.

9. Avoid using the shift operators with the signed number.

10. The *shift-left* operator multiplies a number by a power of 2 (2^n), not simply by 2.

11. The *shift-right* operator divides a number by a power of 2 (2^n), not simply by 2.

15-7   KEY TERMS AND CONCEPTS[3]

afferent modules	efferent modules	*one's complement (~)*
bitwise *and (&)*	fan out	*shift left (<<)*
bitwise *exclusive or (^)*	force to change	*shift right (>>)*
bitwise *inclusive or (|)*	force to one	stepwise refinement
bitwise operator	force to zero	transform analysis
central transform	mask	transform modules

---

[3]Note: Italic terms are bitwise operators.

15-8 SUMMARY

- C is a proper language for system programming because it contains operators that can manipulate data at the bit level. These operators are called bitwise operators.

- There are two categories of bitwise operators: logical bitwise operators and shift bitwise operators.

- The bitwise *and* (&) is a binary operator applied to two operands of integer value. It does a bit-by-bit comparison of the two operands. The result of each comparison is 1 if both bits are 1s. It is 0 otherwise.

- The bitwise *and* operator (&) is used to force masked bits in a variable to 0.

- The bitwise *inclusive or* (|) is a binary operator applied to two integral operands. It does a bit-by-bit comparison of its two operands. The result of each comparison is 0 if both bits are 0s. It is 1 otherwise.

- The bitwise *inclusive or* operator (|) is used to force masked bits in a variable to 1.

- The bitwise *exclusive or* (^) is a binary operator applied to two integral operands. It does a bit-by-bit comparison of its two operands. The result of each comparison is 1 only if the 2 bits are different. If they are the same, the result is 0.

- The bitwise *exclusive or* operator (^) is used to force masked bits in a data item to change.

- The second operand in the bitwise *and,* bitwise *inclusive or,* and bitwise *exclusive or* is called a mask.

- The bitwise *complement* operator (~) is a unary operator. It changes the value of each bit from 0 to 1 or from 1 to 0.

- Bitwise shift operators are binary operators used to shift data to the right or the left. The second operand in these operators is an integer that defines the number of bits to be shifted.

- The bitwise *left-shift* operator (<<) shifts the bits in the first operand to the left as many bits as is defined by the second operand. This effectively multiplies a number by 2^n, where n is the number of bits to be shifted.

- The bitwise *right-shift* operator (>>) shifts the bits in the first operand to the right as many bits as is defined by the second operand. This effectively divides a number by 2^n, where n is the number of bits to be shifted.

15-9 PRACTICE SETS

REVIEW QUESTIONS

1. To change every bit in a variable from a 1 to a 0 or from a 0 to a 1, use the 1s complement operator.
   - a. True
   - b. False

2. The bitwise *and* operator is used to turn bits on.
   - a. True
   - b. False

3. The bitwise _____ is used to force one or more bits to 0.
   - a. *and*
   - b. *exclusive or*
   - c. *inclusive or*
   - d. *shift left*
   - e. *shift right*

4. The bitwise _____ is used to change a bit.
   - a. *and*
   - b. *exclusive or*
   - c. *inclusive or*
   - d. *shift left*
   - e. *shift right*

5. The bitwise _____ is used to divide by a power of 2.
   - a. *and*
   - b. *exclusive or*
   - c. *inclusive or*
   - d. *shift left*
   - e. *shift right*

6. In program design, a function that collects data that are directed toward a central transform is classified as a(n) _____ module.
   - a. afferent
   - b. efferent
   - c. input
   - d. output
   - e. transform

EXERCISES

7. Which of the following operators is used to flip all bits in a variable?
   - a. &
   - b. ^
   - c. |
   - d. ~

8. Which of the following operators is used to flip selected bits in a variable?

   a.   `&`   c.   `|`

   b.   `^`   d.   `~`

9. Which of the following operators is used to set selected bits in a variable to 1?

   a.   `&`   c.   `|`

   b.   `^`   d.   `~`

10. Which of the following operators is used to set selected bits in a variable to 0?

    a.   `&`   c.   `|`

    b.   `^`   d.   `~`

11. Determine the result of the following operations:

    a. `~11011001`   c. `~11110001`

    b. `~11111111`   d. `~00000000`

12. Determine the result of the following operations:

    a. `11111100 & 00111111`

    b. `11111111 & 10101010`

    c. `00000000 & 11111001`

    d. `10101010 & 11100001`

13. Determine the result of the following operations:

    a. `11111100 | 00111111`

    b. `11111111 | 10101010`

    c. `00000000 | 11111001`

    d. `10101010 | 11100001`

14. Determine the result of the following operations:

    a. `11111100 ^ 00111111`

    b. `11111111 ^ 10101010`

    c. `00000000 ^ 11111001`

    d. `10101010 ^ 11100001`

15. Find the complement of the following decimal numbers, assuming that they are unsigned 8-bit integers:

    a. 24   c. 67

    b. 123   d. 4

16. Assuming that all the numbers are unsigned 16-bit integers, find the value of the following expressions:

    a. `4 | 2 & ~ 5`

    b. `3 | 5 | 4 & 255`

    c. `4 ^ 2 & 5`

    d. `123 | 255 & 0`

17. Assuming that all the numbers are unsigned 16-bit integers, find the value of the following expressions:

    a. `13 << 2`

    b. `22 << 4 >> 3`

    c. `5 << 2 & 3 && 3 >> 2 >> 3 | 4`

    d. `6 << 4 >> 4 + 3 & 0`

18. Show the mask and the operator that turn on the most significant bit of an 8-bit integer. (Remember, the bits are numbered from the right, starting with 0.) Give the answer in binary and hexadecimal form.

19. Show the mask and the operator that turn off the most significant bit of an 8-bit integer. (Remember, the bits are numbered from the right, starting with 0.)

20. Find the mask that can complement the values of the first and third bits of an 8-bit integer. (Remember, the bits are numbered from the right, starting with zero.) What operator should be used?

21. Find the mask that when used with the & operator sets the second and fourth bits of an 8-bit integer to zero. (Remember, the bits are numbered from the right, starting with 0.)

22. Find the mask that when used with the | operator sets the second and fourth bits of an 8-bit integer to 1. (Remember, the bits are numbered from the right, starting with 0.)

23. What is the result of the following expression?

    `a & ~a`

24. What is the result of the following expression?

    `a | ~a`

25. What is the result of the following expression?

    `a ^ a`

26. If `a` is an 8-bit integer, what is the value of the following expression?

    `a ^ 0xFF`

27. If `a` is an 8-bit integer, what is the value of the following expression?

    `a ^ 0x00`

28. What is the value of `a` after the following expression?

    `a &= 0xF7`

PROBLEMS

29. Write a function to determine if the right-shift operator on your computer adds 0s or 1s on the left side of the number. Be sure to test it with both a positive and a negative number.

30. Write a function that uses bitwise operators to print the binary representation of a number.

31. Write a function that determines if the bits in a short (16-bit) unsigned integer are alternatively 0 and 1. The first bit can be either 0 or 1.

32. Write a function that returns the largest pattern of consecutive 1s in an unsigned integer. Include 32,766 and −1 in your test data.

33. Write a function that counts the number of one bits in an unsigned integer. Call this function from `main` and then print the answer showing both the number of one bits and the number of zero bits in a value. Calculate the number of zero bits dynamically. Both the function and `main` are to be portable to any hardware platform; that is, you cannot pre-calculate the number of bits in a type.

34. Write a function that determines if a number is even or odd using the bitwise operators. (Hint: The least significant bit can be used to determine odd and even.)

35. Write a function that determines if an integer has an even number of one bits.

36. Rework Problem 35 so that it works for any integer size.

37. Write a *void* function that sets a specified bit in an integer to 1. The function is to have two parameters: The first parameter is the integer to be manipulated and the second is the bit location, relative to the least significant bit, that is to be turned on. Your test program should start with 0 and turn on several bits in turn.

38. Rework Problem 37 to turn off (set to zero) the specified bit.

39. Rework Problem 37 to flip the specified bit.

40. Write a function that flips the bits in an unsigned integer.

41. Modify Program 15-7, "Convert words to uppercase," on page 762, so that it works the same as *toupper,* that is, so that it only changes lowercase letters to uppercase and does not change any other characters.

42. Modify Program 15-8, "Convert words to lowercase," on page 764, so that it works the same as *tolower,* that is, so that it only changes uppercase letters to lowercase and does not change any other characters.

43. Write a function to rotate integer bits to the left. Use a test driver, and test it with at least three values.

PROJECTS

44. Modify Program 15-7, "Convert words to uppercase," on page 762, to convert a whole line instead of just one word. Hint: Check for spaces. Then write a driver program to test the functions.

45. A 32-bit integer (long on most personal computers) can store four characters. Write a program that reads a line in a text file, packs the characters in the line into an integer, and then writes the integers to a binary file. Use separate functions to read the file, pack the data, and write the binary file. The packing function is to use bitwise manipulation to pack the characters. The integrity of the text data is to be preserved; that is, tabs and newline characters are to be packed.

    After the binary file has been written, read it and print the data. This will require a second function to unpack the data. The unpack function is to be called by the print function. Verify the results by using a print utility to print the original text file.

46. Write a function to change an Internet address in decimal–dot notation (x.y.z.t) to its 32-bit binary format. (See Chapter 12, "Internet Addresses," on page 626, for a discussion of Internet addresses.) The address should be read as a string and printed as a binary number. Test it with 153.18.8.105.

47. Write a function to change a binary Internet address to decimal–dot format, such as 153.18.8.105.

ASCII Tables

The American Standard Code for Information Interchange (ASCII) is shown in this appendix. Table A-1 indicates the decimal, hexadecimal, octal, and graphic codes (symbol) with an English interpretation, if appropriate. Table A-2 gives a hexadecimal matrix of all values.

A-1 ASCII CODES (LONG FORM)

Decimal	Hex	Octal	Symbol	Interpretation
0	00	00	null	NULL value
1	01	01	SOH	Start of heading
2	02	02	STX	Start of text
3	03	03	ETX	End of text
4	04	04	EOT	End of transmission
5	05	05	ENQ	Enquiry
6	06	06	ACK	Acknowledgment
7	07	07	BEL	Ring bell
8	08	10	BS	Backspace
9	09	11	HT	Horizontal tab
10	0A	12	LF	Line feed
11	0B	13	VT	Vertical tab
12	0C	14	FF	Form feed
13	0D	15	CR	Carriage return
14	0E	16	SO	Shift out
15	0F	17	SI	Shift in
16	10	20	DLE	Data link escape
17	11	21	DC1	Device control 1
18	12	22	DC2	Device control 2
19	13	23	DC3	Device control 3
20	14	24	DC4	Device control 4
21	15	25	NAK	Negative acknowledgment
22	16	26	SYN	Synchronous idle
23	17	27	ETB	End of transmission block
24	18	30	CAN	Cancel
25	19	31	EM	End of medium
26	1A	32	SUB	Substitute
27	1B	33	ESC	Escape
28	1C	34	FS	File separator
29	1D	35	GS	Group separator
30	1E	36	RS	Record separator
31	1F	37	US	Unit separator
32	20	40	SP	Space
33	21	41	!	
34	22	42	"	Double quote
35	23	43	#	
36	24	44	$	
37	25	45	%	

Table A-1 ASCII codes

Decimal	Hex	Octal	Symbol	Interpretation
38	26	46	&	
39	27	47	'	Apostrophe
40	28	50	(	
41	29	51	)	
42	2A	52	*	
43	2B	53	+	
44	2C	54	,	Comma
45	2D	55	—	Minus
46	2E	56	.	
47	2F	57	/	
48	30	60	0	
49	31	61	1	
50	32	62	2	
51	33	63	3	
52	34	64	4	
53	35	65	5	
54	36	66	6	
55	37	67	7	
56	38	70	8	
57	39	71	9	
58	3A	72	:	Colon
59	3B	73	;	Semicolon
60	3C	74	<	
61	3D	75	=	
62	3E	76	>	
63	3F	77	?	
64	40	100	@	
65	41	101	A	
66	42	102	B	
67	43	103	C	
68	44	104	D	
69	45	105	E	
70	46	106	F	
71	47	107	G	
72	48	110	H	
73	49	111	I	
74	4A	112	J	
75	4B	113	K	
76	4C	114	L	
77	4D	115	M	
78	4E	116	N	

Table A-1   ASCII codes (continued)

Decimal	Hex	Octal	Symbol	Interpretation
79	4F	117	O	
80	50	120	P	
81	51	121	Q	
82	52	122	R	
83	53	123	S	
84	54	124	T	
85	55	125	U	
86	56	126	V	
87	57	127	W	
88	58	130	X	
89	59	131	Y	
90	5A	132	Z	
91	5B	133	[	Open bracket
92	5C	134	\	Backslash
93	5D	135	]	Close bracket
94	5E	136	^	Caret
95	5F	137	_	Underscore
96	60	140	`	Grave accent
97	61	141	a	
98	62	142	b	
99	63	143	c	
100	64	144	d	
101	65	145	e	
102	66	146	f	
103	67	147	g	
104	68	150	h	
105	69	151	i	
106	6A	152	j	
107	6B	153	k	
108	6C	154	l	
109	6D	155	m	
110	6E	156	n	
111	6F	157	o	
112	70	160	p	
113	71	161	q	
114	72	162	r	
115	73	163	s	
116	74	164	t	
117	75	165	u	
118	76	166	v	
119	77	167	w	

Table A-1 ASCII codes (continued)

Decimal	Hex	Octal	Symbol	Interpretation
120	78	170	x	
121	79	171	y	
122	7A	172	z	
123	7B	173	{	Open brace
124	7C	174	|	Bar
125	7D	175	}	Close brace
126	7E	176	~	Tilde
127	7F	177	DEL	Delete

Table A-1   ASCII codes (continued)

A-2   ASCII TABLE (SHORT FORM)

	0	1	2	3	4	5	6	7	8	9	A	B	C	D	E	F
0	null	SOH	STX	ETX	EOT	ENQ	ACK	BEL	BS	HT	LF	VT	FF	CR	SO	SI
1	DLE	DC1	DC2	DC3	DC4	NAK	SYN	ETB	CAN	EM	SUB	ESC	FS	GS	RS	US
2	SP	!	"	#	$	%	&	'	(	)	*	+	,	—	.	/
3	0	1	2	3	4	5	6	7	8	9	:	;	<	=	>	?
4	@	A	B	C	D	E	F	G	H	I	J	K	L	M	N	O
5	P	Q	R	S	T	U	V	W	X	Y	Z	[	\	]	^	—
6	`	a	b	c	d	e	f	g	h	i	j	k	l	m	n	o
7	p	q	r	s	t	u	v	w	x	y	z	{	|	}	~	DEL

Table A-2   Short ASCII table (hexadecimal)

Reserved Words

The C language contains several keywords, or reserved words, that cannot be used for functions, variables, or named constants. They are shown below.

auto	*int*
break	*long*
case	*register*
char	*return*
const	*short*
continue	*signed*
default	*sizeof*
do	*static*
double	*struct*
else	*switch*
enum	*typedef*
extern	*union*
float	*unsigned*
for	*void*
goto	*volatile*
if	*while*

Flowcharting

A flowchart is a tool to show the logic flow of a program. Although it is generally considered a computer programming tool, it can and has been used for many other purposes. Programmers use flowcharts to design a complete program or just part of a program. Depending on the programming language, the parts can be called such things as procedures (Pascal), functions (C), or paragraphs (COBOL). We will use the general term *algorithm* to indicate any part of a program that needs design.

The primary purpose of a flowchart is to show the design of an algorithm. The flowchart also frees the programmer from the syntax and details of a programming language while allowing him or her to concentrate on the details of the problem to be solved.

A flowchart gives a pictorial representation of an algorithm—in contrast to another programming design tool, pseudocode, which provides a textual design solution. Both tools have their advantages, but a flowchart has the pictorial power that other tools lack. A new student of computer science must learn how to think about an algorithm before writing it. A flowchart is a tool for this pictorial thinking.

C-1 AUXILIARY SYMBOLS

A flowchart is a combination of symbols. Some symbols enhance the readability or functionality of the flowchart; they do not directly show instructions or commands. They show the start and stop points, the order and sequence of actions, and how one part of a flowchart is connected to another. These auxiliary symbols are shown in Figure C-1.

Figure C-1 Auxiliary symbols

An oval shows the beginning or ending of an algorithm. When it is used to show the beginning of an algorithm, we write the word START inside the oval. When it is used to show the ending of an algorithm, we write the word STOP or RETURN in the oval.

One of the first rules of structured programming is that each algorithm should have only one entry point and one exit. Thus, a good structured flowchart should have one and only one START and one and only one STOP. Beside the STOP and START, ovals should be aligned to show clearly the flow of the actions in an algorithm. For example, a flowchart for a program that does nothing is shown in Figure C-2. This program starts and stops without doing anything.

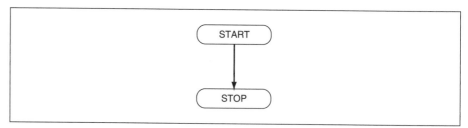

Figure C-2 Use of the oval symbol

FLOW LINES

Flow lines show the order or sequence of actions in a program. They connect symbols. Usually a symbol has some entering and some leaving lines. The START oval has only one leaving line. The STOP oval has only one entering line. We have already shown the use of flow lines in Figure C-2. We will show other flows in the examples that follow.

CONNECTORS

We use only one symbol, a circle with a number in it, to show connectivity. It is used when we reach the end of the page, but our flowchart is not finished. At the bottom of the page we use a connector to show that the logic flow is continued at the top of the next page. The number in the connector can be a simple serial number, or it can be a combination of a page and symbol in the form `page.number`. Figure C-3 shows an off-page connector.

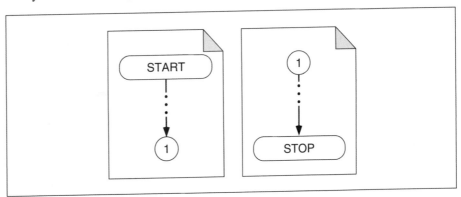

Figure C-3 Use of connectors

C-2 PRIMARY SYMBOLS

Programmers use the primary symbols to show the instructions or actions needed to solve the problem presented in the algorithm. With these symbols, it is possible to represent all five structured programming constructs: sequence, decision, *while, for,* and *do...while.*

SEQUENCE

Sequence statements simply represent a series of actions that must continue in a linear order. Although the actions represented in the sequence symbol may be very complex, such as an input or output operation, the logic flow must enter the symbol at the top and flow out at the bottom. Sequence symbols do not allow any decisions or flow changes within the symbol.

Flowcharts use four sequence symbols: assignment, input/output, module call, and compound statement. They are shown in Figure C-4.

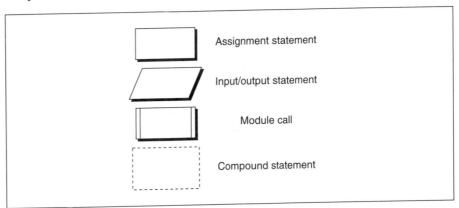

Figure C-4 Sequence symbols

Null Statement

It is worth noting that *do nothing* is a valid statement. It is commonly referred to as a null statement. The null statement is considered a sequence statement, since it cannot change the flow direction of a program. There is no symbol for a null statement. It is simply a flow line. Figure C-2, on page 788 is an example of a null statement.

Assignment Statement

The assignment statement is shown using a rectangle. Within the assignment symbol, the assignment operator is shown as a left-pointing arrow. At the right side of the arrow is an expression whose value must be stored in the variable at the left side. Figure C-5 shows an assignment statement.

Figure C-5 The assignment statement

Input/Output Statement

A parallelogram shows any input or output, such as reading from a keyboard or writing on the system console. For example, an algorithm that reads the value of two variables from the keyboard and then writes their values on the screen in reverse order is shown in Figure C-6.

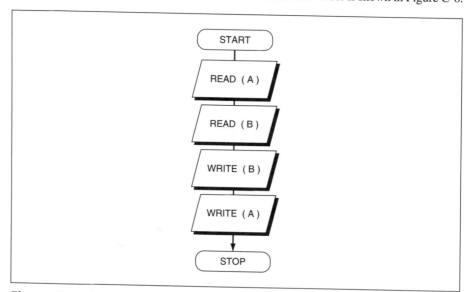

Figure C-6 Read and write statements

Module-Call Statement

The symbol used for calling a module is a rectangle with two vertical bars inside. The flowchart for the called module must be somewhere else. In other words, each time you see a module call statement, look for another flowchart with the module name.

In C programs the module-call symbol is used only for a *void* function. Functions that return values are shown in the assignment statement.

To show how a module call is used in a program, let's design the flowchart for a program that calculates and prints the average of three numbers. This example has two noteworthy points: First, the flowchart for the called module (AVRG) does not begin with START. Rather, it shows the name of the module and the parameter list. Also, the exit oval contains RETURN, indicating that it is not the end of the program but, rather, a return from a called module. The resulting flowchart is shown in Figure C-7.

Compound Statement

Although flowcharts have no actual symbol to show a compound statement, we encapsulate all statements that make a compound statement in a broken-line rectangle. In a C program, compound statements represent a block of code, code that is enclosed in braces. An example of a compound statement is seen in Figure C-9, on page 792.

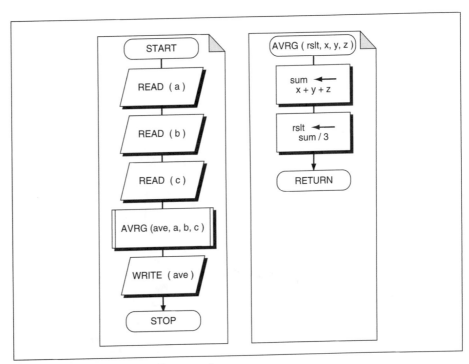

Figure C-7   Module call example

SELECTION STATEMENTS

Unlike the sequence statements, conditional statements can cause the flow of the program to change. They allow the execution of selected statements and the skipping of other statements. Structured programming has two selection statements: two-way and multiway selection.

Two-Way Selection

The two-way symbol is the diamond. When it is used to represent an *if...else* statement, the true condition logic is shown as the right leg of the logic flow, and the false condition, if present, is shown on the left leg of the logic flow. With the *if...else*, there must always be two logic flows, although often one of them is null. (Remember that the null statement is represented by a flow line; there is no symbol for null.) Finally, the statement ends with a connector where the true and false flows join. In this case, the connector has nothing in it.

Although you will often see decisions drawn with the flow from the bottom of the diamond, this is not good style. Even when one of the flows is null, it still must flow from the left or right sides of the diamond.

Figure C-8 shows the use of the decision symbol in the *if...else* statement. As we pointed out above, a decision always has two branches. On each branch, we are allowed to have one and only one statement. Of course, the statement in each branch can be a null or a compound statement. But only one statement is allowed in each branch; not less, not more. Also remember that the whole figure is only one statement, not two or three; it is one *if...else* statement.

Let's design an algorithm that reads an integer. If the integer's value is greater than 10, it subtracts 10 and writes the original number and the result. If the value is less than 10, it does nothing. The flowchart for this program is seen in Figure C-9.

Multiway Selection

The second application of the selection symbol used with structured programming is multiway selection. C's implementation of multiway selection is the *switch* statement. Actually, the multiway selection statement is nothing more than a shorthand notation for the *if...else* statement. If a language does not have a *switch* statement, the same logic is implemented using nested *if...else* statements or the *else-if* construct.

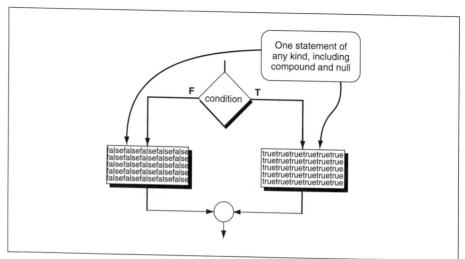

Figure C-8 *if ... else* statement

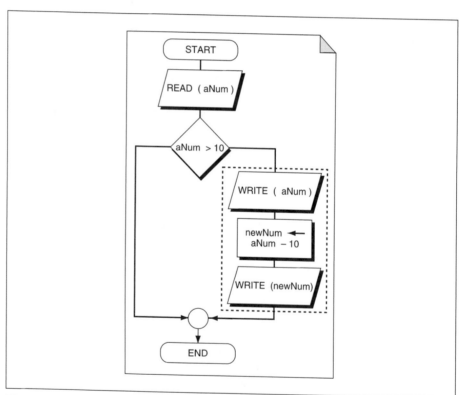

Figure C-9 Example: Read and subtract 10

Figure C-10 shows the use of the *switch* statement. As you can see, we can have as many branches as we need. On each branch, we are allowed to have one, and only one, statement. Of course, the statement in each branch can be a null or a compound statement. But remember that only one statement in each branch is allowed; not less, not more. Also remember that the whole figure is only one statement, not two or three; it is one *switch* statement. (If these rules sound familiar, remember that the *switch* statement is nothing but a shorthand form of *if...else,* so the rules are the same for both.

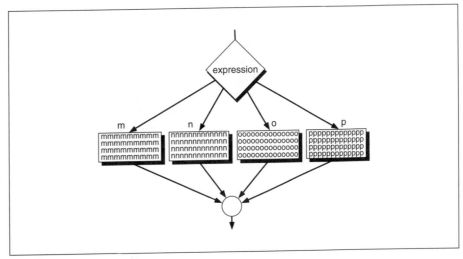

Figure C-10 Multiway selection statement

Let's design an algorithm for a program that reads one character representing a letter grade and prints the corresponding grade point average (GPA). Figure C-11 shows this design.

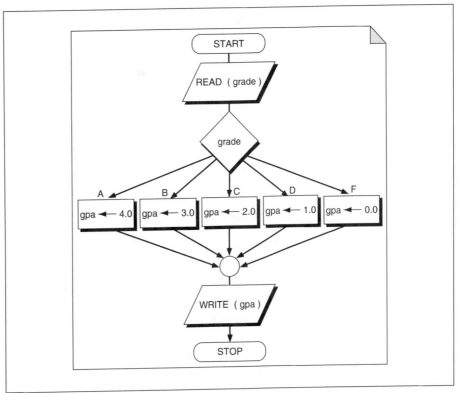

Figure C-11 Example: Design for calculate grade point average

LOOPING STATEMENTS

C has three looping statements: *for, while,* and *do...while.*

for Statement

The *for* statement is a counter-controlled loop. It is actually a complex statement that has three parts, any of which can be null: (1) the loop initialization, which normally sets the loop counter; (2) the limit test; and (3) the end-of-loop action statements, which usually increment a counter. Since the *for* statement is a pretest loop, the loop might not be executed. If the terminating condition is true at the start, the body of the *for* statement is skipped.

As is the case in all structured programming constructs, the body of the loop can contain one and only one statement. As is the case with the other constructs, this one statement can be null or a compound statement. Figure C-12 shows the *for* construct.

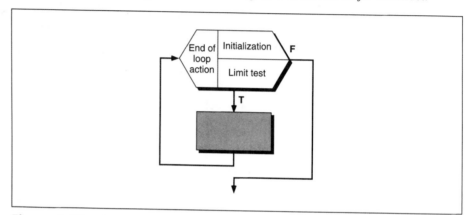

Figure C-12   *for* statement

Figure C-13 shows the flow of actions when the program enters the loop for the first time. The counter is initialized, the condition is tested, and the program enters the loop if the condition is true. If the condition is false, the program does not enter the loop; it executes the next statement, if any.

Figure C-13   *for* statement flow

The actions of the *for* statement are rather complex. Let's trace them through Figure C-13a. When the statement is entered for the first time, the initialization (1a in Figure C-13a) is performed. The limit test (2a in Figure C-13a) is then checked (remember, *for* is a pretest construct) and if the limit test is true, the body of the statement is entered (3a—true in Figure C-13a).

Figure C-13b shows the logic flow at the end of each loop. Note that first the end-of-loop action (1b in Figure C-13b)—usually an increment or decrement of the loop counter—is executed; then the limit condition is tested (2b). If the limit is false (has not been reached), the loop continues for at least one more time (3b—true). If the limit has been reached, the loop terminates (3b—false). Obviously, only one of the two branches can be taken in one loop.

Let's design an algorithm that will read 20 numbers and print their sum. Since the number of times is known in advance, *for* is an excellent choice for the looping construct. The design for this program is shown in Figure C-14.

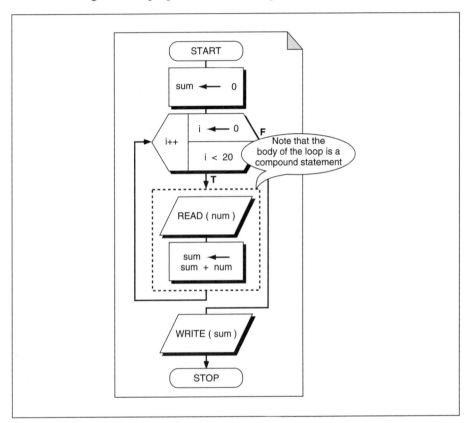

Figure C-14 Example: Design for read 20 numbers

while **Statement**

The second looping construct is the *while* statement. The major difference between the *for* and *while* loops is that the *while* loop is not a counting loop. Both are pretest loops; therefore, like the *for,* the body of the *while* loop may never be executed.

We use the same basic symbol for the *while* loop, but since there is only a limit test, the internal divisions are not necessary. Figure C-15 shows the basic format of the *while* statement.

Let's design another program that reads numbers from the keyboard and prints their total. This time, we don't know how many numbers we may be reading. All we know is that all the numbers are positive. We can therefore signal the end of the numbers by having the user key –1.

Since we don't know how many times we will loop, we need a different construct; the *while* is well designed for this type of logic. The program flow is seen in Figure C-16. Note that in this design, the first number is read *before* the loop. This is known as priming the loop and is common in pretest loops.

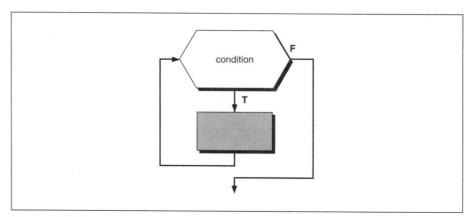

Figure C-15   *while* statement format

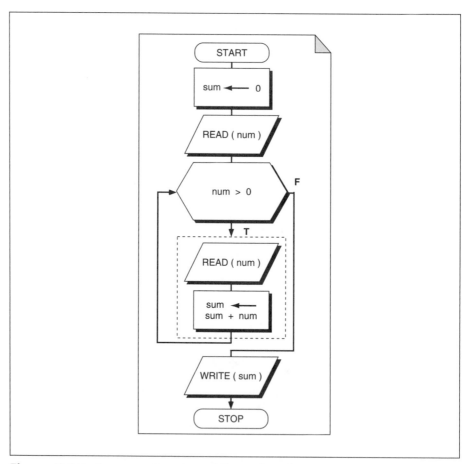

Figure C-16   Program flow for *while* read and total

***do...while* Statement**

The third application of the loop symbol is the *do...while* statement.

Because of the inherent differences between the *for* and *while* loops and *do...while* loop, it must be used differently in a flowchart. There are two major differences between the *while* and the *do...while:*

1. A *while* loop is a pretest loop. The *do...while* loop is a post-test loop.
2. The body of a *while* loop may never be executed. The body of a *do...while* loop is executed at least once.

Figure C-17 shows the use of the *do...while* statement. Note that in this statement, the condition is tested at the end of the loop.

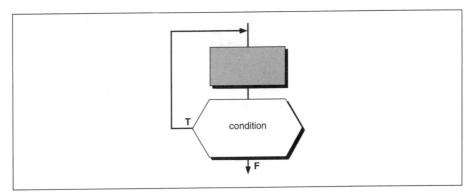

Figure C-17   *do...while* **statement**

Let's design an algorithm that reads and processes a number. In this algorithm, the number must be between 1 and 5. To make the program robust, we use a *do...while* loop that forces the user to enter a valid number. This is a common technique for validating user input. Note that as in previous looping constructs, the *do...while* loop can have only one statement. Therefore, we enclose the prompt and read in a composite symbol. The algorithm is shown in Figure C-18.

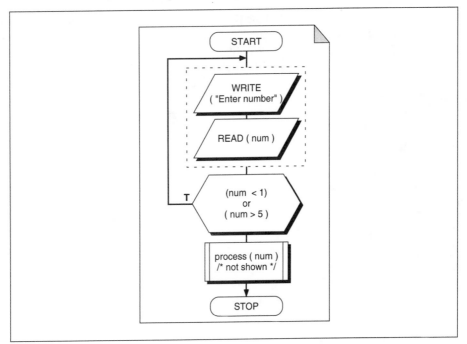

Figure C-18   Example: Algorithm for input validation with *do...while*

Numbering Systems

Today the whole world uses the decimal number system developed by Arabian mathematicians in the eighth century. We acknowledge their contribution to numbers when we refer to our decimal system as using Arabic numerals. But decimal numbers were not always commonly used. The first to use a decimal numbering system were the ancient Egyptians. The Babylonians improved on the Egyptian system by making the positions in the numbering systems meaningful.

But the Babylonians also used a sexagesimal (base 60) numbering system. Whereas our decimal system has ten values in its graphic representations, a sexagesimal system has 60. We still see remnants of the Babylonians' sexagesimal system in time, which is based on 60 minutes to an hour, and in the division of circles, which contain 360°.

D-1 COMPUTER NUMBERING SYSTEMS

Four different numbering systems are used in computer programming. The computer it-self uses a binary system. A binary system has only two values for each number position, 0 and 1. Programmers use two different shorthand notations to represent binary numbers, octal and hexadecimal. And of course, programmers also use the decimal system. Since all these systems are used in C, you will need to have a basic understanding of each to fully understand the language.

DECIMAL NUMBERS

We all readily understand the decimal numbering system. In fact, we have used it so much that it is basically intuitive. But do you really understand why the second position in the decimal system is tens and the third position is hundreds? The answer lies in the powers of the base to the system, which in decimal is ten. Thus, the first position is 10 raised to the power 0, the second position is 10 raised to the power 1, and the third position is 10 raised to the power 2. Figure D-1 shows the relationship between the powers and the number 243.

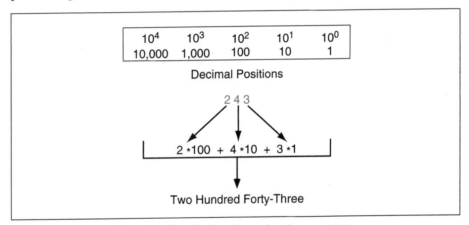

Figure D-1 Positions in the decimal numbering system

BINARY NUMBERS

Whereas the decimal system is based on 10, the binary system is based on 2. The binary system has only two digits: 0 and 1. Binary digits are knows as bits, which is an acronym created from **Binary digIT**.

Figure D-2 shows the powers table for a binary system and the value 243 in binary. In the position table, each position is double the previous position. Again, this is because the base of the system is two. You will need to memorize the binary powers to at least 2^{10}.

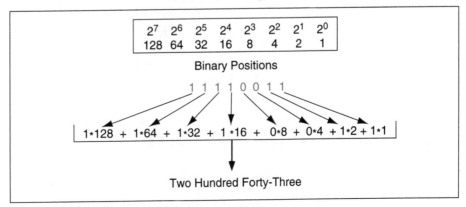

Figure D-2 Positions in the binary numbering system

OCTAL NUMBERS

The base of the octal system is 8. This means that there are eight different symbols: 0, 1, 2, 3, 4, 5, 6, and 7. Although octal is not commonly used in modern computer systems, it is still supported by C and needs to be understood. The octal numbering system is shown in Figure D-3. Again, the number represented is 243.

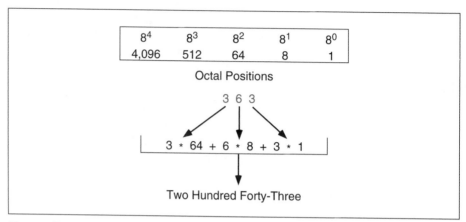

Figure D-3   Positions in the octal numbering system

HEXADECIMAL NUMBERS

The hexadecimal system is based on 16 (*hexadec* is Greek for 16). Thus, the hexadecimal system has 16 symbols: 0, 1, 2, 3, 4, 5, 6, 7, 8, 9, A, B, C, D, E, and F. Since the base is 16, each positional value is 16 times the previous one. This is shown in Figure D-4.

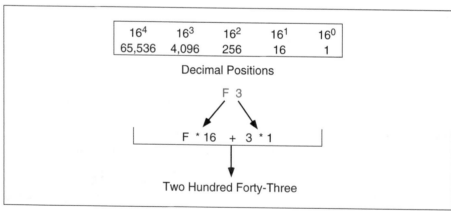

Figure D-4   Positions in the hexadecimal numbering system

Look carefully at the binary, octal, and hexadecimal numbering systems in Table D-1. Some of the values are duplicated, because octal and hexadecimal are simply shorthand notations for binary. Rather than represent a number as a large string of 0s and 1s, programmers therefore can use either octal or hexadecimal.

D-2   INTEGER TRANSFORMATIONS

Since you will work in all four numbering systems when you program in C, you need to learn how to convert to and from binary to the other formats. If you understand the concepts shown in the previous section, you can easily do the conversions.

Decimal	Binary	Octal	Hexadecimal
0	0000	0	0
1	0001	1	1
2	0010	2	2
3	0011	3	3
4	0100	4	4
5	0101	5	5
6	0110	6	6
7	0111	7	7
8	1000	10	8
9	1001	11	9
10	1010	12	A
11	1011	13	B
12	1100	14	C
13	1101	15	D
14	1110	16	E
15	1111	17	F
16	10000	20	10

Table D-1   Decimal, binary, octal, and hexadecimal table

BINARY TO DECIMAL

Let's start by converting a number from binary to decimal. Refer to Figure D-5 for this discussion. To convert from binary to decimal, you start with the binary number and multiply each binary digit by its value from the binary positions table in Figure D-2, on page 799. Since each binary bit can be only 0 or 1, the result will be either 0 or the value of the position. After multiplying all the digits, add the results. This conversion is shown in Figure D-5.

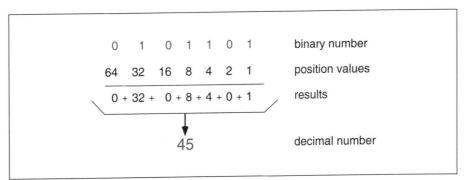

Figure D-5   Binary to decimal conversion

DECIMAL TO BINARY

To convert from decimal to binary, you use repetitive division. The original number, 45 in the example, is divided by 2. The remainder (1) becomes the first binary digit, and the second digit is determined by dividing the quotient (22) by 2. Again, the remainder (0) becomes the binary digit, and the quotient is divided by 2 to determine the next position. This process continues until the quotient is 0. This conversion is shown in Figure D-6.

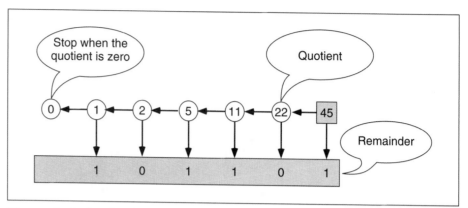

Figure D-6 Decimal to binary conversion

BINARY TO OCTAL OR HEXADECIMAL

The previous section showed a mathematical way to convert from binary to decimal. Converting from binary to octal and hexadecimal is done by grouping binary digits into groups of three for octal and groups of four for hexadecimal. Do you see why we use these groupings? Table D-1 shows the bit configurations for the binary, octal, hexadecimal, and decimal representations of the numbers 1 to 16.

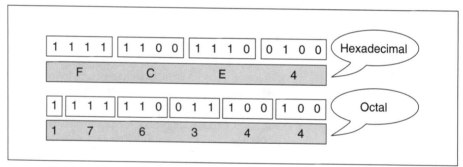

Figure D-7 Converting a large binary number

Now, if we have a large binary number, we can easily change it to a hexadecimal using the above information. We divide the number into 4-bit sections (from the right). Then, to each section, we assign the appropriate hexadecimal digit. This concept is shown in Figure D-7.

If we have a large binary number, we can easily change it to an octal number using the same concept. Divide the number into 3-bit sections (from the right). Then, to each section, assign the appropriate octal digit. This is also shown in Figure D-7.

D-3 STORING INTEGERS

Sometimes when you print out integer values, you get a surprising result. What you thought was a positive number may be printed as a negative number. In another case, what you expected to be a small number turns out to be very large. If you understand how numbers are stored in the computer, you may still be surprised, but you will understand what happened and therefore be able to debug your program easier and faster. So let's study how integers are stored. We will first look at unsigned numbers and then at signed numbers. In all cases, we assume that the size of an integer is 2 bytes (16 bits).

UNSIGNED INTEGERS

Storing unsigned integers is a straightforward process. The number is changed to the corresponding binary form, and the binary representation is stored. For example, an unsigned integer can be stored as a number from 0 to 65,535, as shown in Figure D-8.

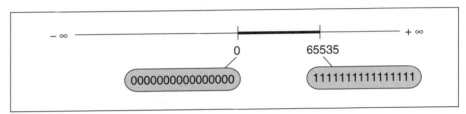

Figure D-8   Storing integers

Figure D-8 also shows the range of an integer stored in a 16-bit word. Another way to show the range is with a circle. In this case, 0 is placed at the top of the circle, and the values are placed around the circle clockwise until the maximum value is adjacent to the first value, 0. This format is shown in Figure D-9.

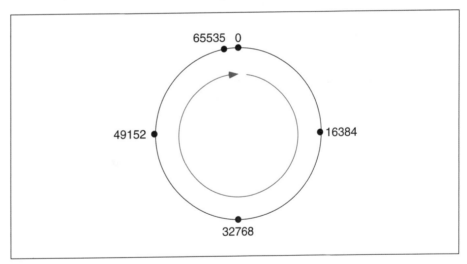

Figure D-9   Range of integer values

In Figure D-9, the number after 65,535 is 0! Why? Part of the reason is that 65,536 requires 17 bits to store its value, and we only have 16 bits. The value is 0 because we start over at the beginning of the circle. In other words, storing numbers is a modulo process. The number to be stored is represented as modulus the maximum number that can be stored + 1, in this case 65,536. This relationship is shown below.

$$65{,}535 + 1 \leftrightarrow 65{,}536 \; \% \; 65{,}536 \leftrightarrow 0$$

To demonstrate this concept, we have included Program D-1.

```
 1  /* Demonstrate circular nature of unsigned integer numbers.
 2         Written by:
 3         Date:
 4  */
 5  #include <stdio.h>
 6  #include <limits.h>
 7
 8  int main (void)
 9  {
10  /* Local Definitions */
11      unsigned int x = UINT_MAX;
12
13  /* Statements */
14      printf("Maximum value:      %u\n", x);
15
16      x++;
17      printf("Maximum value + 1: %u\n", x);
18
19      x++;
20      printf("Maximum value + 2: %u\n", x);
21
22      return 0;
23  }  /* main */
24
```

```
Results:
   Maximum value:      65535
   Maximum value + 1:  0
   Maximum value + 2:  1
```

Program D-1 Demonstrate integer numbers

SIGNED INTEGERS

Storing signed integers is different from storing unsigned integers because we must consider the sign bit. Three methods are used to store signed integers in a computer: sign and magnitude, one's complement, and two's complement.

Sign and Magnitude

Storing an integer in the sign-and-magnitude format uses 1 bit to represent the sign (0 for positive, 1 for negative), which means only 15 bits are left over to represent the absolute value of the number. Therefore, the maximum positive value is one-half of the unsigned value.

Aside from the magnitude of the number that we can store, there are two significant differences between the sign and magnitude and unsigned numbers. First, we can now store negative numbers. Second, there are two zero values, a plus zero and a minus zero. (See Figure D-10.) Since this method is not used to store values in today's computers, we do not discuss it in this text; refer to texts discussing areas where it is used, such as communications systems.

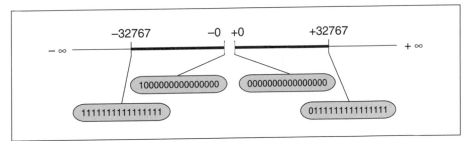

Figure D-10   Sign and magnitude bit configurations

One's Complement

The one's complement differs from the sign and magnitude in two ways: First, negative numbers are stored in their complemented format. Second, the sign bit—zero for positive and one for negative—is propagated from the sign bit to the most significant bit of the value. Like the sign and magnitude, the one's complement has two zero values, plus and minus. Figure D-11 shows the configurations for one's complement values.

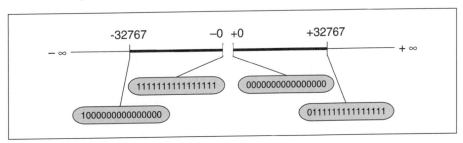

Figure D-11   One's complement format

Let's look at each of these differences in turn. To complement a bit, you simply reverse it as in the one's complement unary operator (~). If it is 0, it becomes a 1; if it is 1, it becomes 0. This is seen in the following example, in which we complement +10. After complementing the value, the sign is propagated as shown below.

```
+10    ⇌  0000000000001010
-10    ⇌  1111111111110101
```

Like the sign and magnitude, the one's complement is not used to store data in general-purpose computers. Therefore, for further discussion, consult textbooks discussing those areas where it is used.

Two's Complement

In the two's complement method, like the one's complement, all the bits change when the sign of the number changes. So the whole number, not just the most significant bit, takes part in the negation process. However, we have only one 0.

Our integer variable therefore can store numbers from –32,768 up to +32,767. Note that because zero belongs to the domain of positive numbers—although it is considered neither positive nor negative—the absolute value of the maximum integer is 1 less than the absolute value of the minimum integer. This range is shown in Figure D-12.

As Figure D-12 shows, there is symmetry between the positive and negative numbers. However, if you complement a positive number using the one's complement

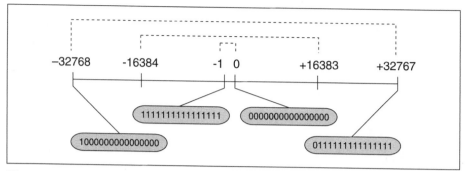

Figure D-12 Two's complement range

operator (~), you will not get the negative number with the same absolute value. The absolute value will be 1 more. In a symmetrical manner, if you complement a negative number, you will get a positive number whose absolute value is 1 less. This concept is demonstrated in Program D-2.

```
1   /* This program demonstrates the two's complement values.
2         Written by:
3         Date:
4   */
5   #include <stdio.h>
6
7   int main (void)
8   {
9   /* Local Definitions */
10      int a = +13422;
11      int b = -768;
12      int ca;
13      int cb;
14
15  /* Statements */
16      ca = ~ a;
17      cb = ~ b;
18      printf("The complement of %6d is %6d\n", a, ca);
19      printf("The complement of %6d is %6d\n", b, cb);
20      return 0;
21  }  /* main */
```

```
Results:
   The complement of  13422 is -13423
   The complement of   -768 is    767
```

Program D-2 Demonstration of two's complement

With a little thought, you should recognize that 0 and –1 are the complement of each other. Likewise, +32,767 and –32,768 are the complement of each other. These facts are apparent from the bit pattern of the number. The range of integers in two's complement format is shown in Figure D-13.

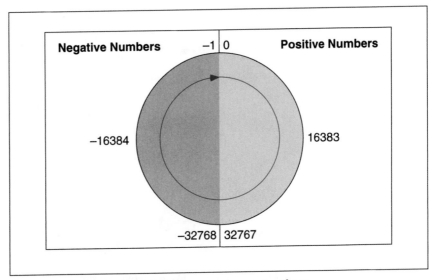

Figure D-13   Range of two's complement values

Converting to Two's Complement

To change a decimal number to its two's complement form, follow these steps:

1. Ignore the sign.
2. Change the absolute value of the number to binary form.
3. Add extra zeros at the left of the number to make the number of bits the same as the size of the integer.
4. If the number is positive, stop; if the number is negative:
   a. Complement the number (change 0 to 1 and 1 to zero).
   b. Add 1 to the number.

For example, let's change +76 to its two's complement.

- Step 1: The absolute value is 76.
- Step 2: 76 in binary is 1001100.
- Step 3: Add extra zeros to make the number 16 bits long.

> 0000000001001100

- Step 4: The sign was positive, so the two's complement is

> 0000000001001100

As another example, let's change –77 to two's complement.

- Step 1: The absolute value is 77.
- Step 2: 77 in binary is 1001101.
- Step 3: We add extra zeros to make the number 16-bits long.

> 0000000001001101

- Step 4: The sign was negative, so the two's complement can be obtained using the following two steps:

a. We complement the number

```
1111111110110010
```

b. We add 1 to the number

```
1111111110110010+
               1
----------------
1111111110110011
```

Did you notice that the two numbers (+76 and –77) are complements of each other? As we said before

```
+76 ⇌  0000000001001100
-77 ⇌  1111111110110011
```

Two's Complement Addition

One of the advantages of the two's complement method is that it makes addition and subtraction very easy.

To add two numbers, just add individual bits.

```
  7      0000000000000111
+10     +0000000000001010
 17      0000000000010001
```

As shown in the next example, the addition works even if one of the numbers is negative.

```
    7        0000000000000111
+(-10)      +1111111111110110
  - 3        1111111111111101
```

If there is a carry from the most significant digit into the sign, an overflow has occurred, and the result is invalid. For example, if we add 10 to 32,767, we get an invalid result, as shown below.

```
+32767     0111111111111111
+ 10       0000000000001010
-32759     1000000000001001
```

What is the value of 1000000000001001 in binary? To understand what happens, refer to Figure D-13, on page 807. First note that 32,767 is at the bottom of the circle. When we add 10, we move clockwise 10 positions, which puts us in the negative portion of the number range. The value at that position is –32,759. Now you should understand why sometimes you get strange output when you print numbers.

Two's Complement Subtraction

Surprisingly, subtraction is also very easy. To subtract a number from another number, we take the two's complement of the subtrahend and then add the numbers, as shown below.

```
  7       7        0000000000000111
-10    +(-10)     +1111111111110110
 - 3    - 3        1111111111111101
```

D-4 STORING FLOATS

In this section, we discuss how to store floating-point numbers in computer memory. A floating-point number is always stored as a signed number. It consists of two parts: a mantissa and an exponent. In a binary system, a floating-point number can be represented as

$$m * 10^r$$

Using this format, the number 235.23 is represented as

$$0.235 * 10^3$$

Most computers use what is called the normalized floating point: First, the mantissa is stored as a decimal fraction, and second, the most significant digit of the mantissa cannot be zero (except for the number 0 itself, which cannot be represented in normalized form). So the value 0.007 is stored as

$$7.0 * 10^{-3}$$

To store the floating-point value, we need store only the mantissa (without the decimal point) and the exponent (without the base). This results in only the 7 and the -3 being stored, as shown in Figure D-14.

Floating-point representations can increase the precision and the range of the numbers stored. The size of the mantissa determines the degree of precision; increasing its size increases the precision. Similarly, increasing the size of the exponent increases the range of numbers that can be represented. This naturally leads to C's three floating-points, *float* (the smallest), *double*, and *long double* (the largest).

There are many different formats for storing the mantissa and the exponent; Figure D-14 is representative. It shows the representation of 0.007 using the formalized notation and two's complement storage.

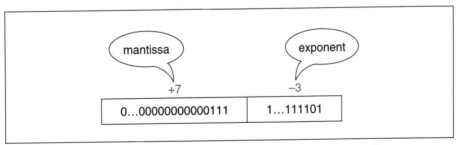

Figure D-14 Storing a floating-point number

Standard Libraries

This appendix documents two of the more important C libraries. Note that the values shown here are representative only and will change from hardware to hardware.

E-1 `limits.h`

Meaning	Identifier	16-bit word [a]	32-bit word [a]
bits in a char	CHAR_BIT	8	8
short char minimum	SCHAR_MIN	(-128)	(-128)
short char maximum	SCHAR_MAX	127	127
unsigned char maximum	UCHAR_MAX	255	255
char minimum	CHAR_MIN	(-128)	(-128)
char maximum	CHAR_MAX	127	127
short int minimum	SHRT_MIN	(-32,768)	(-32,768)
short int maximum	SHRT_MAX	32,767	32,767
unsigned short maximum	USHRT_MAX	65,535	65,535
int minimum	INT_MIN	(-32,767)	(-2,147,483,648)
int maximum	INT_MAX	32,768	2,147,483,647
unsigned int maximum	UINT_MAX	65,535	4,294,967,295
long minimum	LONG_MIN	-2,147,483,648	(-2,147,483,648)
long maximum	LONG_MAX	2,147,483,648	2,147,483,647
unsigned long maxim	ULONG_MAX	4,294,967,295	4,294,967,295

[a]Libraries contain unformatted numbers (no commas), often expressed in hexadecimal.

Table E-1   Contents of `limits.h`

E-2 float.h

Meaning	Identifier	Typical value 32-bit word[a]
digits of precision	FLT_DIG	6
	DBL_DIG	15
	LDBL_DIG	18
size of mantissa	FLT_MANT_DIG	24
	DBL_MANT_DIG	53
	LDBL_MANT_DIG	64
largest integer for negative exponent (float radix)	FLT_MIN_EXP	−125
	DBL_MIN_EXP	−1021
	LDBL_MIN_EXP	−16381
largest integer for negative exponent (base 10)	FLT_MIN_10_EXP	−37
	DBL_MIN_10_EXP	−307
	LDBL_MIN_10_EXP	−4931
largest integer for positive exponent (float radix)	FLT_MAX_EXP	128
	DBL_MAX_EXP	1024
	LDBL_MAX_EXP	16384
largest integer for positive exponent for (base 10)	FLT_MAX_10_EXP	38
	DBL_MAX_10_EXP	308
	LDBL_MAX_10_EXP	4932
largest possible floating-point number	FLT_MAX	3.40282e+38
	DBL_MAX	1.79769e+308
	LDBL_MAX	1.18973e+4932
smallest possible floating-point number	FLT_MIN	1.17549e−38
	DBL_MIN	2.22507e−308
	LDBL_MIN	3.3621e−4932
smallest possible fraction	FLT_EPSILON	1.19209e−07
	DBL_EPSILON	2.22045e−16
	LDBL_EPSILON	1.0842e−19

[a] Libraries contain unformatted numbers (no commas), often expressed in hexadecimal.

Table E-2   Contents of float.h

Function Prototypes

F

F-1   FUNCTION INDEX

In this appendix, we list most of the standard functions found in the C language. We have grouped them by library so that related functions are grouped together. We have also listed them alphabetically in Table F-1 for your convenience. Note that not all functions are covered in the text and that there are functions that are not covered in this appendix.

Function /	Page	Library	Function /	Page	Library	Function /	Page	Library
abort	816	stdlib	fscanf	815	stdio	rand	816	stdlib
abs	816	stdlib	fseek	815	stdio	realloc	816	stdlib
acos	814	math	ftell	815	stdio	remove	815	stdio
asctime	817	time	fwrite	815	stdio	rename	815	stdio
asin	814	math	getc	815	stdio	rewind	815	stdio
atan	814	math	getchar	815	stdio	scanf	815	stdio
atan2	814	math	gets	815	stdio	sin	814	math
atexit	816	stdlib	gmtime	817	time	sinh	814	math
atof	816	stdlib	isalnum	814	ctype	sprintf	815	stdio
atoi	816	stdlib	isalpha	814	ctype	sqrt	814	math
atol	816	stdlib	iscntrl	814	ctype	srand	816	stdlib
calloc	816	stdlib	isdigit	814	ctype	sscanf	815	stdio
ceil	814	math	isgraph	814	ctype	strcat	817	string
clearerr	815	stdio	islower	814	ctype	strchr	817	string
clock	817	time	isprint	814	ctype	strcmp	817	string
cos	814	math	ispunct	814	ctype	strcpy	816	string
cosh	814	math	isspace	814	ctype	strcspn	817	string
ctime	817	time	isupper	814	ctype	strlen	817	string
difftime	817	time	isxdigit	814	ctype	strncat	817	string
div	816	stdlib	labs	816	stdlib	strncmp	817	string
exit	816	stdlib	ldexp	814	math	strncpy	816	string
exp	814	math	ldiv	816	stdlib	strpbrk	817	string
fabs	814	math	localtime	817	time	strrchr	817	string
fclose	815	stdio	log	814	math	strspn	817	string
feof	815	stdio	log10	814	math	strstr	817	string
ferror	815	stdio	malloc	816	stdlib	strtod	816	stdlib
fgetc	815	stdio	memchr	817	string	strtol	816	stdlib
fgets	815	stdio	memcmp	817	string	strtoul	816	stdlib
floor	814	math	memcpy	816	string	system	816	stdlib
fmod	814	math	memmove	816	string	tan	814	math
fopen	815	stdio	mktime	817	time	tanh	814	math
fprintf	815	stdio	modf	814	math	time	817	time
fputc	815	stdio	pow	814	math	tmpfile	815	stdio
fputs	815	stdio	printf	815	stdio	tmpnam	815	stdio
fread	815	stdio	putc	815	stdio	tolower	814	ctype
free	816	stdlib	putchar	815	stdio	toupper	814	ctype
frexp	814	math	puts	815	stdio	ungetc	815	stdio

Table F-1 Standard functions in C

F-2 CHARACTER LIBRARY

The following functions are found in `ctype.h`.

isalnum	int	`isalnum(int a_char);`
isalpha	int	`isalpha(int a_char);`
iscntrl	int	`iscntrl(int a_char);`
isdigit	int	`isdigit(int a_char);`
isgraph	int	`isgraph(int a_char);`
islower	int	`islower(int a_char);`
isprint	int	`isprint(int a_char);`
ispunct	int	`ispunct(int a_char);`
isspace	int	`isspace(int a_char);`
isupper	int	`isupper(int a_char);`
isxdigit	int	`isxdigit(int a_char);`
tolower	int	`tolower(int a_char);`
toupper	int	`toupper(int a_char);`

F-3 MATH LIBRARY

The following functions are found in `math.h`.

ceil	double	`ceil(double number);`
exp	double	`exp(double number);`
fabs	double	`fabs(double number);`
floor	double	`floor(double number);`
fmod	double	`fmod(double number1, double number2);`
frexp	double	`frexp(double number, int *);`
ldexp	double	`ldexp(double number, int);`
log	double	`log(double number);`
log10	double	`log10(double number);`
modf	double	`modf(double number, double *);`
pow	double	`pow(double number1, double number2);`
sqrt	double	`sqrt(double number);`
sin	double	`sin(double number);`
sinh	double	`sinh(double number);`
asin	double	`asin(double number);`
cos	double	`cos(double number);`
cosh	double	`cosh(double number);`
acos	double	`acos(double number);`
tan	double	`tan(double number);`
tanh	double	`tanh(double number);`
atan	double	`atan(double number);`
atan2	double	`atan2(double number1, double number2);`

F-4   STANDARD I/O LIBRARY

We have divided the system input/output library stdio.h by the type of data being read.

GENERAL I/O

General input/output contains functions that apply to all files.

clearerr	void	clearerr(FILE *fp);
fclose	int	fclose(FILE *fp);
feof	int	feof(FILE *fp);
ferror	int	ferror(FILE *fp);
fopen	FILE	*fopen(const char *extn_name, const char*file_mode);

FORMATTED I/O

Convert text data to/from internal memory formats.

fprintf	int	fprintf(FILE *fileOut, const char *format_string, ...);
printf	int	printf(const char *format_string, ...);
sprintf	int	sprintf(char *to_loc, const char *format_string, ...);
fscanf	int	fscanf(FILE *fileIn, const char *format_string, ...);
scanf	int	scanf(const char *format_string, ...);
sscanf	int	sscanf(const char *from_loc, const char *format_string, ...);

CHARACTER I/O

Read and write one character at a time.

fgetc	int	fgetc(FILE *fp);
fputc	int	fputc(int, FILE *fp);
getc	int	getc(FILE *fp);
getchar	int	getchar(void);
putc	int	putc(int, FILE *fp);
putchar	int	putchar(int char_out);
ungetc	int	ungetc(int char_out, FILE *fp);

FILE I/O

These functions work with binary files.

fread	size_t	fread(void *in_area, size_t size, size_t count, FILE *fp);
fwrite	size_t	fwrite(const void *out_data, size_t size, size_t count, FILE *fp);
fseek	int	fseek(FILE *fp, long offset, int from_loc);
ftell	long	ftell(FILE *fp);
rewind	void	rewind(FILE *fp);

STRING I/O

Read and write strings.

gets	char	*gets(char *string);
puts	int	puts(const char *string);
fgets	char	*fgets(char *string , int size, FILE *fp);
fputs	int	fputs(const char *string , FILE *fp);

SYSTEM FILE CONTROL

System commands that create and delete files on the disk.

remove	int	remove(const char *file_name);
rename	int	rename(const char *old_name, const char *new_name);
tmpfile	FILE	*tmpfile(void);
tmpnam	char	*tmpnam(char *file_name);

F-5   STANDARD LIBRARY

The following functions are found in stdlib.

MATH FUNCTIONS

The following math functions are found in stdlib:

abs	int	abs(int number);
div	div_t	div(int numerator, int divisor);
labs	long	labs(long number);
ldiv	ldiv_t	ldiv(long numerator, long divisor);
rand	int	rand(void);
srand	void	srand(unsigned seed);

MEMORY FUNCTIONS

Memory allocation functions.

calloc	void	*calloc(size_t num_elements, size_t element_size);
free	void	free(void *);
malloc	void	*malloc(size_t num_bytes);
realloc	void	*realloc(void *stge_ptr, size_t element_size);

PROGRAM CONTROL

The following functions control the program flow:

exit	void	exit(int exit_code);
abort	void	abort(void);
atexit	int	atexit(void (*) function_name (void));

SYSTEM COMMUNICATION

The following function communicates with the operating system:

system	int	system(const char *system_command);

CONVERSION FUNCTIONS

The following functions convert data from one type to another:

atof	double	atof(const char *real_num);
atoi	int	atoi(const char *real_num);
atol	long	atol(const char *real_num);
strtod	double	strtod(const char *str, char **next_str);
strtol	long	strtol(const char *str, char **next_str , int base);
strtoul	unsigned long	
		strtoul(const char *str, char **next_str , int base);

F-6   STRING LIBRARY

The following functions are found in string.h:

COPYING DATA

The following functions all copy strings or memory:

memcpy	void	*memcpy(void *to_mem, const void *fr_mem, size_t bytes);
memmove	void	*memmove(void *to_mem,
		const void *fr_mem, size_t bytes);
strcpy	char	*strcpy(char *to_str, const char *fr_str);
strncpy	char	*strncpy(char *to_str, const char *fr_str,
		size_t bytes);

strcat	char	*strcat(char *to_str, const char *fr_str);
strncat	char	*strncat(char *to_str, const char *fr_str, size_t bytes);

COMPARING DATA

The following functions all compare strings or memory:

memchr	void	*memchr(const void *mem, int a_char, size_t bytes);
memcmp	int	memcmp(const void *mem1, const void *mem2, size_t bytes);
strchr	char	*strchr(const char *str, int a_char);
strrchr	char	*strrchr(const char *str, int a_char);
strcmp	int	strcmp(const char *str1, const char *str2);
strncmp	int	strncmp(const char *str1, const char *str2, size_t bytes);
strpbrk	char	*strpbrk(const char *str1, const char *str2);
strstr	char	*strstr(const char *str1, const char *str2);

STRING LENGTHS

The following functions return the length of strings or substrings:

strlen	size_t	strlen(const char *str);
strspn	size_t	strspn(const char *str1, const char *str2);
strcspn	size_t	strcspn(const char *str1, const char *str2);

F-7   TIME

The following functions are found in time.h:

clock	clock_t	clock(void);
difftime	double	difftime(time_t time_start, time_t time_end);
mktime	time_t	mktime(struct tm *cal_time);
time	time_t	time(time_t *num_time);
asctime	char	*asctime(const struct tm *cal_time);
ctime	char	*ctime(const time_t *num_time);
gmtime	struct tm	*gmtime(const time_t *num_time);
localtime	struct tm	*localtime(const time_t *num_time);

Preprocessor Directives

The C compiler is made of two functional parts: a preprocessor and a translator. The preprocessor uses programmer-supplied commands to prepare the source program for compilation. The translator converts the C statements into machine code that it places in an object module. Depending on the compiler design, the preprocessor and translator can work together, or the preprocessor can create a separate version of the source program, which is then read by the translator. This is the design shown in Figure G-1.

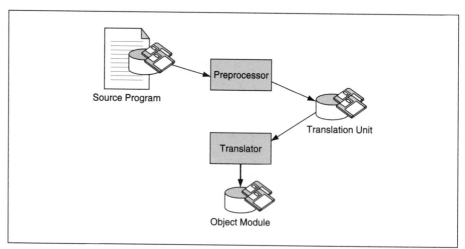

Figure G-1   Compiler environment

The preprocessor can be thought of as a smart editor. Like a smart editor, it inserts, includes, excludes, and replaces text based on commands supplied by the programmer. In this case, however, the commands are made a permanent part of the source program.

All preprocessor commands start with a pound sign (#). Some of the traditional compilers require the pound sign to be in the first column. ANSI/ISO C specifies that it can be anywhere on the line. In addition, preprocessor commands can be placed anywhere in the source program.

The preprocessor performs three different functions. First, as we have seen ever since our first program, it is used to specify which header files are to be included in the program. Second, it is used for macro definition, which enables us to create macros for use in our program. The FLUSH statement is a simple macro definition. Finally, the preprocessor can be used to conditionally include or exclude code from the program.

G-1   FILE INCLUSION

The first and most common job of a preprocessor is to copy the contents of files into programs. The files are usually header files that contain prototype statements and data declarations for the program, but they can contain any valid C statement.

The preprocessor command is *#include*, and it has two different types of operands. The first directs the preprocessor to include header files from the system library. This form places the library name in pointed brackets, as shown below and in Figure G-2.

```
#include <stdio.h>
```

Figure G-2 Include directive

In the second form, the preprocessor looks for the header files in the library that holds the source code. This format is shown below.

```
#include "filename.h"
```

Of course, either case can contain a fully qualified file name that directs the library search. For instance, in a DOS environment in which we have a DOS directory named `project`, which in turn contains a source code directory named `source`, stored on drive K, we use the following include:

```
#include "K:\PROJECT\SOURCE\HEADER.H"
```

The only difference between the two forms is the location of the library. In both cases, the precompiler locates the header file and copies the contents of the file to replace the include command. The result is an expanded source program that contains code written by the program and code from the specified libraries.

G-2 MACRO DEFINITION

The second preprocessor function is macro definition. A macro is formal syntax that can be used to generate statements for use in a program. For the C language, the macro generates C statements.

There are two different macro formats, simple and parameterized. Both use the same command format, as shown below.

```
#define name token(s)
```

Tokens are text that is used to specify the format of the resulting statement and are considered to be the macro body.

Once defined, a macro may be used until it is undefined (deleted). When the preprocessor encounters the name of a macro within the program, it generates the appropriate C statements, as specified by the macro definition using the tokens specified in the definition body. The tokens can be straightforward C code or complex parameterized statements.

SIMPLE COMMANDS

Simple commands are so named because they have no parameters. This does not mean that the code is simple, however; it means that the macro code can be used without modification. For example, each of the following macros is simple:

```
#define  SIZE   9
#define  TRUE   1
#define  OF_MSG "Err 304: Overflow. Call programmer."
#define  LIMIT (234)
#define  FLUSH while (getchar () != '\n')
```

By traditional standard, the names of macros are coded in uppercase to warn the reader that they are macros. There is no syntactical requirement that they be uppercase, however. Figure G-3 shows two examples of simple macros. The first uses macros to define the dimensions of an array. The second uses a macro to define an error code.

You need to remember the following points about macro expansion:

1. Macro expansion does not need an equal sign. Everything following the macro name is simply treated as text to be substituted for the macro name by the preprocessor. If you include an equal sign, it will be included in your generated code.

2. Preprocessor commands are not terminated by semicolons. If you place a semicolon at the end of the statement, it will be included in the expanded code. Both of these situations are common errors. Table G-1 shows examples of the errors that they can generate.

```
#define ROWS 5
#define COLS 4

#define OFMsg "Err 201: List Overflow\n"

int main (void)
{
   int ary[ROWS][COLS];
   ...
   printf(OFMsg);
   ...
} /* main */
```
Before

```
int main (void)
{
   int ary[5][4];
   ...
   printf("Err 201: List Overflow\n");
   ...
} /* main */
```
After

Figure G-3   Define substitution

Code	Result

Example 1
`#define    SIZE = 9;`
...
`a = SIZE;`
	...
	`a = = 9;;`

Example 2
`#define LIMIT 9;`
...
`for (i = 0; i < LIMIT; i++)`
    ...
	...
	`for (i = 0; i < 9;; i++)`
	    ...

Table G-1   Examples of define substitution errors

In the first example in Table G-1, the intent is to assign SIZE to the variable a. Since an equal sign is included, however, the result is an expression that tests a for 9. This is a valid statement, and no error is generated, although no code is generated either.

The first example contains a second error, the semicolon at the end. In this case, this also results in valid code, a null statement, which will not cause a compile error. These types of errors can be difficult to locate, especially when you consider that you normally do not see the expanded code.

In the second example, we are more fortunate. The macro expansion results in a compile error. In this case, the semicolon creates too many expressions in the *for* statement.

PARAMETERIZED MACRO

Often, the macro you are generating needs to contain variable data. In this case, you indicate the variable data through parameters. This capability is very powerful.

To include parameters in the macro, the opening parenthesis must be placed immediately at the end of the macro name; that is, there can be no white space between the macro name and the opening parenthesis of the parameter list. If there is a space, then the opening parenthesis is considered part of the token body and the macro is assumed to be simple.

The identifiers inside the parentheses are formal parameters (as in a function) and are replaced with actual parameters during the expansion. However, the replacement of formal parameters with actual parameters in macro expansion works differently from the substitution in a function. In a function, the formal parameters are replaced with the *value* of actual parameters. In macro expansion, only the token text is replaced. In other words, the actual parameters are replaced by the formal parameters textually. The form is shown below.

```
#define   name(par1, par2, …) replacement-tokens
```

Note that the parameters are separated by commas. The name of each parameter must be unique within the macro.

The parameterized macro expansion takes place in two steps:

1. The actual parameters in the macro are associated with the formal parameters in the macro definition (command).

2. A copy of the macro body, with the actual parameters substituted for the formal parameters, replaces the macro statement.

This substitution is seen in Figure G-4.

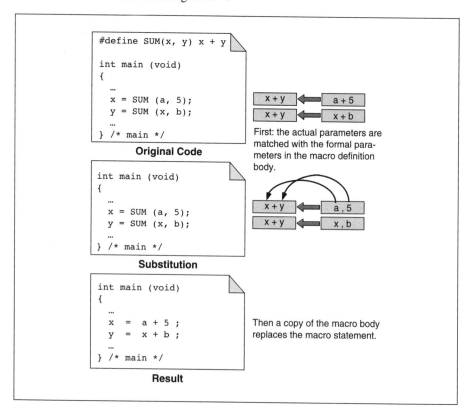

Figure G-4   Macro parameters

Remember that the preprocessor operates much like an editor. This means there is no checking that the expanded statement is valid. Because a macro expansion is a textual substitution instead of a value substitution, it is possible to generate erroneous, but syntactically valid, code. For example, consider the following macro, which sometimes generates what you want and sometimes gives very different results:

```
#define PRODUCT(x, y)    x * y
```

In the following example, the result is as you would expect and want:

```
z = PRODUCT (a, b);
```

The resulting code is

```
z = a * b;
```

Now, however, watch what happens when the same macro is used in the following statement:

```
z =  PRODUCT (a + 1, b + 2);
```

After expansion, we have the following code:

```
z = a + 1 * b + 2;
```

which is undoubtedly not what is wanted. Because of the rules of precedence, this expression becomes, in effect,

```
z = a + b + 2;
```

Therefore, you always enclose the format parameters for the replacement tokens in parentheses. The correct code for PRODUCT then becomes

```
#define PRODUCT(x, y)    (x) * (y)
```

which results in the correct expansion, as shown below.

```
z = (a + 1) * (b + 2);
```

NESTED MACROS

It is possible to nest macros. C handles nested macros by simply rescanning a line after macro expansion. Therefore, if an expansion results in a new statement with a macro, the second macro will be properly expanded. For example, consider the macros shown below.

```
#define PRODUCT(a, b) (a) * (b)
#define SQUARE(a) PRODUCT(a, a,)
```

The expansion of

```
x = SQUARE (5);
```

results in the following expansion:

```
x = PRODUCT(5, 5)
```

which after rescanning becomes

```
x = (5) * (5);
```

Note, however, that the macro expansion will not rescan and reexpand a macro that appears in its own definition.

Finally, note that this rescanning may result in unexpected code. For example, consider the following preprocessor commands:

```
#define SIZE S
#define S    10
```

The preprocessor first scans the text for SIZE and changes it to S. It then scans the text and changes S to 10. This situation is shown in Figure G-5.

```
#define  SIZE  S
#define  S      10

int main (void)
{
  ...
  if  (length < SIZE)
  ...
} /* main */
```
Original Code

```
int main (void)
{
  ...
  if  (length < S)
  ...
} /* main */
```
First Macro Scan

```
int main (void)
{
  ...
  if  (length < 10)
  ...
} /* main */
```
Second Macro Scan

Figure G-5 Example of macro rescanning

MACRO STATEMENT CONTINUATION

Macros must be coded on a single line. If the macro is too long to fit on a line, you must use a continuation token. The continuation token is a backslash (\) followed immediately by a newline. If any whitespace is present between the backslash and the newline, then the backslash is not a continuation token, and the code will most likely generate an error. An example of a macro continuation is shown in Program G-1 Statement 7.

STRING COMMAND (#)

The string command (#) is used to create text enclosed in quotes. This use of the pound sign is not to be confused with the preprocessor command token. In this case, the pound sign appears in front of the formal parameter in the replacement section. The result is the use of actual parameter as a string. This macro command operator is also shown in Program G-1.

```
 1 | /* This program tests string directives
 2 |       Written by:
 3 |       Date:
 4 | */
 5 | #include <stdio.h>
 6 |
 7 | #define PRINT_INT(a) \
 8 |     printf("The variable '" #a "' contains: %d\n", a);
 9 |
10 | int main (void)
11 | {
12 | /* Local Declarations */
13 |     int legalAge = 21;
14 |
15 | /* Statements */
16 |     PRINT_INT (legalAge);
17 |
18 |     return 0;
19 | }  /* main */
```

```
  Results:
      The variable 'legalAge' contains: 21
```

Program G-1 Example of string directive

MERGE COMMAND (##)

Occasionally, it may be necessary to write macros that generate new tokens. With the merge command operator, two tokens are combined. For example, imagine we want to create A1, B3, and Z8 in our program. This can be done easily with the following macro definition:

```
#define FORM(T, N)   T##N
```

Now if we use the following code:

```
int   FORM (A, 1) = 1;
float FORM (B, 3) = 1.1;
char  FORM (Z, 8) = 'A';
```

we get

```
int   A1  = 1;
float B3  = 1.1;
char  Z8  = 'A';
```

UNDEFINE COMMAND

Once defined, a macro name cannot be redefined to change its value. Any attempt to do so will result in a compile error.

It is possible to delete the definition of a macro with the *#undef* command. This command terminates the definition of a macro command. Once a macro has been undefined, it can then be redefined with a new value, as shown in the following example.

```
#define SIZE 20
...
#undef  SIZE
#define SIZE 40
```

G-3 CONDITIONAL COMPILATION

The third use of the preprocessor is to conditionally include or exclude code from the program. For an application programmer, this capability has two common uses: inserting debugging logic in a program and commenting out code. The conditional compilation commands are defined in Table G-2.

Command	Meaning
#if	*if* expression: when true, following code included.
#endif	End of *if* expression: terminates included statements.
#else	Specifies alternate code to be included when expression is false.
#elif	*else-if*: Specifies alternate condition for including text when previous conditional statement is false.
#ifdef	*if* defined: Include following statements when a macro name is defined by *#define*.
#ifndef	*if* not defined: Include the following statements when a macro name is *not* defined.

Table G-2   Conditional compilation commands

if...else
COMMANDS

The precompiler *if...else...endif* commands work just like their C counterparts with two exceptions. First, the expression does not need to be enclosed in parentheses. Using parentheses is permitted, however, and it is a wise thing to do. Second, you do not need to block (use braces) multiple lines of code. All statements from the beginning of the conditional *if* command to its matching *end* command are included. The format of the conditional *if* command is shown in Figure G-6.

Figure G-6   Conditional *if* command

When the conditional expression is true, the statements that follow are included in the program to be compiled. If the condition is false, they are not included. The conditional *if* command *must be terminated by a* conditional *end if* command. If you leave out a matching *#endif,* then all of your program that follows will be part of the conditional compilation! As shown in Figure G-6, you can also use an *else* command. In this case, when the *#if* expression is false, the code following the *#else* is sent to the compilation.

Program G-2 contains an example of a conditional *if* command that you might use while debugging a program. In this example, we are tracing a variable as it changes in different functions in a program. When we are in debugging mode, as determined by DEBUG being set to 1, we will print the contents of the variable at key locations in the program. Since other variables may be displayed for debugging purposes also, we use the PRINT_INT defined macro we described earlier to print the value in the variables.

```
1  #define DEBUG 0
2  #define PRINT_INT(a) \
3      printf("The variable '" #a "' contains: %d\n", a);
4      ...
5      int totalScore;
6      ...
7  #if (DEBUG)
8      PRINT_INT (totalScore);
9  #endif
```

Program G-2   Debug example

CONDITIONAL MULTIWAY SELECTION

When we need a multiway decision, we use the fourth directive, *#elif.* For example, if you are writing a software application that must run at multiple locations, you need to define unique code depending on the location you are compiling for. Each installation needs unique report headings and perhaps other unique code. One way to do this is shown in Program G-3.

```
1  #define Denver   0
2  #define Phoenix  0
3  #define SanJose  1
4  #define Seattle  0
5  ...
6  #if (Denver)
7      /* Denver unique initialization */
8      #include "Denver.h"
9  #elif (Phoenix)
10     /* Phoenix unique initialization */
11     #include "Phoenix.h"
12 #elif (SanJose)
13     /* San Jose unique initialization */
14     #include "SanJose.h"
15 #else
16     /* Seattle unique iniitalization */
17     #include "Seattle.h"
18 #endif
```

Program G-3   Conditional multiway selection

Program G-3 Analysis First, we create a unique header file for each installation. Then, using conditional commands, we select which include file to use based on defined flags for each site. In this example, we have selected San Jose, so only its code is included in the program.

EXCLUDING CODE

Often, when working on a large program, you want to comment out some code while you concentrate on a troublesome block of code. If you have comments in the code being excluded, using the comment token to exclude code can be difficult. (Remember, you cannot nest comments.) An easy way to exclude the code is with an *#if* command, as shown in Figure G-7. In this example, all the code for *locate part* is excluded from the compile. Note that we have used a very simple form of the conditional *if*, *#if 0*. Since we want to temporarily drop the shaded code, we simply set the condition to false (0).

```
/* Locate part */
    ...
    ...
    /* Part not found */
    ...
    ...
    /* Wrong part found */
    ...
/* Process part */
    ...
```

```
#if 0
/* Locate part */
    ...
    /* Part not found */
    ...
    ...
    /* Wrong part found */
    ...
#endif
/* Process part */
    ...
```

Figure G-7 Blocking out code

IF DEFINED
(ifdef/ifndef)

The *if*-defined commands allow us to set conditional compilations based on whether or not a name has been *previously* defined in the compile unit. Its operation is shown in Figure G-8. While this command has many uses, it is most commonly used to prevent

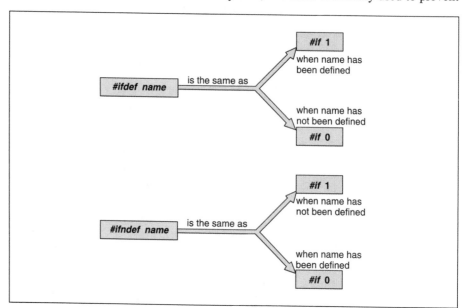

Figure G-8 The *#ifdef* and *#ifndef* commands

multiple definitions for the same name. For example, assume that you are including several different application header files, many of which are also used separately. If we need to define a constant for the size of a name, we would code it as

```
#define NAME_SIZE 25
```

However, if we put this same definition in each of the header files, we will get duplicate name errors. We guard against this by using the *if* defined as shown below.

```
#ifndef    NAME_SIZE
    #define NAME_SIZE 25
#endif
```

Note that we use the same *end-if* command (*#endif*).

In a similar manner, we use the *#ifdef* to ensure that a name has been defined before undefining it.

```
#ifdef    SIZE
    #undef SIZE
#endif
```

Program Standards and Styles

This appendix documents the programming standards and styles used throughout this book. Most companies have their own documented standards and styles. Obviously, when you work for a company, you need to follow its standards.

Our intent with these standards is to suggest some well-proved standards and styles that will enable you to program in a clear and readable form. They form the basis of a discipline that will be needed when you program professionally.

On the other hand, we also encourage you to experiment within the framework of these standards and develop a style that suits you.

For discussion, we have grouped the standard and style comments by program section.

H-1 GLOBAL AREA

Standard   The global area of a program is used only for interprogram and interfunction communication. (See Program H-1.)

1. Place comments at the beginning of the program that document
   a. The purpose of the program.
   b. The author of the program.
   c. The date the program was written.
   d. The date and a description of all changes.
2. Preprocessor commands
   a. All includes are placed at the beginning of the program.
   b. Defined constants are placed at the beginning of the program.
   c. Macros are placed here and within functions as required.
3. All structure definitions are placed either in the global section at the beginning of the program or in a header file.
4. Prototype statements are placed after the structure declarations.

Standard   Variables are not placed in the global section of the program.

1. The only variables allowed in the global section of the program are for external communication. *No internal variables may be placed in this section.*

```
 1  /* This program ...
 2        Written by:
 3        Date:
 4
 5     Change History:
 6         mm/dd/yy: Authority: Change request #nn.
 7                   Program modified to ...
 8  */
 9  #include ...
10
11  /* Defined Constants */
12
13  /* Macros */
14
15  /* Structure Declarations */
16
17  /* Prototype Declarations */
18
19  /* Interprogram Communication Variables */
```

Program H-1   Contents of global program area

H-2 PROGRAM MAIN LINE

Standard   The only statements found in *main* are (Program H-2):

1. A start of program message
2. Function calls
3. An end of program message

```
1  int main (void)
2  {
3  /* Local Definitions */
4
5  /* Statements */
6      printf("\nBegin program <name of program>\n\n");
7
8      <function calls only>
9
10     printf("\nEnd of program <name of program>\n\n");
11  }  /* main */
```

Program H-2   Standards for *main*

H-3 GENERAL CODING STANDARDS

Standard   Do not crowd your code.

1. Provide at least one space before and after every operator.
2. Provide at least one space at the beginning and end of every expression.
3. Align the operator and second operand in a series of assignment statements. This makes for more readable code.
4. Group related statements by placing blank lines before and after them. (Think of a series of statements as sentences in a paragraph, and break them up into small groups that deal with only one process within the function.)

Standard   Only one declaration or definition may be coded on a line.

Standard   With the obvious exception of *for* and the conditional expression, only one statement may be coded on a line.

Style   Group variable declarations by type. Order them alphabetically by type, and place a blank line between types.

Style   Adopt a consistent identifier naming style. The preferred style is lowercase, with the first letter of each identifier segment after the first capitalized.

Style   Adopt consistent naming conventions, such as

1. *fpName* for file pointers
2. *pName* for variable pointers

Style   Abbreviate only when identifiers become long. A good abbreviation style is

1. Remove all vowels unless they start a word.
2. Represent double consonants by a single consonant.

Standard   Minimize the number of statements within a function.

Style   The statement portion of a function should fit on one screen.

Standard   Code that is dependent on a statement is indented at least three spaces. (Exception: Only the first *else if*…is indented.)

Standard   All blocks are terminated with a comment.

1. End a function block with a comment that contains the name of the function. Example: `/* main */`
2. End *if* statements with `/* if */` or `/* if <condition> */`
3. End *else* statements with `/* else */` or `/* else <condition> */`
4. End *while* statements with `/* while */`
5. End *for* statements with `/* for */`
6. Comment intrafunction blocks at the beginning and at the end.

Standard   Avoid using *continue* and *break* statements within loops.

Standard   Never use *goto*.

H-4   VARIABLES AND STRUCTURES

Standard   Use intelligent identifier names.

1. Avoid single character identifiers except for loop counters in a *for* statement.
2. Identifiers should clearly convey their contents and use.

Hint: If you feel that you need to add a comment to explain the name of a variable, the name is inadequate. Change the name.

Style   Indent components within a structure definition to show their relationship in the definition.

H-5   FUNCTION DEFINITION

Standard   Always explicitly code the return type.

Standard   Begin each function, except *main,* with comments that identify its purpose and explain its parameters and return value.

Standard   Within the function definition, place each formal parameter on a different line. Align the parameter types and identifiers.

Style   Place the parameters within a function prototype statement on multiple lines only when there are too many. In that case, place each parameter on a separate line, and align the types and identifiers.

Standard   Clearly document the declarative portion of all functions. (See Program H-2.)

Style   Within a function, use comments only to explain a block of code. Place comments at the beginning of the code that needs explanation. *Do not place comments on lines.*

Standard   Terminate all functions with a return statement.

Style   Avoid multiple return statements within a function.

Standard   Place a visual identifier at the beginning of each function. (See Program H-3.)

Standard   Clearly mark the end of the program. (See Program H-3.)

```
 1  /* ================= <function name> =================
 2     <function purpose>
 3         Pre    <explanation of all parameters
 4         Post   <explanation of all output actions
 5               and return value
 6  */
 7  int doIt (int    p1,
 8            float p2)
 9  {
10  /* Local Definitions */
11
12  /* Statements */
13
14  return 0;
15  }  /* <function name> */
16  /* ================= End of Program ================= */
```

Program H-3   Function format

Command-Line Arguments

All the programs we have written have coded with no parameters. But `main` is a function, and as a function, it may have parameters. When `main` has parameters, they are known as **command-line arguments**.

Command-line arguments are parameters to `main` when the program starts. They allow the user to specify additional information when the program is invoked. For instance, if you write a program to append two files, rather than specify the names of the files as constants in the code, the user could supply them when the program starts. Thus, a UNIX user in the Korn Shell might execute the program with the command line shown below.

```
$appendFiles file1 file2
```

I-1 DEFINING COMMAND-LINE ARGUMENTS

As the programmer, you design the parameter lists for functions you write. When you use system functions, such as *rand,* you follow the parameter design set up by the language specification. Command-line arguments are a little like both. As the programmer, you have control over the names of the parameters, but their type and format are predefined for the language.

The function `main` can be defined either with no argument (*void*) or with two arguments: one an integer and the other an array of pointers to *char* (strings) that represent user-determined values to be passed to `main`. The number of elements in the array is stored in the first argument. The pointers to the user values are stored in the array. The two different formats are shown in Figure I-1.

```
int main (void)

{
/* Local Definitions */


/* Statements */

}    /* main */
```
No command-line arguments

```
int main (int    argc,
               char *argv[])

{
/* Local Definitions */

/* Statements */

} /* main */
```
With command-line arguments

Figure I-1 Arguments to *main*

Although the names of the arguments are your choice, traditionally they are called **argc** (argument count) and **argv** (argument vector). This data structure design, with six string pointers in the vector, is shown in Figure I-2.

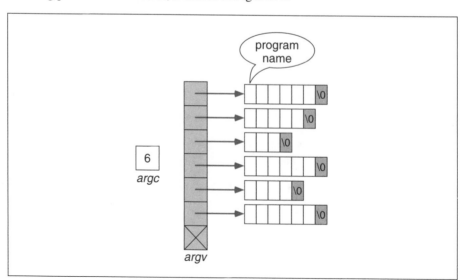

Figure I-2 *argc* and *argv* format

The first argument defines the number of elements in the array identified in the second argument. The value for this argument is not entered from the keyboard; it is provided automatically by the system.

I-2   USING COMMAND-LINE ARGUMENTS

The *argc* array has several elements. The first element points to the name of the program (its file name). It is provided automatically by the program. The last element contains `NULL` and may be used to identify the end of the list. The rest of the elements contain pointers to the user-entered string values.

To fully demonstrate how command-line arguments work, let's write a small nonsense program. It does nothing but exercise the command-line arguments. The code is shown in Program I-1.

```
 1  /* Demonstrate the use of command-line arguments.
 2         Written by:
 3         Date:
 4  */
 5  #include <stdio.h>
 6  #include <string.h>
 7  #include <stdlib.h>
 8
 9  int main (int    argc,
10            char *argv[])
11  {
12  /* Local Definitions */
13     int i;
14
15  /* Statements */
16     printf ("The number of user elements: %d\n", argc);
17     printf ("The name of the program: %s\n", argv[0]);
18
19     for ( i = 1 ; i < argc ; i++ )
20        printf ("User Value No. %d: %s\n", i, argv[i]);
21
22     return 0;
23  } /* main */
```

Program I-1   Display command-line arguments

Now that we've written the program, let's run it with several different arguments. First, let's run it with no user arguments. Even when the user doesn't supply values, the program name is still supplied by the system. (For all of these runs, we assume a DOS environment.)

```
C:>cmdline
The number of elements: 1
The name of the program: CMDLINE
```

For the second run, let's add `hello` to the run command.

```
C:>cmdline hello
The number of elements: 2
The name of the program: CMDLINE
User Value No. 1: hello
```

To make the exercise more interesting, let's run the program with a phrase on the command line.

```
C:>cmdline Now is the time
The number of Elements: 5
The name of the program: CMDLINE
User Value No. 1: Now
User Value No. 2: is
User Value No. 3: the
User Value No. 4: time
```

But what if our intent is to read a phrase? C looks at the user values as strings. This means that the spaces between the words separate each word into a different element. If we want an element to contain more than one word, we enclose it in quotes just like a string in code.

```
C:>cmdline "To err is human" Pope
The number of elements: 3
The name of the program: CMDLINE
User Value No. 1: To err is human
User Value No. 2: Pope
```

The user elements cannot be numbers. If you enter a number, it is taken as a string. However, the string can be converted to a number using a standard function such as *strtod*.

Pointers to Functions

J

Functions in your program occupy memory. The name of the function is a pointer constant to the first byte of memory. For example, imagine that you have four functions stored in memory: main, fun, pun, and sun. This relationship is shown graphically in Figure J-1. The name of each function is a pointer to its code in memory.

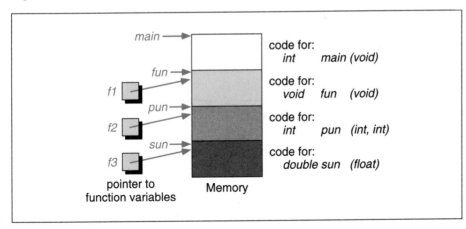

Figure J-1 Functions in memory

J-1   DEFINING POINTERS TO FUNCTIONS

Just as we can with all other pointer types, we can define pointers to function variables and store the address of fun, pun, and sun in them. The syntax for declaring **pointers to functions** is different. To declare a pointer to a function, you code it as if it were a prototype definition, with the function pointer in parentheses. This format is shown in Figure J-2. The parentheses are important: without them, C would interpret the function return type as a pointer. Pointers to function variables are also shown in Figure J-1.

```
                              ┌──────────────────────┐
                              │ f1 is a pointer to a │
                              │ function with no parameters │
                              │   that returns void  │
                              └──────────────────────┘
    ...
    /* Local Definitions */
    void    (*f1) (void);
    int     (*f2) (int, int);
    double  (*f3) (float);

    ...
    /* Statements */

    ...
    f1  =   fun;
    f2  =   pun;
    f3  =   sun;
    ...
```

Figure J-2   Pointers to functions

J-2   USING POINTERS TO FUNCTIONS

Program J-1 shows how our three functions, fun, pun, and sun, can be executed when they are passed as a parameter. Analyze the prototype declaration for strange carefully. The parameter, ptrToFunction, is a pointer to a function that has no parameters and returns nothing. This means that strange expects to receive the address (a pointer) of the function that it will execute. To pass the function's address, we simply use its name as the parameter: The function name is a pointer constant.

```
1   /* Demonstrate use of pointers to functions.
2         Written by:
3         Date:
4   */
5   #include <stdio.h>
6
7   /* Prototype Declarations */
8   void strange (void(*ptrToFunction)(void));
```

Program J-1   Pointers to functions

```
 9   void fun   (void);
10   void pun   (void);
11   void sun   (void);
12
13   int main (void)
14   {
15   /* Local Definitions */
16      void (*f1) (void);
17
18   /* Statements */
19      f1 = fun;
20      strange (f1);
21      f1 = pun;
22      strange (f1);
23      strange (sun);
24      return 0;
25   } /* main */
26
27   /* ================== strange ==================
28      This function will call whatever function is passed
29      to it by the calling function.
30          Pre    ptrFun is pointer to function to be executed
31          Post   requested function has been executed
32   */
33   void strange (void(*ptrToFunction)(void))
34   {
35      (*ptrToFunction)();
36      return;
37   }  /* strange */
38
39   /* ================== fun ==================
40      Prints a simple message about fun.
41          Pre     Nothing
42          Post    Message has been printed
43   */
44   void fun (void)
45   {
46      printf("Fun is being with good friends.\n");
47      return;
48   }  /* fun */
49   /* ================== pun ==================
50      Prints a simple message about pun.
51          Pre    nothing
52          Post   message has been printed
53   */
54   void pun (void)
55   {
56      printf("Pun is a play on words.\n");
57      return;
```

Program J-1 Pointers to functions (continued)

```
58  }  /* pun */
59
60  /* ================= sun =================
61     Prints a simple message about sun.
62        Pre    nothing
63        Post   message has been printed
64  */
65  void sun (void)
66  {
67     printf("Sun is a bright star.\n");
68     return;
69  }  /* sun */
```

```
Results:

Fun is being with good friends.
Pun is a play on words.
Sun is a bright star.
```

Program J-1 Pointers to functions (continued)

Storage Classes and Type Qualifiers

In this appendix, we discuss two attributes of data types, storage classes and type qualifiers. The storage class of a C object defines its spatial territory and its temporal authority. Simply stated, an object's spatial territory defines where it can be referred to in the program. The temporal authority defines when an object is available. The type qualifier adds two special attributes to types: constant (*const*) and shared data (*volatile*).

K-1 STORAGE CLASSES

The storage class of a C object defines two characteristics of that object: its spatial territory and its temporal authority. Spatial territory defines *where* an object is defined. It is also referred to as the **scope**, or **visibility**, of an object. Simply stated, an object's spatial territory defines where it can be referred to in the program.

The temporal authority defines *when* an object is alive. Temporal authority is also referred to as **extent**. When storage is allocated for an object, it is born; when the storage is released for reuse, it dies. These two attributes are visually presented in Figure K-1.

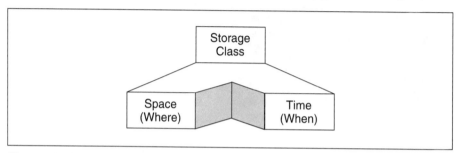

Figure K-1 Storage classes

Although storage classes can be defined for any object in C, we define the storage classes only for variables. The types of storage classes for other objects (like functions) are beyond the scope of this text.

Variables have four different storage classes: *auto, register, static,* and *extern.* They are mutually exclusive: that is, only one storage class can be explicitly used with a variable. Two examples are shown below.

```
auto   int   a;
static float x;
```

The four storage classes are reflected in Figure K-2 and are discussed in turn.

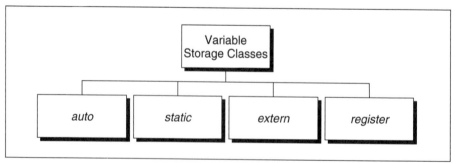

Figure K-2 Variable storage classes

auto

All local variables that are not specifically defined with another storage class are automatically (hence the name) defined as storage class *auto*. Because it is automatic, you do not need to use the term *auto*. All the local variables you have used in your programs have been storage class *auto*.

The storage class *auto* can only be used in a block; it cannot be used at the global level. An *auto* variable has the following characteristics:

1. *Spatial limitation (scope): Local.* An object defined with the *auto* storage class is limited to the block in which it is defined and its subblocks. It is undefined to any other place. In other words, it is local to the block; its authority is local.

2. *Temporal limitation (extent): Mortal. auto* storage class variables are alive only when the block in which they are defined is running—that is, during the time when it is active. Before a block begins execution, the variable does not exist. When the block terminates, such as when it returns, the variable dies.

   When the block is suspended, such as when it calls a subfunction, the variable is suspended but can still be accessed and changed. That is, while the variable is suspended, it can be referred to and changed through a pointer. Then, when the block becomes active again, the variable becomes active.

   If a block is called many times, the variable will be born and die over and over again. This gives *auto* variables their mortal characteristics; they are born and die. They have a short lifetime; however, they can be reborn.

As an example of *auto* variables, consider the block in the *for* statement shown in Figure K-3. Normally, you do not declare variables within a *for* statement block, but it is perfectly legal to do so. In this case, we define two integer variables, a and b. Assuming that the *for* statement is inside a loop, the variables will be born and die each time the *for* statement is executed. Note, however, that while the *for* statement is looping, they are alive and well.

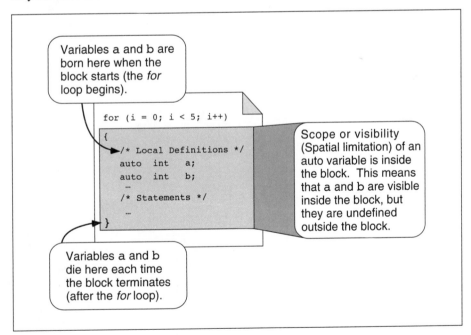

Figure K-3 Storage class *auto* example

Initialization

An *auto* variable can be initialized where it is defined or left uninitialized. If initialized, it receives the same initialization value each time it is born. If it is not initialized, its value will be undefined every time it is born.

Uninitialized *auto* Storage Class

When the *auto* variable is not initialized, its value is unpredictable. The variable holds what is left from the storage location's previous operation.

> The keyword *auto* is not needed; the default for a local variable is *auto*.

static

A *static* variable can be defined inside a block or in the global area of the program. Its characteristics differ slightly depending on where it is defined. We will study each case separately.

Local *static* Variables

When a *static* variable is defined inside a block, it has the following characteristics:

1. *Spatial limitation (scope): Local.* The spatial limitation of a *static* storage class variable is local; that is, it is visible only inside the block in which it is defined. It is undefined everywhere else. Locally defined *static* variables have only local authority.

> Allocation is done only once for static variables.

2. *Temporal limitation (extent): Immortal.* While its spatial limitation is local, its temporal limitation is the whole life of the program. In other words, it lives as though it were a global variable. A *static* variable is born when the program starts running and only dies when the program stops running.

> Static variable values are alive for the whole program.

Locally defined *static* variables are one of the truly significant features of the C language. In many situations, the value in a local variable needs to be maintained between calls to a function. In other languages, these variables must be declared globally, which reduces the benefits of data hiding and isolation. In C, you simply declare the variable as *static* and its values live from call to call. Figure K-4 contains an example of *static* variables.

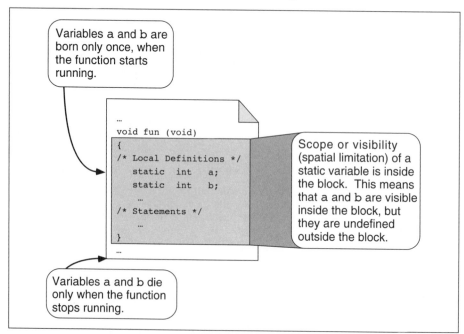

Figure K-4   Storage class *static* example

Initialization

A static variable can be initialized where it is defined, or it can be left uninitialized. If initialized, it is initialized only once. If it is not initialized, its value will be initialized to zero.

Global *static* Variables

Global variables—that is, variables defined outside the scope of all blocks—can be referred to by other compilation units. This is one of their characteristics and is one of the reasons why their use should be limited. To prevent a global variable from being exported to the linker for reference by other compilation units, it can be declared *static*. When a *static* variable is defined in the global section of a program, it has the following characteristics:

1. *Spatial limitation (scope): Global.* A global spatial limitation is visible from its definition to the end of the compile unit. It can be referred to and changed by all the blocks that come after it, unless it is redefined locally.

2. *Temporal limitation (extent): Immortal.* Its temporal limitation is the same as for a locally declared *static* variable.

The initialization of global *static* variables is the same as for local declarations.

> The use of *static* for a global variable guarantees that the scope of the variable cannot extend beyond its spatial area—that is, beyond the current compile unit.

extern

The primary purpose of the ***extern*** storage class is to make variables visible to other compilation units. They can be defined only in the global area of a program; they cannot be defined in a block. In fact, by default, all global variables are *extern*s. If you don't want a global variable to be visible outside the current compile unit, you must declare it as *static*.

The *extern* storage class is exported to the linker so that other compilation units can refer to it or change its contents. Obviously, this makes *extern* variables dangerous: They should be used with caution and only when necessary. This explains our admonition against them throughout the text.

The *extern* storage class has the following characteristics:

1. *Spatial limitation (scope): Global.* It is visible from its definition to the end of the program. It can be referred to and changed by all of the blocks that come after it as well as by other programs that are aware of its existence. It has a global authority.

2. *Temporal limitation (extent): Immortal.* The temporal limitations are the same as for the *static* storage class.

Figure K-5 contains examples of *extern* storage classes.

Initialization

An *extern* variable's initialization rules are the same as for *static* storage classes. They may be initialized when they are defined. If they are not explicitly defined, they are initialized to zero.

EXTENDING VISIBILITY

The C language requires that a variable be defined before it can be used. This presents no problems with local variables, but occasionally, especially in large programs, it may be necessary to refer to a global variable before it has been defined. This situation usually occurs when large systems are built using library files.

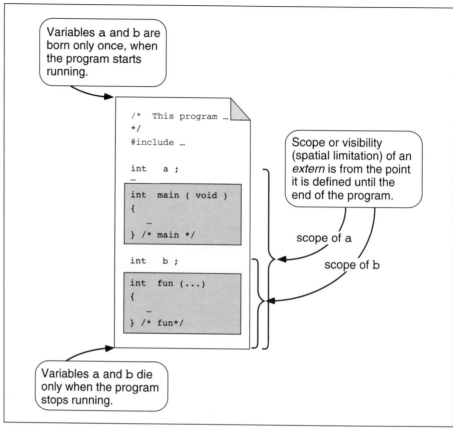

Figure K-5 Storage class *extern* example

Figure K-6 diagrams the use of *extern* to extend the visibility of an external variable. By using the keyword *extern* in a function block, you specify that somewhere in the compile unit the variable a will be defined. Note that this use of *extern* is not a variable definition; it only declares the name of the variable. No memory is allocated. The actual definition comes later.

Study Figure K-6 carefully. Note the spatial limitation of b. It is visible in the second function because it is declared to be external to the function. At the end of the function, however, it is no longer visible. It becomes visible again when it is defined as a global variable later in the compile unit. This is possible because, as an *extern*, the variable's temporal limitation is for the life of the program, even though its spatial visibility is limited.

EXTENDING VISIBILITY TO OTHER FILES

We can extend the visibility of an *extern* variable to other source files. As we will see in the next section, a source file can be decomposed into many source files, compiled separately, and then linked together to form one unit. This is common on large projects. However, all the functions compiled separately later become part of a whole. To facilitate communication among the separate parts, an *extern* variable can be defined in one of them and its visibility extended to the others that need it. As we mentioned before, external references are one of the valid uses for global variables.

Figure K-7 shows how *extern* facilitates communication among separately compiled units. In Figure K-7a, integer a is declared at the global level. Since all global variables are by default *extern* storage classes, the keyword *extern* is not used in its definition. In Figure K-7b, it is declared globally using *extern*; in Figure K-7c, it is declared locally using *extern*. In both Figure K-7b and c, no memory is allocated for it; it is just given spatial visibility.

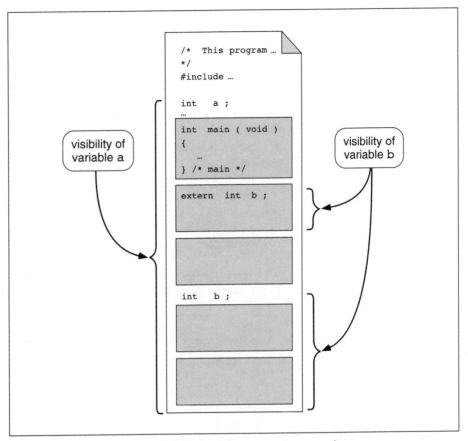

Figure K-6   Extending visibility with *extern* storage classes

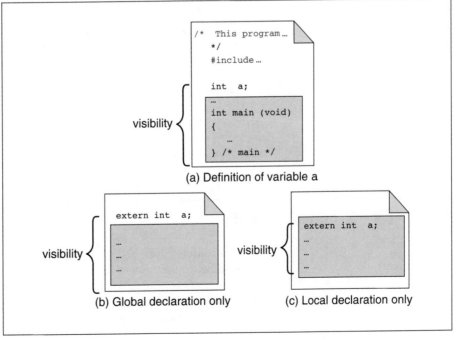

Figure K-7   External references to other compile units

register

A *register* storage class defines a variable with a recommendation to the compiler to use a central processing unit (CPU) register for the variable instead of a memory location. This is done for efficiency. The time required to access a CPU register is significantly less than the time required to access a memory location. The scope and extent of a *register* variable are the same as for an *auto* variable.

Computers have a limited number of registers. This makes them valuable resources that need to be optimally used. We recommend that you never use storage registers for two reasons: First, the standard states that you cannot compute the address of a register. This means that you can't use the address operator and the indirection operator with a register. It also disallows implicit conversions, such as might occur when using a register with mixed mode arithmetic.

The second reason is that the compiler may ignore your recommendation. Registers are scarce resources, and the compiler often needs all of them for the program to run efficiently. Couple this fact with the first reason, which prevents you from using the variable in an efficient manner, and you can see why we recommend against using store registers.

SUMMARY

We summarize the spatial and temporal authority for variable storage classes in Table K-1. How and where they can be used are summarized in Table K-2.

Temporal Authority	Spatial Authority	
	Local	Global
Mortal	*auto* *register*	
Immortal	*static*	*static* *extern*

Storage class temporal and spatial authority

Storage Class	Keyword	Global	Blocks
auto	optional		✓
static	required	✓	✓
extern	mixed[a]	✓	
register	required		✓

[a]Optional but should be omitted in definition; required in declaration.

Table K-1 Definition of storage classes

K-2 TYPE QUALIFIERS

The type qualifier (Figure K-8) is used to add two special attributes to types: *const* and *volatile*. Although their names lead you to believe that they are contradictory, they are not. In fact, they can both be used with the same type definition.

When both a storage class, such as *static,* and a type qualifier are needed, the storage class comes before the type qualifier.

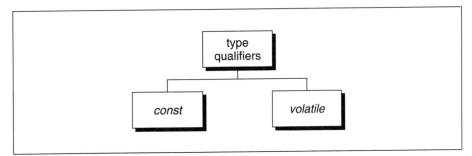

Figure K-8 Type qualifiers

const

A *const* (constant) object is a read-only object; that is, it can only be used as an rvalue. A constant object must be initialized when it is defined because it cannot be changed later. A simple constant is shown below.

```
const double PI = 3.1415926;
```

In addition to the simple types, arrays, structures, and unions can also be defined as constant. In these cases, all their component elements are constants. For instance, in the string constant shown below, none of the individual elements can be changed.

```
const char str[] = "Hello";
```

Also, given a constant structure or a union, as shown below, the individual elements cannot be changed.

```
const struct          const union
   {                     {
    ...                   ...
    ...                   ...
   } x;                  } y;
```

POINTERS AND CONSTANTS

Pointers can also be defined as constants. Depending on how they are coded, however, three different variations can occur.

1. The pointer itself is constant.
2. The object being pointed to is constant.
3. Both the pointer and its object are constants.

Case I: Pointer Constant

When the keyword *const* is associated with the identifier (placed after the type and before the identifier), the pointer itself is a constant. This means that its contents cannot be changed, they can only be initialized.

```
int a;
int *const ptr = &a;
```

In this case, it is an error to use the pointer as an lvalue later in the program.

```
ptr = &b;                   /* Error: ptr is constant */
```

Case II: Object Is Constant

When the keyword *const* is associated with the type (the first term in the definition), then the object being referenced is a constant, but the pointer itself is not. So, while we can change the value in the pointer, we cannot dereference the operator as an lvalue. Consider the following definitions:

```
const int   a = 5;
const int   b = 7;
const int *ptr;
```

In this case, we can assign `ptr` the address of either a or b. But an attempt to change the contents of the constants using the dereference is an error.

```
ptr = &a;                               /* Valid code */
ptr = &b;                               /* Valid code */

But

*ptr = 21;              /* Error: pointing to constant */
```

Case III: Both Pointer and Object Are Constant

To indicate that both the pointer and the object that it points to are constant, use the keyword *const* twice.

```
int                x;
int                *px;
const int          a = 5;
const int *const p = &a;

x  = *p;                 /* Valid assignment */
px = p;                  /* Valid assignment */


*p = 5;                  /* Invalid: a is a constant */
p  = &a;                 /* Invalid: p is a constant */
```

volatile

A *volatile* object is an object that may belong to two different entities. Normally, objects used in a program belong only to the C compiler. When the compiler owns an object, it can store and handle it in any way necessary to optimize the program. As an example, a C compiler may think that it is more efficient to remove an object from RAM memory and put it in cache memory.

However, sometimes objects must be shared between your program and some other facilities outside the C program; for example, some input/output routines. To tell the compiler that the object is shared, we declare it as type *volatile*. In this case, we are telling the compiler that this object may be referenced or changed by other entities.

Programmers use *volatile* objects in advanced system programming; further discussion about *volatile* objects is beyond the scope of this book.

Separate Compilation

All the programs that you have written in this text have been small by industry standards. Large systems require tens of thousands of lines of code. Very large systems require millions of lines of code. When systems are that large, you need more tools. In this section we describe one of those tools, separate compilations.

L-1 WRITING SEPARATE COMPILATION UNITS

Figure L-1 shows the steps to build an object module from one source file. These are the steps you have been following throughout the book.

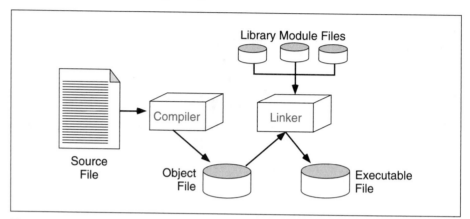

Figure L-1 Single compilation

When a large project is designed, it is broken down into modules that can be developed and unit tested separately. This is a logical concept. It is much easier to write and debug a small module than a large one. This is true even when you consider the driver program that must be written to test the modules being developed separately from the rest of the final program. A driver program is temporary code that is used to debug modules that will later be combined into a large executable program.

After the unit testing is complete, the object files can be linked together to form one executable program. Figure L-2 shows an executable file being built from separate compilations. It is not necessary to compile the source files at the same time. Often, weeks or months pass between their compilation and their being linked into an executable file.

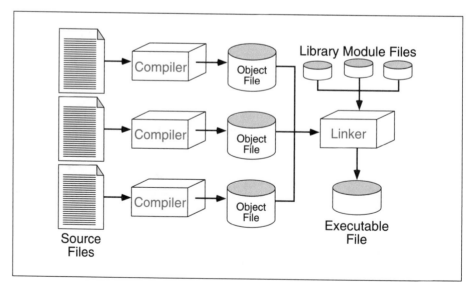

Figure L-2 Separate compilation environment

To build an executable program from separately compiled modules, we use two storage classes defined before: *extern* and *static*. The use of *extern* is a simple extension from communications between functions in the same compilation unit to communications between functions in different compilation units. In this case, it tells the compiler that an object will be shared by more than one source file. The object will be defined in one file and only declared in the others, as shown in Figure K-7, on page 849.

On the other hand, a *static* object defined globally tells the compiler that it belongs to its particular file and that no other files are allowed to access it. This allows different source files to have different objects with the same name; because they are *static,* the objects are not shared, they are private. The concept of *static* global variables with identical names is shown in Figure L-3.

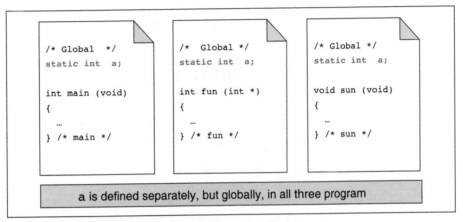

```
/* Global  */          /* Global */           /* Global */
static int  a;         static int  a;         static int  a;

int main (void)        int fun (int *)        void sun (void)
{                      {                      {
   ...                    ...                    ...
} /* main */           } /* fun */            } /* sun */
```

a is defined separately, but globally, in all three program

Figure L-3   Use of *static* in separate compilations

To demonstrate separate compilations, we created three separately compiled units. The first is `main`, which simply prints the values in two variables and then calls two functions, `fun` and `sun`. Note that the calls do not have any parameters. All communications are done through *extern*'s. Figure L-4 outlines the design of the three compilation units. The code is shown in Programs L-1 to L-3.

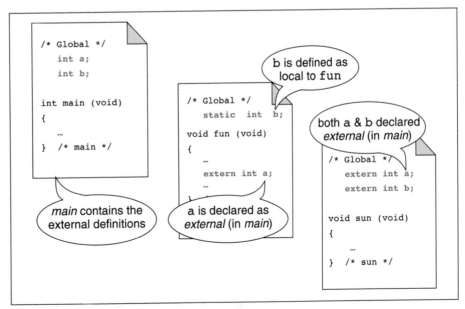

```
/* Global */
   int a;
   int b;

int main (void)
{
   ...
}  /* main */
```

```
/* Global */
   static  int  b;

void fun (void)
{
   ...
   extern int a;
   ...
}
```

b is defined as local to fun

both a & b declared *external* (in *main*)

```
/* Global */
   extern int a;
   extern int b;

void sun (void)
{
   ...
}  /* sun */
```

main contains the external definitions

a is declared as *external* (in *main*)

Figure L-4   Separate compilations

```
1   /* Demonstrate separate compilations.
2          Written by:
3          Date:
4   */
5   #include <stdio.h>
6
7   /* Prototype Declarations */
8      void fun (void);
9      void sun (void);
10
11  /* Global Definitions */
12     int a = 100;
13     int b = 200;
14
15  int main (void)
16  {
17  /* Statements */
18     printf ("The value of a in main is: %3d\n",    a);
19     printf ("The value of b in main is: %3d\n\n", b);
20
21     fun ();
22     sun ();
23
24     printf ("The value of a in main is: %d\n", a);
25     printf ("The value of b in main is: %d\n", b);
26
27     return 0;
28  }  /*main */
```

```
Run results:
The value of a in main is: 100
The value of b in main is: 200

The value of a in fun is : 101
The value of b in fun is :   0

The value of a in sun is : 102
The value of b in sun is : 201

The value of a in main is: 102
The value of b in main is: 201
```

Program L-1 Separate compilations—main

```
1   /* Demonstrate separate compilations.
2          Written by:
3          Date:
4   */
5   #include <stdio.h>
```

Program L-2 Separate compilations—fun

```
 6
 7    static int b;
 8
 9    /* ==================== fun ====================
10        Increments a global variable and prints it
11            Pre    nothing
12            Post   variable incremented and printed
13    */
14    void fun (void)
15    {
16    /* Local Definitions */
17        extern int a;
18
19    /* Statements */
20        a++;
21        printf ("The value of a in fun is : %3d\n",   a);
22        printf ("The value of b in fun is : %3d\n\n", b);
23        return;
24    }   /* fun */
```

Program L-2 Separate compilations—fun (continued)

```
 1    /* ==================== sun ====================
 2        Increments two global variables and prints them.
 3            Pre    nothing
 4            Post   variables incremented and printed
 5    */
 6    extern int a;
 7    extern int b;
 8
 9    void sun (void)
10    {
11    /* Statements */
12    a++;
13    b++;
14
15    printf ("The value of a in sun is : %d\n",   a);
16    printf ("The value of b in sun is : %d\n\n", b);
17
18    return;
19    }   /* sun */
```

Program L-3 Separate compilations—sun

Program Analysis   First, note that there is only one main. Even though we are compiling each function separately, the rule that there must be one and only one main for each program still must be followed. When the resulting program begins execution, it is still main that controls its logic flow.

These three functions share the integer variable, a, and two of them share b. Both of these variables have been defined globally in main. The function fun uses the variable a but defines its own variable b as a *static* global variable. Note that when it prints b, the result is zero. This is because uninitialized *static* variables are automatically initialized to zero. Finally, function sun prints both variables.

L-2   PROCEDURES FOR SEPARATE COMPILATION

The C standard does not specify how separate source files should be combined into a program. Each system is therefore free to develop its own set of rules and procedures. In this section, we describe two of the more common environments, UNIX and Turbo C in a DOS environment. Your installation will provide documentation on how to build programs for your system.

UNIX

Building an executable program file from separate source files is relatively straightforward in UNIX. Your installation will undoubtedly have an even simpler procedure using a command file. The steps without command files are shown below and in Figure L-5.

Figure L-5   UNIX separate compilations

1. Create source files for main and all separately compiled functions just as you would for any program. Remember, a program can have only one main.
2. Compile the individual source files separately using the −c option (for compile only, do not link).
3. Run the UNIX C compiler using the −o option, which specifies that an output (executable) file is to be created. The name of the executable program is the first file parameter. The names of the object modules follow the program name.

You are now ready to test your program. Test it just as you would any other program. Remember, however, that if you make any changes, you need to relink your executable file (Step 3). Just making changes and recompiling an individual source file does not change the executable program.

Turbo C

Turbo C uses a project approach to achieve separate compilations. You create a project file and add source files to it. From that point on, compiling and running are just like a single program environment. The steps to create a project for the programs in separate complication—main are shown below.[1]

1. Create source files for main and all separately compiled functions just as you would for any program. Remember, a program can have only one main.

2. In the Project window, select *Open,* and type the name of the project in the Name box. It is not necessary to add an extension. Turbo will automatically add .PRJ to the name you enter. Use a name that reflects the purpose and use of the program you will create. For this exercise, we used the name SEPCOMP.PRJ.

3. In the Project window, select *Add.*

   a. In the Name box, type the file search command for the source files. For example, if you have the files in a directory called Project on the C drive, you enter C:\project*.c to list all your C source files.

   b. Select the file to be added, and click *Add.*

   c. Repeat Step b for each file to be added.

   d. Click *Done.*

      At this point, your project window should show the source files needed for the compile. The Lines, Code, and Data columns will contain n/a until the source files are recompiled.

4. Double-click on a source file name. This opens the file. Compile the program. Note that Lines, Code, and Data columns now reflect the current data for the file.

5. Repeat Step 4 for each source file.

At this point, your project window should look like Figure L-6.

```
┌─[■]════════════ Project: SEPCOMP════════════1═[ ≠ ]═┐
│ File name Location              Lines  Code  Data  │
│ SEPCOMM.C .                       30    67   131   │
│ SEPCOMF.C .                       25    37    67   │
│ SEPCOMS.C .                       25    41    63   │
│                                                    │
└────────────────────────────────────────────────────┘
```

Figure L-6 Project window for Turbo separate compilations

6. In the Project window, select *Make Project.* This creates an executable (.exe) file.

   At this point, you should save the project. To save the project, select the *Options* window, then select *Save.* In the Save window, click on the Project box. Make sure it is selected (has an X in it). Then click *Save.* Your project file has now been saved.

You should now test your program. You can test it from the DOS Shell or from the Run window. Remember, however, that if you make any changes, you need to rebuild your project. Just making changes and recompiling an individual source file does not change the executable program.

---

[1]These steps follow the procedure using Turbo 3.0++ for DOS. If you have Windows or a later version of the system, there may be some minor differences.

Exercise Solutions

This section contains solutions to selected review questions and exercises at the end of each chapter.

CHAPTER 1

1. b. False
3. b. False
5. a. True
7. a. Database management system
9. a. Assembly/symbolic
11. d. Source file
13. a. Flowchart

EXERCISES

15. The two major components of a computer system are hardware and software. The hardware component of the computer system is made of five parts: The input devices, central processing unit (CPU), primary storage or main memory, output devices, and auxiliary storage devices. The software consists of system software, which includes the operating system, and application software used to solve the user's business requirements.

17. In a time-sharing environment, each user has a terminal that does not have any processing capability of its own; all processing is done by a central computer. In a client/server environment, users have terminals that have some processing capabilities; a portion of the processing is done by the terminal workstation, and a portion is done by a central computer.

19. The operating system provides system services such as a user interface, file and database access, and communication services. Its primary purpose is system efficiency while providing user access to the hardware and applications.

21. General-purpose software can be used for more than one purpose. Examples include word processors, spreadsheets, and database management systems. Application-specific software solves a specific business problem and cannot be used for other purposes. Examples include personal finance systems and general ledger accounting systems.

23. Symbolic languages, often called assembly languages, provide mnemonics for machine instructions, data identifiers, and other objects such as functions. They allow the programmer to write program instructions that basically mirror the machine instructions. High-level languages, on the other hand, are machine independent and allow the user to concentrate on the problem being solved rather than the hardware on which it is being solved. Generally, each high-level language statement generates many machine language statements.

25. The system development life cycle contains six steps:

    a. System requirements: Define the requirements for the system.

    b. Analysis: Evaluate alternative solutions to requirements.

    c. Design: Describe the specific implementation for the problem.

    d. Code: Prepare and unit test programs based on the design.

    e. System test: Verify that the programs integrate and work as a system to satisfy the user requirements.

    f. Maintenance: Keep the system working in production.

27. The four steps to develop a program are:

    a. Understand the problem.

    b. Develop a solution.

    c. Write the program.

    d. Test the program.

29. "Resist the temptation to code" means that the programmer must fully understand the problem and design a solution before beginning the process of writing code. It is human nature to want to get to the coding step as soon as possible, but this often leads to poorly implemented and inefficient programs.

31. Software engineering is the use of sound engineering methods and principles to develop software that works.

CHAPTER 2

REVIEW QUESTIONS

1. b. False

3. a. True

5. b. Declaration sections contain instructions to the computer.

7. e. `$salesAmount`

9. a. Each character has a unique binary value.

11. c. Like variables, constants have a type and may be named.

13. d. `%hd`

15. d. *scanf*

EXERCISES

17. b and c

19. c, d, and e

21. b, c, and e

23. a. String
    b. Long integer
    c. Long double
    d. Float
    e. Character

25. a. Not valid: Hyphen is not a valid character to use in an identifier
    b. Not valid: An identifier may not contain spaces
    c. Valid
    d. Valid
    e. Valid

27. The following lines must be changed to read as follows:
    Line 1:
    ```
    /* This program does nothing */
    ```
    Line 2:
    ```
    int main (void)
    ```

29. The following lines must be changed to read as follows:
    Line 1:
    ```
    #include <stdio.h>
    ```
    Line 4:
    ```
    printf ("We are to learn correct");
    ```
    Line 5:
    ```
    printf ("C language here");
    ```
    Last line:
    ```
    } /* main */
    ```

31. The following lines must be changed to read as follows:
    Before main:
    ```
    #include <stdio.h>
    ```
    Line 7:
    ```
    int     a;
    ```
    Line 8:
    ```
    double  b;
    ```
    Line 9:
    ```
    char    c;
    char    d;
    /* we recommned only one definition per line */
    ```

CHAPTER 3

REVIEW QUESTIONS

1. b. False
3. b. False
5. b. False
7. c. Conditional
9. b. ++a
11. d. Precedence
13. c. An explicit cast on a variable changes its type in memory.
15. c. All compound statements must be terminated by a semicolon.

EXERCISES

17. e

19. b and d

21. a. x = 4, y = 5

    b. x = 4, y = 5

    c. x = 4, y = 6

    d. x = 4, y = 5

    e. x = 2, y = 4

23. a. 22.52

    b. 4.5

    c. 13.33

    d. 0.88

    e. 0.07

25. a. 5

    b. 2

    c. 4

    d. Undeterminable. If a single variable is modified more than once in an expression, the result is undefined.

    e. Undeterminable. If a single variable is modified more than once in an expression, the result is undefined.

27. a. 5

    b. 294

    c. 4

    d. 29

    e. 9

CHAPTER 4

REVIEW QUESTIONS

1. a. True

3. a. True

5. b. False

7. d. The function definition contains executable statements that perform the function's task.

9. a. Empty parameter lists are declared with the keyword *void*.

11. d. Indirection operator (`*`)

13. d. `(rand () % 21) + 30`

EXERCISES

15. This function either must be declared to return an integer or must not return the value of the local variable `z`.

17. Function `sun` is defined inside function `fun`.

19. a. `int  sun (int x, int y);`

    b. `int  sun (int x, int y);`

    c. `void sun (void);`   `(single void parameter)`

    d. `void sun (int x, float y);`

21. a. 9.5
    b. 2.4
    c. 3.4
    d. 7.0
    e. 7.0
23. a. 3.5, 3.5, 3.8, 3.2, 3.5
    b. 3.5, 3.45, 3.76, 3.23, 3.46
    c. 3.5, 3.45, 3.76, 3.234, 3.457
25. -2 2
27. See Figure S-1.

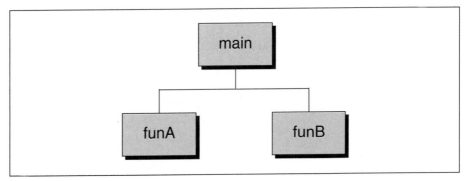

Figure S-1　　Solution for Chapter 4, Exercise 27

Output:
5 0

12 1
10   5 25

CHAPTER 5

REVIEW QUESTIONS

1. a. True
3. a. True
5. b. False
7. c. =
9. e. The selection expression cannot have a side effect.
11. d. *else-if* and *switch*
13. c. The *else-if* requires integral values in its expression.

EXERCISES

15. a. (! ((3 + 3) >= 6))
       (! (6 >= 6))
       (! (true))
       false
    b. (((1 + 6) == 7) || ((3 + 2) == 1))
       ((7 == 7) || (5 == 1))

```
                    ((true) || (5 == 1))      /* Second expression not evaluated */
                    true
                c.  (((1 > 5) || (6 < 50)) && (2 < 5))
                    (((false) || (true)) && (true))
                    ((true) && (true))
                    true
                d.  (((14 != 55) && (! (13 < 29))) || (31 > 52))
                    (((true) && (! (true))) || (false))
                    ((true && false) || false)
                    ((false) || (false))
                    false
                e.  ((6 < 7) > 5)
                    ((true) > 5)
                    (1 > 5)
                    false
```

17. a. 1

    b. 1

    c. 1

    d. 1

    e. 1

19. a. 0

    b. 1

    c. 1

    d. 1

    e. 0

21. $x = 4, y = 1, z = 2$

23. $x = 4, y = 1, z = 2$

25. $x = 2, y = 0, z = 2$

27. $x = 0, y = 0, z = 1$

29. $x = 0, y = 1, z = 0$

31. $x = 1, y = 3, z = 1$

33. a. c (lowercase 'c')

    b. ?

    c. c (lowercase 'c')

    d. 5

35. a.
```
!x || !y && z
!y && z || x
!x && !y && z
x && y || z || y
!x || !y || !z || y || z
```

CHAPTER 6

REVIEW QUESTIONS

1. a. True

3. b. False

5. e. The update for a pretest loop must be a part of the loop body.

EXERCISES

7. e. The number of updates always equals the number of loop iterations.

9. e. Both the *for* and the *while*.

11. d. Both statements include initialization within the statements.

13. b. *case*

15. c. Logarithmic

17. a. On separate lines

12	11	10	9	8

    b. On separate lines

12	11	10	9	8

    c. On separate lines

12	11	10	9	8

19. a. nothing

    b. nothing

    c. 12

21. a.
```
x = 0;
if (x < 10)
   {
    do
       {
        printf ("%d\n", x);
        x++;
       } while (x < 10);
   } /* if */
```
    b.
```
scanf ("%d", &x);
if (x != 9999)
   {
    do
       {
        printf ("%d\n", x);
        scanf  ("%d", &x);
       } while (x != 9999);
   } /* if */
```

23. a.
```
x = 1;
if (x < 100)
   {
    do
       {
        printf ("%d\n", x);
        x++;
       } while (x < 100);
   } /* if */
```
    b.
```
if (scanf ("%d", &x) != EOF)
   {
    do
       {
        printf ("%d\n", x);
       } while (scanf ("%d", &x) != EOF);
   } /* if */
```

25. a.
```
x = 0;
printf ("%d\n", x);
for (x++; x < 100; x++)
    printf ("%d\n", x);
```

b.
```
res = scanf ("%d", &x);
for (; res != EOF;)
      res = scanf ("%d", &x);
```

27. This *for* loop will print the numbers 1 to 10 all on the same line with no spaces. The only correction might be to add a space in the format string of the print statement.

29. a. On separate lines:

20 19 18 17 16 15 14 13 12 11 10

b. On separate lines:

20 18 16 14 12 10 8 6 4 2

31. a.

```
 1
  2
   3
    4
     5
      6
       7
        8
         9
          10
           11
            12
             13
              14
               15
                16
                 17
                  18
                   19
                    20
```

b.

```
                    20
                   19
                  18
                 17
                16
               15
              14
             13
            12
           11
          10
         9
        8
       7
      6
     5
    4
   3
  2
 1
```

CHAPTER 7

REVIEW QUESTIONS

1. a. True
3. b. False
5. a. True
7. c. `stdfile`
9. a. Opens the file for reading and sets the file marker at the beginning.
11. a. Conversion Code.
13. a. *scanf* implicitly casts data to match the conversion code and its corresponding address parameter.
15. e. Terminates the *scanf* function and leaves the invalid character in the input stream.

EXERCISES

17.
```
i1 = 14   i2 = 67 f1 = 67.0   c1 = '.'   c2 = 2
```
27.
```
000123, -00234, -00007
-234, %, ", \t, 123 A 10 a H
```

CHAPTER 8

REVIEW QUESTIONS

1. a. True
3. b. False
5. b. False
7. c. index
9. d. `ary[0] = x;`
11. e. sorting
13. e. sequential
15. a. A two-dimensional array can be thought of as an array of one-dimensional arrays.

EXERCISES

17.
```
2
2
1
2
```
19.
```
after first pass:   7   8   13   44   26   23   98   57
after second pass:  7   8   13   23   26   44   98   57
after third pass:   7   8   13   23   26   44   98   57
```
21.
```
after first pass:   3   7   13   26   44   23   98   57
after second pass:  3   7   13   26   44   23   98   57
after third pass:   3   7   13   26   44   23   98   57
```

23. Bubble sort, because the two smallest elements have been bubbled to the front.

25.

FIRST	LAST	MID
0	7	3
4	7	5
6	7	6
8	7	0

27. In each pass, the first element of the unsorted sublist is picked up and transferred into the sorted sublist by inserting it at the appropriate place. When it locates the correct position, therefore, the data have already been moved right one position, and the current location is empty. So, the sort simply places the saved element in its proper location.

CHAPTER 9

REVIEW QUESTIONS

1. a. True

3. a. True

5. a. Pointers are built on the standard type, address.

7. e. `*p++;`

9. c. `int *ptr = &x;`

11. a. `p`

13. c. It is possible to cast a pointer to integer as a pointer to *float*.

15. b. Runs efficiently on any hardware.

EXERCISES

17. a. True

b. False (because a is not a pointer)

19. a. `++a = 6`

b. `++(*p) = 6`

c. `--(*q) = 6`

d. `--b = 6`

21. a. Not valid. p is an uninitialized pointer to integer, so it cannot hold an integer value.

b. Not valid. p is an uninitialized pointer to integer, so it cannot be dereferenced.

c. Not valid. p is an uninitialized pointer to integer. Even if it were initialized, dereferencing it provides an *int*, not an address of an *int*.

d. No error.

23. a. a pointer to a pointer to a pointer to an integer

b. a pointer to a pointer to an integer

c. a pointer to an integer

d. an integer

25. a. No error

b. Error: `&a[0]` must be stored in p instead of `&p`.

c. Error: q must store `(p+2)` instead of `&(p+2)`.

d. No error

27. `int * spin (int *x, long double **py);`

29. See Figure S-2.

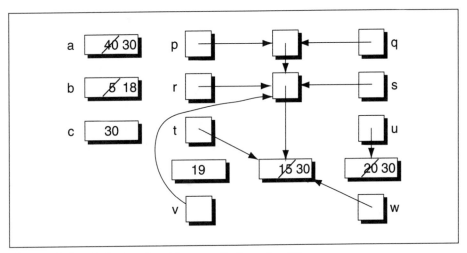

Figure S-2   Solution for Chapter 9, Exercise 29

CHAPTER 10

REVIEW QUESTIONS

1. a. True

3. a. True

5. c. The name of an array can be used with the indirection operator to reference data.

7. b. `int ary[ ] [SIZE2]`

9. a. Allocated memory can be referred to only through pointers; it does not have its own identifier.

11. e. To ensure that it is released, allocated memory should be freed before the program ends.

EXERCISES

13. a. `*(tax + 6)`
    b. `*(score + 7)`
    c. `*(num + 4)`
    d. `*(prices + 9)`

15. If we interpret the sixth element as `ary[5]`, and if p is pointing to `ary[3]`, we can access `ary[5]` using `*(p+2)`, or we can use an index, like so: `p[2]`.

17.
    6 6
    3 4
    6 2
    4 6

19. Prototype: `void fun (int **ary);`
    Call: `fun (table);`

21. See Figure S-3.

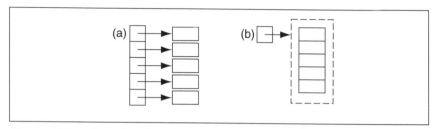

Figure S-3 Solution for Chapter 10, Exercise 21

    a. x is an array of pointers where each pointer can point to an integer.

    b. x is a pointer to an array of integers.

23. See Figure S-4.

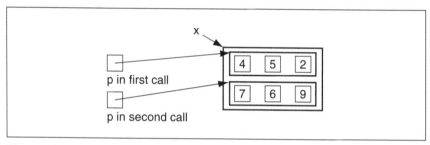

Figure S-4 Solution for Chapter 10, Exercise 23

    4 5 2
    7 6 9

Explanation for the first call:
    p is pointing to the whole first row, so (*p) is the first row itself. Then using the first row, (*p)[0] refers to the first element (4), (*p)[1] refers to the second element (5), and (*p)[2] refers to the third element (2).

Explanation for the second call:
    p is pointing to the whole second row (x+1), so (*p) is the second row itself. Then using the second row, (*P)[0] refers to the first element (7), (*p)[1] refers to the second element (6), and (*p)[2] refers to the third element (9).

25. **a.** e

    b. m

27. **a.** 4

    b. 4

    c. 2147462972 (address of i)

    d. 4

    e. 2147462972 (address of i)

    f. 2147466300 ((address of i) + 8)

29. **a.** num[2]

    b. num[i + j]

    c. num[0] + num[num[1]]

    d. num[j]

    e. num[i] + num[j]

31. **a.** &num[0]

    b. num[0]

    c. num[0] + 1

    d. num[1]

    e. num[j]

33. **a.** not valid: mushem needs two addresses.

    b. valid

    c. valid

    d. not valid: mushem needs two addresses.

    e. valid (but discards return value)

35. 1. 9 4 17

    2. 31 17 10 18 7 19 10

CHAPTER 11

REVIEW QUESTIONS

1. b. False

3. b. False

5. e. string

7. a. String variables cannot be used with the assignment operator.

9. c. gets

11. c. if (strmcp (string1, string2) == 0)

13. a. *strchr*

15. e. functional

EXERCISES

17.
```
*(y)     ==> e
*(y + 1) ==> a space (between e and i)
*(y + 4) ==> a space (between s and b)
```

19. A number > 0 (probably 25, which is the difference between 'z' (90) and 'A' (65))

21. abefgnpanm

    panm

    befgnpanm

    <There is nothing to be printed for the fourth line because the s9 is pointing null.>

23. DOO

    CK

    BOO

    O

    OO

    OBOO

    B

25. argorp

    agrxxx

    Note: xxx on the second line would be anything that exists in memory because p is pointing before the address of the beginning of the string.

CHAPTER 12

REVIEW QUESTIONS

1. b. False
3. b. False
5. a. True
7. d. type definition
9. d. The enumerated values are automatically assigned constant values unless otherwise directed.
11. e. There are three different structure declarations: variable, tagged, and type-defined structures.
13. c. `stu.major`
15. d. *union*
17. a. true
    b. false
    c. false
    d. true

EXERCISES

19.
```
typedef struct
    {
    int    partNo;
    char   *descr;
    int    reOrder;
    int    onHand;
    char   unitMeas[9];
    float  price;
    } ITEM;
```
21.
```
struct ARRAY_ELEMENT
    {
    char *month;
    int  days;
    char *activity;
    };

struct ARRAY_ELEMENT calendar [366];
```
23. a. valid
    b. not valid: **y** is pointer to a character
    c. valid
    d. valid
    e. valid
25. 12.450000
    66
    0

CHAPTER 13

REVIEW QUESTIONS

1. b. False
3. a. True
5. b. False
7. a. Because they are more flexible, binary files are more portable.
9. a. The file is placed in an error state regardless of the file mode.
11. a. *fwrite*
13. d. *fseek*
15. b. Sequential files are often updated in an online environment.

EXERCISES

17.
```
     char *m = "wb"    ==>    char *m = "rb"
```
19. a. No error
    b. Error: *ftell* needs only one parameter, file pointer.
    c. Error: fp must be the first parameter, and the seek code is the last.
    d. No error
    e. No error
21. C (See Figure S-5.)

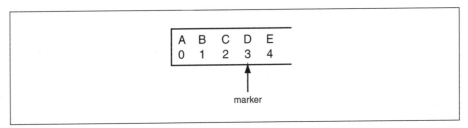

Figure S-5   Solution for Chapter 13, Exercise 21

23. D (See Figure S-6.)

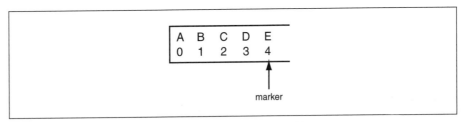

Figure S-6   Solution for Chapter 13, Exercise 23

25. Some garbage data because the file marker is located beyond the data. (See Figure S-7.)
27. 3. See Figure S-8.
29. In the call to *fseek*, it does not move in an increment of `sizeof(int)`, so garbage is printed because the file marker is located at the middle of integer data (second byte of 04). See Figure S-9.

Figure S-7   Solution for Chapter 13, Exercise 25

Figure S-8   Solution for Chapter 13, Exercise 27

Figure S-9   Solution for Chapter 13, Exercise 29

CHAPTER 14

REVIEW QUESTIONS

1. a. True
3. a. True
5. b. False
7. d. The link field in a linked list always points to a successor.
9. e. Traverse the list.
11. a. Atomic data

EXERCISES

13. The variable list will point to the second node. We will lose the first node and never be able to find it again. This problem does demonstrate the need for at least one "walking" pointer (depending on the intended operation) so that we do not lose the beginning of the list.

15. If the first data node is the one to be deleted, pPre will point to the dummy node, and pCur will point to the first data node. The following statements will delete the first data node:

```
pPre->link = pCur->link;
free (pCur);
```

17. If pNew points to the new node, pPre points to the dummy node, and pCur is NULL, then the following two statements will do the job:
    ```
    pNew->link = pPre->link;
    pPre->link = pNew;
    ```

19. Both header pointers (list1 and list2) will point to the second linked list, and the first one is lost forever (not accessible any more) unless there is another pointer with its address.

21. We will append the linked list to itself, creating a circular linked list. This list will include the dummy node.

CHAPTER 15

REVIEW QUESTIONS

1. a. True
3. a. and
5. e. shift right

EXERCISES

7. d. (the one's complement)
9. c. (the bitwise *inclusive or*)
11. a. 00100110
    b. 00000000
    c. 00001110
    d. 11111111
13. a. 11111111
    b. 11111111
    c. 11111001
    d. 11101011
15. a. 11100111   (231 or 255 - 24)
    b. 10000100   (132 or 255 - 123)
    c. 10111100   (188 or 255 - 67)
    d. 11111011   (251 or 255 - 4)
17. a. 52 (shift left 2 bits is multiply by 4)
    b. 44 (22 << 4 is 352 (shift left 4 is multiply by 16) 352 >> 8 is 44 (shift right 3 is divide by 8)
    c. 0 (First add parentheses to show priority.)
       ((5 << 2) & 3) && (((3 >> 2) >> 3) | 4)
       ((5 << 2) & 3) has a value of zero, therefore, the expression is false (zero).
    d. 0 (zero, since the last operand is bitwise and by zero).
19. The mask is 01111111 (0x7f), and the operator is the bitwise *and* (&).
21. 11110101 (0xf5)
23. 0 (all zeros)
25. 0 (all zeros)
    Exclusive or turns off bits, so the *exclusive or* of a variable to itself always sets the value to zero.
27. It is unchanged (the *exclusive or* result is 1 if the bits are different and zero if they are the same).

Glossary

A

absolute value: the magnitude of a number regardless of its sign. In C: *abs*.

abstract data type (ADT): a data declaration and a set of operators that are allowed on the data, encapsulated as a type.

accuracy: the quality factor that addresses the correctness of a system.

actual parameters: the parameters in the function calling statement that contain the values to be passed to the function. Contrast with *formal parameters*.

additive expression: in C, the binary addition and subtraction expressions.

address list: in C: function parameter list that consists of variable addresses.

address operator: in C: the ampersand (&).

afferent module: a module whose processing is directed toward the central transform; that is, a module that gathers data to be transmitted toward the central processing functions of a module.

algorithm: the logical steps necessary to solve a problem in a computer; a function or a part of a function.

algorithmics: the term created by Brassard and Bratley that refers to the study of techniques used to create efficient algorithms.

and **operator (&&):** a binary logical operator with the property that the expression is true if and only if both operands are true.

ANSI/ISO C: the standard for the C language adopted by the American National Standards Institute.

append mode: in file processing, the mode that adds to the end of a file.

application software: computer software developed to support a specific user requirement. Contrast with *system software*.

application-specific software: any application software that can be used for only one purpose, such as an accounting system.

argc (argument count): in C: the parameter in **main** that contains the number of parameters passed to main from the user by the operating system.

argv (argument vector): in C: a list of addresses to the parameters passed to main.

array: a fixed-sized, sequenced collection of elements of the same data type.

array of pointers: an array of addresses, often used to represent a sparse array.

ascending sequence: a list order in which each element in the list has a key greater than or equal to its predecessors.

ASCII: the American Standard Code for Information Interchange. An encoding scheme that defines control characters and graphic characters for the first 128 values in a byte.

assembler: system software that converts a source program into executable object code; traditionally associated with assembly language program. See also *compiler*.

assembly language: a programming language in which there is a one-for-one correspondence between the computer's machine language and the symbolic instruction set of the language.

assignment expression: an expression containing the assignment operator (=) that results in the value of the expression being placed into the left operand.

associativity: the parsing direction used to evaluate an expression when all operators have an equal priority. See *left* and *right associativity*. See also *precedence*.

atomic data: data that cannot be meaningfully subdivided.

atomic data type: see *standard type*.

auto: the default storage class for a local variable.

auxiliary storage: any storage device outside main memory; permanent data storage; external storage.

B

base case: in recursion, the event that does not involve a recursive call and therefore ends the recursion.

batch update: an update process in which transactions are gathered over time for processing as a unit. Contrast with *online update.*

big-O analysis: the analysis of an algorithm that measures efficiency using big-O notation rather than mathematical precision.

big-O notation: a measure of the efficiency of an algorithm in which only the dominant factor is considered.

binary expression: any expression containing one operator and two operands.

binary file: a collection of data stored in the internal format of the computer. Contrast with *text file.*

binary search: a search algorithm in which the search value is located by repeatedly dividing the list in half.

bit: acronym for Binary digIT. The basic storage unit in a computer with the capability of storing only the values 0 or 1.

bitwise operator: any of the set of operators that operate on individual bits in a field.

blackbox testing: testing based on the system requirements rather than a knowledge of the program.

block: in C, a group of statements enclosed in braces {...}.

block scope: see *scope.*

body: the part of a function that contains the local definitions and statements; all of a function except the header declaration. Contrast with *function header.*

body of loop: the code executed during each iteration of a loop.

Boolean: a variable or expression that can assume only the values true and false.

braces: the { and } symbols.

break: a C statement that causes a *switch* or loop statement to terminate.

bubble sort: a sort algorithm in which each pass through the data moves (bubbles) the lowest element to the beginning of the unsorted portion of the list.

buffer: (1) hardware, usually memory, used to synchronize the transfer of data to and from main memory. (2) memory used to hold data that have been read before they are processed, or data that are waiting to be written.

buffered input/output: input or output that are temporarily stored in intermediate memory while being read or written.

buffered stream: C term for buffered input/output.

bug: a colloquial term used for any error in a piece of software.

byte: a unit of storage, usually 8 bits.

C

C standard library: any of the libraries that contain predefined algorithms delivered with the system, such as standard library, (`stdlib.h`) and standard input and output (`stdio.h`).

called function: in a function call, the function to which control is passed.

calling function: in a function call, the function that invokes the call.

case label: the entry point for a value in a *switch* statement.

cast: a C operator that changes the type of an expression.

ceil: the standard C function that returns the ceiling of a floating-point number.

ceiling: the smallest integral value that is larger than a floating-point value.

central processing unit (CPU): the part of a computer that contains the control components—that is, the part that interprets instructions. In a personal computer, a microchip containing a control unit and an arithmetic-logical unit.

central transform: the modules of a program that take input and convert it to output. See also *afferent* and *efferent.*

changeability: the quality factor that addresses the ease with which changes can be accurately made to a program.

char: the C type for character.

character: a member of the set of values that are used to represent data or control operations. See *ASCII.*

character set: the set of values in a computer's alphabet, usually ASCII or EBCDIC.

chronological list: a list that is organized by time; that is, in which the data are stored in the order in which they were received. See also *FIFO* and *LIFO.*

classifying function: a standard C character function that classifies a character according to C's character taxonomy, such as "printable" or "alphanumeric."

clear box testing: see *whitebox testing.*

client: in a client/server network, the computer that provides the basic application computing; the computer residing in the user's physical area.

client/server: a computer system design in which two separate computers control the processing of the application, one providing the basic application computing (the client) and the other providing auxiliary services, such as database access (the server).

close function: the function that concludes the writing of a file by writing any pending data to the file and then making it unavailable for processing.

cohesion: the attribute of a module that describes how closely the processes within a module are related to each other.

coincidental cohesion: the cohesion level in which totally unrelated processes are combined into a module.

column: in a two-dimensional table, the second dimension; the dimension representing vertical columns in the array. Contrast with *row*.

comma expression: the last (lowest precedence) expression in C, used to combine multiple expressions into one expression statement.

comma operator: in C, the operator that connects multiple statements in one expression.

command-line argument: in C, a parameter specified on the run-time execute statement and passed to the program for its use.

comment: in a C program, a note to the program reader that is ignored by the compiler.

communicational cohesion: the processes in a module are related only in that they share the same data.

compilation: the process used to convert a source program into machine language.

compiler: system software that converts a source program into executable object code; traditionally associated with high-level languages. See also *assembler*.

complement: in a logical expression, a change in the code syntax such that a positive statement is stated negatively or a negative statement stated positively, without a change in the value of the expression.

composite data: data that are built on other data structures; that is, data that can be broken down into discrete atomic elements.

compound statement: a sequence of statements enclosed in braces. See also *block*.

computer language: any of the syntactical languages used to write programs for computers, such as machine language, assembly language, C, COBOL, and FORTRAN.

computer system: the set of computer components required for a complete system, consisting of at least an input device, an output device, a monitor, and a central processing unit.

conditional expression: in C, short-hand form of a two-way selection.

const: a storage class that designates that a field's contents cannot be changed during the execution of the program.

constant: a data value that cannot change during the execution of the program. Contrast with *variable*.

content coupling: the direct reference to the data in one module by statements in another module. The lowest form of coupling and one to be avoided.

continue: in C, a statement that causes the remaining code in a loop iteration to be skipped.

control character: a nonprintable character value whose function is to perform some operation, such as form-feed, or that is used to indicate status, such as the start of a transmission.

control coupling: communication between functions in which flags are set by one module to control the actions of another.

conversion code: in formatted input and output, the code in the format specification that identifies the data type.

converting function: a C character function that either converts lower-case alphabetic characters to upper case, or vice versa.

correctability: the quality factor that addresses the ease with which errors in a module can be fixed.

counter-controlled loop: a looping technique in which the number of iterations is controlled by a count; in C, the *for* statement. Contrast with *event-controlled loop*.

coupling: a measure of the interdependence between two separate functions. See also: *content coupling*, *control coupling*, *data coupling*, *global coupling*, and *stamp coupling*.

CPU: central processing unit.

D

dangling else: a code sequence in which there is no *else* statement for one of the *if* statements in a nested *if*.

data coupling: communication between modules in which only the required data are passed. Considered the best form of coupling.

data encapsulation: the software engineering concept in which data are hidden from an application program's access.

data flow: in a structure chart, an indicator identifying data input to or output from a module.

data hiding: the principle of structured programming in which data are available to a function only if it needs them to complete its processing; data not needed are "hidden" from view. See also *encapsulation* and *scope*.

data name: an identifier given to data in a program.

data structure: the syntactical representation of data organized to show the relationship among the individual elements.

data type: a named set of values and operations defined to manipulate them, such as character and integer.

data validation: the process of verifying and validating data read from an external source.

declaration: in C, the association of a name with an object, such as a type, variable, structure, or function. See also *definition*.

default: in C, the entry point to the code that is to be executed if none of the case values match the *switch* expression.

define: in C, a preprocessor command that names and provides the code for a macro.

definition: in C, the process that reserves memory for a named object, such as a variable or constant. See also *declaration*.

definition section: the portion of a block in which variables and constants may be defined. The first section in a block. See also *statement section*.

delimited string: a string terminated by a nondata character, such as the null character in C.

delimiter: the character or token that identifies the end of a structure.

De Morgan's rule: a rule used to complement a logical expression.

dereference: access of a data variable through a pointer containing its address.

dereference operator: in C, the asterisk (*). Used to indicate that a pointer's contents (an address) are to be used to access another piece of data.

derived type: a composite data type constructed from other types (array, structure, union, pointer, and enumerated type).

descending sequence: a list order in which each element in a list has a key less than or equal to its predecessor.

disk: an auxiliary storage medium used to store data and programs required for a computer.

disk drive: the auxiliary storage hardware device used to read and write a disk.

diskette: a removable flexible disk, enclosed in a protective flexible or rigid cover, used to store data for a personal computer.

double: the C type for double-precision floating point type.

drive: an auxiliary storage device that can write and read data, such as the internal hard disk, a floppy disk, or a tape unit.

dynamic allocation: allocation of memory for storing data during the execution of a program. Contrast with *static allocation*.

dynamic array: an array that has been allocated in the heap during the execution of the program.

dynamic memory: memory whose use can change during the execution of the program (The heap).

E

EBCDIC: Extended Binary Coded Decimal Interchange Code. The character set designed by IBM for its large computer systems.

edit set: a list of characters used to validate characters during the formatted reading of a string.

efferent module: a module whose processing is directed away from the central transform; that is, a module that predominately disposes of data by reporting or writing to a file.

efficiency: the quality factor that addresses the optimum use of computer hardware or responsiveness to a user.

else-if: a style (as opposed to syntax) convention used to implement a multiway selection for a nonintegral expression. Each expression in the series must evaluate the same variable.

empty list: a list that has been allocated but that contains no data. Also known as a null list.

encapsulation: the software engineering design concept in which data and their operations are bundled together and maintained separately from the application using them.

end of file: the condition that occurs when a read operation attempts to read after it has processed the last piece of data.

enumeration constant: the identifier associated with a value in an enumeration declaration.

EOF: end of file. In C, a flag set to indicate that a file is at the end.

error report file: in a file update process, a report of errors detected during the update.

error state: one of three states that an open file may assume. An error state occurs when a program issues an impossible command, such as a read command while the file is in a write state, or when a physical device failure occurs. See also *read state, write state*.

error stream: in C, the standard file used to display errors, often assigned to a printer (*stderr*).

escape character: in C, the backslash (\) character used to identify a special interpretation for the character that follows it.

escape sequence: any group of keystrokes or characters used to identify a control character. In C, the backslash (\) used to indicate that the character that follows represents a control character.

event-controlled loop: a loop whose termination is predicated upon the occurrence of a specified event. Contrast with *counter-controlled loop*.

exchanging values: the logic used to exchange the values in two variables.

exclusive or: a binary logical operation in which the result is true only when one of the operands is true and the other is false.

executable file: a file that contains program code in its executable form; the result of linking the source code object module with any required library modules.

explicit type conversion: the conversion of a value from one type to another through the cast operator. Contrast with *implicit type conversion*.

exponential efficiency: a category of program/module efficiency in which the run time is a function of the power of the number of elements being processed.

expression: a sequence of operators and operands that reduces to a single value.

expression statement: an expression terminated by a semicolon.

expression type: one of seven expression attributes that broadly describes an expression's format: *primary, postfix, unary, binary, ternary, assignment,* and *comma.*

extent: the attribute of a field that determines when it can be accessed within a source program. See also *temporal authority.*

extern: the storage class that exports the name of a field to the linker so that it can be used by other programs. Unless otherwise designated, global fields are automatically storage class *externs.*

F

factorial efficiency: a measure of the efficiency of a module in which the run time is proportionate to the number of elements factorial.

false: the Boolean value used to indicate that an expression is not true.

fan out: an attribute of a module that describes the number of submodules it calls.

field: the smallest named unit of data that has meaning in describing information. A field may be either a variable or a constant.

field specification: a subcomponent of the format string used to describe the formatting of data, in the formatted input and output functions.

field width: in a field specification, the specification of the maximum input width or minimum output width for formatted data.

FIFO: First In, First Out.

file: a named collection of data stored on an auxiliary storage device. Compare with *list.*

file mode: a designation of a file's input and/or output capability; files may be opened for reading, writing, appending, or updating.

file state: the operating condition of a file: read state, write, or error state.

file table: in C, the predefined standard structure, FILE, used to store the attributes of a file.

filename: the operating system name of a file on an auxiliary storage device.

fixed-length string: a string whose size is constant regardless of the number of characters stored in it.

flag: an indicator used in a program to designate the presence or absence of a condition; *switch.*

flexibility: the quality factor that addresses the ease with which a program can be changed to meet user requirements.

float: a single-precision floating-point type.

floating-point number: a number that contains both an integral and a fraction.

floor: the largest integral number smaller than a floating-point value.

flowchart: a program design tool in which standard graphical symbols are used to represent the logical flow of data through a function.

force to change: the bit manipuation concept used to force selected bits to change from 0 to 1 or from 1 to 0.

force to one: the bit manipulation concept used to force selected bits to 1.

force to zero: the bit manipulation concept used to force selected bits to zero.

formal parameter: the parameter declaration in a function prototype used to describe the type of data to be processed by the function. Contrast with *actual parameter.*

formal parameter list: the declaration of parameters in a function header.

format string: in C, the first parameter in a formatted input or output function used to describe the data to be read or written.

formatted input/output: in C, any of the standard library functions that can reformat data to and from text while they are being read or written.

frequency array: an array that contains the number of occurrences of a value or of a range of values. See also *histogram.*

front: when used to refer to a list; a pointer that identifies the first element.

function: a named block of code that performs a process within a program; an executable unit of code, consisting of a header, function name, and a body, that is designed to perform a task within the program.

function body: the code within a function that is contained in the function's definition and statement sections.

function call: a statement that invokes another function.

function declaration: in C, a prototype statement that describes a function's return type, name, and formal parameters.

function definition: in C, the implementation of a function declaration.

function header: in a function definition, that part of the function that supplies the return type, function identifier, and formal parameters. Contrast with *body.*

functional cohesion: a module in which all of the processing is related to a single task. The highest level of cohesion.

G

general case: all the code in a recursive function that is not a base case.

general-purpose software: software, such as a spread sheet, that can be used in multiple applications.

global coupling: communication between different modules that uses data accessible to all modules in a program. Considered to be a very poor communications technique for intraprogram communication.

global declaration section: the declaration and/or definition of a variable or function outside the boundaries of any function—that is, before *main* or between function definitions. Contrast with *local declaration*.

global variable: a variable defined in the global declaration section of a program—that is, defined outside a function block.

H

hard copy: any computer output that is written to paper or other readable mediums such as microfiche. Contrast with *soft copy*.

hardware: any of the physical components of a computer system, such as the keyboard or a printer.

header declaration: that part of a function that contains the return type, function name, and parameter declarations.

header file: in C, a file consisting of prototype statements and other declarations and placed in a library for shared use.

head pointer: a pointer that identifies the first element of a list.

heap: see *heap memory*.

heap memory: a pool of memory that can be used to dynamically allocate space for data while the program is running.

hexadecimal: a numbering system with base 16. Its digits are 0 1 2 3 4 5 6 7 8 9 A B C D E F.

high-level language: a (portable) programming language designed to allow the programmer to concentrate on the application rather than the structure of a particular computer or operating system.

histogram: a graphical representation of a frequency distribution. See also *frequency array*.

I

identifier: the name of an object. In C, identifiers can consist only of digits, letters, and the underscore.

implicit type conversion: the automatic conversion of data from one type to another when required within a C program. Contrast with *explicit type conversion*.

include: in C, a preprocessor command that specifies a library file to be inserted into the program.

inclusive or: see *or* operator.

indentation: a coding style in which statements dependent on a previous statement, such as *if* or *while*, are coded in an indented block to show their relationship to the controlling statement.

index: the address of an element within an array. See also *subscript*.

index range checking: a feature available in some compilers that inserts code to ensure that all index references are within the array.

indexing: a process used to identify one element in an array.

indirect pointer: a pointer that locates the address of data through one or more other pointers; pointer to pointer.

indirection operator: in C, the unary operator (*) used to deference a pointer.

infinite loop: a loop that does not terminate.

information hiding: a structured programming concept in which the data structure and the implementation of its operations are not known by the user.

initialization: the process of assigning values to a variable at the beginning of a program or a function.

initializer: in C, any value assigned to a constant or variable when it is defined.

input device: a device that provides data to be read by a program.

input stream: in C, the flow of data from a file to the program.

inquiry: a request for information from a program.

insertion sort: a sort algorithm in which the first element from the unsorted portion of the list is inserted into its proper position relative to the data in the sorted portion of the list.

int: the C data type for integral numbers.

integer: an integral number; a number without a fractional part.

intelligent data name: a software engineering principle that requires the identifier to convey the meaning or use of an object.

interoperability: the quality factor that addresses the ability of one system to exchange data with another.

iteration: a single execution of the statements in a loop.

K

key: one or more fields that are used to identify a record (structure).

keyboard: an input device used for text or control data, that consists of alphanumeric keys and function keys.

keyboard file: see *standard input file*.

keywords: see *reserved words*.

L

leading zero flag: the flag in the format string of a print statement indicating that numeric data are to be printed with leading zeros.

left associativity: the evaluation of an expression that parses from the left to right. Contrast with *right associativity*.

left justification: the orientation of variable-length data in an output format such that trailing null values are inserted and the first data character is at the left end of the print area. Contrast with *right justification*.

length-controlled string: a variable-length string function in which the data are identified by a structural component containing the length of the data.

lexicographical: a textual data order based on the dictionary.

LIFO: Last In, First Out.

limit test expression: in a loop, the expression that determines if the loop will continue or stop. See also *terminating condition*.

linear efficiency: a measure of the efficiency of a module in which the run time is proportionate to the number of elements being processed.

linear list: a list structure in which each element, except the last, has a unique successor.

linear loop: a loop whose execution is a function of the number of elements being processed. See also *linear efficiency*.

linear search: see *sequential search*.

link: in a list structure, the field that identifies the next element in the list.

linked list: a linear list structure in which the ordering of the elements is determined by link fields.

linked list traversal: processing in which every element of a linked list is processed in order.

linker: the program creation process in which an object module is joined with precompiled functions to form an executable program.

list: an ordered set of data contained in main memory. Compare with *file*.

list traversal: any logic that visits and processes all the data in a list.

literal: an unnamed constant coded in an expression.

loader: the operating system function that fetches an executable program into memory for running.

local declaration: a variable or type declaration that is only visible to the block in which it is contained. Contrast with *global declaration*.

local variables: variables defined with a block.

logarithmic efficiency: a measure of the efficiency of a module in which the run time is proportionate to the log of the number of elements being processed.

logarithmic loop: a loop whose efficiency is a function of the log of the number of elements being processed. See also *logarithmic efficiency*.

logical cohesion: a design attribute that describes a module in which the processing within the module is related only by the general type of processing being done. Considered unacceptable design in structured programming.

logical data: data whose values can be only true or false. See *Boolean*.

logical operator: a C operator (`&&`, `||`, `!`) used in a logical expression.

long double: a C data type whose precision may be greater than *float*.

long integer: a C data type whose values may be greater than *int*.

loop control expression: the expression in a loop statement that is used to determine if the body of the loop is to be executed.

loop update: the code within a loop statement or body that changes the environment such that the loop will eventually terminate.

lvalue: an expression that allows the contents of a variable to be modified.

M

machine language: the instructions native to the central processor of a computer and that are executable without assembly or compilation.

main **memory:** see *primary memory*.

mask: a variable or constant that contains a bit configuration used to control the setting of bits in a bitwise operation.

master file: a permanent file that contains the most current data regarding an application.

memory: the main memory of a computer consisting of random access memory (RAM) and read-only memory (ROM); used to store data and program instructions.

memory constant: a C type defined using the type qualifier *const*.

merge: to combine two or more sequential files into one sequential file based on a common key and structure format.

monitor: the visual display unit of a computer system, usually a video display device.

multidimensional array: an array whose elements consist of one or more arrays.

multiplicative expression: an expression that contains a multiply, divide, or modulus operator.

multiway selection: a selection statement that is capable of evaluating more than two alternatives. In C, the *switch* statement. Contrast with *two-way selection*.

N

natural language: any spoken language.

negative logic: an expression that begins with the negation operator (`!`).

nested *if* **statement:** an *if* statement coded as either the true or false statement within another *if*.

nested loop: a loop contained within another loop.

nested structure: a structure that contains other structures.

node: in a data structure, an element that contains both data and structural elements used to process the list.

null *else*: the absence of a false statement in an *if* statement.

O

object module: the output of a compilation consisting of machine language instructions.

octal: a numbering system with a base of 8. The octal digits are 0 1 2 3 4 5 6 7.

offset: in pointer arithmetic, a computed value that is used to determine another index location within an array.

one-dimensional array: an array with only one level of indexing.

one's complement: the bitwise operator that reverses the value of the bits in a variable.

online update: an update process in which transactions are entered and processed by a user who has direct access to the system.

open function: the function that locates and prepares a file for processing.

operability: the quality factor that addresses the ease with which a system can be used.

operand: an object in a statement on which an operation is performed. Contrast with *operator*.

operating system: the software that controls the computing environment and provides an interface to the user.

operator: the syntactical token representing an action on data (the operand). Contrast with *operand*.

***or* operator (||):** a binary logical operator with the property that if any of the operands is true, the expression is true.

ordered list: a list in which the elements are arranged so that the key values are placed in ascending or descending sequence.

output device: a device that can be written but not read in the current state of a file.

output stream: in C, the flow of data from a program to the file.

overflow: the condition that results when an attempt is made to insert data into a structure and there is no room.

P

parameter: a value passed to a function.

parameter list: a list of values passed to a function. (Note: the values may be data or addresses.)

pass by address: in C, the technique used when a pointer is passed to a function as a parameter.

pass by reference: a parameter passing technique in which the called function refers to a passed parameter using an alias name.

pass by value: a parameter passing technique in which the value of a variable is passed to a function.

personal computer (PC): a computer designed for individual use.

plane: the third dimension in a multidimensional array.

pointer: a constant or variable that contains an address that can be used to access data.

pointer arithmetic: addition or subtraction in which a pointer's contents (an address) are changed by a multiple of the size of the data to which it is pointing.

pointer constant: a pointer whose contents cannot be changed.

pointer indirection: the use of a pointer to access data.

pointer to function: a pointer that identifies the entry point to a function. It is used to pass a function's address as a parameter.

polyonymic efficiency: a measure of the efficiency of a module in which the run time is proportionate to the number of elements raised to the highest factor in a polynomial.

portability: the quality factor that addresses the ease with which a system can be moved to other hardware environments.

postfix decrement: in C, the operator (such as a—) that subtracts 1 from a variable after its value has been used in an expression.

postfix expression: an expression in which the operator follows the operand.

postfix increment: in C, the operator (such as a++) that adds 1 to a variable after its value has been used in an expression.

post-test loop: a loop in which the terminating condition is tested only after the execution of the loop statements. Contrast with *pretest loop*.

precedence: the priority assigned to an operator or group of operators that determines the order in which operators will be evaluated in an expression. See also *associativity*.

precision: in the format string of a print function, the maximum number of integral digits, the number of significant digits or fractional digits in a floating-point number, or the maximum number of characters in a string.

precision modifier: the print format string modifier that specifies the number of decimal places to be printed in a floating-point value.

prefix decrement: in C, the operator (such as —a) that subtracts one from a variable before its value is used in an expression. AKA *unary decrement*.

prefix expression: an expression in which the operator precedes the operand.

prefix increment: in C, the operator (such as ++a) that adds 1 to a variable before its value is used in an expression. AKA *unary increment*.

preprocessor: the first phase of a C compilation in which the source statements are prepared for compilation and any necessary libraries are loaded.

preprocessor directives: commands to the C precompiler.

pretest loop: a loop in which the terminating condition is tested before the execution of the loop statements. Contrast with *post-test loop.*

primary expression: an expression consisting of only a single operator; the highest priority expression.

primary storage: the volitile (RAM) memory of a computer.

printable character: a character value that is associated with a print graphic.

printer: an output device that displays the output on paper.

procedural cohesion: a module design in which the processing within the module is related by control flows. Considered acceptable design only at the higher levels of a program.

process-control loops: a continuous loop used to control operating equipment, such as a building air conditioning/ heating system.

processing unit: see *central processing unit.*

program development: the system development activity in which requirement specifications are converted into executable programs.

program file: a file that contains an executable program.

program testing: the process that validates a program's operation and verifies that it meets its design requirements.

prototype declaration: the function header that declares the return type, function name, and parameter number and types without defining the function itself.

prototype statement: in C, the declaration of a function that provides the return type and formal parameter types.

pseudocode: English-like statements that follow a loosely defined syntax and are used to convey the design of an algorithm or function.

Q

quadratic efficiency: a measure of the efficiency of a module in which the run time is proportionate to the number of elements squared. Quadratic efficiency is one of the polyonymic factors.

quadratic loop: a loop that consists of two or more loops, each of which have a linear efficiency, resulting in a loop with quadratic efficiency.

quality: see *software quality.*

query: see *inquiry.*

R

random number: a number selected from a set in which all members have the same probability of being selected.

read mode: the attribute of a file that indicates that it is opened for input only.

read state: one of three states that an open file may assume. The state of a file during which only input operations may be performed. See also *error state, write state.*

real time: processing in which updating takes place at the time the event occurs.

rear: when used to refer to a list; a pointer that identifies the last element.

record: see *structure.*

recursion: a function design in which the function calls itself.

register: the storage class that requests that, if possible, a variable be allocated to a CPU register.

reliability: the quality factor that addresses the confidence or trust in a system's total operation.

reserved words: the set of words in C that have a predetermined interpretation and cannot be used in the definition of an object.

return: the C statement that causes execution of a function to terminate and control to be resumed by the calling function.

return code: the value sent back to the calling function by a called function.

reusability: the quality factor that addresses the ease with which software can be used in other programs.

reusable code: code that can be used by more than one process.

rewind: the C function used to position an open file at the beginning.

right associativity: the evaluation of an expression that parses from the right to the left. Contrast with *left associativity.*

right justification: the orientation of variable length data in an output format such that leading null values are inserted and the last data character is at the right end of the print area. Contrast with *left justification.*

right–left rule: a method of reading complex declarations or definitions that starts with the identifier and alternately reads right and left until the declaration has been fully read.

row: in a two-dimensional array, elements along a horizontal axis. Contrast with *column.*

rvalue: an expression attribute indicating that the expression can be used only to supply a value for another expression.

S

scanset: the set of allowed or disallowed characters when reading a string.

scope: an attribute of a variable that defines whether it is visible to or hidden from statements in a program. See also *temporal authority.*

search: the process that examines a list to locate one or more elements containing a designated value known as a search argument.

secondary storage: see *auxiliary storage.*

security: the quality factor that addresses the ease or difficulty with which an unauthorized user can access data.

seed: the variable used in a random number generator to calculate the next number in the series. In C, the seed is set by the library function *srand.*

selection: see *selection statement.*

selection sort: the sort algorithm in which the smallest value in the unsorted portion of a list is selected and placed at the end of the sorted portion of the list.

selection statement: a statement that chooses between two or more alternatives. In C, the *if...else* or *switch* statements.

self-referential structure: a structure that contains a pointer to itself.

sentinel: a flag that guards the end of a list or a file. The sentinel is usually the maximum value for a key field and cannot be a valid data value.

separate compilation: a capability within a programming language that allows parts of a program to be compiled independently and later assembled into an executable unit.

sequential cohesion: a module design in which the processing within the module flows such that the data from one process are used in the next process.

sequential file: a file structure in which data must be processed serially from the first entry in the file.

sequential search: a search technique used with a linear list in which the searching begins at the first element and continues until the value of an element equal to the value being sought is located, or until the end of the list is reached.

serial search: any search technique that starts at the beginning of the list and continues toward the end.

server: in a client/server system, the centralized computer that provides auxiliary services.

short: the C type for short integer.

short integer: an integer format used for small numbers, generally less than 32,768.

side effect: a change in a variable that results from the evaluation of an expression; any input/output performed by a called function.

sign flag: the flag value (+) in the conversion code of a print format string that indicates that positive numbers must be printed with a plus sign.

signed: a type modifier indicating that a numeric value may be either positive or negative. Contrast with *unsigned.*

size: an indicator (h, l, L) in the conversion code of a format string that modifies integer and *float* types.

slack bytes: inaccessible memory locations added between fields in a structure to force a hardware-required boundary alignment.

soft copy: computer output written to a nonpermanent display such as a monitor. Contrast with *hard copy.*

software: the application and system programs necessary for computer hardware to accomplish a task including their documentation and any required procedures.

software quality: an attribute of software that measures the user's total satisfaction with a system.

sort: the process that orders a list or file.

sort pass: one sort loop during which all elements are tested.

source file: the file that contains program statements written by a programmer before they are converted into machine language; the input file to an assembler or compiler.

space flag: the flag value in the conversion code of a print format string indicating that positive numbers must be printed with a leading space.

sparse array: a two dimensional array in which the rows are only partially filled.

spatial authority: an attribute of a field that determines which functions within a program can refer to it or change its contents.

square brackets: the [and] symbols.

stack memory: in C, the memory management facility that is used to store local variables while they are active.

stamp coupling: the communication technique between modules in which data are passed as a structure; often results in unrequired data being passed.

standard error stream: the text file automatically opened by C for display of error messages (*stderr*).

standard input stream: the text file automatically opened by C for input to a program (*stdin*).

standard library: any of a collection of libraries containing functions required by the C standard provided by an implementation of the C language.

standard output stream: the text file automatically opened by C for output from a program (*stdout*).

standard type: one of the intrinsic C types that are considered atomic; that is, that cannot be broken down (*void, char, int, float*).

statement: a syntactical construct in C that represents one operation in a function.

static: a storage class that designates (a) that a local field must maintain its contents throughout the execution of a program (contrast with *auto*), or (b) that a global variable's name must not be exported to the linker (contrast with *extern*).

static memory: memory whose use (e.g., for a variable) does not change during the running of a program.

static memory allocation: memory whose location is determined by the compiler and therefore preset before run time. Contrast with *dynamic allocation*.

***stderr*:** see *standard error stream*.

***stdin*:** see *standard input stream*.

***stdout*:** see *standard output stream*.

stepwise refinement: a design methodology in which a system or program is developed from the top down; starting with the most inclusive, each module is decomposed and refined until the meaning of a component is intrinsically understood.

storage class: an attribute of a field that determines its spatial and temporal usage. See also *auto*, *extern*, *register*, *static*.

stream: in C, the flow of data between a file and the program; a sequence of bytes in time.

string: in C, a variable-length sequence of characters delimited by a null character.

structure: a named collection of fields grouped together for processing; see *record*.

structure chart: a design and documentation tool that represents a program as a hierarchical flow of functions.

structure variable: in C, a structure definition that cannot be used as a type.

stub: a temporary and incomplete function used to test function interfaces during program development.

subscript: an ordinal number that indicates the position of an element within an array. See also *index*.

suffix: a modifier to a numeric constant that indicates its type when used in an expression.

switch: See *flag*.

switch statement: the C implementation of the multiway selection.

symbolic language: a computer language, one level removed from machine language, that has a mnemonic identifier for each machine instruction and has the capability of symbolic data names.

syntax: the "grammatical" rules of a language. In C, the set of keywords and formatting rules that must be followed when writing a program.

system development life cycle: a model of the steps required to develop software that begins with the need for the software and concludes with its implementation.

system development software: any computer tool used to develop software, such as but not limited to compilers, debuggers, and documentation tools.

system software: any software whose primary purpose is to support the operation of the computing environment. Contrast with *application software*.

T

tagged structure: a C structure in which the structure is given an identifier that can be used to declare variables of the structure type.

tape storage: an auxiliary storage medium that stores data as a sequential file on a magnetic recording surface.

temporal authority: an attribute of a field that determines when a field is alive and active during the execution of a program.

temporal cohesion: a module design in which processes are combined because they all need to be processed in the same time sequence.

terminating condition: in a loop, the condition that stops a loop. See also *limit test*.

ternary expression: in C, an expression that contains three operands (the conditional expression is the only ternary expression in C).

testability: an attribute of software that measures the ease with which the software can be tested as an operational system.

testing: see *program testing*, *blackbox testing*, or *whitebox testing*.

text editor: software that maintains text files, such as a word processor or a source program editor.

text file: a file in which all data are stored as characters. Contrast with *binary file*.

timeliness: an attribute of software that measures responsiveness of a system to a user's time requirements.

time-sharing environment: an operating system concept in which more than one user has access to a computer at the same time.

token: in C, a syntactical construct that represents an operation or a flag, such as the assignment token (=).

top–down design: a program design concept in which a design progresses through a decomposition of the functions beginning with the top of the structure chart and working toward the lowest modules. See also *stepwise refinement*.

transaction file: a file containing relatively transient data that is used to change the contents of a master file.

transform analysis: an analytical process that creates a program design by classifying modules as input, process, or output.

transform module: the function in a program that takes input from the afferent modules and prepares it for processing by the efferent modules.

translation unit: in C, a temporary compilation file used to store modified source code.

translator: a generic term for any of the language conversion programs. See also *assembler* and *compiler*.

traversal: an algorithmic process in which each element in a structure is processed once and only once.

true: a Boolean value used to indicate that an expression is true.

two-dimensional array: an array in which each element contains one array. See also *multidimensional array*.

two-way selection: a selection statement that is capable of evaluating only two alternatives. In C, the *if...else* statement. Contrast with *multiway selection*.

type: a set of values and a set of operations that can be applied on these values.

type qualifier: a modifier used in the definition of an object.

U

unary decrement: see *prefix decrement*.

unary expression: any of the C expressions that contain only one operand.

unary increment: see *prefix increment*.

unary minus: in C, the operator that complements the value of an expression.

unbuffered input/output: input or output that is transmitted directly to or from memory without the use of a buffer.

underflow: an event that occurs when an attempt is made to delete data from a data structure and it is empty.

union: C term for *variable structure*.

unsigned: a type modifier indicating that a numeric value may be only positive. Contrast with *signed*.

update: (1) in array processing, the process that changes the contents of an element; (2) in file processing, a mode that allows a file to be both read and written.

update mode: a file process mode that specifies that the file will be both read and written.

user-defined function: any function written by the programmer, as opposed to a standard library function.

user prompts: monitor messages to a user that request the user input one or more values.

V

value error: an input value that does not satisfy specified criteria.

variable: a memory storage object whose value can be changed during the execution of a program. Contrast with *constant*.

variable structure: a data structure in which two or more types of data may occupy the same positions within the structure. In C, a *union*.

visibility: the temporal authority for a field that designates where in the program it can be accessed or changed; see *scope*.

void: the absence of data.

void **functions:** functions whose return value is *void*.

void **pointer:** a generic pointer type that can hold the address of any data type or structure.

volatile: an attribute of a variable that indicates that it may be accessed or changed by functions beyond the control of the compiler.

W

whitebox testing: program testing in which the internal design of the program is considered; *clear box testing*. Contrast with *blackbox testing*.

whitespace: in C, the space, vertical and horizontal tabs, newline, and form-feed characters.

width modifier: in a format string, a conversion code modifier that specifies the input maximum or output minimum size.

write mode: the attribute of a file indicating that it is opened for output only.

write state: one of three states that an open file can assume. A file in the write state can only be used for output. See also *error state, read state*.

Index